EGYPT
CHILD of AFRICA

Edited by
Ivan Van Sertima

From the Library

of _____

Transaction Publishers
New Brunswick (U.S.A.) and London (U.K.)

JOURNAL OF
AFRICAN CIVILIZATIONS

VOL. 12   SPRING, 1994

EGYPT:
CHILD OF AFRICA

Contents

PART ONE

ACKNOWLEDGEMENTS

Our appreciation to our graphic design specialist, LaCheun L. Patten, whose expertise and assistance for the past five years has facilitated the production of the Journal and its promotional materials.

Our gratitude to William Coston of Philadelphia and James Lucas of Washington, D.C., Friends of the Journal, whose generous donations have helped keep the Journal alive in difficult circumstances.

We also want to thank the scholars, too numerous to mention, from Africa, America, the Caribbean and Europe, who submitted essays during the past two years for inclusion in this issue. Some of these were excellent but inappropriate, some extremely promising but calling for considerable revision or a complete shift of focus, to qualify for acceptance in an anthology of this nature.

We would also like to thank LaSarah R. Patten, secretarial assistant to the *Journal of African Civilizations* for the last ten years, for completing her tasks expeditiously in spite of almost impossible time constraints.

Ivan Van Sertima

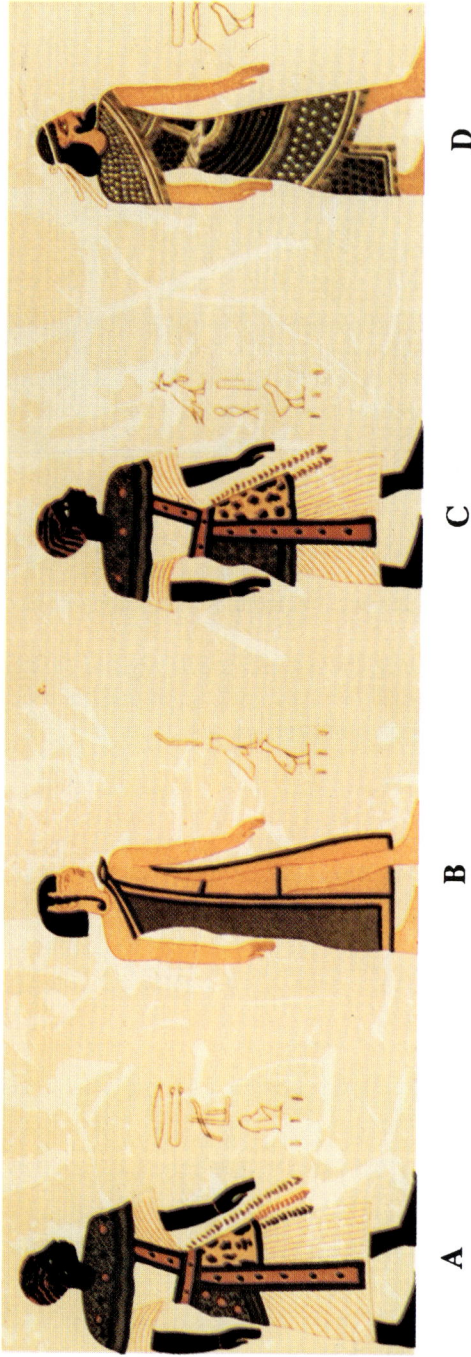

A   B   C   D

This painting from the tomb of Ramses 111 (1200 BC) shows that the Egyptians saw themselves as Blacks, and painted themselves as such without possible confusion with the Indo-Europeans [Caucasoids] or the Semites. It is a representation of the races in their most minute differences, which insures the accuracy of the colors. Throughout their entire history, the Egyptians never entertained the fantasy of portraying themselves by types B or D.

A) The Egyptian seen by himself, black type   C) The other Blacks in Africa
B) The "Indo-European"   D) The Semite

(From K.R. Lepsius: Denkmaler aus Aegypten und Aethiopien, Erganzungsband, plate 48)

EDITORIAL

Of the twelve anthologies issued by the *Journal of African Civilizations,* this is the fourth volume devoted to the study of ancient Egypt. The other three are: *Nile Valley Civilizations* (now discontinued) *Great African Thinkers* and *Egypt Revisited.* Our heavy concentration on this subject is neither accidental nor indulgent. It is the most hotly debated issue in the field of world civilization studies. In 1992 and 1993 alone I was invited to take part in three national debates on this matter. I quote briefly from remarks I made at the opening of one of these debates . . .

"I would like to begin by redefining the question. I think it is very important from the outset that we understand clearly what it is that I seek to establish here today. The question as presented to me: *Were the Ancient Egyptians Black or White?* is not the ideal way in which such an issue should be posed, for, unintentional though it may be, it is a trap. It enables those who seek to undermine the contribution of early Africans to civilization, to appear in this debate as fair and balanced, blessed with a sweet reasonableness, while I, who only seek to set the historical record straight, am, by the very wording of the proposition, encouraged to take stands which, if not racist, are, at the least, simplistic and facile.

What I set out to do here is quite different. I seek to bring to heel the racists of the early nineteenth century and their reasonable-seeming apologists of the twentieth. To do this, it is necessary, as I say, to redefine the question. The question before us is this and it is in this way that it should hereafter be posed:

First, whether the ancient Egyptians were *predominantly* African or Africoid in a physical sense during the major native dynasties *before* the late invasions of the Persian, Greek, Roman and Arab foreigners.

Second, whether—and this is even more important—their language, their writing, their vision of god and the universe, their concept of the divine kingship, their ritual ceremonies and practices, their administrative and architectural symbols and structures, their techno-complex, were quintessentially African (that is, based essentially upon models and patterns developed in the continental heartland of Africa) and *not* (I repeat *not*) in any major particular, projected from those in Europe or Asia in that or any previous time.

Now, let me say one thing further before we proceed with an examination of this question. There was probably no great civilization in the world, be it African, European, or Asian, that was entirely pure and homogeneous. The great Roman historian Pliny, who first saw the Britons in the second century A.D., describes *some of them* as having complexions as dark as the Ethiopian. Claudian, reporting the victory of the Roman general, Theodosius, over the English, mentions a good number of "nimble blackamoors" among them. The Chinese themselves recorded that there were men of black skin among the rulers of the Shang dynasty (1766–1100 B.C.). They actually speak of them as Na-Khi (*Na* in Chinese means black and *khi* means man). Schliemann and Evans, who excavated Minoan Crete, also tell us of the black skins of many of these Cretans who entered Greece in great numbers at an early time. Yet nobody would dare to pose questions such as: Were the ancient Chinese Black or Yellow? Were the ancient Greeks or the ancient Britons White or Mixed? No. No. No. No. No.

Everyone would immediately dismiss that for the nonsense that it is. The Blackamoors in second-century Britain, the black-skinned Cretans in ancient Greece, the *Na-Khi* or Black rulers and noblemen in the Shang Dynasty would be dismissed immediately as minor elements, as being of little or no consequence in the development of the indigenous civilization. But let there be a handful of Europeans or Asians in a vast body of Africans and immediately the question arises. Egypt is in Africa but was Egypt really African? Is the Egyptian Black or White? Why, I ask you, is it not an issue at all in the European or Asian case but becomes the Number One Issue in the African? The reasons for this are twofold. First of all, the Egyptian as we see him today is as different in his racial composition from the Egyptian of dynastic times, as we modern Americans in this room at this moment are from the early peoples who created native American civilization. Second, because we have been fed upon the achievements of European and Asian civilization. We would never dare to question the indigenous basis of their civilization. For we have not come upon them as we have come upon the poor African, his world looted and shattered, his empires in splinters, his peripheral elements focussed upon obsessively as though they were the very center and climax of his cultural development. All through our lived lives we have seen the European and, to some extent the Asian, in the flower of their ascendancy. But we have been trained to see and to imagine only one kind of African—the primitive, the slave, the colonial, the tragic outcast and misfit on the edge of the modern world. If, therefore, we find him at the Center of a Civilization, the matter of its origin and its inspiration becomes highly suspect. The question immediately arises: Are we really dealing with a *true* African? Let us dig up his graves. Let us check out his crania. Let us rip off his mummy wraps. Is the nose of the ancient Egyptian broad enough to be Negro? Are his lips thick enough? Does his jaw jut out far enough? Is his skin Black enough? Is he not just a tanned European? A brown Mediter-ranean? A Eurafrican? A Hamite? An Afro-asian? . . . "

* * *

The new archaeological finds in Africa that Charles Finch brings to our attention in this issue are so astonishing that they force us to review a considerable body of historical data. It means that an accepted and approved model used so far to explain the origin and nature of the African universe in general, and the Egyptian in particular, requires radical modification be-cause a whole new set of data does not fit into it. We now know, for example, using the most refined radio-carbon techniques, that the Great Pyramid was built at least 374 years earlier than we have been led to believe and that the pre-dynastic dynasty of Ta-Seti, excavated in 1962 by the expedition led by Keith Seele and Bruce Williams, is even earlier than had first been calculated, since it shifts backwards in time as a consequence of the shifted timeline of the dynasties of the north,

We are also presented with compelling new data about the Sphinx, the most monumental of human sculptures. It is important for all of us to exam-ine the details of this new data for it is telling us that the Sphinx was not really built by the Pharaoh Khafre but simply renovated by him and belongs to a period that precedes the dynasties of the north by several centuries. The new finds and datings at Katanda and Ishango in northeastern Zaire by an archaeological team (Brooks and Yellen) also make it clear that the womb or placenta-land of Nile Valley culture lies clearly within the continental heartland of Africa. The combination of new data is so momentous that it forces upon us dramatic changes in our vision of things.

Brooks and Yellen, a married team of archaeologists, found in the prehis-toric rubble of a district called Katanda in northeastern Zaire a startling assembly of bone harpoon points, all of which were so finely wrought, so elaborately barbed and polished, that they suggested a sophisticated aquatic culture in that area at some earlier point in time. These harpoons were very much like a type found elsewhere in strata dated 14,000 years ago but at Katanda, using the most refined radiocarbon dating techniques, this team arrived at datings going back 70,000 years.

Because modern homo sapiens appeared in Africa 140,000–200,000 years ago and many millennia separate them from this phase or movement in time, because also we are listening to the cautious voice of a team with impeccable qualifications, who have checked and double-checked every-thing, shocked as they are by these incredible datings, we should not dismiss this evidence lightly. It forces us to realize that serious archeology in inner Africa is only just beginning, that we have so far entered only a few rooms in the half-buried house of humankind.

The finds at Ishango by Jean de Heinzelin, redated by the Yellens (25,000 years old) are no less impressive. They provide links, as do the much earlier

Katanda finds, to the Nile Valley. At Khartoum near the Upper Nile and also at Es Shaheinab, near Khartoum, there are neolithic sites that contain harpoon points bearing the clear imprint of Ishango ancestry. Following another branch, the technology seems to move northward from Khartoum along the Nile Valley to Nagada in Egypt. But it is not just the tools and techniques that connect these places. Markings on a bone at Ishango reveal a familiarity with prime numbers, decimals and addition by duplication. This latter method of addition by duplication appears in the Rhind Mathematical Papyrus from Egypt, dating back 4,000 years ago. It is the oldest mathematical treatise on record. Ishango artifacts date back a lot earlier than that, of course, but the linkages are not nebulous at all. Finch's forging of links between the sites in Inner Africa and those in pre-dynastic Egypt are made with such density and delicacy of detail that I can only pinpoint a few of the conclusions here.

More evidence of significant and hitherto unsuspected connections between Egypt and the Great Lakes region of Africa come to light in Anthony Richards review in this issue of Egypt and the Mountains of the Moon by F.D.P. Whicker (1990). The very early contact between the two regions has been traced by a variety of minerals and parts of at least twenty two plants, all of which are found together in the wild within a small area of the Great Lakes region, at the foot of the Rwenzoris. There is a growing body of evidence, therefore, that makes good scientific sense of Finch's statement that "a well-defined culture, like humanity itself, flowed out of the lacustrine African womb into the rest of the continent" and that "the Nile served as a veritable umbilical cord, connecting the northern tier of the continent to its East African 'placenta-land'."

*   *   *

The misreading and misinterpretation of the skeletal evidence has been the greatest stumbling block to an acceptance of the African origins of the ancient Egyptian but, even more seriously, to an appreciation of the persistence and predominance of the African type during the critical formative dynasties of Egypt. It is difficult for many to understand how the so-called "true Negro" does not even represent the majority of African types on the continent. The African presents a variety of faces or phenotypes. There are at least six variants of the indigenous African whereas most skeletal studies have focussed on the form or fiction of ONE.

Keith Crawford writes on the variants of the Africoid type with the freshness of a wind blowing away the must of millennia from the mummies. He and his former teacher, Shomarka Keita, have helped to bring about a significant shift of thinking on this matter. What really constitutes the Africoid type? What environmental modifications occurred during the movements of this type across the length and breadth of the ancient Nile Valley, modifications removed from the myth of Mediterranean migrations or Mesopotamian mixings? What light do these cast upon the validity of previous studies done on the skeletal remains in ancient Egypt?

Crawford shows us in his essay "Racial Identity of Egyptian Populations based on Analysis of Physical Remains" that the placing of the African into a facile single-type classification to determine the race of the Nile Valley inhabitants has led to the grossest falsifications imaginable. No single myth in this whole field of study has done more damage than the monotypic classification of the African or Africoid.

Native African populations are phenotypically "polytypic", that is, there exists in Africa a variety of phenotypes (faces and/or body shapes) that may differ from the stereotypical "Negro", falsely formed and firmly fixed within the rigid imagination and classification of Eurocentric observers. Crawford outlines six of these variants or types. I shall, lest they be lost to students, highlight the main features of these types. There is the Elongated variant, to which General Aidid, who fought our troops to a standoff in Somalia, belongs. This variant is distinguished by an elongated body build, narrow head, face and nose, dark skin and spiralled hair, thick but not everted lips. They range from long to moderately long-headed, with a narrow nasal opening, long narrow face and mild to absent prognathism (that is, with either slightly protruding or non-protruding upper jaw/lower face). This stands in contrast to the classical Negro type but are indigenous, unmixed Africans. They were living in Africa long before Egypt was born. The Elongated type includes the Fulani, the Tutsi and the Hima (Rwanda) the Masai (Kenya) the Galla (Ethiopia) the Somalis (Somalia) and the Beja (Northern Sudan).

Then there is the Nilotic variant who is taller than the elongated type with a narrower head, a lower and wider nose, a very slender body, with extremely long legs and little fat. These Nilotic types include the Nuer, the Dinka, the Shilluk and the Anuak, all of whom occupy the Nile River basins in the Southern Sudan.

Most popular of all, of course, is that classical variant which innocents and experts alike fondly and foolishly refer to as the "true Negro". This variant is said to have skin color varying from dark brown to black, to be relatively long-armed and long-legged, of tall stature, broad shoulders, narrow hips, black and kinky hair, short, broad face, a considerable degree of prognathism (that is, with a jutting jaw or jutting lower face) flat nose, very depressed at the root, thick and often everted lips. There are also the pygmies, whose skin is reddish-yellow to light-brown, broad-headed with very wide nose. One should also make mention of the so-called "Bushman" variant, which is hard to box and bind into a single phenotype. This variant shows a remarkable degree of heterogeneity or diversity. Their types range from dark to light complexions, long to moderately long heads, pronounced to absent lower face protrusion. There are one or two more but they are fairly localised, hence the above mentioned will suffice.

The point to all these details about heads and noses and jaws and lips and skin color, is simply this. Some of these African variants have elements of their facial appearance that is characteristic of other races. As Crawford puts it "This must be the case since all races evolved from an African prototype and it was necessary that this type possess the potential to express multiple traits which could then be modified by the environment".

But, without the illumination of these scientifically precise classifications and their subtle modifications, and with only the distorting beams from the torch of racism to guide them, the Egyptologists of the 19th and 20th centuries could not see these remarkable ancient Egyptians as related to the peoples who had become Europe's despised colonials and vassals. They could not conceive that in a much earlier time, they had flowed into the Nile Valley from that devastated land which Europe's greed and Africa's despair were later to transform into "the dark continent". Thus the shock of Kemet's glory, shining through the ruins of its ancient graveyards, its monumental pyramids and sphinxes, statues and stelae, could not be seen as connected in any way with a brutalized, depopulated, fragmented and flattened Africa. The contrast between a great ancient empire, practically mummified in stone, with medieval centers in tropical Africa, beaten down and beaten back into the bush by the Holocaust of all Holocausts, was too brutal and blinding for one to see, without multi-dimensional lenses, any racial or cultural relationship. Thus did the peoples of inner Africa come to be excluded from all serious consideration as central players on the stage of ancient Egyptian civilization.

Thus it was, that whenever certain cranial traits characteristically found in Caucasoids were detected in African crania, this was used to show that the African had made spectacular strides only and because he was no longer a true African but a dark-skinned European, a brown Mediterranean, an Afro-European, an Afro-Asiatic, or a new fictitious concoction with a biblical derivation, the mythical "Hamite". Thus could one discount all his claims to unique and spectacular architecture, original discoveries in astronomy, complex and profound philosophical probings into the mystery of Matter and Being, revolutionary breakthroughs in the fields of medicine and mathematics. Such achievement was deemed impossible without generous infusions of the blood and brains of other races. If a single Caucasoid trait, therefore, occurred (such as a narrow nose, which is the product not only of ice but of dry heat) it meant that he had been heavily blended and blessed with imported first-class blood. Thus his *later* invaders could credit themselves with his *earlier* accomplishments.

*   *   *

It is the best of biographers who record not only the strengths and weaknesses of important leaders or thinkers but see them through critical lenses ground and tinted by the context of their place and time. Runoko Rashidi has done this for the late John G. Jackson, and, in this issue, for Chancellor James Williams and William Leo Hansberry.

I remember speaking from the same pulpit, along with Chancellor Williams, in the church of St. Augustine in Washington D.C. It was February, 1980, fourteen years ago. It was a strange and moving encounter. Chancellor was so gracious and gentle, almost avuncular. In spite of his age and infirmity, he stood on the platform like a great tree, swaying a little, slightly gnarled and bent by the winds of time. He spoke for at least an hour. His voice was tremulous but firm, his delivery sometimes slow but flawless, his speech melodiously phrased, the words bubbling effortlessly from his lips, trickles from a decanter of vintage wine. But the great pressures of the mission kept us sequestered thereafter in our separate spaces and studies. We were not to meet again in life.

Rashidi's comment on Chancellor's masterpiece "The Destruction of Black Civilization: Great Issues of a Race from 4500 BC to 2000 AD" is worth quoting: "Totalling uncompromising, highly controversial, broadly sweeping in its range and immensely powerful in its scope, there have been few books published during the past quarter-century focusing on the African presence in antiquity (particularly the Nile Valley) that have so profoundly affected the consciousness of an entire generation of African-Americans in search of their past." What made it so different from previous histories of Black people, Rashidi points out, is that it was specifically concerned "with Black civilization alone—what the Blacks themselves achieved independently of either Europe or Asia". This is what made it, considering both the time of its publication and its bold and novel approach to Black history, a groundbreaking work. Rashidi outlines the key elements in this work and highlights its main objectives.

I myself was influenced by Williams and I do not regret it. But I must point out that I followed one of his errors of judgment too uncritically and have paid for it. Rashidi, himself, is critical of this error. He speaks of Williams' questionable assertions about the predominance of the mulatto elements of the north. This mixing on a major scale was to occur a lot later than Williams thought. But it is quite understandable within the context of the time and does not seriously detract from the value of his work in the main. Shomarka Keita and Keith Crawford, Chatterjee and Kumar, A.C. Berry and R.J. Berry, just to mention a few, had not yet made their skeletal evidence available to us. This evidence in its definitive form was to come much later. But, even with the lack of it, Rashidi clearly shows that Chancellor was ahead on several fronts. Earlier Black historians before him were largely making subjective and rhetorical statements about Egypt, without the same level of supportive counter-evidence.

Rashidi goes on to introduce us to the work of William Leo Hansberry. Hansberry was to have a great influence on Chancellor as well as on Nnamdi Azikiwe, who became the first President of the Federal Republic of Nigeria. It is sad to learn in this brief biography that "Hansberry was slighted and snubbed for much of his life, not only by White Academia, but by many of his Black academic colleagues as well" and that "one of his great consolations was the love, admiration, and respect of his students".

In "Black Land of Antiquity" Rashidi performs a useful service for students who want to have a solid reference guide to what happened in ancient KMT and under what pharaoh and in what time and in what place. This is not the usual kings' list, with the names of the known and unknown rulers, the dates of their ascension to the throne and the dates of their demise. It is not a dramatic reconstruction either, no fictionalization or imaging of events, no faces of the great and famous, few records of their words, wise or foolish. But it is an overview of great events. The lack of extensive detail is no fault of the historian. That is all that we have, as we reach back into the most distant moments of human time. That is all that is passed down to us in the vast majority of cases. The events, however, the bleached and arid bones of antiquity, are fleshed by very detailed notes. Students are advised to pay close attention to these valuable footnotes.

We must remember that this was not the age of the common people. It is therefore the history of gods and kings, not of mere mortals. There are no newspapers recording current events in point-by-point detail. Also, the books that survive time and the sacking of the Library of Alexandria, are not historical novels but medical and mathematical papyri, treatises on the origins of god and the universe, the flow of the stars, the precession of the equinoxes, the motion and revolution of the planets. There are no reconstructions of sensational battles and romances, only the names of God's representatives upon the earth, the divine Pharaohs and their families, and occasional headlines, often scrawled on the walls of monuments and temples, of their divine happenings. Yet it is a valuable resource for all of us, a diary of the highlights of dynastic times. There is also the thread of a theme running through it. Rashidi places emphasis, for example, on the regenerative powers of the south. Several new and important phases in Kemetic history seem to begin with a southern intrusion, a southern inspiration. It is as if the sun goes down at times in the darkened north of Kemet only to rise again in the flame of a new morning on the southern horizon. This is a reference guide which all students should read and master. It is prepared with a comprehensive grasp of events, done with balance, concision and good judgement.

In his third contribution to this issue, Rashidi provides us with a lucid introduction to the Hamitic hypothesis, the subject of a more definitive essay by anthropologist Dana Reynolds-Marniche. The concept of Brown and Mediterranean races was grounded in the racist thinking of the 18th, 19th and early 20th century. Rashidi titles his article "From the Center to the Fringe" for, as he points out, this myth provided the basis for the removal of Black people *from the center of world civilization to the fringe.* This mythical "Brown Mediterranean" race formed the main bulk of the inhabitants of ancient Egypt and has been called the proto-Egyptian type. Strangely enough, when few Europeans were aware of the wonders of ancient Egypt, the mythical sons of Ham were thought of as Blacks but the moment they began to enter Egypt in great numbers following the Napoleonic expedition of 1798, they raised their eyes in incredulous wonder at the marvels of this civilization and there arose, as Rashidi puts it," the historical impetus to transform the Hamites into Caucasians". One of Diop's sarcastic remarks on these myth-makers, who sought to erase the Black from Egyptian history so that they could claim it, is aptly quoted: "They have invented," says Diop "the ingenious, convenient, fictional notion of the 'true Negro,' which allows them to consider all the real negroes on this earth as fake Negroes."

* * *

This introduction is just a curtain-raiser on "The myth of the Mediterranean Race" by Dana Reynolds-Marniche. She explains how this myth sprang up side by side with the myth of the Brown race or Hamite. They both proceed from the same motives of course. They both set out to show that the Aryan and the Eurasian were the originators of all of the earliest complex societies. They therefore had to explain away the problematic skulls and skeletons they found buried in these early civilizations that did not fit in with their schema. In parts of Southeast Asia and Europe were found the remains of a gracile, long-headed type, different from most modern Europeans. Not only that. These types were buried differently, in an embryonic or contracted position, rarely found among the other broad-headed Southwest Asians. To complicate matters, they had some traits normally associated with the so-called "Negro"—a fairly flat nose, a certain measure of prognathism. It did not occur to the investigators (since that was a much later scientific discovery) that the skull of a race is not of a permanent character, that it can undergo modification in a changed environment, and that what they were seeing was just one of several variants of the African.

To establish firm claim to the first civilizations, this type had to be proven Aryan or Eurasian. It could not possibly come from Africa or it would upset the apple-cart of the master-race mythology. Thus, absurdity followed absurdity. The peoples in Ethiopia and Somalia were likened to southern Italians or even Nordics. But a lot of new research methods have helped to dispel these racist notions. Reynolds-Marnische cites the most important of these—the analysis of the statistical frequency of skeletal traits known to be genetically based; fine-tuned studies of the blood and DNA. The conclusions arrived at by these new methods confirm that "the so-called Mediterraneans of Africa and elsewhere were really the result of a long evolution in African eco-systems". Why this is so important to our primary study in this volume is that, to quote her "the evidence from all sides has actually shown that populations related to modern Blacks south of Egypt were representative of the populations from earlier types of Africans".

Dana Reynolds-Marniche deals with all the celebrated racists who were major advocates of this concept—Guiseppe Sergi, Grafton Elliot-Smith, Carleton Coon. She identifies, exposes, and then systematically shatters, with the ammunition of a new science, all the hypotheses these gentlemen have built for over a century to block the African from early civilizations, especially the most revered, that of the ancient Egyptian. I close with her own words: "If these populations have been camouflaged by words that say nothing of the truth, then those words must be seen for what they are—scientific disguises and lies created to keep a mythical view of history and its evolutionary stages in place, and to deny the light stemming from a boundless Black past".

*   *   *

Manu Ampim sees Martin Bernal and Basil Davidson as "insider/outsider" scholars who constitute what he calls a counter school to the "Africentric movement". He is well aware that these scholars part company on important matters with the regular crowd of Eurocentric racists but he contends that, in spite of this, they are reluctant to give Africans their full due for the ancient Egyptian civilization and imply that Egypt, from rather early times, was a very mixed bag of races and that the Black African does not feature as a distinctive predominant element in this multiracial milieu.

Ampim argues that, while one can draw a tentative distinction between the useful aspects of their scholarship and their racism (however subtle or modified), the two elements (subjective racial reflex and scholarly discourse) cannot be separated fully. This is not just a simple black and white distinction, he contends. "All scholarship and ideas", says Ampim, "are based on socio-historical experiences and therefore reflect worldview and social interest. They are formed in a social context, and the very questions raised and the methodologies used are driven by worldview and a working set of assumptions. Thus a study in the sociology of knowledge is necessary to understand fundamental assumptions and motivations which produce scholarship and ideas". Ampim goes a step further and here is where he dives into very clouded water. "African people," he warns, "should be cautious when receiving European ideas, particularly on the African socio-historical experience, because the notion of 'scientific objectivity' is a Eurocentric myth".

As editor of a work, for which I shall be held totally responsible, as though I were the presiding Pen behind the hands of all its authors, whether I agree or disagree with them or not, let me issue a clear note of warning on this kind of critique, which, despite its protestations to the contrary, blends and therefore confuses two issues which should be conceptually separated and separately addressed. There is no question, as Ampim rightly states, that society shapes man as much as man shapes society and one's ideas (initially at least) sprout from the socio-intellectual soil within which one is conceived and nurtured. But man is not genetically glued or connected by his hair or pigment to a socio-intellectual garment or overcoat, be he white, yellow, or black. Man and his world is involved dynamically in an endless debate. Socio-ideological structures and frameworks interpenetrate each other. The sociological horizon of man is only one of the four walls in the house of consciousness and time that fences him in. The mind of man, therefore, is not in a walled prison. It is a river without banks. It is not clothed in Nature's imprisoning epidermis. It cannot be subjected to the melanin dosage test, having no fixed and final color. Ampim's critique has a certain value but only where it pinpoints specific errors of fact, specific conceptual contradictions, and this he does at times with an astute perceptiveness, but, if we were to follow him to the extremes to which he is sometimes driven, we could end up concluding that Frank Snowden, the ultra-conservative African-American historian, by virtue of the socio-ideology of his race, would tend to be more open on these matters than the revolutionary Gerald Massey, born in the lap of "white" privilege (and hence intellectually tainted from the start by his socio-racial environment). Even Ampim would agree that this is patently absurd. Nevertheless, in a world still primitively locked in clichés of race and color, it is hard to escape the imprisoning reflex that still dominates debate on these matters.

Basil Davidson has come a long way. So has Martin Bernal. If Chancellor Williams had lived to study Keita and Crawford and some of our other Journal authors he would no longer share the view of Davidson and Bernal that the north of Kemet was an essentially mixed and mulatto north. Were I not transformed by insights arising from my own work and the school I later founded through this Journal, I myself might be echoing the late Dr. Williams on this matter. Let us accept, and in this respect Ampim helps us, that there are still serious flaws in the approaches of these gentlemen to the study of Egypt, but we can examine and expose these flaws without dumping them neatly into a black/white bag, making the *pros* black and the *cons* white. It may simplify the debate for laymen, who love to settle complex issues with clear-cut polarities, but it can make it more difficult in the end for scholars who need to examine closely the subtleties and contradictions

in the so-called Bernal-Davidson school, which, according to Ampim, com-
promises and undermines the work of "Africentric" Egyptologists. May I
point out here, it is *not* even a school at all (that is, a fairly homogeneous or
conforming body of thought). One can be led to the conclusion that this
intellectual gang of two, after years of training in clever double-talk, skillfully plotted an infiltration into the "Africentric" ranks so that their surreptitiously planted contradictions could undermine the presumed unity of the
movement. What Ampim fails to realize is that there are glaring contradictions within their own ranks. Davidson, in spite of some reservations of his
own about Diop, raps Bernal hard on the knuckles for paying too little
attention to the intellectual achievement of Africans like Diop and his African-American counterparts, who, Davidson asserts, have done as much as
he (Bernal) to "topple the Aryan model". It may even be claimed, says
Davidson, that "this achievement is among the most significant intellectual
advances of the twentieth century". Davidson goes further in his attack on
his own *school* (or should we say his own *schoolmate*): "Bernal's treatment
of this important aspect of his subject," Davidson complains "is disappoint-
ingly deficient" (*Race and Class,* Vol. 29, No. 2, London, 1987).

Ampim, however, uses his critical skills to great advantage in his survey
of potential forgeries in the museums of the world. His brief study in this
volume of the statues of Ra-Hotep and Nofret, who have in all likelihood
been misrepresented as "white Libyans", is remarkably thorough. It is good
detective work. No one has commented with such microscopic rigor on
what so few, for so long, have allowed so many to take for granted.

*   *   *

Asa Hilliard, in his Carter Woodson lecture, acquaints us with the role
played by African and African-diasporan scholars in the study of the race
and ethnicity of the ancient Kamites. It is a roll-call of the Black Valhalla of
Kemetic scholars who have gone before us—Carter G. Woodson, Martin
Delaney, George Washington Williams, Frederick Douglass, William Leon
Hansberry, Druscilla Dunjee Houston, J.C. de Graft-Johnson, W.E.B. du
Bois. Cheikh Anta Diop, St. Clair Drake. John G. Jackson, Chancellor Williams. The list of our living scholars—African, African-American, Caribbean—now devoted to the study of African history in general and Kemetic
history in particular—is just as long and just as significant. Hilliard points to
the disturbance in American conservative circles over the opinion and influence of some of these contemporary scholars. Arthur Schlessinger, for example, the famous Pulitzer Prize winner, foresees their "unauthorized ideas"
about a black Kemet as "threatening the unity of America itself".

One is grateful for the no-nonsense approach that Hilliard brings to bear
on these matters. He points out, for example, that this is no unified school of
thought and that the new data researched and presented is not to be characterized as "Africentric" data. *The data is simply valid or invalid and should*

be dealt with in that way. He attacks the media for focussing on *two queens of KMT who are of foreign descent, Nefertiti (daughter of the Persian king Dushratta) and Cleopatra VII (a descendant of the Ptolemaic line from Macedonia, possibly with some African mixture).* They are almost always selected by the media as the illustrations for articles that discuss KMT, especially articles about the race of the Kemites. May I interject here. *Some* "Afrocentric" commentators, by their superficial approach to these figures of ambiguous racial ancestry, have brought this one down upon themselves. What of Queen Tiye, he asks, and I have asked this a thousand times myself (having initially chosen her as the centerpiece of my anthology on women) what of this unmistakably black-skinned and dark-eyed "lady of both lands", falsely described by the Nazi historians of the thirties as having white skin and blue eyes?

Hilliard also places Bernal's contribution to Egyptology in proper context. "Bernal argues that European nationalist scholars cared deeply about the perceived relationship between KMT and Europe. He contends that it was the emergence of white supremacist scholarship, for the purpose of rationalizing slavery and colonization, and for building the self-esteem of Europeans that led nationalists to attempt to degrade Kemet and to fabricate a mythical past for Europe.

"The degradation of Kemet could not be done easily in the face of texts, architecture, monuments, art work, etc., an overwhelming record of excellence. Therefore some scholars tried to whiten its population, and hopefully, physically and conceptually, to separate KMT from the African continent . . . "

"Bernal has done an excellent job" Hilliard claims "of documenting what he called the fabrication of information about KMT, *not the assertion that KMT was a black nation, a position that he never takes . . .*" The real bombshell of Bernal's Black Athena was not about Africa at all, it was about Greece. He charges that much of our conception of Greece and its relationship to KMT was fabricated, largely by German nationalist scholars during the 18th and 19th centuries. They sought to explain the Civilization of Greece by arguing for northern invasions of Aryans who were supposed to be the culture—carriers or producers. The goal of these historians, according to Bernal, was nothing less than to demonstrate an "immaculate conception of Grecian civilization, free of the taint of Black Africa . . . *That was Bernal's task.*"

One last word of vital importance to us in this discourse. Hilliard emphasizes a number of points on which all participants in the UNESCO debate on the peopling of Egypt found consensus. One stands out above all else. That there was absolutely no evidence of large-scale migration between Kemet and Mesopotamia. No Mesopotamiam loan-words were found at all in Kemetic.

This I wish to emphasize as I close my commentary on the highlights of the Carter G. Woodson address by Asa Hilliard. Nothing has annoyed me more than the almost religious insistence by some scholars that Mesopotamia profoundly affected Egypt in its formative stages, that it gave Egypt the seed for its hieroglyphic system and its pyramids. Not a single shred of evidence exists for this outrageous but persistent assumption. On this matter, the Unesco historians were unanimous. That the two cultures could have had no genetic linguistic relationship or be populated by the same people.

*   *   *

Peggy Brooks-Bertram has done extensive research on the Black Kings of Kush and has come up with such an abundance of half-hidden data that she proposes an entirely new name-change for what we have come to accept all along as the Twenty-Fifth Dynasty of Egypt. This name-change is not suggested simply out of a scholar's fastidiousness. The new data reveals a long line of unknown Nubian kings which leads us into a new understanding of what was happening for centuries south of Egypt. The dynasty of Kush, which conquered Egypt in the 8th century B.C. is not to be seen any longer as a mere interloper dynasty which came into its own because of the waning lights and powers of the North. Five dynasties based at Napata, running parallel and separate in the south, preceded this. The Nubians, then, the princes of Kush, stood in the blaze of their own sun, not just in the borrowed light, the sunset flicker of another empire. We have been habituated into seeing them as lesser than their brothers in the north, as semi-barbarians standing in awe on the broken steps of a grand but fallen house, the twenty-fifth rung of a disintegrating staircase. That is why they have been represented in so many museums under the most contemptuous classifications. All I saw, as I, in my college days, walked through the museums of Britain, looking at these figures, were name-tags screaming "Period of Decline". Enough of this! No more. From now on, this should be known by its corrected name—The Sixth Napatan Dynasty of Kush. It stands in the golden hue of its own primal light. Nubia, after all, was there in the morning of times. *Khenti* is the Egyptian word not only for "south" but for "first". The Nubians (let it be repeated until it rings like bells tolling the death of a myth) the Nubians initiated the first pharaonic dynasty, Ta-Seti. Most Egyptologists are still fearfully silent about this 1962 discovery. The Nubians are still being portrayed as the "colonized", the "tribute-bearers", the "enslaved", the "culture-copiers".

As Brooks-Bertram points out "it is both possible and necessary to extricate the Kushite kings from the shadow of Egypt and view them within the context of their own pharaonic civilization, a civilization distinguished by a history and tradition in some ways different from, although, in its earlier phase, seminal to that of Egypt". Sixteen unknown kings preceded Alara and Kashta, who overthrew Egypt. If you allow thirty years roughly to a generation as constituting a dynasty, she contends, one arrives at a Sixth

Napatan dynasty.

She presents us with a photo gallery of this family of pharaohs. Through her painstaking research, she provides us also with what is probably the most definitive statement so far on the life and times of Taharka, who, in 13 years of peace and 13 years of war, left the most indelible mark on Napatan history. Finally, she identifies the problems which plague archaeological efforts not only to portray this remarkable individual in particular but the Kushites in general.

*   *   *

Our final essay in Part One of this issue is by Wayne Chandler. "Seven Times Seven" takes a comprehensive look at the seven Hermetic axioms of ancient Egypt and their historical impact on science, religion and mysticism. The ancient Egyptians claim that what came to be known as the Hermetic philosophy was originally bequeathed to them in remote antiquity by Tehuti or Thoth. Thoth would later become immortalized as one of the most prominent gods of ancient Egypt. The followers of Thoth-Hermes advocate that, through proper study of the Hermetic principles, one may acquire a complete understanding of universal order and one's relationship to it, thereby enabling one to control one's destiny. In this work, (of which this essay is but an introduction), Chandler examines these principles closely, giving the reader a provocative insight into the way in which religion, history, and the dynamics of personal life were perceived in the Hermetic teachings. The complete work should be published shortly by Black Classic Press.

*   *   *

We have published eighteen issues of the *Journal of African Civilizations* since we launched this historical series in 1979. Twelve of these eighteen issues are anthologies with titles, only two of which have been discontinued. The best of these two issues appear in the anthologies still in print. For example, we revive in this issue a study I did on the influence of an African-Caribbean ritual cult (vodun) on the art of Haiti, from my 1981 anthology *African Presence in the Art of the Americas*. We also reprint in this current issue all the science essays that appeared in *Nile Valley Civilizations* since they are most relevant to our study of the African contribution to ancient Egyptian civilization. Other essays that appear in this discontinued volume are to be found elsewhere—Chiekh Anta Diop on African mathematics in *Great African Thinkers*; Ivan Van Sertima on the *African Presence in Early America* in the anthology bearing that title; Runoko Rashidi on the *African Presence in Early Asia* in the anthology bearing that title; Charles Finch on the origin of the Christ-figure in ancient Egypt and its complex symbolism, in his own collection of essays published by Karnak House, London. We intend to keep the ten anthologies we now have in print in permanent circulation, and to create new titles as time goes on but at a more structured pace.

Our urgent concern over the next five years is to ensure the use of these books as texts in colleges. The audio tapes issued by *Legacies Inc* are equally important since those tapes bearing the book titles summarize and crystallize the most important elements in the texts and give to teachers and students alike, a more thorough understanding of the subject matter. The work of a whole generation of scholars will go to waste unless these works can enter "the curriculum of inclusion" or, as it is known in some places, "the multi-cultural curriculum". To help in this process, we shall be introducing major study guides to these texts, and, in some cases, accompanying videos. These will be published (at the rate of one or two a year, beginning with the fall of 1995) by Van-Patten Productions. They will be announced, both in the reprints of our anthologies (which are constantly being updated, revised, extended, indexed) as well as in our annual Xmas mailings.

This is the beginning of a major revolution in thinking which goes beyond mere protest rhetoric, which attempts, with the utmost seriousness, to change the perception everywhere of the role of people of African descent in the history of the world. This cannot be accomplished without the help of many people. We therefore urge our readers to join in this crusade. You can do this simply by completing your own personal library of the books and the audio tapes (and by securing the forthcoming study guides and videos) by alerting your family and your friends, your local bookstores and libraries, your school systems at all levels, so that we may continue this critical revision of history that we have started.

Ivan Van Sertima

Ivan Van Sertima, Chancellor Williams, Ernest Withers, Jr.

"I remember speaking from the same pulpit, along with Chancellor Williams, in the church of St. Augustine in Washington D.C. It was February, 1980, fourteen years ago. It was a strange and moving encounter. Chancellor was so gracious and gentle, almost avuncular. In spite of his age and infirmity, he stood on the platform like a great tree, swaying a little, slightly gnarled and bent by the winds of time. He spoke for at least an hour. His voice was tremulous but firm, his delivery sometimes slow but flawless, his speech melodiously phrased, the words bubbling effortlessly from his lips, trickles from a decanter of vintage wine . . . But the great pressures of our mission kept us sequestered thereafter in our separate spaces and studies. We were not to meet again in life."

—Ivan Van Sertima

DR. CHANCELLOR JAMES WILLIAMS (1893-1992): AN APPRECIATION OF HIS CONTRIBUTIONS TO THE RECONSTRUCTION OF AFRICAN CIVILIZATION

By Runoko Rashidi

> *I consider myself, and I always emphasize this, that I am a student of history. I've found out that there is so much to be done—so very much to be done—so much yet to be done—such a vast untouched amount—that we are just students.*
> —Chancellor Williams, *Conversation with Jake Beason*

Among the recent preeminent scholars involved in the effort to eradicate the racial myths overshadowing the African origins of Nile Valley civilization, few have had the impact of Dr. Chancellor James Williams (1893–1992). Dr. Williams achieved wide acclaim as the author of *The Destruction of Black Civilization: Great Issues of a Race from 4500 B.C. to 2000 A.D.* In this work, Chancellor Williams "shifted the main focus from the history of Arabs and Europeans in Africa to the Africans themselves—a history of the Blacks that is a history of Blacks."[1]

Dr. Chancellor James Williams

Chancellor James Williams, the youngest of five children, was born in Bennetsville, South Carolina, on 22 December, 1893. His father had been a slave, his mother a cook, a nurse, and evangelist. Williams' elementary education was completed in Bennetsville at the Marlboro Academy. After moving to Washington, D.C. (where he lived for more than seventy years), he attended Paul Laurence Dunbar High School and Armstrong High School, graduating from the latter. Williams received a Bachelor of Arts degree in Education from Howard University in 1930 and a Master of Arts degree from the same institution in 1935. He did post-graduate, non-resident studies at the University of Chicago and the University of Iowa. Williams obtained a Ph.D. in Sociology from American University in Washington, D.C. in 1949.

In 1945, Chancellor Williams joined the faculty of the Howard University History Department. He retired in 1966 but returned in the early 1970s as a distinguished lecturer. It was while at Howard University, first as a student and later as a teacher, that Williams came under the guiding influence of one of the finest Africanist scholars of the twentieth century—William Leo Hansberry.

Dr. Williams was a Visiting Research Scholar at Oxford University, England and the University of London in 1953 and 1954. In 1956, he began direct field studies in African history. He was based at University College in Ghana, which later became the University of Ghana. Williams was actually in that country when it gained independence from Britain on 6 March 1957 under the leadership of Kwame Nkrumah. The final phase of the field studies, which covered twenty-six countries and 105 language groups, was completed in 1964.[2]

The career of Chancellor Williams was multi-faceted and varied: university professor; President of the Log Cabin Baking Company; Vice President and General Manager of Cooperative Industries; Editor of *The New Challenge*; U.S. Government economist; high school teacher and principal; historical novelist and author-historian. He was the father of fourteen children. Blind, and in poor health, the last years of his life were spent in a nursing home in Washington, D.C. He died on 7 December 1992. His legacy, however, remains distinct, vibrant and alive.

Contributions to the Reconstruction of African Civilization

In 1961, Public Affairs Press published one of Chancellor Williams' most important and scholarly works—*The Rebirth of African Civilization* (a study of Africa in transition and programs of actions). In 1965, Pencroft Books published Williams' *Problems in African History: A College Lecture Series*. In *Problems in African History*, Williams wrote: "Africans and persons of African descent must assume the primary responsibility and leadership in historical research. . . . if we are to continue to leave practically all important historical research and writing concerning the black race to the white man, then we must be prepared to accept, uncomplainingly, the white man's point of view."[3]

Chancellor Williams is probably best known as the author of *The Destruction of Black Civilization: Great Issues of a Race from 4500 B.C. to 2000 A.D.* Totally uncompromising, highly controversial, broadly sweeping in its range, and immensely powerful in its scope, there have been few books published during the past quarter-century focusing on the African presence in antiquity (particularly the Nile Valley) that have so profoundly affected the consciousness of an entire generation of African-Americans in search of their past. Dr. Asa G. Hilliard III, one of America's foremost African-centric scholars and educators, describes *The Destruction of Black Civilization* as "the masterpiece by Chancellor Williams that tells a comprehensive story of the development and destruction and suppression of the culture and civilization of the people of Africa."[4] Dr. John Henrik Clarke, a contemporary of Dr. Williams and one of our greatest living scholars, describes *The Destruction of Black Civilization* as "a foundation and new approach to the history of our race."[5]

The Destruction of Black Civilization was first published in 1971 by Kendall/Hunt in Dubuque, Iowa. In 1972, the book won an award "for pioneering work in African History" from the Black Academy of Arts and Letters. In 1974, Third World Press published a revised and expanded edition of *The Destruction of Black Civilization*. The 1971 edition of *The Destruction of Black Civilization* was dedicated to William Leo Hansberry and Carter G. Woodson (research pioneers in African history); the 1974 edition to the Black youth of the 1960s. In 1979, for *The Destruction of Black Civilization*, Chancellor Williams became the first recipient of the *Clarence L. Holte International Biennial Prize* by the 21st Century Foundation.[6] Ivan Van Sertima's *They Came Before Columbus: The African Presence in Ancient America* was awarded the *Clarence L. Holte International Biennial Prize* in 1981.

The Destruction of Black Civilization attempts to answer the question of why the great African civilizations declined. It is the summary of sixteen years of documentary research and field studies, and was originally intended as a two volume history of the African people. Dr. Williams pointedly explained that:

> The writing plan for the two volumes would have required at least another five years, even if the serious impairment of my vision had not occurred. In the meantime there had developed an urgent need for the results of my research which concentrated on crucial areas in the history of the Blacks that had been either unknown, known and misinterpreted, or known but deliberately ignored. My own history classes were only a part of the rebellion against the only kind of textbooks available. It was a general rebellion against the subtle message from even the most 'liberal' white authors (and their negro disciples): 'You belong to a race of *Nobodies.* You have no worthwhile history to point to with pride.'[7]

The Preview to the work itself is a masterpiece. It is both comprehensive and revolutionary in its approach, considering that Dr. Williams was specifically concerned "with Black civilization alone—what the Blacks themselves achieved independently of either Europe or Asia."

This was an entirely new approach to the study of the history of the Blacks. It meant, first of all, segregating traditional African institutions from those later influenced by Islamic Asia or Christian Europe. In this way, and in no other, we can determine what our heritage really is and, instead of just talking about 'identity,' we shall know at last precisely what purely African body of principles, value systems or philosophy of life—slowly evolved by our own forefathers over countless ages—from which we can develop an African ideology to guide us onward. In other words, there can be no real identity with our heritage until we know what our heritage really is. It is all hidden in our history, but we are ignorant of that history.[8]

The Destruction of Black Civilization is undoubtedly a classic and pioneering work with great strengths and few flaws, the flaws including the paucity of footnotes and Williams' rather questionable assertions about the "Mulatto Problem" in African history. But, as Williams noted:

In the 'View from the Bridge' and the final chapters, I make a more definite break from the 'old line' school of historians. To be objective and scientific, this school insists, the research scholar should do no more than present the comprehensive and fully documented results of his investigations. There should be no 'subjective' commentaries, no editorializing. Just present the factual data and leave the work to the readers to interpret or evaluate as they choose.

This may not only be the correct viewpoint, but it is even beautiful for historians who represent the already arrived people who control the world. They can well afford the luxury of historical knowledge for knowledge's sake—the great satisfaction that comes from just knowing how things came to be.

But the Black historian, member of a race under perpetual siege and fighting an almost invisible war for survival, dare not follow in these footsteps of the master. Quite the contrary, after faithfully researching and piecing together the fragmented record of the race's history, the task of critical analysis and interpretation should begin. What were our strengths in the past? In what respects were we most vulnerable? Where did we go wrong? And all this, like the study of history itself, must be for the express purpose of determining what to do now. In short, the Black historian, if he is to serve his generation, must not hesitate to declare what he thinks the results of his studies mean. For even when our history shows us where we have been weak, it is also showing us how, through our own efforts, we can become strong again.[9]

Many of the key elements of the *The Destruction of Black Civilization*, as outlined in the Preview, are stated below:

1. Africa is the native homeland of Black people. The Asiatic peoples who occupy Northern and Eastern Africa, even though they may have been there for centuries, are no more native Africans than are the Europeans who likewise occupy and control the southern regions of the African continent.

2. All *unmixed Africans* are not jet black. For while the great majority are black skinned, countless numbers who have lived for long periods in cool areas have lighter complexions and no "Caucasian blood" at all.

3. African people were among the earliest builders of monumental civilizations, including the development of scripts, sciences, engineering, medicine, architecture, religion, and the fine arts.

4. How such an advanced civilization was lost is one of the greatest and most tragic issues in human annals, and should be the primary thrust of research studies in African history.

5. Asian imperialism, though seldom acknowledged, has been even more devastating for African people than European imperialism; and the Arabs' white superiority complex is not one whit less than that of Europeans, although their strategy of 'brotherhood' deceives naive Blacks.[10]

6. The forces behind the continuous splintering of already small groups and even the breaking up of kingdoms and empires, followed by the equally endless migrations, included the steadily increasing death of the soil and the advance of the deserts; the drying up of lakes and rivers, along with the attending climatic changes and internal strife—combined with foreign invasions and famine to become a way of life.

7. The strength and greatness of African people can be measured by how, in the face of what at times seemed to be all the forces of Hell, they fought through to survive it all and reconstructed kingdoms and empires—some of which endured for centuries.

8. Within the framework of even the smallest surviving states African people maintained the basic principles of the traditional African constitution, and held on through all the passing centuries to the fundamental elements of its ancient democratic, social, political, and economic systems all over the African continent.

9. Africa was the birthplace and cradle of a religious civilization based on the conception of one supreme god, creator of the universe.

10. Irrespective of the remarkable civilizations Africans developed, African people fell far behind in the forward march of the rest of humankind because, in addition to the destructive forces of nature on the continent and the hostile forces from without, African people further enshackled themselves with their own hands through certain aspects of their social institutions and beliefs that stood as roadblocks to progress even where conditions were favorable.

Dr. Williams emphasized and concluded that the reconstruction of African civilization "will call for a new kind of scholarship, a scholarship without any mission other than the discovery of truth, and one that will not tremble with fear when that truth is contrary to what one prefers to believe."[11]

Appendix I

William Leo Hansberry (1894–1965):
Hero and Mentor of Dr. Chancellor Williams

> *Hansberry was my hero. He was the greatest single influence on me.*
> —Chancellor Williams,
> *Interview with George Kent*

Chancellor Williams was profoundly influenced by William Leo Hansberry as a teacher, mentor, and friend.[12] The 1971 edition of *The Destruction of Black Civilization* was dedicated to William Leo Hansberry and Carter G. Woodson. In the Bibliographical Note to *The Destruction of Black Civilization*, Williams wrote that "Standing alone and isolated in the field for over thirty-five years, William Leo Hansberry was the teacher who introduced me to African history and, of equal importance, to the ancient documentary sources. His massive documentation of early Greek and Roman historians and geographers of Africa covered several years of labor, leaving one to wonder how the utterly false teaching that Africa had no written history spread over the world."[13] In 1972, Chancellor Williams noted of Hansberry: "The life and work of this remarkable man influenced mine directly. For while I resolved to take up the work where he left off, I took it up defiantly and with the high resolve that, having slowly and painstakingly carried on the research on the highest level of scholarship as he did, I would not care a snap about what either white or Negro critics think or say about my works."[14]

Professor William Leo Hansberry—one of the most distinguished and determined Africanist scholars of the twentieth century—was born in Gloster, Mississippi on 25 February 1894. He attended Atlanta University in 1916, where he came under the influence of Dr. William Edward Burghardt DuBois (1868–1963). In 1917, Hansberry transferred to Harvard University where he became a student of archaeologist George Andrew Reisner (1867–1942), and a receptor of sympathetic advice from anthropologist Earnest Albert Hooton (1887–1954). In addition to his studies at Harvard, where he received his B.A. degree in 1921 and M.A. degree in 1932, Hansberry conducted research at the University of Chicago in 1936, Oxford University in 1937 and 1938, and the University of Cairo in 1953 and 1954.

After teaching for a year at Straight College in New Orleans, Hansberry joined the faculty of Howard University in September, 1922, where he taught courses on African civilizations and cultures until his retirement in June 1959. In 1922, Professor Hansberry initiated the African Civilization

Section of the Howard University History Department. In June 1925, he organized and coordinated a major symposium and exhibition held at Howard on *The Cultures and Civilizations of Negro Peoples in Africa*, where twenty-eight scholarly papers were presented by his students, sixteen of which were by women.

In August, 1927, Hansberry spoke at the Fourth Pan-African Conference in New York on the topic of archaeological research in Africa and its significance for African people. In 1934, he helped organize the Ethiopian Research Council, of which he became director. The aims of the Ethiopian Research Council were to "stimulate interest in Ethiopia's efforts to resist the Italian invasion," which took place in 1935, "and to disseminate information on Ethiopian history, ancient and modern. Correspondents were located in London, Paris, Rome, and Addis Ababa; affiliates were listed in Ethiopia, France, and Panama, in addition to Chicago, New York, and Philadelphia."[15]

During the mid-1950s, Hansberry engaged in field research in Ethiopia, Egypt, Sudan, Kenya, Uganda, Zimbabwe, Zaire, Ghana, and Nigeria; and visited Tanzania, Malawi, Zambia, and Liberia. In 1955, for the *Journal of Negro Education*, he reviewed George G.M. James' classic—*Stolen Legacy*. In 1955 and 1956, for the *Washington Post* and *Africa Today*, he reviewed Ghanaian scholar J.C. deGraft-Johnson's *African Glory: The Story of Vanished Negro Civilizations*. Although Hansberry produced a number of impressive written works, it is highly unfortunate that his own *magnum opus*, *The Rise and Decline of the Ethiopian Empire*, was never published, although both Kwame Nkrumah and Nnamdi Azikiwe invited him to publish the work in Africa.

Hansberry was slighted and snubbed for much of his life, not only by White Academia, but by many of his Black academic colleagues as well. One of his greatest consolations though, was the love, admiration, and respect of his students. Besides Chancellor Williams, one of Hansberry's most prominent pupils was Nnamdi Azikiwe, who became the first President of the Federal Republic of Nigeria.[16] Lorraine Hansberry, the brilliant playwright, was Hansberry's niece.

On 22 September 1963, Hansberry delivered the inaugural address at the formal opening of the Hansberry College of African Studies at Nsukka, University of Nigeria. In 1964, he became the first recipient of the African Research Award from the Haile Selassie I Prize Trust. On 3 November 1965, at the age of seventy-one, William Leo Hansberry died of a cerebral hemorrhage.

Appendix II

Chancellor Williams on the African Presence in Asia: The Task Ahead of Us

The special character of *The Destruction of Black Civilization* is apparent from the start, beginning with the epigraph, where Dr. Williams reproduces a tantalizingly anonymous Sumer legend. The Sumerians, centered in the fertile valley of the Lower Tigris-Euphrates, were the creators of the earliest known monumental civilization in Asia.[17]

> 'What became of the Black People of Sumer?' the traveller asked the old man, 'for ancient records show that the people of Sumer were Black. What happened to them?' 'Ah,' the old man sighed. 'They lost their history, so they died.'

It is this very epigraph, by the way, simple though it may seem to some, that has captivated and sustained a number of researchers currently engaged in reconstructing the history of the African presence in Asia:

> I only made passing reference in the work to Blacks scattered outside of Africa over the world—not from the slave trade, but dispersions that began in prehistory. This fact alone indicated the great tasks of future scholarship. . . . We are actually just on the threshold, gathering up some important missing fragments. The biggest jobs are still ahead.
>
> Ancient China and the Far East, for example, must be a special area of African research. How do we explain such a large population of Blacks in Southern China—powerful enough to form a kingdom of their own? Or the Black people of Formosa, Australia, the Malay peninsula, Indo-China, the Andaman's and numerous other islands? The heavy concentration of Africans in India . . . opens still another interesting field for investigation. . . . For again, reference is not made to small groups which may have wandered anywhere over the earth; rather, our concern is with great and dominant populations. These are the Blacks who have so puzzled Western scholars that some theorize that Asia or Europe may be the homeland of Africans after all. The African populations in Palestine, Arabia, and in Mesopotamia are better known, although the centuries of Black rule over Palestine, South Arabia, and in Mesopotamia should be studied and elaborated in more detail.[18]

Notes

1. "I have shifted the main focus from the history of Arabs and Europeans in Africa to the Africans themselves—a history of the Blacks *that is a history of Blacks*. They will be coming back—center stage—into their own history at last. But to what end? Will it be just for the intellectual satisfaction of *knowing* our true history? Knowing it, yes—but *so what?* The answer is *nothing*—unless from history we learn what our strengths were and, especially in what particular aspect we were weak and vulnerable. Our history can then become at once the foundation and guiding light for united efforts in serious planning what we should be about now." Chancellor Williams, *The Destruction of Black Civilization,* rev. ed. (Chicago: Third World Press, 1974), 45.

2. "In so far as the study of African history is concerned, I regard direct investigation in the field—and in Africa—as of the highest importance. This field work should be undertaken only after thoroughgoing research in written and other documentary sources. The study of available written sources, their evaluation, and the mounting archaeological records are all the first major phase of African research and, I would say, a prerequisite for field-work" Williams, 27.

3. Chancellor Williams, *Problems in African History* (Washington, D.C.: Pencroft Books, 1965), 6.

4. Asa G. Hilliard III, *A Selected Bibliography (Classified) and Outline on African-American History from Ancient Times to the Present,* rev. ed. (East Point: Hilliard, 1991), 90.

5. John Henrik Clarke, Quoted on the back of *The Destruction of Black Civilization,* rev. ed. (Chicago: Third World Press, 1974).

6. Williams, *The Destruction of Black Civilization,* rev. ed. (Chicago: Third World Press, 1974), 17.

7. "The first three recipients of the prize were Dr. Chancellor Williams in 1979; Dr. Ivan Van Sertima in 1981; and Dr. Vincent Harding in 1983.

Since 1985, the Phelps-Stokes Fund has managed the $50,000 endowment portfolio, and the Schomburg Center for Research in Black Culture has administered the operations for the prize." *Black Bibliophiles and Collectors: Preservers of Black History,* eds. Elinor Des Verney Sinnette, W. Paul Coates and Thomas C. Battle (Washington, D.C.: Howard University Press, 1990), 137.

8. Williams, 19.

9. "In studying the actual records in the history of the race, therefore, the role of White Arabs must not be obscured either by their Islamic religion or by the presence of the Africans and Afro-Arabs among them any more than we should permit white Europeans and white Americans to use Christianity to cover their drive for power and control over the lives of other peoples" Williams, 24.

10. Williams, 22–23.

11. Williams, 44.

12. For comprehensive well-documented accounts of William Leo Hansberry's life and works, see Joseph E. Harris, "Profile of a Pioneer Africanist," in *Pillars in Ethiopian History: The William Leo Hansberry African History Notebook,* vol. 1, ed. Joseph E. Harris (Washington, D.C.: Howard University Press, 1974): 3–30; James G. Spady, "Dr. William Leo Hansberry: The Legacy of an African Hunter," *A Current Bibliography on African Affairs* (Nov/Dec 1970): 25–40; Larry Obadele Williams, comp., *William Leo Hansberry: Pioneer of Africana Studies in the Americas* (Atlanta: Ipet Isut, 1989).

13. Chancellor Williams, *The Destruction of Black Civilization* (Dubuque: Kendall/Hunt, 1971), 223.

14. Chancellor Williams, "William Leo Hansberry, Teacher: As Seen by a Former Student," in *A Tribute to the Memory of Professor William Leo Hansberry* (Washington, D.C.: Howard University Department of History, 1972), 18.

15. Harris, 24.

16. "He was my teacher *in* Anthropology during my undergraduate years in 1928 and 1929. Since then he had become an intimate friend whose wise advice and encouragement sustained me in periods of crisis." Nnamdi Azikiwe, "Eulogy on William Leo Hansberry," *Negro History Bulletin* (Dec. 1965), 63.

17. Runoko Rashidi and Ivan Van Sertima, eds., *African Presence in Early Asia*, rev. ed. (New Brunswick: Journal of African Civilizations, 1988).

18. Chancellor Williams, *The Destruction of Black Civilization*, rev. ed. (Chicago: Third World Press, 1974), 44.

Dr. Chancellor James Williams (1893–1992):
A Selected Bibliography

Compiled by Runoko Rashidi, Yemi Toure,
and Larry Obadele Williams

Books by Chancellor Williams

The Raven. New York: Dorrance & Co., 1943.
And If I Were White. Washington, D.C.: Shaw Publications, 1946.
Have You Been to the River? New York: Exposition-University Press, 1952.
The Principals and Their Tasks: Research Studies in Current Educational Problems in the South. Tuskegee Press, 1954.
The Rebirth of African Civilization. Washington, D.C.: Public Affairs Press, 1961.
Problems in African History: A College Lecture Series. Washington, D.C.: Pencroft Books, 1965.
The Destruction of Black Civilization: Great Issues of a Race from 4500 B.C. to 2000 A.D. Dubuque: Kendall/Hunt, 1971.
The Destruction of Black Civilization: Great Issues of a Race from 4500 B.C. to 2000 A.D. Rev. ed. Chicago: Third World Press, 1974.
The Second Agreement with Hell. New York: Carlton Press, 1979.
The Rebirth of African Civilization. 1961; rpt. Introduction by Anderson Thompson. Chicago: Third World Press, 1993.
The Rebirth of African Civilization. 1961; rpt. Introduction by Baba El Senzengakulu Zulu. Acknowledgment by Dorothy Rose. Hampton: UB & US Communication Systems, 1993.

Chapters in Textbooks

"Sociological Trends in Africa South of the Sahara." In *Contemporary Sociology.* New York: Philosophical Library, 1958.
"Pan African-Asian Movements." In *Contemporary Political Ideologists.* New York: Philosophical Library, 1960.
"The Teaching of African History." In *The Teaching of History.* New York: Philosophical Library, 1967.
"Educational Obstacles to Africanization in Ghana, Nigeria and Sierra Leone." *Journal of Negro Education* (Summer 1961): 261–65.
"William Leo Hansberry, Teacher: As Seen by a Former Student." In *A Tribute to the Memory of Professor William Leo Hansberry.* Washington, D.C.: Howard University Department of History, 1972: 17–18.

Articles in Encyclopedias

"The Empire of Mali." *International Encyclopedia*, New York: 1969.
"Songhay." *International Encyclopedia*, New York: 1969.

Conversations and Interviews with Chancellor Williams

Beason, Jake Patton. "A Conversation with Dr. Chancellor Williams: Black Historian, Author." Chap. in *Why We Lose: An Anthology for Black People's Cultural Survival*. Milwaukee: Beason, 1989: 49–73.
"Black Books Bulletin Interview Chancellor Williams." *Black Books Bulletin* 1, No. 4 (1973): 27–31.
"How Black Civilization Was Destroyed: Why Did It Happen? An Interview With Chancellor Williams." *Tony Brown's Journal* (Apr/June 1982): 11–12.
Kent, George. "George Kent Interviews Chancellor Williams." *The Black Position*, No. 3 (1973): 16–38.

Works About Chancellor Williams

Alexander, Bill. "Chancellor Williams: Keeper of the Flame." *Black Issues in Higher Education*, 28 Jan 1993: 18–22.
"The Amazing Dr. Williams: Distinguished American Historian Studies Nyasaland." *The Times* (Malawi), 17 Mar 1964: 7.
Bailey, A. Peter. "50,000 Prize for Black Literary Excellence." *New York Amsterdam News*, 3 Mar 1979: 13.
Baillou, Charles. "Pan-Africanism Called Cure to Black Troubles." *New Dimensions* 1, No. 24 (1993): 7.
Beason, Jake Patton. "Biographical Sketch: Dr. Chancellor Williams." Chap. in *Why We Lose: An Anthology for Black People's Cultural Survival*. Milwaukee: Beason, 1989: 75–98.
Carr, Greg E. Kimathi. *Chancellor Williams' The Destruction of Black Civilization: Study Guide, Book 2*. Los Angeles: The Association for the Study of Classical African Civilizations, 1993.
Cheatwood, Kiarri. "African Reverence: Chancellor Williams." *Black World* (Dec 1975): 46–47.
Jennings, La Vinia Delois. "Chancellor Williams." In the *Dictionary of Literary Biography*, Vol. 76. *Afro-American Writers, 1940–1955*. Edited by Trudier Harris and Thadious M. Davis. Detroit: Gale Research, 1988: 196–99.
Muhammad, Donald. "Chancellor Williams Remembered: World Loses Great Black Historian." *The Final Call*, 25 Jan 1993: 25, 36.
"Negro Professor to Study SR's History." *Daily News* (Zimbabwe), 19 Mar 1964: 3.
Petrie, Phil W. "Dr. Chancellor Williams: Celebrating Our Glorious History." *Essence* (Dec 1981): 134.
Toure, Yemi. "Elder Statesmen: An Era is Passing for Five Authors Known for Reclaiming the Role of Blacks in History." *Los Angeles Times*, 3 Mar 1991: E1.
Trescott, Jacqueline. "Righteous Brother: Chancellor Williams' Studies in Black Pride." *Washington Post*, 5 Mar 1980: B1.
Williams, Larry Obadele, comp. "Chancellor Williams." In *Towards An African Historiography: A Bibliography*. Atlanta: The Ipet Isut, 1989: 34–35.

Book Reviews

Ayaga, Odeyo Owiti. "Three Book Reviews: *Introduction to African Civilizations*, by John G. Jackson; *The Destruction of Black Civilization: Great Issues of a*

Race from 4500 B.C. to 2000 A.D., by Chancellor Williams; *Black Man of the Nile*, by Yosef ben-Jochannan." in *Black World* (Aug 1973): 51–52, 73–77.

Clarke, John Henrik. Review of *The Destruction of Black Civilization: Great Issues of a Race from 4500 B.C. to 2000 A.D.* In *Your Black Books Guide* 1, No. 3 (1990): 3–4.

Harris, Robert L. Jr. Review of *The Destruction of Black Civilization: Great Issues of a Race from 4500 B.C. to 2000 A.D.* In *Black World* (May 1975): 51–52.

Killens, John Oliver. Review of *The Destruction of Black Civilization*. In *New Directions Magazine* (Apr 1975): 32–36.

Lanier, R. O'Hara. Review of *The Rebirth of African Civilization*. In the *Journal of Negro Education* 31, No. 4 (1962): 479–81.

Peay, Mark. Review of *The Destruction of Black Civilization*. In *Nommo* 24, No. 3 (1992): 10.

Perry, Thelma D. Review of *The Destruction of Black Civilization*. In the *Negro History Bulletin* (Feb 1975).

Thompson, Anderson. "Destruction of Black Civilization: A Review Essay." In *Black Books Bulletin* 1, No. 4 (1973): 14–17.

This unusual photograph of the Sphinx was taken by Dr. Willard Johnson of M.I.T. It should be compared with a startlingly identical line drawing of a facial reconstruction of the Sphinx by New York Detective, Frank Rigo. The drawing, establishing the Africoid features of the Sphinx, appears in a *New York Times* Op-Ed article by John Anthony West.—*The Editor*

NILE GENESIS:
CONTINUITY OF CULTURE
FROM THE GREAT LAKES TO THE DELTA

Charles S. Finch III, M.D.

There is a concept that is used in contemporary physics called the "paradigm shift." Fundamentally, it means that an accepted and approved model explaining the physical nature of the universe requires radical modification because a whole new data set does not fit into it. Paradigm shifts can be momentous or modest but they often compel dramatic changes in our vision of things. The concept seems applicable to any scholarly or scientific pursuit and, in recent years, our understanding of ancient history has been undergoing a paradigm shift. We are being forced to radically readjust our optic on ancient history because more and more we are stumbling upon evidence that shows that Africa is the real crucible of modern human culture. Tidy little categories such as "paleolithic," "neolithic," and "prehistoric" no longer seem adequate to explain the emerging evidence for the extreme antiquity of advanced culture in Africa.

Physics is largely free of "political" biases; not so the study of ancient history. Though paradigm shifts in physics may engender intense intellectual struggles, the weight of accumulating evidence usually carries the day. A paradigm shift affecting our image of ancient man is another matter; too much racial mythology and ideology are wrapped up in it. Often, new empirical evidence in the fields of ancient history, no matter how compelling, is ignored or rejected without a hearing. Still the tendency is clear: the more we explore the archaeology of Africa, the more we find that modern human culture took root there first. Since the human species was born in Africa, the unfolding of the traits of advanced human culture there seems entirely consistent.

Ishango and Katanga: Cradlelands of African Culture

Alison Brooks and John Yellen are a married team of archaeologists from

George Washington University who have been working for some years in northeastern Zaire along the shores of Lake Edward, in the neighboring districts of Katanda and Ishango.[1] Their scientific credentials are impeccable and they are the embodiment of methodical, meticulous field researchers. Yet their findings among archaeological populations in the lake districts of Zaire have somewhat strained their natural caution. The artifacts they are uncovering and testing by the most refined radiocarbon techniques are giving them results that may force the jettisoning of the conventional chronology of paleolithic East African culture. This is not a situation that, from a scholarly point of view, is to be taken lightly.

From the prehistoric rubble of Katanda where the team was working, Yellen, in 1988, extracted a finely-wrought, fossilized bone harpoon point.[2] This was the first of several such finds:

> . . . two more whole points and fragments of five others turned up, all of them elaborately barbed and polished. A few feet away, the scientists uncovered pieces of an equally well-crafted daggerlike tool. In design and workmanship the harpoons were not unlike those at the very end of the Upper Paleolithic, some 14,000 years ago. But there was one important difference. Brooks and Yellen believe the deposits . . . were at least *five times that old* (my emphasis).[3]

Their conviction that a relatively advanced culture existed in east-central Africa 70,000 years ago is underscored by earlier work by Brooks on the related Ishango site. This site, just four miles from Katanda, was first excavated by the Belgian, Jean de Heinzelin, in the late 1950s, where he found a harpoon-rich "aquatic civilization," as he called it.[4] His original date for the site was 8,500 B.P. but Brooks redated the site more than 25 years later with more sensitive radiocarbon instruments and found, instead, that the site dates back to 25,000 B.P., making it three times older than original estimate![5] Furthermore, the stratigraphy of the Katandan deposits is much deeper than that of the adjacent Ishango and, as the above quotation indicates, the Brooks-Yellen team thinks that the artifacts there are more nearly 70,000 years old. These dates are perplexing because they mean that these cultures had already reached a level of technical development not achieved outside Africa until 54,000 years later.

Storms of controversy persist around the locus of modern human origins; several researchers continue to look for sites outside Africa for evidence of modern human beginnings.[6] But the most compelling evidence fixing the geographic region where humanity first appeared continues to trickle in from the lacustrine regions of east-central Africa. Even where Africa's role as the biological womb of humanity is conceded, many still assume that complex culture evolved elsewhere.[7] However, this recent work by Brooks and Yellen more firmly situates the cultural cradle of humanity in Africa.

Indeed, Brooks's redating of the Ishango site puts the famous Ishango Bone in an entirely new perspective.

When De Heinzelin first excavated the Ishango site with its cache of bony harpoon heads, he came across a bone tool carrying groups of peculiar markings on it. A close examination convinced him that these markings represented an arithmetic system revealing a familiarity with prime numbers, decimals, and addition by duplication.[8] The Harvard archaeologist, Alexander Marshack, could not bring himself to accept evidence of "mesolithic" mathematics in central Africa but he did become convinced that the marks on the bone represented notations marking the lunar cycle.[9] Very likely, there is truth in both explanations and, therefore, the evidence of the Ishango Bone reveals an intellectual sophistication that no one would have accorded mesolithic populations living in east-central Africa some 9,000 years ago.

Brooks' recent radiocarbon datings have fermented the brew even more: since Ishango dates back 25,000 years, these people were not mesolithic but *paleolithic*. De Heinzelin had noted that the Ishango artifacts seemed archaic by comparison to other mesolithic populations and Brooks' datings cleared up the mystery. But mathematics and lunar calendars in Africa in the Upper Paleolithic period? With a tantalizing possibility that such skills in that region might be older yet? The conventional model of cultural evolution advanced by Marshack may have to be reconsidered.

Brooks and Yellen are not unmindful of the minefield they have to cross. Brooks herself has said, "It is precisely because no one believes us that we want to make our case airtight before we publish. We want dates confirming dates confirming dates."[10]

De Heinzelin's study of the harpoon heads and the Ishango Bone convinced him of something else: the culture revealed by these artifacts was carried virtually intact northward into the Nile Valley region of Africa. Thus, De Heinzelin tells us,

> From central Africa the [harpoon] style seems to have spread northward. At Khartoum near the upper Nile there is a site that was occupied considerably later than Ishango. The harpoon points found there show a diversity of styles . . . [other harpoons] have the notches that seem to have been invented first at Ishango. Near Khartoum, at Es Shaheinab, is a Neolithic site that contains harpoon points bearing the imprint of Ishango ancestry; from here the Ishango technique move westward along the southern border of the Sahara.[11]

De Heinzelin goes on to say,

> The technology also seems to have followed a secondary branch northward from Khartoum along the Nile Valley to Nagada in Egypt. This

site has both bone and copper harpoons. Made in the Neolithic period
before the Egyptian dynasties began, many of them are notched at the
head. Others show the influence of the Near Eastern Natufian technique
and the Fayum technique which is closely related to it.[12]

It would seem, if De Heinzelin is correct, that a well-defined culture, like
humanity itself, flowed out of the lacustrine African womb into the rest of
the continent. The Nile seemed to serve as a veritable umbilical cord, connecting the northern tier of the continent to its East African "placenta-land."
It has to be wondered if this is the reason why one of the ancient Egyptian
names for Africa south of the Nile Valley was *Ta-Kenset*, literally "placenta-land."

The reference to the Natufian harpoon technique in the above quote is of
interest because the Natufian culture of Syrio-Palestine can be dated back
10-12,000 years and the human fossil remains associated with this culture
denote a clear Africoid type.[13] The similarities of Nile Valley and Natufian
harpoon manufacture probably indicate a broader cultural kinship and if the
source of these harpoon styles is the Lake Edward horizon, it is not implausible to assume that the Ishango/Katandan culture radiated beyond Africa
directly into Western Asia.

The peopling of the Nile Valley from the Africa's Great Lakes region
must have occurred over and over again in waves. The population wave
from the Great Lakes directly ancestral to the historical Nile Valley peoples
probably began to settle north of the second cataract no later than 15,000
years ago. This settlement did not pre-empt later migrations, of course, but
most of these probably came in from the west, that is from the Sahara,
beginning about 10,000 years ago.[14] Another line of migration apparently
trickled in intermittently from the horn of Africa along the Blue Nile from
10 to 6,000 years ago. The dynastic Egyptians' never-ending fascination
with *Punt*, their name for the Horn of Africa, and clear attestations from
them regarding their kinship with the Puntites, compel us to look in that
direction for an ancestral lineage of the peoples who created pharaonic
culture. There seems to have been a touch of religious awe associated with
Punt since it was also referred to as *Ta-Neter*, i.e., "Land of the God."

One last word regarding the Ishango Bone: De Heinzelin thinks that the
Bone demonstrates a knowledge of addition by the method of duplication.
This is of surpassing interest because the very same method of addition is
utilized in the Rhind Mathematical Papyrus from Egypt, dating back nearly
4,000 years ago.[15] It is the oldest mathematical treatise on record. Is it possible that this mathematical procedure reached the Nile Valley directly from
the lacustrine horizons of East Africa?

The Cultural Horizons of the Nile Valley During
the Pre-Dynastic Epoch

The founder of pre-dynastic Nile Valley archaeology was William Flinders Petrie whose excavations at Nagada and Ballas in Upper Egypt nearly 100 years ago unearthed the first artifactual evidence of the cultures pre-existing historical pharaonic society. Petrie eventually excavated more than 1,200 pre-dynastic graves. Other pre-dynasticists, such as Quibbell, De Morgan, Brunton, and Caton-Thompson, refined and extended his research considerably during the next 40 years but Petrie established the basic principles of pre-dynastic archaeology and worked out a dating method that is still used.[16]

At Nagada and Ballas, Petrie found an almost invariant burial scheme: (1) the body was contracted into the fetal position, (2) the head positioned toward the south, and (3) the face pointed toward the west. Moreover, the graves always contained the personal possessions of the deceased. On the strength of this artifactual evidence alone, it seems clear that many of the ideas featured in later pharaonic religion existed in prototype among these predynastic people at Nagada. The fetal position evokes the idea of rebirth. The southward orientation of the body echoes the dynastic references to the south as *Khenti*, "the land of beginnings." The south is also *Ta-iakhu*, "the land of the spirits," where the souls of ancestors dwell. The face pointing west is reflected in the place name *Amenta*, "the hidden land," for *Amenta* is the western region where the soul of the departed journeys after it quits the body. Finally, dynastic Egypt was proverbial for the amount of worldly goods interred with the deceased. The elaborate funerary cult of dynastic times seems to have evolved directly from pre-dynastic practices.

Petrie found thousands of vases and pots of varying styles in these Nagada graves. After six years of continuous work, Petrie, in 1900, managed to group all the pottery into nine classes and, more impressively, assign a correct temporal sequence to each class. This became known as his famous *Sequence Dating*, a method still in use. Sequence Dating allows the determination of the time relationship among different pre-dynastic vases—and therefore of the cultures that produced them—but *not* the absolute dates of their manufacture. Petrie created Sequence Dates (S.D.) from 20 to 79, with 30 representing the earliest pre-dynastic pottery styles in his sample and their associated culture(s), and 79 representing the 1st Dynasty. He very sensibly reserved Sequence Datings under 30 for pottery sequences and cultures yet to be discovered. Petrie assigned a tentative date for his earliest pottery sequences, e.g. S.D. 30, of 8,000 B.C. This chronology was, within his lifetime, downdated considerably to 5,500-4,500 B.C. Petrie, to the end, never accepted such low dates.[17] The low dates, nonetheless, have held sway up to now, though recent research has been compelling a reconsideration.

The names given by Petrie to the two pre-dynastic cultural sequences delineable by his pottery classes were "Amratian" and "Gerzean." Modern pre-dynasticists often use the terms Nagada I and Nagada II to refer respectively to Petrie's Amratian and Gerzean. These and other predynastic cultural horizons extended into the Sudan.

As more and more pre-dynastic material was recovered in Egypt and Nubia, it became clear to Petrie at least that there was a uniformity of culture that spanned Egypt and Nubia. It was Petrie's conviction that there was "a peaceful, if not a united, rule all over Egypt and Nubia" during the entire pre-dynastic period.[18] More recent research has tended to confirm that assessment. In fact, there is evidence that this predynastic cultural unity encompassed all of the lands hugging the Nile from the confluence of the White and Blue Niles at Khartoum to the apex of the Delta.[19] That parts of this Nile Valley culture-complex can be traced to Africa's Great Lakes region has already been touched upon.

Though pre-dynasticists such as De Morgan and Quibell found and excavated additional graves at Nagada and Ballas, no older cultures were unearthed until the excavations of Brunton and Caton-Thompson in 1928 at Badari, 100 miles north of Nagada. The artifacts discovered were clearly pre-dynastic and eventually determined to be more archaic than those recovered from Nagada and Ballas. These cultures became known respectively as "Tasian" and "Badarian" and were assigned Sequence Datings between 20–29. Though at first they seemed to be distinct horizons, with the Tasian being older and more primitive, they were eventually linked together as the same culture in different phases, e.g., the "Tasian-Badarian" sequence. Under Petrie's schema, this cultural sequence would be at least 12,000 years old (10,000 B.C.), but modern dating, though not consistent, takes it back maximally to 5500 B.C. and minimally to 4,000 B.C.[20]

The Badarians were culturally a thriving people, most renowned for their hand-made pottery. Their vases were fashioned with a durability, finish, and extraordinary thinness that were never to be surpassed. They were also notable for well-turned ivory utensils and the use of copper. Theirs is the longest pre-dynastic sequence in the Nile Valley.

The Amratians succeeded the Badarians and their pottery was characterized by distinctive red bodies with black tops and also a style with white, crossed-lines. It is in the Amratian sequence that stone vases appear for the first time. In an advance over the Badarians, the Amratians not only worked extensively and more variously in copper but also in gold. Faience and blue glazing of quartz appears with them.

The Gerzeans, the last distinct cultural sequence preceding the dynasties, reveal themselves to have been a people on the brink of formal civilization. Their pottery shows unique features: buff coloration with red zigzag lines and spirals, designs of many-oared boats, and representations of flamingoes and sometimes of people. Stone vases are more varied in shape and fashioned from more diverse materials. Copper use is general, as is gold, and small quantities of silver—probably imported from Western Asia—appear. Ornamental iron beads are present and glass-making appears for the first time in the Nile Valley.

Given the received 1st Dynasty date of 3100 B.C., the extremely low dating of 4,000 B.C. for the entire pre-dynastic era recently advanced creates a crowding phenomenon.[21] If accepted, we are then required to assume that three successive, well-defined cultural horizons took root and then vanished in the Nile Valley in the space of 900 years. When, as will be noted below, evidence surfaces that pushes the dynastic period back to 3500 B.C., the crowding becomes even more severe, leaving only 500 years for the entire pre-dynastic era.

A word should be said about the pre-dynastic horizons discovered in Lower Egypt. The first was found near Merimde, just west of the Delta, and dated to 4880 B.C.[22] The Merimdens were a mixed farming and hunting people, roughly contemporaneous with the Badarians to the south, but culturally very different from them. The difference seems so pronounced that the Merimdens have seemed "un-Egyptian" to some. Phenotypically, they were of small stature and rounder of head than the dolicocephalic Badarians, but more significant was their very different burial practices. The Merimdens buried their dead inside their settlements instead of in separate graveyards and included no personal belongings or food offerings with the deceased. As will be discussed below, a high proportion of mother-child burials among the Merimdens seems to reflect a "matristic" or matrilineal cultural focus, but this element seems to have originated from a place very different from where the Badarians came from. Since their manner of house-building and their agriculture shares similarities with Neolithic Near Eastern societies, many have looked toward Palestine for the original home of these people. But there exists an older horizon in the Nile Valley that furnishes clues to the provenance of the Merimdens.

About 150 miles south of Merimde, as the crow flies, lies the Fayum depression. In antiquity, it served as a water reservoir in the dry season for dynastic Egyptians but it is also significant for two related pre-dynastic cultures discovered there. In archaeological terms, these horizons are called "Fayum A" and "Fayum B," confusing because Fayum B is actually older, dated to 6300 B.C. The Fayum horizons seemed to have distinct affinities with Neolithic Saharan cultures, known to have been in existence as early as 8100 B.C.[23] The Fayum, Merimde, and Near Eastern horizons all seemed to share certain traits and may all have been extensions of the Saharan cultural complex.

As noted, the Lower Egyptian pre-dynastic horizons at Fayum and Merimde appear markedly different from the Upper Egyptian/Nubian ones.

In fact, they are not strictly considered pre-dynastic at all but rather late Neolithic horizons existing at a lower cultural stage than the Badarian or Nagadan sequences. Lower Egyptian pottery is very crude by Badarian standards and neither Fayum nor Merimde, unlike the Badarians and Nagadans, knew of metal. The consensus is that the civilizing impulse leading to dynastic pharaonic culture emerged in the south. It might be said that classical Nile Valley civilization evolved primarily in the region between Assiut (Badari) and the 2nd cataract (Ta-Seti).

Despite clear and unequivocal indicators, the geo-ethnic provenance of the creators of Nile Valley civilization continues to be a contentious issue. For this reason, some space must be devoted to a discussion of it. As we have seen, Petrie was of the opinion that there was a kind of cultural unity linking the pre-dynastic horizons of Egypt and Nubia. Sir Alan Gardiner shared this opinion:

> However striking the change from the one stage to the other may appear, the continuity of the evolution as a whole must be affirmed with all emphasis . . . there was an affinity between Libyans, Egyptians, and Nubians which confirms our description of the earliest culture of the Nile Valley as *essentially African* (my emphasis).[24]

Others echo this assessment. The noted pre-dynasticist Fekri A. Hassan asserts:

> The earliest Neolithic levels in the Nile Valley . . . shared a common Saharan-Nilotic base, as well as some Near Eastern affinities . . . These regional cultural differences are not associated with biological differences. Investigations of crania from Badarian settlements indicated that they were similar to those from Nagada, Abydos, El-Amrah, and Hu.[25]

Petrie himself observed that the numerous female figurines found at Nagada—associated with the early Amratian and Gerzean sequences beginning S.D. 34—showed the steatopygy typical of the southern African Khoisan type.[26] While it is doubtful that these early Nile Valley dwellers were pure Khoisan, it seems evident that their place of origin is to be sought in Africa's southerly regions. Moreover, skull studies of the Badarians after their discovery by Brunton and Caton-Thompson have almost unanimously identified them as southern in origin.[27]

Recently, an excellent review of the data on the "skull metrics" of Nile Valley/North African populations by S.O.Y. Keita has shed additional light on these questions.[28] Keita notes that previous studies of the Badarian and Nagada I (Amratian) series of skulls when compared to those disinterred from Kerma in the northern Sudan, show nearly identical phenotypes.[29] Keita conducted his own multi-variate analyses of 10 skull series from

North Africa (west of Egypt), the Nile Valley, East Africa and West Africa to ascertain phenotypic clusterings on a broader continental scale. The Nile Valley series included 72 pre-dynastic skulls, 22 from Badari and 50 from Nagada. Keita duly noted the interpretive problems occasioned by the small sample size but he still found, consistent with earlier data, that both the Badarian and Nagadan skull series clustered phenotypically around those of Kerma (Nubia), East Africa (Kenya), and West-Central Africa (Gabon).[30] This phenotypical clustering extended to dynastic Abydos, the mythical home of Osiris:

> The Nagada and Kerma [Nubia] series are so similar that they are barely distinguishable in the territorial maps; they subsume the first dynasty series from Abydos.[31]

In a follow-up article, Keita discussed the 1st Dynasty Abydos series more fully, finding that 57% of the skulls in that series could be assigned a southern origin.[32] But throughout his writings, Keita expressed a caveat also articulated by the late C.A. Diop, to wit: a "monotypic" classification cannot be used to determine absolutely the pre-dominant ethnicity of the dwellers of the Nile Valley.[33] In this case the monotype of the oft-caricatured "Negro," that is the type possessing an elongated cranium, jutting jaw, crispy hair, flaring nostrils, everted lips, bandy legs, and black skin, cannot be considered fully representative of native Africans. As Keita suggests, native African populations are phenotypically "polytypic," that is, there exists in tropical Africa a variety of phenotypes that deviate significantly from the caricature. A casual perusal of almost any indigenous African group can convince even an untrained observer of the truth of this assertion. Dolicocephalic skulls and sub-nasal prognathism, as seen in many pre-dynastic Nile series, do establish a southern provenance but a modification or absence of this distinct phenotype in certain Nile Valley skull series do not necessarily "de-Africanize" them.

Another feature of the pre-dynastic graves, from the Badarian epoch down through the Gerzean, that points to a southern origin is the unmistakable "matrifocal" ethos. A number of pre-dynasticists have noted the superior wealth of women's graves and the feminine gender of the greater number of pre-dynastic figurines.[34] Fekri Hassan gives us the clearest exposition of the implications of the feminine "bias" of these artifacts:

> Ritual and supernatural beliefs associated with agricultural life must have emerged with the beginnings of the Neolithic. A study of figurines and mortuary goods from the Nagada region indicates that such beliefs and rituals were closely related to women. Lineage was probably matrilineal as indicated by the exclusive internment of women and children at Merimda. This may have been because women were associated

with grinding grain and making bread and gruel as well as brewing beer and, perhaps, initially planting grain.[35]

Thus, even the Lower Egyptian horizons, like the one at Merimde, evince a definite matristic character. As is well-attested, this matrifocality/matrilineality, at least in social and domestic relations, continued in Egypt to the end of dynastic history. Matrilineality, in fact, was the almost invariable rule of succession governing the pharaonocracy. The custom undoubtedly derived from African antecedents.[36] Since a linkage between the Merimden and Saharan horizons is evident, it can be inferred that the custom was more or less general throughout Neolithic Africa.

Early in this essay, evidence was brought forward linking the Ishango/Katandan horizons with those in the Nile Valley, Sahara, and Syrio-Palestine. In fact the Natufians of 10,000 years ago in Palestine shared phenotypic affinities closer to the Badarians than they did the Merimdens, whose culture is said to have been more closely related to those of the Near East. It has been customary to separate the Near East from Africa. Ethno-culturally though, in the light of increasing Neolithic evidence, it is perhaps more nearly correct to consider the lands between Khartoum in the south and the Tigris-Euphrates in the north as constituting one broad horizon in the period between 10,000 and 5,000 B.C. This broad horizon was composed substantially of "Saharo-Nilotic" ethno-cultural elements. Regional differences and variations were certainly evident in this larger cultural complex, but on-going techno-commercial relations linked the various groups of this horizon.

It is certainly true that what is known as the Near East is more properly thought of as Africa's "Northeast Extension," because geologically and geographically that is in fact what it is. It was the main corridor of human migration out of Africa into the rest of the world beginning 100,000 years ago and it makes sense to find that the earliest definable Near Eastern Neolithic populations, the Natufians, are indisputably Africoid. There seems to be no good reason not to believe that prior to 5,000 B.C., this "Northeast Extension" participated in the various cultural horizons of Africa. Thus when we look at the Neolithic Near East, we are looking culturally at a "province" of Neolithic Africa.

Radiocarbon Dating of Nile Valley Horizons:
Old Arguments, New Finds

As has already been intimated, the absolute chronology of the Nile Valley is a hotly contested subject. Despite his status as the founding father of pre-dynastic Nile Valley studies, Petrie's chronology very early underwent criticism and revision, resulting in considerable downdating of his original estimates of pre-dynastic time. Recent work by Fekri Hassan, based on extensive radiocarbon datings of pre-dynastic sites, has pulled the Badarian epoch down to 4400-4000 B.C. Even these dates are not consistent with thermoluminescent tests giving a Badarian date of 5500 B.C. Nonetheless, Hassan, a respected authority, published no fewer than six radiocarbon studies of predynastic sites between 1980 and 1988. High resolution radiocarbon instruments have brought much greater precision to dating technique but anomalies still persist, judging from other work.

One such anomaly has arisen from recent radiocarbon datings of organic materials extracted from the Great Pyramid and numerous other pyramids, temples, and tombs in the Giza\Sakkara area by Herbert Haas and his colleagues.[37] Sixteen organic samples were extracted from the Great Pyramid, 13 of these were of charcoal. After instruments in the two testing laboratories were calibrated, results were obtained on the 16 samples that gave a range of ages the researchers found startling. The oldest radiocarbon date on the Great Pyramid came from a charcoal fragment from the 198th course, giving a date of 3809 B.C. The youngest date came from a mortar of limestone from the second course giving a date of 2853 B.C. Averaging all the dates on the 16 samples together, Haas and his team determined that, by radiocarbon testing, the pyramid was *minimally* 389 years older than the given "historical date," that is, it was built around 2978 B.C. In fact, all 10 of the monuments/temples evaluated were older than the received "historical" dates by an average age of 374 years. If, in round numbers, it can be said that these Old Kingdom monuments are about 400 years older than previously believed, then the beginning of the 1st Dynasty goes back *minimally* to 3500 B.C. As we have seen with other evidence adduced above, it is hard to reconcile these monumental radiocarbon data of Haas's with Hassan's radiocarbon readings giving a date for the beginning of the predynastic era of 4,000 B.C. Even a somewhat remoter allowable date of 4400 B.C. (Hassan) for the Badarian period hardly seems plausible. The thermoluminescent date given by Hoffman of 5500 B.C. for the Badarian period at least has the virtue of creating more chronological space for the pre-dynastic era.

Ta-Seti and the Beginning of Nile Valley Civilization

Complicating matters is the seldom-referred-to work by Bruce Williams concerning the Ta-Seti kingdom discovered at Qustul.[38] The site was excavated for the first time in 1962 by Keith Seele who, even then, thought that the size and wealth of the tombs marked them as royal.[39] Systematic analysis of the artifacts, however, did not take place until 15 years later by Bruce Williams at the Oriental Institute, adding a hitherto unknown chapter to Nile Valley history. In one sense, however, the Qustul artifacts confirmed what Egyptian annals had already attested: there were whole dynasties that immediately preceded the 1st Dynasty under Menes.

Qustul lies in Nubia, more than 100 miles south of Aswan and the 1st cataract, and is now covered over by Lake Nasser. Qustul was a well-known site for what is known as A-group Nubian culture, contemporaneous with and related to the Gerzean pre-dynastic complex of Upper Egypt. The archaeological context of the tombs found in a burial spot known as "Cemetery L" showed clearly that they were older than the 1st Dynasty. When the tombs were opened, a startling variety of goods and materials were present, including five different kinds of pottery, expensive, finely-crafted jewelry, copper weapons, gold bracelets, and incense burners. All or parts of 1,000 separate ceramic vases and 100 stone vessels were recovered. As Williams said,

> The range of these and other fragments from the plundered cemetery began to indicate a wealth and complexity that could only be called royal.[40]

The place and date of this find contravened all accepted models for the appearance of pharaonic civilization in the Nile Valley and since Williams' original article in 1980, an intransigent myopia has relegated the Qustul finds to the fringes of academic Egyptology:

> Tombs of this size, wealth, and date in Egypt would have been immediately recognized as royal. Their extraordinarily varied contents would have been taken as evidence of a complex culture exposed to wide outside connections. But because the discovery was made in Nubia at a time and a place when kingship was thought impossible, further proof of royalty is necessary.[41]

Hieroglyphic signs on a seal from another related find at Siali, also located in Nubia just above Aswan, furnished a name for the kingdom to which this royal tomb belonged: Ta-Seti, "Land of the Bow." Inscribed scenes from the seal and from an incense burner show Ta-Seti kings engaged in military campaigns in Upper Egypt and Libya. Moreover, some of the vases in the tomb were of Syrio-Palestinian manufacture. These pieces of evidence give a picture of a powerful regional kingdom conducting far-flung commercial, diplomatic, and military activities as far as 1,000 miles away, even beyond Africa itself.

A sequence of tombs affiliated with 12 pharaohs comprise Cemetery L at Qustul. This complex of royal tombs led Bruce Williams to believe that the ruling dynasty of Ta-Seti stretched back 300 years prior to the 1st Dynasty. What Williams didn't categorically say, but what logically follows from the evidence, is that Ta-Seti represents the beginning of pharaonic civilization and is truly a founding dynasty, segueing directly into the unification dynasties inaugurated by Aha-Menes. The line of pre-dynastic pharaohs mentioned in certain annals must be that of Ta-Seti and therefore Ta-Seti belongs in the scheme of "proto-dynasties" that governed early Nile Valley history. Bruce Williams himself implies something of the sort in the original article on the subject:

> Apparently, the demise of Qustul coincides with the campaign of Aha in Nubia, the first king of the Egyptian First Dynasty, who recorded the smiting of Ta-Seti.[42]

Ta-Seti was therefore brought down by its successor dynasty, that of Aha-Menes, the one that unified Egypt and inaugurated the formal dynastic era. Ta-Seti can be said to represent the transition between the late pre-dynastic Gerzean cultural sequence and the formal dynastic period.

The temporal relationship of Ta-Seti to the 1st Dynasty is ascertained by the same contextual analysis that gave rise to Petrie's sequence dating. Thus, we have no absolute chronology for Ta-Seti; its dating is relative to that of the 1st Dynasty. Evidence has been adduced above that pushes the 1st Dynasty back to 3500 B.C. Thus, if Ta-Seti is known to have appeared 300 years before the 1st Dynasty, its date of origin goes back to 3800 B.C. With the appearance of Ta-Seti, true civilization ascends the stage of history in the Nile Valley. These additional chronological facts compress the pre-dynastic era too severely to entertain a Badarian date of 4400 B.C.

Chronology and the Calendar

The other factor bearing on the complexities of early Nile Valley chronology is that of the calendar. Since the author has treated this question at length elsewhere, it is only necessary to devote but a little space here to this aspect of the problem.[43] It is enough to say that the earliest identifiable calendar date we have is 4241 B.C. from Egypt's famed Sothic calendar, the one still in use today. The existence of such a sophisticated calendar, a seamless calendric interdigitation of the solar and Sirian movements, presupposes an equally sophisticated culture creating it. Though it is possible that a late, relatively advanced predynastic culture/such as the Gerzean, was capable of such an astronomical feat, it seems more plausible that such a calendar was the product of a true civilization. It is just another conundrum among many that chronologists and historians of the Nile Valley have wrestled with.

New Dates for the Sphinx: New Dates for Nile Valley Civilization?

In spite of the contradictory mass of facts introduced so far, more recent evidence yet threatens to blow *all* the carefully contrived schemes of Nile Valley chronology out of the water. This evidence comes from a wholly unexpected source that has sat literally in front of the very eyes of travellers, writers, and scholars for as long as there has been an Egypt; that is to say, the enigmatic and legendary Sphinx. One is reminded of the remonstrance of Sherlock Holmes to Watson: "You see but you do not observe." However, an amateur Egyptologist named John Anthony West, acting on a clue from the writings of Schwaller de Lubicz, did see *and* observe. What is more, from what he saw and observed, West drew the obvious conclusion.

The late R.A. Schwaller de Lubicz, the aforementioned mentor of John Anthony West, was a decidedly heterodox metaphysician and antiquities scholar who boldy challenged some of the most cherished principles of Egyptology. Predictably, the academic Egyptologists have reacted to the ideas of Schwaller de Lubicz and his school with derision. Among other things, this school holds that Egyptian civilization is millennia older than the textbook Egyptologists claim and West found a startling confirmation of this conviction in and around the Sphinx.[44]

The evidence for a greater antiquity of Nile Valley civilization has been "hiding in plain sight," as it were. The Sphinx reposes in an enclosure or quarry just below and to the east of the plateau of Giza, the site of the three great pyramids of Egypt. Even a casual visitor to the Sphinx cannot fail to notice the deep and numerous fissures on the wall of the ditch surrounding it and similar patterns of wear on its body. What could have caused such wear? To answer this question, West enlisted the aid of a team of geologists led by Robert M. Schoch of Boston University who had this to say about the erosive patterns present on the Sphinx and the surrounding enclosure wall:

> Geologists date landforms (including huge sculptured statues) by ana-
> lyzing weathering features and correlating them with the region's cli-
> matic history. In the case of the Sphinx, the sides of its body and the
> walls of its enclosure clearly exhibit a rolling, undulating vertical pro-
> file on the horizontal rock layers, which in turn are cut by vertical
> crevices. *These are textbook examples of rain-induced weathering* (my
> emphasis).[45]

The question that Schoch had to pose, once he got a good look at the Sphinx and its surrounding ditch, was how could the Sphinx and the walls of its enclosure sustain such deep, rain-induced weathering when Old Kingdom tombs immediately to the south of them and cut from the same limestone rock showed only wind-weathering? Nothing like the deep, vertical fissuring caused by coursing water could be found on *any other* monument, temple, or statue in the vicinity of the Sphinx. The only reasonable conclusion—the one West arrived at 20 years ago—is that the Sphinx was built in an entirely different epoch than those other well-known Old Kingdom structures.

Northeast Africa has not always been subjected to desert-like conditions.

From 10,000 B.C. to 3,000 B.C., the Nile Valley experienced the "Nabtian Pluvial," a period of relatively heavy rainfall, before succumbing to an extremely arid climate with very sparse precipitation.[46] It is only during this pluvial period that sufficient rain could have fallen on the quarry, where the Sphinx sits, to have caused the deep fissuring present on the surrounding quarry walls and on its body. Since this pluvial period effectively ceased by 3,000 B.C., the Sphinx must have been built prior to that time, well before the conventional date of 2500 B.C. usually given for its construction.

Schoch and his colleague Thomas Dobecki, a seismologist from Houston, accumulated data from their study that helped them arrive at a more definite age range for the Sphinx. They found that their seismic readings showed sub-surface water penetration in the bedrock of the Sphinx, six to eight feet deep in the front half of the Sphinx and four feet deep in rear.[47] This differential could only be explained by presuming that the Sphinx had been carved in stages; the head and forepart first and the hind-quarters last.

It is known from the work of Lehner and Gauri that the Sphinx had been renovated and repaired at least three times in history, and West and Schoch convincingly argue that the first repair occurred during the Old Kingdom.[48] The masonry and construction technique evident on the rump of the Sphinx undoubtedly derive from Old Kingdom building methods and an inscription on the rump, datable to the Old Kingdom, confirms this assessment.[49] There is every reason to believe that these Old Kingdom repairs and the carving of the hinderpart of the Sphinx, were undertaken by Khafre (a.k.a. Cephren), which accounts for the tradition linking Khafre with the Sphinx. If this first repair, along with the sculpting of the hinderpart, occurred during Khafre's reign, conventionally given as 2500 B.C., Schoch points out that it has taken 4,500 years—from Khafre's time until now—for water to penetrate to a depth of four feet into the bedrock of the Sphinx's rear.[50]

Concerning the bedrock under the forepart of the Sphinx, it is known that the pace of water penetration slows the deeper it seeps into the bedrock. Allowing for the slowing of water penetration to the profounder depths of six to eight feet, Schoch has proposed dates between 5,000 and 7,000 B.C. for the initial construction of the Sphinx.[51] He considers these estimates conservative.[52] It must be borne in mind that the bedrock upon which the Sphinx sits, was freed from over-lying rock by human hands. Thus any water penetration measured from the surface of this bedrock *must* date from the time of human construction, not before.

According to Schoch, the original Sphinx was built so that the head and forepart jutted outward from the limestone cliff. The rump did not exist and the effect was not dissimilar to the one created by the presidential busts at Mount Rushmore. The rump was sculpted later and in the process, a rectangular ditch was completed around the body as the limestone was removed from the quarry.

Expectedly, conventional academicians dismiss this work out of hand. There have been numerous knee-jerk academic rejections unsupported by any counter-evidence but a few have endeavored to mount serious critiques of the work of the West-Schoch team. One line of argument contends, correctly, that there have been recurring, though infrequent, rainfalls in the Nile Valley since the end of the Nabtian pluvial period 5,000 years ago. These downpours, uncommon though they are, would be sufficient to account for the water erosion on the Sphinx. Cited as an example of the effect of these intermittent downpours in Egypt is a mud-brick wall recently washed away by rain.[53] This argument is easily met. Mud-brick is the most ubiquitous building agent in Egypt precisely *because* rainfall is so infrequent. If rain was more frequent in Egypt than it is, it would be impossible to use mud-brick because it so readily dissipates when exposed to water. Thus, the washing away of a mud-brick structure by one of the *occasional* downpours that occur in Egypt cannot be compared to the deep and persistent fissuring in the limestone from which the Sphinx was constructed, caused by frequently recurring rainstorms at a remoter period.

Another argument brought forth to confute the West-Schoch demonstration involves discussion of the deterioration of the limestone due to condensation of moisture and precipitation of salt.[54] This line of reasoning fails to account for the deep vertical fissuring evident in the enclosure walls and on the body of the Sphinx. Nor does it explain the differential water penetration into different parts of the Sphinx's bedrock. Furthermore, why isn't the same pattern of water wear exhibited on any of the other Old Kingdom structures near the Sphinx built from the same formation of limestone?

Finally, the weathering patterns on the limestone body of the Sphinx are attributed to 50 million years of deterioration of the native limestone by the effects of the underground water table and accounts for the need, in the time of Khafre, for the sculptor to encase the body of the Sphinx in granite blocks.[55] Zahi Hawass, the author of this theory, insists that other unweathered limestone edifices on Giza were not constructed from stone quarried from the immediate vicinity but from nearby areas at a higher elevation. This assertion flies in the face of Schoch's evidence which shows that the Sphinx and its neighboring Old Kingdom structures were constructed from blocks of the same limestone formation. Moreover, if the limestone in the quarry where the Sphinx was built had deteriorated so badly from the effects of the water table, why would they use it at all? Why not use undamaged limestone so widely available from nearby formations? Moreover, the water table explanation still does not account for the deep external fissures on the walls of the ditch and on the body of the Sphinx.

Taken as a whole, the objections to this elegantly simple geological study seem facile and obtuse. They simply do not refute the work or the derived conclusions. What is unusual about this particular debate, though, is that its issues are intelligible to the lay public:

> It's not often that a scientific breakthrough is easily understood by nonscientists, still rarer that it makes good spectator sport. The quest to unriddle the Sphinx is an exception. Most of the evidence involves no microscopes, telescopes, or particle accelerators. All that's needed is a naked eye and the ability to follow an argument. And most of the action takes place not in the lab, but in Egypt, in public view.[56]

The Sphinx is one of the architectural and artistic wonders of the world. Sculpting such a marvelous piece of statuary could only have been realized in a civilization equal to the task. There was nothing "prehistoric" or "primitive" about the Sphinx or the culture that created it. The Sphinx thus seems to represent *prima facie* evidence of the existence of a full-fledged, flourishing Nile Valley civilization no later than *7,000 years ago!* Quite possibly it is as old as *9,000 years!* If the evidence holds up, the entire edifice of antiquarian scholarship will be faced with the prospect of revising *all* historical chronology and the attendant models of the emergence of civilization. Everything would have to be re-thought: the pre-dynastic sequences, the chronology of unification, the date of Ta-Seti and other ancient facts too numerous to mention. Much of the terminology, such as "neolithic," would have to be redefined or discarded. No wonder no self-respecting academician wants to touch it. West put it this way,

> The theory, if correct, upsets the entire apple-cart of ancient history, and I could hardly expect enthusiasm from people who make a living selling apples.[57]

Epilogue

Where do all these developments leave us? In spite of 100 years of consistent work, pre-dynastic Egyptian archaeology remains a hodge-podge of often contradictory facts and interpretations. What we can say is that the received chronology of the Nile Valley, to which academic Egyptology tenaciously clings, is hopelessly obsolete. But then it never did make much sense.

New evidence is gradually bringing into focus a northeast African civilization existing farther back in antiquity than had ever been imagined. It may be plausibly presumed that this high culture evolved out of a confluence of migrations and influences coming down the Nile from the Great Lakes merging with those moving eastward out of the Sahara. But the Saharan horizon itself is ultimately traceable to the East African Great Lakes, exemplified by the Ishango-Katandan complex. Ultimately, that region must be considered the cradle land of all African culture, specifically that derivable from the Saharo-Nilotic complex.

John Anthony West is convinced that there were one or more Nile Valley civilizations preceding that of dynastic Egypt by thousands of years. This is entirely consistent with Manetho's account of Egyptian history, recorded more than 2200 years ago.[58] Fragments of evidence show that cultures of greater technical sophistication than previously assumed might have existed in paleolithic Africa between 50-12,000 years ago.[59] We also know that fewer than 10% of the *known* archaeological sites on the continent have even been surveyed, let alone excavated. Archaeologically, Africa is still largely *terra incognita*. When the mammoth task of systematically exploring the archaeology of old Africa is at last undertaken, West's suppositions concerning "neolithic" and "paleolithic" African civilizations may come to seem less and less farfetched.

Glossary

Horizon: An archaeological cultural complex.

Lacustrine: Of or pertaining to lakes.

Mesolithic: A word meaning "Middle Stone Age," not strictly applicable to Africa since it refers primarily to a European cultural stage between the Paleolithic and Neolithic. The time span of the European Mesolithic extends from about 7,000 to 2700 B.C.

Neolithic: Means "New Stone Age" and generally refers to a cultural stage in Africa and the Near East existing between 8,000 B.C. (or earlier) and 4500 B.C. Neolithic cultures were characterized by small farming villages and pottery, through little or no utilization of metals. Europe entered the Neolithic period later than Africa or the Near East.

Paleolithic: This term refers to the "Old Stone Age," encompassing the period between 2.5 million years ago and 10,000 B.C. The Paleolithic was divided into the three sub-periods, "Lower," "Middle," and "Upper." The Upper Paleolithic was the final phase of the Paleolithic, beginning about 40,000 years ago. Paleolithic peoples were pre-agricultural hunters and gatherers.

Pluvial: Extended era of moderate to heavy rainfall.

Radiocarbon Dating: Method of determining the age of non-living organic materials by measuring the amount of decay of carbon isotopes in the sample.

End Notes

1. See Shreeve J, "The Dating Game," *Discover*, September 1992, pp. 76–83.
2. Ibid., p. 78.
3. Ibid.
4. See De Heinzelin J, "Ishango, " *Scientific American* (106), June 1962, pp. 105–16.
5. Shreeve, op. cit., p. 82.
6. Kittles, R, *Mitochondrial DNA and Human Origins: Assessing the Debate*, Spring 1993, Unpublished.
7. Shreeve, op. cit., p. 80.
8. De Heinzelin, op. cit., p. 111
9. See Marshack A, *The Roots of Civilization*, Mt. Kisco: Moyer Bell Limited, 1991, pp. 21–32.
10. Shreeve, op. cit., p. 82.
11. De Heinzelin, op. cit., p. 109.
12. Ibid.
13. See Diop CA, "Processus de Semitisation," *Parente Genetique de l' Egyptien Pharaonique et des Langues Negro-Africaines*, Dakar: Nouvelle Editions Africaines, 1977, pp. xxix–xxvii .
14. See Wendorf F, Close AE, and Schild R, "Prehistoric Settlements in the Nubian Desert, " *American Scientist* (73), March–April 1985, pp. 132–141, for a discussion of archaeological evidence of a pottery-making, cattle-rearing Neolithic people inhabiting the lands west of the Nile as far back as 8,000 B.C.
15. See Gillings R, *Mathematics in the Time of the Pharaohs*, New York: Dover Publications, Inc., 1982 .
16. See Flinders Petrie WM, *Prehistoric Egypt*, London: Quaritch, 1920, pp. 3–6.
17. See Jones WD, *Venus and Sothis*, Chicago: Nelson-Hall, 1982, p. 80.
18. Flinders Petrie, op. cit., p.3.
19. De Heinzelin, op. cit., p. 109 and Wendorf, Close, and Schild, op. cit. passim.
20. See Hoffman, MA, *Egypt Before the Pharaohs*, London: Ark Paperbacks, 1980, p. 142 for evidence of the higher Badarian date of 5500 B.C. and Hassan, FA, "The Predynastic of Egypt," *Journal of World Prehistory* (2)2, June 1988, pp. 138–41 for dating results of the Badarian period of 4000 B. C.
21. Hassan, ibid .
22. Hoffman, op. cit., p. 169.
23. Wendorf, Close, Schild, op. cit., p. 132 .
24. Gardiner A, *Egypt of the Pharaohs*, New York: Oxford University Press, 1964, 1978, p. 395 .
25. Hassan, op. cit., p. 159.
26. Flinders Petrie, op. cit., p. 8.
27. Vid. Gardiner, op. cit., p. 392.
28. Keita SOY, "Studies of Ancient Crania from Northern Africa," *American Journal of Physical Anthropology* (83), 1990, pp. 35–48.
29. Ibid., pp. 36–8.
30. Ibid., 38–46.
31. Ibid., p. 40.
32. Keita, SOY, "Further Analysis of Crania From Ancient Northern Africa: An Analysis of Crania From First Dynasty Egyptian Tombs, Using Multiple Discrimi-

nant Functions," *American Journal of Physical Anthropology* (87), 1992, p. 250.

33. Vid. both articles by Keita, passim (notes #28 and #32).

34. Cf. Hoffman, op. cit., p. 328 and Hassan, op. cit., p. 170.

35. Hassan, ibid., p. 169.

36. Cf. Finch CS, *Echoes of the Old Dark Land: Themes from the African Eden*, Decatur: Khenti, Inc., pp. 57-87 .

37. Haas H, Devine J, Wehnke R, Lehner M, et al., "Radiocarbon Chronology and the Historical Calendar in Egypt," *Chronologies in the Near East*, Evin J and Hours F, editors, BAR International Series, 1987, pp. 585–606.

38. Williams B, "The Lost Pharaohs of Nubia, " *Archaeology* (33) 5, September/October 1980.

39. Ibid., p. 14.

40. Ibid.

41. Ibid., p. 16.

42. Ibid., p. 21.

43. Finch, op. cit., pp. 115-127.

44. The story of West's efforts to have his theory confirmed appears in the February 1993 issue of *Conde Nast Traveller*, in a cleverly written and illustrated article entitled "Civilization rethought," pp. 100–05; 168–77 .

45. Schoch RM, "One Geologist's review, " *Conde Nast Traveller*, February 1993, p. 103.

46. Cited in Schoch, RM, "Redating the Great Sphinx of Giza, " *KMT* (3) 2, Summer 1992, p. 55.

47. Schoch, ibid., pp. 56-7.

48. Cited by West, op. cit., pp. 170–1.

49. Schoch, "Redating the Great Sphinx . . . ", op. cit. pp. 56–7.

50. Cited in West, op. cit., p. 176.

51. Schoch, "Redating the Great Sphinx . . . ," op. cit., p. 57.

52. Ibid., p. 58.

53. See "On the other hand . . . ", *Conde Nast Traveller*, February 1993, p. 105 for a synopsis of the counter-arguments put forward against the conclusion of the West-Schoch team.

54. Ibid.

55. Ibid.

56. West, op. cit., p. 177.

57. Ibid., p. 170.

58. Vid. Waddell WG, translator, *Manetho*, Cambridge: Harvard University Press, 1940, 1980 for fragments of Manetho's history that record king lists going back to about 5500 B.C. and legendary dynasties going back to nearly 37,000 B.C.

59. See Finch CS, *Africa and the Birth of Science and Technology* (pamphlet), Decatur: Khenti, Inc., 1993, pp. 2–5.

THE RACIAL IDENTITY OF ANCIENT
EGYPTIAN POPULATIONS BASED ON
THE ANALYSIS OF PHYSICAL REMAINS

Keith W. Crawford

The following article was condensed from a soon to be published book entitled: "The Racial Identity of Ancient Egyptian and Nubian Populations: A Review of Studies Analyzing Physical Remains."

Population Variation and Theories on Race in Africa

Wilson et al. studying mitochondrial DNA showed more differentiation in Africa than anywhere else, which indicated that man had been evolving there for the longest period of time (Cavalli-Sforza, 1991). Observed differences occurring in populations can be the result of multiple evolutionary factors including mutations (changes in genetic material), gene flow (migrations and admixture with differing populations), environmental selection of specific traits (natural selection) or genetic drift (population sampling error). The validity of the concept of an ancestral group from which present African populations are descended is supported by both genetic studies and skeletal comparisons. Brauer (1990) demonstrates a remarkable overlap of features between Paleolithic skeletons from North Africa (35,000–3,000 B.C.), sub-Saharan Africa (20,000–3,000 B.C.) and "modern"* humans from the Nile Valley (Nazlet Khater man, 35,000 B.C. and Wadi Kubbaniya man, 20,000 B.C.; see discussion below) and points out difficulties in distinguishing between these early sub-Saharan skeletons and North African skeletons. This suggests that an ancient ancestral population in Africa was subject to natural selection and other evolutionary processes thereby producing the diversity in modern day populations. Studies calculating the degree of relatedness between world populations based on genetic similarities for certain proteins reveal that present day African populations with markedly

---

*Students should note that Dr. Crawford is not using the word 'modern' to refer to present-day populations in Egypt but to "homo sapiens sapiens" the human being in its most evolved or "modern" stage. (Editor)

different physical traits emerge as a group distinct from other world populations. Sanchez-Mazas et.al. (1986) show Senegalese from sub-Saharan West Africa and Ethiopians from the Horn of Africa forming a distinct grouping. This study examined genetic similarities in five blood group and HLA systems between 14 populations, Similarly, Nei (1978) shows West Africans from Ghana and Bantu Africans from Southeastern Africa emerging together, again distinct from the other European, Asian, and American populations. These relationships were based on gene frequency data for 11 protein and blood group genes and compared 12 populations for which this data was available. Cavalli-Sforza et. al (1988) presented a study of gene frequencies for 120 alleles (genetic variations of a particular trait) in 42 World populations. Africans, including Mbuti Pygmies, West Africans, Ethiopians, Bantu speakers, Bushmen, and NiloSaharan speakers, formed a cluster (Africoid) distinct from all other world populations. They also show that all these African populations speak languages from African linguistic families (see also Blench, 1993).

A critical point to understand when studying the racial makeup of Nile Valley populations is that the full diversity of Africoid variants was not often appreciated by the early anthropologists. What Anthropologists called the "Negro" identified only one form of Africoid variant common to the forest zone of West Africa. This variant became familiar to the European as the type primarily involved in the slave trade, and the ancestral group to Blacks in the American diaspora. Because of the extreme racist prejudice that grew against this group, and its role as the primary source of labor in the U.S. and European colonies, there was a conscientious effort to minimize the influence of this variant (or variants with close affinities) in Nile Valley populations. Other Africoid variants are important to our discussion of Nile Valley populations because their range of distribution overlaps or is in close vicinity with the Nile valley. Their physical traits were likely present in ancient Egyptian populations.

The Elongated African variant is distinguished by a generalized elongated body build, narrow head, face and nose, dark skin and spiralled hair, thick but not everted lips. Morphometrically they range from dolicranic to mesocranic, (long to moderately long headed) mesorhine to leptorrhine (low nasal index = narrow nasal opening), low facial index (long narrow face) and mild to absent prognathism (protruding upper jaw/lower face) (fig. 1). Thus, this variant stands in contrast to the Broad African variant (the so-called Negro) that is dolicranic (long-headed), platyrhine (high nasal index = wide nasal opening), high facial index (short broad face), and moderately to markedly prognathous (see Keita, 1992) (figs. 2,3). *The Elongated types*, all of which possess the above traits, include the Fulani (wide range extending from West Africa to the Sudan just below the Sahara), the Tutsi, the Hima (both in Rwanda), the Masai (Kenya), the Galla (Southern Ethiopia),

Tigreans, Amharas (both from Ethiopia), Somalis (Somalia) and the Beja (Northern Sudan) (Hiernaux, 1976). Hiernaux stresses that there is evidence for the continued presence of Elongated traits since Pleistocene times, with no evidence of gene flow from populations outside of Africa. He postulates that the constellation of Elongated traits arose as an adaptation to dry heat.

The Nilotic variant described by Hiernaux, when compared to the Elongated variant are noted to be taller with a narrower head (a much lower cephalic index), a lower and wider nose (a higher nasal index), a very slender body, with extremely long legs and little fat. Nilotic types include the Nuer, Dinka, Shilluk and Anuak, all of whom occupy the Nile river basins in the southern Sudan. An example of the differences that exist between the cranial morphology of "Negroes" and other Africoid populations is seen in a study conducted by Strouhal (1971) where he compares the metrical values representing a population of X-group Nubians from Wadi Quintna (described as Negroes) with those of modern Nilotic populations.

> "When examining individually all Negroid skulls from Wadi Quintna" he concludes "not one specimen was found showing characteristic features of Nilotes . . . " (see Greene, 1981).

Coon (1965) displays a picture of a Shilluk man with Black skin, ulotrichous (wooly) hair and somewhat thickened lips. Under the photo of this unquestionably "Negroid" person is the caption "A Shilluk with European features" (fig. 4). To the lay person such a statement is most puzzling. Understand that Coon is referring to features of the cranial anatomy, erroneously thought to have resulted from Caucasoid admixture.

Comas (1950) has described the traits of various African ethnic groups and he demonstrates a phenomenal degree of variability. He describes *the "true negro"* as having skin color varying from dark brown to black, relatively long armed and long legged, tall stature, broad shoulders, narrow hips, black and kinky hair, dolichocephaly (cranial index 74-75), frequently a considerable degree of prognathism, platyrrhine (flat) nose, very depressed at the root, thick and often everted lips. He describes the Hausa of Northern Nigeria as being very black, essentially *dolichocephalic* (cranial index 76.4) markedly less prognathous, less platyrrhine and less muscular than the West coast "negro". He describes Nilotic types typified by the Dinka and the Shilluk as being typically very tall, black, dolichocephalic (cranial index 72), thin lips, a nose with a high bridge and non-flaring nostrils, a long narrow face with medium prognathism. Some Bantu-speaking groups are identified which have light skin, thin lips, higher and less broad nose; while others, typified by the Tetela are *brachycephalic* (cranial index 81-84). The Akkas and Babingas are *"negrillos"* (*pygmies*) whose skin is reddish-yellow to light brown, a cranial index approaching brachycephaly (79) and a very wide nose. The "Bushman" (Khoisan) variants exhibit a remarkable degree of heterogeneity. Their types include dark to light complexions, dolichocephals to mesocephals (long to moderately long heads), leptorrhine to platyrrhine (narrow noses to flat wide noses), low to high brow ridges, and prognathous to orthognathous types (i.e., marked to absent lower facial protrusion). One type has been termed Europoid because it possesses traits found in European populations such as leptorrhiny and orthognathism.

The preceding discussion should make it clear that African populations display an entire spectrum of phenotypes including those attributed to being characteristic of other races. This must be the case since all races evolved from an African prototype and it was necessary that this type possess the potential to express multiple traits which could then be modified further by the environment. The so-called "true Negro" does not even represent the majority of African types on the continent.

A Caucasoid presence was assumed in some ancient Nile Valley populations when certain cranial traits characteristically found in Caucasoids were also detected in these African crania. The conclusion was that the African populations were Caucasoid or had Caucasoid admixture. In fact, until rather recently, it was assumed that practically all African populations had experienced significant admixture with Caucasoids based on their possession of certain "Caucasoid" traits (Coon, 1964; Seligman, 1966). The term Hamitic described the presence of "Caucasoid" traits in African populations.

Rightmire (1976) has critically examined the data used to substantiate the existence of Caucasoid populations in East Africa during post-Pleistocene periods. These Caucasoid theories were introduced by Leakey (1931, 1935) based on his analysis of the early East African skeletal remains. He concluded,

> "The present review indicates that at least some of the Rift crania have been inappropriately labeled as representative of a Mediterranean Caucasoid population. When carefully measured and subjected to multiple discriminant function analysis, many of the skulls are excluded from probable membership in Egyptian (Caucasoid) test populations in no uncertain terms. Much firmer ties can be established with one or another of the several African Negro groups."

It is important to point out that the Egyptian skulls Rightmire uses that he labels "Caucasoid" come from the Delta region in Lower Egypt *from the 26th-30th dynasties.* During this period, Egypt was successively invaded by Assyrians and Persians and later by the Greeks, thereby introducing a Caucasoid element into the population. Nevertheless, other researchers have shown that these skulls also have affinities with populations from tropical Africa, and other regions of the Nile valley (discussed below). The series E crania were a poor choice to represent a Caucasoid group.

Racial classification takes factors into account that cannot be assessed from the skeleton alone. For example, Batrawi (1935) published photos of a skull in profile from the X-group Nubian cultural phase with ulotrichous (woolly) hair still attached. The accompanying caption states, "typical negro hair". Next to this photo is displayed a facial view of the same skull with the caption, "face of the same; not typically negro" (fig. 5). There are no Caucasoid populations with ulotrichous hair, yet the facial features are identified as not typically negro. Consider what the conclusions about the skull would have been in the absence of the hair. Coon et. al (1950) reports populations with "Mediterranean" cranial features coupled with stereotypical negro soft parts, but they have not observed the reverse (Keita, 1990).

Hiernaux (1976) employs a scientific approach to this Hamitic question as follows,

> "Many authors have used some measured or observed external characters (mostly facial features such as long, narrow and prominent noses) as indicators of a Caucasoid element in Sub-Saharan Africa. In the anthropological literature this element is very often called `Hamitic', extending this originally linguistic term to the field of physical anthropology. In *Races of Africa*, a widely known work by C.G.Seligman (1966), a large number of populations of sub-Saharan Africa are seen as `Hamiticized' to a greater or lesser extent, only the bushman and the populations of the West African forest belt are said to be free from Hamitic admixture".

These observations are significant because they indicate that most African populations have some cranial features that are considered to be "Caucasoid" from a typological approach. Is it biologically accurate to assume that these features are Caucasoid? Hiernaux explores this question, using an example;

> "The Tutsi and the Hutu have intermixed to some degree, but, as groups, they remain strikingly different. The Tutsi exhibit `Hamitic' facial features to a marked degree. Do they systematically differ from the Hutu in the direction of Caucasoids?
>
> The Tutsi are taller than the Hutu by ten centimeters; the average male stature is 176 cm. Such tallness is by no means characteristic of North Africa or Western Asia: For example, the inhabitants of the central plateau of Yemen have an average stature of 164 cm. In skin colour, the Tutsi are darker than the Hutu, in the reverse direction to that leading to Caucasoids. Lip thickness provides a similar case: on the average the lips of the Tutsi are thicker than those of the Hutu. In most instances, they are not everted as most West Africans. Like that of the Hutu, the hair of the Tutsi is spiralled (perhaps less tightly so but this has not been quantified)."

Later he continues,

"In cephalic index the Hutu are nearer to Yemenites than are the Tutsi, whose long narrow head makes the index lower than the other two groups. Existing serologic data based on a rather small sample are equivocal; the Tutsi are Higher in the M frequency, but do not differ from the Hutu in Ro frequency, nor the frequency of transferrin Dl.
    These comparisons do not lend support to the idea that the Tutsi are a mixture of Caucasoids and West Africans. If the West African element, introduced recently by the mixing with the Hutu, were subtracted, their physique would differ even more from North Africans and West Asians. Apparently 'Hamitic' features developed in the Tutsi's ancestral line independently of any exotic source or, if an exotic element really was introduced, it was such a long time ago that selection has thoroughly remodelled the resulting gene pool. Even if the second hypothesis were correct, the physical appearance of the Tutsi would result from evolution that took place in sub-Saharan Africa."

In early studies, Egyptian populations were identified racially as "Hamitic" or "Mediterranean". The work of Rightmire and Hiernaux was important in challenging the assumptions and methodology used in studies with African populations. Studies on the effects of climate on cranial morphology suggested that environmental influences were responsible for certain "Caucasoid" traits and not influence from Caucasoid populations. Using appropriate comparative groups and statistical methods, "Hamitic" populations can be shown to be related to other African populations and not to Caucasoids from Europe or Asia. Additionally, it is important to remember that modern populations considered to be "Hamitic" (e.g., some Ethiopians) have been shown genetically to cluster with other Africoid variants and not racial groups or populations outside of Africa.

Many of the earlier researchers used a typological approach to analysis of Nile Valley populations. Typology assumes races can be characterized and distinguished by mutually exclusive features that are stable through time. Researchers who have used a cluster of specific traits for defining a race encounter the problem of marked heterogeneity within the race for the presumed defining traits. We have seen how Africoid populations display a great deal of variation in the expression of "diagnostically Negroid" traits.

Newer paradigms in human variation do not assume that all populations lumped together in a racial class are homogeneous in their characteristics. A more scientific approach, the evolutionary approach, involves selecting as many independent characteristics as possible from different skeletal subsystems, comparison of the population under study with other relevant populations close in time and locale, and analysis by statistical tests that remove the effects of correlation between characteristics (which will hopefully identify a range of traits controlled by independent genetic loci). This provides a more accurate method for assessing racial affinity between the groups compared. Unlike typological models which assume traits are stable through time, the evolutionary model assumes that population characteristics change over time and there may be difficulty in comparing ancient populations with modern populations. Populations are therefore dynamic entities continuously being modified by environment and gene flow (Greene, 1981).

Early Skeletal Remains in the Nile Valley

The earliest modern human fossil found in Egypt was the skeleton of the Nazlet Khater man found near Tahta, Egypt which was dated to 35, 000-30, 000 B.C. (upper Paleolithic period). Regarding the racial affinity of this skeleton, Thoma (1984) concludes,

"Strong alveolar prognathism combined with fossa praenasalis in an African skull is suggestive of Negroid morphology. The radio-humeral index of Nazlet Khater is practically the same as the mean of Taforalt (76.6). According to Ferembach (1962) this value is near to the Negroid average."

In 1982, Wendorf discovered a skeleton at Wadi Kubbaniya, located 10-15 km north of Aswan in Egypt. This skeleton dated to approximately 20,000 B.C.. The wide nasal aperture, lower nasal margin morphology (presence of the sulcus praenasalis), wide interorbital distance and alveolar prognathism demonstrate affinities with Broad African variants (i.e. "Negroid" traits) (Stewart, 1985).

Greene and Armelagos (1964) analyzed a collection of crania from Wadi Halfa dating from 13,000 to 8,000 B.C. The skulls were dolichocephalic with bun-shaped occiputs, and they displayed extreme facial flattening in the orbital and nasal regions, massive browridges, sloping foreheads, great alveolar prognathism, large teeth and large, deep mandibles. Rightmire (1975) notes a similarity between this population and skeletons from West Africa (Tamaya Mellet, Niger and El Guettara, Mali).

These studies indicate the presence of populations with Broad African traits (Negroid) as the earliest inhabitants of Egypt.

Predynastic Egyptian Populations

The earliest predynastic cultural period that has been described is that of the Badarian culture, believed to have developed around 4500 B.C. One of the earliest and most thorough characterizations of Badarian crania was undertaken by Stoessinger (1927), examining two series of Badarian skulls. This type was characterized by doliocrania (long heads), chamerrhine with a high nasal index (broad nose) and prognathous; all of these being characteristically found among populations with Broad African traits. Morant (1935) reports,

"Comparisons between the Badari means for single characters and those available for other ancient Egyptian series have been made by Miss Stoessiger, and it has been shown that the Badari type diverges slightly from them in being more prognathous and in having a higher nasal index. In these respects it is more negroid."

Strouhal (1971) not only demonstrated affinities with Broad Africans in Badarian crania, but he conducted analyses on hair that was preserved with some of the specimens. He observed that Cross-sections of the hair displayed flattened outlines with indices of 35-65, which corresponds to hair with a wooly to kinky type consistency.

Most recently, using improved statistical analysis, Keita (1990) observed,

"The Badarian crania have a modal metric phenotype that is clearly 'southern'; most classify into the Kerma (Nubia), Gaboon, and Kenyan groups."

He further reports,

"No Badarian cranium in any analysis classified into the European series, and few grouped with the 'E' series."

The Nagada cultural period that followed the Badarian period has also been shown to have consisted of populations with affinities to Broad African populations. One of the earliest studies to characterize Nagada crania was conducted by Fawcett (1902). She identifies the characteristics of the Nagada race commenting,

"We are dealing therefore with a long-headed narrow-faced race with a flat nose and rather round orbits."

Nutter (1958) compared Nagada, Badarian and Kerma (Upper Nubia) skulls and concluded the three groups were almost identical, all of them possessing Broad African phenotypic traits (see Keita, 1990).

Crichton (1966) observed that a combined Nagada series diverged towards a tropical African series from Kenya but they were more similar to a series of crania from Abydos spanning the 3rd to 30th dynasties. In general, Crichton observed a decrease in the "Negroid" traits present in Egyptian crania as one progressed in time from early predynastic periods late into the dynastic era. But Crichton's conclusions about changes in racial affinities of Egyptian populations over time were almost certainly influenced by the region of origin of the population sample. Carlson and van Gerven (1979) carefully note,

"With regard to Crichton's (1966) analysis, it is important to consider that his earliest Egyptian groups were spatially separated 432 km. to the south of his most recent series. There is therefore the distinct alternative possibility that the differences detected between the earliest and latest groups reflect geographical variation. The nasal aperture, for example, appears to be adaptively responsive to climatic variation (Wolpoff, 1968; Glanville 1969) and appears to be clinally distributed. Interestingly, metric variation in the nasal aperture figured most prominently in distinguishing Egyptian from East African crania. Crichton's results demonstrate that the East African crania are smaller than the Egyptian series and have a broader nasal aperture. The Egyptian series presents a similar continuum, with the crania from the upper Nile being smallest and having the broadest nasal aperture. That distribution is consistent with a geographical, ecological hypothesis."

Carlson and van Gerven illustrate in this passage how environmental influences can affect cranial morphology.

Other osteological analyses have been conducted on Nagada skeletons. A study of proportions of the long-bones on Nagada skeletons conducted by Robbins (1986) identified them as "super negroid". Morant (1925) and Fawcett (1902) make reference to research by Warren (1897) examining Nagada long bones identifying them as Negroid. A high brachial or femoral index, indicating a greater relative length of the forearm/femur to the total arm/leg, is characteristic of tropical African populations. This is consistent with Allen's rule which predicts that high ratios for these limb indices would be found in peoples originating in tropical regions as an adaptation for loss of heat.

Keita (1990) concludes from a largescale analysis of North African crania,

"The upper Nile valley series show close affinities to one another and to tropical African series . . . The Badari and Nagada I cranial patterns emerge as tropical Africans (with Kerma) . . . Notable Nagada/Kerma metric overlap is observed with the first dynasty series, which share the pattern to a lesser degree, as indicated by its centroid values."

The Nagada predynastics and A-Group Nubians (3800 B.C.–3000 B.C.) both established pharaonic systems of kingship and possessed other religious concepts that later became the foundation for Dynastic Egypt (Williams, 1986, 1991).

The Dynastic Period

Since many African populations were erroneously assumed to have Caucasoid influence, most studies assessing racial affinities of ancient

Egyptians looked only for the presence of "Negroid" traits. Researchers seldom compared Egyptian crania with Elongated or Nilotic populations.

Narmer-Menes is the ruler credited with initiating the entire dynastic sequence by unifying Upper and Lower Egypt, and founding the First dynasty. He was a southerner (Upper Egyptian) and his depictions on artifacts show Broad African features (see Chandler, 1989).

Montet (1965) describes the Old Kingdom rulers (Dynasties III–VI) as having,

> " . . . unusually large, almost flat noses, thickish lips and somewhat low foreheads. Such were without exception the kings of Egypt at the time of the Old Kingdom."

Keita (1992) has conducted a thorough analysis of First dynasty (Archaic period) crania from Abydos. He has demonstrated,

> "The predominant craniometric pattern in the Abydos royal tombs is 'southern' (tropical African variant), and this is consistent with what would be expected based on the literature and other results (Keita, 1990). This pattern is seen in both group and unknown analysis. However, lower Egyptian, Magrebian, and European patterns are observed also, thus making for great diversity. The Magrebian affinities may be difficult to interpret, given that this series contains a range of variation from tropical African to European metric phenotypes (Keita, 1990)."

He further reports,

> "The strong Sudanese affinity noted in the unknown analysis may reflect the Nubian interactions with Upper Egypt in predynastic times prior to Egyptian unification (Williams, 1980, 1986)."

Keita also cites the work of Petrie (1939) who was convinced that the rulers from Third dynasty royal tombs in Lower Egypt were of Sudanese origins based on their portraiture which showed "Negroid" traits.

The preceding study comparing morphometric characteristics clearly indicate affinities with Broad African populations in cranial series from the Archaic-Old Kingdom, early dynastic period. The studies of Keita (1992) and Crichton (1966) also suggest biologic continuity of populations from the predynastic period into the early dynastic era in Egypt. Data from nonmetrical studies presented below will further support this conclusion.

During the Middle Kingdom period (Dynasties XI, XII), Egypt again was the pinnacle of civilization in the ancient world. The origins of the Middle Kingdom, as with the Old Kingdom, were from the south or in Upper Egypt. The dynasties of the Middle Kingdom were established by ruler/conquerors with Broad African features who originated in Upper Egypt (Drake, 1987, p.

189 discussing Mentuhotep's southern origins and founding the 11th dynasty, Bernal, 1991, p. 189 for a description of Sesostris I coming from the extreme south and founding the 12th dynasty). Barnard (1936) analyzed several series of skulls that had been previously analyzed by other researchers including a late predynastic series, the 6th–12th dynasty series from Denderah in Upper Egypt, the 12–13th dynasty Kerma sample (Upper Nubia) and a Ptolemaic series (Greek rule in Egypt, after the 30th dynasty). Barnard observed that by her statistical method, the Ptolemaic series was significantly different from the other three series. The late predynastic series when compared with the 6–12th the dynasty Egyptian series and the 12-13th dynasty Nubian series just reached the 0.05 level of significance (i.e., the groups are not different from one another). Barnard states,

"The Sixth to Twelfth and Twelfth to Thirteenth dynasty show definitely no difference inter se. If these results are compared with those obtained by the method that was commonly in use, i.e. that based on the Coefficient of Racial Likeness (C.R.L.), it will be found that judged by the latter method, the differences between the series are consistently more significant than they are according to the method used in this paper."

She further points out that by the method of the C.R.L., the 6–12th Egyptian dynasty series and the 12–13th dynasty Nubian series are significantly different, whereas there is no difference by her method. The C.R.L. was commonly used to compare populations in earlier studies (e.g., Morant, 1935). Several researchers have shown this method to be inappropriate for racial comparative studies (e.g., Seltzer, 1937). The C.R.L. analysis was sometimes the source of erroneous conclusions about the degree of relatedness between different Nile Valley populations.

Keita (1990) has shown that Kerma crania share characteristics with tropical African populations. Collett (1933) identified the Kerma skulls as "Negroid", a view shared by Eliot-Smith (1910), who reported earlier that the Middle Kingdom Nubian population was "distinctly Negroid" (Nielson, 1971).

With reference to the physical proportions of Middle Kingdom Egyptians, we gain additional evidence of their African character. Robins and Schute (1983) report,

"Robins (1983) has recently analyzed Warren's data on predynastic bones and has measured photographs and X-rays of some dynastic skeletons from the Middle Kingdom. She has shown that, for males at least, plausible estimates of stature that are reasonably consistent when different long bones are used only result from negro equations, and that the most satisfactory equations are those of Trotter and Gleser (1958)."

The establishment of the New Kingdom after a period of rule by the Asiatic Hyksos kings of the Delta in Lower Egypt came about as a result of the military campaigns of the southern ruler Sequenre Tao, a seventeenth dynasty king. Harris and Weeks in "X-Raying the Pharaohs" write of Sequenre Tao,

> "His entire facial complex, in fact, is so different from other pharaohs (it is closest in fact to his son Ahmose) that he could be fitted more easily into the series of Nubian and Old Kingdom Giza skulls than into that of later Egyptian kings. Various scholars in the past have proposed a Nubian- that is, non-Egyptian-origin for Sequenre and his family, and his facial features suggest that this might indeed be true."

Note also that their work supports the close relationship between the Nubian and Old Kingdom Egyptian populations. Ahmose I, the son of Sequenre Tao by his full blooded sister succeeded in expelling the Hykssos rulers from Egypt and establishing the 18th dynasty. Ahmose's wife-sister, Ahmose-Nefartari was the most venerated queen in Egyptian history and thus we see the foundations of the 18th dynasty originating from the south, very possibly Nubia.

Robins and Schute (1983) examined the physical proportions of New Kingdom Pharaohs. They conclude,

> "It can be seen that all the pharaonic values, including those of 'Smakhare', lie much closer to the negro curve than to the white curve. Since stature equations only work satisfactorily if the individuals to whom they are applied have similar proportions to the population group from which they are derived, this provides justification for using negro equations for estimating stature from single bones of the New Kingdom pharaohs, reinforcing the previous findings of Robins (1983). Furthermore, the Trotter and Gleser white equations for the femur, tibia and humerus yield stature values that have a much wider spread than those from negro equations with mean values that are unacceptably large."

Their study included the 18th dynasty pharaohs Amenhotep I, II, III, Ahmose, Thutmose I, II, III, IV, Smenkhkare and Tutankhamen; and 19th dynasty pharaohs Merneptah, Rameses II, Seti I, II and Siptah. Since the estimation of stature takes into account limb proportions, the data from the studies of stature in Middle Kingdom and New kingdom Egyptians indicate that they possess the same adaptations as Africans in tropical climates.

Photographs of 18th dynasty and some 19th dynasty royal mummies clearly demonstrate the presence of Broad African traits. Prognathism can be observed in the X-ray profiles of the cranium for some of these rulers (see Harris and Weeks; El-Madhy, 1989; van Sertima, 1991) (fig. 6).

The series E crania from Gizeh, Lower Egypt from the 26th to 30th dynasty were shown by Howells (1973) to cluster with Europeans in some analyses but with tropical Africans in other analyses. This suggests that they possessed traits from both populations. During this period Lower Egypt was successively invaded by Assyrians and Persians. Brauer (1976) did a morphological and multivariate analysis comparing African cranial series from all over the continent and encompassing all periods from the predynastic era to the present. Overall, The series E crania cluster with other Northeast African groups including Nubians (Group C, X, Meroitic, Christian), Nagada, Galla/Somali (Elongated African). In one of the analyses, the Gizeh skulls are apart from most of the Nile valley populations, but still cluster with crania from Jebel Moya in Upper Nubia/Sudan. This study supports the assertion that so-called Caucasoid features in Egyptian populations may actually result from interactions with other African groups that have erroneously been assumed to possess Caucasoid ancestry (i.e., some Nubian groups, Elongated Africans). In reference to this study, Keita (1993) states,

"In a study of East African crania, Brauer (1976) used a range of other African crania for comparison; his analyses, using Penrose distances, show Nubian and early Egyptian series to generally cluster with more southern Africans. The Nile valley series did not cluster apart, as series did by geography in Howell's (1973) study, or form a major distinct group unto themselves, as a racial 'type' model would predict which assumed they were very different, of a different 'race', than more southern Africans."

Berry et al. (1967) observed close relationships between a Badarian series and an Old Kingdom series from Abydos by analyzing frequencies of non-metrical (genetic) cranial traits. Further, they found no difference between the Badarian series and the population at Gizeh. There was additionally no difference noted between a Nagada series and populations of Tarkhan and Abydos from the post-archaic period (third–sixth dynasties; 2700–2200 B.C.). This similarity between predynastics and early dynastic populations from Upper Egypt and other regions was also observed by Keita in his metrical studies (1990, 1992) of crania from these periods and locations. Hence, there appears to be biologic continuity in Predynastic and Upper Egyptians through the Old kingdom, demonstrated by both metrical and non-metrical methods.

Strouhal (1979) demonstrates a tremendous degree of overlap in the range of frequencies for non-metric traits between ancient Egyptian series studied by Berry et. al. (including samples from Badari, Nakada, Hierankopolis, Abydos, Tarkan, Hawara, Giza, Qurna, and Qua) and modern southern African "Negroes" studied by Rightmire (1977). These observations support the relatedness of the ancient Egyptians to the other populations of Africa.

Borgognini-Tarli and Paoli (1972) determined ABO blood groupings of

Dynastic Egyptians by analysis of marrow collected from the femurs of skeletons. In comparing the distribution of blood types within the Egyptian population, a pattern was established which was shown to be most similar to a present-day Haratin population living in the Algerian Sahara desert. The Haratin are believed to be the descendants of ancient populations that inhabited the Saharan region before its desiccation. The Haratin have been termed "Black Berbers" and share affinities with tropical African populations. The Egyptian samples came from various sites in Upper Egypt representing the entire dynastic period.

Diop (1981) devised a method for quantifying the melanin content of the epidermis from dynastic Egyptian mummies. The preservation of the skin did not interfere with the detection of melanin. Diop demonstrated that the melanin content from the mummies was comparable to the quantity in the skin of present day tropical African populations. These findings take on added significance when we consider how the ancient Egyptians actually looked.

Conclusions

Egyptian populations from the Paleolithic period (35,000 B.C.) to the predynastic period (4th millennium B.C.) display physical features common to Africoids with Broad traits ("Negroid"). Features in African populations that were thought to indicate a Caucasoid influence may be attributable to natural selection and reflect the wide range of variability among "true" Africoid types. Morphometric analysis of crania, cephalometric studies (X-ray), estimates of stature, genetic analysis of both non-metric traits and blood groups, and studies of hair and pigmentation show that dynastic Egyptians are related to other Nile Valley and tropical African populations more closely than to any population outside of Africa. Gene flow from outside of Africa may have introduced Caucasoid genes particularly during the First and Second Intermediate periods (dynasties 7-10 and 13-17, respectively) and the late dynastic period in Lower Egypt. Remains from Archaic/Old Kingdom, Middle Kingdom and New Kingdom rulers show affinities to Broad Africoid populations (Negroids). Future studies should focus on examining the presence of other Africoid traits (e.g., Elongated, Nilotic, Bushmanoid) in Egyptian populations.

Acknowledgment

Special thanks are extended to my mentor, Shomarka Keita, MD, professor of Anthropology at Howard University and the University of Maryland. His outstanding research in physical anthropology has produced a change of attitudes and perspectives with regard to the African identity of the Ancient Egyptians.

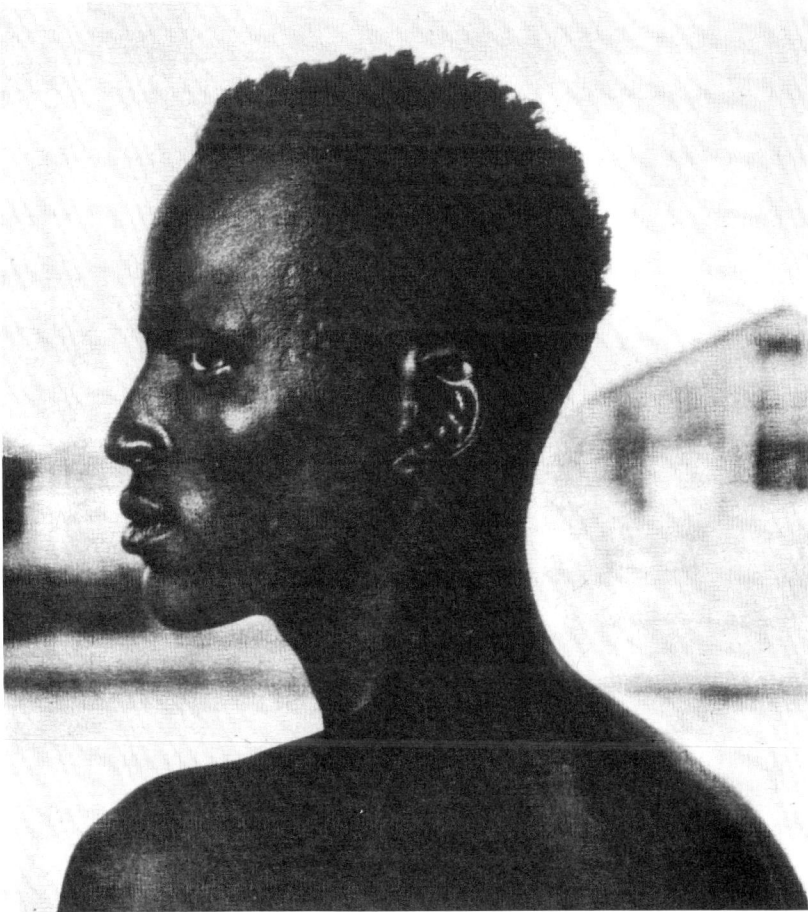

123. A Somali.

Figure 1. An Africoid of the "Elongated" variety. Africans with these facial features were labelled "Hamitic" and were thought to have Caucasoid admixture or even to belong to the Caucasoid race. Genetic analysis and ancestral relationships show many populations with these features to cluster with other African populations and emerge distinct from European or Asiatic races (From Coon, C., 1965).

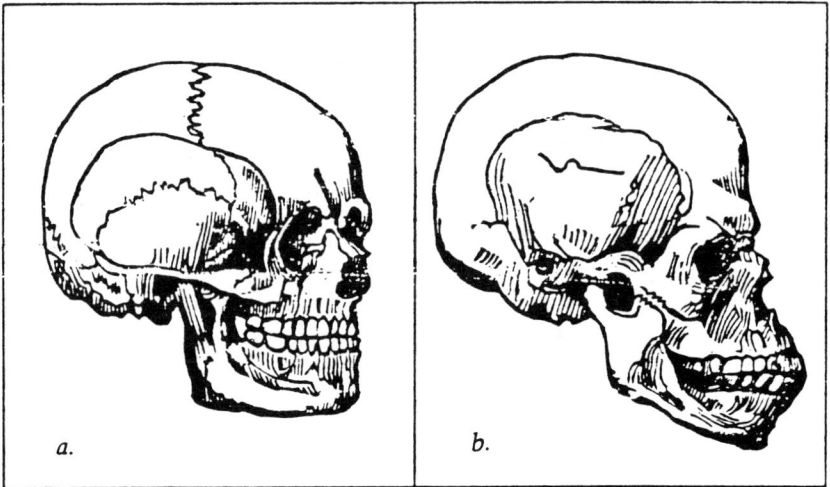

FIGURE 1. ALVEOLAR PROGNATHISM IN TWO SKULLS. Reprinted from
Nott and Gliddon, *Types of Mankind* (1855).
a. GREEK SPECIMEN
b. WEST AFRICAN SPECIMEN

Figure 2. Prognathism (lower facial protrusion) is evident in the skull from
West Africa. The European skull, which lacks this feature, is termed
orthognathous. Prognathism is generally not found in Caucasoid populations,
but there are also numerous Africoid variants that lack prognathism. This led
some early researchers to postulate Caucasoid influence in these African
populations (From Drake, 1987).

Figure 3. An Africoid of the "Broad" variety (A Nuba chief from Kenya). Africans with these features were termed "Negroes" and populations with these characteristics were often assumed to represent the only "pure" unmixed members of the race. In actuality, this is only one of many "true" Africoid variants. Africoids display a tremendous degree of variability but are more closely related to each other than to any populations outside of Africa (From Van Sertima, 1979).

Figure 4. An Aricoid of the Nilotic variety. Models on racial differentiation that are scientifically invalid attribute certain facial features to Caucasoid influence, yet these modern populations show no blood group characteristics or any other genetic features that would relate them to Caucasoid populations (From Coon, C., 1965)

X – GROUP – IBRIM

Fig. 1.   Typical negro hair.   ♂   193 : 33 K   Fig. 2.   Face of same ; not typically negro.

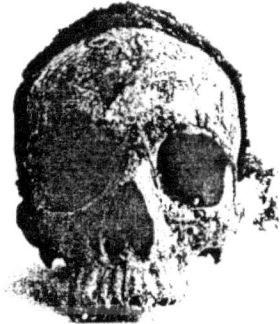

Figure 5. This figure illustrates a major problem in the racial analysis of ancient Nile Valley skeletal remains. The Nubian skull has hair attached that is clearly characteristic of Africoid variants. Yet, in the absence of the hair, this skull would probably have been classified as Caucasian, based on typological models (From Batrawi, A., 1945).

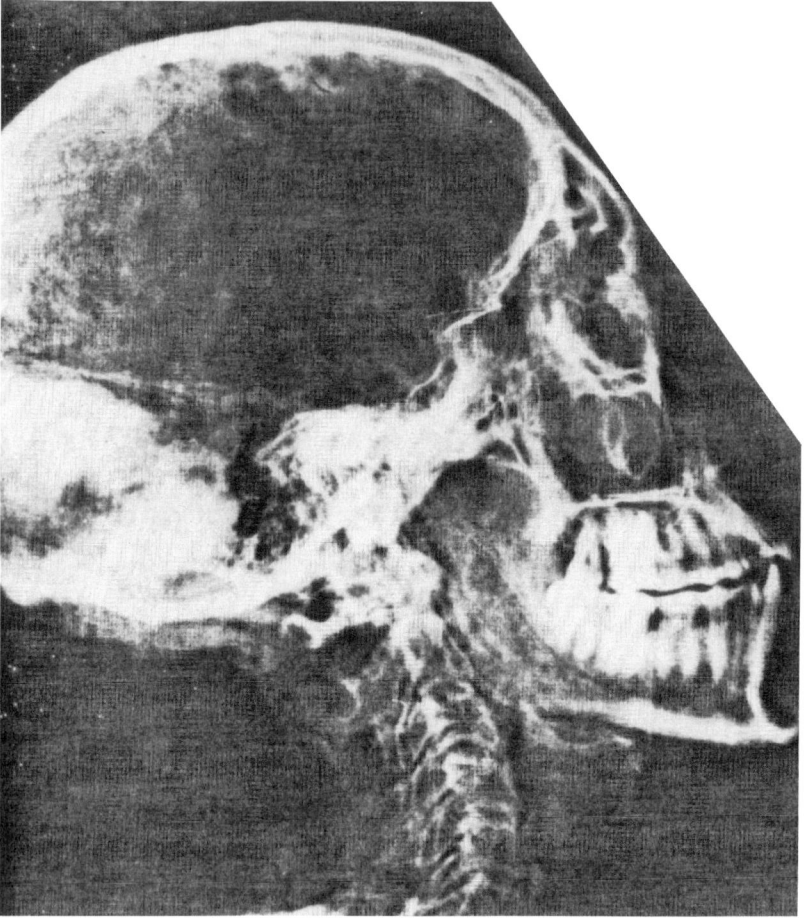

Figure 6. Facial prognathism is clearly visible in this X-ray profile of the mummy of Pharoah Thutmose IV (18th Dynasty, from Harris and Weeks, 1973).

EGYPT IS IN AFRICA
BUT WAS ANCIENT EGYPT AFRICAN?

Ivan Van Sertima

I would like to begin by redefining the question. I think it is very important from the outset that we understand clearly what it is that I seek to establish here today. The question as presented to me: *Were the Ancient Egyptians Black or White?* is not the ideal way in which such an issue should be posed, for, unintentional though it may be, it is a trap. It enables those who seek to undermine the contribution of early Africans to civilization, to appear in this debate as fair and balanced, blessed with a sweet reasonableness, while I, who only seek to set the historical record straight, am, by the very wording of the proposition, encouraged to take stands which, if not racist, are, at the least, simplistic and facile.

What I set out to do here is quite different. I seek to bring to heel the racists of the early nineteenth century and their reasonable-seeming apologists of the twentieth. To do this, it is necessary, as I say, to redefine the question. The question before us is this and it is in this way that it should hereafter be posed:

First, whether the ancient Egyptians were *predominantly* African or Africoid in a physical sense during the major native dynasties *before* the late invasions of the Persian, Greek, Roman and Arab foreigners.

Second, whether—and this is even more important—their language, their writing, their vision of god and the universe, their concept of the divine kingship, their ritual ceremonies and practices, their administrative and architectural symbols and structures, their techno-complex, were quintessentially African (that is, based essentially upon models and patterns developed in the continental heartland of Africa) and *not* (I repeat *not*) in any major particular, projected from those in Europe or Asia in that or any previous time.

Now, let me say one thing further before we proceed with an examination of this question. There was probably no great civilization in the world, be it

---

Excerpt from an address to the Brooklyn Museum on July 13 in a symposium entitled "Were the Ancient Egyptians Black or White?"

African, European, or Asian, that was entirely pure and homogeneous. The great Roman historian Pliny, who first saw the Britons in the second century A.D., describes *some of them* as having complexions as dark as the Ethiopian. Claudian, reporting the victory of the Roman general, Theodosius, over the English, mentions a good number of "nimble blackamoors" among them. The Chinese themselves recorded that there were men of black skin among the rulers of the Shang dynasty (1766–1100 B.C.). They actually speak of them as Na-Khi (*Na* in Chinese means black and *khi* means man). Schliemann and Evans, who excavated Minoan Crete, also tell us of the black skins of many of these Cretans who entered Greece in great numbers at an early time. Yet nobody would dare to pose questions such as: Were the ancient Chinese Black or Yellow? Were the ancient Greeks or the ancient Britons White or Mixed? No. No. No. No. No.

Everyone would immediately dismiss that for the nonsense that it is. The Blackamoors in second-century Britain, the black-skinned Cretans in ancient Greece, the *Na-Khi* or Black rulers and noblemen in the Shang Dynasty would be dismissed immediately as minor elements, as being of little or no consequence in the development of the indigenous civilization. But let there be a handful of Europeans or Asians in a vast body of Africans and immediately the question arises. Egypt is in Africa but was Egypt really African? Is the Egyptian Black or White? Why, I ask you, is it not an issue at all in the European or Asian case but becomes the Number One Issue in the African? The reasons for this are twofold. First of all, the Egyptian as we see him today is as different in his racial composition from the Egyptian of dynastic times, as we modern Americans in this room at this moment are from the early peoples who created native American civilization. Second, because we have been fed upon the achievements of European and Asian civilization. We would never dare to question the indigenous basis of their civilization. For we have not come upon them as we have come upon the poor African, his world looted and shattered, his empires in splinters, his peripheral elements focussed upon obsessively as though they were the very center and climax of his cultural development. All through our lived lives we have seen the European and to some extent the Asian, in the flower of their ascendancy. But we have been trained to see and to imagine only one kind of African—the primitive, the slave, the colonial, the tragic outcast and misfit on the edge of the modern world. If, therefore, we find him at the Center of a Civilization, the matter of its origin and its inspiration becomes highly suspect. The question immediately arises: Are we really dealing with a *true* African? Let us dig up his graves. Let us check out his crania. Let us rip off his mummy wraps. Is the nose of the ancient Egyptian broad enough to be Negro? Are his lips thick enough? Does his jaw jut out far enough? Is his skin Black enough? Is he not just a tanned European? A brown Mediterranean? A Eurafrican? A Hamite? An Afro-asian?

I am not simply being melodramatic, ladies and gentlemen. This is what has actually been happening. It is still going on. It has been going on now for more than two hundred years.

Let us look at what they found or claimed to have found when they opened the graves. An Oxford team—David Thomson and Randall McIver—declared in 1905 that only 25 percent of the ancient Egyptians were Negroid. Sir Arthur Keith challenged this, showing that if these parameters were used, then 30 percent of England's population would be classified as Negroid. Then came Professor Falkenberger who, using his parameters, decided that 36 percent of Egyptians before the dynasties were Negroid, 11 percent were Cro-Magnoid (that is European) and 20 percent were mixed. He also used a category that had become popular with all the racists trying desperately to de-Africanize Egypt—a category known as "Mediterranean". He placed as many as 33 percent in this "Mediterranean" box. Cheikh Anta Diop, the great Senegalese physicist, showed how unscientific this category was, since, using it as Falkenberger did, he could classify 90 percent of modern Africans as Mediterranean. In other words, not to mince matters, these paleoanatomists (as they call them) were playing the fool.

Two more recent studies make it clear that we are dealing with a type that is predominantly African even though the African, like other peoples, cannot be confined to one single cranial type or phenotype. In 1973 an analysis was done of what they call "non-metrical variation" in skulls. This study was done by A.C. Berry and R.J. Berry. The Egyptian skull samples show a gentic continuity from pre-Dynastic times right through the Old and Middle Kingdoms—a span of two thousand years. There is a shift in the New Kingdom where we still have very powerful African figures in control (witness the 17th—19th dynasties) but there seems to be some serious mixing going on. There is a considerable infiltration of new people into the Nile Valley. The study by the Indian team, Chatterjee and Kumar, in 1965, had come up with roughly the same results. Over a span of two thousand years they found skulls which, in respect to "long head, broad face, low orbit and broad nasal aperture, have the same characteristic features of the Negroid type." Allow me, before I leave this matter, to cite also a body of findings brought to my attention by an exhaustive and meticulous appraisal of the latest work of physical anthropologists done by Dana Reynolds. Work done on cranial and dental traits of the ancient Egyptians show a remarkable homogeneity (a great amount of sameness) right up until the period just before the dynasties of the Ptolemies. The Ptolemies are very late in the day, when the Greeks and Romans have invaded Africa. The findings of Greene, Carlson, Armelagos, Ucko and others are very important because they show that these Egyptians (even though some of them did not have all the expected classical Negroid traits) were misclassified as "Mediterranean" and falsely linked with Southern European types. They were descended, the findings show, from a type known as Mechtoid, a type which usually possessed the prognathism and broad-nosed traits we usually associate with the African type. This type was in no way allied to the type we have come to call Europoid or Caucasoid.

A very interesting test has been done on Egyptian mummies by the late Senegalese physicist, Cheikh Anta Diop. The melanin level in the skin between the derm and the epiderm varies with racial types and since mummies were preserved for thousands of years and the melanin granules flare and can be counted under a certain light, Diop was able to gauge the melanin level in the skin of mummies in the museum of Man. It was of a level only known in African man. This test is known as the Melanin Dosage test and it has been accepted by American science. Some years ago I was lecturing to doctors at the Center for Disease Control in Atlanta. I complained then that Egyptian authorities had refused my friend Diop permission to take tiny samples of skin from the mummies in the Cairo Museum so that he can extend his work in this field. Two specialists came forward, suggesting that I use their good offices to get permission for Diop to continue his work. Unfortunately Diop died less than a year afterwards and the matter was forgotten. I would like it to be recorded also that I was informed by a skeletal radiologist at Howard University that, in an examination of 11 Egyptian mummies, 2 were found to have carpal fusion. Carpal fusion is an unusual fusion of bones in the wrist. It is so rare in Europeans that an occurrence of 2 in 11,000 would raise medical eyebrows. It is considered in fact to be an almost exclusive African disease. Yet, after finding an incidence of 2 in a random sample of 11, the dishonest team of examiners in Cairo concluded that the mummies were either European or, at least, Semitic.

But why should we turn only to the witnesses of the dead? There were living witnesses who saw these Egyptians with their own eyes. Native Egyptians who had not yet lost the color of their skin nor the texture of their hair. Their flesh had not yet melted into the frame of their bones. True, they were not as obsessed as we are today about color and race. The Greeks did not see themselves pathologically as "white" people nor did the Egyptians see themselves pathologically as "black" people.

No stigmata was attached to color until much later in history when it came to determine one's status and even one's fate. But they were not blind to the fact that humans came in different colors. Herodotus travelled in Egypt. He speaks of them as being black in color and having wooly hair. He is not alone in this. We can cite Aristotle, Lucian, Appolodorus, Aeschylus, Achilles Tatius of Alexandria, Strabo, Diodorus of Sicily, Diogenes Laertius, Ammianus Marcellinus. They were not going into the graves. They were not measuring skulls. They were not testing for melanin in the skin. They were right there, looking into the faces of these people, talking with them, fighting with them, making love to them. And the Egyptians themselves used words to distinguish themselves that clearly makes you aware that they knew the color of their skin. Thank God though, they were far away from this sad sick time, so that they could be proud of it or ignore it altogether. . . .

BLACK LAND OF ANTIQUITY:
A BRIEF HISTORICAL OUTLINE OF DYNASTIC KMT

By Runoko Rashidi

From the beginning of the First Kemetic Dynasty and through the greater part of her Dynastic Period, African people with dark complexions, full lips, broad noses, and tightly-curled hair were overwhelmingly dominant in both the general population and the royal families.[1] By the latter portion of the fourth millennium B.C., the forces of the Black Land of Upper Kmt, probably during the reign of Narmer (the historical king often equated with the legendary Menes), had completed the task of coupling Upper Kmt in the South (the borders of which extended from the vicinity of the first cataract to the apex of the Delta), with Lower Kmt in the North (essentially the Delta) into a single unified state.[2] Although the history of the struggle for the unification of the *Two Lands* is lacking in many details, it is highly significant that Narmer, the first Lord of the Two Lands of Kmt, came from the South. On this point, it has been written:

> The southern Kingdom, Upper Egypt, was clearly conceived as the dominant of the two regions. It was from the south that the most enduring influences in Egyptian society came and without doubt most of its greatest leaders were southerners too. Throughout her long history Egypt constantly needed to return to the south to refresh herself and to restore her institutions, even perhaps her soul, when the weight of years or of external pressures laid too heavily upon her.[3]

According to the preeminent British Egyptologist of the late nineteenth and early twentieth century, William Mathew Flinders Petrie (1853-1942): "It is remarkable how renewed vitality has always come into Egypt from the south. . . . Each of the great stages of Egyptian history seems to owe its new energy to a southern conquest."[4] And as Dr. Cheikh Anta Diop (1923-1986) explained, "We also understand better now why the Egyptian term designating royalty etymologically means: (the man) 'who comes from the South' = who belongs to the South = who is a native of the South = the king of Egypt, not only the king of Upper Egypt."[5] Indeed, the establishment of the very early kingdom of Ta-Seti, based at Qustul in Lower Nubia, preceded

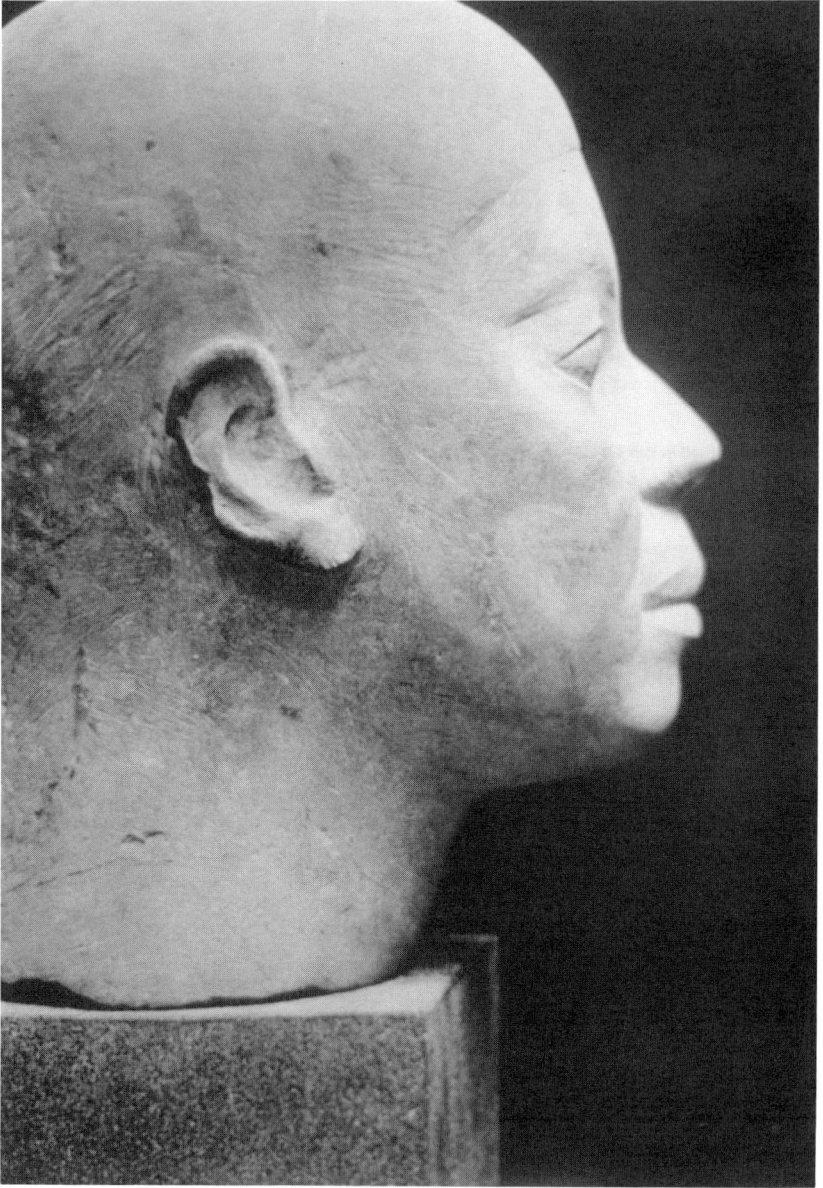

Figure 1. Portrait Head of a Princess of Dynasty IV.

the unification of Kmt and may have been the seat of Kmt's founding dynasty.[6] It should also be pointed out, that while Narmer is generally regarded by modern historians as Kmt's first true monarch, he likely saw himself as the culmination of an historical epoch rather than the beginning. Narmer was the heir to thousands of years of African achievement, and assumed charge of an already advanced and well-evolved society.

Ushered in by the conquests of King Narmer, Dynasties I and II (ca. 3200?–2686 B.C.E.), usually designated the *Early Dynastic* or *Archaic Period*, reflect the practical consolidation of Kmt as a nation-state. It was during the Early Dynastic Period that the White Wall—referred to by the Kamites as *Ineb-hedj* and designated in Graeco-Roman tradition as *Memphis*—at the frontier between Upper and Lower Kmt, was established as Kmt's administrative capital. The White Wall would remain one of Kmt's foremost centers through the length of the Dynastic Period.

Following Narmer, other important royal personages of the Early Dynastic Period include: Hor-Aha, perhaps Narmer's son, under whom major temples were erected and dedicated to the neters Ptah and Neit; Djer, who occupied the throne of Kmt for 47 years and celebrated far into Kemetic history as a superb physician; Mer-neit, who may have been Dynastic Kmt's first female monarch; Den, who conducted experiments with stone as a building material; and the last king of Dynasty II—Khasekhemui, another Southerner who strove aggressively to irrevocably cement the foundations of a strongly centralized Kemetic state. Of King Khasekhemui, Michael Rice notes that:

> It is probable that he, at least as much as Menes-Narmer, deserves the name of the Unifier of Egypt. If he was a giant in stature he remained a giant in the recollection of the people, for his memory was venerated profoundly over many centuries. The two statues from Hierakonpolis, the first from Egypt to show the King enthroned, are amongst the greatest works of art to survive from the earliest period.[7]

After the reign of Khasekhemui, Kmt's Early Dynastic Period gave way to the historical era known as the Old Kingdom (2686–2181 B.C.E.). The Old Kingdom, comprising Dynasties III through VI, was perhaps Kmt's First Golden Age. The Old Kingdom is chiefly appreciated as the famous epoch of Kemetic pyramid building. These monuments, particularly the three built over a seventy year period that dominate the Giza plateau, are arguably the world's most enduring expressions of architectural prowess, and remain a source of awe, wonder and inspiration.[8] The pyramid of Khufu itself—the purest geometric form in human architecture, has the distinction of being the largest single building ever constructed by man.[9]

From the Old Kingdom emerged such luminaries as: Netjerykhet Zoser, the first recognized royal personage to commission the construction of a

Figure 2. King Sahure of Dynasty V.

large monument in hewn stone; Bedjmes, the noted African ship-builder; the phenomenal Imhotep, architect, administrator, astronomer, author, magician, physician, and high-priest; Nae-maet Sneferu, the benevolent king during whose reign the classic pyramid form appeared; Khufu, builder of the Great Pyramid ('Khufu on the Horizon'); Khafre, who built the Second Giza Pyramid ('Great is Khafre') and may have had the face of Hor-m-akhet (the 'Great Sphinx') rendered in his own likeness; Menkaure, builder of the third Giza Pyramid ('Divine is Menkaure'); Hesyre, 'Chief of Dentists and Physicians'; Sahure, who launched the first recorded Kemetic expedition to Punt ('God's Land') in Inner Africa; Ptah-hotep, author of profound precepts of morality and ethics; Unas, whose tomb chamber was the first to be inscribed with the religious literature now known as the *Pyramid Texts*; and Pepi II, another Southerner, whose 94 years on the throne is the longest documented reign in human annals.

By 2180 B.C.E., increasingly arid climatic conditions and accelerating political decentralization had resulted in a drastic decline in Kemetic fortunes. Incursions of Asiatics into the Delta and social revolution hastened the decline.[10] Mer-en-Jehuti (Manetho) wrote that "The Seventh Dynasty consisted of seventy kings of Memphis, who reigned for 70 days."[11] Kmt's mines and quarries grew silent, and great temples were no longer constructed. River transport along the Nile came to a virtual halt, and poverty became widespread. This relatively obscure age of prevailing instability and popular discontent, known as Kmt's *First Intermediate Period*, lasted about 140 years and comprised Dynasties VII through X. It was during the First Intermediate Period that the Kemetic religious literature known as the *Coffin Texts* appeared.

During Dynasties IX and X (ca. 2160–2040 B.C.E.), domestic order was partially restored to much of Kmt through the authority of an African family based at Henen-nesut (Herakleopolis). Mer-en-Jehuti described the first king of Dynasty IX, who may have been a governor of the Twentieth Nome of Upper Kmt, as "more cruel than all his predecessors, and visited the whole of Egypt with dire disasters."[12] Of the eighteen monarchs of Dynasties IX and X, the best known members include: Kheti I, Kheti II, Neferkare, Kheti III, and Merikare.

Ancient Kmt's Second Golden Age, the *Middle Kingdom*, the significant period in Kemetic history encompassing Dynasties XI (ca. 2134–1991 B.C.E.) and XII (1991–1786 B.C.E.), was founded by the Mentuhoteps and Intefs—a distinguished and aggressive family of African nobles from Waset, the then unheralded city in Kmt's Scepter nome that the Greeks were to call *Thebes*. When Nebhepetre Mentuhotep II assumed the Upper Kemetic throne around 2060 B.C.E., his house was only able to claim hegemony over Southern Kmt. Under his determined and able leadership however, this situation changed dramatically and quickly, and early in his reign

Figure 3. King Nubkaure Amenemhet II of Dynasty XII.

the Southerners began their most sustained and ultimately successful drive for the reunification of all Kmt. This was accomplished in 2040 B.C.E., along with reestablishment of a strong central monarchy. Kmt, once again, was united under a single royal house, with Nebhepetre Mentuhotep II proclaimed as the nation's undisputed king.[13]

In 1991 B.C.E., another Southerner, Sehetepibre Amenemhet I (1991–1971 B.C.E.) founded Kemetic Dynasty XII. During his reign, for administrative purposes, the capital of Kmt was transferred from Waset north to It-Tawy ('Holder-of-the-Two Lands'). Of the eight monarchs of Dynasty XII, the first six each had reigns of more than nineteen years. Nubkaure Amenemhet II (1929–1895 B.C.E.) dedicated a temple in Sinai to the goddess Heru, and sent an expedition to Punt. Khakaure Senusret III (1878–1843 B.C.E.) was a formidable militarist. Nymare Amenemhet III (1843–1797 B.C.E.) raised two Pyramids and commissioned the construction of the monument that came to be called the 'Egyptian Labyrinth.' The Labyrinth must have been one of the largest buildings in antiquity, and contained three thousand individual rooms—fifteen hundred below the ground and fifteen hundred above the ground.

Herodotus (ca. 485–425 B.C.E.)—author of the first significant prose work in European literature—wrote that the Labyrinth surpassed the pyramids, and noted that, "I have seen this building, and it is beyond my power to describe; it must have cost more in labor and money than all the walls and public works of the Greeks put together."[14] Petrie, who excavated the site in 1888, provided additional information on this extraordinary African edifice:

> These mere figures will not signify readily to the mind the vast extent of construction; but when we compare it with the greatest of the other Egyptian temples it could be somewhat realised. On that space could be erected the great hall of Karnak, and all the successive temples adjoining it, and the great court and pylons of it; also the temple of Mut, and that of Khonsu, and that of Amenhotep III at Karnak; also the two great temples of Luxor; and still there would be room for the whole of the Ramesseum. In short, all the temples on the east bank of Thebes, and one of the largest on the west bank, might be placed together in the one area. . . . Here we certainly have a site worthy of the renown which the labyrinth acquired.[15]

Following Dynasty XII, Kmt experienced her *Second Intermediate Period*. It has even been suggested that the Dynasty XIII kings were actually elected as rulers for indefinite Periods of time.[16] Dynasty XIII was based at Waset. Even more obscure than Dynasty XIII, Kemetic Dynasty XIV was based at Ineb-hedj (Memphis). Mer-en-Jehuti provides a combined total of 136 monarchs for both dynasties.[17] The end of Dynasty XIV coincided with the general collapse of Kmt's central government. A disorganized Kmt was

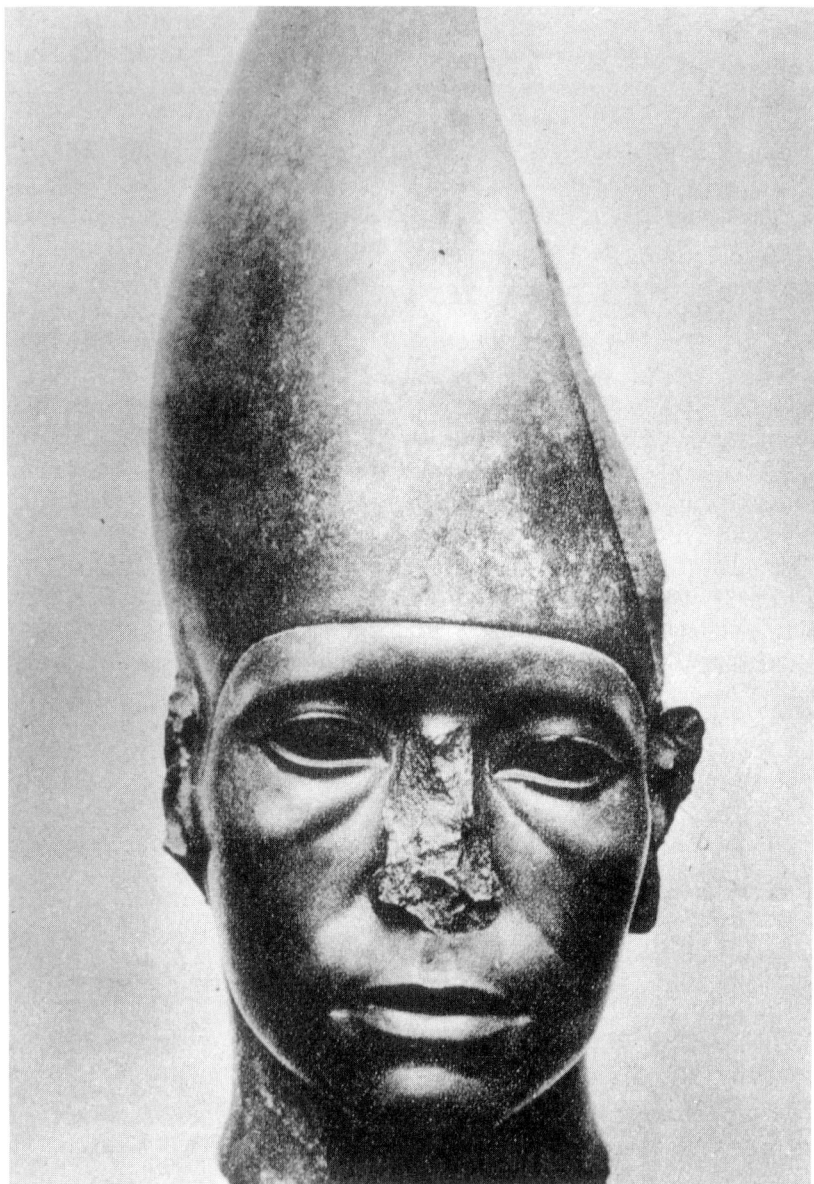

Figure 4. King Nymare Amenemet III of Dynasty XII.

obviously not prepared for its national defense and unfortunately the Second Intermediate Period occurred at a time of serious upheaval and migrations in Western Asia. Capitalizing on Kmt's internal disarray were the Hyksos— the Rule*rs of Foreign Lands,* who proceeded to occupy the country in force. According to Mer-en-Jehuti:

> Unexpectedly, from the regions of the East, invaders of obscure race marched in confidence of victory against our land. By main force they easily seized it without striking a blow; and having overpowered the rulers of the land, they burned our cities ruthlessly, razed to the ground the temples of the gods, and treated all the natives with cruel hostility, massacring some and leading into slavery the wives and children of others. Finally, they appointed as king one of their number.[18]

The Hyksos occupied Kmt for more than a century, and constituted Dynasties XV and XVI. During Dynasty XVII they remained dominant in northern Kmt, while in southern Kmt the Blacks were intensifying their national liberation struggle. Among the principal leaders of this struggle were: King Seqenenre Tao I, Queen Tetisheri, King Seqenenre Tao II, Queen Ahhotep I, and King Wadjkheperre Kamose. Generally speaking, and in this period in particular, it should be stressed that the women of the royal Kemetic families exercised considerable influence and occupied positions of great authority.[19] Queen Tetisheri of Dynasty XVII is one such example:

> Tetisheri must be looked upon, therefore, as in every way a predecessor of that remarkable line of XVIIIth dynasty queens whose rights and prerogatives were so high that they were virtual rulers of the country. Presumably it was in them that the family strain was purest and through them that the inheritance passed. Most of them survived their husbands, and in widowhood held enhanced influence. For about a century the royal family was to all intents and purposes a virtual matriarchate. The active, warlike functions and the ritualistic offices were the men's, and officially they took precedence, but a large share in actual government lay in the hands of this line of women.
>
> Tetisheri is not only the earliest of this line whose name has survived—she must have actually headed it. ... She was the ancestress of a line of women famous in Egyptian history: Ahhotep, Ahmose-Nefretiri, Ahhotep II, Ahmose and finally Hatshepsut with whose ambitions the female line of the royal family reached its climax and suffered its eclipse.[20]

Under the inspired leadership of Ahmose I and his wife and queen, Ahmose-Nefertari (whose veneration continued for more than six hundred years after her death), the Africans finally marshalled the strength to eject the Hyksos. King Ahmose I and Ahmose-Nefertari are hence recognized as the founders of Dynasty XVIII—the beginning of Kmt's Third Golden Age.

Figure 5. King Nebmare Amenhotep III of Dynasty XVIII.

Usually referred to as the *New Kingdom*, sometimes designated as the *Age of Empire*, this epoch comprised Dynasties XVIII through XX , and lasted from about 1570 B.C.E. to 1080 B.C.E. Based at Waset, it was during Dynasty XVIII that Kmt, out of a desire to guarantee its national security, established itself as a militant world power with the status of a large empire. Undoubtedly, Dynasty XVIII was probably the apogee of Kemetic might and influence. There were major expeditions to Punt and important economic relations were maintained with Minoan Crete, Bronze Age Cyprus, and Myceanean Greece. Much of Southwest Asia was subjugated and reduced to vassalage.

In addition to Ahmose I and Ahmose-Nefertari, Dynasty XVIII was the age of: Makare Hatshepsut, the determined and capable female sovereign who sent an expedition to Punt; Senenmut, 'Overseer of Works' during the reign of Makare Hatshepsut and the architect of Hatshepsut's mortuary temple at Waset; Menkheperre Thutmose III, the redoubtable warrior-king who personally directed seventeen military campaigns and extended the Kemetic empire from the Upper Nile to the Upper Euphrates; Menkheprure Thutmose IV, who excavated Hor-m-akhet (the 'Great Sphinx'); Nebmare Amenhotep III ('The Magnificent'), who reigned for thirty-eight years at the peak of Dynasty XVIII; Queen Tiye, 'Great Royal Wife' of Amenhotep III; Amenhotep (son of Hapu)—scribe, government official, and architect during the reign of Nebmare Amenhotep III; Akhenaten, who orchestrated one of the world's most dramatic religious reformations and during whose reign the Kemetic empire was allowed to wither and decay; and Nebkheprure Tutankhaman ("King Tut"), the famous "boy-king," who held the throne for only nine years but the contents of whose tomb the world continues to marvel at.

Kemetic Dynasty IXX was founded by Menpehtyre Ramses I, who reigned only briefly. Ramses I was succeeded on the throne by his son, Menmare Seti I, under whom efforts were made to revive the Empire. Clearly though, the single most towering figure of Kemetic Dynasty IXX was Usermare Ramses II— commonly known as "Ramses the Great." The sixty-seven year reign of Ramses II was for Kmt an era of general prosperity, stable government and exceptional construction projects.[21] The dominance of Amen was restored and his priests firmly reinstated. Ramses II was actually deified in his own lifetime, and it was largely through the unrelenting projection of his own personality that both Dynasties IXX and XX are often simply referred to today as the "Ramesside Dynasties."

Following Ramses II, the stature of Kmt, once again, began to deteriorate. Baenre Merneptah, the thirteenth son and successor of Ramses II, was forced to repel a major foray into Kmt by a violent confederation of Sea Peoples—the perpetrators of rampant devastation in the eastern Mediterranean and northern Africa during the later portion of the second millennium

Figure 6. Queen Tiye of Dynasty XVIII.

B.C.E. During Dynasty XX, Usermare-Meryamen Ramses III led Kmt's defense against three desperate invasions of Libyan tribesmen and the nomadic Sea Peoples. Shortly thereafter, Kmt experienced prolonged labor troubles among government workers and an inflationary rise in wheat prices. During the middle of Dynasty XX occurred a sharp decline in the value of copper and bronze, accompanied by a gradual weakening of central authority. Kemetic royal tombs were apparently robbed with impunity by high officials, and the country may have experienced a severe famine. It is probably no coincidence that it was in Dynasty XX that the craft of mummification reached its zenith.

At the beginning of Dynasty XXI, the power in Kmt was apportioned between the priesthood of Amen, which ruled over Upper Kmt, and northern princes who ruled Lower Kmt from the eastern Delta. Dynasty XXII was a Libyan dynasty.[22] Its first ruler, Hedjkheperre Sheshonq I (946–925 B.C.E.), invaded Palestine and plundered Jerusalem. During Dynasty XXIII, local rulers proliferated in Kmt. In Dynasty XXIV, the Libyan prince Tefnakhte of northern Kmt made a treaty with Hosea of Samaria against Assyria; his son, Bakenrenef (Bocchoris), supported the king of Israel against Assyria. This turbulent era, comprising Dynasties XI through XXIV, during which civil wars were waged intermittently, lasted about three centuries and constituted Kmt's *Third Intermediate Period.*

It was only with the rise and enthronement of the Kushite rulers of Dynasty XXV that a powerful movement of cultural revival and economic resurgence in Kmt was sparked.[23] Dynasty XXV, Kmt's Fourth Golden Age, was based at Napata, near the fourth cataract. The entire line of Dynasty XXV kings were men of great piety, confident in the belief that they were the true seat of Kemetic sovereignty. About 750 B.C.E., the Kushite king Kashta made a Pilgrimage to the Amen Temples at Waset, where he was hailed 'King of Upper and Lower Kmt.' A daughter of Kashta, Amenirdas I, was installed in Waset with the title of 'Divine Wife of the God Amen.' In 730 B.C.E., Kashta's son and successor, Piye (Piankhi), conquered Upper and Lower Kmt, but chose to govern from Kush (Upper Nubia between the third and sixth cataracts). Finally, about 715 B.C.E., Shabaka, Piye's brother and successor, completed the total reunification of Kmt and ruled from Waset, the head of a stupendous Kushite empire that extended from the Mediterranean southwards to the confluence of the Blue and White Niles. It was during this time that the ancient creation story currently known as the *Memphite Theology* was copied on a granite slab.[24] During the reign of Shabaka's successor, Shabataka, the demotic script was introduced.

Perhaps the most outstanding sovereign of Dynasty XXV was Taharqa (690–664 B.C.E.). As a prince he is believed to have led an African expedition to Spain. As King, he commanded military campaigns in Western Asia

Figure 7. King Usermare Ramses II of Dynasty IXX.

to save his Jewish allies from destruction at the hands of the Assyrians[26]. As "A loving son, Taharqo at one point sent for his mother, resident in far-off Napata, to visit him, so that she could enjoy the sight of her son on the throne of Upper and Lower Egypt."[27]

It is regrettable that so much of the focus of the Dynasty XXV monarchs had to be directed towards fending off a menacing nation of foreign aggressors—the Assyrians. The Assyrians equipped their armies with iron weapons and, unlike many nations of antiquity, placed no heavy dependence on foreign mercenaries whose loyalties might shift at any time. The bulk of the Assyrian armies consisted of archers, heavily armed spearmen, shield bearers, horsemen, and heavy chariotry. The Assyrian armies were well trained and utilize battering rams and formidable siege machines. For several decades the Africans held their own against the Assyrians, but in 671 B.C.E. Assyrian legions invaded Kmt and ransacked Ineb-hedj (Memphis). In 663 B.C.E., Assyrian armies again invaded Kmt and this time pillaged Waset, massacred its inhabitants, and emptied the temples of their treasures. According to Diop:

> The fall of the most venerated city of all Antiquity aroused deep emotion in the world of that time and marked the end of the Nubian Sudanese or Twenty-fifth Ethiopian Dynasty. That date also marked the decline of Black political supremacy in Antiquity and in history.[28]

In 658 B.C.E., Psametik I, initially an Assyrian vassal, established Kemetic Dynasty XXVI. With the intervention of Greek mercenaries, he eventually managed to successfully discard the yoke of Assyrian domination. The kings of Dynasty XXVI, which was based at Sau (Sais) in the western Delta, tried to restore Kmt's former grandeur by promoting commercial expansion. Large numbers of foreigners, particularly Greeks, settled in Kmt during Dynasty XXVI. Dynasty XXVI was also a period in which numerous foreign scholars, including Thales (ca. 636–546 B.C.E.) and Pythagoras (ca. 582–507 B.C.E.), studied in Kmt.[29] Additionally, it was during Dynasty XXVI that the prophet Jeremiah (ca. 628–586 B.C.E.) sojourned in Kmt, a bronze statue bearing the name of King Sendji of Dynasty II was made, and the near-legendary Imhotep of Dynasty III was deified as a god of science and medicine.

Dynasty XXVI was an era of martial conflicts in which Kmt was largely inadequate. During the long reign of Psametik I, the entire military garrison at Abu (Elephantine) deserted to the the king of Kush, who is said to have provided them with land grants and wives in the southern portion of the kingdom. In 605 B.C.E., the Kemetic military was soundly defeated by the Babylonians at the battle of Carchemish. The Babylonians never successfully occupied Kmt, but they remained a constant threat to the security of

Figure 8. King Taharqa of Dynasty XXV.

the country until the Babylonians themselves were eclipsed by the rising strength of Persia.

In 525 B.C.E., the Persians, under Cambyses II, invaded, conquered, and incorporated Kmt into the Persian Empire. It was during Dynasty XXVII—the time of the Persian occupation, that Hecataeus of Miletus (ca. 510 B.C.E.) and Herodotus of Halicarnassus (ca. 450 B.C.E.) visited Kmt. The short-lived Dynasty XXVIII (404–399 B.C.E.), which consisted of only one king—Amyrtaeus, was based at Sau (Sais). It was in Dynasty XXIX that Plato (428–347 B.C.E.) studied in Kmt, while Democritus (ca. 460–370 B.C.E.) pursued his education in Kmt in Dynasty XXX.

In 343 B.C.E., King Nectanebo II was defeated by the Persians under Ataxerxes III. In 332 B.C.E., came the invasion and occupation of Kmt under Alexander of Macedon (356–323 B.C.E.) and the Ptolemaic Dynasty (305–30 B.C.E.). As for Alexander himself, 'Records say he wanted to be buried in Egypt's Siwa Oasis, near Libya, but finally was encased in a gold coffin in Alexandria, the Mediterranean city he founded.'[30]

One of the most brilliant and influential intellectuals of the early period of Ptolemaic rule in Kmt was the celebrated African scholar and priest—Mer-en-Jehuti—more widely known as Manetho of Sebennytos (ca. 275 B.C.E.). The Lower Kemetic city of Sebennytos had been the nation's capital during Dynasty XXX. Manetho, whose authority has been acknowledged several times in this essay, is credited with having written in Greek *The Sacred Book, An Epitome of Physical Doctrines*, and *Aegyptiaca (The History of Egypt)*. It was in the latter work—still the primary fabric connecting Kemetic history—that the famed African scholar organized the monarchs of Kmt into its present dynastic structure.[31]

Notes

1. Among the most unrelenting twentieth century advocates of this view has been Dr. Yosef Alfredo Antonio ben-Jochannan, to whom this essay is dedicated. Born 31, December 1917 in Gondar, Ethiopia, "Dr. Ben" has devoted the better part of his life to the illumination of the African origins of Nile Valley civilizations. In 1939, ben-Jochannan went to Egypt for the first time, and moved to Harlem, New York in 1945. Since 1957, he has coordinated regular study tours and pilgrimages to the Nile Valley, directly exposing thousands of African people to the still visible splendors of ancient Kmt. Professor Emeritus at Cornell University's Africana Studies Department, ben-Jochannan has also been a professor-at-large at Al Azar University in Cairo. Dr. ben-Jochannan remains uncompromising in his views, an active public speaker and a prolific writer, and has probably done more to popularize African history than any living scholar. Dr. Ben has brought African history to life for the masses of African people. This is perhaps his greatest legacy and gift.

Among the most acclaimed nineteenth century advocates of the African origin of Nile Valley civilizations were Martin Robison Delany and Edward Wilmot Blyden. Delany (1812–1885), often called "the father of Black nationalism," might also be regarded as a nascent Kemetologist. As early as 1879, Delany wrote that, "This admission of the hieroglyphic representations to be found on the temples and monuments of Egypt of the advanced status of the negro race, settles at once the controversy, and leaves only to be proven the fact, that the earliest settlers, builders of the pyramids, sculptors of the sphinxes. and original god-kings, were blacks of the negro race." Martin R. Delany, *Principles of Ethnology: Origins of Races and Color with an Archaeological Compendium of Ethiopian and Egyptian Civilization, From Years of Careful Examination and Enquiry* (Philadelphia: Harper & Brother, 1879; rpt., Baltimore: Black Classic Press, 1991), 64. Delany's 'historicizing racial consciousness was reflected in the names he gave his children, which included . . . Ramses Placido (after both the pharaoh Ramses and a Cuban poet and hero of the struggle for liberation)."

Edward Wilmot Blyden (1832–1912), who popularized the slogan "Africa for the Africans," wrote and travelled extensively. During a visit to Egypt in 1866, Blyden recorded that, "Feelings came over me far different from those which I have felt when looking at the mighty works of European genius. *I felt that I had a peculiar heritage in the Great Pyramid* built . . . by the enterprising sons of Ham, from which I descended. The blood seemed to flow faster through my veins. I seemed to hear the echo of those illustrious Africans. I seemed to feel the impulse from those stirring characters who sent civilization to Greece—the teachers of the father of poetry, history, and mathematics—Homer, Herodotus, and Euclid. I seemed to catch the sound of the 'stately steppings' of Jupiter, as, with his brilliant celestial retinue, he perambulates the land on a visit to my ancestors , the 'blameless Ethiopians'. I felt lifted out of the commonplace grandeur of modern times; and, could my voice have reached every African in the world, I would have earnestly addressed him . . . : 'Retake your Fame.'" Edward W. Blyden, *From West Africa to Palestine* (Freetown: T.J. Sawyer, 1873), 112.

2. The chronologies and dates given for each of Kmt's major periods, dynasties, and kings, are approximate calculations from Manetho, the *Royal Annals of the Palermo Stone*, the *Table of Karnak King-List*, the *Table of Abydos King-List*, the *Table of Sakkara*, the *Turin Canon of Kings*, and other ancient and contemporary sources, and are the subjects of continuing debate and controversy.

3. Michael Rice, *Egypt's Making* (London: Routledge, 1991), 25. "The culture which grew and flourished in the Nile Valley was wholly autochthonous. It grew out of the lives and preoccupations of the cattle-rearing African peoples (black Africans, it must certainly be acknowledged) who were the true ancestors of the Pharaohs, in all their majesty and power. The Egyptians long held on to the recognition of their essentially African character. . . . Egypt's decline began when these essentially African characteristics became diluted by incursions from outside the Valley." Rice, 221.

4. W.M. Flinders Petrie, "The Origin of the XIIth Dynasty," *Ancient Egypt* (June 1924), 42.

5. Cheikh Anta Diop, *Civilization or Barbarism*, eds. H.J. Salemson and M. de Jager, trans. Yaa-Lengi Meema Ngemi, (Westport: Lawrence Hill, 1991), 108.

6. "Later king lists refer to whole dynasties before the unification of Egypt, but the names cannot be connected to any specific monuments, events or people. They are dynasties without substance preceded by the entirely mythological kingship of the gods. Until now, the lack of direct evidence has made the study of these early sovereignties largely speculative. Direct evidence for kings in the Nile Valley before the reign of Narmer has finally emerged in context . . . Qustul in Lower Nubia, very near the present-day border of Egypt and the Sudan." Bruce Williams, "Lost Pha-

raohs of Nubia," *Archaeology* 33, No. 5 (1980), 13. In a more recent report, Williams reaffirmed that "The persons buried in the great tombs of Cemetery L at Qustul were pharaohs." Bruce Williams, *The A-Group Royal Cemetery at Qustul: Cemetery L* (Chicago: Oriental Institute of the University of Chicago, 1986), 163.

7. Rice, 145

8. Says an Arab proverb, "All the world fears Time, but Time fears the Pyramids." Cited by Will Durant, *Our Oriental Heritage* (New York: Simon & Schuster, 1954), 150. Napoleon Bonaparte calculated that there was enough stone in the Giza pyramids to build a wall surrounding the entire country of France. "According to his calculations, the three pyramids on the Giza plateau contained enough stone to build a wall, measuring 10 feet in height and 1 foot in width, around the whole of France. The mathematician Monge, who was among the savants accompanying Napoleon on this campaign, is alleged to have confirmed this calculation." I.E.S. Edwards, *The Pyramids of Egypt* (New York: Viking, 1972), 82.

9. "Egyptian architectural work implies mechanical and technical knowledge that specialists have not yet finished discussing. The scholars know that nobody is yet capable of giving a satisfactory explanation of the manner in which the Egyptians proceeded with the construction of the Great Pyramid of Khufu (Cheops)." Diop, *Civilization or Barbarism*, 285.

10. "During the VIth Dynasty; a general paralysis of the state's economy and administration resulted in the cities as well as in the countryside. Thus, the end of the VIth Dynasty saw the first people's uprising of certain date in universal history. The destitute of Memphis, the capital and sanctuary of Egyptian royalty, sacked the town, robbed the rich, and drove them into the streets. There was a true reversal of the social conditions and the financial situations. The movement rapidly spread to other cities. It appears that the city of Sais was temporarily governed by a group of ten notables." Diop, 141.

11. *Manetho*, trans. W.G. Waddell (Cambridge: Harvard University Press, 1940), 55. Manetho's claim is almost certainly an exaggeration, but it is nevertheless a dramatic assertion of the weakness and uncertainty of the formerly stable nation-state. The Kemetic nomes, once the official administrative districts of a strong centralized government, had returned to their original status as small independent states. Mass unrest and anarchy became the order of the day. The Prophecies of Neferti reflect the turmoil and despair of the times: "Every mouth is full of 'how I wish.' All happiness has vanished; The land is ruined, its fate decreed, Deprived of produce, lacking in crops, What was made has been unmade. One seizes a man's goods, gives them to an outsider, I show you the master in need, the outsider stated, The lazy stuffs himself, the active is needy. One gives only with hatred, To silence the mouth that speaks; To answer a speech the arm thrusts a stick; One speaks by killing him." Miriam Lichtheim, *Ancient Egyptian Literature*, vol. 1 (Berkeley: University of California Press, 1975), 142.

12. *Manetho*, 61–63.

13. Nebhepetre Mentuhotep II was the dominant personality of the early Middle Kingdom. In describing a statue of this king, art historian Jules Taylor wrote that: "The eyes stare out with hypnotic intensity from the black painted face. Its bodily proportions are compact, yet massive, so that the arms which are folded across the chest, and the fists which clutch the royal staffs, the crook and the flail, seem indeed capable, if they were invested with life, of joining and holding together the Two Lands, from the cataracts to the Delta. Under the short white cloak he wears, Mentuhotep's legs are disproportionately large and muscular, as though to dramatize their owner's unquestionable and timeless steadfastness to the ground he occu-

pies." Jules Taylor, 'The Black Image in Egyptian Art," *Journal of African Civilizations* 1, No. 1 (1979), 36.

14. Herodotus, *The Histories*, rev. ed., trans. Aubrey de Selincourt (Harmondsworth: Penguin, 1972), 188. Herodotus also wrote that, "The Egyptians who live in the cultivated parts of the country, by their practice of keeping records of the past, have made themselves the most learned of any nation of which I have had experience." Herodotus, 158.

15. Petrie, *Hawara, Biahmu, and Arsinoe* (London: Field & Tuer, 1889), 5.

16. John Van Seters, *The Hyksos* (New Haven: Yale University Press, 1976), 95.

17. *Manetho*, 75.

18. *Manetho*, 79.

19. "The foremost and most significant fact to bear in mind when dealing with the issue of women and leadership in ancient Kemet (Egypt) is simply that there was equality between men and women. The woman had political power as well as a general voice in running the country, as did her sisters in other parts of Africa. The woman had the opportunity to hold high office and was often very wealthy and prosperous. This was in contrast to the situation of her counterpart, the woman of the Near East and Asia." Diedre Wimby, "The Female Horuses and Great Wives of Kemet," *Black Women in Antiquity*, ed. Ivan Van Sertima (New Brunswick: Journal of African Civilizations, 1988), 36.

Probably the most consistently eloquent and scholarly of all the writers who have addressed the extraordinarily prominent role of African women in world history is Dr. John Henrik Clarke.

20. Herbert E. Winlock, "On Queen Tetisheri, Grandmother of Ahmose I," *Ancient Egypt* (lst Qtr. 1921), 16. 'Hatshepsut came from a long line of dynamic women. Among these was Queen Ahmose-Nefertari, wife of Ahmose, founder of the Eighteenth Dynasty. Ahmose-Nefertari was given considerable authority in the cult of the King of the Gods when she was made God's Wife of Amon, a position that held a chief role as a priestess in the national cult center and was provided with goods and property legally documented and published for all to see on a monumental stela set up in the temple of Amon at Karnak. . . . Her royal titles included the exceptional Female Chieftain of Upper and Lower Egypt, which makes it likely that after her husband died she ruled as regent for her son, Amenhotep I. . . . Ahmose-Nefertari outlived Amenhotep and was honored as well by his picked successor, Thutmose I, when he set up a colossal statue of the old queen in the court he built at Karnak." Barbara S. Lesko, "Women's Monumental Mark on Ancient Egypt," *Biblical Archaeologist* 54, No. 1 (1991), 12.

21. Some of the world's most outstanding African-centric scholars have placed pronounced emphasis on Kemetic Dynasty XIX, with major focus on the almost larger than life Ramses II. Drusilla Dunjee Houston (1876–1941), wrote that "Rameses II . . . was the Sesostris of the Greeks. He reigned sixty-seven years. The temple of Abydos records the names of sixty daughters and fifty-nine sons. He built two magnificent temples in Nubia and part of the temples of Karnak and Luxor." Drusilla Dunjee Houston, *Wonderful Ethiopians of the Ancient Cushite Empire* (1926; rpt. Baltimore: Black Classic Press, 1985), 105.

Chancellor Williams wrote that, "In 1320 B.C. the Age of Ramses began. This time, a line of great leaders was not followed by a line of weaklings. This was the Nineteenth Dynasty 1320–1200 B.C." Williams, 117. John Henrik Clarke emphasizes that the pharaohs of the l9th Dynasty, especially Rameses II, restored Egypt's building-age and took it to the apex of its achievement as the best-known state of the ancient world." John Henrik Clarke, Foreword to *The African Called Rameses*

("The Great") II, by Yosef A.A. ben-Jochannan (New York: Ben-Jochannan, 1990), 13

The venerable cultural historian John G. Jackson observed that, "The Nineteenth Dynasty began with the reign of Hormhab, but the great ruler of this dynasty was Rameses II. In a reign of sixty-six years this monarch conquered extensive territories in Western Asia and built colossal temples in the Nile Valley." John G. Jackson, *Ages of Gold and Silver* (Austin: American Atheist Press, 1990), 53. According to Yosef A.A. ben-Jochannan, "If there is one solitary 'pharaoh' I must qualify it is Rameses II." Yosef A.A. ben-Jochannan, *The African Called Rameses ("The Great")* II. 25. Harmonizing with ben-Jochannan, Cheikh Anta Diop wrote that "The highest point of Egyptian history was the Nineteenth Dynasty of Ramses II." Cheikh Anta Diop, "The Beginnings of Man and Civilization," *Great African Thinkers*, eds. Ivan Van Sertima and Larry Obadele Williams (New Brunswick: Journal of African Civilizations, 1986), 341.

22. Dr. Chancellor Williams (1893–1992), former professor of African History at Howard University and the author of *The Destruction of Black Civilization*—a classic work based on sixteen years of documentary field research in which he addressed the controversial question of the ethnicity of the Libyans. According to Williams, "They were, first of all, Western Ethiopians, then heavily Berber, Mongolian, Arab, a sprinkling of Hebrews and other Asiatic peoples, and then, of course, the resulting Afro-Asians. The ethnic composition of the Libyan was about the same as that of early Egypt, with the exception that there were fewer Europeans and more Mongolians. Libya was once so nearly all black that to be called a Libyan meant Black. So the Libyan dynasties during this period could have been predominantly white, Black, Afro-Asian or a combination of all three, depending upon what faction was in ascendancy at the time." Chancellor Williams, *The Destruction of Black Civilization,* rev. ed Chicago: Third World Press, 1974), 118-19.

23. "Around 750 BC, the Napatan dynasts of Cush under Piankhy and his immediate successors took a giant leap forward onto the world spotlight by their pacification and reunification of Egypt. At this juncture in history, that part of Upper Egypt south of Thebes had become a part of Cush but the rest of Egypt had disintegrated into mutually warring petty kingdoms. We cannot delve into this chapter of Egyptian history in any detail but suffice to say that when Piankhy undertook to reunify Egypt he was not looked upon as a usurper or foreign conqueror but rather as a deliverer. As a pious and devoted follower of Amon-Ra, his intercession was, for the most part, welcomed. With the entrance of the kings of Cush into Egyptian history we have the inauguration of the 25th or 'Ethiopian' dynasty of Pharaohs. The 25th dynasty sparked a renaissance in an otherwise moribund Egyptian culture, with some of Egypt's most vigorous art and monument building emerging in this period. There is evidence too of a program of world-wide commerce and exploration that was initiated during the 25th dynasty." Larry Williams and Charles S. Finch, "The Great Queens of Ethiopia," *Black Women in Antiquity*, ed. Ivan Van Sertima (New Brunswick: Journal of African Civilizations, 1988), 21.

24. "The text called the *Memphite Theology*, transmitted by the stela of Shabaka, is an essay on philosophical and theological reflection of Ptah's priests in his Memphis sanctuary." Theophile Obenga, *Ancient Egypt and Black Africa* (London: Karnak House, 1992), 25. "It is actually a text recopied during the reign of Shabaka in the 25th Dynasty and is concerned primarily with the divine basis for governance. The extant text is badly damaged and only a small part of the original is intelligible." Jacob H. Carruthers, "The Wisdom of Governance in Kemet," *Kemet and the African Worldview* (Los Angeles: University of Sankore, 1986), 6.

25. "The second major intrusion of an African army into Spain before the Moors, occurs sometime around 700 B.C. during the period of the 25th dynasty in Egypt, when the Ethiopian Taharka was a young general, but before he had been ceded the throne by his uncle Shabataka.

It is this same Taharka (referred to in early Spanish chronicles as Tarraco) that led a garrison into Spain and invaded it during this Period. We have a clear and indisputable reference to this in a manuscript by Florian de Ocampo *Cronica General* published in Medina del Campo in 1553. The name of the invading general is given as Tarraco. He is not only identified as head of the Ethiopian army. The reference is more specific. It says he was later to become a King of Egypt. The name, the period, the historical fact of his generalship and his later kingship of Egypt, his Ethiopian origin and the wide-ranging trade and exploration of the Ethiopian in this period, all attest to the validity of this reference." Ivan Van Sertima "The Moor in Africa and Europe," *Golden Age of the Moor*, ed. Ivan Van Sertima (New Brunswick: Journal of African Civilizations, 1992), 2.

Megasthenes (ca. 300 B.C.E.) may preserve a similar tradition concerning Taharka in Europe. Megasthenes wrote that "Tearcon (Tabarka?) the Ethiopian, extended their conquests as far as Europe . . . and carried his arms as far as the Pillars: to which also it is said Tearcon arrived." *Indian Fragments,* in *Ancient Fragments,* ed. I.P. Cory (Minneapolis: Savage, 1975), 227.

26. Taharqa may have been the only king of Dynasty XXV to be mentioned in the Bible: "And then he heard say of Tirhakah, king of Ethiopia, Behold, he is come out to fight against thee." 2 Kings 19: 9. "And he heard say concerning Tirhakah king of Ethiopia, He is come forth to make war with thee." Isaiah 37: 9.

27. Timothy Kendall and Susan K. Doll, *Kush: Lost Kingdom of the Nile* (Brockton: Brockton Art Museum, 1982), 10. "In the Sudanese part of their empire the entourages of Kushites frequently included their mothers, wives, sisters and female cousins. This was not so in Egypt proper, though the Kushite Pharaohs were assisted at Thebes by the divine votaresses—princesses vowed to virginity with the god Amon as their only spouse. Conceded quasi-royal privileges, the Amenirdises and Shepenoupets formed a kind of parallel dynasty with succession from aunt to niece." Jean Leclant, "The Empire of Kush: Napata and Meroe," *UNESCO General History of Africa*, vol. 2, ed. G. Mokhtar (Berkeley: University of California Press, 1981), 283.

"In our look at the 25th dynasty, we can get a sense of the very real prominence, both politically and religiously, of the queens of Cush during this Period. They seemed to wield power that was almost unprecedented in Egyptian annals and are instrumental, even after Cush has retired from Egypt, in the transition to the 26th dynasty." Williams and Finch, 27

28. Cheikh Anta Diop, *African Origin of Civilization*, ed. and trans. Mercer Cook (Westport: Lawrence Hill, 1914), 221.

29. "Greece owes everything to Egypt. Egypt was teacher to Greece in its infancy. The Greeks themselves, their most eminent scholars, admitted it. . . . It was Thales who began the cycle by going to Egypt and he admits it. He then told Pythagoras who followed in his footsteps." Cheikh Anta Diop, *Great African Thinkers,* 232.

30. Mimi Mann, "Egyptian Desert May Hold Untold Treasures on the Scale of Tut's Tomb," *Los Angeles Times*, 6 Aug 1989, A7.

31. "If it had been my purpose to mention the early historians on Africa in order of importance, Manetho, the African historian, would have headed the list." Chancellor Williams, 385. Although Manetho's original books have been lost, numerous

fragments are preserved, and are found principally in the works of Jewish historian Flavius Josephus (ca. 70 C.E.), and Christian writers Sextus Julius Africanus (ca. 220) and Eusebius (ca. 340), "with isolated passages in Plutarch, Theophilus, Aelian, Porphyrius, Diogenes, Laertius, Theodoretus, Lydus, Malalas, the Scholia to Plato, and the *Etymologicum Magnum*." W.G. Waddell, Introduction to *Manetho*, vii. Subsequent writers modified Manetho's work by adding a thirty-first dynasty, a subdivision of the period of Persian domination.

References

Ben-Jochannan, Yosef A.A. *The African Called Rameses ("The Great") II and the African Origin of "Western Civilization."* Foreword by John Henrik Clarke. New York: Ben-Jochannan, 1990.

Ben Jochannan, Yosef A.A., and John Henrik Clarke. *New Dimensions in African History: The London Lectures of Dr. Yosef ben-Jochannan and Dr. John Henrik Clarke.* Edited with an Introduction by John Henrik Clarke. Trenton. Africa World Press, 1991.

Ben-Levi, Amaziyah Yosef. "The First and Second Intermediate Period in Kemet." *Kenet and the African Worldview: Research, Rescue and Restoration.* Edited by Maulana Karenga and Jacob H. Carruthers. Los Angeles: University of Sankore Press, 1986: 55–69.

Bernal, Martin. *Black Athena: The Afroasiatic Roots of Classical Civilization.* Vol. 2: *The Archaeological and Documentary Evidence.* New Brunswick: Rutgers University Press, 1991.

Brunson, James E. *Predynastic Egypt: An African-centric View.* Introduction by Runoko Rashidi. DeKalb: Brunson, 1991.

Diop, Cheikh Anta. *African Origin of Civilization: Myth or Reality.* Edited and translated by Mercer Cook. Westport: Lawrence Hill, 1974.

Diop, Cheikh Anta. "Origin of the Ancient Egyptians." *UNESCO General History of Africa.* Vol. 2, *Ancient Civilizations of Africa* Edited by G. Mokhtar. Berkeley: University of California Press, 1981: 58-82.

Diop, Cheikh Anta. *Civilization or Barbarism: An Authentic Anthropology.* Translated from the French by Yaa-Lengi Meema Ngemi. Edited by Harold J. Salemson and Marjolijn de Jager. Foreword by John Henrik Clarke. Westport: Lawrence Hill, 1991.

Durant, Will. *Our Oriental Heritage.* New York: Simon & Schuster, 1954.

Herodotus. *The Histories.* Translated by Aubrey de Selincourt. Rev. ed. Harmondsworth: Penguin, 1972.

Hilliard, Asa G. III. "Waset, The Eye of Ra and the Abode of Maat: The Pinnacle of Black Leadership in the Ancient World." *Egypt Revisited.* Edited by Ivan Van Sertima. Rev. ed. New Brunswick: Journal of African Civilizations, 1989: 211-38.

Hilliard, Asa G. III. "Ancient Africa's Contribution to Science and Technology." *NSBE: National Society of Black Engineers Magazine* 1, No. 2 (1990): 72-75.

Hilliard, Asa G. III. *A Selected Bibliography (Classified) and Outline on African-American History From Ancient Times to the Present: A Resource Packet.* Rev. ed. Atlanta: Hilliard, 1991.

"Interview with Dr. Yosef A.A. Ben-Jochannan." *Color* 1, No. 2 (1991): 9-16.

Jackson, John G. *Ages of Gold and Silver and Other Short Sketches of Human History.* Foreword by Madalyn O'Hair. Austin: American Atheist Press, 1990.

Kendall, Timothy, and Susan R. Doll. *Kush: Lost Kingdom of the Nile*. Brockton:
 ✗   Brockton Art Museum, 1982.
Leclant, J. 'The Empire of Kush: Napata and Meroe." *UNESCO General History of
    Africa*. Vol. 2, *Ancient Civilizations of Africa*. Edited by G. Mokhtar. Berkeley:
    University of California Press, 1981: 278-97.
Lesko, Barbara S. "Women's Monumental Mark on Ancient Egypt." *Biblical Ar-
    chaeologist* 54, No. 1 (1991): 4–15.
Manetho. Translated by W.G. Waddell. Cambridge: Harvard University Press,
    1940.
Mann, Mimi. "Egyptian Desert May Hold Untold Treasures on the Scale of Tut's
    Tomb." *Los Angeles Times*, 6 Aug 1989/ Pt. 1: 7.
Newsome, Frederick. "Black Contributions to the Early History of Western Medi-
    cine." *Journal of the National Medical Association* 71, No. 2 (1979): 189-93
Obenga, Theophile. *Ancient Egypt and Black Africa: A Student's Handbook for the
    Study of Ancient Egypt in Philosophy, Linguistics and Gender Relations*. Edited
    by Amon Saba Saakana. London: Karnak House, 1992.
Petrie, W.M. Flinders. *Hawara, Biahmu, and Arsinoe*. London: Field & Tuer, 1889.
Petrie, W.M. Flinders. "The Origin of the XIIth Dynasty." *Ancient Egypt* (June
    1924): 38-42.
"Report of the Symposium on 'The Peopling of Ancient Egypt and the Deciphering
    of the Meroitic Script.'" *UNESCO General History of Africa*. Vol. 2, *Ancient
    Civilizations of Africa*. Edited by Gamal Mokhtar. Berkeley: University of Cali-
    fornia Press, 1981: 55–82.
Taylor, Jules. "The Black Image in Egyptian Art." *Journal of African Civilizations*
    1, No. 1 (1979): 29-38.
Van Sertima, Ivan. "The Moor in Africa and Europe." *Golden Age of the Moor*. Ed-
    ited by Ivan Van Sertima. New Brunswick: Journal of African Civilizations,
    1992: 2-24.
Van Seters, John. *The Hyksos*. New Haven: Yale University Press, 1976.
Williams, Bruce. "Lost Pharaohs of Nubia." *Archaeology* 33, No. 5 (1980): 12-21.
Williams, Chancellor. *The Destruction of Black Civilization: Great Issues of a Race
    from 4500 B.C. to 2000 A.D*. Chicago: Third World Press, 1976.
Williams, Larry, and Charles S. Finch. "The Great Queens of Ethiopia." *Black
    Women in Antiquity*. Edited by Ivan Van Sertima. New Brunswick: Journal of
    African Civilizations, 1987: 12-35.
Wimby, Rekhety. "The Female Horuses and Great Wives of Kemet," *Black Women
    in Antiquity*, Edited by Ivan Van Sertima. New Brunswick: Journal of African
    Civilizations, 1988: 36–48.
Winlock, Herbert E. "On Queen Tetisheri, Grandmother of Ahmose I." *Ancient
    Egypt* (lst Qtr. 1921): 14–16.

FROM THE CENTER TO THE FRINGE:
THE PERSISTENCE OF RACIAL MYTHS
IN PHYSICAL ANTHROPOLOGICAL THEORY

By Runoko Rashidi

Introduction

The *Hamitic hypothesis* and the anthropological concepts of *Brown and Mediterranean races* are grounded in the racist thinking of the late eighteenth, nineteenth and early twentieth centuries—the heyday of European imperialism and manifest destiny. During this period—it is well known, Black populations in Africa, Asia, Australia, the South Pacific, and the Western Hemisphere were essentially divided, dispossessed, colonized, and thoroughly dominated by competing White nations. These concepts have effectively provided the basis for the removal of Black people from the center of world civilizations to the fringe. The Sumerians—the illustrious Blackheaded people of ancient Iraq—are a prime example. Of the physical anthropologists who have examined actual Sumerian remains and published the results, the works of L.H.D. Buxton, Mario Cappieri, Henry Field, Arthur Keith, and T.K. Penniman stand out. The reader should be aware, however, that none of these scientists was honest enough to call a Black a Black; resorting instead to the use of ridiculous ethnic euphemisms, and for Sumerian physical types presented us with "Hamites, Mediterraneans, and members of the Brown race." In reference to a skull found during the course of excavations at Kish, for instance, Buxton wrote that:

> It undoubtedly belongs to the same type as that which Grafton Elliot Smith has called the Brown race and which Sergi has termed Mediterranean. This type is widely spread throughout the whole region and extends from the Mediterranean to India. It formed the main bulk of the ancient inhabitants of Egypt and has been called the Proto-Egyptian type."[1]

The Hamitic Hypothesis

"Ham was the middle child of Noah's three sons, Shem, Ham, and Japheth. The name 'Ham' means 'hot,' 'heat,' and by application, 'black . . . '. The name 'Ham' is patronymic of his descendants."[2] The four sons of Ham were: Ethiopia, Kmt, Libya, and Canaan. The lines of Ham's

descendents, as described in Genesis, represent a kind of mythologized ethnology. Until the late eighteenth century, it was generally accepted that
Hamites were Black people. The extraordinary results of Napoleon
Bonaparte's expedition to Egypt in 1798, however, became the historical
impetus for Europeans to transform the Hamites into Caucasians.

Briefly stated, according to Edith Sanders, "The Hamitic hypothesis
states that everything of value ever found in Africa was brought there by the
Hamites, allegedly a branch of the Caucasian race."[3] Charles G. Seligman
(1873-1940) explained the civilizing role of the Hamites in Africa in the
following manner: "The civilizations of Africa are the civilizations of the
Hamites, its history the record of these peoples. . . . The incoming Hamites
were pastoral 'Europeans'—arriving wave after wave—better armed as well
as quicker witted than the dark agricultural Negroes."[4] As recently as 1987,
St. Clair Drake noted that, "The term 'Hamitic' is still used by Africanists
whose attempts to purge it of racist implications have not yet been entirely
successful."[5]

The Brown Race

In 1966, Wyatt MacGaffey wrote that, "Recently the term Hamite for the
Caucasoid ideal has fallen into disfavor, but certain authors speak of the
Brown Race. This concept is without scientific value, and must be regarded
as a myth with specific ideological functions related to the colonial situation."[6] The Brown race has a dual ancestry. Although originally created by
Giuseppe Sergi, the notion of the Brown race was substantially modified by
G. Elliot Smith.[7] Australian born Grafton Elliot Smith (1871-1937), who
was eventually knighted, was a prominent anatomist and a hyper-
diffusionist who believed that most, if not all, of the world's early monumental high-cultures, from Sumer to China to the Western Hemisphere,
were rooted in the Nile Valley. Included within Smith's Brown race were
the ancient Kamites, Sumerians, Elamites, and Dravidians. Smith was an
outspoken racist who believed that "The Negro and the Australian are more
primitive than any other living peoples."[8]

The Mediterranean Race

The term *Mediterranean Race* may have been coined by Giuseppe Sergi
(1841–1936), Professor of Anthropology in the University of Rome. In
1901, Sergi's book *The Mediterranean Race: A Study of the Origin of European Peoples* was published by Walter Scott of London. Sergi's views were
at least as racist as those of Smith. According to Sergi, "The most degraded

of existing races, such as the Australians, Tasmanians, Papuans, Veddahs, Negroes, Hottentots, and Bosjemen, as well as the aboriginal forest tribes of India, are typically dolichocephalic."[9]

Anthropologist Carleton S. Coon, the author of numerous works on physical anthropology and a fierce and ardent champion of the concept of the Mediterranean Race, was extremely influential in shaping the views of physical anthropologists in the twentieth century. With Coon's researches, writings and viewpoints, however, Cheikh Anta Diop was not impressed, and commented: "Coon's work contributes nothing new. If all the specimens of races and sub-races described by him lived in New York today, they would reside in Harlem."[10] Diop, in his most eloquent and scholarly manner, adequately summarizes the matter for us:

> Anthropologists have invented the ingenious, convenient, fictional notion of the 'true Negro,' which allows them to consider, if need be, all the real Negroes on earth as fake Negroes, more or less approaching a kind of Platonic archetype, without ever attaining it. Thus, African history is full of 'Negroids,' Hamites, semi-Hamites, Nilo-Hamites, Ethiopoids, Sabaeans, even Caucasoids! Yet, if one stuck strictly to scientific data and archaeological facts, the prototype of the White race would be sought in vain throughout the earliest years of present-day humanity. The Negro has been there from the beginning; for millennia he was the only one in existence. Nevertheless, on the threshold of the historical epoch, the 'scholar' turns his back on him, raises questions about his genesis, and even speculates 'objectively' about his tardy appearance.[11]
>
> If the African anthropologist made a point of examining European races 'under the magnifying glass,' he would be able to multiply them *ad infinitum* by grouping physiognomies into races and sub-races as artificially as his European counterpart does with regard to Africa. He would, in turn, succeed in dissolving collective European reality into a fog of insignificant facts.[12]

Notes

1. L.H.D. Buxton, cited by Stephen Langdon, *Excavations at Kish*, vol. 1 (Paris: Paul Geuthner, 1924), 58-59.

2. Walter Arthur McCray, *The Black Presence in the Bible*, vol. 1 (Chicago: Black Light Fellowship, 1990), 54.

3. Edith R. Sanders, "The Hamitic Hypothesis; Its Origin and Functions in Time Perspective," *Journal of African History* 10, No. 4 (1969), 532.

4. Charles G. Seligman, *The Races of Africa* (New York: Henry Holt, 1930), 96.

5. St. Clair Drake, *Black Folk Here and There*, vol. 1 (Los Angeles: Center for Afro-American Studies, UCLA, 1987), 129.

6. Wyatt MacGaffey, "Concepts of Race in the Historiography of Northeast Africa," *Journal of African History* 7, No. 1 (1966), 16.

7. MacGaffey, 3.

8. Grafton Elliot Smith, *Human History* (New York: Norton, 1929), 123.

9. Giuseppe Sergi, *The Mediterranean Race: A Study of the Origin of European Peoples* (London: Walter Scott, 1901), 22.

10. Cheikh Anta Diop, *African Origin of Civilization: Myth or Reality*, trans. and ed. Mercer Cook (Westport: Lawrence Hill, 1974), 238.

11. Diop, 274.

12. Diop, 275.

THE MYTH OF THE MEDITERRANEAN RACE

Dana Reynolds-Marniche

Introduction

The anthropological concept of a *Mediterranean Race* or *Mediterranean type* has long been used to denote long-headed gracile types of men anciently inhabiting the lands around the Mediterranean, and alleged by some of its more extreme proponents to be ancestral to modern Europeans and Caucasoid types in Asia and Africa. It is a concept that has been predicated upon erroneous ideas, and sustained by fallacious notions of the processes involved in human biological evolution and morphological variation.

The concept of the *Mediterranean Race*, like the *Hamitic Hypothesis*, emerge contiguous to certain Orientalist ideas regarding the origins of civilization in Europe, North Africa, and Southwest Asia. It sought to attribute Eurasian and Aryan origins to all of the earliest complex societies. Archaeologists, however, had discovered through comparative studies of crania and technology, that many of the cultures of Southwest Asia and Europe during the Mesolithic and Neolithic periods were frequently associated with the remains of particularly gracile, long-headed types of men, different from most modern Europeans. They were typically buried in an embryonic or contracted position, rarely found among the broader-headed types in Southwest Asia. More often that not, too, they displayed, in slight to moderate degrees, the prognathism, platyrrhine noses, and other traits normally characterized as *Negroid*.

Much of the problem lay in the fact that scholars believed that the form of the human skull, as indicated by cephalic index, was a permanent racial character. The result of these beliefs was the formulation of another unwarranted anthropological concept—the *Brown race*—often referred to as the *Hamite*. The Hamites were proclaimed as early migrants from Asia, but since the osteological relationship of Hamites with ancient peoples in North Africa, the Nile Valley, and the Arabian Peninsula (places where the inhabitants are no longer *Brown*) was recognized and undeniable, a new terminology was called for. The designation employed was the *Mediterranean Race* or *Mediterranean type*, and frequently, depending on the writer, closely related to the *Eurafrican*, the *Hamite*, and the *Brown race*.

Ancient Egyptians, as well as many modern East Africans, were considered to fall into this category of man. They had been discovered to have cranial and facial traits typical of "Caucasoid" crania. Their noses were often narrow and their profiles frequently *orthognathous**. Because of craniofacial morphological traits, the Hamite was acknowledged as having a special connection to long-headed types of men inhabiting both sides of the Mediterranean in antiquity. These in turn were thought to have been essentially "Caucasoid" populations that had migrated from Central Asia and gradually modified in Africa through intermingling with already present "Negroids" during the late and middle stone ages.

Like the *Hamite Hypothesis* the concept of the *Mediterranean Race* likened peoples in Ethiopia, Somalia (i.e., the Tigrai-Amhara, Galla, Bedja, Beni Amer, and other peoples of similar morphology in northern Sudan and the Sahara), to southern Italians, or even Nordics, primarily because of the occurrence of moderate dolichocephaly (long-headedness) among some of the latter groups. Indeed, before the 1980s it was difficult to pick up a book on Ethiopia or Somalia without being informed of the Hamitic and Caucasoid origins of the majority of the inhabitants of these countries. These notions, of course, have only served to perpetuate confusion over the matter of the biological affinities and external appearances of the people under discussion. Even more importantly, it had for nearly a century deprived several African populations of their biological heritage and cultural genesis.

Such theories should have been invalidated long ago by new discoveries, research methods, and studies on Nilotic and North African populations. Some of the most important of these deal with the analysis of the statistical frequency of skeletal traits known to be genetically-based (as opposed to just functionally-related indices), while others have dealt with blood factors and DNA. They have enabled specialists in physical anthropology to make a new assessment of the relationship of ancient Mediterraneans to other Africans. The conclusions that they have arrived at have tended to confirm that the so-called "Mediterraneans" of Africa and elsewhere were really the product of a long evolution in African ecosystems, where dietary factors and other stresses during the late stone ages led to more gracile or slightly built types of Africans. The evidence from all sides has actually shown that populations related to modern Blacks south of Egypt were representative of the populations of ancient Egyptian and Nubian populations from earlier, more archaic-looking and larger-built types of Africans.

This paper attempts to show how the use of the term *Mediterranean* by anthropologists and historians has created misconceptions about the origins of ancient North African populations, and had tended to conceal the relationship of these ancients and those in other parts of the world classified under the term *Mediterranean* with modern Blacks in Africa and elsewhere.

Major Advocates of the Mediterranean Race Concept

Guiseppe Sergi

Guiseppe Sergi (1841–1936), Professor of Anthropology in the University of Rome, was perhaps the earliest major proponent of the concept of a Mediterranean Race. Sergi was one of the first to become convinced that modern Europeans around the Mediterranean, Italians, and other south Europeans, along with some of the populations located in prehistory in Northeast Africa (represented particularly by the ancient Egyptians and most of the people in the Horn of Africa), were descended from a single type of ancient Mediterranean. Sergi, according to one writer, was inspired, like others in his day, to "counter the Aryan ideology associated with the growing German influence in Europe, to reject all classifications which did not fix a great gulf between the Italians and Germans."[1] The Mediterraneans, as opposed to Eurasian Aryans, were said to be the harbingers of such ancient European civilizations as Greece and Rome, which, according to Sergi, were destroyed by the influx of more or less "barbaric Eurasiatics."[2]

On the basis of craniometric data, Sergi taxonomized the Mediterranean or Eurafrican into three subgroupings, one of which included the African branch or "Hamites," another the "true Mediterranean" (in which he included modern southern Italians and other relatively "olive-colored" or brunette Europeans), and still another—the so-called *Nordic race*.[3]

The closest living representative of the African "Mediterranean" seemed to be with peoples directly to the south of modern Egypt extending into the Horn of Africa. This so-called *Hamite* or *Abyssinian man* was immediately inducted by scholars into the Caucasoid branch of mankind. Because of the nearly total reliance on analysis of craniometric data, Sergi saw no irony in portraying such phenotypically diverse people as the Ba-Himas of Uganda, long-headed Russians, Scandinavians, Italians, and Arabs, as representative of his superfamily of Eurafricans.[4] Phenotypical characteristics like skin coloring and hair form were proclaimed "external traits without diagnostic value" because they were "subject to environmental influence."[5] At the same time, for Sergi, cranio-facial measurements were not viewed as subject to such influence.

Sergi discovered that most of the early dolichocephalic, gracile types from Mesolithic and Neolithic populations of Europe, as well as many of the dolichocephalic people of early Southwest Asia and Northern Africa, were accustomed to distinctive funeral practices. Especially marked were the resemblances in such features as: burial in a contracted or foetal position, the use of red ochre to cover the body, and the removal of front parts of the dentition (e.g., the incisors or molars). These same features—which are now known to have been extremely archaic practices widespread in Africa and elsewhere—were designated as characteristic of "long-headed Mediterraneans."

Grafton Elliot Smith

Sir Grafton Elliot Smith (1871–1937) was another major advocate of the *Mediterranean Race* concept. From 1901 to 1909 Smith was Professor of Anatomy at Cairo's Egyptian Museum, where he was able to examine many thousands of human bodies (skeletons and mummies) belonging to both the royal classes and commoners of predynastic and dynastic Egypt. He found that the Egyptians, for the most part, consistently displayed the osteological or morphometric characteristics found particularly among living peoples south and southeast of Egypt. He described the type as having: effeminate and frail build, with eyebrows poorly developed, occiput bulging, a small, but relatively broad nose, and often a slight projection of the jaws.[6]

Smith initially designated this type the *Brown race* on the basis of the coloring in ancient Egyptian iconography and, secondly, because of what he considered to be the close osteological and cranial affinities with the mainly Cushitic-speaking peoples of East Africa, now called Bedja, Somali, Beni Amer, and Oroma (Galla) in Sudan, Ethiopia, and Eritrea. Smith concurred with Sergi in concluding that:

> Even if the burial customs did not supply us with conclusive evidence of a confirmatory nature, the bones alone would provide sufficient data to enable us to assert that the whole Mediterranean littoral, the Iberian Peninsula, Western France and the British Isles before the coming of copper were united by the closest bonds of affinity.[7]

Smith, like Sergi, who was convinced that many of the early long-headed Neolithic populations were genetically connected to East African "Brown" or "Hamitic" populations. Being acquainted also with Neolithic remains in Europe, he wrote that:

> The family likeness between present-day populations of East Africa and Egypt and the ancient neolithic inhabitants of the British Isles and Mediterranean was such that the description of the bones of an early Briton of that remote epoch might apply in all essential details to an inhabitant of Somaliland.[8]

From his analysis of crania, Smith concluded that the majority of the populations of Arabia, Palestine, and Syria, stretching along the coasts of Asia Minor and extending around the Persian Gulf into India and Indonesia in prehistoric and early historic times, exhibited traits typical of the *Brown* race. Unlike Sergi or Carleton Coon, who comes to call the Nordic "a pigment phase of the Mediterranean," Smith was not ready to admit a direct or immediate relationship between modern Scandinavians or Norwegians to his "Mediterranean" or B*rown* type of East Africa. At the same time, he rejected the thought of a Negroid or Black affiliation of the type generally called *Hamitic* or *Brown*, and asserted that there was only a minute Negroid element in the earliest Egyptians; and claimed that an "intimate look" at the structure of the bone, the architecture of the skull, the nature of the asymmetry of the body of the West and Central Africans could convince one that "there is a profound gap that separates the Negro from the rest of mankind, including the Egyptian." For that reason, he harshly criticized William Z. Ripley, the author of the 1899 publication—*The Races of Europe*—for asserting that the entire ancient "Mediterranean race" was descended from "African Negroes."[9]

Carleton S. Coon

Carleton S. Coon had his own disconcerting version of what constituted the *Mediterranean Race*. He described several types of *Mediterraneans* based on the metric analysis of crania. The *Mediterranean proper*, is described by him as: a man of short stature with a cranial index of 73–75, browridges and bone development weak, short face, variable nasal form, paedomorphic and sexually undifferentiated "with a slight negroid tendency." He found it to predominate in early Egypt. It was, according to Coon, present in France, Italy, and around the Swiss Lakes. To this Mediterranean, he adds an early "Danubian" type, dolichocephalic to mesocephalic, with nasal form messorhine or chamerrhine (that is moderate to very broad in width), extending from central Europe and resembling some of the skeletal remains from Kurgans in southern Russia (Anau) and Anatolia.[10]

Some types further west in Europe from the late stone age appeared to Coon to be affiliated with Nile dwellers from Egypt and further south, not only on the basis of skeletal evidence, but on pottery types. The thick black ware, decorated by incision, of the early Neolithic Fayum and Merimde Delta, resembled early ceramic types of Neolithic western Europe and Anatolia, particularly the Danubian Mediterraneans. Coon adduced that the predynastic inhabitants of Egypt represented the people who brought the Neolithic economy (with emmer, flax, and swine) to the Swiss Lake and the Rhine. He stated that, "Their appearance in the Fayum and the Delta is dated at about 5000 B.C., and their disappearance about 4000 years B.C. . . . One millennium later they, or people like them appeared in western Europe."[11] Sergi also felt that the ancient Swiss Lakes people and their manner of burial were of African derivation.

The Range and Location of Physical Types Designated Mediterranean

Physical anthropologist Wilton Marion Krogman, another employer of the Mediterranean taxonomy, recorded that:

> The Mediterranean type was earliest and basic to north and northeast Africa and the eastern Mediterranean area, Asia Minor and Iran. . . . It seems warranted to conclude that the longheaded Mediterranean cranial type had priority in the vast area comprising southern Europe, northern Africa, Asia Minor, and possibly the entire Middle East.[12]

In his *Cranial Types at Chatal Huyuk*, Krogman notes that the Mediterranean type was "basic to the entire area of the Middle East," including North Africa, well into the historical period and before the coming of rounderheaded "Alpine" types.[13] According to Robert Wenke, the artistic representations and analysis of skeletal remains indicate that the early people of Mesopotamia were a "typical Mediterranean population with relatively long skulls."[14] The long-headed people, who, judging particularly from the research of Ernest Mackay, were the predominant types in Mesopotamia, and made their way to the Indus Valley through Baluchistan and areas further south and east, were very probably dark in color, as suggested by certain Dravidian tribes who seem to have originated in those areas.[15]

Now that several prominent scholars have come to feel that Elamite, and possibly even Sumerian, are early Dravidian dialects, there should be less reason to resist the notion that Black people once inhabited the areas of Iran, Mesopotamia, and the Indus Valley, where artistic depictions in paint and sculptured figurines show the presence of Blacks, and where the long-headed "Mediterranean" skeletal types, with decidedly "Negroid" traits, predominated throughout the early historical period.

When one understands that the Mediterranean type of Asia was nothing other than a black-complexioned man who migrated in neolithic times out of Africa, the cultural connection between Dravidian-speakers to some Black African groups, as pointed out by some Dravidian and African scholars, is better understood.

In the *Historical and Cultural Dictionary of Saudi Arabia*, published in 1972, one can read the following unqualified statement:

> The basic population of Saudi Arabia (as is true of the peninsula as a whole) is a Mediterranean variety of Caucasian. There had been over the centuries considerable admixture of Negroid elements . . . the genetic picture is rather confused. Highest incidence of Negroid features appear in the Tihama, while the Beduin, especially in the Nejd, tends to the more classic Mediterranean type, though there is Negroid admixture in some areas.[16]

All Negroid traits are ascribed in this synopsis to outside biological elements attributable to slavery, while heterogeneous populations invariably more gracile and darker, than the average European type are, as usual, haphazardly thrown into the all-encompassing *Mediterranean* category, which is determined to be Caucasian.

The Mechtoids

Due to the general use of the term *Cro-Magnon* for many of the varied Upper Paleolithic populations of Europe, and the recognition that North Africans of the same era (currently called *Mechtoids*) presented similarities to some of them, it has often been erroneously presumed that the *Mechtoids* of the Paleolithic North Africa, and all populations that were in Europe during the late Paleolithic, were directly ancestral not only to modern-day Europeans in Europe, but "European types" in Africa as well. The prevalence of this belief, until recently, is illustrated by Coon's often repeated suggestion that modern Berbers and Guanches are descendants of a square-jawed ancient Nordic or Europoid type indigenous to North Africa.

Even more recently, Jean Jiernaux adopted the view that the Upper Paleolithic populations in North Africa (whom he admits resembled certain populations in Europe during the same period) were not at all ancestral to sub-Saharan Africans of succeeding periods.[17] Thus, the Upper Paleolithic peoples of North Africa, regardless of the characteristically Negroid traits seen with some frequency among them, came not only to be categorized as Cro-Magnons but misnomered "Caucasoids."[18]

It has previously been suggested however, by various authors (including Coon) that these Mechtoids or Ibero-Maurusians were biologically associated with later types in the North African region—that of the gracile Mediterranean type which was found to be associated with the Capsian blade tradition of Algeria and Tunisia. Not surprisingly, both have been mentioned as "Cro-Magnon Mediterraneans" possessing Negroid traits due to some hypothetical intermixture with a presumedly true "Negro" type.

Thus, even the Mechtoid was early on considered part of the *Mediterranean* type populations as a consequence of the indications of its affinity with later Mesolithic and Neolithic types in the North African region. The first phase of the Capsian in North Africa, called the Upper Capsian and Typical Capsian, belonged to the Mesolithic, and was mainly the work of a Mechta-Afalou population[19] The Libyco-Capsian, beginning approximately 10,000 years ago, continued into the Neolithic and was accompanied by men of the more gracile type in this later period.

Arabians and Berbers, whose phenotypical diversity Coon recognized, are said to be, for the most part, *Mediterranean* in type. Discounting the most plausible causes for red hair and green eyes appearing among inhabit-

ants of the Yemen (e.g., the Turkish settlement there, the slave trade, ancient colonization of the area by Iranians), when Coon finds that a quarter of
the beards of a series of Yemenis showed hues divided between brown and
red, he proclaims "the hair of the basic Mediterranean stock contains a
considerable amount of red pigmentation."[20]

The Berbers too are neither metrically nor morphologically uniform.
Even among the light-skinned Berber speakers, Coon was able to designate
several groups with differing complexions, cephalic indexes, and eye coloring. The Riffians are one Berber group of Morocco which Coon had described as having pinkish white skins, 23 percent with freckles, and the
children possessing an infantile dominance of blondism. Many beards are
light brown and over half had mixed or light eyes. Greenish-brown eyes
were the commonest mixed form, while another group possessed a high
incidence of red hair. Except for the Riffians, the majority of Berbers studied were mesocephalic, as opposed to the dolichocephalic ancient inhabitants of North Africa. Another major light-skinned Berber group, known as
the Ghomara, according to Coon, trace their ancestry to an ancient invasion
from the south. They are described as mesocephalic, while the Senhaja
Sghir are darker-skinned, with an element of sloping forehead. Coon was
convinced, perhaps because of the rather infrequent incidence of blondism
in Berber infants, that the major "Mediterranean" strain in the Berber-speak-
ers is a Nordic one. For him, the most "troublesome factor in the whole
North African racial problem lies in the necessity of explaining the origin of
the local Nordics."[21] He felt that there were two possible explanations, one
being that they were a mixture of brunette Mediterraneans of tall stature
with survivals of the Afalou-bou-Rhummel (Mechtoid type) which passed
down blondism to the Berbers; or there must be admitted a Nordic invasion
of North Africa from Europe or Asia as early as the second millennium
B.C.[22] Thus, Coon formed the opinion that Paleolithic North Africans—as
represented by the Mechtoids—were most likely blonds, disregarding the
plausibility of the influence from a more recent influx of Europeans into
North Africa. It is in large part due to the wishful thinking of Coon and
other anthropologists that many have been misled into thinking that the
early Upper Paleolithic types in North Africa were blond, or the ancestor of
the "square-jawed Nordic" types in North Africa that Coon described in his
Races of Europe.[23]

Besides Coon, Louis Leakey (1903–1972) found certain resemblances
between North African Paleolithic populations and types found at
Elmenteita in East Africa. Coon reported that excavations in Kenya and
Tanganyika had uncovered the remains of a tall, extremely long-headed
Mediterranean type with a tendency to great elongation and narrowness of
face. Recognizing the morphometric similarities, with characteristic abandon, Coon pronounced the area of late stone age sites in East Africa, such as

Elmenteita and Naivasha, "a second southern periphery of the white racial stock: peripheral in this case to the world of the African Negro."[24] He speaks of the East African "Hamite" as being "without doubt derived from this Palaeolithic racial type."[25]

Sonia Cole, another specialist on African prehistory, described the tall dolichocephalic peoples of Gamble's Cave, Naivasha, and Olduvai, as Caucasoids.[26]

The Natufians

Natufian settlements have been found from the Egyptian Delta to southern Turkey. The earliest settlers of the Natufian sites resembled the early Mechta-man of the Ibero-Maurusian and Capsian cultures of North Africa. Although late Natufians are of the smaller, more gracile Mediterranean sort, the early Natufians, according to Marie-Claude Chamla, seem to be typical of the tall proto-Mediterraneans found at Upper Capsian Mesolithic sites with Mechta-man in North Africa, from Morocco to Tunisia, during the seventh and sixth millenniums B.C. resembling the Libyco-Capsian further to the east.[27]

Sir Arthur Keith (1865–1955), who noted the similarity between the cultures of the Shukbah dwellers and that of the Capsian midden-dwellers, also remarked on the resemblance of the practice of the removal of the front incisors, especially by the Natufians, to the practices of certain modern day "Negro" tribes. He designated the Natufians "Mediterraneans with a distinct bias toward the African variety of that stock represented by the predynastic people of Egypt."[28]

Other nave found Natufian crania to bear close resemblance to the early inhabitants of Malta and the Tagus, in Portugal.[29] They were both considered to be slightly "Negroid" in skull and face. Sergi even asserted that the Maltese crania were of "undoubted African origin."[30] Coon, in typical fashion, ruled out the plausible Negroid or Black African affiliation, calling it a principal misconception, and saying that there is no greater "negroid" tendency than is commonly found among many living Europeans of Mediterranean extraction.[31]

The Nile Valley

The ancient predynastic Egyptian skull has usually been described as: long, narrow and coffin shaped; pentagonoid; the face short and narrow; the eyebrows poorly developed; the occiput bulging; the nose small but relatively broad; often with a slight projection of the jaws. This is not to say that there were not non-Africoid populations present in ancient Egypt. In fact, a number of distinctly mesocephalic types of stockier build do appear during the oldest dynastic era in a few North Egyptian towns, though in small numbers. These people are apparently represented by the four or five nearly white skinned scribes and maidservants that are displayed over and over in so many books in an apparent attempt to foster the notion of Old Kingdom Dynastic Egyptians being an essentially European-like people, or at the very least, of mixed "Oriental" origins. According to Smith, however, this type, found at Giza and other Egyptian towns during the oldest dynastic period, was distinguishable morphologically from the so-called "proto-Mediterranean" race that dominated Egypt, and were, for the most part, absorbed by the Fifth Dynasty into the majority population.[32]

Even Coon once commented on the resemblance of the profiles of modern-day Oroma Cushites (Galla) and others designated "Hamitic" to those on paintings depicting the early Egyptian nobility. But for Coon and others, these and the Nilohamites (Masai, Samburu, etc.) were typologically "Mediterraneans," strongly "Hamiticized," and only slightly or moderately Negroid due to past intermingling. As a consequence, the study of the history of the Lower Nile, from the Delta to Nubia, had been the study of the degree of Negroid penetration of a "Mediterranean Caucasoid" or Europoid population.[33]

The prevailing opinion in the time of Coon and Krogman was that these skulls, like those of the Indus and prehistoric Egypt, were devoid of Negroid characteristics, even though such features as platyrrhine nose, long head, short face, and retreating forehead are equally common among so-called "Negroes." Skulls from the much later, but prehistoric, Ubaid culture of Mesopotamia are described similarly as hyperdolichocephalic, with retreating foreheads, prominent browridges and wide cheekbones, with the nose extremely platyrrhine, broad and flat. These in turn have been compared with early Indus Valley crania, as well as the Natufian crania.

Of late, several studies of anthropologists focusing on discrete cranial and dental traits have also come to disprove the long held theories of a Europoid or Caucasoid neolithic invasion of North Africa or Egypt.[34] Analysis of 16 discrete dental variants in Nubian populations from the Mesolithic through the early Christian periods in the Meroitic and Wadi Halfan areas of Nubia by David L. Greene of the University of Colorado did not show differentiation sufficient enough to warrant speaking of racial intrusions. Such rare cusp variants as split hypocene, which were present in Mesolithic remains from Wadi Halfa, were also present in later Nubian populations. According to Greene, this "constitutes strong evidence for genetic continuity in the area over a period of 10,000 years."[35]

Most important is the fact that such features as glabellar protrusion, gonial eversion, and large complex tooth form, have come to be seen as plastic, or functionally-related, as opposed to genetic, and indicative of a heavy masticatory musculature. Discrete or discontinous traits of the skull and dentition have been found to have greater reliability and significance in determining genetic relationships than do analyses using craniometric and morphometric indices.

In a study done by A.C. Berry, R.J. Berry and P. Ucko on the non-metrical, or discrete, variations in the skulls from various predynastic and dynastic Egyptian sites from Lower and Upper Egypt, over thirty variants were employed in determining the degree of biological affinity among the populations in Egypt, Nubia, the Punjab, and southern Palestine. In their paper, it was stated that there was "considerable genetical continuity" between the pre-dynastic population of Egypt and dynastic Egyptian populations, and that the remarkable homogeneity continued until the last native dynasties. In general, the archaic dynastic series from places like Abydos and Tarkhan were found by the Berrys and Ucko to be undifferentiated from predynastic groups at Nagada. The results of the study showed, in their words, an "impressive unity over the period covered by the study" (which was 5,000 years), and more remarkably, an amazing closeness to the iron age Jebel Moya Nubian population—which Strouhal, Cole Arkell and others had described as "Negro."[36]

Jean Hierneaux offered another explanation for the tendency toward narrow noses, extremely narrow heads, and orthognathy of many Africans. Their high and narrow noses and their generally elongated proportions are, in his view, genetic adaptations to dry heat. He mentions that they should not be "considered closely related to Caucasoids of Europe and western Asia, as they usually are in literature.[37]

Bruce Williams, an instrumental figure in illuminating the presence of pharaonic tombs among the A-group in Nubia, saw a continuity between pharaonic elements of this population and the pharaonic elements involved in the rise of the first dynasties at Nagada.[38] The A-group culture is now known to have derived its elements primarily from the preceding Abkan culture, while the Abkan lithic assemblage appears to have developed from the Terminal Paleolithic Nubian Qadan Industry, which dates back over 10,000 years.

The archaeological evidence thus correlates well with the newer speculations by physical anthropologists, who theorize that there was a biological evolution of gracile Nilotes (both Egyptian and Nubians) from earlier and much more robust populations of the Nile Valley.

Conclusion: The Demise of the Mediterranean Race?

Most Egyptologists, anthropologists, and historians have not dealt squarely with the occurrence and impact of migrations after the native Egyptian dynasties into northern Africa, particularly Egypt. Most still find it hard to accept the fact that Egypt was once a predominantly Black civilization. Historians have been satisfied in portraying light-skinned modern day North Africans near the Mediterranean as an exotic type of man indigenous to Africa, somehow representative of "proto-Mediterranean type" populations present in ancient North Africa and Southwest Asia, as well as modern Europe; while at the same time claiming them to be ancestors of East Africans. This kept alive Sergi's hypothesis that Europeans now living along the Mediterranean littoral were the representative of ancient "Mediterranean" types. It is, however, a most remarkable thing that ancient writers and ancient artists, in combination with modern linguistic and archaeological interpretations, provide incontestable evidence of the presence of Black populations in the very same areas where the remains of people of the so-called "Mediterranean type" of ancient times had been discovered. The term "Mediterranean" has no scientific basis when used in this sense. Dr. Cheikh Anta Diop (1923–1986) was among the first to point out that the use of term was a way of glossing over the Africanness and Blackness of ancient Egyptians and populations in other continents, just as the term "Hamite" had been.[39]

The modern and predominantly mesocephalic or brachycephalic populations of southern Italy, Greece, Spain, and the Levant (though probably possessing their share of "Afro-Mediterranean" or "proto-Mediterranean" blood) have been falsely presented as representative of the ancient dolichocephalic "Mediterranean" types described by G. Elliot Smith as allied to East Africans, and which numerically predominated in Southwest Asia and North and East Africa during the late stone ages and as late as the first part of the second millennium B.C.

Obviously, it had not been very palatable for European academicians of the last few centuries to think of southern Europeans or inhabitants of Biblical lands as peoples who have absorbed Black African types. There are, however, more than enough historical writings on "black-skinned" Maures during the days of the Romans and Byzantines occupying various areas of Sicily, southern Italy, Portugal, France and the Mediterranean to suggest that this was the case even after the Christian and Islamic eras.

Modern European populations inhabiting the Mediterranean littoral are not so much "Mediterranean" in the anthropological sense as in a geographical sense; and perhaps (as with most Europeans), mainly the result of amalgamation of various light-skinned mesocephalic and brachycephalic types with dolichocephalic Africans once numerous in those areas. It is highly unlikely that the colonization of Greeks, Romans, and more recently, of Turks and merchant colonies from Syria, Iraq, and Iran, have left no impression on the genetic pattern of North Africa.

New interpretations of biological evolution along the Nile have helped to dispel the myth of the ancient Mediterranean as a type affiliated with modern Europeans or Caucasoids. They are in accord with the theory of a direct evolution of the ancient Egyptian and other Africans (misclassified by

Sergi, Krogman, and Coon) from the robust Paleolithic populations who possessed the prognathism and broad-nosed traits characteristically assigned to the Negroid type of humanity. These conclusions have arisen mainly because of two developments that have taken place in the study of biological and cultural evolution along the Nile.

First, the detailed analysis of physical anthropologists, including Angel, Greene, Carlson, Armelagos, Ucko, and others, who have done work on discrete discontinous cranial and dental traits, have pointed to a remarkable homogeneity of the Egyptian population until the period directly preceding the Ptolemaic era; as well as a noticeable connection with the more robust Nilotes further south from earlier and contemporary periods.[40] Secondly, the new discoveries of archaeologists increasingly confirm the long-suggested theory that Egyptian cultural complexes emerged from, and were directly linked to, cultures of the desert areas directly to the west, south and east of Egypt.

The "Mediterranean" type, depending on where and when he lived, often retained the typical Mechtoid features, including the Natufian, Tasian, Badarian, Al Ubaidian (El Obeid), and Indus Valley "Mediterranean." The incidence and degree of the so-called "Negroid" features varied then, just as they do now among modern Ethiopians and Nilotes. But the perceived lessening of "Negroid" attributes does not nullify the fact that the ancient type designated "proto-Mediterranean" or "Brown Mediterranean" since the turn of the century, was in no way allied to, nor descended from the type now designated Europoid or Caucasoid. On the contrary, it is today indisputable that the early Mediterraneans—who appear to have been among the first settled agriculturalists of Europe, Africa, and Southwest Asia—were direct genetic and cultural descendants of the Upper Paleolithic hunter of the Nile and North Africa. We can say with equal certainty that the latter's lesser modified descendants further to the south and west, who gave rise to the Khartoum variant and Saharan-Sudanese traditions between the ninth and fourth millennia B.C., were those that were to make up the greater part of what are considered to be the Black populations of Africa.

It is time that all interested in understanding the legacy of Egypt and other areas where "Mediterranean" types were said to have been numerically predominant, recognize that those types were of African derivation, and that the culture of the Nile was not the result of confluence of people from the Middle or Near East and Africa, but arose over a long period from a culture stemming from the remote past belonging to the same stock of people that gave birth to other "Black African" types and Blacks in ancient Asia and Europe. If these populations have been camouflaged by words that say nothing of that truth, then those words must be seen for what they are—scientific disguises and lies created to keep a mythical view of history and its evolutionary stages in place, and to deny the light stemming from a boundless Black past.

Notes

1. Wyatt MacGarrey, "Concepts of Race in the Historiography of Northeast Africa," *Journal of African History* 7, No. 1 (1966), 3.
2. MacGaffey.
3. Guiseppe Sergi, *The Mediterranean Race: A Study of the Origin of European Peoples* (London: Walter Scott, 1901).
4. Sergi.
5. MacGaffey, 3.
6. Grafton Elliot Smith, *The Ancient Egyptians and the Origins of Civilization*, 2d ed. (New York: Harper & Brothers, 1923), 56, 66.
7. Smith, 66–77.
8. Smith, 65.
9. Smith, 79.
10. Carleton S. Coon, *The Races of Europe* (New York: Macmillan, 1939), 82–113.
11. Coon, 93.
12. Wilton Marion Krogman, "Ancient Cranial Types at Chatal Huyuk and Tell Al-Judaidah, Syria from the Late 5th Millennium B.C. to the Mid-Seventh Century," in *Turk Tarih Kur. Bas. Belleten* 13 (1949), 452.
13. Krogman, 452–54.
14. Robert Wenke, *Patterns in Prehistory* (Oxford University Press, 1980), 415.
15. E.J. Mackay, *Further Excavations at Mohenjo-Daro*, vol. 1 (New Delhi: Government of India Press, 1938).
16. Carroll Riley, *Historical and Cultural Dictionary of Saudi Arabia* (Scarecrow, 1972), 16.
17. Jean Hiernaux, *Peoples of Africa* (New York: Scribner's, 1970), 87.
18. Hiernaux.
19. David W. Phillipson, *African Archeology* (Cambridge: Cambridge University Press, 1985), 94.
20. Coon, 405.
21. Coon, 488.
22. Coon.
23. Coon, 467, 483.
24. Coon, 444.
25. Coon.
26. Sonia Cole, *The Prehistory of East Africa* (Harmondsworth: Penguin, 1963).
27. Marie-Claude Chamla, "The Settlement of Non-Saharan Algeria from the Epipaleolithic to Modern Times," *Physical Anthropology of European Populations* (The Hague: Mouton, 1980).
28. Cited by Krogman, 435.
29. Coon, 63.
30. Sergi.
31. Coon, 85.
32. Smith.
33. Coon.
34. D.L. Greene. G.H. Ewing, and G.J. Armelagos, "Dentition of a Mesolithic Population from Wadi Halfa, Sudan," *American Journal of Physical Anthropology* 27 (1976), 41–56; D.L. Greene, "Dental Anthropology of Early Egypt and Nubia." *Journal of Human Evolution* 1 (1972), 315–24.
35. D.L. Greene, *Dentition of Meroitic, X-Group and Christian Populations*

from Wadi Halfa, Sudan (Salt Lake City: University of Utah Press, 1967).
36. A.C. Berry and R.J. Berry, "Origins and Relationships of the Ancient Egyptians. Based on a Study of Non-metrical Variations in the Skull," *Journal of Human Evolution* 1(1972), 203–206.
37. Hiernaux, 126.
38. Bruce Williams, "The Lost Pharaohs of Nubia," *Archaeology* 33, No. 5 (1980), 12–21; Bruce Williams, *The A-Group Royal Cemetery at Qustul: Cemetery L* (Chicago: Oriental Institute of the University of Chicago, 1986).
39. Cheikh Anta Diop. *African Origin of Civilization: Myth or Reality*, ed. and trans. Mercer Cook (Westport: Lawrence Hill, 1974).
40. J.L. Angel, "Biological Relations of Egyptian and Eastern Mediterranean Populations During Pre-dynastic and Dynastic Times," *Journal of Human Evolution* 1 (1972), 307–13; D.L. Greene, *Definition of Meroitic, X-Group and Christian Populations from Wadi Halfa, Sudan* (Salt Lake City: University of Utah Press, 1967); D.L. Greene, "Dental Anthropology of Early Egype and Nubia," *Journal of Human Evolution,* 1 (1972), 315–24; D.L. Greene, G.H. Ewing, and G.J. Armelagos, "Dentition of a Mesolithic Population from Wadi Halfa, Sudan," *American Journal of Physical Anthropology* 27 (1976), 41-56.

Glossary

A-group: Indigenous Nubian population; shared a manner of burial and physical type often claimed to be identical to predynastic populations of southern Egypt.

Abkan: Stone industry and culture in Nubia thought to be ancestral to the later A-group population.

Abyssinian type: Basically refers to gracile types of men especially represented in Northeast Africa; often accompanied by narrow nose and lacking prognathous aspect.

Al Ubaid (Obeid): Period and wide-spread ceramic culture of Mesopotamian area dating between 5300–3600 B.C.; associated with skeletons of *Mediterranean* type.

Amratian: The earliest neolithic and food producing culture of Egypt; thought to have had a connection to Ghassulian of Palestine and Sinai.

Badarian: A predynastic culture of southern Egypt affiliated with the Amratian.

Berbers: Name used to designate various peoples of Northern Africa varying in culture and biological origination.

Brachycephalic: Short and broad-headed.

Capsian: Mesolithic culture of North Africa centered in Algeria and Tunisia.

Chatal Huyuk: A site located in southern Turkey; one of the earliest known "complex cultures" of the Mediterranean area; associated with skeletons of *Mediterranean* type.

Craniometric: The comparison and contrast of crania and cranial features based on metric measurements.

Cro-Magnon: Anatomically modern man present in late Paleolithic Europe and long acknowledged as similar to Mechtoids in physical morphology.

Cushite: Linguistic group found mainly in the Horn of Africa and closely related to dialects of ancient Arabia, Akkadian, and the indigenous dialects of ancient North Africa.

Dolichocephalic: Long head with an index of less than 75.

Elmenteitan: Pastoral culture of Kenya dating from ca. 1200 B.C. to 1000 A.D. The site in Kenya where were found tall types of men once thought to be akin to Mesolithic North African types and from the same period.

Epi-genetic: Traits that are not genetically determined.

Kenya Capsian: Also known as Eburran; dating back at least 15,000 years in Eastern Africa, typologically resembling the Capsian of North Africa.

Lithic: Tool industries.

Mechtoids: Hunters of robust build once populating North Africa and the Nilotic area mainly during the Upper Paleolithic and Mesolithic periods; now believed to have been ancestral to several African types.

Mesolithic: The stone age period between the Paleolithic and the Neolithic; the prefixes indicate *Old, Middle*, and *New* stone ages.

Morphological: Refers to the form and structure of the body.

Natufian: A Mesolithic and Neolithic industry of the Levant; name for settlements stretching from Turkey to the delta area of modern Egypt.

Nordic: A name used generally to designate the types of blonde, and (normally) moderately long-headed types found in Scandinavia; blond peoples of Europe.

Orbit: Referring to the bony socket of the eye.

Paleolithic: Early stone age period preceding the beginnings of the Mesolithic era.

Platyrrhine: Inclining to flatness in regard to nasal index.

Prognathous: Jaws projecting beyond the upper face.

Qadan: Culture found at Jebel Sahaba in Nubia associated with Mechtoid type of man thought to be directly ancestral to modern Nubians.

Red Sea Hills: Located in the eastern part of Egypt.

Taxonomy: Classification.

Wada Halfa: Site in Nubia where large groups of skeletons were found dating from between 12,000 to 14,000 years before present.

BRINGING MAAT, DESTROYING ISFET:
THE AFRICAN AND AFRICAN DIASPORAN
PRESENCE IN THE STUDY OF ANCIENT KMT

Asa G. Hilliard III

> *"I made everyman equal to his fellow*
> *and I forbade them to do Isfet*
> *But their hearts disobeyed what I had said."*
> (Coffin Texts Spell 1130)

Currently, there are controversies in the study of ancient KMT. K-M-T, a name written in MDW NTR (Ancient Egyptian Hieroglyphics), a writing system without vowels, means "The Black Place," or "place of the blacks," following Cheikh Anta Diop,[1] and is one of three primary names that native African people in the northern Nile Valley used to refer to their nation. Today that nation is referred to as "Egypt", even by the scholars who study it as a specialty. The name "Egypt" is the foreign name given to KMT by the Greeks, nearly two thousand years after the nation was established. Most scholars who study KMT today call themselves "Egyptologists."

Carelessness rather than fidelity to the actual Kemetic names and language is not a minor matter. It is hard enough to understand a 6,000 year old foreign language and culture, even with the highest quality of contemporary scholarship. The Greeks who renamed KMT did not read the MDW NTR. Therefore, using their terminology when we can read the texts directly, creates unnecessary distortion.[2] More rigor in the use of the Kemetic language is desirable, because there is a natural tendency for foreigners to *project* their meanings onto Kemetic. Why then should we use Greek in place of English and have double distortions? Ideally, we would use the native language itself.

This problem offers a parallel for our topic today. What other meanings from the present are projected onto the ancient past, inappropriately? Controversial matters require fidelity to documentation.

In addition to KMT, two other names that natives used were Ta-Mrry (meaning "The Beloved Land") and Tawi (meaning "The Two Lands"— Upper and Lower KMT). When discussing KMT, academic accuracy would dictate, in every case possible, that we use the native names. It can be very misleading to our understanding of KMT to use foreign names, since the Kemetic names are filled with meanings that help to clarify what would otherwise be obscure.

The controversy to which I refer is about the "race," or more properly the phenotype, and ethnicity of the Ancient Kemites. It is in this sense that I use the term race. At its base the controversy is over the true place of African people in world history. The focus of this struggle boils down to the matter of whether the greatest recorded civilization of ancient times, KMT, belongs to Africa proper, or to Asia, or to Europe, or even to an unknown people of unknown origins. At least we hear little lately of the idea that people from outer space constructed the pyramids.

Some newspaper and magazine accounts, and some professional media organs as well, have presented the controversy in simple-minded black/ white terms, or as one between a new group of "African centered," "non mainstream," or even "pseudo scholars," and the "legitimate," old (read white) mainstream scholarly establishment. Of course, this is a gross over-simplification of what is really happening, even a falsification of what is really happening. There are African and non-African, mainstream and non-mainstream, new and old scholars on both sides of the question. For example, there are African and African Americans who are formally trained as Egyptologists, anthropologists (including, specialists in physical anthropology), linguists, biologists, etc. who use their disciplines to address the topic of the Kemites. They are now breaking new ground as scientists.

While it is not my purpose here to describe the contending groups by category, I cannot help but wonder at the widespread reporting of false information in the popular mass media. For example, both of the two most publicized queens of KMT are of *foreign descent*, Nefertiti (daughter of the Persian King Dushratta)[3][4] and Cleopatra VII (a descendant of the Ptolemaic line from Macedonia, possibly with some African mixture). They are almost always selected as the illustrations for articles that discuss KMT, especially articles about the race of the Kemites. Writers seldom show the truly power-ful ruling queen Tiy,[5] Nefertiti's mother-in-law, a bust of whom is in the same Berlin Museum with Nefertiti. Though the powerful Queen Tiy is unmistakably black skinned and dark eyed, in the 1930s in Germany, she was described as having white skin and blue eyes![6]

Why use foreigners to represent natives? Why turn natives into white people? It is a not so subtle attempt to prove that the Egyptians were actu-ally white.[7] Even scholarly magazines follow this pattern.[8] While either Nefertiti or Cleopatra may have been part African, (The Royal families of KMT of the 18th dynasty frequently took the daughters of Asian royal families as wives), neither Nefertiti nor Cleopatra (the last Queen) had anything to do with the development of the civilization of KMT. Apparently journalistic and even some academic standards now tolerate gross levels of error, inaccuracy, and irrelevancy.

Challenges to current "mainstream" conclusions about the phenotype and ethnicity of the Ancient Kemites have been labeled as false, as misinterpretations, and even as fabrications and fantasies. One hysterical Pulitzer Prize winner even foresaw such "unauthorized" ideas as "black KMT," taught by African scholars, as threatening the unity of America itself![9] Of course, this particular writer has a pattern of challenging mainstream African scholars who challenge the fabrication and falsification of the historical record.[10, 11] Schlesinger defended the historical novel written by William Styron, on Nat Turner, even though Styron filled in the blanks with fiction. The African scholars were challenging Styron's fabrication. Schlesinger also is quoted by Stuart Jones as justifying the practice by the state to tell a "royal lie." Apparently, myth can be used to serve national purposes. The African scholars who challenged Styron were arguing for a factual account, just as they do in the study of KMT.

Scholarly arguments and documentation in support of KMT as the product of indigenous African people:

1. are not new
2. are not exclusively or even unanimously the catechistic view of African and African diasporan scholars, since many European scholars of note have long argued the same thing, and some African Diasporan scholars disagree.[12, 13, 14, 15, 16, 17]

and should be dealt with in that way.

The shrill challenges to the idea of native African KMT that are widely publicized, mainly in the mass media;

1. *Characterize* (mainly by perjorative name-calling, burlesque, and ridicule) the scholars who challenge the very recent view of KMT as a "white" and even European civilization.
2. *Characterize* the scholarship, but do not offer scholarly critiques of the empirical
3. are not simply the uninformed opinions of non-scholars
4. are not in and of themselves arguments for or against any political or ideological view or "ism," but are arguments that can and will be pursued for their scientific validity. Their social or political utility is a secondary matter.
5. are not "Afrocentric" data, although African centered scholars may find the valid data and conclusions interesting and useful, just as may other scholars. The data are simply valid or invalid and should be dealt with in that way.

The shrill challenges to the idea of native African KMT that are widely publicized, mainly in the mass media:

1. *Characterize* (mainly by perjorative name-calling, burlesque, and ridicule) the scholars who challenge the very recent view of KMT as a "white" and even European civilization. *Characterize* the scholarship, but do not offer scholarly critiques of the empirical data or documentation that African scholars and others present to support the idea of native African KMT. As such, the critiques can hardly be regarded as authoritative.
2. Rely heavily on journalists, rather than on the published research of scholars.
3. Do not invite and may not even permit rebuttals to the few academic specialists who may respond in academic journals.
4. Seem to share a private (political and social) network that is funded by right wing think-tanks. The think tanks fund propaganda on the topic but do not fund research and publish technical scientific papers on the topic.
5. Sometimes come from scholars who say that they are afraid to be named along with their quotes. Therefore it is impossible to determine if they have done research and publication on the topics of the phenotype and ethnicity of the ancient Kemites, topics nevertheless on which they still express "authoritative opinions," without citations of the technical literature.

This situation is not new. KMT has held a central place in the minds of European populations for centuries. There have been at least two periods in time where Europeans were virtually, as some writers have labeled them, "Egyptomaniacal." They were fascinated and overwhelmed in a positive way by the grandeur of this great African civilization. The periods were the Greek and Roman Classical periods, from Homer to Constantine, and the Renaissance period. Homer was fascinated and laudatory, as were later Greek students who spent long years of study in KMT, by their own account.[18] [19] This period spanned the better part of a millennium.

The early students of KMT, during times closer to the Renaissance, and at the beginning of the formal study of "Egyptology," were equally awe struck. Jean François Champollion, who is credited with translating the MDW NTR (hieroglyphics) in 1922, after studying at Waset (Luxor), reading the texts, was quoted as saying that, "The Egyptians of old thought like men a hundred feet tall. We in Europe are like Lilliputians."[20] John Anthony West quotes German Egyptologist Heinrich Brugsch, who was convinced that the animal-headed gods, monsters and other strange manifestations of Egypt were *symbolic* expressions of a profound spiritual science, which was of course the view handed down by all the ancients and traditionally asserted by the Hermetic, Masonic orders and the Renaissance Neoplatonists."

In fact, as Bernal has shown, we need to understand the political sociology of the times in order to evaluate the European scholarship on ancient KMT, especially the scholarship that represents a radical change in opinions about KMT from the positive to the negative, the scholarship of the 1700s and the 1800s. The changes in European opinions that are significant are changes in opinion about the phenotype of the Kemites and about the influence of Kemetic civilization on world civilization, including that of the West.[21]

In other words, Bernal argues in Chapter Four that European nationalist scholars cared deeply about the perceived relationship between KMT and Europe. He argues that it was the emergence of white supremacist scholarship, for the purpose of rationalizing slavery and colonization, and for building the self esteem of Europeans that led nationalists to attempt to degrade KMT and to fabricate a mythical past for Europe.

The degradation of KMT could not be done easily in the face of texts, architecture, monuments, art work, etc., an overwhelming record of excellence. Therefore some scholars tried to whiten its population, and hopefully, physically and conceptually, to separate KMT from the African continent. Then they tried to place KMT physically and culturally in the "Middle East," even before there was a Middle East. Only the post KMT spread of Arabic Language and culture and the religion of Islam justifies our present use of the term "Middle East." There simply was no "Middle East" in the ancient world. Even the term "Mediterranean" needs strong qualification to have any meaning in relationship to ancient cultures of the third and second millennia B.C.E. These terms suggest a cultural unity between and among the Aegean, Mesopotamia, and KMT where this was not at all the case.[22]

Bernal has done an excellent job of documenting what he called the fabrication of information about KMT, not the assertion that KMT was a black nation, a position that he never takes. But the real bombshell of Martin Bernal's *Black Athena* was not about Africa at all, it was about Greece. He charges that much of our conception of Greece and its relationship to KMT was *fabricated*, largely by German nationalist scholars during the 18th and 19th centuries! They sought to explain the Civilization of Greece by arguing for northern invasions of Aryans who were supposed to be the culture carriers or producers. The goal of these historians, according to Bernal, was nothing less than to demonstrate an "immaculate conception" of Grecian Civilization, free of the taint of black Africa, and other "Orientals." But that was Bernal's task, not mine.

It is my purpose here to treat briefly merely one small part of this discourse. I already hold an opinion about the phenotype and the ethnicity of the ancient Kemites, as I am certain some here do also. However, my purpose is not to present the documentation for that view here either. Rather, *I am interested in the role that African and African diasporan scholars have played in the study of the race and ethnicity of the ancient Kemites*, especially since that role has been misrepresented in many recent newspapers, magazines, and even in some academic publications, and especially since one of our greatest scholars, Dr. Carter G. Woodson himself, studied this very topic and provided an opinion about it. As such he was in the center of the mainstream of African and African Diasporan scholars who gave serious attention to that subject.

The work of African Diasporan scholars has been substantial, and in at least, two cases, the work of the Africans represents the most comprehensive and complete scientific treatment of the subject. This particular empirical and historical work was done by two Africans, Cheikh Anta Diop and Theophile Obenga, who were trained formally as "Egyptologists" and were also trained in other related scientific disciplines, in Europe, disciplines such as anthropology, physics, chemistry, etc.[23, 24]

Parenthetically, rarely does the voluminous work of these two well prepared scholars, work done over several decades, receive a competent critique from their peers. Even more rarely are their peers and critics as well prepared in a multidisciplinary way as are Diop and Obenga.

Two words in the title of this paper are probably unfamiliar to some. "MAAT" is a Kemetic word that has been translated roughly and inadequately as "truth," "justice," "righteousness," "order," "balance," "reciprocity," etc. MAAT was the fundamental guiding idea, value and divine purpose of Kemetic society. Its opposite was "ISFET" which means "falsehood", "disorder," "injustice," etc. Honest scholarship on KMT that addresses one of the central topics, the "race" and ethnicity of the Kamites, is, hopefully, a contribution to MAAT. Whether or not we accept the arguments of certain scholars of African descent, at the very least we ought to know what the arguments are, by whom and when they have been made, and something of the quality of the arguments.

By no means can we say that the pro and con sides on this topic are divided by the race of the scholars. For example there is a long tradition among some Egyptologists that the Kemetic civilization was thoroughly African. In fact there is little controversy when we move beyond the question of the Kemetic phenotype to cultural comparisons between Kemet and her southern neighbors. Therefore, my isolation of scholars of African descent for this presentation is done mainly to show what the mainstream scholarly arguments in the African and African diasporan community have been, and to provide some information that will speak to the power and legitimacy of their work.

The Sociology and Politics of Scholarship

Clearly the question of the antiquity of KMT and its influence on Europe has not been merely an academic question for European scholars. It has been and still is highly political. It has been very hard for some Europeans to accept the idea of the humanity, the civilization, and especially of the world leadership role of African people, and that this African role predates "Classical Civilization" and even the concept of Europe itself.

We cannot minimize the scientific importance of the fact that Egyptology emerged as a scientific study during the period when Africans were being enslaved by Europeans, during the colonization of the entire continent by Europeans, during the period of segregation and apartheid designed by Europeans, and through the period of racism and white supremacy that persists till this very day. During these periods, the study of KMT, "Egyptology" which most scholars agree began with the Napoleonic expedition in 1798–99, has been almost totally dominated by European scholars. These scholars were not immune to the politics of the times, although a few were able to avoid and even to confront falsehood that derived from white supremacy, racism and chauvinism.

These basic conditions would lead a prudent person to be vigilant and skeptical when reviewing the opinions of such scholars on matters involving the highly charged "race" question. Moreover, few of the scholars, Egyptologists included, who hold and publicly express opinions about the race of the Kemites have actually studied that specific subject systematically. To know the religion, the architecture, the astronomy, the pottery or other parts of the Kemetic experience, does not automatically qualify a scholar as an expert on "race" or phenotype and African continental culture.

The sociology and politics of knowledge in times of oppression has been thoroughly documented.[25, 26, 27, 28, 29, 30, 31] The gross negligence, ignorance and outright fraud and propaganda from within the community of scholars, including many of the leading influential scholars, are the topics of many scholarly investigations and critiques, too numerous even to consider here.[32] [33] In other words, there is much more to be considered here than a simple academic disagreement among scholars.

Therefore, one cannot have blind trust in any apparent contemporary consensus of scholars, mainstream or other. This is especially true when there are too few effective academic checks and balances against chauvinistic scholarship, and especially when so few of the Egyptologists have ever studied the question of phenotype and ethnicity, and published their findings.

A former president of the Organization of American Historians has made a telling point in public before his peers, without a challenge.

"Speaking at the annual meeting of the Organization of American Historians, Leon Litwack, Professor of History at the University of California, Berkeley, and outgoing president of the organization, indicted past
historians for perpetuating racism. He called on his present-day colleagues to heal that wound . . .

   "No group of scholars was more deeply implicated in the miseducation of American youth and did more to shape the thinking of
generations of Americans about race and blacks than historians
. . . whether by neglect or distortion, the scholarly monographs and
texts they authored, perpetuated racial stereotypes and myths."[34]

This was a broad indictment by a courageous historian. But the historian
can bring either MAAT or ISFET, and Litwack was firmly committed to
MAAT. We cannot simply ignore the implications of this for the study of all
human history.

Woodson on KMT

Carter G. Woodson's work can be said to have addressed at least two
primary points.

1. He dealt directly with invalid history deriving from *neglect* of African
   people. He demonstrated that there was a massive amount of materials that were available to provide a valid picture of the experiences of
   African people.
2. He confronted directly the hidden seamy side of scholarship in a society that had slavery, colonization and racism as central forces, resulting in *distortion, fraud,* and *fabrication* of information through invalid scholarship about people of African descent. Carter Woodson's
   books, *The Education of the Negro prior to 1861*[35] and *The Miseducation of the Negro*[36] were direct challenges to and documentation of
   the *deliberate and strategic* attempts by white supremacists, including
   some scholars, not only to falsify records, but to use the falsification
   of information to control independent thought by people of African
   descent, with the intent to create mental slavery among Africans.

We will see that these same two themes are present in the work of most
African and African Diasporan scholars who studied ancient KMT and their
"race" and ethnicity.

Carter G. Woodson was clear about the African racial and cultural origin
of the Kemetic people. He was also clear about European Chauvinistic
mythology that passed for scholarship.

" . . . The Aryan theory of the evolution of culture from the preeminent
Asiatics who in migrating covered both Europe and Africa with new

ideas has been generally rejected by thinkers of our day. The thought that the long-headed Nordics came southward to civilize the rest of the world has also been abandoned as unscientific . . .

. . . The civilization of the Nile started among the blacks of Ethiopia and passed on to influence the mixed breeds of Egypt, which later came under Asiatic influences. In Book III of Diodorus Siculus it is said, "The Ethiopians conceive themselves to be of greater antiquity than any other nation; and it is probable that born under the sun's path its warmth may have ripened them earlier than other men. They suppose themselves also to be the inventors of divine worship, of festivals of solemn assemblies, of sacrifices, and every religious practice. they affirm that the Egyptians are one of their colonies." The Egyptians, too, asserted that their civilization came from the black tribes to the south, and "at the earliest period in which human remains have been recovered Egypt and Lower Nubia appear to have formed culturally and racially one land."

Among the later Egyptians developed octoroons, quadroons, samboes and blacks, the same types which developed as a result of race admixture in America. Berbers, Semites, and Negroes went into this melting pot to make up what we call the Egyptians who led the world in government, industry, science, architecture, literature, and art. In the early period, the predynastic epoch, however, Egypt was mainly Negroid.[37]

So when I say that the African and African Diasporan challenge to a "White KMT" is not new, we can prove it by reference to scholarly works of Dr. Carter G. Woodson. The early work of this Harvard educated historian led him to the conclusion that the ancient Kemites were mainly native, black, Africans.

Perhaps that was one of the reasons why this genius had so much trouble with the philanthropists. They were not eager to support his search for truth.[38, 39, 40] I might add, the same is often true today.

Woodson understood the African heritage and the continuing relationship of it to Africans in all the diaspora. He also understood the relationship of KMT to the rest of Africa.

Woodson was not alone among his contemporaries. In 1917, his newly established *Journal of Negro History* contains an article by George Wells Parker. It was entitled the "African Origin of Grecian Civilization."[41] It is interesting to note that this article should have stimulated a broader search by African and African diasporan historians for the truth about KMT. Why did so many of them ignore this challenge over the past 70 years?

Pre-Woodson African and African American Scholars on KMT

Carter G. Woodson was not the first African American Historian to assert the fact that KMT was African. Serious historians, both African and European, had done the research and had announced their findings.

As early as 1830, the fiery David Walker, born in North Carolina, and a Boston businessman, after years of research, in his famous *Appeal* confronted the question of the race of the ancient Kemetic people directly.

> . . . Some of my brethren do not know who Pharaoh and the Egyptians were—I know it to be a fact, that some of them take the Egyptians to have been a gang of *devils*, not knowing any better, and that they (Egyptians) having got possession of the Lord's people, treated them *nearly* as cruel as *Christian Americans* do us, at the present day. For the information of such I would only mention that the Egyptians were Africans or coloured people, such as we are—some of them yellow and others dark—a mixture of Ethiopians and the natives of Egypt—about the same as you see the coloured people of the United States at the present day."[42]

In 1879 Harvard educated physician Martin Delaney wrote explicitly about the race of the ancient Egyptians.

> "To determine the race representatives of the Egyptian gods, will go far toward deciding the disputed questions as to who were the first inhabitants of Egypt and builders of the pyramids, catacombs and sphinxes . . .
>
> And yet we are told by his Lordship, that "the Negro knows no higher position even to this day, than to kneel at the feet of Sethos, in utter servitude." Would the priesthood, who among them in those days were always of the royal stock and nobility, be chosen from the Negro race, if that race had only been subordinate and thus degraded? Would the whole group of people represented on those pillars at Beyt-el-Welee, in Nubia, have been of the race of any other people than those who designed and placed them there? No such thing. And the fact is, that the Negro race comprised the whole native population and ruling people of the upper and lower region of the Nile—Ethiopia and Egypt—excepting those who came by foreign invasion; and the entirety of the Negro group in this important historical representation, can be readily accounted for from the fact of the columns being found in Ethiopia, a part of this country—Africa—where foreigners did not so frequently reach, and therefore did not deface and erase, as was common in regard to those for centuries found in Egypt."[43]

In 1883, the great historian George Washington Williams wrote a book with a chapter that was entitled, "The Negro in light of philology, ethnology, and Egyptology," and another chapter entitled "Primitive Negro Civilization." In the latter he wrote the following:

> Before Romulus founded Rome, before Homer sang, when Greece was in its infancy, and the world quite young, "hoary Meroe" was the chief city of the Negroes along the Nile. Its private and public buildings, its markets and public squares, its colossal walls and stupendous gates, its

gorgeous chariots and alert footmen, its inventive genius and ripe scholarship, made it the cradle of civilization, and the mother of all. It was the queenly city of Ethiopia,—for it was founded by colonies of Negroes. Through its open gates long and ceaseless caravans, laden with gold, silver, ivory, frankincense, and palm oil, poured the riches of Africa into the capacious lap of the city. The learning of this people, embalmed in the immortal hieroglyphic, flowed down the Nile, and, like spray, spread over the delta of that time-honored stream, on by the beautiful and venerable city of Thebes,—the city of a hundred gates, another monument to Negro genius and civilization, and more ancient than the ancient glory of Ethiopia! Homeric mythology borrowed its very essence from Negro hieroglyphics; Egypt borrowed her light from the venerable Negroes up the Nile. Greece went to school to the Egyptians, and Rome turned to Greece for law and the science of warfare. England dug down into Rome twenty centuries to learn to build and plant, to establish a government, and maintain it. Thus the flow of civilization has been from the East—the place of light—to the West; from the Orient to the Occidental."[44]

In 1884 Frederick Douglass asserted that the Ancient Kemites were black in a commencement speech before the literary societies of Western Reserve College in Rochester. The speech was titled, "The Claims of the Negro Ethnologically Considered." In it Douglass said the following:

"The fact that Egypt was one of the earliest abodes of learning and civilization, is as firmly established as are the everlasting hills, defying, with a calm front the boasted mechanical and architectural skill of the nineteenth century . . . Greece and Rome—and through them Europe and America have received their civilization from the ancient Egyptians. This fact is not denied by anybody. But Egypt is in Africa. Pity that it had not been in Europe, or in Asia, or better still in America! Another unhappy circumstance is, that the ancient Egyptians were not white people; but were undoubtedly, just about as dark in complexion as many in this country who are considered genuine Negroes; and that is not all, their hair was far from being of that graceful lankness which adorns the fair Anglo Saxon head."[45]

Many other African scholar/leaders preceded Carter G. Woodson in asserting the Africaness and the blackness of the ancient Kemites.[46]

Contemporary and Post Woodson African and African American Scholars on KMT

Many African American, African Carribean, and African scholars followed Woodson. Professor William Leo Hansberry, graduate of Harvard, professor at Howard University, and the "Father of African Studies," did extensive work on this topic, traveling to Egypt for a first hand view of the primary evidence in museums and on the monuments. However, only a few of his extensive notes have been published.[47] Significantly, Hansberry followed the pattern of other African diasporan scholars by his appeal to ancient texts. He mastered the Greek record and describes Africa through their eyes.

In 1926, Drusilla Dunjee Houston, struggling virtually alone at her home in Oklahoma, wrote a comprehensive story of African people in the world, including histories of Ethiopia and Kemet. She called all of the people of north east Africa by their ancient name, "Cushites."[48]

In 1954, the African scholar Dr. J.C. deGraft-Johnson wrote to set the record straight. His work which situated KMT properly is now a classic.[49] That was the same year that African American Professor George G.M. James, of Guyanese descent, published his now famous classic *Stolen Legacy*, a book that was to inspire Martin Bernal's writing of *Black Athena*, and which has now been complemented and extended by the work of Egyptologist Theophile Obenga.[50] Obenga brought his fluent knowledge of the MDW NTR (hieroglyphic writing and primary texts), and his extensive first hand knowledge of African cultures generally, to the comparative study of Greece and KMT. James did not have a background in the Kemetic language. These authors had no doubt about the African race and ethnicity of the Kemites.

The great W.E.B. Du Bois made his views explicit, not only about the race and ethnicity of the Ancient Kemites. Like Carter G. Woodson, he wrote as well about the falsification problem tying it directly to the need to rationalize the slave trade and colonization.

> "The Egyptians, however, regarded themselves as African. The Greeks looked upon Egypt as part of Africa not only geographically but culturally, and every fact of history and anthropology proves that the Egyptians were an African people varying no more from other African peoples than groups like the Scandinavians vary from other Europeans, or groups like the Japanese from other Asiatics. There can be but one adequate explanation of this vagary of nineteenth-century science: it was due to the slave trade and Negro slavery. It was due to the fact that the rise and support of capitalism called for rationalization based upon degrading and discrediting the Negroid peoples. It is especially significant that the science of Egyptology arose and flourished at the very time that the cotton kingdom reached its greatest power on the foundation of the American Negro slavery. We may then without further ado ignore this verdict of history, widespread as it is, and treat Egyptian history as an integral part of African history."

Du Bois continues:

> "We conclude, therefore, that the Egyptians were Negroids, and not only that, but that by tradition they believed themselves descended not

from the whites or the yellow, but from the black people of the south. Thence they traced their origin, and *toward the south in earlier days they turned the faces of their buried corpses . . .* ".[51]

St. Clair Drake, distinguished anthropologist, studied the question of world racism and the race of the Ancient Kemites. Like Du Bois, he found racism to be a major influence on opinions about the race of the natives of KMT. He expressed the following opinion:

"Racism has put such blinders on people of the contemporary Western world that most tourists visiting Cairo today can take their camel rides around the Sphinx without ever noticing what struck Volney and Denon so forcefully, namely, that an ancient pharaoh was the same type of man who today walks the streets of Kingston, Harlem, Birmingham, and the South Side of Chicago. Likewise, most of the Arab population of Egypt is probably unaware that millennia before their ancestors arrived on the scene after A.D. 700, most of the Egyptians resembled the Sphinx, and that Blacks not Arabs, were once the dominant type in Egypt. Today Aswan, far up the Nile, or even Khartoum in the Sudan, presents a more accurate picture of Early Egypt's population than does Cairo."[52]

The years of research by Professors John G. Jackson, Chancellor Williams, John H. Clarke and Yosef ben-Jochannan paved the way for a whole new generation of scholars.[53, 54, 55, 56, 57, 58] Dr. Yosef ben-Jochannan has spent virtually his entire scholarly life on a study of the documentation of the race of Kemites and on the problem of falsification of data, apart from being one of the greatest teachers of the subject.

We must not fail to note that several scholars of African descent were prepared as Egyptologists in the traditional formal way. Dr. Cheikh Anta Diop and Dr. Theophile Obenga were formally trained in traditional Egyptology. Their works have been voluminous and multidisciplinary. Diop's masterpiece, *Civilization or Barbarism*[59] has no competitor in the research on the race of the ancient Kemites. Moreover, his multidisciplinary training in Egyptology, physics, chemistry, mathematics, cultural anthropology, history, linguistics is unlike that of any other Egyptologist. He integrated all of these disciplines and applied them to the study of KMT. A sample of his works will convince the reader that this is true.[60] Similarly, Dr. Obenga's masterpiece of history, anthropology, mathematics, and linguistics, *African Philosophy of the Pharaonic Period*,[61] stands as a unique contribution to our understanding of KMT as an African culture.

We cannot fail to mention that Drs. Diop and Obenga faced 18 of their peers in world Egyptology, in Cairo, in 1974 under the sponsorship of the United Nations. This was the only multinational, multiracial, multidisciplinary meeting of Egyptologists to date to focus on the topic of the race of the ancient Kemites. I believe that any honest reading of the minutes of that momentous meeting showed no support for a white KMT at all, and showed a massive amount of empirical scholarship by Diop and Obenga in support of black KMT. The European recorder at the symposium gave the debate to Diop and Obenga. Yet there has been virtually no mention in the popular media of this telling scientific debate.[62]

The study of KMT and its African origins has been proliferating rapidly during the past thirty years. The new scholars are too numerous to mention. However, they include such stalwarts as Jacob Carruthers, Charles Finch, Maulana Karenga, Runoko Rashidi, Larry Obadele Williams, Legrande Clegg, Tony Browder and Ivan Van Sertima.[63] Special mention must be made of Sister Rekhty Diedre Wimby, who completed her coursework for the doctorate at the University of Chicago Department of Oriental Studies in Egyptology. She has produced several scholarly works and also concludes that Ancient KMT was African.[64]

More recently, a new generation of scholars in related scientific disciplines have added even more relevant data to this study. For example, Dr. Keita, a physical anthropologist at Howard University, had done extensive empirical work on First Dynasty skulls, and he has done an exhaustive, state-of-the-art, critical review of the physical anthropology literature on KMT.[65] He finds that the "race" of the ancient Kemites was Africoid and that the debate about "race" has been conducted using few scientifically valid criteria.

Bringing MAAT: Destroying ISFET

The 1974 Cairo Symposium under the sponsorship of the United Nations and Dr. Molefi Asante's Temple University Symposium on Martin Bernal's *Black Athena*, in October of 1990, were examples of what has to be done in order to bring MAAT into being.

- Open dialogue in a scientific setting is basic.
- *Evidence* should be provided by those who hold diverse points of view.
- Expertise must come from diverse interests and points of view, national, ethnic, academic disciplines.

Anyone who reviews the proceedings of either of these meetings will see that, even when disagreements remained, the open forum imposes a discipline of its own. Wild speculations are eliminated or at least moderated. Chauvinistic pontifications are exposed to the scrutiny of peers and the public, with the certainty of competent rebuttal. Points of view offhandedly expressed by experts will be given the value that they deserve, rather than being automatically canonized as truth.

For example, in the Cairo Symposium mentioned above, Professor Jean Vercoutter, well known Egyptologist from Paris, made the statement that the ancient population of Kemet was made up of "black skinned whites." His remark was treated by his peers as trivia.

In a scientific forum such opinions are unlikely to be expressed, and if expressed, they will be unable to compete with data-based arguments. For, example, Dr. Diop presented eleven categories of evidence to support his argument for a native black African KMT, including eye witness testimony of classical writers, melanin levels in the skin of mummies, Bible history, linguistic and cultural comparisons with the rest of Africa, Kemetic self-descriptions, Kemetic historical references, physical anthropology data, blood type studies, carvings and paintings, etc.[66] That is why the reporter at the Cairo Symposium wrote the following in the minutes of the meeting:

> "Although the preparatory working paper ... sent out by UNESCO gave particulars of what was desired, not all participants had prepared communications comparable with the painstakingly researched contributions of Professors Cheikh Anta Diop and Obenga. There was consequently a real lack of balance in the discussions."[67]

At this conference, there was either expressed or implied consensus on the following points. (No objections were raised to them.)

1. In ancient KMT the south and the north were always ethnically homogeneous.
2. Professor Vercoutter's suggestion that the population of KMT had been made up of "black skinned whites" was treated as trivia.
3. There were no data presented to show that Kemetic temperament and thought were related to Mesopotamia.
4. The old Kemetic tradition speaks of the Great Lakes region in inner-equatorial Africa as being the home of the ancient Kemites.
5. There was no evidence of large scale migration between Kemet and Mesopotamia. There were no Mesopotamian loan words in Kemetic: (therefore the two cultures could have no genetic linguistic relationship or be populated by the same people.) For comparison purposes, mention was made of the fact that when documented contact with Kemet was made by Asian Hyksos around 1700 B.C.E., loan words were left in ancient Kemet.
6. No empirical data were presented at the conference to show that the ancient Kemites were white. (Generally, there is a tendency for some historians to *assume* that developed populations are white, but to require proof of blackness.)
7. Muslim Arabs conquered Kemet during the 7th century of the Common Era. Therefore, Arabic culture is not a part of Kemet during any

part of the 3,000 years of dynastic Kemet.

8. Genetic linguistic relationships exist between the African languages of Kemetic, Cushitic (Ethiopian), Puanite (Punt or Somaliland), Berber, Chadic and Arabic. Arabic only covered territory off the continent of Africa, mainly in adjacent Saudi Arabia, an area in ancient times that was as much African as Asian.

9. Dr. Diop invented a melanin dosage test and applied it to royal mummies in the Museum of Man in Paris, mummies from the Marietta Excavations. All had melanin levels consistent with a "black" population. The symposium participants made a strong recommendation that all royal mummies be tested. To date there is no word that this has been done. Dr. Diop struggled for the remaining years of his life to have access to the Cairo museum for that purpose, but to no avail.

Significantly, it was at the urging of African scholars, led by Dr. Cheikh Anta Diop, that this UNESCO sponsored scientific gathering was convened. Interestingly, the reporter's comments quoted above actually used one of the aspects of MAAT, "balance," to describe Diop and Obenga's work. Truly open dialogue brings MAAT and destroys ISFET. We know this but have not required the open dialogue.

More multi-disciplinary, multi-racial, multi-national, meetings of scholars are required, if ISFET is to be banished and MAAT restored. The results of the work of African and African diasporan scholars mentioned above is living proof of the uniqueness and validity of the contributions to be made. We cannot allow a massive research and publication effort about African people and culture to go forward in the absence of the African voice. This is an issue of scientific correctness, not political correctness.

Research is not now, nor has it ever been, a neutral enterprise. We must make conscious efforts to bring MAAT into being. Scholars can no longer pretend that the political world around them has no bearing on the quality of science that they practice.

Conclusion

African scholars the world over will continue to struggle in the glorious and courageous tradition of Dr. Carter G. Woodson for truth, justice, righteousness, balance, order and reciprocity, in other words for MAAT. We hope that seekers of the truth from all groups will be able to have their say. We can and must live with whatever true, honest and competent studies reveal, no matter how it affects anyone. We cannot, we must not, substitute one chauvinism for another. We must let the chips fall where they may. But we will not suffer falsehood and miseducation in silence. Woodson, our mentor, is our model for bringing MAAT and destroying ISFET. It is that aspect of his memory that gives us the greatest cause to honor him on this date.

Notes

1. Diop, Cheikh Anta (1974) *The African Origin of civilization: myth or reality.* Westport: Lawrence Hill.

2. Massey, Gerald (1992) *Ancient Egypt: Light of the world (a work of reclamation in twelve books).* Baltimore: Black Classic Press (First published 1907) "An ignorant explanation of the Egyptian sign language was begun by the Greeks, who could not read the hieroglyphics. It was repeated by the Romans, and has been perpetuated by "classical scholars" ever since. But, as the interpretation of Egypt, that kind of scholastic knowledge is entirely obsolete. Ignorance of primitive sign language has been and is a fertile source of false belief." p. 4 It was Massey's argument that the ancient African sign language from the interior of the continent was the source of Kemetic signs or MDW NTR (glyphs). The reader should also see, Churchward, Albert (1913) *The signs and symbols of primordial man: the evolution of religious doctrines from the eschatology of the Ancient Egyptians.* (Reprinted 1978) Westport: Greenwood Press, Publishers.

3. Vandenberg, Philipp (1978) *Nefertiti: an archaeological biography.* London: Hodder and Stoughton.

4. Moret, Alexander (1972) *The Nile and Egyptian Civilization,* New York: Barnes and Noble (First published 1927) p. 316 (Moret even argues that the famous bust that is thought to be Nefertiti "is almost certainly not Nefertiti." p. 217 The bust is not positively identified. It was out of circulation immediately after it was found in 1912, up until 1920. (see Vandenberg, Philipp (1978) and *Nefertiti: an Archaeological Biography.* London: Hodder and Stoughton) We do not really know what the bust looked like when it was found, before it was restored. And so we have, a foreign woman, of unknown race, with only the temple paintings and a few little known carvings to tell us what she looked like.

5. Hilliard, Asa G., III (1989) "Waset, the eye of Ra: The Pinnacle of black leadership in the ancient world" In Van Sertima, Ivan *Egypt revisited: Journal of African Civilization.* 10, pp. 211–238.

6. Kozlof, Arielle P. and Bryan, Betsy M. (1992) *Egypt's Dazzling Sun: Amenhotep III and his world.* Cleveland: Cleveland Museum of Art, p. 23 (See especially the beautiful full color bust of Queen Tiy on page 192) (See page 87 for references to the common practice of importing foreign women to KMT, paid for in gold.)

7. *Newsweek.* September 23, 1991, (See cover, "Was Cleopatra Black?: Facts or fantasies—a debate rages over what to teach our kids about their roots.")

8. Young, Peter A. (1992) "Was Nefertiti Black?" *Archaeology.* 45, 5, p.2

9. Schlessinger, Arthur Jr. (1991) *The disuniting of America.* New York: American Express

10. Jones, Stewart (1972) "The Schlesingers on Black History." *Phylon.* 33, 2, pp. 104–111

11. Carruthers. Jacob (1992) *Carruthers on Schlesinger: critical commentaries.* Los Angeles: The Association of the Study of Classical African Civilization (ASCAC Foundation 3624 Country Club Drive, Los Angeles, California, 90019)

12. Volney, C.F. (1793) *The ruins or meditation on the revolutions of empires: and the law of nature.* New York: Truth Seeker Press (reprint 1950) (Volney visited and studied in KMT. He was overwhelmed. He referred to the Ancient Egyptians as

follows. "Those piles of ruins, said he, which you see in that narrow valley watered by the Nile, are the remains of opulent cities, the pride of the ancient kingdom of Ethiopia. Behold the wrecks of her metropolis, of Thebes with her hundred palaces, the parent of cities, and monuments of the caprice of destiny. There a people now forgotten discovered while others were still barbarians, the elements of the arts and sciences. A race of men now rejected from society for their *sable skin and frizzled hair*, founded on the study of the laws of nature, those civil and religious systems which still govern the universe." p. 16–17

13. Massey, Gerald (1881) *A book of the beginnings: containing an attempt to recover and reconstitute the lost origins of the myths and mysteries, types and symbols, religion and language, with Egypt for the mouthpiece and Africa as the birthplace, Vols. I and II*. Secaucus: University Books (reprint 1974) Massey, Gerald (1907) *Ancient Egypt: Light of the world (a work of reclamation and restitution in twelve books) Vols. I and II*. Baltimore: Black Classic Press

14. Heeren, A. (1833) *Historical researches into the politics, intercourse, and trade of the Carthaginians, Ethiopians, and Egyptians*. London: Henry G. Bohn

15. Steegmuller, Francis (1972) *Flaubert in Egypt: A sensibility tour. A narrative drawn from Gustave Flaubert's travel notes and letters translated from the French*. Chicago: Academy Chicago Publishers. Flaubert is quoted as follows: "Sphinx. We sit on the sand smoking our pipes and staring at it. Its eyes still seem full of life: the left side is stained white by bird droppings (the tip of the Pyramid of Kekphren has the same long white stains); it exactly faces the rising sun, its head is gray, ears very large and protruding like a negro's, its neck is eroded: from the front it is seen in its entirety thanks to a great hollow dug in the sand; the fact that the nose is missing increases the flat, negroid effect. Besides, it was certainly Ethiopian; the lips are thick." p. 55

16. Snowden, F. Jr. (1971) *Blacks in antiquity*. Cambridge: Harvard University Press

17. Macgaffey, Wyatt (1991) "Review article: Who owns Egypt?" *Journal of African History*. 32, pp. 515–519

18. Obenga, Theophile (1992) *Ancient Egypt and black Africa*. London: Karnak Press

19. Sauneron, Serge (1960) *The priests of Ancient Egypt*. New York: Grove Press (See especially pages 113–170 on The Sacred Wisdom)

20. West, John Anthony (1985) *Traveler's key to Ancient Egypt*. New York: Alfred A. Knopf p. 40

21. Bernal, Martin (1987) *Black Athena: The Afroasiatic roots of classical civilization. Vol 1. The fabrication of ancient Greece*. New Brunswick: Rutgers University Press (see especially Chapter 4)

22. Diop, Cheikh Anta (1978) *The cultural unity of black Africa: the domains of patriarchy and matriarchy in classical antiquity*. Chicago: Third World Press (First published 1959)

23. Diop, Cheikh Anta (1990) *Civilization or barbarism: an authentic anthropology*. New York: Lawrence Hill

24. Obenga, Theophile (1992) Ancient *Egypt and Black Africa*. London: Karnak

25. Weinreich, M. (1946) *Hitler's professors: the part of scholarship in Germany's crimes against the Jewish people*. New York: Yiddish Scientific Institute

26. Diop, Cheikh Anta (1978) *The African Origin of civilization: myth or reality*. Westport: Lawrence Hill (see especially chapter on "The modern falsification of history")

27. Hilliard, Asa G., III (1991) "Fabrication: the politics and sociology of knowledge in the study of ancient Kemet," Paper presented at Temple University Symposium on Martin Bernal's B*lack Athena*, Philadelphia

28. Du Bois, W.E.B. (1973) *Black reconstruction in America: 1860–1880*. New York: Atheneum (See especially Chapter 17, "The propaganda of history.")

29. Montagu, Ashley (1968) *The concept of the primitive*. New York: The Free Press

30. Conrad, Earl (1966) *The invention of the negro*. New York: Paul Eriksson, Inc.

31. Stanton, William (1960) *The leopard's spots: scientific attitudes toward race in America, 1815–59*. Chicago: University of Chicago Press

32. Benedict, Ruth (1959) *Race: science and politics*. New York: Viking

33. Hilliard, Asa G., III (1992) Bibliography on Racism and Scholarship, unpublished manuscript.

34. *Black Issues in Higher Education. (1987)*

35. Woodson, Carter G. (1919) T*he education of the Negro prior to 1861: a history of the education of the colored people of the United States from the beginning of slavery to the Civil War*. Washington, D.C., Associated Publishers (Reprinted by A & B Publishers, Brooklyn, New York, 1933)

36. Woodson, Carter G. (1977) *The miseducation of the Negro*. New York: AMS Press (First Published, Washington, D.C., Associated Publishers, 1933)

37. Woodson, Carter G. (1936) *The African background outlined: or Handbook for the study of the Negro*. Washington, D.C.: The Association for the Study of Negro Life and History (Reprinted by Greenwood Press, Westport, Conn., 1968) pp. 16 and 25–26

38. Hunter, Clarence (1991) "The financial woes of Carter G. Woodson," Mississippi Library. 55, 3, pp. 71–73

39. Scally, Sister Anthony (1991) "Phelps-Stokes confidential memorandum for the trustees of the Phelps-Stokes Fund Regarding Dr. Carter G. Woodson's Attacks on Dr. Thomas Jesse Jones," *The journal of Negro history*. 76, 1–4, pp. 48–60

40. King, Kenneth (1971) *Pan Africanism and education: A study of race philanthropy, and education in the southern states of America and East Africa*. Oxford: Clarendon Press

41. Parker, George Wells (1917) *The journal of negro history*. "The African origin of the Grecian Civilization," 2, 1, pp. 331-344

42. Walker, David (1830) *David Walker's Appeal, in four articles; together with a preamble, to the coloured citizens of the world, but in particular, and very expressly, to those of the united states of America, third and last edition, revised and published by David Walker, 1830*. (Reprinted with a new introduction by James Turner, by Black Classic Press, Baltimore, 1993) pp. 27–28

43. Delaney, Martin (1879) *Principia of ethnology: the origin of races and color, with an archaeological compendium of Ethiopian and Egyptian Civilization, from years of careful examination and enquiry*. Philadelphia: Harper and Brother, Publishers (Reprinted by Black Classic Press, Baltimore, 1990) pp. 60 and 69

44. Williams, George W. (1883) *History of the Negro race in America: from 1619 to 1880. Negroes as Slaves, As Soldiers, and as Citizens; together with a preliminary consideration of the unity of the human family, an historical sketch of Africa, and an account of the Negro governments of Sierra Leone and Liberia*. New York: G.P. Putnam's Sons, p. 22 (Reprinted 1989, by Ayer Company Publishers, Inc., Salem, New Hampshire

45. Brotz, Howard (1992) (Ed.) *African American social and political thought:*

1885–1920. New Brunswick: Transaction Publishers, p. 233

46. Williams, Larry Obadele and Hilliard, Asa G., III (1992) *The struggle to bring true African history into being*. Los Angeles: Association for the Study of Classical African Civilizations, (ASCAC Foundation)

47. Harris, Joseph E. (1977) *Africa and Africans as seen by classical writers: the William Leo Hansberry African History Notebook, volume II*. Washington, D.C.: Howard University Press

48. Houston, Drusilla Dunjee (1985) *Wonderful Ethiopians of the ancient Cushite Empire*. Baltimore: Black Classic Press (First published 1926)

49. deGraft-Johnson, J.C. (1986) *African Glory: the story of vanished negro civilizations*. Baltimore: Black Classic Press (First published 1954)

50. James, G.G.M. (1988) *Stolen legacy*. San Francisco: Julian Richardson (First published 1954 by Philosophical Library)

51. Du Bois, W.E.B. (1965) *The world and Africa: an enquiry into the part which Africa has played in world history*. New York: International Publishers (First published 1946) pp. 99 and 106

52. Drake, St. Clair (1987) Bla*ck folk here and there: an essay in history and anthropology, volume I*. Los Angeles: Center for Afro-American Studies, University of California

53. Huggins, Willis N. and Jackson, John G. (1937) *An introduction to African civilizations: with main currents in Ethiopian History*. New York: Negro Universities Press

54. Jackson, John (1972) *Man, God and civilization*. Secaucus: Citadel

55. Williams, Chancellor (1974) *The destruction of black civilization: great issues of a race from 4500 B.C. to 2000 A.D.* Chicago: Third World Press

56. Van Sertima, Ivan (ed) *Egypt Revisited*. New Brunswick: Transaction Publishers, 1989

57. ben-Jochannan, Yosef (1988) *Africa mother of western civilization*. Baltimore: Black Classic Press

58. ben-Jochannan, Yosef (1989) *Black man of the Nile and his family*. Baltimore: Black Classic Press

59. Diop, Cheikh Anta (1990) *Civilization or barbarism: an authentic anthropology*. New York: Lawrence Hill

60. Van Sertima, Ivan and Williams, Larry (Eds.) (1986) *Great African Thinkers: Cheikh Anta Diop*. New Brunswick: Transaction

61. Obenga, Theophile (1990) *La philosophie Africaine de la period pharaonique: 2780–330 avant notre ere*. London: L'Harmattan See also Obenga, Theophile (1992) *Ancient Egypt and black Africa*. London: Karnak House

62. "Annex to chapter I: report of the symposium on "The peopling of Ancient Egypt and the Deciphering of the Meroitic Script," In Mokhtar, G. (Ed.) (1981) *General history of Africa-II: ancient civilizations of Africa*. Berkeley: University of California Press pp. 58–83.

63. Carruthers, Jacob (1984) *Essays in Ancient Egyptian Studies*. Los Angeles: Timbuctu Publishers. Finch, Charles (1991) *Echoes of the old darkland: themes from the African eden*. Decatur, Georgia: Khenti Inc. Karenga, Maulana (Ed.) (1990) *Reconstructing Kemetic culture: papers, perspectives, projects*. Los Angeles: University of Sankore Press. Karenga, Maulana and Carruthers, Jacob (Eds.) (1986) *Kemet and the African Worldview: research rescue, and restoration*. Los Angeles: University of Sankore Press. Van Sertima, Ivan (Ed.) (1989) *Egypt revisited*. New Brunswick: Transaction. Van Sertima, Ivan and Williams, Larry Obadele (Eds.) (1986) *Great African Thinkers: Cheikh Anta Diop*. New Brunswick: Transaction

Publishers. Rashidi, Runoko (1992) *Introduction to the study of African Classical Civilizations.* London: Karnak. Clegg, Legrand H., II "Black rulers of the golden age," (1977) (In) Ivan Van Sertima (Ed.) *Great black leaders: ancient and modern.* New Brunswick: Transaction Publishers. Browder, Anthony (1992) *Nile Valley contributions to civilization: exploding the myths, vol. I.* Washington, D.C.: Institute of Karmic Guidance

64. Wimby, Rekhty Diedre (1984) "The female Horuses and Great Wives of Kemet," *Black women in Antiquity: Journal of African Civilizations.* 6, 1, pp. 36–48

65. Kieta, S.O.Y. (1990) "Studies of ancient crania from northern Africa," *American journal of physical anthropology.* 83, pp. 35–48. Kieta, S.O.Y. (1992) Further studies of crania from ancient northern Africa: an analysis of crania from First Dynasty Tombs, using multiple discriminant functions. *American journal of physical anthropology.* 87, pp. 245–254. Kieta, S.O.Y. (1993) *Studies and comments on ancient Egyptian biological relationships.* (in press in *History of Africa*)

66. Diop, Cheikh Anta (1981) "Origin of the ancient Egyptians" In Moktar, G. (Ed.) *General history of Africa: volume II, Ancient Civilizations of Africa.* Berkeley, California: University of California Press, pp. 27–57

67. UNESCO, (1978) *The peopling of ancient Egypt and the deciphering of Meroetic script: The general history of Africa, studies and documents I, Proceedings of the symposium held in Cairo from 28 January to 3 February, 1974.* Paris: United Nations Educational, Scientific and Cultural Organization, p. 102.

THE SIXTH NAPATAN DYNASTY OF KUSH

Peggy A. Brooks-Bertram

It has been nearly six years since I was first exposed to some to the history of the Kushite Kings of what was known as Ethiopia but which is now known as the Northern Sudan. My earliest encounter was through Chapter 8 in Van Sertima's *They Came Before Columbus*, "The Black Kings of the 25th Dynasty."

> *"Here lay the black princes of the 25th Dynasty*
> *who from circa 751 to 654 B.C., threw their*
> *shadow across the length and breadth*
> *of the Egyptian empire, from the shores*
> *of the Mediterranean to the borders*
> *of modern Ethiopia, almost a quarter*
> *of the African continent. They were*
> *among the last of the great sun*
> *kings of the ancient world."* (Van Sertima, 1976)

Fascinated with "the last of the great sun kings," I have begun to examine and reconstruct highlights of their lives so that the popular reader can grasp a better understanding of a brilliant piece of ancient African history, often distorted, disjointed and rarely if ever presented from an African perspective.

Earlier stories of the "great sun kings" are told through ancient Greek travelers who stumbled across their civilizations, by their contemporaries to the North, East and West of them and particularly by their North African neighbors in Egypt with whom they not only shared a border (Lower Nubia) but before whom they established the world's first known kingship, setting into place a pharaonic system which preceded that of their northern neighbor by at least 300 years (Williams). This pharaonic structure not only began in Nubia, but ended with the Napatan dynasty of Nubia. Yet, almost without exception, the story of the Napatan kings of Nubia is contained within and made subordinate to the history of Egypt. This treatment has led to both a misrepresentation and minimization of their contributions to both Egyptian and world history; and has relegated their epoch (1200 uninterrupted years of rulership in both Egypt and Nubia) to the margins of Egyptian history and to the distortion of valuable aspects of their own unique history. Most perplexing of all is the erratic and peculiar treatment by archaeologists and historians of the racial classification of these indigenous Central African people.

The purpose of this paper is to review the achievement of the rulers of the Napatan dynasty of Kush, painting them in fuller and brighter colors; to propose a much needed name change which would be more representative of this independent civilization, which was not simply an appendage to Egypt. I would also like to construct a more complete picture of one of the most outstanding members of the Napatan kings, King Taharka; to identify some of the problems which plague historical and archaeological efforts to portray this remarkable individual and the Kushites in general, and to propose new areas for research in Nubian studies in general and Napatan studies in particular.

In the Nubian section of London's British Museum, the red granite sphinx of King Taharka from the Amun Temple of Kawa is a commanding presence. His high cheek bones, full fleshy lips and pronounced furrows at each side of the nose, the so-called "Kushite folds," are distinctive Nubian features.

Napata, the home of this king, was the capital of Kush, which was located in Nubia or the Northern Sudan in what was then called Ethiopia. Nubia played an extraordinary role in Egypt, first as its creator and later as its unifier and conqueror in the 8th century B.C. and was the cultural preserve of classical Egyptian culture (Van Sertima). It was one of the most important regions of the whole of the African continent and was the corridor from Central Africa to the Mediterranean. It flourished more than 500 years before the building of the great pyramids of Egypt and continued on after Columbus's voyages to the New World. Nubia is a 5,000 year heritage. *"If such a culture rose up today it would be the year 7400 before it ran its course."* (Botuwinick).

It was known in ancient times as "the Land of Gold" and took its name from ancient Egyptians who called gold 'nub.' Ancient Nuba lay in both Egypt and the northern Sudan. Lower Nubia (Wawat) lay between Shellal and Adindan in Kmet on the Nile and Upper Nubia (Kush) between Adindan and Dongola, part of the Sudan, primarily the area from the Second Cataract southward as far south as the Dongola Reach (going southward into central Africa) (Adams, UNESCO, Arkell). Much of this area remains archaeologically unexplored. The area in which Kush was located was known as Napata, which lay at the far end of the Dongola Reach just downstream of the Fourth Cataract. However, the very earliest Kushite settlements are believed to have been located in ancient Kerma, just below the Third Cataract. Napata itself, the ancient headquarters of the Kings of Kush, was an area rather than a single town and embraced the country on

both sides of the Nile. It is here in the 8th century B.C. that the Kushite
Kings of the Napatan Dynasty, or the Kings of Kush came to power (Arkell,
Adams).

Name Change: The Sixth Napatan Dynasty, Restoration Age of Kush

There is no question but that the ancient Kushites have a fascinating and
extraordinarily important history. Our most popular knowledge of them is
through the Old Testament where one king is mentioned by name. (Old
Testament) Historians and archaeologists, however, generally portray them
within the context of ancient Egyptian history as the "colonized," "tribute
payers," "enslaved," "culture copiers," and people for whom
Egyptianization lessened the threat of attack from these black men from Ta-
Seti, The Land of the Bow. Early travelers, especially the Greeks, described
them as the "people whom the Gods favor" (Homer). Within the context of
ancient Egyptian pharaonic history, they are known as the 25th Dynasty,
constituting the Late Kingdom, Fourth Golden Age or the Revival Age of
Egypt. More recently, this Late Period is named the Third Intermediate
Period. Kitchen's reasoning for this is given thus: "*Because the problems attending on late dynasties 22/23 plus 24 are inseparable from issues affecting the 24th or Nubian Dynasty, the latter had been included in this book as
part of the 'Third Intermediate Period' chronologically, even though in
other aspects (e.g., art) it would be better considered as an age of transition
between the Libyan and Saite epochs.*" (Kitchen) By this designation, the
Napatan dynasties are relegated to an "interloper" status much like that of
the Hittites and the Hyksos. In other words, the Nubian kings are seen as
'transitory' outsiders meddling in affairs not their own.

But in a rather extraordinary reversal of historical fortune attributed to a
1962 find in Qustul on the border of Egypt and the Northern Sudan (ancient
Nubia), a new light weakens substantially the "interloper theory." In a place
where kingship was thought impossible (no doubt because of its closeness
to Central Africa) an incense burner inscribed with serekhs, definitive symbols of Egyptian royalty, was found in a cemetery dating back to pre-dynastic times. This burner and other artifacts found in the cemetery furnishes the
earliest definite representation of a king in the Nile Valley or anywhere.
(Williams) The people at Qustul in Nubia were obviously kings of considerable wealth and had far wider cultural contacts than had ever been thought
possible for such a remote place. To the north of Qustul, a seal impression
from Siali reveals that Nubia, Ta-Seti or the Land of the Bow, was not only
a kingship but a territorial state and possessed sophisticated advanced political order (Williams). The activities recorded from the Siali, Gebel Sheikh,
Suleiman and Qustul finds leave no doubt about a pharaonic Nubia even
before the unification of Upper Egypt, a civilization that rose out of both

Egyptian and Sudanese heritages and had contacts as far away as Lybia and Western Asia. It appears that twelve kings at Qustul participated with other kings in Upper Egypt in the creation of a unified culture. These kings helped fashion pharaonic civilization and left a legacy for Egypt's First Dynasty. For Nubia, they established an early political unity which led to that country's first cultural distinction (Williams).

It is believed that after the A-group culture at Qustul ceased to exist in lower Nubia, this culture moved to Upper Nubia, south, beyond the reach of First Dynasty conquerors, possibly to Kerma (striking parallels exist between the Kerma cemetery remains and those of Cemetery L at Qustul). They then moved on to Nubia. It is in ancient Napata that we find centuries later the Napatan Kings who, in a meteoric rise, become ruler of both Upper and Lower Egypt and Kush for nearly one century. And this rise was not, as some would have us believe, merely "a classic example of a barbarian people turning the tables on its former overlords and oppressors" (Adams).

Because of this reversal of historical fortune, it is both possible and necessary to extricate the Kushite kings from the shadow of Egypt and view them within the context of their own pharaonic civilization, a civilization possessing a history and tradition in some ways different from, although, in its earliest phase, seminal to that of Egypt. The final phase of Nubian ascendancy, known formerly as the Twenty-Fifth Dynasty of Egypt, will be referred to herein as the Sixth Napatan Dynasty, Restoration Age of Kush. Using Reisner's chronology, which includes 16 unknown kings of Napata who preceded Alara and Kashta, the initiators of the overthrow of Egypt, and attributing 30 years roughly to each generation as constituting a dynasty, one arrives at a Sixth Napatan Dynasty. (Reisner) This sequence of dynasties begins with the period after Herihor, the last known Egyptian viceroy of Ethiopia (1090 B.C.) and closes with the reigns of Alara, Kashta and Pianhky.

The title, *6th Napatan Dynasty, Restoration Age of Kush* implies therefore that the Napatan kings were not interlopers, as the business of Egypt and indeed the known world was very much their business; that theirs was not an "ephemeral empire" which constituted a "final flash in the pan," and that there existed an independent political unity and cultural distinction which must be discerned separately from that of Egypt. And, finally that ancestors of the Napatan dynasty ruled contemporaneously with pharaonic Egypt and indeed longer than pharaonic Egypt and, if the work of the Nubian archaeological expedition under Bruce Williams is to be respected, preceded Dynastic Egypt by at least six generations (Williams). Additionally, though referring to a later period, we know from both the First and Second Kamose stele that there was a Nubian Kingdom during the last 2nd Intermediate Period and that it was one of three independent Kingdoms: Northern Egypt under the Hyksos King, Upper Egypt between Cusae and

Elephantine under Kamose and Kush under a Nubian ruler who is known as Ndh. (T. Save-Soderbergh) We therefore reject Toynbee's description and Adams' acceptance of this description of this Napatan period as "heroic" because heroic here implies that this was an "ephemeral empire," or a "short-lived barbarian successor state scampering upon the ruins of older civilizations" (Toynbee). In Adams' own words "the rulership of the Kushites was exceptionally hardy and persisted without significant interruption for 1,000 years, not only surviving a number of foreign invasions but achieving a notable renaissance in its late centuries."

There were two branches of the Kushite Kingdom, the Napatan and the Meroitic (Adams). The focus of this paper is on the rulers of the Sixth Napatan Dynasty, Restoration Age of Kush with specific emphasis on the sixth ruler, King Taharka. And while it is primarily a personal and dynastic history, it does not undermine its importance to history in general. The Napatan branch with its capital at Napata is divided into at least five divisions with the first two representing rulers who initiated the overthrow of Egypt and those who ruled over both Egypt and Kush. The first three divisions reigned from 806–653 B.C. ruling both Egypt and Kush. The third division consisted of descendants of Taharka and ruled from 655–533 B.C. ruling only over Kush. These included Atlanersa, Senkamaniseken, Anlamani, Aspelta and three other kings. This third division ruled simultaneously with the Saites, led by Psammeticus II and having rulership only over Kush or Nubia. The fourth component also claiming descent from Taharka ruled simultaneously with the Persians (525 B.C.) and ruled only over Kush. The fifth and final rulership division occurred from 453–308 B.C. where their primary enemy were the Bedouin nomads or the Meded. There were eight kings in this division. All but one was buried with Taharka at Nuri. One naned Piankhlara was buried beside Pianhky at El-Kurru. A final King, Nastasen, though from the Meroitic branch, was buried also at Nuri (Smith).

But it was the rulership of those kings in the first three divisions (806–653) which attracted the most attention. This prominence can be attributed, in the main, to the fact that the "colonized" were now the rulers but mostly it seems because they were black. Toynbee described this reversal of fate of pharaonic Egypt as "when a growing civilization breaks down through the deterioration of an actively creative into an odiously dominant minority . . . the ex-proselytes' attitude changes from an admiration expressing itself in "cultural imitation" to a hostility breaking out into warfare . . . between the disintegrating civilization and its alienated external proletariat" (Toynbee).

It is within the first three divisions that we find King Taharka. While extensive work on the chronology has been treated by others elsewhere, I will list these kings and very briefly describe them here. The first personal-

ity we encounter is Alara. Though shadowy, this is the first of the royalty of
Napata about who we know little if anything. He is however, known, from
the comments of his descendants, as one who trusted in Amun, who conquered his enemies and was chosen 'king' by the God and who had a long
and prosperous reign (the actual length is unknown). We also know that his
wife Kasaqa was buried next to him at El Kurru. He is also equated with the
unidentified King Ary, known from a stele at Kawa (Macadam). A brother,
Kashta, succeeded Alara, and was also considered to be a shadowy figure.
Though we know little of Kashta's reign, we do know that he was the first
Napatan pharaoh to rule in Thebes and held both upper Egypt and Thebes.
He traveled to Thebes (Waset), was recognized by the priests of Amon, and
had his daughter Amernardis I adopted as a successor to the High Priestess
Shepenupet I, daughter of Osorkon III (Arkell). He also formalized an alli-
ance between the monarchy and the Amon cult at Thebes. This power base
is believed to have set the stage for the Napatan rapid rise to power (Priese).
He died about 751 B.C., having reigned for approximately 19 years and was
succeeded by Pianhky or 'Peye' his son (Baer). It is with Kashta that actual
images of the Napatan dynasty emerge. Kashta's features, for example,
though rough, appear on a fragment of a relief recovered at Elephantine
(Leclant). Maspero described Kashta as a semi-Negroid type with a snub
nose, receding chin, and thick prominent lips (Maspero). Kashta was also
the father of Shabako and died relatively young (Bauer).

The third king in this first division is *Peye, popularly known as Pianhky*,
or "Pianhky the Conqueror," who reigned for 40 years (Greene). He is
credited with bringing under Kushite rule the numerous nomes or kinglets in
lower Egypt which materialized on the demise of the 23rd and 24th Libyan
dynasties. Although these nomes retained much of their power under 'Peye,'
he is credited with their initial overthrow (Kitchen). He is remembered most
for his Victory Stele, which details the existing political structure of Egypt
during these times and is one of the longest and most detailed of ancient
Egypt. In 159 lines, this illustrious king details the political situation of
lower Egypt under Tefnakht of Sais, his victory over the Saites and personal
information such as his deep concern and love for the starved horses in the
stables of Nimrod of Hermopolis and for his initiation of horse burials at El
Kurru. He left another record of his overthrow of Upper Egypt on the walls
of the great temple of Amun at Napata (Petrie), contributed to the temples in
his native Nubia and left other buildings as well (Reisner 1917, 1920).
Leclant laments that images of Pianhky "are meagre, indistinct documents
for so glorious a king." (Leclant)

The next Kushite to mount the throne was Shabaka, brother to Peye and
also a son of Kashta. Under his rulership, all of Egypt and the Nile Valley
from Napata to the Mediterranean was under Kushite rule. At least one
writer mentions Shabaka and his successor Shebitku in the same breath and

describes them as "somewhat shadowy figures, neither of whom left an important personal statement" (Adams). This is a misrepresentation of these two kings. Between them they ruled for twenty-two years. Shabaka established Kushite administration over the whole of Egypt and is known for his "tenuous peace" with Assyria. He ruled for 14 years and is credited with erecting and refurbishing temples, and maintaining the language of the inscriptions of the temples from the Old Kingdom as well as the architecture of these buildings (Kitchen). This is an enormous contribution to our later understanding of the history, particularly the religious history of Egypt preceding the Napatan rulership (Lavard). Kitchen also accredits numerous accomplishments and contributions to this Shabaka. Rawlinson credits him with the construction of hydraulic irrigation systems in Egypt and described him as a ruler with great humanity and deep respect for Egyptian customs and religious beliefs (Rawlinson). Winifred Brunton described Shabaka thus: *"he showed, like a true Ethiopian, great interest in religious matters, and we owe it to him that one of the most interesting known theological documents had survived because he had it transcribed from the leather roll on which it had been written in the Old Kingdom, and which had already much suffered, onto a granite stele . . . It is called the "Philosophy of a Memphite priest—really the text according to which certain scenes from the myths of Horus and Set were enacted by the priests"* (Brunton).

Shebitku, also known as Shabataka, came to power on the death of Shabako in 696 B.C. and is credited with encouraging Hezekiah of the Kingdom of Judah to resist the Assyrians (Old Testament, Chronicles). In a radical departure from the Napatan dynasty foreign policy of Shabaka and even Peye, Shebitku broke the peace with Assyria by interfering in Palestine against Assyria. Earlier his brother Shabaka had "remained a friendly neutral toward Assyria, unlike his Libyan predessor in 720 B.C., in so far as he complied with the Assyrian demand for extradition of the fugitive Iamani of Ashod" (Kitchen). The political climate was now changed and Shebitku became a supporter of the King of Ekron and Judah against Assyria. By this action, the Napatan dynasty was catapulted into what became a long-standing military confrontation with three generations of Assyrian warlords, an enormous military might. And though the Kushite political and military influence extended from Napata to the Delta and nearly one half of the Mediterranean Levant from Tanis up to Tyre including the Isle of Cyprus (Trigger), the Assyrians would turn out to be mighty adversaries. Shortly after becoming king, Shebitku, in light of the impending threat of Assyrians on the doorstep of Egypt, commanded his younger brothers (the most talented of whom was the young prince Taharka) to leave Napata and travel to the Delta to face the Assyrians on behalf of Judah (Arkell, Kitchen). In response to this call, the young Taharka was introduced early to what later became a long history of military confrontation with Assyria during his reign.

Taharka

The reign of Taharka (690–664) is the focus of this paper. His name looms large in the Bible where the terror caused by the black warriors of the land of Kush is evident. He stands out among Napatan rulers as evidenced by his devotion to maintaining a Napatan cultural unity and cultural continuity, primarily through temple and monument building in honor of his god Amun; his involvement in international political intrigue and his foreign travels and conquests. He was 32 when he became king on the death of Shebitku, probably usurping another older brother Khaliut (Macadam). He was called to Thebes with his brothers where an election process, probably using the divining oracle, took place and he was chosen to go to Memphis with his uncle Shebitku possibly in the Spring of 701 B.C. (Kitchen) He took the unusual prenomen Khu-Nefertem, whom Nefertem and Re Protect. He was known also as both Horus and Nebty, *was "Exalted of Epiphanies* and as Golden Horus, Protector of the Two Lands (Leclant). He was the first and only member of the Napatan dynasty who turned seriously from the task of conquest to that of consolidation. Issues regarding his travels and conquests will be addressed later.

While little is known about his early life, it is possible to reconstruct what life must have been like living with the royal Napatan family. As a boy he was away from Nubia for as many as 18 years, a time in which he had not seen his mother. Upon his coronation he arranged for her to visit him in Memphis in the sixth year of his reign. It was customary for the Queen Mother to pay a ceremonial visit to the new King after the coronation, "thereby impersonating Isis after the installation of Horus in his father's seat" (Macadam). Brunton suggests that *"Professor Griffith had already remarked, when the stele was discovered, that the insistent comparisons of Taharka and his mother to Horus and Isis may be camouflaged references to dissensions within the royal family"* (Brunton). However, this was not an isolated comparison, as the same comparisons were made to Tanwetamani. Taharka reigned for twenty-six years, a reign characterized by 13 years of peace and 13 years of war with Assyria (Kitchen).

Years of Peace

During the thirteen years of peace, Taharka was busy building throughout Egypt and this was most notable in Thebes as evidenced by stele and fragments of buildings. At Karnak there is evidence of a noble colonnade which today still evokes admiration and awe in visitors to the area. Wenig, for instance, speaks of Taharka as "a great builder approaching the scale of Ramses II" (Wenig). Taharka was an intensely religious man and loyal to the local god Amon. He expressed this belief through generous attention to the temples. Temple architecture accredited to Taharka's reign include a Temple of Amon at Gebel Barkal where a room was rebuilt by Taharka to house his grey granite altar which served as a support for the Bark of Amon. It was also in this temple that he ordered the construction of a rock temple dedicated to Amon and another sanctuary in honor of Amon's consort, Mut (the Temple of Mut). Also, in Gebel Barkal, he set up the first and finest of a series of large statues in the Temple of Amon in the forecourt (Smith). At Sanam and Tebo on the Isle of Argo he had temples built for the worship of Amun and dedicated them to the local god Amon. Sanam was across the river from Gebel Barkal and housed sunken reliefs in the style of Pianhky's triumphal scene. In one of the few, if not the only one, a scene on a Taharka stele depicting men riding donkeys and six wheeled carts was carved (Griffith). Taharka's love, however, was the temples of Kawa which he had seen early in his youth. In passing it on the Nile headed north, he made a vow to restore them. These temples are believed to be finer in detail than the other temples he had constructed. Macadam reported that Taharka sought sculptors who probably belonged to the workshops which produced the reliefs in the Theban tombs of officials of the reign of Taharka and the beginning of the Saite dynasty. It is in this temple that we find raised reliefs decorating the Hypostyle Hall, and sunken reliefs copied after, or reviving, Old Kingdom reliefs. Scholars cite the style of these reliefs as evidence of "archaizing" or Kushite imitation of the art of Egypt. The use of Old Kingdom royal models at Kawa is the most striking and one of the earliest examples of this type of relief (Macadam). In the temple of Kawa, Taharka was also responsible for the revival of the Pyramid Texts in literature and the old text of the Memphite Theology (Wilson). Not only were the Kawa Temples a treasure trove of Nubian royal inscriptions second only to Jebel Barkal. Kawa was a local centre of considerable importance and it was a favorite site of state visits and received considerable endowments to the temples.

At Qasr Ibrim, a temple with some of the few extant frescoes from this epoch was also constructed (Plumley). At Karnak in Upper Egypt, Taharka is remembered for the work he had undertaken in the building of the monuments there. The best known of these has long been the single column which alone remained standing of the five pairs with open papyrus capitals that lined the central axis of the First Court at Karnak (Leclant). He built also at Buhen (Jakoblielski). As a devout believer in Amun, with whom he appears on many reliefs, especially at Kawa, Taharka had his son Nesishutefnut installed as second Prophet of Amun (Parker) and his daughter Amenirdis II was adopted into the powerful religious Thebaid as the daughter to the God's Wife of Amun Shepenupet II (Leclant, Bauer). He was also a traveler and conqueror known to have traveled as far as Gibraltar in his conquests.

Years of War

But things were not to remain peaceful. When Taharka had been summoned to Memphis by Shebitku, he was the titular head of a Nubio-Egyptian expedition. Together with his brothers and an army force brought from Nubia, they marched to face Sennacherib who was threatening Judah. This summons is recorded on a stele at Kawa: *"Now his majesty had been in Nubia as a goodly youth in the company of goodly youths whom his Majesty King Shebitku had sent to fetch from Nubia, in order that he might be there with him, since he loved him more than all his brethren."* (Macadam) Reisner says a battle with Sennacherib could not have taken place at this time because Taharka was then only eight years of age. Others disagree with Reisner on this point. Leclant and Kitchen for example establish his age at 20 years and place Taharka in the Delta at this time but assert that this force did not actually engage the Assyrian King Sennacherib. They conclude, like others, that Sennacherib's troops were actually stricken with an epidemic and were forced to return to Assyria and Nineveh. However, Taharka's location in the Delta with armed troops at this time does open the avenue for another area of inquiry (that is, other travels and conquests which will be discussed later). In 674 B.C. Taharka defeated Sennacherib's son Essarhaddon who was attempting to invade Egypt (Kitchen).

After this defeat, there were three years of silence from Assyria. But in 671 B.C. Essarhaddon returned to the boundaries of Egypt and this time defeated Taharka, driving him from Memphis and capturing members of his family and all in his royal court. While some historians paint a picture of a cowardly Taharka fleeing to Napata, it must be remembered that the Assyrians had had tremendous help. Essarhaddon, for example, was able to cross the Sinai Desert because agreements with the Bedouin were concluded. This meant that the life-sustaining wells would be available for Assyrian troops. Additionally, the Assyrians had access to a large number of camels provided by other nomads who were in alliance with the Bedouin (Budge, Breasted). After losing Memphis, Taharka retreated to Thebes but was not pursued by Essarhaddon.

In commemoration of his victory over Taharka, Essarhaddon immortalized the king (actually Taharka's son) on a stele at Sinjirli (Syria) depicting Taharka as a captive. However, the captive was later borne out to be the heir of Taharka, his son Ushanahuru. Essarhaddon explains this in the stele where he says *"Memphis his royal city, in half a day, with mines, tunnels, assaults, I besieged, I captured, I destroyed, I devastated, I burned with fire. His queen (lit., woman of his palace), his harem, Ushanahuru, his heir (lit., son of his begetting), and the rest of his sons and daughters, his property and his goods, his horses, his cattle, his sheep in countless numbers, I carried off to Assyria."* (Luckenbill) (Plate 1)

Plate 1. SINJIRLI STELE Stele of Assyrian king, establishing the triumph of his forces over the Nubians.

But Taharka had a score to even with the Assyrian giant. In 667 B.C. Essarhaddon returned to Egypt because the resilient Taharka, responding to pleads from cities in the Delta, had reestablished Napatan rule in Upper Egypt by recapturing Memphis in what Brunton terms *"three murderous battles resulting in a massacre which left the entire Assyrian garrison dead."* (Brunton) Essarhaddon was furious when he heard this news and rushed off to Egypt but died en route (Arkell).

Assurbanipal, son of Essarhaddon, picked up the gauntlet and set out in 667–666 to reestablish Assyrian overlordship of the Delta Kinglets. *"The Assyrians were bearing oversized shields covered by complete panoplies. Some were equipped with targe and dart, they had an iron-clad cavalry."* (Brooks-Bertram). In this third battle, Taharka's forces were defeated and he managed to escape first to Thebes and later to Napata. The Assyrians reestablished overlordship of the Delta chiefs, who, because of their conspiracy with Taharka, were later executed for their attempted revolt (Arkell).

The ultimate defeat of Taharka is attributed in part to the widespread use of iron by the Assyrians and the greater discipline of their armies (Arkell). However, most scholars of this era overlook or minimize the fact that the Delta kings often cowered in the face of Assyrian attacks thereby not providing Taharka with needed support and that the Assyrians had secured enormous support from outside sources (Redford). In 664 B.C., having *"fought the father, the son and then the son of the son"* (Brooks-Bertram, 1988), Taharka died and was buried with the splendor befitting the ruler of two lands. Even his selection of Nuri, in the most well placed pyramid in the field, has to be considered as a contribution to further understanding of the individual personalities of the Napatan kings (Dunham). His choice of Nuri signalled a major break with burial tradition of earlier Napatan Kings and established a tradition of burial at Nuri which ran for more than 300 years, thereby making it possible to discover artifacts which could further establish an historical chronology of these kings as well as establish evidence of the cultural continuity of the Napatan dynasties.

The defeat, and later death, of Taharka was in effect the end of Napatan rule in Egypt and although Taharka's successor, Tanwetamani, promptly invaded the northern Kingdom, guided by a dream to reunite Upper and Lower Egypt, he enjoyed only a brief triumph (Arkell). He too was defeated by the Assyrians. But this time the city of Thebes (Waset) the home of the Amon priesthood, was sacked and resulted in the loss of 14 centuries of treasures, including two solid gold electrum obelisks (Leclant). Depleted of manpower and resources, Tanwetamani retired to the South. Despite the disastrous defeat, the gold mines and the trade routes of that country remained capable of making Kush prosperous again. He was succeeded by a series of strong rulers who maintained their capital at Napata and continued to be buried with their ancestors at the pyramid sites of El Kurru and Nuri. Of the immediate descendants of Taharka the most important were Atlanersa, Senkamanishen, Analamani and Aspelta in that order and finally Nastasen (Smith).

Thus, for about three hundred and fifty years, from the beginning of the Saite period until well along into the reign of the first Ptolemy, the successors of Kashta and Pianhky maintained an undivided rule over the country, from the district just south of Aswan to the region around Khartoum (Smith). This disaster at Thebes signalled the end of Napatan rule in Egypt. While the next three hundred years find the Napatan rulers concentrating mainly on affairs within their southern domains, even as late as 650–640 B.C., the Napatan successors of Tanwetamani, (Atlanersa, for example), were still making threatening rumblings in Nubia which resulted in Psammethichus, the Saite king, establishing a garrison at Aswan. Again, in response to Nubian rumblings, Necho, the son of Psammethichus, dispatched troops to Napata in 593 B.C., resulting in a bitter clash. In retaliation Necho removed the names of former Nubians from monuments throughout Egypt (Yoyotte).

Early Life: Up Close and Personal

While much had been written about this Napatan dynasty, these efforts have been directed more toward establishing chronology and at the same time, developing a story about the race of the Napatan kings. What is sorely missing, though, is the creation of a more complete picture of individual Napatan rulers. Taharka, for example, we can well imagine to have been a sensitive, deeply religious man, strong in character and resolve and surrounded by a close-knit and loving family. Instead we get bits and snippets about various episodes in his life, mostly military exploits. As a result, we are left with a character who appears to lack depth. Adams describes the history of Nubia as "episodic" (Adams). So it certainly is with the history of the individual personalities in the Napatan dynasty. Episodism can be attributed in part to limited textual and archaeological remains but also to the actions of historians and archaeologists who, for reasons known only to themselves, selectively emphasize, distort, or ignore parts of this history. Episodism and historical selectivism not only obscure the view of cultural unity and cultural continuity which was a distinctive hallmark of life under these kings, it impedes the development of close-up, personal and sensitive views of these remarkable individuals. For an "up-close," sensitive, personal, view of King Taharka, we can look first at his family tree. (Plate 2)

If we accept Kitchen's reasoning for dating this family, and the reports of the excavations at Nuri, Jebel Barkal and Kawa, Taharka would have known his father and possibly his grandfather and would have received his early education under the tutelage of his father. From earliest historical times, the

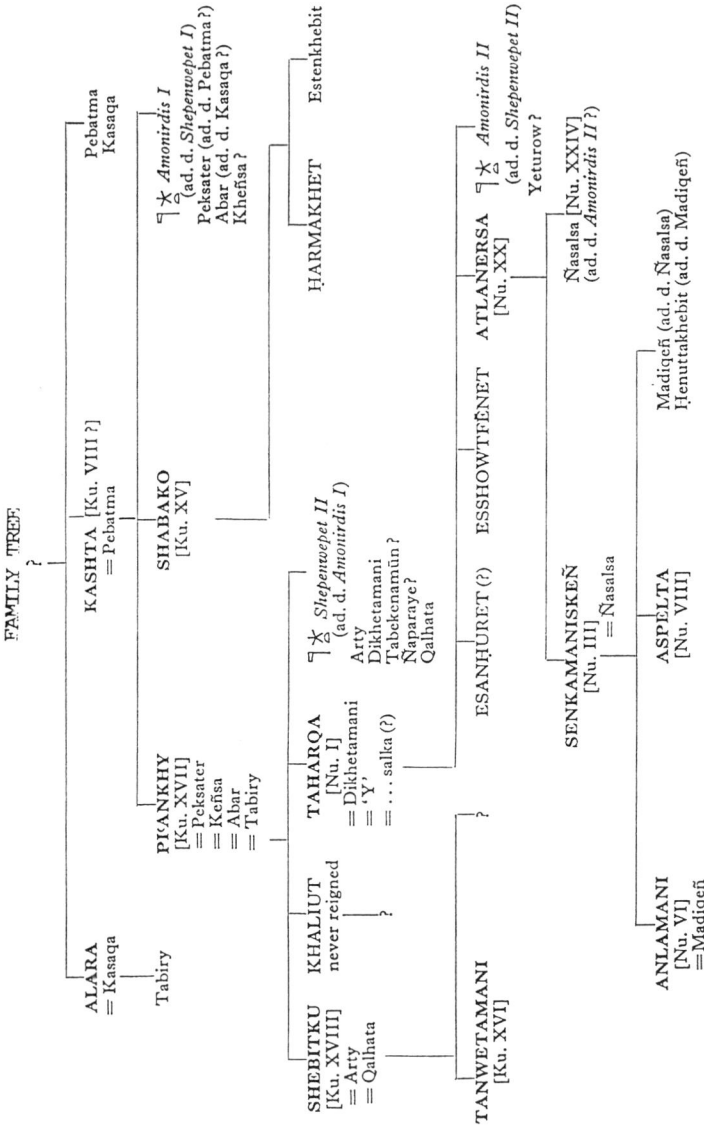

PLATE 2

Plate 2. Family tree of the Sixth Napatan dynasty of Kush.

rule of the royal secession at Napata seems to have dictated that a king should be succeeded by one of his brothers and then, if possible, by one of his sons (Torok). Alara was succeeded by Kashta, Peye by Shabako and Shebitku by his brother Taharka (Macadam). This implies that a close family relationship was possible, not only of father and son but of grandfather, great uncles and so on. He knew his mother and is pictured with her and his wife, Diketamani, on a stele found at Kawa, an important work which has received little if any attention. In this family, he might also have surrounded by his children, his nephews, nieces and grandchildren (Kitchen). The group might even have included some direct descendants of Taharka, possibly Atlanersa, and Senkamanishen. Through his immediate predecessors, he would have been exposed to a vitally rich cultural legacy provided by all of the kings before him. One can image that he would have had access to an entire line of images representing his family as far back as Alara, his great grand uncle.

While little is known about his early life, it is possible to reconstruct what it might have been like living with the royal Napatan family. He was born in 722/721 B.C. in the month of February (Kitchen). As a young boy, Taharka would have been nursed by his mother for nearly three years and might well have gone about nude during the first years of his childhood. He would have worn the short plaited lock on the right side of the head following the example of the youthful god Horus who was supposed to have worn this sidelock. As a royal child, he may also have worn a broad band instead of the lock (Lepsius). In his very early years he might have been affectionately called "little wise one," i.e., a good child. He might have played with toys in the royal nursery such as the naughty crocodile and the good little man who would jump (Erman). Royal children like Taharka may have had flowers and pet birds in their nursery. Boyhood followed a loving childhood after 4 years. From that period on, a boy dressed differently and his education was in the charge of his father. At a tender age, royal children, especially boys, were either brought up in the palace with royal children (Erman), sent away from home or to a special school to prepare for a career. We know also from Taharka's own stele at Kawa (known also as Gematen) that he left home early as he hadn't seen his mother in many years (Macaddam).

As a member of the royal family he would wear a seal ring with his name (Reisner), arm bracelets (Macadam), and a special covering for his head (Leclant and Plumley). Most often royal men were pictured in a tight fitting skull cap. It is a cap which had enormous religious significance. So significant is this royal headgear that it is shown being handed by the God Amun to Peye (Piankhi) on a stele. This is the only known representation of its kind to signify royal insignia's connection to the God Amon. (Plate 3)

As king he would have worn the double urea over the skull cap with the uraeus on the front of the crown as proof of a kingship, of the right to rule,

Plate 3. God Amun presenting King Piankhy (Peye) with a cap and the Red crown of Lower Egypt.

and symbol of kingly protection. The cobra was believed to possess magical and religious significance. Both admired and feared, the cobra was the manifestation of divine power and was identified with the protection of the goddesses and, as a powerful amulet, became the insignia of Egyptian kingship (Kendall).

As an equally awesome badge of honor King Taharka would also have as part of his attire (especially as an adult) the walking stick which all men carried. It would be used as an aid when walking or as a support when standing. In manhood, he would also carry a staff as a symbol of command (Erman).

As a man of means he would have required oils for his body—imported oils—probably from the south coasts of the Red Sea, which supplied the precious *Qemi*, ointment used for oiling the dead as well. Like other royals, he might have one of his servants or couriers anointing him with Qemi (Erman). And if he gave into vanity, to maintain the blackness of his hair he might have subscribed to the physicians remedies of *"anointing the head with the blood of a black calf that has been boiled in oil"* (Erman). One can also imagine that as a young man, he must have been deeply religious and felt a great obligation to build anew, restore and protect the temples. He is credited with erecting numerous temples dedicated to his god Amun. These include his temple at Sanam (Griffith) and the Temples of Kawa. Perhaps the most well known are those at Kawa and Gebel Barkal. Kawa along with Gebel Barkal became the great religious centers of the Napatan kings. He built also at Semna, and at Qasr Ibrim in Lower Nubia (Dunham, Plumley). It is reported for example, that Taharka first saw and became enamored with the temples at Kawa on his way north in the service of Shebitku. On his stele at Kawa he expressed sorrow on the ruinous condition of these temples and vowed to care for them. He kept that promise and as a result these temples would later provide a treasure trove of Napatan royal inscriptions second only to Jebel Barkal (Macadam). Taharka's attentions and offerings to these temples is indeed a love story begging for attention, and one which provides even more insight into this extraordinary man. Many generations later, another of the descendants of Taharka would return to Kawa, and, noting their unattended condition much as Taharka had done centuries earlier, would also promise to restore them, this time in the name of Taharka. Such a story has not yet been written and clearly indicates Napatan efforts at cultural unity and cultural continuity.

As a child and young man, Taharka would have grown up in a society which while heavily influenced by Egypt, would have meticulously returned to the iconography of Egypt under the Old Kingdom and Middle Kingdoms, no doubt remembering when Kush gave birth to Egypt. While some scholars (Kitchen, Adams, Breasted) term this behavior *"archainizing"* which they interpret to mean mimicry, this author attributes this behavior to reclamation of Old and Middle Kingdoms iconography and religious ideology as Napatan devotion to cultural continuity, which recognized Napatan or Kushite rulership beginning at a still unknown time in history up to their own rulership of Egypt. The Qustul finds further strengthen the concept of cultural continuity and subsequent Napatan practices of remembering their past.

As a husband and father he must have known great pain when in a second clash with Essarhaddon in 671 B.C. Taharka lost that part of his family residing at Memphis. Luckenbill's translation of the text of the Essarhaddon Stele at Sinjirli and that of Budge in a fascinating little book entitled, *"Essarhaddon,"* provide a chilling version, even if exaggerated in some parts, of a great loss to Taharka. Essarhaddon writes: *"His queen (lit., woman of his palace), his harem, Ushanahuru, his heir (lit., son of his begetting), and the rest of his sons and daughters, his property and his goods, his horses, his cattle, his sheep in countless numbers, I carried off to Assyria . . . I had a stele made with my name inscribed (thereon) and on it I caused to be written the glory of the valor of Assur, my lord."* (Luckenbill) On this stele Essarhaddon is depicted standing and holding a pair of reins attached to a ring which goes through the nose or lips of a pair of kneeling individuals. The largest figure is Ba'al, the King of Tyre, and the other is Ushanahuru, the son of Taharka.

Another stele called the Dog River Stele, near Beirut, is a second monument commemorating the victory over Taharka. Essarhaddon recounts: *"Amidst gladness and rejoicing I entered Memphis, the royal city of Taharka which was covered with gold."* In this stele Essarhaddon counts his booty from Memphis as Taharka's queen, his harem, Ushanahuru, his heir . . . his courtiers, ivory, vessels of gold, the property of the harem women, his son-in-law, his family, the princes, physicians, seers, the goldsmiths, the son of Bin-juki (?) . . . (Luckenbill).

Two other stele, with images of Ushanahuru, though less clear, depict two kneeling figures in chains before Essarhaddon. The triumph over Taharka was so significant for Essarhaddon that these four stele were erected at strategic places within Assyria (F. Thureau-Dangin).

The loss of his family must have been tremendous but nowhere in the discussions of the reign of Taharka is any humanity accorded to these events even though they must have had an enormous impact on his future ideas about the Assyrian threat on the doorstep of Egypt. No doubt they account for what Brunton describes as Taharka's murderous siege when he returned to Memphis. Within a year he had gathered an army and returned to massacre the Assyrian garrison left by Essarhaddon. Memphis was retaken (Brunton). Regrettably Brunton does not cite this material so that further study can be conducted.

Problems

If the historian is "the keeper of the text," "the ventriloquist that balances corpses on its knee," "the worker of mute mouths" and one who "gives speech to silence," and "transforms bones and blood into reminiscences" (Mariani), then perhaps we must return to the corpses, the bones and the mute mouths for a fuller and more comprehensive history of this extraordinary Napatan dynasty. To say the least, the history of this dynasty, like that of the history of Nubia, is, as Adams suggests, *episodic*. He attributes this episodism as one propounded by Reisner, and endorsed by most of his successors. Additionally, he attributes episodism to several factors: "lack of systematic knowledge of Nubia beyond the second cataract; the general absence of archaeological information forcing scholars to rely heavily on the textual record of Nubian history; and a certain residual influence of pre-scientific historical thought which contributed greatly to misunderstanding about cultural change; and, objectivity overridden by zeal for particular historical themes" (Adams). He adds further that what Nubian history lacks today is not so much historical fact "as an intelligible and coherent point of view around which to arrange the known facts" (Adams). It seems therefore that if there is ever to be a more correct understanding of Nubian history and therefore that of the Sixth Napatan Dynasty, both archeology and history must be rearranged around known facts about which ventriloquist archeologist-historians have been silent or to which when speaking, they have rendered confusing and baffling explanations. Due to limitation of both space and time only two such areas will be briefly addressed.

The first addresses racism in the reporting of Napatan history. Adams, for example, stopped short in his analysis of the problem in Nubian history when he failed to identify specifically the racist ideology of both early archaeologists and Nubian scholars and its effects on both early and later reporting of this history. It is this ideology which has significantly affected both historical and archaeological research on the racial identification of the Napatan dynasties and their contributions to Sudanese, Egyptian and indeed world history. Racist ideology is evident in the demeaning language used to describe these people; in the creation of racial designations which confound all known and generally accepted categories of racial groupings, e.g., semi-negroid; or black white people; attempts to relegate these people to the backwater of civilization by denial of or failing denial, dimunition and denigration of their contributions by relegating such accomplishments to the margins of history; the development of classificatory schemes which diminish their role in civilization emphasizing those aspects of their history which represent a "low tide" while ignoring or attributing to the influence of others their cultural and political "high tides"; and by a pictorial representation which demeans those racial characteristics; e.g., big nose, lips and hair which distinguished them from their immediate neighbors and indeed other civilizations on the planet.

The pictorial representation of a people is critical to understanding their origins. These were African people and while Reisner's earlier ascription to them as having Libyan or Mediterranean ancestry, no doubt because such groups were believed to possess strains of "white blood," has been discredited, the spectre of the racism in this racial assignment is reflected in work nearly 80 years later. While acknowledging that the earliest tombs were thoroughly Nubian in form, he nevertheless sought to deny the Nubian origin of the dynasty by using specious evidence to construct a theory that his kings were of Libyan (i.e., light-skinned) origin and perhaps related to the Egypto-Libyan 22 Dynasty.

His primary evidence was actually no more than his own racial bias (Kendall). Considering the still persistent refusal to identify these people for what they were, any serious discussion of the 6th Napatan Dynasty must return to the scene of the original crime and work carefully forward. Perhaps Drucilla Dungee Houston said it best: "*Archeologists dig up the proofs, ethnologists announce their origins, but history refuses to change its antiquated and exploded theories.*" (Dungee)

On this matter we need only to turn to archaeological remains where the old adage that a picture is worth a thousand words is a propos. When faced with the images of these kings, e.g., Taharka, some scholars recognized with no problem the racial background of these people and called them as they saw it. In 1927, for example, Taharka was described from an image on an Assyrian stele from Sinjirli, "*from the left hand extend the ropes ('reins') which pass through the lips of the two figures at his feet. The first of these figures is clearly Taharka, who is represented with strongly marked Negroid features.*" *This was later found to be Taharka's son, Ushanahuru.* (Luckenbill) (See Plate 4.)

In 1930, Taharka is described from this same stele as: "*there one see the powerful figure of Essarhaddon holding two ropes in his hands, one runs through the nose of the kneeling figure of the King of Tyre, the other through that of a yet more pitiful personage, a little negro with fettered legs, wearing a small skullcap with a uraeus: Taharka!*" (Brunton). Brunton also provides a drawing of how she conceived Taharka to look as an adult. (Plate 5)

Breasted says of this same portrait that " . . . *and the other, as his negroid features indicate, is the unfortunate Taharka*" (Breasted). As further attestation to scholars' identifying Taharka (his son) as a Negro, Breasted says: "*He was the son of a Nubian woman and his features, as presented in contemporary sculpture show unmistakable negroid characteristics.*" (Breasted)

Then there are those scholars who cannot see Taharka's negroid features,

Plate 4. Ushanaru (kneeling figure on left-Sinjirli stele).

Plate 5. Brunton's Portrait of Taharka.

adding to the relentless trek of historians and archaeologists alike, toward denial of the incalculable contribution of this African dynasty to Egyptian and indeed world civilization. Of that same Senjirli stele, Shinnie, scholar of ancient Mero says *"this is probably not a portrait, but more likely merely the Assyrian artists conventional representation of a man from the far south"* (Shinnie). My question is: Why a "conventional representation" when you have the real thing before you? In 1946, Smith describes Taharka again from that same stele. *"Taharka is shown mistakenly as negro by Assyrian sculptors"* (Smith). Now the *ancients* have made a mistake! The Assyrians have been accused of many things but never of not recognizing and accurately describing their enemies!

In 1975, eminent French scholar Jean Leclant dismisses Brunton summarily with these words, *"The fact is that Taharka was not a negro but a Kushite. In any case, we cannot accept the reconstruction of the negroid Taharka proposed by Brunton."* (Leclant) Clearly, Leclant gets roasted on his own pitard here because in his own article he displays a picture of those precious little ivory carvings from the inlaid ivory carvings of the Tomb of Shebitku. He reports that in these carvings, *"Shabataka had allowed himself the satisfaction of putting the characteristic image of a Negro in contrast to those of peoples of the North."*

Clearly, Leclant is imposing upon Shabataka (Shebitku) his very own racist biases which were not operable in ancient times. Additionally, it is impossible to decide that the two figures that are shown are from different racial stock. Both are obviously negro. Further, the figure that is identified as a negro (I categorize them both as negro) has exactly the same features of Ushanahuru, Taharka's son. From another carving, Leclant describes a royal lion-cub getting ready to devour a Kushite with Negroid features and kinky hair. (Leclant). If we match the head of this "Kushite with Negroid features" to that of Ushanahuru, we get the same image. This is the same image from the so-called negro head in the Shabaka ivories. Smith, in describing these ivories said: " . . . little figures brandishing weapons probably come from a hunting scene which is more clearly native Ethiopian, bearing even on its tiny scale a close relationship to the reliefs of Taharka. . . . Those (other figures, sic.,) represent figures of foreign prisoners in the same attitude and with the same careful details of costume as in the faience tiles of Ramsees III. Only Libyans and Negroes are represented." (Smith) Isn't it possible to assume that the same careful detail shown the costumes was evident in the facial images as well? The head of the negro of which Smith spoke (from the Sinjirli stele) is the same type of image that we find on fragments from the Barkal Temples (Dunham). One can only become more confused at Leclant's assignment of differences between a Kushite and a Negro. Differences he never bothers to explain. And worse yet, that he should impose upon the ancients his own biases about racist distinctions.

Plate 6A. Kushite on Shakaba ivories.

Plate 6B. Libyan on Shakaba ivories.

Plate 7. Brunton's Portrait of Taharka (repeated for comparative purposes).

Plate 8. Ushanaru on Sinjirli stele (repeated for comparative purposes).

Plate 9. Relief of Taharka from Kawa Temples.

In 1977, Adams, another eminent Nubian scholar, describes his overall approach to Nubian history thus: "If I deplore the earlier tendency of Egyptologists to see the Nubians as nothing more than second-class Egyptians, I am equally resentful of efforts to place them in another historical pigeonhole as "Africans" or "blacks" (Adams). Why pray tell is being what one is a "historical pigeonhole"? The fact is, we need only to view side by side those images which support the Africanness of King Taharka, images created by the ancients themselves. These would include the Sinjirli stele, (Plate 1) the Shabaka ivories where a Kushite (which represents Taharka's background) is clearly described (Plate 6A), a relief of Taharka from Kawa, (Plate 9) as well as Brunton's drawing of Taharka. (Plates 5 and 7)

Even scholars like Kitchen, who have added significantly to Napatan chronology ignores the issue of race and even worse, in his well-researched work, portrays these kings as transitory and incompetent interlopers in Egyptian affairs and suggests that they would have done well to have stayed at home.

Perhaps the most troubling of the racial identification of the Napatan kings is scholars' efforts to present through imagery a "Europeanized" version of the Napatans by depicting, emphasizing and opening for study only those artifacts which minimize an "Africoid" appearance. This is the remaking of history through "disrepresentation." By disrepresentation I mean the selective use of archaeological artifacts, which tell only part of a story if not indeed a different story. This is certainly what has happened with the physical image (particularly facial images) of King Taharka. The "disrepresentation" is centered around the lips, nose and head shape of these kings. In other words, those facial features which designate them as African people no matter where one would find them on the globe. This type of treatment suggests the need for a family photo or a photo gallery of these kings if for no other reason than to depict family likenesses, and to compare likenesses around the world.

In all that has been written about this dynasty, Leclant comes closest to creating such a photo gallery (without trying) but this effort is mired first in his non-acceptance of their race and second in his distaste and dislike of those images which emphasize their indigenous central African origins. One cannot understand how such a scholar can square such inconsistencies with himself. Nonetheless, it is possible to construct a royal family photo gallery from stele, temple reliefs, building fragments, frescoes and statues beginning with Alara and ending with Tanutamon. First, is Alara. (I am informed by personal discussion with the Assistant Curator of the Boston Museum of Fine Arts that the stele of "Ary" in the Temples of Kashta is really to be attributed to Alara.) The second in this gallery is a fragment stela depicting Kashta. While the image is unclear he is identified by inscription and one can make out the characteristic insignia of the diadem and the double uraeus of the Napatan kings. Equally visible is his large bulbous nose. However, Leclant is unable to discern the nose. Peye (Piankhi) lost to us in colossal statue, faded, obscured, unclear on stele, appears with his favored horses on the Victory Stele found at El Kurru. There are, however, numerous statues, fragments and other likenesses of Napatan kings which remain unnamed, anyone of which might be an image of Peye. Fourth, a likeness of Shabaka, which is one of the oldest securely dated sculptures of this time. Fifth, a likeness of Shebitku displaying the classic Kushite folds.

But King Taharka is a man of many faces, whether in relief; as a sphinx (Amon Temple at Kawa); as a colossi (Gebel Barkhal); on temple shrines (Kawa) looking into the face of his god Amun who the Napatan kings depict as possessing the same facial features as his royal subjects; on temple fragments (Kawa) or on fresco (Quasm Ibrim). Those elements of his facial features which define him as an African man are unmistakable. And last, there is Tanwetamani (in relief and on fresco) who succeeded Taharka.

Scholars' treatment of the image of Taharka requires comment. While his image occurs on many extant statues, reliefs, stele, frescoes and shrines, the images of him which have received the greatest attention and praise are those which do not reflect the characteristic Kushite bulbous nose, the prominent folds around the nose, the large lips, round head and short neck. Some scholars, Leclant for example, describe as "unflattering" those portraits of Taharka which depict him with a prominent nose, thick lips and drooping eyes (Crypt Room E of the Edifice of Taharka of the Lake, Temples of Kawa).

Leclant describes these characteristics thus: *"frankly, this unflattering type of iconography was developed to emphasize the Kushite origin of the King."* (Leclant) He goes on to identify at least three other images of the king which he deems unflattering (one at the Temple of Amon-Ra-Montu at Karnak North, another on a small object such as a menat in the Metropolitan Museum of Art and another on amulets discovered by G.A. Reisner).

What Leclant does consider to be a proper image of Taharka is another relief of which he says "a real elegance distinguishes this series, so regular that despite vandalism and the damage wrought by time, the identification is beyond *question. "The slightly hooked nose, the sensual mouth, cheekbones salient but not exaggerated, wilful chin..."* (Leclant). If anything, this is the most uncharacteristic image of this king and is so different as to raise suspicions as to its assignment to King Taharka except to portray him as something other than African.

In fact, if Leclant's goal was, as he implied, to accurately portray the image of the Napatans, especially King Taharka, he missed that opportunity because he failed to present those images which best represented a king of Sudanese ancestry. These would have at least included such images as: 1) a relief titled "King in the Care of a Goddess" Catalogue #71 in Wenig; 2)

Plate 10. Kashta.

Plate 11. Piankhi.

Plate 12. Shabaka.

Plate 13. Shebitku.

image of Taharka on a loose block found in the First Court of Temple T, in the Kawa Temples, plate lxiii of Kawa, and 3) Brunton's reconstruction of the image of Taharka from existing archaeological material. Brunton describes Taharka thus: " . . . *Taharka's physiognomy remains strong and isolated in the long portrait gallery of the pharaohs; the magnificent black granite head in Cairo, as also a couple of small bronzes, show a leader of one of the energetic East African people, cattle-owners and warriors, of mixed Hamitic and Negro stock.*"

That "little negro" portraiture that Brunton describes from the Senjirli stele provides a perfect comparison to portraiture of Taharka found all over Nubia and particularly in the area of Napata. However, such comparisons have never been made. If indeed scholars still cannot make up their minds about Taharka's African or negroid characteristics, they have only to compare the image of his son Ushanahuru with that of his father and indeed that of Kashta, where despite difficulty, we can clearly make out the presence of a bulbous nose. (Fragment of a stela with Kashta in profile from Elephantine.) Like father, like son.

Scholars have also tried to attribute modern racist attitudes to the ancients. This is evident in assertions that the Assyrians gave negroid characteristics to Taharka's son in order to insult the Kushites. Not only did this kind of racist mentality not exist at that time, it is highly unlikely that a Napatan king would see such characteristics as demeaning. Otherwise, they would not have depicted themselves in this way. It is these facial characteristics which were to be found throughout the temples, especially at Jebel Barkal and at Kawa. Even on loose stones we find tiny faces on fragments, each bearing the bulbous nose and full lips. Particularly intriguing are the entire shrines, especially from the Temple of Kawa, Shrine of Taharka (now in the Ashmolean Museum) where even the Gods on the shrine with Taharka sport a big nose and lips, looking just like the Napatan family members.

Travels and Conquests

Secondly, scholars are curiously silent on the travels of the Napatan kings outside of Egypt and Kush and their conquests along the way. Though Trigger reports their influence throughout the Mediterranean Levant, including Cyprus (Trigger), it is only in a little known, seldom quoted, but exciting little book by Drucilla D. Houston that we find these kings described as having left their footprints all over the globe. This is especially true of King Taharka. Closely aligned, though never explored, is the relationship between Taharka's early travels and conquests and his dedication to the God Amun. It was truly a religious mission. It is significant to note that on Taharka's stele of his 6th year, from Kawa he writes that "*I received the*

Plate 14. Red granite sphinx of Taharka.

Plate 15. Colossus of Taharka.

Plate 16. Tanwetamani.

Plate 17. Taharka (from Leclant).

Plate 18. Taharka, king in care of a goddess.

crown in Memphis after the Hawk (Shebitku) had soared to heaven, and my
father Amun commanded me to place every land and country beneath my
feet southward to Re Retehu-Qabet (the known world in the South, possibly
Buhen), northward to Qebh-Hor, eastward to the rising sun and westward
to its setting." (Lines 15 and 16 from the Kawa Temples, stele of 6th year.)
Here Macadam says that the context in which Qebh-Hor is mentioned confirms the view of MacIver and Breasted that this locality marks the northern
limit of the Egyptian Empire if not the known habitable world (Macadam).

In effect, this ancient text informs us that the king got his marching
orders from the God Amun himself. He was ordained by his God to travel
and conquer! Essentially he was to have no borders. In the north, for example, we learn from Luckenbill of Taharka's influence all along the Mediterranean Levant as it was his conspiracies with Ba'al of Tyre which triggered an Assyrian invasion from the East. This influence included the cities
around the mouth of the Levant including the Isle of Crete. (Luckenbill)
Further north, Makharri, writing on the History of The Mohammedan Dynasties of Spain, cites a 15th century Spanish chronicle which places
Taharka in Spain sometime around 700 B.C. He is described as the invading
general heading an Ethiopian army to the South of Spain which he is said to
have entered. (Makkary) On this matter we have to return to Taharka's
earlier military adventures when first summoned by his uncle Shebitku
where he was called to command an army against Sennacherib in 702 B.C.
We know also that this engagement probably never took place because of a
plague which afflicted the Assyrian troops forcing their return to Assyria
thereby sparing the young general a fight. Additionally, we know that
Taharka was leading a Nubio-Egyptian army force which was probably
spoiling for a fight especially after having earlier left Thebes where the
oracle of Amon had identified Taharka as the younger brother to usurp the
crown-to-be from older brother Khalihut. When it became clear that the
military expedition was cancelled, it is highly probable that Taharka, in
possession of men who were seasoned travelers, and in possession of arms
and ships, merely turned his sites to Southern Spain. The young prince
anxious to show himself worthy of Amon's blessings and the Napatan
crown, set sail for Spain. Their embarking would have been the second time
Africans had come to Spain or Andalus as it was then known. The first time
was by a North African king, Batrikus (Al-Makkary). The later Nubian
scenario is supported in a review by Van Sertima of a manuscript by Florian
de Ocampo, Cronica General, published in Medina del Campo in 1553. He
found reference to an Ethiopian garrison which invaded Spain. He writes
that *"the name of the invading general is given as 'Tarraco,' (note the*
Spanish spelling). He is not only identified as head of an Ethiopian army,
the reference is made more specific. It says he was later to become a King
of Egypt" (Van Sertima).

For the territories in the East, Drucilla Houston places the Kushites in

Plate 19. Another relief of Taharka from the Kawa Temples.

Arabia, saying that *"the extended conquests of the Egyptian kings do not seem at all impossible when we remember that they were recovering and reclaiming regions anciently their own."* Further, regarding the east, Dungee quotes Baldwin, *"in the oldest recorded traditions, Arabia is the land of Kush,"* and that *"in the early traditions and records of Greece, Arabia was described as Ethiopia,"* and *". . . we would decide that the old race of the Upper Nile early sent colonies across the sea, which built up the cities and communities along the opposite Arabian coast. This happening before the founding of Memphis or the colonizing of Chaldea."* (Dungee) According to Dungee, Strabo reports that Taharka rivalled Ramsees II in his conquests, which extended westward to the Pillars of Hercules and eastward to the Assyrian domains (Dungee).

Conclusion

Though the textual and artifactual remains of these kings relate to a dynastic history only, this should not diminish the importance of this epoch in African history. It is evident from their ancient cemeteries and temple stele that the Napatan dynasty kings possessed a fierce loyalty to their old gods and traditions pre-dating ancient Egypt. Long after Egypt's old kingdom fell silent, the Napatans returned to their long-held traditions and revitalized the artistic and linguistic systems of predynastic Old and Middle Kingdom rulers. They were responsible for the continuity of ancient Egypt's religious and cultural practices (which were in reality their own from the earliest times) and which they shared with Egypt. At Thebes the Kushites continued the politically and ideologically useful office of 'God's Wife,' and the high priesthood was revived. They exploited traditional religious ideas concerning kingship and stressed symbolic unity and recalled the form if not actuality of the great periods of centralization. They were generally devoted to Ma'at. In the Temples of Kawa, for instance, there is evidence of the revival of the Pyramid Texts in literature and the old text of the Memphite Theology (Van Sertima).

The Napatans, especially King Taharka, were great builders as evidenced by the contribution of temples the length and breadth of Egypt, their restoration of numerous temples and the reinstitution of pyramid building especially the particularly Napatan tradition of step-pyramids found only in the Northern Sudan and Central America (Van Sertima).

Under their rulership royal mummification was restored and pyramid building, though on a smaller scale, found new life and form. Both of these had lapsed for centuries. Royal incest known as "solar blood" was reinstituted to assure only the pure bloodline of the Kushites would rule from the throne. Additionally, Egyptian architecture was given fresh impetus. In all, Egypt under the Napatan dynasty, especially King Taharka became one strong ruling power ruling all of the known world at that time.

If it is that the character of any civilization is determined in the final analysis by three factors: its technology, institutions, and ideology (Trigger) then, there is irrefutable evidence of the character of the 6th Napatan Dynasty, Golden Age of Kush.

Implications for Further Research

There remains, however, considerable work to be done on this epoch, primarily in the area of "distortion-removal," rewriting this history from a truly Nubiocentric perspective and remedying the episodism by filling in the gaps from one era to another. We need research in those areas which explore issues raised by some of the Nubian scholars themselves. First and foremost has to be the continuation of research at Qustul, hopefully examining the relationship between the finds at Qustul, Nuri, El Kurru and Jebel Barkal with particular emphasis placed on the common threads provided, for example the horse burials of the Napatans, found first at El Kurru, then Nuri and now Qustul.

Second, Professor Leclant had raised considerable questions about 6th Napatan dynasty remains which have never been adequately studied. He states: "*a sketchy note published by G.A. Reisner, Known and Unknown Kings of Ethiopia, . . . mentions a few fragments of bones, but these are not mentioned in Reisner's other report published that year.*" About Shabaka he says: "*While we do not have many portraits of this king, on the other hand we may have some of his remains: a few fragments of bone, notably of the skull, have been found in the descending shaft of the pillaged sepulcher at El Kurru. No detailed study has yet been made of them.*" (Leclant) And, of Alara he says, "*It may be, however, that two skulls discovered at El Kurru by the American Excavation team should be regarded as belonging to Alara and his twin sister.*" In a personal communication with the Assistant Curator of the Boston Museum of Fine Arts, it was reported that some of the bones of King Taharka are also in their possession. In a Preprint from Meroitica 16, Kendall states: "*Besides having the original objects to examine, I also had access to the unpublished skeletal material from Kurru. Reisner had had all the bones from each tomb wrapped in linen cloth, the corners of each tied to form a closed bag. These bags were placed in boxes. Unfortunately, somehow, labels were not included with all of the bones, so some of the bags lost their identities . . . some of it was never identified by sex or age. This I was able to accomplish with the assistance of Dr. Lane Beck, Director of Harvard's osteological collections, with interesting results.*" Imagine that with such a rare opportunity to do so, there was no analysis of the remains for racial designation!! This is a very critical area of needed research because of the possibility of answering the question of the race of

Kushites. Perhaps for example, with new technology, we can even reconstruct the face of Taharka and study the bone fragments for racial clues.

Third, another area of needed inquiry is that of the many faces of Taharka, particularly those which emphasize his Sudanese origins, features which continue to unsettle eminent Nubian scholars. Perhaps here we can begin comparisons of various images to establish Kushite likenesses within the Napatan family and with their immediate neighbors so favored by historians and archaeologists alike: the Libyans. Fourth, there is a critical need to examine museum politics and the resulting territorialism surrounding certain artifacts which has rendered many Napatan artifacts inaccessible and therefore unavailable for indepth research.

At the very least, these areas of Napatan history cry for attention if we ever hope to correct and enhance our knowledge about those men whom the Gods favored and whom Houston described as having left their footprints all over the world.

Bibliography

1. Van Sertima, Ivan. *They Came Before Columbus*, Chapter 8, pp. 122–141, Random House, 1976.
2. Williams, Bruce. "The Lost Pharoahs of Nubia." *Archeology*, 33, 1980, pp. 12–21, September/October.
3. Van Sertima. African Presence in Early America, pp. 35, *Journal of African Civilizations*, 1989.
4. Botuwinik, Bruce. *Africa In Antiquity, I*. The Arts of Ancient Nubia and The Sudan, 1978, p. 9.
5. Adams, Nubia, Corridor to Africa, Princeton, pp. 13–43, 1977.
6. UNESCO, *General History of Africa II*, Ancient Civilizations of Africa. (ed.) G. Mokhtar, 1981.
7. Arkell, A.J., *A History of the Sudan From the Earliest Times to 1821*, pp. 110–113, 1961.
8. Reisner, G.A. "Excavations at Napata, the Capital of Ethiopia", *Bulletin of the Museum of Fine Arts*, Boston, Vol. XV., No. 89, June 1917, pp. 25–34, Boston.
9. Arkell, Ibid., p. 110–113.
10. Adams, Ibid., pp. 13–43.
11. Old Testament, 2 Kings, xix, 9.
12. Kitchen, Kenneth. *The Third Intermediate Period in Egypt* (1110–653 B.C.) Warminster, p. 148, 1973.
13. Williams, Ibid., p. 19.
14. Ibid., p. 21.
15. Ibid., p. 21.
16. Adams, p. 247.
17. Reisner, G. "Known and Unknown Kings of Ethiopia." *Bulletin of the Museum of Fine Arts.* 16, No. 97 (1918), 67–81.
18. Williams, Ibid., P. 21.
19. Soderbergh, T. Save, "The Nubian Kingdom of The Second Intermediate Period." *Kush: Journal of the Sudan Antiquities Service.* Khartoum, 1956, Vol. 4, pp. 54–61.

20. Toynbee, A. *A Study of History,* Vol. 5, pp. 268–70, 1962, New York.

21. Adams, p. 249.

22. Ibid., 246–332.

23. Smith, William S. "Ancient Egypt as Represented in The Museum of Fine Arts." *MFA* Boston, 1946, pp. 174–75.

24. Toynbee, Vol. 8, p. 1.

25. MacAdam, M.F. Laming. *The Temples of Kawa.* Vol. 1, The Inscriptions (2 Vols.) Oxford University Excavations in Nubia. London, 1949.

26. Arkell, p. 121.

27. Priese, Karl-Heinz, "The Napatan Period." Chapter 6, pp. 75–105, *Africa in Antiquity I. The Arts of Ancient Nubia and The Sudan,* 1978.

28. Bauer, Klaus, "The Libyan and Nubian Kings of Egypt: Notes on the Chronology of Dynasties XXII to XXVI." *JNES.* Jan.-April, 1973, Vol. 32. No. 1 and 1, Ninetieth Year, pp. 20–21.

29. Leclant, J. "Kashta Pharoah, en Egypte," *ZAS* 90 (1963): 74–78.

30. Maspero, G. *ASAE* 10 (1909): 10.

31. Bauer, p. 20.

32. Greene, *Fouilles executees a Thebes,* British Museum, Mummy Babdage 660, No. ix 54, 114–15, 117.

33. Kitchen, pp. 362–367.

34. Petrie, Flinders,. *History of Egypt,* II, 1905, 269, Figure 109.

35. Reisner, G.A. *JEA* 4 (1917), P. 225.

36. Reisner, *JEA* 6 (1920), 2610264.

37. Leclant, Jean. "The Image of The Black in Western Art." p. 90, Vol. 1, *Kushites and Meroites: Iconography of The African Rulers in the Ancient Upper Nile,* pp. 89–1132, 1976.

38. Adams, p. 263.

39. Kitchen, pp. 380–382.

40. Lavard, A.H. *Discoveries in Nineveh and Babylon,* 1853, p. 156.

41. Kitchen, pp. 380–382.

42. Rawlinson, George. *History of Ancient Egypt.*

43. Brunton, Winifred. *Great Ones of Ancient Egypt.* New York. Charles Scribner's Sons, 1930, p. 162.

44. Old Testament, 2 *Kings* xix, 35.2, *Kings* xviii, m, xix; *Isaiah* xxxvi, xxxvii.

45. Kitchen, p. 155.

46. Trigger, B.G., B.J. Kemp, Di O'connor and A.B. Floyd. *Ancient Egypt, A Social History.* Cambridge University Press. Cambridge, 1983, pp. 242–245.

47. Arkell, p. 26.

48. Kitchen, p. 383.

49. MacAdam, Vol. 1, p. 17.

50. Kitchen, p. 158.

51. Leclant, J. "The Empire of Kush." *The Unesco Courier,* February to March, 1980, 33rd Year, p. 55.

52. MacAdam, *Kawa Temples,* Vol. 1, p. 19.

53. Brunton, Ibid., p. 168.

54. Kitchen, p. 388–393.

55. Wenig, Steffen. *Africa in Antiquity* II. "The Arabs of Ancient Nubia and The Sudan." The Brooklyn Museum, 1978, pp. 45–48.

56. Griffith, F.L.I., *Liverpool Annals of Archeology and Anthropology,* 9, 1922, 67ff.

57. Smith, Stevenson W., *The Art and Architecture of Ancient Egypt.* Penguin Books, 1958, p. 238.

58. MacAdam, *Kawa Temples,* Kawa Stele of Taharka, IV, lines 7–10, V., lines 13, 15.

59. Wilson, *Near Eastern Texts,* 4.

60. Plumley, J. Martin, "Qasr Ibrim," Journal of Egyptian Archaeology. Vol. 61, 1975, pp. 5–26 (Plate XII).

61. Leclant, J. *Orientalia,* 22, 1953; 85.

62. Leclant, J. *BIFAO,* 53, 1953, p. 113.

63. Jakoblieslski, 1973.

64. Parker, R.A. A Saite Oracle, Papyrus 1962, part II, 1967.

65. Leclant, p. 101.

66. Bauer, p. 20–21.

67. Kitchen, p. 158–159.

68. Budge, E.A. *The History of Essarhaddon, Sons of Sennacherib, King of Assyria* BC 681–668, London, Trubner and Co., Ludgate Hill, 1988.

69. Breasted, J.H. *A History of Egypt: From the Earliest Times to The Persian Conquest,* pp. 555, New York, 1916.

70. Luckenbill, Daniel. *Ancient Records of Assyria and Babylonia: From Sargon to the End.* Greenwood Press, New York, Vol. 11, p. 228, 1927.

71. Brunton, Ibid., p. 169–170.

72. Arkell, p. 128.

73. Brooks-Berram, P. "The Battles of Taharka." (Chapter in an unpublished work) 1988.

74. Arkell, p. 128–9.

75. Ibid., p. 130.

76. Redford, Donald B. *Egypt, Canaan and Israel in Ancient Times.* Princeton University Press. 1992, p. 350.

77. Brooks-Bertram, P. "The Battles of Taharka," 1988.

78. Dunham, Dows. *The Royal Cemeteries of Kush.* Vol. 2, Nuri, Boston, 1955.

79. Arkell, p. 134.

80. Leclant, Jean, in *The Role of the Phoenicians in the Interaction of Mediterranean Civilizations,* (ed. W.A. Ward) 1967.

81. Smith, p. 175.

82. Ibid.

83. Yoyotte, BIFAO, 51 (1952), pp. 15027.

84. Adams, pp. 4–5.

85. Torok, L. "On the Foundations of Kushite Kingship Ideology in the Empire of Kush . . . " *Seventh International Council for Meroitic Studies.* Berlin, 1992. pp. 2-4.

86. MacAdam, pp. 120–131.

87. Kitchen, p. 149–150.

88. Ibid., pp. 162–172.

89. Lepsius, C.R. *Denkmaeler, Aus Aegypten und Aethiopien . . . Abt. V, Aetiopische Denkmaeler,* Berlin, 182–45, p. iii, 106.

90. Erman, Adolf, *Life in Ancient Egypt.* Trans., by H.M. Tirard. Dover Publications, Inc., New York, 1971, p. 164.

91. Erman, p. 165.

92. MacAdam, *Temples of Kawa,* pp. 443, vol. 3.

93. Reisner, G.A. *BMFA,* Vol. XXI, April 1923, No. 124, p. 19.

94. MacAdam, M.F.L. *Temples of Kawa, History and Archeology of the Site,* p.

177, Vol. 2, London, 1955.
95. Leclant, p. 92, 96.
96. Plumley, J. Martin. "Qasr Ibrim." *The Journal of Egyptian Archaeology,* Vol. ⤴
61, 1975, pp. 5–26.
97. MacAdam, Plate XXIIa, Vol. 11.
98. Kendall, Timothy. *National Georgraphia.* Nov. 1990, pp. 96–124.
99. Erman, p. 228.
100. Ibid., p. 231.
101. Ibid., p. 232.
102. Griffith, University of Liverpool Annals of Archaeology and Anthropology,
Vol. IX (1992), pp. 79–90.
103. MacAdam, Vol. 1, 119–30.
104. Dunham, D. and Janssen. *Semna Kumma, Second Cataract Forts,* Vol. 1
(1960), pp. 12–13.
105. Plumley, pp. 19–20. ⤴
106. MacAdam, Vol. 1.
107. Adams, pp. 246–293.
108. Breasted.
109. Kitchen.
110. Luckenbill, pp. 227–229.
111. Luckenbill, p. 229.
112. Thureau-Dangin, F. *Til-Barsib.* 1936, pp. 151–155, plates XII and XIII.
113. Brunton, p. 170.
114. Krueger, Barbara. (Introduction, pp. ix-xi) *Remaking History, Discussions
in Contemporary Culture.* Dia Arts Foundation.
115. Adams, p. ?.
116. Kendall, p. 4.
117. Houston, pp. 15–16.
118. Luckenbill, p. 224.
119. Brunton, p. 170.
120. Breasted, p. 556.
121. Shinnie, p. 154.
122. Smith, p. 137.
124. Leclant, p. 104.
125. Smith, p. 155.
126. Dunham, Dows. "Barkal Temples" #c8860, Pl III. *MFA* Boston. 1970.
127. Adams, p. 8.
128. Leclant, p. 104.
129. Leclant, p. 105.
130. Wenig, Cat. 71.
131. MacAdam (Kawa Plate lxiii).
132. Trigger, p. 269.
133. Houston, (?).
134. MacAdam, Vol. 1, p. 28.
135. Ibid.
136. Luckenbill, pp. 221–231.
137. Ibn-l-Khattib al-Makkary. *The Mohammedan Dynasties in Spain.* Translated
by Pascual de Gayangos, London, W.H. Allen and Company, 1884, and reprinted
New York, Johnson Reprint, 1964.
138. Fell, Barry. "A Cartouche of Shishonq from Almunecar Spain," in *Journal
of the Epigraphic Society,* Vol. 7, No. 171, April 1979.

139. Van Sertima, ibid., p. 136.
140. Houston, p. 110.
141. Ibid., p. 127.
142. Ibid., p. 127.
143. Van Sertima, ibid., p. 136.
144. Leclant, p. 100.
145. Trigger, p. 243.
146. Trigger, p. 243.
147. Leclant, p. 96.
148. Kendall, Timothy. *Meroitica,* 16, 1997.

THE PROBLEM OF THE BERNAL-DAVIDSON SCHOOL[1]

Manu Ampim

This paper is a summary of my work, *Egypt As A Black Civilization: The Counter School* (1992). It examines one of the critical issues confronting Africentric Movement activists and scholars. That is, the critical problem of the Martin Bernal-Basil Davidson School. This School has become a solid component within the Africentric Movement, even as it argues for a mixed race origin of the ancient Egyptian population, and thus undermines the work of Cheikh Anta Diop and other Black scholars working in the field of Classical African Studies.

Introduction

For the past decade Black scholars of the current Africentric Movement have correctly celebrated the new explosion of information about the power and primacy of classical African civilizations. This information is now becoming common knowledge among a small but increasing number of people in the African American and international community. With the works of such pioneers as Cheikh Anta Diop, Théophile Obenga, Chancellor Williams, Yosef ben-Jochannan, and with such publications as the *Journal of African Civilizations*, Black scholars are re-establishing the African origin, inspiration, and context of ancient Egyptian high culture and civilization. This celebration of classical African civilizations, particularly ancient Egypt, has fueled the Africentric Movement and serves as a foundation for the *entire* Movement. I summarize the main aspects and focus of the Movement in my pamphlet, *The Current Africentric Movement in the U.S.: The Centrality of Ancient Nile Valley Civilization* (1990).[2] Africentrism offers an important corrective to Eurocentrism, which promotes many racist illusions, myths, and the crude and conscious falsification of African and human history.

In the process of rescuing and restoring Egypt as a Black civilization, and thus correcting world history—which has been systematically falsified by misguided Eurocentric scholarship—Black scholars have welcomed within the Africentric Movement certain outside scholars and their research contributions. However, in welcoming these outside scholars and their contributions, Africentric scholars and writers have often unwisely overlooked these outside scholars' arguments and conclusions of a multiracial identity of the indigenous ancient Egyptian population. Thus, even as the Africentric Movement is at its height of influence and is fueled by the project of the restoration of Egypt as a Black civilization, there is a group of these insider/ outsider scholars who constitute what I call a counter school, or more specifically the *Bernal-Davidson School*. This School is active and effective and operates *within* the Movement. If not checked, the *Bernal-Davidson School*—which sees Egypt as a fundamentally multiracial society—will continue to undermine the Movement's progress in restoring classical African civilizations. I address the problem of the *Bernal-Davidson School* in my work, *Egypt As A Black Civilization: The Counter School (1992)*. *The Counter School* is the first part of my two-volume analysis of *Critical Issues in the Current Africentric Movement*.[3] I wrote in *The Counter School* that

> it does African people no good to celebrate white thinkers all of whom are bound by their primary socialization and European worldview— regardless of their sensitivity to our cause of correcting, reconstructing, and reinterpreting African and world history. As Chancellor Williams points out in his seminal work *The Destruction of Black Civilization* (1974), "There is still too much dependence on white scholars to do the work for us. . . . They write from the Caucasian viewpoint, and we are naive indeed if we expect them to do otherwise—all the ballyhoo about 'scientific objectivity' to the contrary notwithstanding."[4]

As the problem of the *Bernal-Davidson School* confronts the Africentric Movement, there are several white scholars who have already achieved remarkable success in dominating discussion and interpretation of the more recent periods of the African historical experience.[5] However, given the radically different historical experiences between Africans and Europeans there is a fundamental contradiction in European scholars being considered (either by the Eurocentric establishment or the African American community) the "authorities" on African/African diaspora culture and history.

Racial Views of Popular Egyptologists

Before discussing the view of the *Bernal-Davidson School*, it is necessary to point out that there are several European Egyptologists who are also popular within the Africentric Movement, but who express negative and/or racist views about African people. However, they are read widely, and in some cases even admired, by Movement scholars and activists. I discuss this problem in *The Counter School*.[6] Schwaller de Lubicz, John Anthony West, Wallis Budge, and Alan Gardiner are popular within the movement, but all agree (in one way or another) that African people did not have the intellectual capacity to create the Egyptian high culture. While we can draw a tentative distinction between the useful aspects of their scholarship and their racism, the two cannot be separated fully. All scholarship and ideas are based on socio-historical experiences and, therefore, reflect worldview and social interest. They are formed in a social context, and the very questions raised and methodologies used are driven by worldview and a working set of assumptions. Thus, a study in the sociology of knowledge is necessary to understand fundamental assumptions and motivations which produce scholarship and ideas. Consequently, African people should be cautious when receiving European ideas, particularly on the African socio-historical experience, because the notion of "scientific objectivity" is a self-negating Eurocentric myth.

The anti-Black views of these popular European Egyptologists are not as supportive of the arguments of the *Bernal-Davidson School* as are those views of Hermann Junker, who denies that African people were even in the vicinity of Egypt until the 18th dynasty (1600 B.C.E.)! In 1921, Dr. Junker published an influential essay, "The First Appearance of the Negroes in History," in which he argued that from the oldest period of Egypt, up to the beginning of the first dynasty, "we find no evidence whatsoever of Negroes in the vicinity of Egypt."[7] He even states that, "Representations of Negroes are wholly absent in the Old Kingdom" (Dynasties 1–6—the Pyramid Age) (see figs. 1–3 to refute Junker's statements). According to Junker, "true" Africans ("Negroes") appeared for the first time in the lower Nile Valley (Egypt) only from the 18th dynasty onwards, around 1600 B.C.E. What is important here is that Junker makes these statements even after acknowledging that Egypt "is a part of Africa." It should be noted, however, that the creation and definition of a "Negro" is an artificial construction and its meaning conveniently changes to suit the particular white supremacist theory being advanced. This process is nothing more than a European tactic devised to unnaturally separate and misclassify African people. Junker's general views—which may seem extreme at first glance—are not only accepted by most mainstream Egyptologists, even though these statements are in complete contradiction to all known facts about Egypt, but they resemble the views of the *Bernal-Davidson School* discussed below.

Of course, Junker's "scholarship" is not taken seriously by the Africentric Movement. The question remains whether some of the *Bernal-Davidson School*'s conclusions will meet the same fate.

The Cairo Symposium and the Bernal-Davidson School

At the historic 1974 UNESCO-sponsored international conference on "The Peopling of Ancient Egypt," held in Cairo, Cheikh Anta Diop,

Théophile Obenga and eighteen other of the world's most prominent
Egyptologists convened to debate the question of the racial identity of the
ancient Egyptians.[8] The two African scholars, Diop and Obenga, emerged
triumphant against the world's most formidable opposition, as they argued
successfully that Pharaonic Egypt was linguistically, culturally, and racially
an African civilization. They were academically lethal as they tore through
the arguments of the European and Arab professors. A summary of the
conference proceedings indicates the dominance of the African scholars,
particularly Diop. It also indicates that mainstream Egyptologists share the
same ideas as Junker, and reveals the current state of standard Egyptology
and the defensive reaction to the idea of "Blackness." Moreover, many
participants, after having their arguments for a "white" or "mixed" Egypt
met with stronger arguments by Diop and Obenga, decided instead to (1)
abandon all discussion about race, arguing that the concept of "race" was
now outmoded and too subjective; or (2) abandon the old theory of a
"white" Egypt and retreat to positions of a mixed Egypt. This latter defense
of Egypt as an African culture but racially mixed is significant because it is
the same position taken by the *Bernal-Davidson School* discussed below.

This latter argument was raised at the conference by the French scholars
Vercoutter and Lecant, and is of particular relevance in relation to the ideas
of the *Bernal-Davidson School*. Professor Vercoutter stated that Egypt was
African in its way of writing, in its culture and in its way of thinking, but
nevertheless the population had always been mixed. Professor Lecant also
acknowledged the African character in the Egyptian style and way of thinking, but said that the unity of the Egyptian people was only cultural, not
racial.

Nevertheless, the fact that the African scholars, Diop and Obenga, dominated the proceedings is clearly indicated in the conference's final report,
which states that "not all participants had prepared communications comparable with the painstakingly researched contributions of Professors Cheikh
Anta Diop and Obenga. *There was consequently a real lack of balance in
the discussions.*[9]

The views expressed at the Cairo Symposium on the multiracial origin of
the Egyptians are essentially the same as the *Bernal-Davidson School*.
Therefore, this School is just as much in opposition to Diop's arguments as
the Egyptologists whom he humbled in Cairo.

The Bernal-Davidson School

Before commenting on the *Bernal-Davidson School*, which has indeed
penetrated the Africentric Movement, it should be pointed out that the following discussion is not to suggest that the work of this School has no
importance to the Movement—which would be absurd—but rather to ana-

lyze its positions on questions affecting the Movement. Given the significant influence of the *Bernal-Davidson School* within the Africentric Movement, it seems difficult for many Movement activists and scholars to understand the complicity of this School in the conceptual imprisonment and denigration of African people. The *Bernal-Davidson School* is popular despite the fact that it differs with the fundamental ideas and scientific positions held by the Movement.

This crafty inside/outside School includes a *principal, a popular graduate,* and an up-and-coming *Ph.D. candidate.* The first two figures are well known within the Africentric Movement, and the third figure is on his way to becoming another popular alumnus of this School. Predictably, all three of these figures are white males, and neither of them are considered scholars of Egyptian civilization.

In *The Counter School,* I discuss the basic assumptions of two of the members of this School on the question of the racial identity of the Egyptians. I show that their arguments resemble Junker's and are the same as those made by Diop's and Obenga's opposition at the Cairo Symposium. Secondly, I discuss all three members and their shameful treatment of Professor Diop, the pharaoh of African Studies, and other Black scholars working in the area of Classical African Studies. Following is a summary of these arguments and the problems with the *Bernal-Davidson School.*

The Popular Graduate

The *popular graduate* of this counter school is none other than Martin Bernal, the author of the multi-volume work *Black Athena.*[10] Bernal's contribution in volume I of *Black Athena* (1987) is to expose the vicious racism of 18th and 19th century European scholarship and how it systematically falsified ancient history to deny the African (Egyptian) contribution to civilization, in order to elevate the European society of Greece to almost divine status. Bernal examines two models of ancient Greek society, one viewing Greece as essentially of European or Aryan origin, which Bernal calls the "Aryan Model"; and the other viewing Greece arising from major Egyptian and Phoenician cultural influence, which he calls the "Ancient Model."

The "Ancient Model," which was the conventional view among the ancient Greek writers, was the accepted view of Greek history for two millennia until it was overthrown in the first half of the 19th century by German nationalist scholars, who invented the racist "Aryan Model." Bernal's documentation of this Aryan fabrication has given African people important historical ammunition, but which has unnecessarily earned Bernal a respected place *within* the Africentric Movement.

Bernal does discuss the central role of Egypt in civilizing Greece. However, concerning the race of the Egyptians, he writes similar to mainstream

Egyptologists at the Cairo Symposium that, "I am very dubious of the utility of the concept 'race' in general because it is impossible to achieve any anatomical precision on the subject." He adds, "I am even more skeptical about the possibility of finding an answer in this particular case." Yet he states, "I am convinced that, at least *for the last 7000 years the population of Egypt has contained African, Southwest Asian and Mediterranean types.*"[11] Thus, Bernal makes it clear that he believes the Egyptians to have been a fundamentally mixed population from the earliest time. "It is also clear," Bernal continues his statement, which brings his position closer to Junker's, "that the further south, or up the Nile, one goes, the Blacker and more Negroid the population becomes, and that this has been the case for the same length of time [i.e., for the last 7000 years]." Bernal continues to write within the Aryan Model—which he ironically condemns—when he states that "few scholars would contest the idea" that civilization first began in Mesopotamia, and that this region "in some way triggered" the development of Egyptian civilization.[12] This latter assertion is a strange contention by Bernal. Of course, he offers no evidence to show that Mesopotamian culture "triggered" Egypt's development. It is clear from the available evidence that Africans were quite capable of creating their own civilization and did not need help from Bernal's "Semites." Indeed, it is ironic that Bernal has offered his Semitic interpretation of antiquity—via the Phoenicians—on the heels, success, and momentum of the Africentric Movement, which offers an African interpretation.

He admits that the native Egyptian population was African—simply because Egypt is in Africa—but he would add that not all of them looked like "today's West Africans."[13] He seems to stereotype all West Africans as having a full Black color and being "Negroid," implying therefore that they are the "true" Blacks or Africans. Bernal's "West African" stereotype is analogous to Junker's racist construction of the true "Negro." It is not certain if Bernal's stereotyped notion of the "West African" is due to his general ignorance of the physical and color variety among native West African people, or to racism which would prevent him from admitting this range and, by logical extension, admitting that Egypt (as in ancient Nubia and other traditional African societies) was an African civilization, with its base population also ranging in black and brown skin colors.

Bernal's treatment of Black scholars, particularly the late Cheikh Anta Diop, is disgraceful. He confines his discussion of Black scholarship on Egypt to only two and one-half pages in his lengthy 575 page book, while at the same time claiming to place his work within "the spectrum of Black scholarship."[14] Actually, this bold claim is probably true in that Bernal is now often mentioned in the same sentence with the Black scholars whom he openly disrespects. His mistreatment of Black scholars by downplaying and distorting their contributions is a clear example of why Bernal's motives must be questioned. Euro-American academics like Bernal, and the mainstream publishing world, refuse to give an in-depth look at serious Black scholarship and research. The irony is clear. While Bernal argues for the restoration of the Ancient Model, he glosses over the work of Black scholars, a group which has always written within the context of Bernal's Ancient Model.

No one sincere in addressing scholarship on Egypt can give Diop such inadequate attention, given his pivotal role in re-directing the interpretation of Egypt as an African high civilization.[15] Professor Diop almost singlehandedly toppled Eurocentric scholarship and forced it to retreat on its stand that the Egyptians were white. Yet Bernal reduces the historical impact of Diop's work and avoids making any reference to the Cairo Symposium.

Bernal presents the multi-faceted Diop as only a "nuclear physicist" writing about Egypt, and no longer a historian, Egyptologist, mathematician, and linguist. After misrepresenting Professor Diop's wide range of training and fields of expertise, Bernal reduces his research on the Black identity of the Egyptians to Diop's *faith* that the Egyptians were . . . Black.[16] Bernal conveniently overlooks Diop's profound scientific demonstrations on proving the Black identity of the Egyptians. Actually, Bernal certainly must have been aware that Diop fashioned an eleven category methodological framework to scientifically determine the race of the Egyptians, and thus did not have to rely on, as Bernal calls it, "faith." Bernal lists in his bibliography Diop's *African Origin of Civilization* (1974), in which Diop presents most of this framework. He also presented this entire framework at the 1974 Cairo Symposium, the proceedings of which were published in UNESCO's *General History of Africa, vol. II: Ancient Civilizations of Africa* in 1981, six years **before** *Black Athena* was published.[17] Given the fact that *Black Athena* is so thoroughly researched, it is difficult to imagine that Bernal was not aware of this major UNESCO publication, which partly focuses on Egypt—one of Bernal's main concerns.

Perhaps Bernal's underlying reason for not discussing Diop's work is indicated in his 25 September 1991 lecture at John Hopkins University. Bernal made the following significant admission concerning his dismissal of Diop's research:

> "Cheikh Anta Diop, who was a Senegalese scientist who wrote extensively on the African nature of Egypt, for a long time had been saying that his language, Wolof (spoken in Senegal), had close relations to ancient Egyptian. *And my reaction for the first fifteen years (that I counted it) was nonsense!*"

Bernal also indicated he now concedes that Diop's assertion may be "possible, but I wouldn't go any further than that!"[18]

Other Black scholars who have made valuable contributions toward reclaiming the African origin of Egyptian civilization receive the same mistreatment as Diop in *Black Athena*.[19] One must question Bernal's motives because most of these Black scholars, whom he arrogantly overlooks, had *already anticipated every aspect* of Bernal's main thesis of the Ancient Model of civilization long before the publication of *Black Athena*. Nevertheless, Bernal gives little indication of this fact.

The Ph.D. Candidate

The up-and-coming Ph.D. candidate in this counter school is Chris Gray, the author of *Conceptions of History in the Works of Cheikh Anta Diop and Théophile Obenga* (1989).[20] Gray's book is published by Karnak House, the main Africentric publishing house in Britain, which makes it likely that Gray will have little trouble further penetrating the Africentric Movement.

The value of Gray's *Conceptions of History* is that it is the first published book in English which examines the historical and linguistic arguments of Cheikh Anta Diop and Théophile Obenga. Gray emphasizes the methodology and pan-African objectives of these two great African thinkers. Their historical project and objectives have been to reconnect the Black civilization of Egypt to its African roots, so that it can serve as a foundation for a future culturally independent Africa. Gray shows that Diop and Obenga focus on the commonality within African historical identity and group consciousness, which is the foundation of a potential multinational federated state of Africa. This historical project, Gray shows, is in direct opposition to western Africanist historians, who view things from the exterior and are irresistibly inclined to break the fundamental unity of African culture in what Diop calls an "explosive micro-analysis" of petty details.

However, when Gray's work is closely examined, it becomes apparent that not only are many of his arguments superficial and poorly developed, but that he is critical of Diop throughout his book.

The first example is that Gray consistently attempts to reduce Diop's genius and diminish his ideas. He endlessly searches for a white intellectual mentor for Diop. According to Gray, Karl Marx was one such European thinker who influenced Diop. He writes,

> One need only read Diop's major works to get an idea as to his notions of materialism and the importance of Marx to his thinking.[21]

Gray also asserts that Diop is "interested in using Marx and Marxist ideas as a basis for his notion of materialism." However, he has to qualify his statements and admit that Diop did not espouse Marxism-Leninism, and that some of Diop's "application of materialism are unorthodox and brings into play a different method of seeing."[22] Gray also unsuccessfully attempts to set up the Swiss linguist Ferdinand de Saussure as a white intellectual predecessor of Diop. However, again, Gray has to qualify his assertions and state that Diop's ideas of African languages being relatively stable "appear to run counter to notions developed by de Saussure.[23]

After failing to find a white mentor for Diop, Gray's second approach to diminishing and lessening the power of Diop's work is to state on numerous occasions throughout the book that Diop's protegé, Théophile Obenga, "is more cautious and less polemical [confrontational] than his teacher," that he has "a deeper knowledge" of linguistics than Diop, and that he seeks "to refine some of Diop's linguistic arguments." Or that "Obenga's tone is more measured than Diop's and his historical argument more refined." Not surprisingly, the outsider Gray attributes Obenga's "more measured" tone to his writing of poetry as an "outlet for his 'passion.' "[24]

Gray's attack on Diop is equally apparent when he agrees with Diop's detractors, who criticize Diop for his polemical style and "passionate tone." However, Obenga would remind Gray and others that, "Ordinarily, when one denounces the tone adopted by a particular author, it's that one is incapable of getting at the author from a deeper level . . . .A serious critique is thus that which endeavors to examine the content of a work and to give an account of it in the most objective manner possible."[25] Gray is also critical of Diop's use of the words "irrefutable" and "obvious" while drawing "unshaken conclusions" from his linguistic data.[26] At the same time however, Obenga, who uses the exact same terms as Diop ("irrefutable" "impossible" and "absolutely impossible") in his demonstrations, escapes Gray's criticism.[27] Gray's double standard aimed at reducing Diop's work again emphasizes his effort to dismantle Diop before the reader. The inconsistent treatment of Diop and Obenga could be Gray's strategy to first reduce and discredit Diop and later to attack Obenga. For example, it should be noted that Gray is scheduled to travel to Africa and study under Obenga as part of his doctoral fieldwork at Indiana University, thus positioning himself to become the white "authority" on Obenga and Diop.

Lastly, Gray's Eurocentric views on Diop's and Obenga's project for reconstructing African history is made plain in the statements below. Quoting comments made by Jean Duvignard to voice his own criticism, Gray writes:

> "The utopian rationalization of the past and the creation of the myth of 'Africanness' are probably necessary to help man to respond to the demands of modern life. No nation has taken up this revolution without first having created the phantom of its 'great past'."[28]

After shrinking Diop's and Obenga's scientific demonstrations to "utopian rationalizations" and pulling rabbits out of the hat, Gray elaborates on this point by amazingly comparing their work to the 19th century German nationalist movement, which created Bernal's Aryan Model. Bernal shows in *Black Athena* that this nationalist movement was fueled by racist ideas, covered with a thin wrapping of truth and a package of historical lies. It is evident that the outsider Gray does not accept Diop's and Obenga's project as being based on historical facts, but largely on creating "the phantom of its [Africa's] 'great past'" in the same manner as white supremacist writers of 19th century Germany.

The Principal

The principal and main teacher in the counter school is the well respected Basil Davidson, who is also being promoted from *within* the Africentric Movement. Davidson's noted contribution over the years has been to highlight the accomplishments and humanity of African people in his many writings.[29] He has done this in the face of the rampant racism within the ranks of European scholarship, which has sought to deny the historical facts of African high culture.

However when Davidson, the so-called "dean of today's historians of Africa," turns to the subject of the racial identity of the Egyptian population, his arguments are no different than those raised at the Cairo Symposium in opposition to Diop and Obenga. For example, Davidson wrote in *Lost Cities of Africa* (1959) that the origin of Egyptian civilization "had been African as well as Asian"; in other words a mixed population.[30]

Several years later, in *The African Past* (1964) he explicitly states that the Egyptians were not Black or "Negro." According to Davidson, the reaction against a non-African interpretation of Egypt has gone "to the other extreme." His views move closer to Junker's when he openly remarks, "One recent writer would have it that Egypt of the Pharaohs was a Negro state; another would trace the Akan of modern Ghana to ancestral parents on the banks of the Lower Nile. *These are romantic views.*"[31] Davidson's position is in the middle of these two "extreme" arguments.

In his later writings, Davidson expresses this middle position more subtly. In *Africa in History* (1974) he states "it now seems perfectly clear that the vast majority of predynastic Egyptians were of continental African stock," but according to Davidson this group included incoming migrants from the "Near East," suggesting that they were not Black. He does make it clear that "whatever their pigmentation or physical appearance" the Egyptians must be assigned to African history.[32] He makes no claims about the racial affiliation of the Egyptians other than that the vast majority were "African," a term which Davidson *does not* translate to mean Black. The term "African" for Davidson and Bernal only refers to people who reside in Africa and does not imply any particular ethnic group or physical type. In fact, Bernal now concedes that a more accurate title of his work would have been *African Athena*.[33]

Davidson even more subtly expresses his interpretation of a multiracial Egyptian society in a 1987 review of Bernal's *Black Athena,* which has been republished in the *Journal of African Civilizations*.[34] In his review, Davidson's ideas of a mixed Egypt are only slightly expressed, which makes him a very skillful insider/outsider. In his review of *Black Athena*, he indicates that one of his major points of disagreements with the traditional European Egyptologists and historians, is namely their assertion that the ancient Egyptians were not Black and therefore not African. Davidson makes two interesting remarks in reference to this denial by his European colleagues, which expose his multi-racial views. He states, "The Ancient Egyptians, by that orthodoxy [traditional European scholarship], were not only not Black—*in whatever pigmentation variant of non-white that Nature may have provided*—but they were also not Africans."[35] Secondly, "That the Ancient Egyptians were Black *(again, in any variant you may prefer)*— or, as I myself think it more useful to say, were African—is a belief which had been denied in Europe since about 1830, not before."[36] Davidson finds "it more useful to say . . . African" than Black, because he agrees with French Egyptologists Lecant and Vercoutter, that Egyptian people were a mixture of groups rather than "Black Africans" or "Negroes." We can read from Davidson's other statements "in whatever pigmentational variant of non-white that Nature may have provided" or "any variant [of Black] you may prefer" that despite the evidence to the contrary he still believes that the native population of Egypt was a racial combination of various groups. This is consistent with his earlier comments in *Lost Cities of Africa, The African Past*, and *Africa in History*.

Davidson echoes the remarks by Bernal and Professor Vercoutter of France who stated at the Cairo Symposium that there needs to be a more scientific definition of the Black race, that the terms "Black" and "Negro" should be more clearly defined. But Davidson goes further in the most recent edition of *Africa in History* (1991) and states that the old categories of "Black" and "white" should be dismissed.[37] As long as these terms were used to fuel the agenda of white supremacist scholarship, there was no significant opposition to the use of these terms. However, as soon as Black scholars use the term "Black" in reference to the Egyptians as an African people, suddenly it is no longer useful and should be more clearly defined or abandoned.

Davidson, in part I of his 1984 8-part television series on "Africa," again offers a direct view of his fanciful ideas on the mixed race identity of an indigenous population of Egypt , an he is devastating in discrediting Cheikh Anta Diop in the process.[38] Davidson shows Diop explaining a painting scene in the tomb of Ramses III (fig. 4) in which the Egyptians are depicted as jet Black and identical to other Africans. After Diop's presentation, Davidson immediately attacks his work and remarks, "That particular painting, however, is a rare exception. The only one, as far as I know, that so clearly makes the professor's point." Davidson continues, "For the most part the Ancient Egyptians had themselves portrayed as 'reddish-pink', but of course they intermarried with Asians and even more with other Africans. Many of their noble ladies were [Black-skinned] Nubians and ... handmaidens ... just as surely white" (fig. 5). In effect, Davidson argues here that the Egyptians were a mixture of Africans, Asians, and Europeans. With this being Davidson's view, the only reason for him to present Diop's ideas, which run counter to Davidson's, was to discredit Diop before millions of viewers. Davidson presents no other scholar's ideas on the identity of the Egyptians.

Furthermore, Davidson in his recent book *African Civilization Revisited* (1991) makes this same point, as he quotes ancient sources with introductory commentary. He again re-affirms that ancient Egypt was essentially an African civilization, but this time he adds that it remains an issue as to whether the Egyptians were as black or brown as other Africans, but that "probably they were both."[39] Here, Davidson seems to almost change his long held racial position. However, he states as he did in previous writings that the Neolithic Sahara was the "birth arena" from which came the people and culture of Ancient Egypt and the Nile Valley.[40] We know from Davidson's work, *Africa in History* (1974) that he believes that in the Sahara and Egypt there was a "fruitful mixture" of several racial types.[41] Thus, from his earliest writings Davidson has been consistent on his stand that the Egyptians were racially mixed.

Conclusion

The *Bernal-Davidson School* shares the same misguided views as mainstream Eurocentric Egyptologists on the "mixed" race identity of the indigenous Egyptian population. This School therefore has fundamental differences with the views of Cheikh Diop and Africentric Movement scholars. As a result, it is a basic contradiction for the Africentric community—which is exerting an extraordinary amount of energy re-establishing and promoting the African (i.e. Black) identity of classical Egyptian civilization—to widely praise and promote the *Bernal-Davidson School*, which is advancing the identical views that the Africentric community is struggling against!

The *Bernal-Davidson School*'s inability to acknowledge the demonstrative fact that Egypt, the greatest of all high civilizations of antiquity, was solely a Black creation is a perfect example, and should be a warning sign, indicating that even the most progressive European thinkers are unable to move beyond the imprisonment of Eurocentric thinking. Lastly, the critical issue confronting the Africentric Movement is how to negate the influence of the inside/outside *Bernal-Davidson School*, which has gained much notoriety and respect *within* the Movement, even as it undermines the Movement's objective of restoring classical African civilizations. In *The Counter School* I give specific recommendations on how to accomplish this task.[42]

Notes

1. I am indebted to my colleague, Femi Biko, for introducing me to the concept of the "counter school" in 1990, while I was in London.
2. Manu Ampim, *The Current Africentric Movement in the U.S.: The Centrality of Ancient Nile Valley Civilization* (Baltimore, Morgan State University, 1990).
3. Manu Ampim, *Critical Issues in the Current Africentric Movement,* vol. I: *Egypt As A Black Civilization: The Counter School* (Oakland: Advancing The Research, 1991).
4. Ibid., p. 14.
5. Ibid., p. 4–5.
6. Ibid., p. 6–10.
7. Hermann Junker, "The First Appearance of the Negroes in History," *Journal of Egyptian Archaeoloqy* 7 (1921): 122.
8. UNESCO, *The Peopling of Ancient Egypt and the Deciphering of the Meroitic Script: Proceedings of the Symposium held in Cairo, Egypt from 28 January to 3 February 1974* (The General History of Africa, Studies and Documents, no. 1, 1978).
9. Ibid., p. 102.
10. Martin Bernal, *Black Athena*, vol. 1: *The Fabrication of Ancient Greece 1985–1985* (New Brunswick, NJ: Rutgers University Press, 1987).
11. Ibid., pp. 241–42. Emphasis added.
12. Ibid., pp. 12, 15.
13. Ibid., p. 437.
14. Ibid.
15. The papers given by Maulana Karenga, "The Contested Terrain of Ancient Egypt: Diop, Bernal and Paradigms in Africana Studies," and Jacob Carruthers, "The Other Side of *Black Athena*" at the "Challenging Tradition Conference," held at Temple University, October 19–20, 1990, offer insightful analyses of *Black Athena*.
16. Bernal, *Black Athena*, p. 435.
17. UNESCO, *General History of Africa*, vol. II: *Ancient Civilizations of Africa*, ed. G. Mokhtar (Berkeley, University of California Press, 1981), pp. 27–57. Also see: UNESCO, *The Peopling of Ancient Egypt and the Deciphering of the Meroitic Script*.
18. Martin Bernal lecture at John Hopkins University, 25 September 1991. Video tape in author's possession. Emphasis added.
19. M. Ampim, *The Counter School*, p. 19.
20. Chris Gray, *Conception of History in the Works of Cheikh Anta Diop and Théophile Obenga* (London: Karnak House, 1989).
21. Ibid., p. 24
22. Ibid., p. 43
23. Ibid., p. 83

24. Ibid., p. 135, fn. 25.
25. Ibid., p. 59.
26. Ibid., p. 84
27. Ibid., p. 96; UNESCO, *The Peopling of Ancient Egypt and the Deciphering of the Meroitic Script*, p. 69.
28. Gray, *Conceptions of History*, p. 56.
29. Basil Davidson is well known as an author on African history. His works include *Lost Cities of Africa* (Boston: Brown, Little & Co., 1959); *The African Past* (Boston: Little, Brown & Co., 1964); *Africa in History* (New York: Macmillian Publishing Co., 1974); and *African Civilization Revisited* (Trenton, NJ: Africa World Press, Inc., 1991).
30. B. Davidson, *Lost Cities of Africa*, p. 36.
31. B. Davidson, *The African Past*, p. 43. Emphasis added.
32. B. Davidson, *Africa in History* (1974), pp. 21–22.
33. Alex Bream, "Who Invented the Greeks?" *Baltimore Sun*, 21 August 1991, p. 13A.
34. B. Davidson, "The Ancient World and Africa: Whose Roots?" in *Egypt Revisited* (*Journal of African Civilizations, vol. 10*), ed. Ivan Van Sertima (New Brunswick, NJ: Transaction Publishers, 1989), pp. 39–52. Originally published under the same title in *Race and Class* 29 (1987).
35. Ibid., p. 39. Emphasis added.
36. Ibid., p. 40. Emphasis added.
37. B. Davidson, *Africa in History* (New York: Macmillian Publishing Co., 1991 edition), pp. 11; also see p. 26.
38. B. Davidson, "Africa" television series, part I: "Separate But Equal" (Britain, 1984).
39. B. Davidson, *African Civilization Revisited*, p. 49.
40. Ibid., p. 12.
41. B. Davidson, *Africa in History* (1974), p. 9.
42. M. Ampim, *The Counter School*, p. 32.

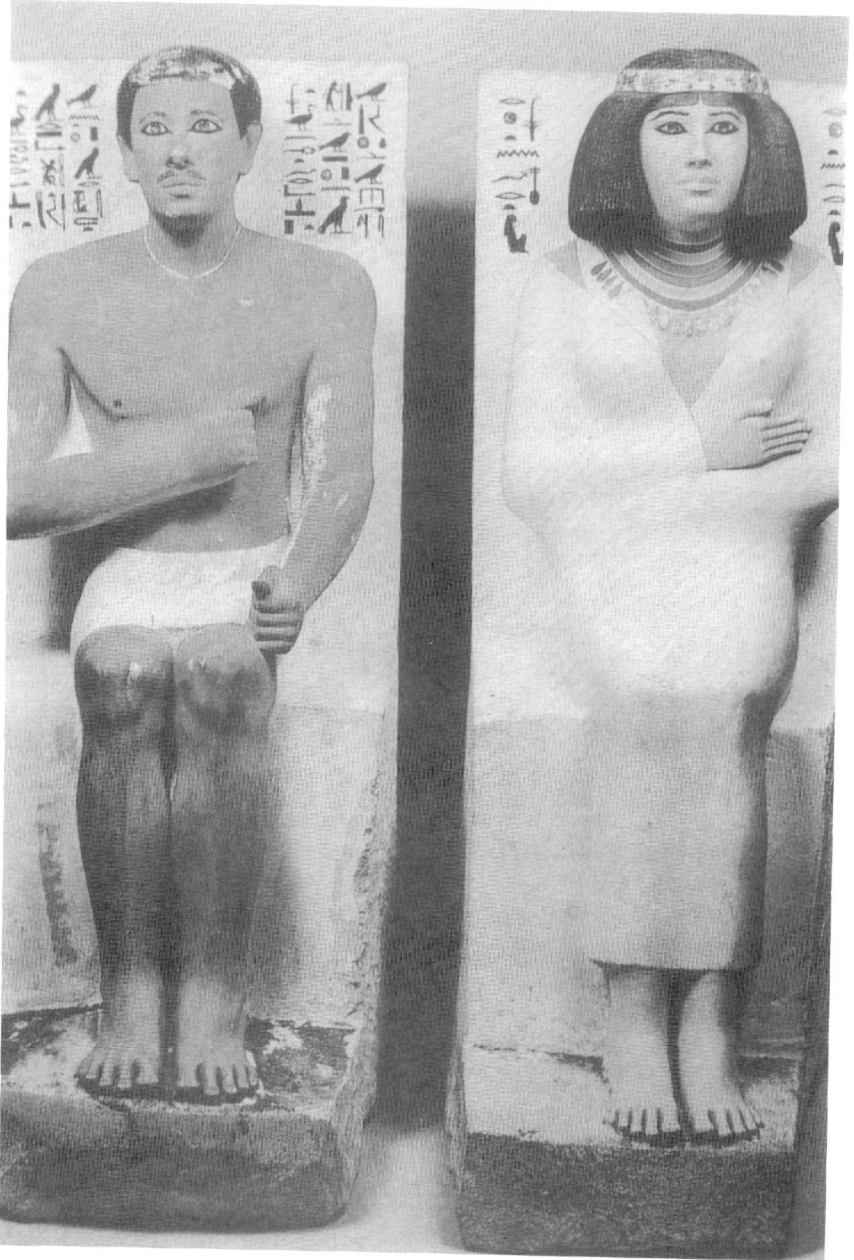

Two statues depicting mixed Libyan types, figures are Rehotep and his wife Nofret, circa 2630 B.C.

RA-HOTEP AND NOFRET: MODERN FORGERIES IN THE CAIRO MUSEUM?

Manu Ampim

Egyptologists are well aware that a large number of items from Egypt, originally thought to be of ancient Egyptian production, have later proven to be modern forgeries. The reasons for such forgeries have been both racial and commercial. Since the 1830s, fake ushabti figures have been popular souvenirs, forged by enterprising Egyptians, and there is now an increasing number of forged (and authentic) artifacts being sold for profit on the burgeoning underground antiquities market. Modern Egyptian forgeries have also had significant racial implications. For example, the famous and well-publicized seated statuette of Seventeenth Dynasty Queen Tetisheri (number 22558, purchased by the British Museum in 1890) is now considered to be a modern forgery.

The "Tetisheri" statuette was first suspected to be a forgery in 1984 by Mr. W.V. Davies, Keeper of Egyptian Antiquities at the British Museum. Davies in a *British Museum Occasional Paper* (no. 36, 1984) compared the forged Tetisheri with other statuettes, including an original Tetisheri statuette once held in the French Institute in Cairo. Davies was able to show that there is a number of inscriptional, iconographic and chemical problems with the forged "Tetisheri," and was produced by "the hand of modern man." I was able to see the famous "Tetisheri" displayed in the British Museum's 1990 special exhibit, "Fake? The Art of Deception."

The "Tetisheri" image is one of the most famous of ancient Egyptian small sculpture, and it owes its popularity to several factors. First, for 100 years the fabricated "Tetisheri," because its facial features are typical of most Europeans, has been published and promoted in a long list of scholarly literature. Second, the statuette has been considered a significant piece of art because it was thought to be an extremely rare sculpture of a royal figure to have survived intact from the transitional Second Intermediate Period (1786–1570 B.C.E.). Third, Tetisheri was the queen mother and great ancestress of the powerful line of rulers of the Seventeenth and Eighteenth dynasties. Queen Tetisheri along with her husband, Senakhtenre Tao, founded a line of rulers who not only liberated Egypt from foreign Hyksos domination, but also revitalized Egyptian culture and inaugurated the great age of temple building. Thus, the implications of the Tetisheri fabrication are enormous. The international celebration of the forged Tetisheri image has caused great distortions of Egyptian (African) and world history, as the false image of a powerful white queen of Egypt has been promoted throughout the world for a century.

The British Museum exhibition of forgeries gave me further confidence to expose an Egyptian forgery which may be greater than the fabrication of Tetisheri. That is, to expose (what I believe are) the forged famous statues of Prince Ra-Hotep and Princess Nofret in the Cairo Museum (room 32, case 223), found at Meydum, in 1871, by French Egyptologist Mariette. Ra-Hotep was a general, high priest of Ra at Iunu ("Heliopolis"), and son of Pharaoh Sneferu, founder of the Fourth Dynasty. Nofret was the wife of Ra-Hotep. Their pair of seated limestone statues rank among the most famous of all Egyptian images. These statues have been published and commented upon in a wide body of literature, mainly because of their light skin and European appearance. Cyril Aldred in *Egyptian Art* (1980) commented that Ra-Hotep and Nofret "reveal the family face of the ruling class whose authority directed the prosperity of this age of the great pyramid builders" (p. 58). Irmgard Woldering in *The Art of Egypt* (1963) remarked that, Ra-Hotep's "facial features express sturdiness, energy and intelligence" (p. 102). Margaret Murray in *Egyptian Sculpture* (1930) described Nofret as having "a rather sensual face, a woman aware of her own beauty, accustomed to and enjoying a luxurious life" (p. 53).

Many writers have commented about the "superior" quality of the Ra-Hotep and Nofret statues, and all have accepted their authenticity. However, upon viewing these statues a couple of years ago, I was immediately struck by a number of abnormal characteristics, which led me to develop a list of iconographic and contextual problems with each of these statues. A few of these oddities were detected nearly a century ago by French Egyptologist Gaston Maspero, who wrote in his *Guide to the Cairo Museum* (1903) that, Nofret "is distinguished by extreme freedom in handling, and has several characteristics *which are entirely original*" (p. 67) (Emphasis added). Maspero mentioned the unique rendering of the neck, breasts, and wig with a diadem. Following is a summary of my list of "original" characteristics, and *preliminary* arguments against the authenticity of the Ra-Hotep and Nofret statues in the Cairo Museum. This summary should be read with the following statement in mind, made by Margaret Murray in her study of *Egyptian Sculpture*: "In taking a general view over the art of the Old Kingdom, it is evident that convention had already set its seal on the artist. The statues are posed *according to definite rules*" (p. 46) (Emphasis added).

Problem 1: Historical Context

1. Ra-Hotep and Nofret are depicted as a European couple in the Egyptian royal family of the Fourth Dynasty, a time when the undisputed rulers of the country came from southern Egypt. In this region, there were no white-skinned groups of any consequence, and there is no sufficient evidence at this early date to suggest there was interracial mixing in the royal family, which remained Black.

Problem 2: Family Portrait

1. Ra-Hotep is depicted with much darker brown colors in tomb reliefs in the Cairo, British, and Berlin museums.
2. Nefermaat (Ra-Hotep's brother) and his family are depicted in medium and dark brown colors in tomb reliefs.
3. Pharaoh Sneferu (Ra-Hotep's father) and his immediate relatives are depicted as a Black royal family.

Problem 3: Facial Features

1. Ra-Hotep has a moustache. This phenomena is unusual in Egyptian art and may not occur outside of a few select statues in the Cairo Museum.
2. Both Ra-Hotep and Nofret have *complete* holes to represent their nostrils, which is very odd. The common practice was to cut only slight recesses in the nose to represent the nostrils, which was probably done to keep the statue sealed and thus aid in its preservation.
3. Both statues have *gray* inlaid eyes. This occurrence is extremely rare, and the several other Old Kingdom statues with this rare feature are all visibly damaged or touched up around the eyes. The rule in Egyptian art is that the iris of the eye is represented as dark brown or black. This rule is applied on inlaid and all other represented eyes. Also, it should be noted that there are frequent examples in the Cairo Museum and other locations of otherwise well-preserved items, *which appear to have undergone deliberate lightening of the eyes in order to give them a grayish or white appearance.*
4. Both statues have *gray* eyes yet their hair is *black*. This is a rare genetic exception within the human population, and may not occur elsewhere in Egyptian art, with the exception of the unnamed scribe in the Louvre Museum. It should be pointed out that the neighboring Libyans had the normal combination of *blond* hair and *blue* eyes, and even the Greeks and Romans are consistently shown with *black* eyes in Egyptian art.

5. Both statues, particularly Ra-Hotep, have very thick lips which are extremely rare among European types. This attribute or the otherwise "Negroid" appearance of Ra-Hotep and Nofret have been noted by Egyptologists Margaret Murray, Flinders Petrie, and William Stevenson Smith.

Problem 4: Paint/Color

1. According to the conventional view (although I have strong personal reservations), the "standard colors" used on Egyptian statuary and paintings was reddish-brown for men and yellowish-white for women. Earlier twentieth century writers consistently described Ra-Hotep and Nofret as having been decorated with these "standard colors." However, both statues are now much lighter than these "standard colors." Ra-Hotep is a palish-tan color and Nofret is an off-white, although faint traces of yellow can be seen around Nofret's nose and outer portion of her face.
2. The paint application on Ra-Hotep is of notably poor workmanship. Ra-Hotep's paint seems to have dried unevenly, and his palish-tan skin is of different colors on his chest, arms and legs, while black paint is dripping from his hairline. This sloppy workmanship is completely contrary to the standards of Fourth Dynasty (Pyramid Age) royal art, which reached a high level of artistic perfection.

Problem 5: Attitude and Dress

1. Prince Ra-Hotep is a royal figure who is not wearing a wig. Instead he is depicted with an Afro. Throughout dynastic Egypt, wigs were commonly worn by men of all social groups. If not wigs, white skull caps covering the entire head were worn. The actual hair of male royal figures and high officials is not shown on Old Kingdom Egyptian statues. They are all decorated in a headdress. One may possibly find exceptions to this rule in the Late Period when a host of foreigners imitated Egyptian art.
2. Ra-Hotep's entire kilt-belt is shown on his lap, rather than the universal Egyptian standard of having one belt-end protruding from the waist line.
3. Ra-Hotep does not have the usual cloth or other item in the clenched fist (left) resting on his leg. This item was never present.
4. Nofret has on a wig which is unusually short and thick and is different from other Old Kingdom wigs. The wigs of this period are usually pleated at the ends, or much thinner and long enough to fall in both the front and back of the shoulders.

5. Nofret has on a diadem with painted flowers. This is an extremely rare, if not the only, Old Kingdom example.
6. Nofret has very prominent nipples. The usual Old Kingdom statuettes show no nipples, or if they do appear they are flat and not very noticeable upon initial observation. In other words, they are rarely highlighted, as are Nofret's.
7. Both figures are wearing rare emblems around their neck. Ra-Hotep has a very unique six-pointed gray pendant, and Nofret has on a necklace with a row of petals across her chest.

Problem 6: Structure

1. Nofret is seated noticeably off-center to her left. Egyptian proportional rules enabled them to avoid such an obvious error.
2. Both statues have backrests which extend as high as the crown of their heads. The rule on individual seated statues is for the backrests to be made into a narrow strip and blended into the back of the seated person's headdress. If it is a wide backrest, it may sometimes extend as high as shoulder length, but not above. This rule is suspended only on *group* statues, and is done for practical reasons to support two or more joined statues.

Problem 7: Inscriptions

1. The hieroglyphic inscriptions on both statues are near the top of the backrests on either side of their heads. However, the common practice on individual seated statues, throughout the Old Kingdom and later periods, was to write the inscriptions on the side of the seat, or on the lower front of the statue on the clothing, or near the calves or footboard around the feet.

These *preliminary* observations concerning the authenticity of the Ra-Hotep and Nofret statues highlight the numerous problems with these statues, as they seem to violate quite a number of Egyptian artistic rules. The construction of these unique statues may indicate an incompetent imitation by modern conspirators. This is the concern of T.G. Wakeling in *Forged Egyptian Antiquities* (1912). The suggestion of a major forgery of Egyptian royal figures is not unreasonable in light of the recent disclosure of the Tetisheri forgery, which may rival that of "Piltdown Man."

The following areas of investigations can determine the authenticity of the Ra-Hotep and Nofret statues in the Cairo Museum:

1. A detailed and systematic study of all sculpture of the Old Kingdom,

particularly Ra-Hotep's immediate family and the Fourth Dynasty in general, both royal and private. I plan to further investigate this area and publish my findings in a future study.

2. A scientific analysis of the pigments to determine if the paint is an ancient or modern application.

Figure 1. Sphinx and Pyramid as the All Seeing Eye

SEVEN TIMES SEVEN
COMPREHENSIVE DISCOURSE ON THE SEVEN
HERMETIC PRINCIPLES OF ANCIENT EGYPT

Wayne B Chandler

Part I—Introduction

> *"The Principles of Truth are Seven; he who knows this, understandingly possesses the Magic Key before whose touch all the doors of the Temple fly open."*
> —Kybalion

Before the dawn of the present era was a period known to the ancient historian as antediluvian, or "world before the flood." Much of what the Western world knows of this period comes through biblical tradition. A passage from Genesis 6:4—"there were giants in the earth in those days and also after that when the sons of God came in unto the daughters of men, and they bear children to them, the same became mighty men which were of old, men of renown"—speaks of this era which predated the great flood associated, in the biblical tradition, with Noah. This and several other biblical phrases allude to the fact that the races of the Earth during this age were truly omnipotent or God-like in every way.

Mythological tradition holds that during this *antediluvian* period was born the great Egyptian sage *Thoth*, or *Tehuti*. Thoth, known to the Greeks as Hermes, became the principal law-giver of Egypt, or in the tongue of the Blacks of that land, *Kmt* (pronounced Kemit), and through his axioms he would allow humanity a comprehensive analysis of the nature of creation and of the Universe.

Most of what transpired during this period is considered by Western civilization to be pure mythology; and because the influence of the West dominates the present era, the races of mankind have fallen prey to a superficial, linear approach to investigative research. This perspective on ancient history has left a substantial void in our vast ancestral cultural legacy, much of which is located in what we now call myth.

The outset of the twenty-first century demands a redefinition of much of our present terminology. Such a redefinition will, in time, allow for a much broader historical perspective than is presently employed by traditional historians. The term myth as understood through a Eurocentric perspective pertains to fantasy and fable in the realm of the surreal. Mythology as it pertained to antiquity was an ancient mode of thinking, early thought. It was founded on natural facts, still verifiable in phenomena. Therefore it was not then, nor now, a mechanism based on insane or irrational perspective. Mythology is the repository of man's most ancient science and when myth is examined within the context of an African belief system it becomes a dynamic vehicle for the transmission of truth:

> "The importance of mythology is, of course, that it is a form of documentation which transcends the human record as much as it states truth rather than fact. Myth can be considered a form of reasoning and record keeping by providing an implicit guide for bringing about the fulfillment of the truth it proclaims. It connects the invisible order with the visible order . . . thought reflected in myth is inseparable from the laws of nature. . . .As a reflection of the thought and experience of a people, the analytical value of myth is that it serves as a measure and/or reflection of the human possibilities, PROBABILITIES, and potentialities of a people."[1]

Thus, an examination of the origin, development, and contributions of an entity such as Thoth from the African myth perspective makes the incomprehensible comprehensible and allows a true understanding of what would have become an historical enigma. Speculation on the historical reality of Thoth is subject to the nature of the present state of the study of history, which is tainted with disbelief, superstition, immorality, anger, and racial superiority, the hallmarks of Western civilization. So regardless of fact, fiction, documentation, or myth, this particular examination of Thoth will consist of what little testimony exists on his actual life, his own account of the divine revelation of his seven basic axioms, and a study of these illuminated laws of the Universe and the higher message therein.

Thoth, or Tehuti, is the personification of universal wisdom and truth. Egyptian tradition holds that he imparted this truth first to the old race, the Kushites, who would later be identified by the Greeks as the Ethiopians. The Greeks, who considered Thoth "the Scribe of the Gods," would also change his name to Hermes, or more accurately *Hermes Mercurius Trismegistus* which means "the thrice-great," "the great-great," "the greatest-great," and "master of masters " With the spread of Western influence, this appellation remained globally intact and his teachings have become known as the Hermetic Philosophy.

The writings of Thoth/Hermes have been known to the West since the fifth century B.C.E. Some of the more popular translations have been those of Hargrave Jennings, 1884, a reprint of Everhard's English version; the

Greek text of C Parthey Berolins, 1854; a German edition by J Scheible, 1855; and the earliest Latin edition of Marsilius Ficinus, in 1471. It was long assumed that the earliest translation from the Egyptian text was done in Arabic during the conquest and occupation of Egypt by the Moors in the ninth century C.E. But many fragments contained in the *Liber Hermetis,* a Latin translation of Greek origin, are traceable to the third or fourth century B.C.E. The West presently acknowledges Walter Scott and Andre-Jean Festugiere as the contemporary experts on Hermetica. It was they who distinguished the "popular" occultist or secret writings attributed to Thoth/ Hermes from the so-called "learned" or "philosophical" treatises; the latter being more prominent in most modern translations of the Hermetica. The problem that confronts us with these recent translations that flooded the West is that they have been little more than an exercise in academia. Esteemed more for the period in which they were originally written than their content, the Hermetic Philosophy gave way to the overt mundane material-ism that presently saturates the Western hemisphere. It has always been vogue for Western academicians to stand on the periphery of what they examine, thinking somehow that they may osmotically engender the experi-ence without actually involving themselves in it. This has been the *raison d'etre* from the outset of Greek civilization to our present period. It is interesting to note the acknowledgement of this pattern regarding the West-ern mind-set by Imhotep, student of Thoth/Hermes, about the ancient Greeks. *"For the Greeks have empty speeches . . . that are energetic only in what they demonstrate, and this is the philosophy of the Greeks, an inane foolosophy of speeches. We, [the Egyptians] by contrast, use not speeches but sounds that are full of action."*[2] Because of this fact, the author has uti-lized the conventional or "philosophical" writings as well as "popular" and rare non-traditional sources in Hermetic academia, to unveil the truths therein.

The Hermetic Teachings are found in all lands among all religions but are never identified with any particular creed or religious sect, rising above them all. These ancient mystery systems were imparted to India and Persia by their indigenous Black inhabitants but degenerated with the influx of the Indo-Europeans. In time they were lost because of the merging of theology and philosophy when teachers became pagan priests who aspired for power amidst religious superstition, cults, and creeds.

In regard to Hermes himself, history has provided several suppositions, much legend, and many myths. Hermes has been associated with many of the early sages and prophets such as Cadmus and Enoch, the latter identified as the "Second Messenger of God." Iamblichus averred that Hermes was the author of 20,000 books; the Egyptian priest/historian Manetho increased that number to more than 36,000. Because of the astounding number of books attributed to Hermes, many feel that he was an array of various personalities or an entire secret society dedicated to the evolution of the human race.

According to records retained by Syncellus, a Byzantine monk of the ninth century C.E., records which he believed were written a thousand years earlier by *Mer-en-Jehuti (Manetho)*, Egyptian High Priest of Sebynnetos, there were two gods named Hermes. The first was Thoth whose legacy extends to the very dawn of African civilization. It was he who originally carved what became the sacred writings on stelae in hieroglyphics for the "old race," the Anu. The second Thoth, who became Hermes Trismegistus, was the son of *Agathodaimon*, who seems to have ruled during the time of Imhotep, ca. 2700 B.C.E., called Asclepius by the Greeks. Syncellus, quoting a portion of text written by Manetho and addressed to Ptolemy II Philadelphus (282–229 B.C.E.), states, "Manetho knew stelae in the land of Seiria . . . inscribed in the sacred tongue in hieroglyphic letters by Thoth, the first Hermes, and translated after the flood from the sacred tongue into the Greek language and set down in books by the son of Agathodaimon, the second Hermes, father of Tat, in the sanctuaries of the temples of Egypt; [Manetho] dedicated [them] to . . . Ptolemy . . . writing thus: ' . . . since you seek to know what will come to be in the cosmos, I shall present to you the sacred books that I have learned about, written by our ancestor, Hermes Trismegistus . . .' This is what he says about the translation of the books written by the second Hermes" (*Hermetica*. Copenhaver, 1992) If indeed this information is historically accurate it would explain much of what has become the dilemma of Thoth/Hermes and his immense literary undertaking. There are other accounts which can be categorized as legend or myth that enunciate the ability of Thoth/Hermes to survive such an ample accomplishment. It is the nature of legend that its many parts support one another, and so it is with the legend of Hermes. Though he is given credit for an astounding number of published works, he is also reported to have lived 300 years, which, if true, would easily allow for such a prolific literary undertaking.

Certainly most would find this life expectancy of three centuries totally incomprehensible. Biblical references to people living to advanced age are often interpreted as symbolic simply because they are considered impossible to believe. The Bible states that Abraham and Sarah had their son, Isaac, when they were both around a hundred years old, and after Sarah's death at 127 years, Abraham fathered six more sons before his own death at age 175 (Genesis 23–25). The question remains—how could people have lived to such ages in antiquity but barely survive to a meager 70 years in the present time? The answer is quite simple. While Hermes still walked the Earth with human beings, he entrusted to his most esteemed disciples and chosen successors his sacred book. The Book of Thoth contained information which explained the process of biological regeneration which allowed the various biochemical and physiological systems in the human body to undergo physical and mental restoration. This axiom was based on the premise that all of the soft tissue systems within the human body are subject to this process of revitalization every seven months and the more fundamental or substantial tissue systems every seven years. The work also contained the secret process by which the regeneration of humanity was to be accomplished.

According to legend, the Book of Thoth was kept in a golden box in the inner sanctuary of a temple dedicated to Thoth. In order to protect it from the encroaching Christian traditions and resulting decay of the mysteries, the highest initiate of what came to be known as the *Hermetic Arcanum,* took the Book of Thoth to an undisclosed location in another land and it was lost to the ancient world. According to Hermetic tradition, this book is still in existence and continues to lead Hermetic disciples of the present age into the presence of the immortals. The traditions of vital regeneration contained in the book are still practiced in India and China.

Using the aforementioned concepts of biological regeneration, one doctor, Deepak Chopra, is revolutionizing the way science and the medical establishment perceives the aging process. South Asian by birth, Dr. Chopra taught at Tufts University and Boston University Schools of Medicine before becoming chief of staff at New England Memorial Hospital. Seeing the shortcomings of Western medicine, Dr. Chopra combined the ancient Indian tradition of Ayurvedic medicine with Western science, achieving remarkable results. Through unfailing example, Chopra has begun to prove that within the human biological framework exist the awareness of immortality. "The new paradigm tells us that life is a process of constant transformation, not decline, and therefore is full of potential for unlimited growth."[3] With the success of Dr. Chopra's research, even staunch adherents to the old paradigm concur that automatic biological degeneration is not programmed into our bodies and that human life is more resilient than previously imagined.

Using genetics and pioneering new avenues in cytology, Dr. Chopra asserts that "humans have the capacity to think about being immortal."[4] Deepak Chopra's findings corroborate the ancient traditions of longevity recorded by Thoth/Hermes in his many writings.

Of the 42 fragmentary writings believed to have come from the stylus of Hermes only two remain: *The Emerald Table* and *The Divine Pymander.* The loss of the balance of his works was truly a great and senseless tragedy to the philosophic world. In his *Stromata,* Clement of Alexandria makes repeated reference to these 42 Hermetic works which were housed in the magnificent Egyptian Library of Alexandria, so named after Alexander the Great. In the years which followed the inevitable demise of the once glorious Egyptian civilization, the Romans, and later the Christians, found themselves in an ongoing struggle to nullify the Egyptians as a cultural and philosophical force. Since the very hub of Egyptian culture was inextricably connected to these ancient doctrines of Thoth, the unwavering treachery of the Romans and Christians finally culminated in one of the most diabolic and nefarious acts in all of history. In the year 389 A.D., the Christian Emperor Theodosius gave the order for the burning of the great Library of Alexandria, knowing that the only way to ensure the collapse of a culture and the enslavement of its people was the total obliteration of their history—and so it was done! Tradition holds that the volumes of the Hermetic Philosophy which managed to escape the fire were buried in the desert and their location was known to only a few initiates of the secret societies. Whatever the nature of the being or concept which has become known as Thoth, the races of mankind unequivocally owe to him the very foundations of all scientific and philosophical traditions, for his philosophies have had an impact on every high civilization born from Earth.

An appropriate introduction to a discussion of the various axioms which constitute the present Hermetic Philosophy is an examination of the legend/ myth of the vision which bequeathed to Thoth/Hermes the mysteries of the Universe and creation. *The Divine Pymander* of Hermes Mercurius Trismegistus is one of the earliest of the Hermetic writings now extant. Though it is not in its original form, having been restructured during the first centuries of the Christian period and incorrectly translated several times since, this work still contains several of the original concepts of the Hermetic Doctrine. *The Divine Pymander* consists of 17 fragmentary writings which were collected and put forth as one work. The second book of Pymander is known as *Poimandres*—*"the vision"*—and is the most famous of all the Hermetic fragments because of its ability to endure virtually unchanged through the ages.

Poimandres: The Vision of Hermes

Within each aspiration dwells the certainty of its own fulfillment.

Hermes, in search for divine truth, found himself seeking solitude in a rocky and desolate place. He came to a place of rest and gave himself over to meditation. Following the secret instructions of the Temple he gradually freed his higher consciousness from the bondage of his bodily senses; and, thus released, his divine nature revealed to him the mysteries of the transcendental spheres. As this process of unfoldment began to climax, Hermes beheld a figure which seemed awe-inspiring and beyond approach. It was the Great Dragon, with wings stretching across the sky and light streaming in all directions from its body. The Great Dragon called Hermes by name and asked him why he thus meditated upon the World Mystery. Immensely humbled by this spectacle, Hermes prostrated himself before the Dragon, beseeching it to reveal its identity. The great creature answered that it was Poimandres, the Mind of the Universe, the Creative Intelligence, and the Absolute Emperor of all things. Hermes then besought Poimandres to disclose unto him the nature of the universe. The Great Dragon nodded its magnificent head and its form immediately changed.

Where the Dragon had stood was now a glorious and pulsating radiance. Then Hermes heard the voice of Poimandres but his form was not revealed. 'I, thy God, am the Light and the Mind which were, before substance was divided from spirit and darkness from Light. And the Word which appeared as a pillar of flame out of the darkness is the Son of God, born of the mystery of the Mind. The name of that Word is Reason. Reason is the offspring of Thought and Reason shall divide the Light from the darkness and establish Truth in the midst of the waters. Understand, O Hermes, and meditate deeply upon the mystery. So it is that Divine Light that dwells in the midst of mortal darkness, and ignorance cannot divide them. The union of the World and the Mind produces that mystery which is called life . . . Learn deeply of the Mind and its mystery, for therein lies the secret of immortality.'

The Dragon again revealed its form to Hermes, and for a long time the two looked steadfastly one upon the other, eye to eye, so that Hermes trembled before the gaze of Poimandres. At the Word of the Dragon the heavens opened and the innumerable Light Powers were revealed . . . Hermes beheld the spirits of the stars, the celestials controlling the universe . . . Hermes realized that the sight which he beheld was revealed to him only because Poimandres had spoken a Word. The Word was Reason and by the Reason of the Word invisible things were made manifest. The darkness below, receiving the hammer of the Word, was fashioned into an orderly universe. The elements separated into strata and each brought forth living creatures. The Supreme Being—the Mind—manifested male and female, and they brought forth the Word and the Word suspended between Light and darkness, was delivered of another Mind called the Workman, the Master-Builder, or the Maker of Things. 'In this manner it was accomplished, 0 Hermes: The Word moving like a breath through space called forth the Fire by the friction of its motion. Therefore, the Fire is called the Son of Striving. The Son of Striving thus formed the Seven Governors, the Spirits of the Planets, whose orbits bounded the world; and the Seven Governors controlled the world by the mysterious power called Destiny. Then the downward-turned and unreasoning elements brought forth creatures without Reason. Substance could not bestow Reason, for Reason had ascended out of it. The air produced flying things and the waters things that swam. The earth conceived strange four-footed and creeping beast, dragons, composite demons, and grotesque monsters. Then the Father—the Su-

preme Mind—, being Light and Life, fashioned a glorious Universal Man in its own image not an earthly man but a heavenly Man dwelling in the Light of God. The Supreme Mind loved the Man it had fashioned and delivered to Him the control of the creations. Man, too, willed to make things, and his Father gave permission. The Seven Governors [Planets], of whose powers He partook, rejoiced and each gave the Man a share of its own nature.

The Man longed to pierce the circumference of the circles and understand the mystery of Him who sat upon the Eternal Fire. Having already all power, He stooped down and peeped through the seven Harmonies and breaking through the strength of the circles, made Himself manifest to Nature stretched out below. The Man, looking into the depths, smiled, for he beheld a shadow upon the earth and a likeness mirrored in the waters, which shadow and likeness were a reflection of Himself. The Man fell in love with his own shadow and desired to descend into it. Coincident with the desire, that divine or intelligent aspect of Man united itself with the unreasoning image or shape. Nature, beholding the descent, wrapped herself about the Man whom she loved, and the two were mingled. For this reason Man is a composite. Within him is the Sky Man, immortal and beautiful; without is Nature, mortal and destructible. Thus suffering is the result of the Immortal Man's falling in love with his shadow and giving up Reality to dwell in the darkness of illusion; for being immortal, Man has the power of the Seven Governors—also the Life, the Light, and the Word—; but being mortal, he is controlled by the rings of the Governors—Fate or Destiny.

Of the immortal man it should be said that He is hermaphrodite, or male and female, and eternally watchful. He neither slumbers nor sleeps, and is governed by a Father also both male and female, and ever watchful. Such is the mystery kept hidden to this day; for Nature, being mingled in marriage with the Sky Man, brought forth a wonder most wonderful—seven men, all bisexual, male and female, and upright of stature, each one exemplifying the natures of the Seven Governors. These, O Hermes, are the seven races, species, and wheels. After this manner were the seven men generated. Earth was the female element and water the male element, and from the fire and ether they received their spirits, and Nature produced bodies after the species and shapes of men. They reproduced themselves out of themselves, for each was male and female. But at the end of the period the knot of Destiny was untied by the will of God and the bond of all things was loosened. Then all living creatures, including Man, which had been hermaphroditical, were separated, the males being set apart by themselves and the females likewise, according to the dictates of Reason.

Then God spoke the Holy Word within the soul of all things saying: 'Increase and multiply in multitudes, all you, my creatures and workmanships. Let him that is endowed with Mind know himself to be immortal and that the cause of death is the love of the body; and let him learn all things that are, for he who has recognized himself enters into the state of Good.'

And when God had said this, Providence, with the aid of the Seven Governors and Harmony, brought the sexes together...He, who through the error of attachment loves his body, abides wandering in darkness, sensible and suffering the things of death; but he who realizes that the body is but the tomb of his soul, rises to immortality.

Then Hermes desired to know why men should be deprived of immortality for the sin of ignorance alone. The Great Dragon answered: 'To the ignorant the body is supreme and they are incapable of realizing the immortality that is within them. Knowing only the body which is subject to death, they believe in death because they worship that substance which is the cause and reality of death.'

Hermes bowed his head in thankfulness to the Great Dragon who had taught him so much, and begged to hear more concerning the ultimate of the human soul. So Poimandres resumed: 'At death the material body of Man is returned to the elements from which it came, and the invisible divine man ascends to the source from whence he came, namely the Eight Spheres. The senses, feelings, desires, and body passions return to their source, namely the Seven Governors, whose natures in the lower Man destroy but in the invisible spiritual Man give life. After the lower nature has returned to the brutishness, the higher struggles to regain its spiritual estate. It ascends the Seven Rings upon which sit the Seven Governors and returns to each their lower powers in this manner. Upon the first ring sits the Moon, and to it is returned the ability to increase and diminish. Upon the second ring sits Mercury, and to it are returned machinations, deceit, and craftiness. Upon the third ring sits Venus, and to it are returned the lusts and passions. Upon the fourth ring sits the Sun, and to this Lord are returned ambitions. Upon the fifth ring sits Mars and to it are returned rashness and profane boldness. Upon the sixth ring sits Jupiter, and to it are returned the sense of accumulation and riches. And upon the seventh ring sits Saturn, at the Gate of Chaos, and to it are returned falsehood and evil plotting. Then being naked of all the accumulations of the Seven Rings, the soul comes to the Eighth Sphere, namely, the ring of the fixed stars. Here, freed of all illusion it dwells in the Light which only pure spirit may understand.

The path to immortality is hard, and only a few find it. The rest await the Great Day when the wheels of the universe shall be stopped and the immortal sparks shall escape from the sheaths of substance. Woe unto those who wait, for they must return again, unconscious and unknowing. Blessed art thou O Son of Light, to whom of all men, I Poimandres the Light of The World, have revealed myself. I order you to go forth, to become as a guide to those who wander in darkness, that they may be saved by my Mind in you. Establish my Mysteries and they shall not fail from this earth.'

Hermes heard and replied, 'THE SLEEP OF THE BODY IS THE SOBER WATCHFULNESS OF THE MIND AND THE SHUTTING OF MY EYES REVEALS THE TRUE LIGHT. MY SILENCE IS FILLED WITH BUDDING LIFE AND HOPE, AND IS FULL OF GOOD, FOR THIS IS THE FAITHFUL ACCOUNT OF WHAT I RECEIVED FROM MY TRUE MIND, THAT IS POIMANDRES, THE GREAT DRAGON THE LORD OF THE WORD THROUGH WHOM I BECAME INSPIRED WITH THE TRUTH.[5]

The Vision of Hermes is significant in several ways. Theologians will invariably discover that many Hermetic precepts would appear in, and obviously influence, the Christian Bible several centuries later. Orientalists familiar with the symbolic iconography of China and India will discover the origin of the Dragon in Chinese mythology and culture, not to mention the philosophical profundities inherent in the Yogic, Hindu, Jaina, and Buddhist traditions of South Asia.

The Vision of Hermes, like so many of the Hermetic writings, is an allegorical exposition of great philosophic and mystic truths. The intention here is to unravel, or in the words of the ancients "to lift the Veil of Isis," to expose the practical and fundamental function of the axioms therein.

The great Hermetic Principles or laws that have been left to us are seven in number. Seven is not just an arbitrary figure, but a powerful and extremely significant symbol of divine or universal cohesiveness that permeates the core of our very existence. The following will dramatize this point:

1. There are *Seven Days* in a week and *Fifty-Two Weeks* in a year (5+2=7). The Earth was created in six days and on the *Seventh Day* God rested.
2. Psychologists state that *Age Seven is the Age of Reason*; twice that, *Fourteen, is Puberty*; thrice that, *Twenty-One, is Maturation*.
3. There are *Seven Cardinal Colors* in the solar spectrum—violet, indigo, blue, green, yellow, orange, red—from which all other colors are derived.
4. There are *Seven Key Notes* in the musical scale.
5. There are *Seven Continents,* as there are *Seven Seas,* as well as *Seven Planets,* called the *Seven Governors* by the ancients, also referred to as the *Seven Angels* in Revelations in the Christian Bible.
6. There are *Seven Holes Which Lead Into the Human Body*—ears, nostrils, mouth, anus, and vaginal or penile orifices. The human brain, heart, eye, and ear are each divided into *Seven Parts*. The skin has *Seven Layers*.
7. There are *Seven Virtues*—faith, hope, charity, strength, prudence, temperance, justice—and *Seven Deadly Sins*—pride, avarice, luxury, wrath, idleness, gluttony, envy.

It is not by chance that so many components of human life are connected to expressions of seven. The ancients held that seven was the most spiritually inclined of all the numbers, therefore it is befitting that there are seven Hermetic Axioms.

The Hermetic Axioms of Thoth/Hermes

1. The Principle of Mentalism
   "The All is Mind; The Universe is Mental."[6]

This principle embodies the truth that All or God is Mind. It explains that the All is the Substantial Reality underlying all the visible manifestations and appearances which we categorize as the material Universe: matter, energy, and all of that which is apparent to our material senses. This entity, the All, is pure Spirit which is unknowable and undefinable, but is regarded in the most ancient traditions as a Universal, Infinite, Living Mind. Human beings, in futile attempts to describe the All, attribute to it characteristics which fall within the realm of what is comfortable and comprehensible. This is theology: the assigning of human qualities to the Supreme in order to comprehend the incomprehensible. Thus, the All is always depicted as a man—God, the Father—and is actually given a personality. In reality this axiom explains that the Universe is a mental creation of the All, that is to say that the All is everything and everything is the All. This principle also explains the true nature of energy, power, and matter, and how these are subordinate to the mastery of the Mind.

2. The Principle of Correspondence
   "As above, so below; as below, so above."[7]

This axiom explicates the constant correspondence between the various planes of life, whether recognized or not. When we perceive our solar system, vast and mystifying, with the Sun at its center and the planets in orbit around the Sun, we may acknowledge the same patterns on a much smaller scale: the atom, with the nucleus at its core, and the protons, electrons, and neutrons, which, like the planets, orbit around the nucleus. The understanding of this law provides a key to unlocking the enigma of the multidimensional reality in which we exist on all planes: mental, material, and spiritual.

3. The Principle of Vibration
   "Nothing rests; everything moves; everything vibrates."[8]

This principle embodies the truth that everything is in constant motion. Whether this motion is perceivable is irrelevant, for this law affirms that everything vibrates and that nothing is ever at rest. Modern science may now attest to this fact but it should be kept in mind that this is a fact that was known thousands of years ago in ancient Kmt (Egypt) and India. The higher the vibration, the higher the form or entity which exists within that particular frequency. Therefore the vibrational connection between some of the grosser forms of matter, such as a rock and a human being, is very great. Spirit has the highest vibrational frequency of all, vibrating at such a phenomenal speed that it seems to be at rest—just as a rapidly moving wheel seems to be motionless. It is said that those practitioners of the Hermetic teachings who are able to grasp this principle will be able, with the appropriate formulas, to control their own mental vibrations as well as those of others. So, as stated by one of the old masters: "He who understands the Principle of Vibration, has grasped the scepter of power."[9]

4. The Principle of Polarity
   "Everything is dual; everything has poles; everything has its pair of opposites; like and unlike are the same; opposites are identical in nature, but different in degree; extremes meet; all truths are but half-truths; all paradoxes may be reconciled."[10]

This law exemplifies the truth that for every extreme there is another equally as valid and that the extremes thus opposed may have the effect of balancing each other. Though there are two sides to everything, and every truth may also be false, humans experience this duality throughout life. For example, a woman who lives by a particular reality may find that a year later she has matured, grown, and her perspectives have changed, thus making her prior truth or reality no longer valid. Hermes states that everything is broken down or divided into opposites, yet these opposites are identical in their nature, different only in their degree. To illustrate: hot and cold are the same thing—temperature; they simply occupy different places on the temperate scale. The same may be seen with short and tall, light and dark, or large and small, all of which reflect opposite extremes of the same scale. One commonly experienced duality is love and hate. These are two mental states which reflect opposing degrees of emotion, but which often fade into and out of one another to such a degree that they are barely distinguishable. The old saying—there is a thin line between love and hate—could not be closer to the truth. How often do we move from love to hate and back again. Within this principle we can uncover the art of polarization, a kind of mental alchemy which allows one to change his own individual polarity, from hate to love or evil to good.

5. The Principle of Gender
   "Gender is in everything; everything has its Masculine and Feminine Principles; Gender manifests on all planes."[11]

This axiom embodies the truth that gender is manifested in everything; the masculine and feminine principles are always at work. This is not only true of the physical plane but of the mental and spiritual planes as well. This principle has an affinity to the axiom which precedes it, polarity. On the physical plane, the principle manifests as sex, but on higher planes it takes higher forms. No creation, whether physical, mental, or spiritual, is possible without this principle. Within our own individual spheres of existence we know that every male has elements of feminine energy, and every female carries the components of the masculine. When this law is employed, we see the creation of planets, solar systems, as well as animal life of all kinds.

6. The Principle of Rhythm
   "Everything flows out and in; everything has its tides; all things rise and fall; the pendulum swing manifests in everything; the measure of the swing to the right is the measure of the swing to the left; rhythm compensates."[12]

The principle of rhythm can explain the cycles of life, the truth that everything has a tide-like ebb and flow. Hermes states that the ebb of the tide is equal to its flow and is set in motion and maintained by the rhythm of the Universe. There can be no better example than that of the various races of mankind and their civilizations. Once there were opulent and great empires which were created, maintained, or influenced by the Black race. For thousands of years these civilizations flourished as a pinnacle of cultural influence, even over those nations that they did not touch directly. But just as the great swing of the pendulum brought about their ascension, so it brought about their demise. Within every great experience, whether related to race, culture, civilization, or individual magnanimity, the tide must eventually turn. This principle is eternally united with the concept of the great awe-inspiring cycles or ages of humankind as well as those of the Earth, which forever dictate upheavals as well as periods of tranquility. There is always an action and a reaction, an advance and a retreat. This law therefore manifests in the creation and destruction of worlds, the rise and fall of nations, and ultimately in the mental states of humanity.

7. The Principle of Cause and Effect
"Every cause has its Effect; every Effect has its cause; everything happens according to Law; Chance is but a name for Law not recognized; there are many planes of causation but nothing escapes the Law." [13]

This law purports that everything happens according to law—that nothing just merely happens. Chance and coincidence do not exist; these are terms human beings choose, or are forced to use because of an ignorance of the principle at work. The masses of the Earth are governed by a herd instinct—the many are led aimlessly by the few—destined to be carried along, obedient to the wills and desires of others stronger than themselves. Because they are basically unconscious, they are forever subject to the effect of environment, heredity, suggestion, and other outward causes moving them about like pawns on a chessboard. Once this principle is understood and practiced, one becomes a mover as opposed to the moved, playing the game of life, as opposed to being played by it.

This is the introduction to a larger work to be published shortly by Black Classic Press. For further information, contact Wayne Chandler (see address in biographical note)

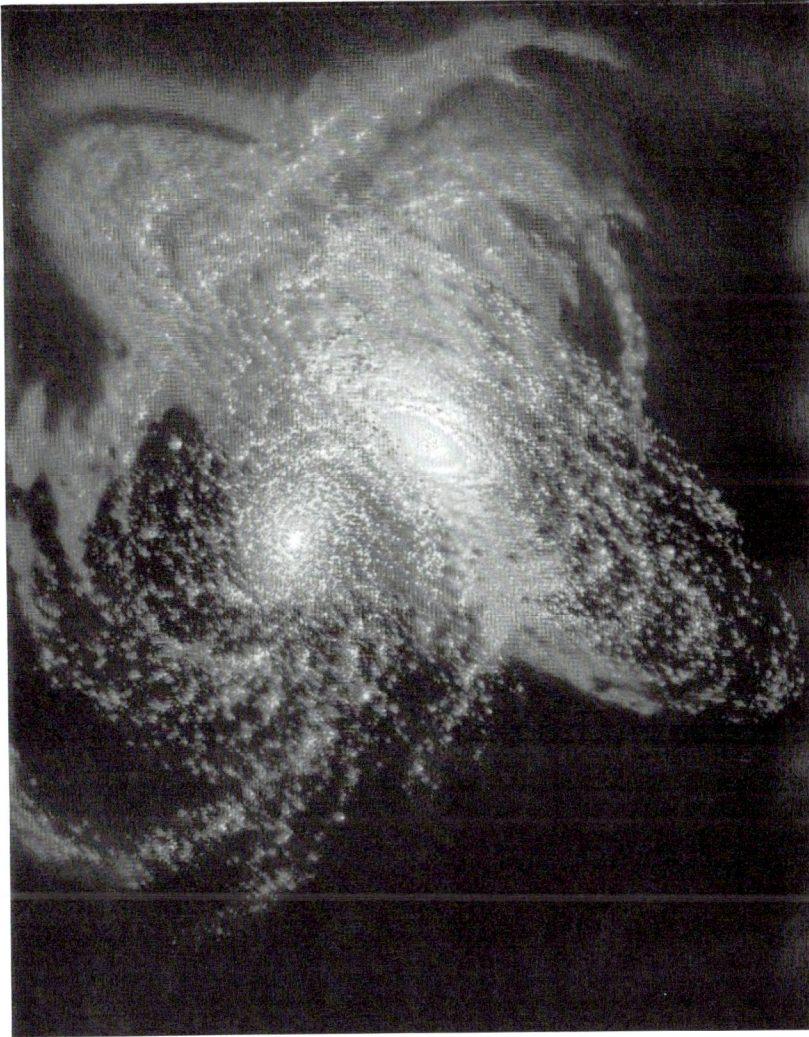

Figure 2. This photo exemplifies one of the great phenomena in the material Universe. Science recognizes that most galaxies belong to groups bound together gravitationally resisting the overall tendency to fly apart. But there are instances when two galaxies will merge without sustaining damage to one another, creating a new galaxy. Astronomers have been astounded for years by this marvel of generation, stating that the stars in these galaxies "have less chance of hitting one another than do a couple of gnats flying around in the Grand Canyon." The Hermetic Philosophy would explain that these galaxies are charged with either positive or negative force or yin and yang energy. Therefore, we see in this example, creation through gender, in one of its most abstract manifestations.

Contents

PART TWO

CORRESPONDENCE

THE SCIENCES OF ANCIENT EGYPT

EDITOR'S CORNER

(Essays on African survivals in New World Language, Myth
and Ritual from a work in progress)

EDITORIAL—PART TWO

The sections introduced in Part Two of this anthology are new departures for the Journal—*Reviews* of books by some of our contributors and of anthologies I have edited: *Correspondence*, which gives a forum for heated disputes on matters that deeply concern us, *Research News and Notes* that highlight new discoveries and seek to settle lingering questions about old ones. There is also another well-deserved tribute to a departed scholar—Alexander Von Wuthenau—who died in January of this year. He was a regular contributor to the Journal and provided support in many countries, particularly Mexico, for my controversial thesis on the African presence in Early America. Most important in Part Two, however, are the essays on the science of ancient Egypt which were presented at the Nile Valley Conference. These essays are absolutely vital reading for students of ancient Egyptian civilization. They were read to the Nile Valley Conference held in Atlanta from September 26–30, 1984. I introduce them as I did in that Journal *Nile Valley Civilizations* (Vol. 6, No. 1) which has been discontinued. Nothing, therefore, is lost and nowhere could they appear more appropriately than in this issue.

. . . What happened in Atlanta must rank as one of the turning points in the great struggle to revise the early history of the world in general and the history of Africa's classical civilizations in particular. It is the first conference on African history that drew as many as two thousand, five hundred people to one of its sessions, witness to a new and profound interest in Africa's past, a new and profound effort to illuminate the dark and forgotten rooms in which the mummies of our ancestors lie.

For five days people came from far and wide to file past the body of an Africa that seemed to breathe again because of the transmitted vitality of their awakened memory and interest. The shadows of our greatest men and women walked among us again so that we could hear the muffled thunder of their footfalls, the whisper of their voices in the great hall of the Martin Luther King International Chapel. We could feel connected again to the flow of an ancient electricity that still runs to us, it seems, from the currents of that time.

We felt for a moment a sense of loss when we learnt that Dr. Cheikh Anta Diop, the pharaoh of African studies, would not be able to sit among us in person to celebrate this event. According to Diop's own words, the plane taking him from Dakar, Senegal, had been forced to return after the discovery of a fractured wing one thousand miles out from base. It had almost crashlanded on its return to Dakar, blowing out all the tires. The shock of this experience, perhaps, kept Dr. Diop home. News of this, however, cast but a temporary chill over the proceedings. It soon became clear to us all that we had gathered there because of his presiding spirit, because of the essence and purpose of his work, which it was our duty to continue even as we would be forced one day to continue without his physical presence. His spirit was the real catalyst. And even if the wings, upon which his body flew, were broken, his spirit had already flown to us . . .

Pappademos

John Pappademos shows how Newton, perhaps the greatest figure in European science before Einstein, drew directly and indirectly upon the early sciences of the Nile Valley. Newton achieved a synthesis of three lines of development—astronomy, mathematics and mechanics—and this success rested directly upon his predecessors Kepler, Copernicus, Descartes and Galileo. Pappademos contends that the work of these scientists would have been impossible without the foundation laid centuries earlier in Egypt. He traces the influences of these men upon Newton and the influence of Egypt, both in the classical and later Muslim period, upon these men. Even Newton himself admits on several occasions his debt to the ancient Africans. He attributes for example the first atomic theory to the Egyptians and the Phoenicians. "That all matter consists of atoms was a very ancient opinion . . . I think the same opinion obtained in the mystic philosophy which flows down to the Greeks from Egypt and Phoenicia, since atoms are sometimes found to be designated by the mystics as monads". Newton also admits that his law of universal gravitation had been anticipated two thousand years earlier by the Pythagorean philosophers and that this was the real meaning of their doctrine of the "harmony of the spheres." Pythagorus spent twenty-two years in Egypt studying Egyptian science and it was there, according to Newton, that the Greek mathematician learnt this doctrine. Newton also saw an Egyptian anticipation of his own heliocentric theory (theory of the rotation of the earth and other planets around the sun). In addition to this study of the roots of the Newtonian laws, Pappademos lists all the discoveries of the Egyptians in the field of astronomy, many of which are deliberately ignored by the historians of science.

Lumpkin

Mathematician Beatrice Lumpkin highlights Nile Valley pre-eminence in mathematics for four millennia and the leading role this played in building the foundations of modern science. The first cipherization of numbers took place in Egypt where hieroglyphic numerals used special symbols for the powers of 10. Fractions also became necessary very early in Africa because of the vast construction of pyramids, irrigation works, temples and obelisks, which required accurate measurements of lengths, areas and volumes. These fractions were at the heart of Egyptian arithmetic. They enabled the scribes to perform complex operations and they were used by scientists for thousands of years, right up to the modern period. Lumpkin demonstrates, from the surviving papyri, Egyptian breakthroughs in trigonometry, algebra (the *aha* calculus) and geometry. She reclaims Euclid for African mathematics and wonders how a man born and raised in Africa, showing no evidence of an alient parenthood, feeding upon all the mathematical texts available to him in Egypt at the time, could be represented as fair and Greek in all the textbooks. Euclid's *Elements*, containing 13 books and 465 propositions, has dominated the teaching of geometry for 2000 years. She also spotlights the Moorish period when inferior European mathematics was lifted to the level of the African and the Asian by Muslim arithmetic and algebra, the transfer from India of the Hindu numerals (at first resisted by European superstitions about numbers) and the works of the great Egyptian mathematicians like Abu Kamil.

Akbar

In our section on Nile Valley as source of world philosophy, we have provocative essays by Na'im Akbar, Richard King, and Asa Hilliard. Akbar attempts to outline the nature of the Egyptian contribution to the science of psychology. The Greek word *psyche* is derived from the Egyptian in which *khe* is the soul and *su* is she, hence, the feminine nature of the Greek *Psukhe*. Omitting the initial Greek P, we have the root of the word—*sakhu*. This, in Egyptian, means the understanding, the illuminator, the eye or soul of being. Akbar points up the difficulty of trying to identify a psychology of ancient Egypt in any explicit sense but he focuses on the doctrine of self-knowledge, wherein lies, in a simplified form, the initial psychology of consciousness. The seven dimensions of the self or soul (*Ka, Ba, Khaba, Akhu, Seb, Putah* and *Atmu*) are discussed. These constitute the natural form of the human being's psychology as well as his evolution. "The challenge of man," says Akbar "was to become knowledgeable of these souls [or forms of the self] and achieve a crystallization of them into an Eighth or Divinely permanent form." This eighth form, according to Gerald Massey, was the Horus or the Christ.

King

Richard King in his essay "The Symbolism of the Crown" sees the study of the crown, the jewels and the tableau found in the tomb of the 18th dynasty pharaoh Tut as excellent examples of symbolic reference to a historical stream of ancient African philosophical thought that runs through classical Egyptian civilization. His analysis of that symbolism and its underlying philosophy leads to more than an introduction to an African psychology of the unconscious. He touches on controversial issues that relate to the pineal gland and melanin with clarity and certitude. He cites items of physical evidence of "the African knowledge of biological psychiatry and depth psychiatry thousands of years before the rediscovery of the same bodies of knowledge by Europeans." Egyptians, he claims, had knowledge of the location and function of the pineal gland. They knew it was located anatomically at the posterior end of the third ventricle of the brain. The pineal gland is a modified eye. It is an actual eye in lower forms, like the lizard, but it withdrew into the head of mammals like man and became a light converter, whose hormonal signals can actually change levels of consciousness. He shows that the black pupil in the eye of Horus, through which rays of light are made to enter in certain Egyptian representations, corresponds to the black dot or pineal eye, the *locus coeruleus,* the uppermost in a chain of twelve pigmented black nucleii in the brain stem.

Hilliard

Asa Hilliard discusses the classical expression in ancient Egypt of the African system of education which was "the parent of other systems of education, especially early European education in Greece and Rome." He selects for his study of this system a peak period of Egyptian development—the eighteenth dynasty—and a major center of government in that dynasty—Thebes (today's Luxor) where stand two gigantic temples that contain the most highly developed education system on record from ancient times. One of these great temples of Luxor housed an elite faculty of priest-professors and at one time catered to an estimated 80,000 students at all grade levels. Temples were at the center of religion, politics and education.

This temple-university had a huge library and its faculty, called "teachers of mysteries," were divided into five major departments: astronomy and astrology; geography; geology; philosophy and theology; law and communication. Hilliard introduces us to the steps in this process of education, which is not seen simply as a process of acquiring knowledge but the transformation of the learner, who progressed through successive stages of rebirth to become more godlike. Hilliard underlines the fact that this education was a blend of the theoretical and practical, a holistic education. The educational concepts of Egypt did not die when the last college at Philae was closed by Justinian in 527 A.D. Some remained in disguised form in the educational systems of the European conquerors.

ALEXANDER VON WUTHENAU
Photography by Jacqueline L. Patten-Van Sertima (1985)

TRIBUTE TO A DEPARTED SCHOLAR
—ALEXANDER VON WUTHENAU—

The *Journal of African Civilizations* pays solemn tribute to Alexander Von Wuthenau, who died soon after a telephone conversation with the editor in January of this year.

He sounded pleasantly surprised at first (I had not spoken with him for three years). "O yes?" he said, rather softly, when I told him the good news, and then he chuckled, breaking into a raspy cough, catching his voice for a moment and then losing it, fading into silence. I had just told him that the Smithsonian press was about to publish my 1991 address, an update on the evidence for the presence of Africans in the Americas before Columbus. I was calling him, I said, to get photographs of nine of the pieces from his collection. Alex, I must point out, was in his early nineties. He had spent a great part of his life pursuing evidence in the field of American art history for this thesis. It had been a source of animated discourse and sometimes, perhaps, of amused incredulity and courteous indulgence among the elite and pretentious circles he frequented. It was an honor, of course, for professors, potentates, and presidents alike, to have a baron as a guest, especially a celebrated diplomat and scholar from the last royal house of Germany, even if he was a bit eccentric and seemed to some of his conservative hosts to be promoting a lunatic theory. He actually chuckled with an irrepressible mirth in that last conversation and though it led to coughing and his final silence, I got the impression that he had got the last laugh on some of these hypocrites. He died, I would like to believe, suffocated in a surfeit of exhilaration.

Von Wuthenau had spent nearly half a century excavating and classifying ancient and medieval terracotta in Mexico. He was among the first to sequence-date them into Pre-Classic, Classic, and Post-Classic periods. He was also the first to introduce pre-Columbian clay portraits of African types into Mexican museums, particularly those of Diego Rivera and Josue Saenz. He did several programs with me, translating my commentary into Spanish for Mexican television. He was the author of *The Art of Terracotta Pottery in Pre-Columbian South and Central America* (Crown Publishers, 1970) and *Unexpected Faces in Ancient America* (Crown, 1975).

He also published essays in three of the Journals: "African Representations in Ancient American Art" in Vol. 3, No. 2 (November 1981)

"Nestesen—Forgotten King of Kush" in Vol. 4, No. 1 (April, 1982) and "Unexpected African Faces in Pre-Columbian America" in Vol. 8, No. 2 (December, 1986).

His mother was Countess Marie Antoinette Chotek, sister of the wife of the Archduke Franz Ferdinand, whose assassination at Sarajevo triggered a series of events that hastened Europe's inevitable lurch towards the Second World War. Alexander von Wuthenau was Secretary for cultural and legal affairs to the German legation in Buenos Aires, Argentina. He was later appointed Secretary of the German Embassy in Washington D.C. just before the outbreak of the war. He renounced diplomatic service, however, when Hitler insisted that all ambassadors should sign a statement that they were pure Aryans. Von Wuthenau refused to sign, pointing out in a letter that infuriated the Nazi government that there was no such thing as a pure Aryan and that racial purity and racial superiority were myths. He fled to Mexico after this potentially fatal impertinence.

There he played many roles—art lecturer at the University of the Americas, architect of a church, a city square, a museum, an engineer who altered the course of a river to irrigate large tracts of land, builder of his own chateau and studio at San Angel.

Visitors to Mexico in search of pre-Columbian American art featuring the African, especially those I took to Mexico with me in 1984, are advised that the Von Wuthenau studio housing his terracotta has now been removed from San Angel to Tepoztlan. The sculptures Von Wuthenau excavated and collected for half a century are protected from seizure and acquisition by the Mexican government under a special arrangement negotiated before his death.

I close this tribute to my good friend of many years with a quote from the Introduction to my book *They Came Before Columbus:*

"Terra-cotta sculpture of faces was the photography of the pre-Columbian Americans and what Von Wuthenau had done was to open new rooms in the photo gallery of our lost American ages. No longer was the African chapter in American pre-Columbian history an irrecoverable blank because of the vicious destruction of American books. Here were visible witnesses of a vanished time and they were telling us a new story."

Ivan Van Sertima

BOOK REVIEWS

Introduction to the Study of African Classical Civilizations, by Runoko Rashidi, London: Karnak House, 1992

African-centered scholarship hails the advent of a major work by cultural historian and lecturer of international standing, Runoko Rashidi. Rashidi has created a textbook devoted to the study of "That Other African:" Earth's original human, the creator of the first civilized Earth cultures, and the first explorer of Asia, Europe, and the Americas. The title of the work—*Introduction to the Study of African Classical Civilizations*—highlights two of its most important elements. Rashidi juxtaposes the words "classical" and "African" which challenges the Western reflex association of "classical" with the Greco-Roman roots of Western civilization. Long overdue is the presentation of scholarship on African civilization on par with that of the roots of Eurocentric thought.

The second distinctive and functionally critical feature of this book is its organization in textbook format. The four chapters of Part One look at Nile Valley Civilizations, flourishing in the Upper Nile Valley of Northern Africa, now variously called Ethiopia and ancient Egypt, but known in the ancient tongue of our ancestors as *Kmt*. Rashidi recounts, with startling detail, the dynastic history of Kmt with a litany of black African rulers dating from 3200 B.C.E., giving special attention to the golden age of Kmt under the reign of Ramses the Great. Rashidi's astounding ability to condense with great accuracy and comprehensiveness, the histories of these periods is indispensable to those academicians whose research leads them into these eras of African history.

In Part Two, Rashidi turns to Asia, using the seminal research of the late eminent historian Cheik Anta Diop to assert that Asian peoples and civilizations are an extension of Africa. Rashidi clearly stands apart as a strong advocate for the recognition of the African presence in early as well as contemporary Asia. The first chapter of this section discusses the 90,000 year history of Africans in Asia and the African roots of Asian civilizations and religions. For a long time Asia was considered the cradle of humanity, but Diop's work has proven that the first Asians actually journeyed there from the Great Lakes region of East-Central Africa, where was born the first Homo erectus and Homo sapiens sapiens.

Particularly striking in this section are the photographs of Africoid Persians, Phoenicians, Arabians, Indians, Chinese, Jews, Filipinos, and Malaysians. Photographs of stone carvings and statues reveal that the Buddha himself was of Africoid origin.

Chapter Six is devoted to the Dalits, a large but relatively unknown member of the global African community and a particular interest of Runoko Rashidi's—he dedicates his book to them with the imperative "Know Thyself." Since his 1987 sojourn to South India as the honored keynote speaker at the first *All Indian Dalits Writers Conference* in Hyderabad, Rashidi's mission had been to bring into our global vision the Blacks of India, known as the Untouchables, who are socially and politically oppressed, and denied the very basic of human rights at the hands of non-native Aryan invaders. He documents in detail the atrocities committed against them throughout Aryan/Hindu history and continues their history up to the present day involvement with Dalit writers, historians, and civil rights reformists. Rashidi makes a striking point: despite a series of holocausts and calamities, Africans survive in Asia today at a population of almost two-hundred million. His attention to the Dalits is rounded out by a provoking essay by V.T. Rajshekar, a Dalit militant, who likens the struggle of the Untouchables to that of African Americans: two black populations struggling in the suffocating web of Western civilization.

Part Three is a discourse on theories of the origins of American civilizations, tracing them from Asia, that is, *from Asians of African descent.* Rashidi exhibits great thoroughness of study, reaching back to the roots of history—archeology—to fill in a gaping hole in American history with the archaeological work and theories of Harold Sterling Gladwin. Rashidi points out that the 2000 B.C.E. migration of Mongoloid people into the Americas was so large that it absorbed three previous migrations of various African and Asian peoples, and became the amalgamated race now called the "American Indian" (which includes populations of "Indians" in North, Central and South America). As a result of the modern historical view, and resulting popular concensus, that the "American Indian" is the "Native American," the very first Americans—Black Africans—have faded "into the shadowy realms of fairy tales, myths and legends." Rashidi issues an important challenge: "the history of the Western Hemisphere will remain incomplete and misunderstood until the presence of Black people . . . is acknowledged by both scholars and the general public."

Chapter Eight studies the African presence in the ancient British Isles, leaning heavily on the works of nineteenth century historian/anthropologists Gerald Massey and David MacRitchie. Rashidi discusses the origins of the "dark white" Briton, black Vikings, and the role of the Moor in western Europe. He includes several reproductions of British family crests in which African visages figure prominently.

Both scholars and the general public will be influenced by this book which, while a scholarly textbook aimed at the serious student, is also lively and lucid reading. The book is divided into manageable sections that can be read by a group in a classroom for discussion or on the subways for pondering and digestion during work hours.

Each topic is approached in a manner which lends itself to study and learning. The author had skillfully dissected the complexities of African history and broken them down into practicable sections. Each part of the book is followed by a helpful summary for easy reference, or review before a test. Also indispensable is the list in table form of geographical names which translate ancient African location from their modern and Greco-Roman names into Kemetic names. The reader is grateful for the extensive glossary, detailed references, and a comprehensive bibliography. Rashidi is incredibly well-read and traveled, and overwhelmingly knowledgeable; both academia and the armchair scholar should be grateful to him for sharing his wisdom, and especially appreciative of his ability to break it down in such a comprehensible manner.

Runoko Rashidi truly succeeds in his effort to promote Pan-Africanism by trying to "reunite a family that has been separated for too long."

Wayne B. Chandler

Predynastic Egypt: An African-centric View, by James E. Brunson III. Introduction by Runoko Rashidi. DeKalb: KARA, 1991. 150 pages; 31 illustrations and two maps. $10.00 paperback.*

A clear African-centric perspective on Predynastic Kmt (Ancient Egypt) is absolutely fundamental to the overall redrafting of global history, including the chronicle of the early Nile Valley. This is cardinal to the view that art historian James E. Brunson had taken in his expanding collection of writings on the Black presence in antiquity and today. In his quality new work, *Predynastic Egypt: An African-centric View*, Brunson concentrates on the origins and evolution of Predynastic and early Dynastic Kmt. This is an area in African studies that deserves far more attention than it has received up to this point. As Brunson explains in the Foreword to the book, *Predynastic Egypt: An African-centric View* was created for the sole purpose of addressing a specified and neglected area of ancient Kemetic studies."[1] He puts forth that, "The term *Predynastic* is used to characterize the era which anticipates the first recognized historical dynasty of Egypt. This period, which is generally dated between 5000–3200 B.C.E., saw the development of significant social, cultural, political, and economic institutions."[2]

The brilliant young cultural historian Runoko Rashidi, one of Brunson's closest collaborators, contributed the Introduction to *Predynastic Egypt*. In the Introduction, entitled "Dr. Cheikh Anta Diop and the Primacy of Africa," Rashidi—a specialist on the African presence in Asia—seeks to demonstrate the primacy of Nile Valley civilization over that of Western Asia. Rashidi, like Brunson himself, places considerable emphasis on the ancient Western Asian civilization of Sumer. Rashidi explains to the reader that:

> Flourishing during the third millennium B.C.E., Sumer seems to have constructed the general framework, and established the basic patterns for the kingdoms and empires which gradually succeeded her.[3]

In relationship to the Nile Valley, while referencing and incorporating the work of the late Dr. Cheikh Anta Diop, Rashidi writes that:

> The dynastic phase of Kemetic civilization, however, was already in full motion by 3200 B.C.E., and thus it is little wonder that Diop re-

*For information, write to: James E. Brunson, P.O. Box 0962, DeKalb, IL 60115–0962.

gards the synchronization of Kemetic and Mesopotamian history as a political necessity 'resulting from ideology, not from fact.' The apparent objective of this strategy is to endeavor to explain Kemetic origins through Mesopotamia, and thus deny Kmt its African roots and character. On the other hand, says Diop, 'if we remain within the realm of authentic facts, we are forced to view Mesopotamia as a belatedly born daughter of Egypt.'[4]

The first two chapters of *Predynastic Egypt* deal with the Badarian and Naqada cultures. Brunson places the Badarian culture between 5000 B.C.E. to 4000 B.C.E., and states that:

> The Badarians used copper ore (malachite) for face paint, pointing to a basic knowledge of smelting techniques.
> It is also significant to point out that agriculture in the Nile Valley, and the creation of the calendar, coincides with the Badarians. So we see that Egypt was already propelled toward civilization and any external influences in the Nile Valley at this time may be seen as minimal.[5]

The Naqada I culture (4000 B.C.E.–3500 B.C.E.) is known as the Amratian phase. "Naqada II, or the Gerzean phase (3500–3200 B.C.E.) of the Naqada culture, is characterized by accelerated culture contacts, both direct and indirect with Ta-Zeti (Nubia), the Sahara, the island of Crete, and Western Asia."[6]

Brunson devotes four of the nine chapters in the book to an exploration of cultural connections between Predynastic Egypt and the island of Crete in the Aegean Sea, the Sahara, Western Asia, and the Nubian 'A' Group, where he relies particularly upon the work of Bruce Williams.[7] Although modest in size (170 miles east to west, thirty-five miles north to south), Crete exercised immeasurable influence on the early Aegean archipelago and Mycenaean Greece. Brunson seeks to put forth evidence supporting the southern origins of some of the primary components of the high-culture of early Crete, illustrating Crete as a conveyor of African culture to Europe and the Mediterranean. Brunson is not the first writer to make this connection. Historian John G. Jackson, for example, writes that:

> The first civilization of Europe was established on the island of Crete. It is sometimes called the Minoan Culture, after King Minos, an early legendary ruler of the island. The ancestors of the Cretans were natives of Africa, a branch of western Ethiopians. They dwelt in the grasslands of North Africa before that area dried up and became a great desert. As the Saharan sands encroached on their homeland, they took to the sea, and in Crete and neighboring islands set up a maritime culture.[8]

Brunson also references the researches of British excavator Arthur Evans, responsible for much of the early archaeological work on the island. Evans was strongly convinced of African migrations to neolithic Crete, and wrote that:

> The multiplicity of these connections with the old indigenous race of the opposite African coast, and with which we undoubtedly have to deal with in the predynastic population of the Nile Valley, can in fact be hardly explained on any other hypothesis than that of an actual settlement in Southern Crete.[9]

Some of the most important sections in *Predynastic Egypt* focus on the Anu. Anu is a name found seemingly everywhere that ancient Black populations have been found. The *Anu Seti*, for example, lived on the banks of the Upper Nile Valley and related areas. The *Anu-Tehennu* were the early inhabitants of Libya. The ancient people of Arabia Petraea were called the *Anu*. In Western Asia, Anu was the great father of the gods, including Ishtar and Enlil, in Sumerian religious mythology. Early on recognized as the highest power in the universe and the sovereign-lord of the Sumerian pantheon, Anu was "older than all the other gods and the source of all existence." Probably the major cult center of Anu was the city-state called Uruk, known to the Sumerians as *Eanna—the House of Anu*. According to Brunson:

> During the Third Dynasty of Uruk, King Lugalzagissi of Uruk (2340–2316 B.C.E.) conquered all of Sumer in the name of Anu. Gudea, Governor of the city-state of Lagash and high priest of Anu (2150–2100 B.C.E.) revived the glory of Sumer's past, again elevating the deity to a supreme position.[10]

The longest, the most substantial, and last chapter in *Predynastic Egypt* is entitled "Evidence in the Artifacts." In this concluding chapter, Brunson employs his expertise as an art historian in an examination of such ancient artifacts as painted pottery, predynastic standards and ceremonial palettes. This chapter, in particular, captures, in this reviewer's estimation, the real value of *Predynastic Egypt: An African-centric View* to both the lay persons and advanced students—Brunson's ability to utilize art history at the core of multi-disciplinary approach in providing a coherent synthesis of views on an extremely important early phase in the evolution of African civilization.

Regina Blackburn

Notes

1. James E. Brunson, *Predynastic Egypt: An African-centric View*, (DeKalb: KARA, 1991), 9.
2. Brunson, 21.

3. Runoko Rashidi, Introduction to *Predynastic Egypt: An African-centric View*, by James E. Brunson (DeKalb: KARA, 1991), 16.

4. Rashidi.

5. Brunson, 28.

6. Brunson, 38.

7. Bruce Williams, "The Lost Pharaohs of Nubia," *Archaeology* 33, No. 5 (1980), 12–21; Bruce Williams, "Latest Research on Nubia: A Letter to the Editor," *Nile Valley Civilizations*, ed. Ivan Van Sertima (New Brunswick: Journal of African Civilizations, 1984), 44–46; Bruce Williams, *The A-Group Royal Cemetery at Qustul: Cemetery L* (Chicago: Oriental Institute of the University of Chicago, 1986).

8. John G. Jackson, *Introduction to African Civilizations* (Secaucus: Citadel Press, 1970), 76–77.

9. Arthur Evans, "The Early Nilotic Libyan and Egyptian Relations with Minoan Crete," *Journal of the Royal Anthropological Institute of Great Britain and Ireland* (1925), 225.

10. Brunson, 44.

Exploding the Myths, Volume I. Nile Valley Contributions to Civilization, by Anthony T. Browder, 1992, Institute of Karmic Guidance, 288 pages: *80,00 Words of Text, *14,000 Words of marginal notes, *200 Photographs, *150 Illustrations, *10 Maps, *7 Tables, *Timeline, *Glossary, *Bibliography. Paperback $16.95, Hardcover $29.95.

Tony Browder's newest book, *Nile Valley Contributions To Civilization* is marked by two compelling characteristics: *usefulness* and *readability*. They serve this book well. The surge of broad interest in the origins of Egyptian civilization makes this an important work *now*. Egyptology until recent days has been the narrow province of scholars and specialists among whom there has been considerable debate as to where the roots of Egypt's highly developed civilization lay. With Browder's book, a reader of mild or curious interest can come away artfully informed on two issues: first, that Egypt is, in fact, in Africa, and second, the foundations for the Pharaohs were laid in the ancient cradlelands of Africa. This issue is carefully explored and settled by Browder's scholarship and painstaking research.

The Nile Valley is appropriately established as the primary source of the culture and civilization that in the public mind is always associated with present-day Egypt. That is proven to be serious error in Browder's exposition as he meticulously documents the locus of the ancient Egypt as being centered more than 400 miles "up" the Nile. No distinction was made between the people who populated ancient Egypt in what is present day Sudan and Egypt. Is is more than a romantic notion that these people were Black people as evidenced in the description of themselves both in hieroglyph and images discovered in archaeological research. All of Browder's sources on this issue are scholars with impeccable credentials. The passage following is the launching pad of the author's inquiry upon which his sound foundation is laid:

"It is in the Nile Valley where one can find the greatest primary evidence of the earliest beginnings of agriculture, architecture, engineering, language, writing, philosophy, science and religion. In short, all of the essential components that would lead to the development of a great civilization."

Browder introduces the reader of this volume to Qustul, the world's oldest monarchy, a Nubian civilization that paralleled the development of ancient Egypt or Kemet. Its date is ca. 3800 B.C. This work clearly establishes a highly organized political structure that antedates the First Dynasty in Egypt (Kemet) by more than two centuries. Most of the continuing data on the Nubian civilization was lost forever with the construction of Lake Nasser and the consequent flooding of the primary areas of investigation. The point that Browder makes explicitly with these references is that the Nubians were as sophisticated in building cities, roads and temples comparable to the people of ancient Egypt (Kemet). Browder concludes on the basis of his well documented theories that *Nubia was the lifeline of ancient Kemet, and the source of its language, philosophy and religion.* In some respect, Kemet was the daughter nation of the ancient Nubia. At one point during the 25th Dynasty, Nubian rulers remained in control of Kemet until they were finally overrun by the Assyrians. Browder's fundamental thesis is sound and carefully argued that whatever Egypt became, the primary influence was from the south, the direction from which the Nile flows to the Mediterranean.

I have just returned from another of more than a dozen visits to Egypt with a tour group of sixty persons. One of our guides came to me quizzically on the second day and remarked that a tour member had inquired, "Is Egypt in Africa?" Any American over forty might have that same mind-set given the slant of Eurocentric geography and social studies texts of the United States. The intentional distortion of history by Europeans to assign the civilization of the Nile Valley to Asian and/or European origin has been pronounced. Browder, with this work, joins the pioneers J.A. Rogers, William Leo Hansberry, George G.M. James, Charles Wesley and others who spent their lifetimes setting the record straight. *Nile Valley Contributions To Civilization*'s singular significance is that it de-mythologizes the many attempts to wrest Egyptian civilization from the heartland of the African continent. To be sure, this volume complements the work of John Henrik Clarke, Asa C. Hilliard, Ivan Van Sertima and Yosef ben-Jochannan who have been Browder's mentors academically and personally.

In addition to a splendid chapter devoted to detailing The Historical Accomplishments of Kemet (Chapter 3, Part I) in which the reader is informed on the Nile Valley roots of architecture, astronomy, agriculture, philosophy and religion, Part II is probably of more significance to someone educated in the West. Part II, *The Stolen Legacy,* traces carefully and with full documentation the persistent attempts to Europeanize Egypt's history and culture. Browder is in full agreement with W.E.B. Dubois who asserted a century ago that Europeans began questioning the race and color of Egyptians to provide the rationale and justification for the Atlantic slave trade and its horrific de-humanization of African people in the American slave system. The attempt was made to re-write history in order to support a racist ideology. Four generations later, that re-writing reveals itself in changing the physical images of ancient African Pharoahs despite the countless representations that supported an African origin of the Nile Valley civilization. There is also the matter of the Greeks appropriating the *mystery systems* of the Nile Valley civilization and fusing these with later Greek philosophy. Browder is uncompromising in setting the record straight. Chapter Five, *The Rape of Egypt*, discloses historically the route by which many of the great treasures of Egypt have found their way around the world, occupying celebrated museums without any recompense whatsoever to the country from which they were seized. Much of this "rape" took place during the Napoleonic invasion and the subsequent occupation by the British. Browder underscores the importance of the discovery of the tomb of the boy king, Tutankhamen, in 1922.

In summary fashion, Browder demonstrates the clear manner in which the Nile Valley civilization has touched all of our lives, both in Europe and America. The very currency with which we conduct business on a daily basis betrays the far-ranging influence of the Nile Valley. Along the way, this young scholar makes a strong and definitive case for *Afrocentrism* that has been under attack and debate by some reputable scholars. This is a volume of considerable significance.

In all candor, as well done as this work is, it contains one glaring flaw. As a Christian theologian, I take strong exception to Browder's assertion " . . . it was not the Roman army that ultimately brought Egypt to her knees and destroyed her, it was the newly emerging religion of Christianity." Though there is some validity to this assertion, it is both exaggerated and overly simplistic. The author provides no clear definition as to how Christianity "brought Egypt to her knees and ultimately destroyed her . . . ". Browder makes no reference to Islam's presence and impact on the demise of Egyptian culture. The glaring omission of the reality that Egypt is today an Islamic nation and not Christian somehow seems to suggest some imbalance in Browder's conclusion. This reviewer feels that the stance of the author on this issue is untenable.

Some word should be said about the book's design which feeds the readability cited earlier. The artful and informative marginal notes make this work friendlier without robbing it of its careful scholarship. *Nile Valley Contributions To Civilization* is thus insulated from the charge of being "dry reading" with the frequent contemporary references made by the author to ancient Africa's influence in our world. A scanning of the Table of Contents reveals the balanced overall treatment of the subject matter. This is a significant and persuasive work that commends itself to broad readership whether scholar or layperson. It is a *must* for the reading lists of our nation's public and private schools.

Wyatt Tee Walker

African Presence in Early America, Ivan Van Sertima, Editor. Transaction
Publishers: New Brunswick and London, 1992.

This is an interesting series of essays on the question of Africans in
America. Van Sertima is the leading Africanist, the more balanced and
broadest of a group that even he says contains extremists. In contrast to the
strident, poorly informed approach, Van Sertima strives for a scholarly, as
far as possible a detached, view of the problem. And it is a problem both as
to the facts, though they are the least of the problem, and of attitude, a huge
problem indeed.

Van Sertima opens the series of chapters with an introduction looking
back fifteen years to the appearance of his They Came Before Columbus:
The African Presence in Ancient America., (Random House 1977). He discusses the narrative style that he used in that volume as a useful device for
reconstructing a past time and circumstances. It became a point of criticism
that obscured much of the factual data presented. This is typical of some of
his academic critics throwing the baby out with the bath water.

In an introduction he states what he had added or is adding in this volume
to the case. This involves much deeper consideration of the Olmec Stone
Heads. Von Wuthenau's marvelous collection of terracotta representations
of racial types in America, especially Mexico, presentation of the skeletal
evidence, the testimony of the ancient maps, much discussion of dating and
much on Jaraizbhoy, some linguistics with very pertinent comparisons with
Egyptian words, unfortunately usually single words, but in contexts that
gives them real meaning. For example, amoxaque (Nahuatl), amouta,
(Quechua), Egyptian Am and Ym carry the same meanings. Also Ra (sun)
and yarur (paradise), Egyptian Ra, (iaro or yrao) have the same meanings.

There are two interesting reviews of pioneers in the field. Leo Wiener
wrote voluminously on African contacts. Van Sertima is critical but sympathetic. Then, Harold Gladwin's book, Men Out of Asia is reviewed, again
critically but sympathetically. There is much on specific peoples and traits.
The Mandingo of the Guinea area of West Africa are indicated as particularly important for the contacts with America. Of special interest is a bit of
epigraphy: a North African Tifinag inscription in the Virgin Islands. Finally
a claim for an Asiatic-African fusion of cultures in America for which Van
Sertima has some reservations. All of this in an introduction.

This is followed by an address that Van Sertima gave for the
Smithsonian. It was an hour length presentation and richly illustrated, but

unfortunately the slides were not included here, but will appear in a forth coming publication. It is an interesting address, reviewing much that he has presented before and that is included in the papers to be reviewed in more detail below. In this address he takes off the gloves at times and exposes some of his critics. A good case is that of Comas of Mexico who said of Von Wuthenau's terracottas that there were no such terracottas. A Dr. Kelley, not further identified, criticized Van Sertima's defense of Leo Wiener by attacking Wiener's linguistics. Van Sertima replies that he is aware of many of the shortcomings of Wiener's work and especially the linguistics, but still thinks that there are things of value in Wiener's work. Of special interest to me he introduces considerable plant geography, cotton, tobacco, jackbeans (Canavalia sp.) And on this topic more later.

Finally we turn to the individual chapters. The first concerns the Egypto-Nubian presence in ancient Mexico, which Van Sertima opens by explaining that he is well aware of other contacts but that here he is going to concentrate on the Olmec. Some extremely important points are made. First that the Olmec heads clearly portray Africans, their helmets are comparable to those of Nubian-Egyptian military, and that the date that they appear at La Venta is quite in keeping with known Nubian activity in Egypt. He then takes up the supporting evidence. This includes the Wuthenau terracottas with their vivid portrayal of classic negro types, the Polish physical anthropologist, Wircinski, finding clear evidence of the total Negroid pattern of Physical traits, and even identifying male Negroid skeletons in graves with Native American female types. Van Sertima then inserts a disclaimer that he thinks that the Olmec culture was African. Absolutely not, he says, but he insists that it was influenced by Africans, he considers it a clear case of an injection of an outside influence, and by a people from the Egyptian cultural world and able to convey important knowledge.

A most interesting comment is inserted here. Since a Phoenician type is also represented, the usual contention is that the Phoenicians must have brought a boat load of black slaves. This type of conclusion crops up with considerable regularity whenever there is evidence of Africans in America. It is of course not only pure assumption, but a case of colossal cheek. The status of these Black Africans is clearly indicated by the fact that it is their heads that are sculptured in colossal size in hard stone and placed in positions dominating the ceremonial plaza at La Venta. Van Sertima develops the Nubian, Egyptian, Phoenician relationships as well, and makes it clear that such an association, common around the Mediterranean, would be quite expectable elsewhere. As for the means of getting here, he reviews Hyerdahl and the reed boat, Ra, and other evidence and finds little difficulty in the voyaging area.

He then takes up the evidence of a meaningful contact. Monarchic traits, the double crown, the royal flail, sacred boat, royal purple, artificial beard,

feathered fan of a specific type and with specific colors, ceremonial um-
brella, hand shaped incense spoons, the Four Bacabs that hold up the sky,
the opening of the mouth ceremony, human headed bird figure emerging
from the tomb, and so forth. For lengthier lists, see Jairazbhoy. Some of
these traits can be elaborated considerably beyond Van Sertima's treatment
and given added certainty that an Egyptian presence is indicated.

One of the tribulations of the diffusionists' work has been establishing
the contemporaneity of the alleged cultural influences from overseas. This
plagued the early work on trans Pacific contacts. In America the usual
criticism of the comparisons of pyramids of Mexico with those of Egypt had
been: they are not synchronous! Van Sertima, in a revealing presentation,
demonstrates that the Nubians picked up the pyramid building trait late and
then perpetuated it almost indefinitely. Thus any contact that involved
Nubians could carry the pyramid traits at exactly the necessary time to make
the Mexican and Egyptian-Nubian pyramids contemporaneous. This seeing
of things in two cultural time frames has been sorely lacking in a great deal
of archeology which is more often marked by narrow specialization than
breadth.

There is a good bit more. When pyramids appear in America in the
Olmec culture, they are oriented astronomically, they are associated with
colossal sculptures which are also making their first appearance on the
American scene, and the whole complex is to be found in the Nile area. Van
Sertima is most careful to state that it was the ideas that followed, carried by
a minority of incomers, and that the American natives put their own stamp
on the work. It takes a heroic effort not to see the evidence, and not to reach
Van Sertima's conclusion.

Van Sertima continues to pile up the evidence. Guanin amongst the
Mandingo with variants means gold, and that is also the meaning reported in
the Caribbean at the earliest contact. Cotton was picked up by the Portuguese in West Africa about 1450 and according to Van Sertima this was
Gossypium hirsutum var punctatum, an American cotton. This of course fits
M.D.W. Jeffrey's contention that the Portuguese at this time also got maize
in West Africa. The banana fits in here also and Van Sertima gives convinc-
ing linguistic evidence for the name of the banana in South America and
Africa being closely related. Carl Sauer and others have repeatedly noted
that probability of the pre-1500 A.D. presence of the banana in America,
and banana leaves have been found in pre Colombian graves in Peru, but are
seldom mentioned.

I can add to this a set of things that may fall into the same category of
pre-1500 introductions from America into West Africa. The American
Guinea Pig is oddly named. On the Guinea coast one also finds maize called
Guinea Wheat, the American pepper (Capsicum) called Guinea Pepper, the
American Turkey confused with the African Guinea Hen. Add cotton and

one is possibly looking at a whole complex of American plant introductions. Van Sertima suggests that the banana and the Canavalia bean were carried from that area into the Americas. It was Jeffreys contention that it was the Arabs that were responsible for this, and it may be so. But the main point is that the evidence has been very largely ignored. Jeffreys for instance was more often attacked ad hominen than his facts checked. Van Sertima has suffered a bit of this also, and his reaction is evident in his Smithsonian lecture. Some bitterness is justified, for the evidence is there for any unbiased scholar to see.

Van Sertima continues with a chapter on the Egypto-Nubian presences in Ancient Mexico. He opens with a consideration of the Olmec and deals at length with the colossal stone heads. As before, it is obvious to any unbiased observer that they represent negro heads and of course the Von Wuthenau clay sculptures simply reinforce this in extension. Again and again Van Sertima denies that he has ever said that the Olmec were entirely African. Rather he calls for an African influence, and input, and a race mixture that fades with time. In this he could cite classic cases. The Norman invasion into England was traceable for only about three generations in skeletons. Near at home in my part of Texas, Chinese imported to pick cotton, merged with the local Negro population and are no longer discernable. At Zuni in New Mexico Father Garces stated in 1775 that there were two races present, but one cannot see them in the present Zuni population.

Van Sertima devotes considerable space to the relationships of the Phoenicians and the Africans. It was close and based on trade, shared shipping, and so on. Then there is considerable data on ships and trans Atlantic crossings in varied craft. Van Sertima seems too conservative here, for the evidence indicates much more purposeful contact than accidental contacts. The long lists of very specific cultural traits shared with Egypt and the Olmec indicate deep penetration of the Olmec culture. What I miss here is the clear evidence of the presence of Asiatic traits in the Olmec. See Betty Meggers paper on this and the works of Gunnar Thompson. It is not an either/or situation. Rather it would appear that there were two sets of influences, one from across the Atlantic and one from across the Pacific. The pity of this situation is that fossilized opinion in the anthropological world has effectively blocked serious study of the situation. Heine-Geldern, Ekholm, Covarubias, Shao, and Thompson have concentrated on the Pacific and Asiatic contacts. Van Sertima presents the African case. What is needed is a careful sorting out of which is which with denial of neither.

For the epigraphic work it is important that this African background be understood. Fell's work with the Micmac writing, and the Atakapa language, the obvious presence of Egyptian influence in the Anubis Cave, and in the petroglyphs in Utah which depict a soul departure with accompanying

Old World animals, are but straws in the wind indicating that the influences are complex, in time and in space. They have been shamefully neglected.

There is a chapter by Von Wuthenau on Unexpected African Faces in Pre-Columbian America. The visual impact is overwhelming. For this publication Von Wuthenau has emphasized the African portraits in clay. Elsewhere he presents a broader picture with many obvious Asiatic and some Europeans portrayed. Of Von Wuthenau's material one can only comment: There are none so blind as those that will not see.

There is a chapter on evidence from physical anthropology indicating an African presence. This is by Keith Jordan. It reviews the Wiercinski study referred to earlier and also considers some of the criticism, especially that of Comas. An addendum on the evidence for Africans in the United States finds Hooton's material on Pecos unsatisfactory. Unsatisfactory is not necessarily wrong. Mention of the Mound Builders distinguishes between Adena, Hopewell, and Mississippian and warns that there are fakes. Fell's support of the Davenport Tablet is used as an example of unwise support of a fake. One wonders. If the Atakapa speak an Egyptian-influenced language and the Micmac write, using Egyptian hieroglyphs, and if Anubis is portrayed in western Oklahoma, there may be more validity for the Davenport table than the opposition wants to admit.

Joan Covey presents an interesting article on ancient maps. There is clear evidence that someone was making maps of considerable sophistication prior to 1500. Somehow they could measure longitude. This skill was thereafter lost. But for that matter, we do not even know how the portolano maps were constructed. We went from quite good ancient maps to miserable maps and only with the invention of accurate chronometers were we able belatedly to begin to get longitude right. The difficulty with this material is that we do not know who had this knowledge. But it seems clear that whoever they were they had been mapping the New World at some very early time.

Beatrice Lumpkin writes on pyramids. It is interesting and the most important item is the one already mentioned. The Kushite kingdoms revived pyramid building and were building them at a time that overlaps the Olmec pyramids. It is a key point, for the disparity of the dating of the Egyptian pyramids and the Olmec-Mayan ones has always been a sticking point. If there were Africans from the Egypto-Nile kingdoms amongst those that reached America, then there is a logical answer to the time problem. For Olmec it is most significant that there was a whole complex that appeared at that one time and place. Pyramids, astronomical observatories and great stone heads are key elements.

David Muffet pleads for a re-consideration of Leo Wiener's work concerning African influences in America in early times. It is difficult material to use, for Wiener was sometimes wrong, often overly selective, and yet he surveyed an immense amount of material and a thoughtful student could find many interesting avenues of research suggested by Wiener's work. We are not very good at seeking the good, but are much more adept at picking flaws and rejecting the whole.

Harold Lawrence discusses the evidence for Mandingo crossings to the New World. The Mandingo are from the Guinea Coast and, as noted earlier, there are strong suggestions from bio geography of contacts between that coast and America. Lawrence adds much more, including historical descriptions of Blacks in America and linguistic evidence especially concerning gold and its alloys common to Central America and West Africa. Startling evidence is presented of the number of boats amongst the Mandingo. Fleets of 2000 are mentioned. While there has been a tendency to dismiss these as just dugouts, large dugouts with planks added to their edges quickly become ships. Further, the importance of size in Atlantic crossings has been very much overstated.

Then comes a review by Runoko Rashidi of Harold Gladwin and his Men Out of Asia. He followed Hooton in suggesting that the first men into America were small blacks. It is an interesting idea, but one most difficult to document. Currently the 11,000 year, Clovis First barrier has been breached. The earliest Americans may now possibly have to be reckoned as entering on the 100,000 year time level. Calico, in the Mojave desert, uranium date, 200,000 years. Nearby Manix Lake has artifacts in fine silts, 20 feet beneath a volcanic ash layer K/A dated at 185,000 years. Brazilians are now reporting a site with abundant evidence of man with two different laboratories reporting dates of 200,000 to 300,000.

It is factual that China was still populated in the south by diminutive blacks as late as the Chou dynasty and southeast Asia is sprinkled today with populations of small Blacks. It is quite possible that they once lived farther to the north and were in position to enter America very early. Possible is not proof. The further thought though is also interesting. The small Blacks are still present in mixed form in dominant cultures. For instance they are in the south of China, an area long a leading region in shipping, merchant trading and a major source for advanced ideas for northern China. Almost totally overlooked, this is another potential source for Black people reaching America. If the Olmec had both African and Asiatic roots Blacks could have been amongst the bearers of both sets of influence.

However, the Blacks in America can be overdone. Hooton saw traces of most of the races of mankind at Pecos. This seems to me to be nearer to the case. The Norse were certainly here and had much more influence than is usually thought. For instance some suggestions of exchanges include Norse cats to America, the game of lacrosse from Scandinavia to America, the sweat bath either way but more probably to Scandinavia, New England soft shell clams to Denmark, and the North Sea marine snail Litornia to America. The Kensington Rune Stone so long debated is now totally verified, (Hall, Nielsen) and the stones from Spirit Pond in the Casco Bay area of southern Maine are now demonstrated as genuine. The more recently found Narraganset Bay stone is still another valid find. The Heavener, Oklahoma inscription is even more startling for its deep interior location and its seemingly greater age than the other examples.

The Norse at one point mention the presence of Irish settlements to the south of them. The presence of ogamic writing widely in America and some of it specifically Irish and Christian, signals another north European presence. The Bat Creek finds signal the presence of a Hebrew group and their influence was such that a Hebrew ceremony (Succoth) persists into the present as The Green Corn Ceremony of the Euchi who formerly lived in the area. Excellent portraits of Eastern Indians show them as strongly europoid and a reconstruction of Adena skulls, by standard forensic means, develops long nosed, long faced European faces. The gist of this is that the peopling of America was complex. All races were involved.

I have little difficulty then with L.H. Clegg's article on the first Americans. He obviously is not as far out on the dating frontier as I am, but very few are. I do like the notion of Australoids in America and very early, though probably not the first. At the University of California at Berkeley in the early 1930s, graduating seniors had to write comprehensive final exams. On a free choice essay question I wrote on the Australoids in America. I noted that there were physical resemblances, that the La Jollans of Southern California used the spear thrower, the curved throwing stick, had initiation ceremonies for boys, women excluded, warned away by the twirling of a bull roarer, and that there were ground paintings involved, all of which traits are in Australia. I would now add that the artifacts of the La Jollan people are virtually indistinguishable from those of the Kartan culture of Australia. Truly, quite a series to be just coincidence.

The final article is by Wayne Chandler. It concerns trait comparisons. He sees both the Atlantic and the Pacific influences. However, it is, as perhaps it had to be, a very brief review of an immense topic. I miss seeing Covarubias, Heine Geldern, Eckholm, Shao, Thompson, Meggers, not to mention, perhaps, some of my nearly fifty papers on trans oceanic transfers. Nor is Heyerdahl with his huge book, *American Indians in the Pacific*, mentioned. It is a rich source with much on race and culture and voyaging. Nor do I see Tolstoy on bark paper making, and so on. Well, no one can do everything, but this is really quite thin coverage of an immense literature on the Pacific and other contacts. Key papers should include some from *Man Across the Sea*, for instance D. Randall Beirn's study on axe types around the world. Most American Indian axe types have Mediterranean prototypes and one in Peru is specifically Egyptian. Even my paper on pre 1500 A.D. chickens in America might be mentioned. They are largely Asiatic in race, designated at times by Asiatic names, used in Asiatic rituals and now (1993) we have the archeological bones to complete the case. People were carrying chickens across the Pacific. They just may have been carrying guinea pigs and turkeys across the Atlantic. . . .

I was impressed with Van Sertima's comments on the parallel between the nearly recordless American civilizations and the African ones, Egypt excluded. He contrasts this with China and India and the west European countries where there is a long continuous historical record. For Africa and America we have to painfully try to reconstruct history from bits of pottery and ruined cities, from pyramids and projectile points. In America we puzzle over what gave rise to the Adena culture and what became of it. In Africa we face the same problem. Even from my slight knowledge of Africa I am aware that there was an important thrust of civilization down the east side of Africa. What happened to it? West Africa also had important civilizational beginnings that were aborted. When, how, by whom? South Africa recently has made a huge beginning toward civilization, though a flawed one, and now threatens to fly to pieces. Is this the model of the past?

Despite the immense effort in the Americas our knowledge of prehistory is slight and in my view distorted by a chauvinism that attempts to preclude any overseas influence on the Amerind civilization growths. Because of our peculiar history in relation to the Black Africans, we have taken a flawed view of early African influences in America. Nowhere is this more obvious than in the case of the Von Wuthenau clay models of Black Africans and in the (immensely important for cultural understanding) huge Olmec heads. When seemingly sane and sober scholars can look at these and deny the presence of Black Africans, it is obvious that we have problems of huge magnitude.

George F. Carter
Texas A&M University, College Station, TX.
in *Journal of the Epigraphic Society* (1994)

Egypt and the Mountains of the Moon, F.D.P. Whicker, Braunton, Devon: Merlin Books, Ltd., 1990. 83 pp. with 40 illustrations (28 in colour) and 4 maps.

This work proposes the wholesale transfer of Protodynastic culture from Central East Africa to the first cataract by a migration.

The author argues that the earliest dynastic Egyptian culture recorded a ritual requirement for raw materials which are exotic to modern Egypt and Sudan, so engendering the necessity for the journeys to Kush, Yam, and Punt, in later times. If the ancient Egyptians had developed their culture in the Lower Nile Valley, they would have remained ignorant of these commodities. The materials include certain minerals, ivory and parts of at least 22 plants which can be found together in the wild within a small area of the Great Lakes region, at the foot of the Rwenzoris. It is this close geographical association between the items which makes the region a more likely site than Sudan for the evolution of the civilization that we find in Archaic Egypt. In the tradition of Wallis Budge, he then shows how the Book of the Dead can be read as tribal lore, describing navigation on these 'ancestral' lakes. Moreover, he reminds us that this region is archae–ologically interesting, having yielded the Ishango bone

The main argument is similar to that employed by others who used proto-linguistic reconstructions to locate the origin of the Bantu (and the Indo-European) languages and to describe their probable early environment. He shows, therefore, that some wild animals recorded in the hieroglyphic writings and paintings of the ancient Egyptians have been wrongly identified by non-biologists and are actually to be found in the tropics. Notably, images of the god Seth are said to be of a mythological animal, but could have been inspired by the aardvark (African ant-bear).

A fatal omission, however, is Dr. Whicker's failure to refer to the climate of the Sahara and Sudan in Predynastic times when several of his listed tropical plants and animals would have flourished in Sudanic zones where they are now extinct. Instead he perfunctorily states that there were no major climatic changes during dynastic times. This lapse is surprising since he devotes space to the climatic history of the Lakes, showing that tectonic activity has probably forced migrations from that region in the past, as suggested by Arkell. It is perhaps because of this omission that the thesis seems to have received little attention, not even a hostile response, from the Egyptological mainstream.

In a subsidiary argument designed to show that the Ancient Egyptians were Black, Whicker presents evidence that modern East Africans share a number of traditions in common with those of New Kingdom Egypt (boat design, the arched harp, headrests, harpoons, braid hairstyles, circumcision); that Bantu languages share some vocabulary and structural features with Middle Egyptian; and that the long horned cattle of the Old Kingdom resemble those herded in western Uganda today. However, he admits that these could be the result of cultural diffusion up the Nile and from the coast in more recent times. In any case most of these coincidences have been variously addressed by previous authors.

The most intriguing feature of the work is the original treatment of ecology, which is derived from the author's research speciality, and long experience as a settler-farmer in Kenya. While this emphasis is fully in line with the current fashion in archaeology, Whicker shows an unusual genius for lateral thinking about the original uses of objects which later held symbolic value. In his fifth chapter, he demonstrates how heraldic symbols of kingship may have evolved from economically significant activities in the livelihood of early African herdsmen, farmers and fishermen. Thus, falcons may have originally been useful as scarecrows, and so encouraged to alight on poles erected in fields in order to protect seed crops, as apparently illustrated in some *nomic* standards. He derives the Blue Crown, *kprs*, from the carapace of a tortoise, and the Red Crown is convincingly manufactured, in pictorial steps, by folding the hide of a calf. He observes that certain African herdsmen deceive their cows into giving milk by wearing similar turbans of hide to simulate the calf's scent.

In accord with this usage of natural objects, the sun-bleached nests of weaverbirds may have inspired the White Crown, perhaps as a ritual symbol of power over the production of linen, a material which was in use from predynastic Egypt onwards. Flax and the early methods for the production of cloth form the fruitful basis of several further speculations of this type, including a reinterpretation of the function of the Narmer palette.

Finally, the WS sceptre and SHEN ring (cartouche) might represent a type of oar/boat-pole and oar-ring respectively. One figure illustrates how such a WS staff can be cut from the branch-point of a rain forest understory tree. Similar devices are reportedly in use on some *sutured boats* in Europe today! These acute observations and the approach of seeking down-to-earth tropical African parallels for heraldic symbols deserve further attention, whether or not the immediate predecessors of Ta-Seti, Ta Shema and Ta-Meh are to be found at the Source of the Nile.

For me, this work is most important as a record of the range of indigenous technologies practised in regions of Uganda which are not easily accessible today.

Anthony Richards

Blacks in Science: Ancient and Modern, Edited by Ivan van Sertima, *Journal of African Civilizations*, Softcover, 325 p. $20.00

The world of scientific and inventive endeavor has at some point in our lives been both intriguing and astounding, which is as it should be, because the discoveries and creations of man are the basis of our civil and technological understanding. The source of much of the scientific information available to us is in the form of books. In these books we read about the glory and greatness of past civilizations based, in part, on their scientific achievements. Therefore, it is essential that we all have some understanding of science so we can more effectively relate to our environment and most importantly ourselves. It is also just as important to keep in mind that many science books were written from an outdated European and American point of view. A point of view that has tainted scientific history every since race, as a negative stigma, has been introduced into writing. The fact that racism is imbedded in writing should not come as a surprise. All literate people have a tendency to promote the achievements of their culture and collective racial grouping through literature. It is when that promotion grows out of hand due to intentional omissions, inaccuracies and far fetched assumptions that a problem begins. This problem is: miseducation and cultural ignorance.

There is, however, a change taking place which will eventually rid some future scientific publications of the inaccuracies and omissions, which have been all too common, in historical scientific evolution. Within the past few years more and more books are appearing which state the facts of scientific evolution based solely on concrete data without the burden of racial, political, or self serving limitations. For years far reaching and even ridiculous explanations of invention and discovery have been published in direct contradiction to known facts and findings. Often authors claimed ignorance of information which convincingly challenged their assumptions. Impudent approaches included unrealistic assessments of facts and adherence to the tunnel vision concepts of past times. We are finding that much of what was postulated as fact was in reality the invention of some overactive imaginations and conjecture based on insufficient and/or fraudulent information. In short, many of the inventions/discoveries which did occur do not coincide with the historical who, what, and where of these scientific milestones. As a more detailed analysis of ancient artifacts becomes more wide spread much of what has not been put forth on strong scientific ground will crumble, giving way to new insight toward current knowledge and better understanding. *Blacks in Science:* examines new and old facts with a critical eye toward the reevaluation of the evolution of science.

This book is a collage of Afro-American and African achievement. Multiple fields of science are covered in an approach which is both interesting and informative. It addresses the missing chapters of books on invention and scientific progress. I call these chapters missing because with the exception of a very few Afro-American inventors, thousands of other talented Black men and women are rarely written about. This book assigns responsibility and proper credit to the Black inventors and co-inventors of important scientific discoveries. In addition Blacks in Science does what no other book on invention/science has previously done—it examines technology prior to the Egyptian dynasties and clearly shows that the foundation of the vast Egyptian technological era was built on African sciences which developed outside Egypt.

Anthropological evidence has shown that advances in engineering, mathematics, navigation, physics and other fields of science occurred in purely African societies long before it was previously believed possible. The discovery of steel-smelting ovens in Tanzania from 1,500 to 2,000 years ago, an observatory in Kenya dated to 300 years before Christ, cereal cultivation in the Nile Valley preceding all other civilizations, the use of fire for domestic purposes 1,400,000 years ago (Kenya) the use of tetracyclene 14 centuries ago (Nubia) and a 2,300 year old African glider have all contributed to a new and awe-inspiring review of ancient African achievement. In short, man's achievement has been shown to have a much broader base than is usually taught in our school systems.

Blacks in Science also brings us 77 pages of Black involvement in technological advancements during modern times. By 1913 alone, as many as 1000 inventions by Blacks were patented. Consider what this number could have been had ideal social and economic conditions existed for Blacks. One of the causes for so few patents being held by Blacks was that in 1858 the U.S. Attorney General ruled that slaves could not have a contract with the United States Government due to their lack of citizenship. This ruling alone limited the ability of most Blacks to acquire patents. It did not, however, stop the flow of Black creative thought. It merely added another obstacle to be overcome in obtaining recognition and financial reward for inventive expression.

The following are examples of the creative genius of Blacks Ancient and Modern: (a.) Between 1,500 to 2,000 years ago Africans produced carbon steel. The temperatures achieved in their steel-smelters reached approximately 1,800 degree centigrade. This figure is 200 to 400 degrees higher than the highest temperature reached in European cold blast bloomeries during the early days of steel production. The importance of this discovery lies in the time frame in which it was done—hundreds of years prior to steel production anywhere in the world Africans were making carbon steel for utensils, ornaments, and weapons. Anthropology Professor, Peter Schmidt and Professor of Engineering, Donald Avery, both of Brown University, informed the world of this information, with proofs, in 1978. (b.) Scientists M. Lynch and L. H. Robbins of Michigan State uncovered an astronomical observatory in Kenya on the edge of Lake Turkana. From this observatory an accurate calendar system was developed by the first millennium B.C. (c.) Great Zimbabwe is a large stone city in Zimbabwe. It is 800 plus years old. The engineering of this city was an enormous and complex feat. Yet when this great stone city was found Europeans who wrote books about it have been trying to prove that this architectural site, which is right in the heartland of Africa, 500 miles away from the sea coast, was built by Persians, Phoenicians, Portuguese, Arabs, or Chinese. The fact that there are no prototypes for Zimbabwean architecture and art among any of these foreign peoples does not seem to bother these historians. (d.) Bantu-speaking peoples use the bark of salix capensis to treat musculoskeletal pains. This family of plants yields salicylic acid, the active ingredient in aspirin. In Mali, kaolin is used to cure diarrhea, the active ingredient in Kaopectate. A traditional Nigerian doctor used Rauwolfia root to treat severe psychotic episodes in a patient. The plant contains reserpine which was first used as a major tranquilizer. In Liberia a smallpox vaccine was developed centuries before Jenner using the same principle developed vaccines in Europe. (e.) Robert E. Shurney as a scientific engineer designed space laboratories for skylab as well as eating utensils for space vehicles. James West, an experimental physicist, co-invented foil electrets (the electrical equivalent to a permanent magnet). Thomas Cannon Jr. wrote mathematical equations that described the mechanical response of a cable when pulled, bent, or subjected to other physical forces. Earl Shaw co-invented a laser important in demonstrating optical energy can be tuned within wave lengths and Dr. Lloyd Quarterman, a nuclear scientist, performed work essential to the production of the Atomic Bomb. He also initiated work on "synthetic blood" in 1967.

Detailed information can be found on each topic mentioned and more in—*Blacks in Science*. This book was edited by Ivan Van Sertima and is the collective work of the many authors. Some of them are: Hunter H. Adams III, Fred Wendorf, Angela E. Close, Bayard Webster, Charles Finch, Claudia Zaslavsky, Debra Shore, Stewart C. Malloy, Robert Hayden, Kirstie Gentleman, and James G. Spady. It is hoped that our readers will become familiar with the names and contributions of each of the authors mentioned as well as the others who contributed to *Blacks in Science*. They have all made significant gains in amassing a more complete picture of scientific evolution. Each article is extremely well written. The authors have gone to great pains to present evidence which speaks for itself and one can ask for little more than that. The photographs and illustrations used in this book act as a guide to further strengthen the reader's understanding of the material presented.

J.W. Gunn, Jr.

SKULL IN ETHIOPIA LINKED TO EARLIEST MAN

Ivan Van Sertima

This note is based on a front-page article in the *New York Times* by John Noble Wilford published on March 31, 1994. It is highly condensed. For more detailed information, readers are advised to secure a complete copy from the New York Times since we have not been granted permission to use any of the two maps nor the photograph of what is probably the first complete human skull that has survived intact from the dawn of upright humans to our own time.

The first complete skull of our earliest human ancestors has been found near the bank of a dry riverbed in Ethiopia. It is that of a large male who lived at least three million years ago. He is a contemporary of the famous "Lucy" skeleton found by Dr. Donald Johannson but, whereas Lucy was reconstructed by Dr. Johannson and colleagues from a wide assortment of pieces, this was almost complete and gave a face at last to the parent of the human species.

The discovery could settle the great debate over whether man belongs to a single species, whether the fossils of man dating from between 3.9 and 3 million years really belong to one type, known as Australopithecus afarensis. This is the most decisive find in a long debate between those who claim all humans are mutations from a single African ancestor and those who insist that the African, the European and the Asian could not possibly be so intimately related as to consider themselves members of the same specie.

The Journal *Nature,* published on the same day as the New York Times article, said that this skull confirmed "the taxonomic unity of Australopithecus afarensis". That is, to put it in layman terms, the find establishes the existence of one specie and not two, as some paleontologists have contended. Drs. Donald Johannson, William Kimbel, and Yoel Rak described the skull not only as the youngest and largest but also the only relatively intact one of the afarensis species, which lived in the region from Ethiopia in the north to Tanzania in the south. In a place called Laetoli in Tanzania, they have found the footprints of two upright humans, an adult and a child taking a walk three and a half million years ago.

A paleontologist at University College, London, Dr. Leslie C. Aiello, said that the skull and other recent findings should "go a long way to settle some of the most heated controversies surrounding the earliest species in the human lineage . . . it would now take compelling evidence to start the pendulum of opinion swinging back toward the idea that there were several species".

Figure 1. Ivan Van Sertima and Donald Johannson discussing the origin of man, on the grounds of the University of Texas at Austin in February 1988.

Research News and Notes — 2

ON THE NAMING OF CONTINENTS

Ivan Van Sertima

Mr. Abdul Khaliq,
New Orleans, Louisiana.
                                                            Nov. 24, 1993
Dear Mr. Abdul Khaliq,

You had written to inquire about the true name for the continent of Africa since there was a dispute among the brothers about the various names suggested. Let me say, quite emphatically, that no people ever named their continent. Before the era of continental travel, the advent of the steamship or the aeroplane, it was impossible for human beings to see immeasurable land spaces (which they could neither traverse on the ground or inspect from the air) as one unbroken territory. And so all sorts of names sprang up for *parts of continents* and some of these names, although intended for other purposes, were eventually accepted as names for vast land spaces. America could not be seen as a unified landspace by human ants crawling over its vastnesses in a trek of several centuries from one end of the planet (the North Pole) to the other end (the South Pole). It was much later, much much later that man began to see it as North America and South America. The Panama Canal, as you know, is a later artificial separator. Most people believe that America was named after *Amerigo* Vespucci and that is probably the origin of the word as a place name. But, as I say, no people named their continent. Some people believe Europe was named after an Ethiopian princess, *Europa*, but I am not sure of that nor is anyone. Asia was certainly not named by itself because it would be impossible in early times for anyone to see Asia as an integral or unbroken landmass occupied by a specific racial milieux.

Strangely enough, in spite of its later partitioning and dismemberment, Africa is probably the only continent that has a name that was thrown up by itself. The name, however, did not grow out of a desire to name a continent because man could not think in those terms when names like these arose (Imagine an ant, confined from birth to death to the limb of a tree, trying to conceptualise the dimensions of the entire forest in which the tree grows). Early man could only envision parts of continents. The early Egyptians, according to Gerald Massey, used the sound or word *Af-rui-ka* to signify "beginnings". It could also mean, by inference, "land of beginnings". The Romans, like the Persians and Assyrians before them, conquered the Egyptians and may have picked up that word or those sounds. Thus in the Roman language—Latin—we have the word *Af-ri-ka*. We also have the adjective *Afer*, meaning Black. It was in all likelihood influenced by the Egyptian with whom they were in contact for centuries. The Arabs later conquered Roman-controlled Egypt and they later used the word *If-fri-quia* to encompass a great part of Africa. Some people make a distinction between the spelling *Afrika* and *Africa*, believing that Afrika is more correct and more African. It is not. The symbol *k* is not African. Neither is *c*. Nor are they English. English has no alphabet it can call its own. These are Roman symbols—both the *c* and the *k*. We have found as many as half a dozen writing systems originated in Africa before the European invasions but, because of the long colonisation, only one or two of them are still in use. So, let me repeat, for those who are making a fuss now about the spelling of *Africa/ Afrika* and *African/Afrikan*—both *c* and *k* are Roman. *C* is usually soft in English, as in the words *acid* and *ascend,* but it is also as hard as *k* as in *acrid* and *acoustic*. *K* and *c* therefore are easily interchangeable. Neither of them are African symbols. Since a great deal of Africa came under English and French influence, the Africans now use the Roman alphabet, which almost all peoples of the world now use, including those Europeans whom the Romans conquered and who, before the Romans, had no alphabet— ancient illiterates like the English, the French, the Germans and the Spanish, to mention just a few.

One last word. I spoke of man as an ant in earlier times, crawling across vast spaces of land which he could not then conceptualise as a discrete mass. But even now, when we have space ships and can study the planet as one mass, we still have not come up with a common name for this planet. "Earth" is not a name. It is just a vague term for a mass of matter and, just as many peoples of Africa (or Europe or Asia or America) could not come up with one name for a vast continent, so the human family has no agreed name as yet for the global house it shares.

Research News and Notes — 3

AFRICAN SMALLPOX INOCULATION INTRODUCED INTO EARLY EIGHTEENTH-CENTURY AMERICA

Ivan Van Sertima

The Boston Gazette of May 1, 1721, reported the widespread outbreak of smallpox in the Boston area. The epidemic produced 5,889 known cases of the contagious disease and 844 deaths in just a few months. A Boston doctor, Dr. Zabdiel Boylston of Boston began experimenting with a new method of African origin to prevent the disease. His experiments came about as a result of prompting by Rev. Cotton Mather who learned of the method of developing a resistance to smallpox by inoculation from his African slave Onesimus.

The slave described to Mather how Africans would develop immunities to smallpox after having been deliberately infected with a dose of the disease. At Mather's urging, Dr. Boylston consulted the slave for the details of the method. The doctor then inoculated his own son and two slaves. This was so successful that, as the epidemic continued, he inoculated 240 more people. All but six of those who underwent the treatment survived. Rev. Mather began to preach from his pulpit about his slave's vaccine, urging the widespread use of it. But many were left to die, for his appeal was largely ignored.

Research News and Notes — 4

AFRICAN-AMERICAN SCIENTISTS PLAYED MAJOR ROLE IN ATOMIC BOMB DEVELOPMENT

Ivan Van Sertima

In the fall of 1979, while lecturing in Chicago, I was introduced to the African-American nuclear scientist, Dr. Lloyd Quarterman. Dr. Quarterman had been awarded a certificate of appreciation by the U.S. Secretary of War for "work essential to the production of the Atomic Bomb, thereby contributing to the successful conclusion of World War II". During that interview, fragments of which were published in the 1983 journal *Blacks in Science,* Dr. Quarterman stated "there were six of us".

There were far more than six actually but he probably referred to the secret circle of six African-American scientists that he personally knew and worked with on his end of the project. The names of some of these gentlemen, therefore, *may* still be unknown to us. However, the Pittsburgh Courier of August 18, 1945, revealed the name of more than a dozen of them. Since this clipping does not mention two of the colleagues Dr. Quarterman named in confidence we are at a loss as to whether some of them were deliberately omitted from the publication at that time because of America's fears that the Russians or other communist governments would bribe, kidnap, or lure them, thereby gaining the advantage that the Rosenbergs, as well as Britain's Burgess and McLean, seem to have given them after the war.

The Pittsburgh Courier, however, names the following: (1) Dr. William J. Knox of New York City, a prominent chemist who played a significant part at Columbia University in conquering the atom secret. (2) one of the chief aides of Dr. Knox, Sidney Thompson, born in Ann Arbor, Michigan, but taken by his parents to Toronto at an early age. He secured an A.B. and M.A. in chemistry from the University of Toronto and worked in industrial and mining engineering in northern Ontario, and done geological surveys for the Canadian government. He returned to the United States in 1939 and taught at Samuel Houston College. He later inspected explosives for the War Department and was assistant to the manager of a war production plant. (3) Another of Dr. Knox's associates on the Manhattan Project was George W. Reed, a Howard University graduate with a A.M. and M.A. degree in chemistry. (4) Dr. Lloyd Quarterman, (for details, see my interview in Vol.

From "Dr. Lloyd Quarterman—Nuclear Scientist" by Ivan Van Sertima (*Blacks in Science*, 1983).

5 of the JAC, now in its 11th printing). (5) Clarence Turner, who did graduate work at Columbia University before going on to work on the riddle of the atom. (6) Dr. Moddie Taylor, who received his B.S. degree, majoring in chemistry, from Lincoln University in Jefferson, Missouri and his Masters and doctorate in chemistry at the University of Chicago.

(7) Robert J. Omohundro, a native of Norfolk, Virginia, a mathematics and physics major at Howard University, and former radio tester for Western Electric. (8) Sherman Carter, a Lincoln University (Pennsylvania) graduate with a major in biology and chemistry. (9) Jasper Jeffries, a graduate of West Virginia State College, with a Masters degree from the University of Chicago, where he taught electronics before entering into the work on the atomic bomb. He also taught chemistry at Winston-Salem, North Carolina and Gary, Indiana. (10) Benjamin Scott, a graduate of Morehouse College, Atlanta, where he majored in chemistry. While doing his Masters degree at the University of Chicago, he became associated with the bomb project. (11) Dr. Ernest J. Wilkins, a major figure like Drs. Knox and Quarterman, but missing paragraphs from the 1945 document sent to me contained the only details I could find on him. Others mentioned, as having lent support to the scientific phase of the project, are *Ralph Gardner* and *Clyde Dillard* of New York and *Harold Evans* of Chicago. Their educational background and area of specialization is omitted.

I would like to thank Joan Gordon, Professor Emeritus of Savannah State College, for providing me with information for this research note. She is the mother of Robert A. Gordon, an astrodynamicist at Goddard Flight Space Center, who developed the equations used to locate maximum and minimum earth reference points in the orbit of satellites. His discovery streamlined the process of predicting the orbit of satellites.

Research News and Notes — 5

WORLD'S OLDEST PAVED ROAD FOUND IN EGYPT

Ivan Van Sertima

This information is taken from the New York Times of May 8, 1994. Once again, it is condensed from a report by the distinguished science writer, John Noble Wilford. Readers are advised to consult the records of the New York Times for more detailed information and for a copy of the map showing the course of the road from the quarry to the quay.

* * *

The demand for building stones for pyramids and temples led to the opening of many quarries in the low cliffs near the Nile. To make it easier to transport these heavy stones from one of the quarries, the Egyptians built what is probably the world's first paved road.

Geologists have found a seven and a half mile stretch of road covered with slabs of sandstone and limestone. They have also found logs of petrified wood. The pavement was probably made to help move sleds loaded with basalt stone from a nearby quarry to a quay so that it could be shipped by barge across the lake and on the Nile to places where pyramids and temples were being built.

Dr. Harrell (professor of Geology at the University of Toledo, Ohio) and Dr. Thomas Bown (research geologist at the U.S. Geological Survey in Denver) mapped the road last year. The site was dated by pottery fragments to between 4,600 and 4,200 years ago. The oldest road ever found before this, was in Crete and that was at least 200 years later than the latest date for this and more likely 600 years later, roughly half a millennium.

The road was on average six and a half feet wide and ran across the desert about 45 miles from modern Cairo. It ran from a quarry of dark volcanic stone to the northwest shore of an ancient lake—Lake Moeris—which is no longer in existence. The two geologists said that there were no deep grooves or other marks on this stone road, which suggested that wooden logs were laid over the stone surface of the road when the great blocks of basalt were moved.

This ancient Egyptian road was actually found in the early years of this century but its significance and extent were not recognized until Drs. Harrell and Bown came across a large basalt quarry at one end of the road.

Research News and Notes — 6

ROYAL SHIPS OF THE PHARAOHS

Runoko Rashidi

Ships have occupied an important place in the society and art of Nile Valley civilizations from a remote period. From the Kingdom of Ta-Seti (ca. 3800–3100 B.C.E.), Bruce Williams of the University of Chicago's Oriental Institute, in 1980, reported that the surface of an incense burner from the Nubian A-Group royal burial ground at Qustul's Cemetery L, Tomb 24, is incised with a "procession of three ships with their tall sterns and bent prows going toward a palace facade."[1] Plastered mud-brick pits in the form of ships have been found near the Dynasty I royal tombs in Lower Kmt at Sakkara, including the tombs of King Aha and Queen Mer-neit (who may have been Dynastic Kmt's first female monarch), and the Dynasty I and Dynasty II tombs across the Nile at Helwan as well.

From the Old Kingdom, Kmt's First Golden Age, the British Museum has a red granite, seated statute of Bedjmes a noted African ship-builder of early Dynasty III—holding an adze over his shoulder. Around 2600 B.C.E., King Nae-maet Sneferu of Dynasty IV sent a fleet of forty ships to the Phoenician city of Byblos on the eastern Mediterranean seaboard to obtain cedar and other valuable woods. Forty vessels returned to Kmt with enough logs to construct three 170-foot-long ships and a number of barges. In Dynasty V, King Sahure (ca. 2485 B.C.E.) launched the first known sea expedition to the sacred African land of Punt ("God's Land"), believed to be located along the coast of Somalia. The fleet returned from Punt with 80,000 measures of myrrh, 6,000 units of electrum, 2,600 units of wood, and 23,020 measures of unguent.

Several large boat-pits have been identified from Dynasty IV at ancient Khem (modern Giza) and Abu Rawash during the successive reigns of Khufu (Cheops), Dedefre, and Khafre (Chephren). Three other boat-pits lie besides the tombs of queens at Giza. In the 1950s, two enormous pits dug into the rock and covered with huge limestone slabs, each weighing eighteen tons and measuring five to six feet, joined with thick mortar, were discovered along the southern side of the Great Pyramid of Khufu (ca. 2575 B.C.E.) at Giza. In one of the pits was a partially disassembled cedar ship, complete with oars, rudders, and cabin. Its detection was called the most significant event in Egyptian archaeology since the revelation of the intact tomb of King Nebkheprure Tutankhamen of Dynasty XVIII in the 1920s. A second ship has been located in the other boat-pit besides Khufu's pyramid, but has not been excavated.[2]

The first of Khufu's ships was restored during a process that encompassed ten years. The restored ship, which consisted of 1,224 pieces of wood which had been partly dismantled and stacked in thirteen successive layers in the pit, measured 142 feet in length, more than sixteen feet in width, with a capacity of about forty tons. The ship was built without any nails; the pieces of wood are held together solely by the use of tenon and mortise joint. It was identified as the world's oldest intact ship, and has been described as "a masterpiece of woodcraft" that could sail today if put into water. Whether these vessels served as part of a pharaoh's royal fleet in the afterlife, or were utilized in a more practical manner, such as ships of state used for transporting the remains of King Khufu, is the source of much controversy.

In 1894, French engineer, geologist, and archaeologist Jacques Jean Marie De Morgan (1857–1924), Director of the Service of Antiquities; while excavating the pyramid complex of the powerful Dynasty XII King Khakaure Senusret III (ca. 1860 B.C.E.) at Dahshur, uncovered three well-preserved cedar ships, each about thirty-two feet long. The Cairo Museum has two of the ships. The Chicago Natural History Museum has the other. Three additional ships from the same complex were subsequently found. With these ships was a large wooden sledge, which had been used to transport them from the water to their burial place.

The Abydos Fleet

Until 1991, only the pyramid complexes of King Khufu of Dynasty IV and King Khakaure Senusret III of Dynasty XII had yielded large intact ships. During September and October of the fall 1991 field-season, however, a team of archaeologists from the University Museum, the University of Pennsylvania, excavating in the desert near the ancient and holy Kemetic city of Aabdju (modern Abydos), 280 miles south of Cairo in Upper Kmt, made a sensational new discovery—an entire royal fleet of at least twelve large wooden ships, each fifty to sixty feet long, buried in the sand eight miles from the Nile River, near the site of the Shunet Ez-Zebib.

Dating from the early third millennium B.C.E., the Shunet Ez-Zebib is a monumental, enclosed, mud-brick funerary structure principally associated with King Khasekhemui, the last sovereign of Kemetic Dynasty II. Each of the Abydos ships had been individually encased in mud-brick graves that follow the contours of the wooden hulls. These boat-graves, which rose a few feet above ground-level in antiquity, measure between 78 and 95 feet in length, and lie side by side in a row that extends more than 185 feet. After

the wooden ships were situated within the mud-brick graves, offering pottery was placed inside the vessels. The remaining space inside and around
each wooden ship was then filled solid with mud brick, in most cases and
sand in others, and the top and sides of each grave was coated with mud
plaster and whitewashed, so that the vessel inside was completely encased
by the huge boat-shaped brick structure. Where sections of the mud-brick
casings have eroded, numerous ceramic offerings can be seen around the
hulls, which appear to be strong and seaworthy.

According to David O' Connor, curator of the Egyptian section of the
University Museum, and field director of the Abydos excavations:

> The final effect must have been quite extraordinary. Each grave had
> originally been thickly coated with mud plaster and whitewash, so the
> impression would have been of twelve (or more) huge white 'boats'
> moored out in the desert, gleaming brilliantly in the Egyptian sun.[3]

A multi-disciplinary team consisting of archaeologists, experts in ancient
ship construction, and conservators are coordinating the excavation of at
least two of the twelve vessels.

Notes

1. Bruce Williams, "The Lost Pharaohs of Nubia," *Archaeology* 33, No. 5
(1980), 17–18. In a more recent report, Williams reaffirmed that "The persons
buried in the great tombs of Cemetery L at Qustul were pharaohs." Bruce Williams,
The A-Group Royal Cemetery at Qustul: Cemetery L (Chicago: Oriental Institute of
the University of Chicago, 1986), 163. See also Bruce Williams, *Nubia: Its Glory
and Its People* (Chicago: Oriental Institute of the University of Chicago, 1987), 4.
2. Farouk El-Baz, "Finding a Pharaoh's Funeral Bark," *National Geographic*
(Apr 1988), 514–33.
3. David O' Connor, "Boat Graves and Pyramid Origins," *Expedition* 33, No. 3
(1991), 11.

Royal Ships of the Pharaohs: A Selected Bibliography

"5,000-Year-Old Ships Found in Egypt." *Los Angeles Times*, 21 Dec 1991: A10.
"Ancient Fleet Discovered in Abydos Desert." *KMT* 3, No. 1 (1992): 48–49.
"Egyptian Fleet Found." *Archaeology* (Sep/Oct 1992): 24.
El-Baz, Farouk. "Finding a Pharaoh's Funeral Bark," *National Geographic* (Apr
    1988), 514–33.
Jenkins, Nancy. *The Boat Beneath the Pyramid: King Cheop's Royal Ship*. New
    York: Holt, Rhinehart & Winston, 1980.
Mann, Mimi. "Egyptian Ghost Fleet Found; Entombed for 5,000 years." *Birming-
    ham News*, 21 Dec 1991: 3A.
Mann, Mimi. "Boats in Desert May Help Solve Pyramids Mystery." *Birmingham
    News*, 22 Jan 1992: 3A.

Miller, Peter. "Riddle of the Pyramid Boats." *National Geographic* (Apr 1988): 534–50.

O' Connor, David. "Boat Graves and Pyramid Origins," *Expedition* 33, No. 3 (1991): 5–17.

Revkin, Andrew C. "Heirlooms and Old Air: A Sealed Egyptian Crypt Tantalizes Scholars in Several Fields." *Science Digest* (Feb 1986): 24.

Figure 1. King Khufu's Royal Ship.

Research News and Notes — 7

THE INFANT MUMMY OF UAN MUHUGGIAG

Michael J. Carter

3150 Laurel Canyon Blvd.
Studio City, California 91604-4215
March 8th, 1991

Dear Professor Van Sertima,

It was a pleasure to attend your lecture at California State University, Los Angeles on the evening of February 1st, 1991. During our brief conversation, I mentioned a reference which appears to considerably extend the date of the Fezzan Mummy you cited in your lecture.

The reference to the mummy is contained in Aidan and Eve Cockburn's (editors) of *Mummies, Disease* and *Ancient Cultures* (1980) Cambridge CB2 1RP: Cambridge University Press, which on page 224 discusses the infant Mummy of Uan Muhuggiag. The Infant Mummy was so-named because it was unearthed from beneath the Uan Muhuggiag (figs: 13.1, 13.2) natural rock shelter located in the Tagzelt Valley. This Mummy, I assume, is the same or co-temporal with the one referenced in your volume.

The Infant Mummy of Uan Muhuggiag was spontaneously preserved, flexed, eviscerated and insulated with vegetable fibers within an animal skin. The Infant's gender was indeterminable because of the disintegration of the soft tissue; although its age is estimated to have been thirty months. A personal and/or status symbol may be inferred from the necklace fashioned from ostrich shells around the Infant's neck.

There were associative artifacts located in the western portion of the cave site which included fragments of animal bones and bone tools. Indicative of other cave shelters in the region the walls and ceilings contained over one-hundred rock paintings of religious iconography. The nature and profusion of the iconography within the shelter intimates that it was known and frequented.

Professor Mori's carbon[14] date of the Infant Mummy was 3,500 B.C. However, Professor E. Tongiorgi of the University of Pisa's carbon[14] assays extended the age of the Mummy. His bracketed chronologies were deduced from two sampling venues: the lowest coal level of the entombment and the animal skin envelope. The coal layer was dated at 7,438 (+–220) B.C. and the envelope of the animal skin was dated 5,405 (+–180) B.C.

In summary, and in addition to your commentary, the Infant Mummy of Uan Muhuggiag is significant because it is evidence of an advanced culture. The mummy was probably prepared in accordance with established religious and medical traditions that would antedate Professor E. Tongiorgi's chronologies.

Sincerely,
M. J. Carter

Figure 1. The shelter of Uan Muhuggiag. (Courtesy of F. Mori)

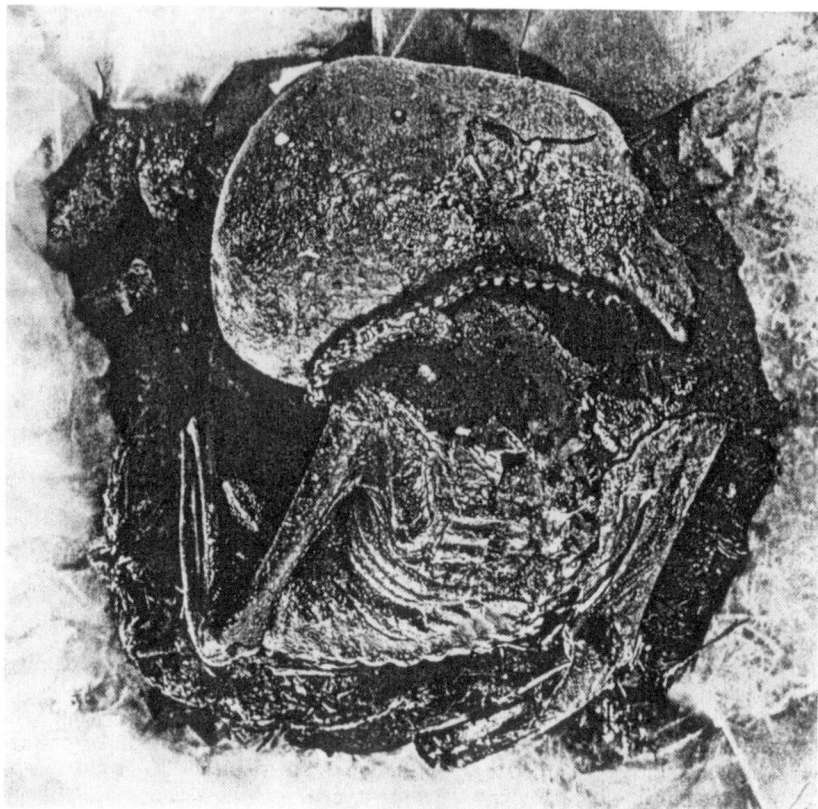

Figure 2. The infant mummy of Uan Muhuggiag. (Courtesy of F. Mori)

Research News and Notes — 8

REDATING THE SPHINX

Manu Ampin

Mainstream Egyptologists have attributed the carving of the Great Sphinx of Giza to the Old Kingdom Pharaoh Khafre, ca. 2500 B.C.E. However, this attribution is based on several pieces of purely circumstantial evidence and unproved assumptions. Four of their most basic assumptions include: (1) the alleged resemblance between the face of a preserved statue of Khafre in the Cairo Museum and the face of the Sphinx. Only dogmatic Egyptologists continue to ignore the facial details of the two statues and assert that they resemble; (2) an ambiguous (now effaced) inscription on a New Kingdom stele of Thutmosis IV (ca. 1400 B.C.E.) which makes a vague reference to Khafre; (3) the physical proximity of the Sphinx to Khafre's pyramid; and (4) a statue of Khafre found in the nearby Valley Temple. However, all of this evidence is superficial and none proves that the Sphinx was carved by Khafre. Several decades ago Selim Hassan in his work, *The Sphinx: Its History in the Light of Recent Excavations* (1949), correctly stated that, "As to the exact age of the Sphinx, and to whom we should attribute its erection, no definite facts are known, and we have not one single contemporary inscription to enlighten us upon this point" (p. 75).

John Anthony West in *Serpent in the Sky: The High Wisdom of Ancient Egypt* (1979), based on a clue from R.A. Schwaller de Lubicz, first presented the hypothesis that the limestone body of the Sphinx and the surrounding enclosure wall are not weathered by wind and sand but *by precipitation*. If true, this would indicate that the Sphinx was carved prior to the last period of major precipitation in the Giza region, which was thousands of years before the conservative Old Kingdom date of 2,500 B.C.E. and thousands of years before the beginning of the Egyptian state. West has been able to advance his thesis in recent years with the assistance of Boston University geologist Robert M. Schoch. Schoch argues for a greater antiquity of the Sphinx on the basis of geological, seismological, Egyptological, and related evidence. He estimates that the Sphinx was originally carved approximately 7,000–5,000 B.C.E., more than twice the age of the accepted Old Kingdom date. (It should be noted, however, that J.A. West believes the carving date to be far older, perhaps 15,000 B.C.E.).

Schoch presented his Sphinx hypothesis at the recent annual conference of the American Research Center in Egypt (ARCE) in Toronto, Canada. The reaction was mixed. Some participants found Schoch's data to be persuasive while others, predictably, found his hypothesis totally implausible.

A geologist from the University of Toledo observing Schoch's ARCE presentation argued during the question and answer period that the Sphinx was buried with sand for most of its existence and that there is good reason to believe that this sand has been wet for most of the time. He further argued that this wet sand was responsible for the Sphinx's accelerating weathering, and he assumed that Schoch had not considered this counter argument. However, the Toledo geologist seems not to be familiar with (although his argument is similar to) the work of K.L. Gauri, G.C. Holdren and W.C. Vaughan, ["Cleaning Efflorescences from Masonry," in J.R. Clifton, ed., *Cleaning Stone and Masonry*, (1986), pp. 3–13] nor of Schoch's response to their conclusions. Specifically, K.L. Gauri, et al. argue that the deterioration on the Sphinx and the enclosure wall are due to the limestone rock being in contact with the wet sand which dried and formed salt crystals that caused the weathering of the stones.

At the ARCE conference, Schoch responded to this counter argument and reiterated his conclusions (presented in previous articles) that the different layers of rock on the Sphinx have different levels of erosion, and that generally, although the upper layers of the rock are harder and more durable, *they are more eroded and recede further back than the less eroded bottom layers.* Yet, these are the opposite results of what one would expect if the salt crystal argument were true. If salt crystals formed from an underground water table was the main cause of the weathering (as the Toledo geologist and Gauri, et al. argue) one would logically expect (1) the bottom layers of the Sphinx (exposed to the wet sand and salt crystals much longer) to be more eroded than the upper layers and (2) the other Old Kingdom tombs and structures (made of the same limestone as the Sphinx) in the Giza plateau to exhibit a similar weathering pattern to that of the Sphinx. Unfortunately for the geologist and others at the conference who totally rejected Schoch's thesis, neither of these results have occurred. These facts strengthen the argument that the weathering of the Great Sphinx indicates that this structure was probably carved during a very earlier period prior to the time that there was major precipitation in the Giza region.

Research News and Notes — 9

"THE" SCIENTIFIC METHOD:
FROM KEMET TO GREECE

Technical terms of Egyptian mathematics dealing with the formal divisions of a problem. This method (*tp*) served as example to Greek mathematicians.
(circa 1,500–2,000, B.C.E.)

Technical terms of Greek mathematics the formal divisions of a proposition, of a problem: the Greek *logos* needs such procedure.
(circa 300–600, B.C.E.)

(I)	tp n irt / tp n hsb	the **enunciation** — it is the question of a problem, of a calculation	Πρότασις (I)
(II)	1st grt	the **setting-out** — the position of a problem	ἔκθεσις (II)
(III)	mi dd n.k	with the **definition** or **specification**	διορισμός (III)
(IV)	irt mi hpr	the **construction** — the exact procedure with the result (hpr.hr)	κατασκευή (IV)
(V)	smt	the **proof**	ἀπόδειξις (V)
(VI)	n3 pw, na pou / gm.k nfr	the **conclusion**	συμπέρασμα (VI)

(Source: Amhose (Rhind) and "Moscow" Papyri)

Nowadays, the scientific mind deals with *analysis* and *synthesis*.

The Greek *logos* is in fact the power with which every question is handled.

Obenga, Theophile. PhD. Egyptologist, Linguist, Philosopher, Historian. (1993). Morehouse College Lecture.

CORRESPONDENCE

February, 1993

Professor Frank J. Frost
University of California at Santa Barbara
Goleta, California

Dear Sir:
We have elected to direct this missive to you rather than Peter Young, the editor of *Archaeology*, because he made his general posture known on the critical debates surrounding the re-interpretation of ancient history in his editorial in the November/December 1992 issue. For him, "the book"—and indeed his mind—is not only closed but locked.

Having said that, your article in the current issue of *Archaeology* seems to be an exercise of setting up straw men to knock down. What is more, your argument loses a lot of steam by its apparent "split-personality:" the reader is wrenched precipitously from an anti-diffusionist essay on ancient sea-faring to the Americas to a rather tangential discussion of Francis Drake's California landing. I do not understand how anything done by Francis Drake disproves pre-Columbian sea voyages to America from various parts of the Old World.

One tends to find over the long-term in scholarly matters that the truth of history represents a balancing of forces. Thus every great culture can be shown to arise from some combination of external influences plus its own native capacity for invention. Moreover, cultural traits and/or techniques diffusing in from outside almost never retain exactly their original form or character. Citing but one of scores of examples, one need only look at what happened to the massive inflows of Chinese cultural traits to Japan. Among that island people, Chinese culture became "Nipponized" and therefore completely distinctive. There is probably no recognizable culture in history that in some way has not absorbed influences from outside itself; it is difficult, in fact, to ascertain how *any* culture can rise to a high level of complexity without some external stimulus or influence. Distances, whether by land or by sea, were no bar to ancient movements of culture. After all, all human populations are descendants of ancestors that diffused out of Africa 50–100 millennia ago and, no later than 40,000 years ago, they arrived in New Guinea and Australia, accessible *only* by the sea route.

There are numerous problems raised by your essay. There is the issue of what is to be deemed "acceptable proof." We need not say that there is no consensus here and the "conservative archaeologists" that you invoke cannot be presumed to speak for anyone but themselves; in point of fact, their minimalist criteria, as you state it, create a kind of self-induced myopia that has them, in effect, describing an elephant only by the part of it they can feel. There is a way, as you should well know, of building up a web of evidence that allows one to draw accurate conclusions with or without identifiable artifacts from the Old World in the New. Such artifacts are not required for the development of a plausible model of contact and contrary to your assertion, observed cultural similarities, particularly when there is a complex web of them, will do! They will do very well. When closely similar, and sometimes identical, beliefs, techniques, methods, iconographs, architectural edifices, etc., are shown in two widely spaced locations, the statistical probability of independent invention falls to nearly zero. These correspondences *have* been shown time after time by many writers.

"Simple co-incidences," as you call them, are seldom simple or co-incidental and to invoke them merely allows one to explain *away* rather than explain. Indeed, theoretical physics denies the very existence of co-incidence and one tends to find that those who use it as an explanation of complex phenomena invariably do so when confronted with inconvenient realities that they cannot understand or refuse to accept. We are in the middle of a paradigm shift where history is concerned and that means that the received "truths" of the past will be revised or discarded.

On the issue of a "conspiracy of silence": we find it incomprehensible that you could write an essay such as this one without a single reference to the work of Ivan Van Sertima or Alexander Von Wuthenau. If you have not read their books, why not? And if you have, how could you, in good faith, pretend they don't exist? Their evidence is difficult to dispense with. You would have to, for example, explain why there are scores and scores of busts, sculptures, and statues depicting individuals with explicitly Negroid features dating from Olmec times in Meso-America. The Michael Coe argument, i.e., the Olmecs were working with "blunt tools," is the truest example of that which will not do. How does one explain these self-same portraits in stone with hair braided in the African style, wearing lip plugs and earrings, and tattooed with tribal markings? How do you explain the existence of American diploid cottons with African genotypes? Finally, how do you explain Columbus's explicit reference in his own diary to African sea-men who had preceded him to America, having gotten hold of some of their gold-tipped spears? Speaking of documents, are you not familiar with an annal describing a 14th-century king of Mali commissioning a voyage westward across the Atlantic, not once but twice?

Nor can one point to primitive watercraft as a reason against pre-

Columbian voyages from either Africa or Asia. The business of Japanese fishermen in antiquity making a voyage across the sea without food or water is a non-argument. One of the things that Heyerdahl showed is that food, that is to say edible fish, literally jumped onto his reed boat, the *Ra*, every day; recurrent squalls provided enough water for both drinking and washing. And it *was* important for Heyerdahl to prove that such a voyage could be successfully completed in simple craft because that was, and still is it seems, one of the arguments used to "disprove" such voyages, i.e., the primitive craft of antiquity could never have made a transoceanic crossing. By proving it *possible*, Heyerdahl was half-way to proving it *probable*.

You will also have to explain how it is that Melanesian and Polynesian sailors in catamaran canoes could and did voyage over thousands of miles of open ocean, apparently because they knew how to "read" ocean waves. How did the original Hawaiians get to Hawaii, after all? If they got that far over the Pacific, they could have just as well landed anywhere on the American west coast. Indeed, the first landings from the South Pacific to America apparently occurred *before* 6,000 B.C. Very recently, Douglas Wallace of Emory University did a comparative analysis of the mitochondrial DNA of numerous Amerindian groups and found that they clustered mostly around Asian mtDNA groups, as expected, *and* around groups belonging to people who today inhabit New Guinea, Melanesia, and Polynesia. His study led him to postulate a date as early as 34,000 B.C. for the first human migrations into the Americas and 6,000 B.C. as the latest date for the last wave of migrations. One route of migration had to have been across the Pacific Ocean. Those contributors to *Man Across the Sea*, postulating Pacific voyages to America, knew what they were about.

Finally, there is the matter of the Piri Reis map. And indeed, one is also perplexed that Charles Hapgood, author of *Maps of the Ancient Sea Kings*, was not mentioned in your article. According to Hapgood, that map must be pre-Christian and the map-maker was sitting at the 1st cataract in Upper Egypt when he drew it. Since it shows the west coast of Africa and the east coast of South America, not to mention Antarctica and Central America, in correct scale proportion using plane trigonometry, clearly there is more to ancient knowledge about the world, its topography, and its dimensions than conservative scholars are prepared to credit. That does not make them sober scholars, that makes them blind.

The idea that the Vikings and then Columbus were the first to make significant land-falls in America by the sea route has not been admissible for some time now. Von Wuthenau's *Unexpected Faces in Ancient America* shows clearly the presence of Chinese, Japanese, Egyptians, Nubians, Phoenicians, and perhaps even Celtics well before the Vikings. The world's oceans didn't become transcontinental highways when the Portuguese and Spanish started sailing them, they had been for hundreds of years, perhaps even millennia, previously. Dismissing the clear evidence as a "tall tale" is not scholarship but ideology.

Long-range sea-faring activity in the Indian Ocean is well-attested from antiquity; Chinese, Indians, Arabs, Egyptians, Phoenicians, and East Africans have been plying those waters for thousands of years. A voyage between East Africa and China in the 14th century, which *is* attested, is much longer than a trans-Atlantic Africa-to-America voyage. Why then is an Africa-to-America voyage in the Medieval period—earlier even—unthinkable? The surprise is not that Africans and Asians voyaged to the New World prior to Columbus but rather in the assumption that they did not and could not, even in the face of all evidence to the contrary.

Finally, we repeat: there is no compelling reason to hinge an entire argument solely on the presence (or absence) of datable artifacts from the home cultures of the early voyagers. After all, the Spanish and Portuguese stole, burned, or destroyed every conceivable facet of pre-Columbian civilization within their means. Perishable trade items would never survive archaeologically anyway and if there were precious metals and other such goods from lands across the sea, they would have been carted away or perished under the Ibernian slash and burn policy toward native cultures. In spite of that, clear and unambiguous traces of these early Old World voyagers are there for all the world to see in statuary, architecture, and even in known documents.

To make all of these issues more intriguing yet, there is an Amerindian scholar by the name of Jack Forbes who thinks that pre-Columbian peoples may have voyaged eastward across the Atlantic and made one or more African land-falls. The evidence for this is admittedly slim but one can at least entertain it as a possibility that must await further corroboration.

Respectfully submitted,
Charles S. Finch III, M.D.
Office of International Health
Richard Campbell, Ph.D.
Department of Pharmacology
Morehouse College,
Atlanta, Georgia.

March 12, 1993

Professor Frank J. Frost
Department of History
University of California, Santa Barbara
Santa Barbara, California 93106-9410

Dear Sir:

We must frankly admit that we did not expect a response to our recent letter, certainly not in so timely a fashion. We do thank you for corresponding with us so promptly.

We find, actually, that the second paragraph of your letter is most remarkable in terms of the evidence you bring forward supporting a pre-Columbian Polynesian presence in South America. It seems to fly right in the face of the "tall tales" posture concerning pre-Columbian, non-Viking American voyages you have adopted. Why wasn't this evidence mentioned in the article? You state that this article was a shortened version of an earlier presentation but was this still a case of selective editing by the magazine? While we do not wish to fall into the easy trap of brow-beating *Archaeology*, there is a definite editorial slant there and it may mean that some of its contributors are "showcased" in such a way that they seem to be advocating points of view that belong more properly to the editors than to the contributors themselves.

As regards New World sweet potatoes in Polynesia, what about the African diploid cottons in the New World before Columbus and vice-versa?

You will excuse us if we find your dismissal of the Piri Reis Map and the work of Von Wuthenau unconvincing. In this kind of correspondence, perhaps a systematic refutation—which is what is required—is not possible. Nevertheless, you have not falsified either Hapgood or Von Wuthenau and *still* haven't even mentioned Van Sertima. This latter individual has rather more than the somewhat arbitrary "eight" correspondences that you mention between Egypto-Nubian and Meso-American cultures at his disposal. Again, where Von Wuthenau is concerned, those terra-cottas, sculptures, and stone heads are very ethnically detailed and there are whole lots of them! One wonders what is required to draw the obvious conclusion, a bunch of pre-Columbian "real-time" snapshots? These sculptures are the nearest and best thing; a virtual "photo gallery" of the various peoples from around the world present in the Meso-American world. I might add that Von Wuthenau is still alive and living in Mexico City. It is easy enough to walk in on him and look at his private museum; the only one of its kind in the world. He is an extraordinarily accessible man.

There is more that could be said but it would be more appropriate for authorities like Van Sertima and Von Wuthenau to take up these discussions.

Again, we thank you for your response and if there is anything that is certain, these debates are going to continue for a good long while. One finds increasingly that it is impossible to look back at history through the same lens we have inherited from 19th century scholarship . . .

> Respectfully,
> Charles S. Finch III, M.D.
> W. Richard Campbell, Ph.D.

Mr. Charles Touhey
Pine West Plaza Building 2
Washington Avenue Extension
Albany, New York 12205

March 31, 1992

Dear Charles,

Thank you so much for passing on the latest instalment in the "Mumblings of de Montellano". In case you are not aware of it, his letter to you provided me with another opportunity, which I have been eagerly awaiting, to set the record straight.

Point 1. Dr. de Montellano claims that an indigenous American woman is the spitting image of the colossal stone heads, that these are roughly of one type and that she is the perfect model for them all. He suggests also, by inference, that all portrait sculpture in America in the pre-Columbian era can be accounted for by this phenotype. I have prepared a series of photographs which show some of the stone heads, especially those found at Tres Zapotes, with characteristics that make such a statement patently absurd. The one with a seven-braided hairstyle is particularly worth noting since neither Bernal nor Coe nor the National Geographic have dared to publish it. It was found in 1984 in the files of the Smithsonian and returned to public scrutiny in my edition of *Nile Valley Civilizations,* after a blackout of 50 years.

Beatriz de la Fuentes, in *Las Cabezas Colosales Olmecas* says of this head: "If in some moment one happened to ponder on the existence of negroes in early Mesoamerica, such a thought would surely occur after you have seen the head at Tres Zapotes (Tres Zapotes 2) the most remote in physiognomy from our indigenous ancestors. The elevated position of this personage is revealed in the headdress, from the back of which dangles seven bands which figure braids that taper off into rings and tassels".

I have also published a series of photographs of continental African types, which display the epicanthic fold to demonstrate how little de Montellano and most Americanists know about racial types in Africa. De Montellano read Bernal who claimed that "the migration [of Africans to pre-christian America] is improbable though not impossible, and *even more improbable is the combination of epicanthus fold with Negroid faces*" (see page 27 of *The Olmec World,* University of California Press, Berkeley, 1969). Neither of these gentlemen, it appears, ever went to study in Africa nor have ever read eye-witness accounts of Africans with epicanthic fold (see Evans-Pritchard and C.G. Seligman in the Sudan and the British ethnologist C.K. Meek in Northern Nigeria). Apart from that, the epicanthic fold can be acquired in nine months. My first cousins have the epicanthic fold because my uncle married a Chinese woman in Guyana with epicanthic fold. In the case of the Olmec, intermarriage between native females and newly-arrived foreign males would not be an exceptional phenomenon. It is less the exception than the rule in culture contacts.

Point 2. De Montellano claims that since C14 datings at San Lorenzo go back to 1200 B.C. the stone heads must have been carved out around that time. This is either sloppy scholarship or dishonesty on de Montellano's part. Since he has read Coe and Bernal cover to cover, as I have, I cannot let him get away with the lesser charge. Anyone who has followed up this matter closely is aware of the fact that Coe and Bernal are agreed that, although C14 datings at San Lorenzo are much earlier than at other major Olmec sites, they have nothing to do with the dating of the stone heads. They are both agreed that the first sequence of the heads are at La Venta, which is a much later site.

See page 54 of my book—*African Presence in Early America*—where I quote Coe's letter to Bernal ... "The sequence would begin with the La Venta heads ... then the San Lorenzo ones, and finally the Tres Zapotes ones ... " (see Bernal, *The Olmec World*, p. 57). Major structures such as these are seldom related to the initial occupation or settlement of a site and the carbon datings at San Lorenzo relate simply to the initial movement of people into the area and to phases long prior to the apogee of the culture or civilization. *Dr. de Montellano knows this!!!* The reason why archaeologists were able to establish a relative dating of the stone heads at La Venta was because they are rooted in a wooden platform which went through at least three phases of construction. In one such phase it was apparently altered to accommodate the sculptures. *Dr. de Montellano knows this!!!.*

Even if, for the sake of argument, the datings were as early as the era of Ramses III (circa 1200 B.C.) the figure of the Egyptian would still be predominantly Negroid and the cultural elements suggested as influences still fundamentally the same in that period (see the color photo in one of the books I edited—*Egypt Revisited*—which shows how the Egyptian saw himself circa 1200 B.C. in relation to the Nubian and other blacks of Africa). My emphasis on the 25th dynasty as the most likely of all periods for the pre-Christian contact, was explained in the 1986 anthology I edited and I made allowance in this later work for both sides of the dating equation. (814 plus or minus 134 B.C.) Jairazbhoy's emphasis on the 1200 B.C. date, unlike my own, lay in his insistence that the outsiders came in during the very first phase and "founded" Olmec civilization. I disagree with his motive for this choice of period though not with some of the meticulously researched details of his thesis. I do not believe anyone but the natives founded Olmec civilization, regardless of whether the outsiders came in the first phase (as in the Jairazbhoy model) or in the later phase of the dating equation (as in the 1977 Van Sertima model). The evidence certainly suggests the influence of outsiders (see my Smithsonian address on the extraordinary ritual parallels between the Olmec and Egyptian). But while one may argue for an influence and in such an argument an apparent identity is put forward, only some of them will pass the acid test. But I have never claimed that the Egyptians or the Egypto-Nubians created Olmec civilization.

Nor have I claimed, as the mendacious de Montellano has claimed, that they gave the Mexicans their calendar. I made passing reference to a calendar described by a priest—the Abbé Hervas—that he pointed out had gone out of use well before Spanish times and was far removed from the Aztec calendar we found in the European contact period. Mexico was not always, as Cortez found it, a fairly centralised state. We found the peoples speaking fourteen languages. It is not impossible for them to have had more than one time-keeping model simultaneously in vastly diverse provinces centuries before the coming of the Conquistadors. The Egyptians themselves had more than one. The Stele of Canopus shows this. Dr. de Montellano, picking on me for mentioning a defunct calendar observed by the Abbé Hervas, claimed that I said the Mexican calendar was the same as the Egyptian. This is a naked and nasty lie. The Aztec 52-year cycle (which I discuss in Chapter 5 of my book) bears absolutely no resemblance to any Egyptian time-keeping model. Its indigenous and unique nature would be obvious even to an idiot. The statement made by Abbé Hervas on a defunct calendar in a part of pre-Spanish America, which he claimed conformed with an earlier Egyptian model, was deliberately cited out of context to make me appear like a facile diffusionist. *De Montellano knows this!!!.*

Point 3: He is not only interested, however, in a debate on the question of pre-Columbian contacts. He is intent on misrepresenting my position on the matter of race in order to slander me. He claims, for example, that I think *native Americans were too stupid to create their own civilization and it required diffusion from superior black people.* This is not based on anything I said but pure personal venom. It misrepresents everything that I am, everything that I have said, everything that I have done.

Let me quote from statements I have made about the native American both in *They Came Before Columbus* (1976) in *African Presence in Early America* (1986) and in my *Testimony to a Congressional sub-committee* overseeing the work of the Christopher Columbus Quincentenary Commission (July 7, 1987).

(a) "I think it is necessary to make this clear—since partisan and ethnocentric scholarship is the order of the day—that the emergence of the "Negroid" face, which the archaeological (i.e. skeletal and iconographic and cultural) data overwhelmingly confirms, in no way presupposes the lack of a native originality . . . " *They Came Before Columbus*, p. 147.

(b) "By the time any outsiders came in any significant numbers, the Olmec would already have had some kind of home-grown civilization. A priest-caste would have emerged, an elite group that governed the rural villages and started to put a stamp, a distinctive stamp, upon the culture, like the jaguar motif, for example. This motif is already in evidence in the 1200 B.C. find at Copalillo (by my colleague at Rutgers, Dr. Hammond). I have never argued that this was brought to America by outsiders. Whatever the arguments of some of my colleagues, and I say this with the deepest respect, they are too apt to assume a native vacuum in pre-Christian America . . . I cannot subscribe to the notion that civilization suddenly dropped onto the American earth from the Egyptian heaven." *African Presence in Early America*, page 16.

(c) "Although it is fashionable to make a special case for one's racial or national identity, I want to point out that I am a cosmopolis of almost all old world and new world races. I am therefore concerned that our vision of the world, of these Americas, take full cognizance of all these peoples and all these ancestors so that one does not live in constant war and uneasiness with the other.

"The European side of me is insulting the Native American side of me by calling these voyages "voyages of discovery", also insulting the African side of me by insisting that these voyages to America were the first, when there is so much evidence to suggest that the Atlantic coastal peoples (the African) made significant contact with the American long before the era of Columbus.

"I came here before you to correct this myth, to present a more objective vision of our plural American legacy."

–Van Sertima before Congress
(July 7, 1989)

This man has read everything I have officially written on this subject. Whatever his disagreement with my views, he knows full well that I am no racist. He knows full well that I have edited a dozen anthologies, displaying the best essays on African civilization history not only by African-American and Caribbean but European, Jewish, African and European-American scholars. He must know that I am beyond racist thinking, having come from a family that has married into every major race of the world. As I intimated before and let me spell it out now in personal detail—my uncle, Alick Van Sertima married a Chinese woman and my first cousins—Sheila Van Sertima (London) and Anita (New York)—have the epicanthic fold which he argues cannot appear on Africans living among native Americans of a

Mongolian cast of feature. The epicanthic fold on the eyes of my cousins was acquired in nine months.

Also, art styles, even when responsive to novel facets of alien physiognomy, do not always abandon every aspect of their earlier formalisation of faces. Thus Nefertiti (who is daughter of the Persian king Dushratta) is represented with the striking prognathism and full-lipped features of her Afro-Egyptian husband, Akhnaton, and their two very African-looking daughters. We are practically looking at his feminine twin in the Temple of Nefertiti. Yet the Berlin bust shows clearly she is no African. Again, the bust of Buddha is presented by the Greeks in an art style so formalized that, were it not for the labelling of the sculpture, we would certainly pronounce him European.

The stone heads do not stand by themselves. As Andrez Wiercinski and A. Vargas Guadarrama have shown, the craniological and skeletal evidence corroborates the Africoid presence suggested by some of these heads. I can go on for days on this matter, Charles, but I must close now. It is a pity one has to waste so much time to deal with the venom and malice of this little man with the big name. As you know, he is a professor of anthropology at Wayne State University in Michigan. He also pretends to comment with authority on the *guanin* complex of words and their linguistic identities in the Caribbean and some parts of Mexico when he knows absolutely nothing about African languages. But I am grateful to him in a way. He has made such a notorious celebrity of me in Michigan that a book chain there has just ordered 3000 copies of my book for the schools. I think you will enjoy my comment on this gentleman and his intellectual pretensions in Note 6 of my address to the Smithsonian which is to be published by the Smithsonian Press in 1993*.

Please keep me informed of his future underhand attacks on my reputation since he circulates these letters surreptitiously in many places. Pay particular attention to the selection of stone-heads and terra cotta which follow. De Montellano claims they are *all* "spitting images of the [American] native."

Ivan Van Sertima

---

*This publication was delayed to 1994.

Figure 1(a). Among the first stone heads found, with Africoid features. *Front view*. Tres Zapotes. This was found in 1862. It is now located at Tuxtla.

Figure 1(b). *Side-view* of the Tres Zapotes head.

Figure 1(c).   Back of the Tres Zapotes head, showing Ethiopean-type braids. This unusual photo, taken in the 1930s, was reintroduced by Wayne Chandler and Gaynell Catherine.

Figures 2(a) and 2(b). Compare (a) *Head of Nuba chief from Kenya* with (b) *Olmec Negroid stone head (Tres Zapotes F).*

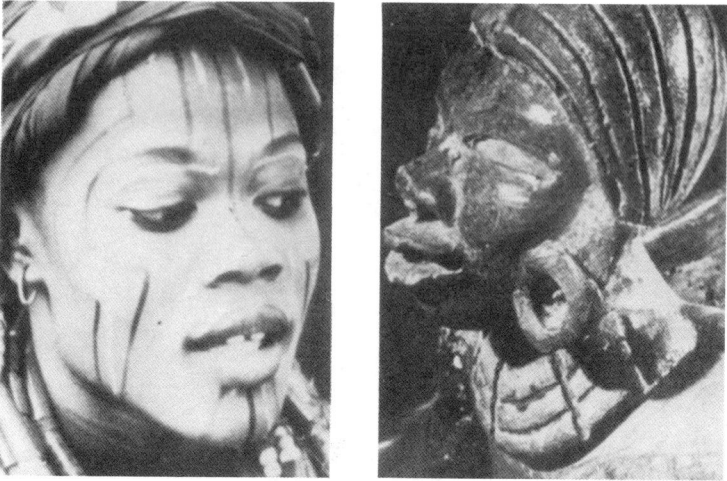

Figures 3(a) and 3(b). *African women in pre-Columbian Mexico.* Compare (a) modern Nigerian woman with (b) Negroid Teotihuacán head (Classic period).

Figure 3(c). *Mandingo head in fourteenth-century Mexico.* Made by the Mixtecs, from Oaxaca. Josue Saenz collection, Mexico City.

Figure 4(a). *Negroid head with vivid sacrification.* Vera Cruz. Classic period. Note headdress.

Figure 4(b). A classic Mochica Negroid portrait vessel from Peru, circa A.D. 900.

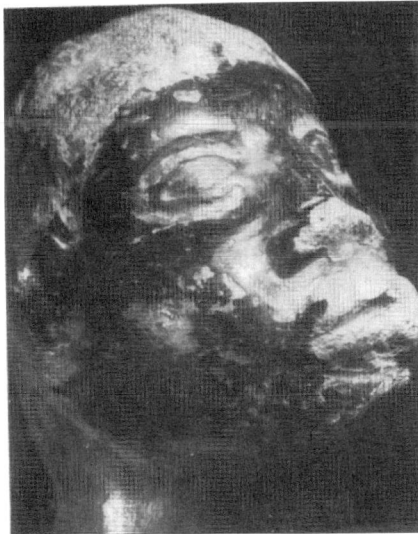

Figure 4(c). *Negroid head.* Worshipped by Aztecs as representation of their god Tezcatlipoca because it had the right ceremonial color.

? th of September

Letter to the Editor
The New York Times
229 West 43rd Street
New York, NY 10036

Dear Sir/Madam:

I have read John Baines' attempted refutation of *Black Athena*, in the August 11 Book Review of the *New York Times*, but must confess to having found little of immediate pertinence to Bernal's etymologies or to his analysis of historiography. Tamara Green (in *Arethusa's* Fall 1989 issue) warns against the susceptibility of critics to polemic, to the extent that "issues raised in his [Bernal's] book will dissipate into countless trivial disputes about this or that historical, linguistic or archaeological fact, an argument that may generate a lot of heat but not much light." Considerably greater weight must be given to the endorsement of Bernal's case by Gary Rosenburg, himself an etymologist, than to Baines' refutation. On the matter of historiographical bias, Baines' opposition to Bernal's work is to be expected; he has made his premise quite clear:

> "It is a striking feature of native Egyptian culture at all periods that it is not technically innovative. Possibly the very prodigality of the land and its water has not encouraged invention." (Baines & Malek: Atlas of Ancient Egypt, p. 14)

> "Until this time [18th Dynasty] Egypt had been technologically backward in comparison with the Near East; during the New Kingdom the two were roughly on a par." (*ibid*, p. 42)

Such statements reek of unreason, but do reveal the real nature of Egypt's *Orientalization*, by which I refer to the tendency of nineteenth century scholars to attribute Egyptian achievement to Mesopotamian example or inspiration, at the same time transforming the Africoid Egyptian into an Asian Caucasoid. Baines only lends greater credence to a central proposition of the (Revised) Ancient Model, wherein this *Orientalization* of Egypt is to be correlated with the rise of European imperialism and slave based society, and that furthermore, the process called for the negation of a wealth of ancient testimony suggesting Egypt's profound and seminal influence on surrounding Mediterranean peoples.

Baines fails to challenge any substantive specifics, either of Bernal or of Diop. For example, he attributes to them both "a defense of the myth of Atlantis as fact," when in reality both authors simple try to make historical sense of a "legend", based on the fact that an authentic event, namely the Thera eruption, did take place at about the time when, according to Egyptian sources, Greek civilization suffered a terrible calamity fitting the description of a huge volcanic eruption. Many legends derive from some real experience, and indeed it is often astonishing how little a myth may vary over the centuries. Such an event as the Thera eruption must surely have had a momentous physical and psychological impact throughout the entire Mediterranean region. Baines disdainfully refers to Diop's *Civilization or Barbarism* as "not a work of original research, but an assembly of studies," as if one scholar or research team could possibly cover such an expanse of academic terrain. He seems to regard what he calls "the much criticized theory known as diffusionism" as erroneous by definition—it is sufficient simply to point to diffusionist arguments in order to discredit them. Sinking to a nebulous low, he seeks to dismiss Bernal with pretentious innuendo: "Like others who come to new fields from outside, [Dr.] Bernal is adept at spotting weaknesses in traditional opinions, . . . " But he is at his deceitful worst when he suggests (to the unsuspecting reader) that Bernal is naively at fault for taking literally Herodotus' statement that there was a black population at Colchis on the eastern side of the Black Sea. The truth is that the Greek historian went to great pains to demonstrate the thoroughness of his investigation of the subject, not only by citing cultural and physical traits common to both the Egyptians and the Colchians, but by consulting Egyptian *and* Colchian sources and cross-examining the information thus gleaned. Bernal stands accused of "taking seriously the ancient Greeks' legends that portrayed much in their civilization as originating in the Middle East, especially in Egypt." In the final analysis, then, the controversy is rooted in the peculiar gall of latter day Aryanist scholars, who presume that they can far better speak for the ancient Greeks about their own history than can the Greeks themselves.

On the question of ethnicity, I think that it is tongue in cheek, and contradictory, to regard physical identity (race?) as unimportant to archaeology, while at the same time insisting on a false distinction between Egyptians and other peoples of East and West Africa. Given the vast pool of iconographic data from which the characteristic image(s) of the Ancient Egyptian can be assessed, such a distinction is no less ludicrous than one between Italians and Norsemen, both patently Caucasoid. It is very unfortunate, therefore, and quite ironic, that the obsolete social historians who place Ancient Egypt in the Oriental sphere of race and culture have caused the Africanist response to seem to emanate from some ethno-political bias. Modern genetics has put paid to the anthropological usage of such essentially geo-political terms as *Negro*. Hopefully, the findings of mtDNA and male Y chromosome research will help Egyptologists in particular to recognize the numerous Nilo-sub-Saharan phenotypes as but varied expressions of the same diverse African gene pool. This original gene pool has the capacity to produce Fulah, Batutsi and Xhosa with acquiline noses and thin lips, as well as short steatopygic types, like the Aka, or the tall savannah osteology so often represented on ancient Saharan rock paintings. The real racists are those who, like Frank Snowden, deny any "Negro" presence in Egypt prior to the 18th Dynasty, based on their own convenient definition.

So much for Baines and bias. However, there are also important factual errors in his commentary. He states, for example, that the Egyptians "would not have known the meaning of the term Africa," whereas in fact the word probably derives from the Egyptian *af rui ka*, literally *born of the primordial [first, original] soul*, or as a toponym, *birthplace*. Disputing Diop's iconographic basis for characterizing the Egyptians as black Africans, Baines is unaware that, in order to focus on realistic portraiture and not to cloud the analysis with the Egyptians' religious usage of yellow and the so called reddish-brown color, Diop deliberately excluded painted materials from the vast mass of evidence that he presented at the 1974 UNESCO symposium on the peopling of ancient Egypt. It should suffice to quote the general conclusion of the proceedings of that symposium:

> "Although the preparatory working paper . . . sent out by Unesco gave particulars of what was desired, not all participants had prepared communications comparable with the painstakingly researched contributions of Professors Cheikh Anta Diop and Obenga. There was consequently a real lack of balance in the discussions."

Furthermore, Diop invited these participants to examine the results of melanin tests he had performed on skin samples from early dynastic mummies of the Mariette excavations, all of which had levels of melanin indicative of black skin like that of Sudanic peoples, confirming Elliot Smith's earlier findings.

Where Egyptian paintings expressly sought to distinguish the various physical types known to them, they showed themselves identical or almost identical to the blacks of inner Africa. Perhaps the best example of this is in the tomb of Ramses III (see plate 48 from K.R. Lepsius: *Denkmaler uas Aegypten und Aethiopen, Erganzungsband*). Bas-reliefs on the tomb of Senwosre I, as well as on other royal tombs, show Africans of the interior being a subtle shade darker in complexion than Egyptians. Champollion the Younger reports extensively on these reliefs in his letters to his elder brother. In *The African Origin of Civilization*, Diop quotes his thirteenth letter:

"I hastened to seek the tableau corresponding to this one [i.e., in the tomb of Senwosre] in the other royal tombs and, as a matter of fact, I found it in several. The variations I observed fully convinced me that they had tried to represent here the inhabitants of the four corners of the earth, according to the Egyptian system, namely: 1. the inhabitants of Egypt, which, by itself, formed one part of the world . . . ; 2. The inhabitants of Africa proper: Blacks; 3. Asians; 4. finally (and I am ashamed to say so, since our race is the last and the most savage in the series, Europeans,. . . . This manner of viewing the tableau is all the more accurate because, on the other tombs, the same generic names reappear, always in the same order. We find there *Egyptians and Africans represented in the same way* [Diop's italics], which could not be otherwise; but the Namou (Asians) and the Tamhou (Europeans) present significant and curious variants."

For these and other reasons, Baines' review, if it may be called that, must be placed in the category of "heat, but not much light."

Sincerely,
Peter R. Gray
13631 Castle Cliff Way
Silver Spring, MD 20904

THE NEWTONIAN SYNTHESIS IN PHYSICAL SCIENCE AND ITS ROOTS IN THE NILE VALLEY

John Pappademos

Sir Isaac Newton is conventionally considered today to be the founder of the science of mechanics, the co-inventor of the calculus, discoverer of the binomial theorem, important pioneer in the science of optics, and discoverer of the law of universal gravitation. He has been frequently termed "the greatest scientist that ever lived".[1] Born in England in 1642, he lived there until his death in 1727. His greatest work, published in London in 1867, was the *Philosophiae Naturalis Principia Mathematica,* or *"Principia"* for short. In this treatise, he not only set forth and applied the law of universal gravitation, but stated the now-famous three laws of motion—the so-called Newton's Laws.

In Isaac Newton's work, there was achieved a synthesis of three lines of development,[2] each of which started in ancient times. These were astronomy, mathematics, and mechanics. Newton's success rested directly on his predecessors Kepler, Copernicus, Descartes, and Galileo in the fields of astronomy, mathematics, and mechanics. In this article we will show that the work of Newton's predecessors would have been impossible without the basis laid centuries earlier in Egypt, so that Egyptian science, after a thousand years, indirectly motivated Newton through his European predecessors such as Kepler, Descartes, Copernicus, and Galileo. Furthermore we will show that Newton was, in addition, directly influenced by ancient Egyptian science.

Galileo

First, we should note that the Italian scientist Galileo (1564–1642) exerted a profound influence on Newton, who, in his *Principia,* assigned the honor of discovery of the first two laws of motion to Galileo,[3] and while still an undergraduate student, was led in the course of solving a problem set by Galileo to a proof that gravity was the force holding the moon and planets in their orbits.[4]

It is not difficult to trace the influence of the scientific writings of the ancients on the young Galileo. He, like other Europeans of the 13th through the 17th centuries A.D., would have made far less progress had it not been for the legacy of thought bequeathed to them by the Egyptian, Greek and Muslim authors of various nationalities. As a student at the University of Pisa and later as a professor at the same institution (1589–92), Galileo studied assiduously the works of Euclid, Ptolemy, Archimedes, Pappus, and literally dozens of other Greek, Muslim, and Egyptian scientists.[5] His knowledge of the ancient philosophers, as evidenced in his notes taken at the time, is remarkable. One of Galileo's particular heroes was Archimedes,[6] who is reported to have spent time at the University of Alexandria.[7] According to Reymond,[8] "Archimedes must have sojourned for some time in Egypt, or he would not have brought out his works in Alexandria, dedicating them to Eratosthenes, Conon, and Dosithenes who lived in that city . . . . It is likewise in Egypt, if Diodorus of Sicily is to be believed, that Archimedes discovered the screw which bears his name. . . . It is doubtful whether such an apparatus had not been used in Egypt before the time of Archimedes".

Another name mentioned many times in Galileo's notebooks was that of the Alexandrian philosopher Philoponus, whose theory of impetus led to Galileo's mechanics.[9] Philoponus, who, like most of the other Alexandrian philosophers, can be taken to be of Egyptian origin, showed by experiment the falsity of the Aristotelean dogma that heavier objects fall more rapidly than lighter objects a thousand years before Galileo, who conventionally gets the credit for proving the dogma false by his reputed experiment of dropping two balls of different weights from the Leaning Tower of Pisa.[10,11]

The influence of the ancient Greek and Egyptian students of mechanics was also effected indirectly through Galileo's university studies of his European 14th and 15th century precursors such as Jordanus, Tartaglia, Bradwardine, Bundan and a number of others. The work of Jordanus and his followers, for example, constituted a discipline known in the later Middle Ages in Europe as the Science of Weights, and belonged to a tradition stemming from texts on mechanics written by Heron, an Egyptian.[12] Furthermore, Stillman Drake has shown[13] how Galileo's famous studies of accelerated motion depended on the theory of proportions developed by Eudoxus, a Greek philosopher trained by the Egyptians.[14]

The influence of Africa also made itself felt in Galileo's experimental work. In his experiments on motion, he used a water clock, an Egyptian invention,[15] to measure time intervals; his measurements of length were based on the Egyptian unit of length (the cubit—braccio in Italian). Although Galileo is commonly credited with the invention of the thermoscope (effectively a thermometer without a scale), it has been noted by Bedini[16] that "the principle of the thermoscope had been noted . . . in the works of Hero of Alexandria (end of first century A.D.), in which the nature of the

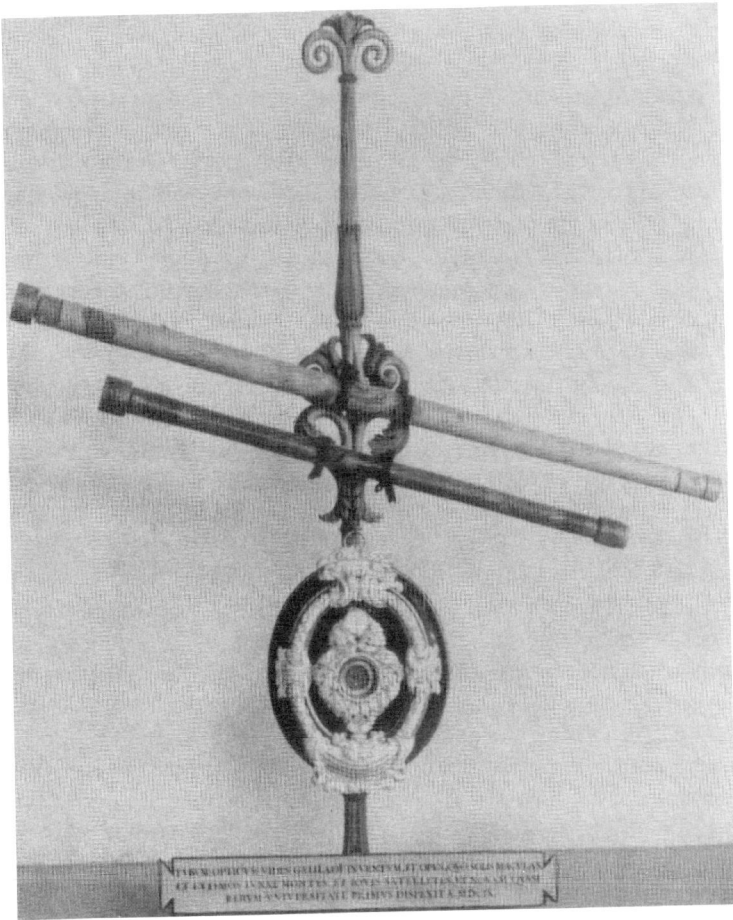

Figure 1. Galilean telescopes.

vacuum and the elasticity of air were discussed. Hero's work as well-known, or at least available, in Italy by the end of the 16th century . . . Galileo was certainly familiar with this work and had studied it . . . "[16] Galileo certainly helped to establish the validity of the heliocentric theory of the solar system by using the telescopes he constructed to observe the phases of Venus as well as the phenomenon of sunspots, but seldom have the prior experiments of Ibn-al-Haytham (Alhazen) of Egypt on lenses been given credit. Alhazen (died in Cairo in 1039 A.D.) was one of the greatest students of optics of all time. The Latin translation of his book *Optics* exerted a profound influence on European science, and included studies of the magnifying power of lenses.[17]

Copernicus

Nicholas Copernicus, astronomer, was born in Poland in 1473 and died in 1543, 21 years before Galileo was born. His major work, *De Revolutionibus Orbium Coelestium,* published the year of his death, is generally credited with causing a revolution in science, and which led through Kepler to Newton's *Principia. De Revolutionibus* was modelled on Ptolemy's *Almagest,* which was published in Alexandria, Egypt, 13 centuries earlier.[18] In *De Revolutionibus* Copernicus set forth the heliocentric theory of the sun and planets. (In the *Almagest,* on the other hand, the sun, stars, and planets were taken to rotate about the earth as center.) The notion that the earth moves and is not the center of the universe was hardly a new one, however; various theories involving a moving and rotating earth had been advocated by a number of ancient philosophers, including Aristarchus of Samos, Plato in his later years, the Pythagoreans, Heraclides of Pontus, Seleucus of Seleucia,[19] and Democritus.[20] To this list should be added the still more ancient astronomers of Egypt, according to Macrobius (circa 400 A.D.),[21] Cicero,[22] Tannery (the French historian of science of the late 19th century),[23] and Newton himself, who believed that the most significant astronomical beliefs of the ancient Greeks were derived from the Egyptians.[24] We will have more to say about Newton's views later on in the article.

Copernicus thoroughly studied the works of the ancient astronomers that were available to him, and acknowledged his debt to them.[25–29]

We do not claim here that Copernicus' theory was just a repetition of the earlier heliocentric theories. It represented a distinct advance over the earlier theories, which were lacking in quantitative arguments. After all, Copernicus had the advantage of access to the fruit of centuries of work. He used the *Almagest* itself,[30] which, although it was based on the geocentric theory, still contained a wealth of astronomical data. Copernicus also made extensive use of the data published by the great Muslim astronomers such as al-Battani (d. 929 A.D.),[31] who refined and extended the data of the *Almagest,* as well as making other important and original contributions.

Kepler

The method used by Newton to justify his law of gravitation was to prove that with it he could derive Kepler's three laws of planetary motion. Kepler, a German astronomer, deduced these laws between 1600 and 1620. Thus Kepler's work was vital to the success of Newton's theory of gravitation and motion.

It is well known that Kepler was a Copernican since his student days. Thus having been freed of the intellectual shackles of believing that the earth was the center of the universe, he was in a position to make his own

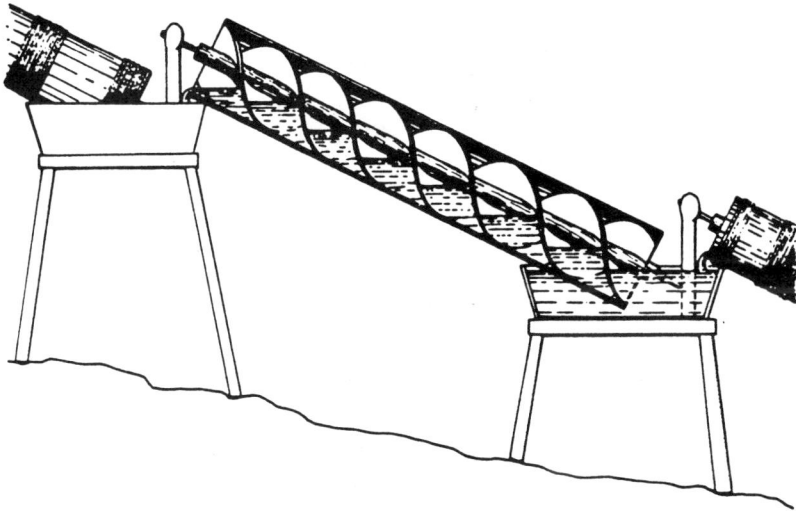

Figure 2. Archimedean screw for raising water. A whole series of such hollow screws could be geared together and used for delivering water up a considerable incline.

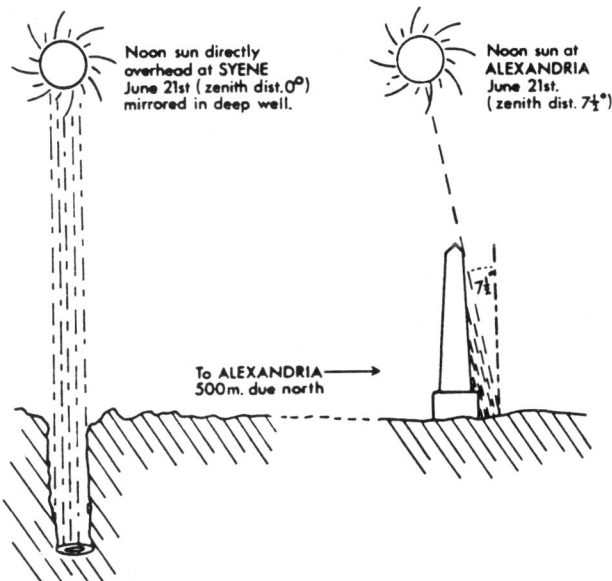

Figure 3. Erasthothenes method of measuring the Earth. He noted that a Syene the sun was directly overhead on Midsummer's Day, while at Alexandria the sun's rays were $7^{1}/_{2}°$ from the vertical, a value calculated from the length of a shadow cast by a column of known height. From this, and knowing the distance between the two places, he calculated the circumference of the Earth to be 250,000 stades (about 24,000 miles).

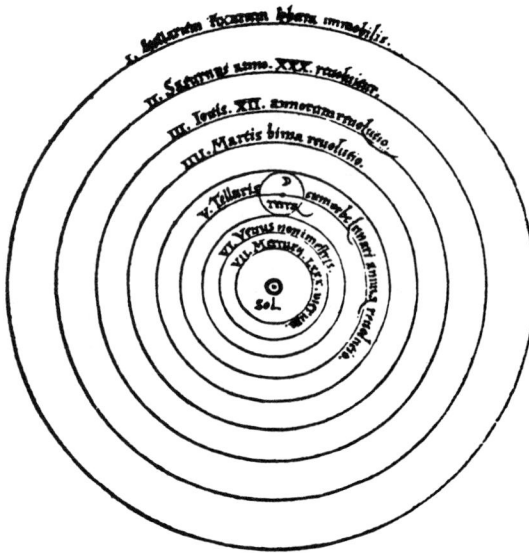

Figure 4. The universe as illustrated by Copernicus in *De revolutionibus orbium coelestium* (1543). I. Sphere of the Fixed Stars. II. Orbit of Saturn. III. Orbit of Jupiter. IV. Orbit of Mars. V. Orbit of the Sun and Moon. VI. Orbit of Venus. VII. Orbit of Mercury: the sun in the center.

contributions; namely, to eventually show that the planetary orbits are elliptical rather than circular (Law 1), that any planet's orbital radius sweeps out equal areas in equal times (Law II), and that the squares of the planets' periods are proportional to the cubes of their mean distances from the sun (Law III). A very good discussion of the background to Kepler's work has been given by Fritz Krafft,[32] who also augments the list given above of ancient opponents of the geocentric hypothesis.

Most accounts of Kepler's life adhere to what Westman[33] has called the "apostolic" or "hagiographic" approach to the history of science. As Westman has put it, "According to this view, the proper subject of historical investigation is the Great Man, for he alone produces the truly revolutionary insights. With some exceptions, the intellectual predecessors of Kepler, excluding Copernicus and Tycho Brahe (the Danish astronomer whose data Kepler used-jp), have not been given sufficient treatment with respect to their influence on him . . .". Westman goes on to cite some recent exceptions to this prevailing view. One of these exceptions is a paper by Fritz Krafft,[34] who has shown the "transmission and modification of Aristotle's aether physics from Sosigenes' (an Egyptian astronomer, circa 45 B.C.-jp) proposals for a non-homocentric physical astronomy (meaning no one center for all celestial circles and spheres), through the mechanical models of

Figure 5. Pen-and-ink drawing of Galileo's legendary experiment at the Leaning Tower of Pisa.

Ptolemy's (another Egyptian scientist -jp) *Planetary Hypotheses,* Alhazen's "naturally" self-moving spheres (Alhazen was born in 965 A.D. in Basra and flourished in Egypt -jp), and Copernicus' inheritance of the tradition of Sosigenes in his rejection of the equant . . ."[33] Krafft's work thus gives new insights into Africa's influence on Copernicus, and thus, indirectly, on Kepler and Newton.

Descartes

In 1637 there appeared in print a book destined to have a great influence on the developing Newton. This was René Descartes' *Discourse on Method,* which contained an appendix entitled "La Geometrie" (Geometry). As a student in Trinity College, Newton mastered Descartes' so-called analytic geometry,[35] the understanding of which was so important to his own later invention of the calculus. Without in any way belittling the creative genius of Descartes, and in fact to understand the context of his contribution all the better, it must be pointed out that the mathematicians of Alexandria were his primary sources of inspiration.[36] We will mention just three of the most important names: Pappus, Apollonius, and Euclid. More often than not, historians of science regard these as Greek and belonging to the "Greek" math-

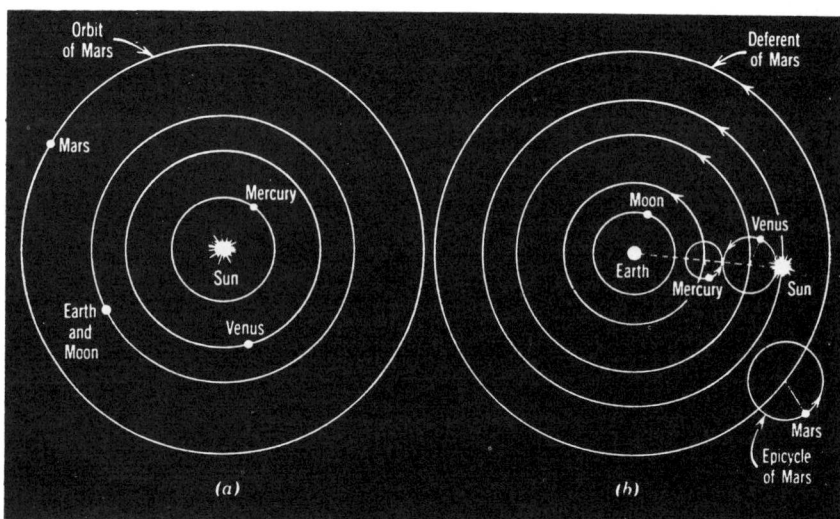

Figure 6. (a) The Copernican view of the solar system. The planets move in concentric orbits with the sun at the center. (b) The Ptolemaic view of the solar system. Each planet undergoes two simultaneous circular motions. For example, Mars travels about an epicycle while the center of the epicycle travels along a deferent. The earth is at the center of the system. Only the moon and sun have no epicycles.

ematical tradition, in utter disregard of the fact that mathematics flourished on Egyptian soil long before the Greek contributors; Egypt continued as the world's leading center of mathematics and astronomy until the death of Hypatia (c. 415 A.D.), and for another six centuries, at least until the death of Alhazen (1039 A.D.), it was one of the leading scientific centers of the world. There is no evidence that the Alexandrians Euclid and Pappus were of Greek origin; Apollonius was born about 262 B.C. in Perga (Asia Minor) but studied in Egypt and spent most of his life in Alexandria.[37] James Gow, the English historian of science, has argued that most of the mathematicians of Alexandria and other contemporary scientific centers such as at Pergamon (Asia Minor) were of Egyptian or Semitic origin.[38] The fact that Descartes drew so heavily on the work of such Alexandrian mathematicians as Apollonius has led some to ascribe credit for the invention of analytic geometry to them, rather than to Descartes.[39]

The Scientific Contributions of Other Non-European Peoples

It should be clear from the above that the work of Newton would have been unthinkable without the prior work in Africa by Egyptian or Egyptian-trained scientists as transmitted and expanded upon by Newton's immediate

Figure 7. It is known that Egyptian temples were properly aligned at a ceremony called "The stretching of the cord." Astronomical objects were used to establish the reference lines. Here, the king and goddess grasp mallets and stakes, around which the cord is looped, and lay the foundation stone.

predecessors Descartes, Galileo, Kepler and Copernicus. We have almost exclusively emphasized the importance of the Nile Valley culture in tracing the genesis of Newtonian mechanics primarily because historians of science have, with few exceptions, allowed the influence of racism to distort their scholarship to such an extent that the importance to science of the Black civilization of the Nile Valley has been neglected and denied. It should not be supposed that the contributions of other non-European peoples (the Arabs, Persians, Jews, Indians, and Chinese, for example) were of no importance in forming the tradition leading to Newton and in general the explosive advance of science in 17th century Europe. Like Africa's contributions, those of other non-European peoples have been belittled, although to a lesser extent.

In our next section, we turn our attention to some writings of Newton himself which bear closely on our subject.

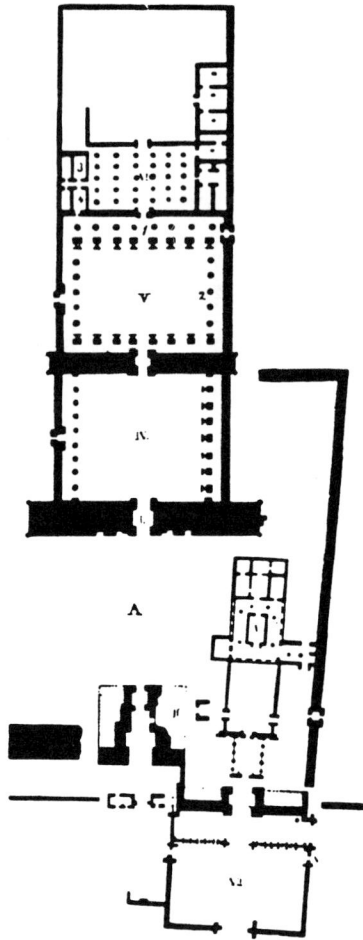

Figure 8. Lockyer interpreted the reorientation of the later buildings (upper) at Medinet-Habu, on the Nile's west bank, across from Luxor, as an Egyptian response to the precession of the equinoxes.

How Newton Himself Recognized That His Work Had Been Anticipated in Ancient Egypt

That Newton drew heavily upon the work of Galileo, Descartes, Kepler, and other Europeans is generally admitted by prevailing historical opinion. However, it is seldom stressed that Newton also was thoroughly familiar with the scientific works of much more ancient writers, especially those of Africa, whose opinions he held in high esteem and from which he drew to support his own arguments. To support this contention, let us let Newton speak for himself. In attributing the first atomic theory to Egypt and Phoenicia, Newton says:[40] "That all matter consists of atoms was a very ancient opinion. This was the teaching of a multitude of philosophers who preceded Aristotle, namely Epicurus, Democritus, Ecphantus, Empedocles, Zenocrates, Heraclides, Asclepiades, Diodorus, Metrodorus of Chios, Pythagoras, and previous to these Moschus the Phoenician, whom Strabo declares to be older than the Trojan War. For I think that the same opinion obtained in that mystic philosophy which flowed down to the Greeks from Egypt and Phoenicia, since atoms are sometimes found to be designated by the mystics as monads." (Newton is not usually thought of in connection with the atomic theory of matter. However, in deriving his results for the gravitational attraction between bodies of macroscopic size, Newton was led to the far-reaching conclusion that the inverse square law governs the force between bodies of atomic size.)

Furthermore, in an early edition of the *Principia,* in justifying his use of the heliocentric theory, Newton says:[41] "It was the most ancient opinion of those who applied themselves to Philosophy, that the fixed stars stood immovable in the highest parts of the world, that under them the planets revolved about the sun, that the earth, as one of the planets, described an annual course about the sun, while by a diurnal motion it turned on its axis, and that the sun remained at rest in the center of the Universe. This was the philosophy taught of old by Philolaus, Aristarchus of Samos, Plato in his riper years, the whole set of Pythagoreans, and that wisest king of the Romans, Numa Pompilius. As a symbol of the round orb with the solar fire in the center, Numa erected a round temple in honor of Vesta, and ordained a perpetual fire to be kept in the middle of it. The Egyptians were the earliest observers of the heavens and from them, probably, this philosophy was spread abroad. For from them it was, and from the nations about them, that the Greeks, a people more addicted to the study of philology than of Nature, derived their first, as well as their soundest, notions of philosophy; and in the Vestal ceremonies we can recognize the spirit of the Egyptians who concealed mysteries that were above the capacity of the common herd under the veil of religious rites and hieroglyphic symbols".

This passage is of extreme importance, because it bears directly on the most central part of Newton's theory of motion and gravitation. For as Westfall notes,[42] "From the observed phenomena of the heliocentric system, Newton argued the necessity of attractive forces to hold bodies in closed orbits, or inverse-square attractive forces to sustain orbits stable in space, and systems that conform to Kepler's Third Laws, and finally of a single inverse-square attractive force that arises 'from the universal nature of matter.' " Newton's firmly held belief that the ancient Egyptians anticipated both the Copernican (heliocentric) theory as well as universal gravitation is corroborated in a memorandum of David Gregory, one of Newton's associates.[43]

Elsewhere, in a set of draft scholia planned for inclusion in a second edition of the *Principia,* Newton makes an effective argument that his own major result—the law of universal gravitation—had been anticipated two thousand years earlier by the Pythagorean philosophers, and that this was the real meaning of their doctrine of the "harmony of the spheres".[44] (It is of course well-known that Pythagoras spent as much as 22 years in Egypt studying Egyptian science and religion, where it is likely he learned this doctrine. This, in fact, is what Newton believed.)

Some Western authors[44] have attempted, in a sophisticated way, to deny validity to Newton's arguments for an Egyptian anticipation of the heliocentric and gravitational theories by relating his ideas to those of a contemporary philosophical trend in Europe typified by the school known as the "Cambridge Platonists". According to McGuire and Rattansi,[44] this Neo-Platonist trend, and much earlier a number of Alexandrian philosophers such as the early father of the Christian Church, Clement of Alexandria (d. 213 A.D.),[45] established a "cult of Egyptian wisdom," attributing all of pagan (i.e., Greek) philosophy to having been plagiarized from the Egyptians or the Hebrews. But the modern critics of Newton and Clement of Alexandria (such as McGuire and Rattansi[44]) do not adduce any evidence to refute Newton, Clement of Alexandria, and the many others. (From the many we could choose, let us mention just three. Simplicios, the 6th century A.D. commentator on Aristotle, conjectures that Thales (the earliest of the Greek philosophers, who studied in Egypt -jp) derived his ideas from myths current in Egypt. Paul Tannery (the 19th century French historian of science - jp) pointed out the similarity between Thales' view of the origin of the world and that contained in ancient Egyptian papyri.[46] And still more recently, the thesis of Egyptian priority has been masterfully set forth in a book by George G.M. James.)[47] They rely instead on the overwhelmingly prevalent tacit acceptance (in Europe and the U.S. at least) of the "Europeanized" version of the history of science to make Newton and Clement look foolish.

Since the rise of slavery with its offspring the doctrine and practice of racism, the Black civilization of the Nile Valley has had its detractors. As recently as 1975, Otto Neugebauer, the well-known historian of ancient science, had this to say: "Egypt provides us with the exceptional case of a highly sophisticated civilization which flourished for many centuries without making a single contribution to the development of the exact sciences."[48] Although Neugebauer's statement might not be fully accepted by the majority of other historians of science, it is nevertheless true that it is a somewhat extreme reflection of an attitude which prevails among the professional U.S. historians of science. Interestingly enough, in the same book from which the above question was taken, Neugebauer makes the following observation: "(in our study of Babylonian astronomy-jp) . . . we have authentic source materials . . . exactly as they were written. Only for papyri (the writing surface used by the Egyptians-jp) could the same be said, but their number and deplorable state of preservation places them far below the cuneiform tablets. It is particularly fortunate that these Babylonian documents were preserved because they allow us to study a type of mathematical astronomy the existence of which we would never have deduced from our Greek sources."[49] This statement by Neugebauer himself, which indirectly admits that most Egyptian scientific writings have been lost to us (unlike those of the Babylonians), shows that his belittling of Egyptian astronomy is hardly justified.

A few historians of science have been able to make a fairer assessment; for example, E.C. Krupp states: " . . . but for all the knowledge we have about ancient Egypt, most Egyptian astronomical lore is lost to us . . . the genuine accomplishments of the Egyptian astronomers, for example, the tropical year and the alignment of the pyramids, are relatively unappreciated by historians of science."[50] George Sarton also had a high opinion of the astronomical ability of the early Egyptians.[51]

Egyptian Achievements in Astronomy

In order to help counteract such negative views of Egyptian science as those cited above, in this section we will give an admittedly incomplete listing of Egyptian achievements in astronomy. This, as mentioned previously, is one of the three main currents which were eventually synthesized by Newton in his *Principia,* where he set forth his theories of gravitation and dynamics.

Egyptian astronomy has been termed "primitive" or "non-existent" far too many times: it is appropriate to assemble the actual achievements of Egyptian astronomy and let the facts speak for themselves. The ancients unencumbered by racism, could take a more honest view of the matter: for example, Aristotle wrote: " . . . the Egyptians and Babylonians have studied these matters (i.e., planetary and lunar astronomy-jp) thoroughly since time immemorial, and through whom we have many reliable reports about each of the stars."[52]

The other two currents, mathematics and mechanics, will not be dealt with here, leaving them to others or to a later paper. The elements of the following compendium have all been separately discussed in the literature, but have not received sufficient emphasis nor have they ever been assembled together. They are listed in roughly chronological order.

The invention of the 365-day calendar, based on astronomical observations. Mankind's first scientific measurement of time. This development probably took place at least as far back as 3000 B.C.[53]

The development of instruments for quantitative astronomical measurement. These included the sundial, water clocks, and the merkhet[54] (which, used a straight-edge and a plumb line, enabled measurements of stellar azimuths).

The precise alignment of temples and pyramids from astronomical observations.[50]

Knowledge of stellar constellations. At least 43 constellations were familiar to the Egyptians in the 13th century B.C.[55]

The writing of astronomy texts. Clement of Alexandria gives the titles of four Egyptian astronomy books[56] (which have not survived): a) On the Disposition of Fixed Stars and Stellar Phenomena, b) On the Disposition of the Sun, Moon, and Five Planets, c) On the Syzygies and Phases of the Sun and Moon, d) On Risings. These texts may not have been intended for publication, but were available only to the priesthood. James[57] has stressed that the Egyptian religion forbade the general disclosure of their philosophy. This may help to explain why so little of Egyptian science has come down to us directly from the Egyptians, but rather indirectly from Greeks such as Pythagoras, who was initiated into the Egyptian mysteries.

Tables of star culminations and risings.[51, 56]

Knowledge of planetary astronomy. Five planets were known to the Egyptians[55]; the retrograde motion of Mars was known[55]; the revolution of Mercury and Venus around the Sun was known.[55, 22]

Prediction of eclipses.[55]

Discovery of the occultations of the stars and planets by the dark side of the half-moon.[58]

Discovery that the earth is spherical. The first measurement of the radius of the earth was made by Eratosthenes (b. 275 B.C.), who was head of the great library of Alexandria.[59] He was born in Cyrene, in what is now Libya. It seems likely that the ancient Egyptians, much before Egypt's conquest by Alexander the Great, had already grasped the idea of a spherical earth,[60, 61] and it was from them that this doctrine was adopted by Pythagoras, who, as we know, spent many years of study in Egypt.

Discovery of the obliquity of the ecliptic. Diodorus Siculus (70 B.C.) reports that the Egyptian priests claimed it was from them Oenopides of Chios learned the sun moved in an inclined orbit and oppositely to the motion of the other stars.[62] In this connection, it should be noted that the priority of Oenopides' claim to this discovery is disputed by Pythagoras.[62] In view of the fact that both Pythagoras and Oenopides went to Egypt to study astronomy,[63, 64] it would seem only fair to give their Egyptian teachers at least some of the credit.

Discovery of the precession of the equinoxes. The "precession of the equinoxes" refers to the very slow, cyclic changes in the coordinates of the fixed stars that takes place with a period of some 26,000 years. The discovery of this phenomenon can be divided into three stages. The first stage took place in Egypt, where the successive realignment of the axes of symmetry of various temples noted by Lockyer[65] showed that the Egyptians were aware of the change in positions of stars over the course of centuries. (The orientations of Egyptian temples were set with extreme precision by astronomical observations in accordance with their worship of the stars or the sun.) The second stage consisted in the measurement of the rate of rotation of the celestial sphere. Hipparchus (b. circa 190 B.C.; d. 125 B.C.) is generally credited with the first measurement, although some have given priority to the Egyptian astronomers.[66] The third stage consisted in a dynamical explanation of the effect, first given by Isaac Newton in the *Principia.*

First proof that the angular diameters of the sun and moon are unequal. Sosigenes (second century A.D.), the Egyptian astronomer who gave Europe the Julian calendar, showed that the angular diameters are unequal by adverting to the phenomenon of annular eclipses of the sun.[67]

First use of the clepsydra (water-clock) to measure the angular diameter of the sun.[67]

Discovery of the conjunction of the planets with each other as well as with the fixed stars. This is on the testimony of Aristotle in his *Meterology.*[68]

The heliocentric theory of the rotation of the earth and other planets about the sun. Elsewhere we have discussed Newton's belief that the heliocentric hypothesis originated in Egypt. Here we will add the remark that most historians of science credit Aristarchus of Samos with this discovery. About Aristarchus' life, little is known other than that he was born in the Greek island of Samos and lived circa 310–230 B.C.; just where, it is not known. He is also known to have been a pupil of Straton of Lampsacus,[69] an Alexandrian scholar who helped found the Museum there.[70] The principle basis for crediting Aristarchus with this discovery seems to be a passage from Archimedes, quoted in full by Heath.[71] But a careful reading of the passage shows that although Aristarchus is charged with backing a heliocentric theory (Archimedes was opposed to this theory), nowhere is he said to be the first to advance such a theory. So Heath's argument for Aristarchus' priority seems pretty thin. It is quite possible, in fact probable, since Alexandria was the leading center for astronomy, that Aristarchus worked in Egypt in Alexandria, where his teacher Straton had been, and there heard of, and became convinced of the truth of this Egyptian theory. At any rate, we choose to follow Newton in assigning credit to the Egyptians as the probable originators of the heliocentric theory.

Ptolemy's Almagest. This was the treatise which became the Bible of world astronomy for over a thousand years. Written in Alexandria about 150 A.D. by an Alexandrian, in all probability an Egyptian.

Conclusion

In the preceding sections, we have set forth arguments supporting the thesis that Newton's theories of motion and universal gravitation were not born simply as a result of Newton's Great Intuition, but rather were the fruition of an intellectual tradition whose origins can be traced back to the African science that flourished millennia earlier in dynastic Egypt. To emphasize the extraordinary vitality of that Egyptian science, we have highlighted some of its achievements in astronomy, one of the important components of that tradition leading to the Newtonian Synthesis. As we have seen, each stage in the transmission of this tradition featured the work of scientists (like Aristarchus, Eratosthenes, Alhazen, Copernicus, and Newton himself) who both inherited the work of the past, and made additional contributions of their own.

In closing, we should note that there is another aspect of the analysis of the origins of scientific advances such as those made by Newton as well as the scientists who paved the way for him. This other aspect, which we will not attempt to explore here, concerns the economic factors which help to propel scientific research forward. A number of authors have discussed the economic and social roots of the *Principia,* starting with the pioneering work of Boris Hessen.[72] Similar studies made for the case of the Nile Valley culture would be of great value in understanding the genesis of Egyptian science.

The author is indebted to Janet Harden and Beatrice Lumpkin in the preparation of this paper.

Notes

1. The New Columbia Encyclopedia. New York: Columbia University Press, 1975, p. 1929.
2. B.L. van der Waerden, *Science Awakening*, Vol. II. New York: Oxford University Press, 1974, p. XV.
3. Louis T. More, *Isaac Newton,* p. 326.
4. Richard S. Westfall, *Never a Rest: A Biography of Isaac Newton.* New York: Cambridge University Press, 1980, p. 151.
5. Wm. A. Wallace (Tr.), *Galileo's Early Notebooks.* Notre Dame, Ind.: University of Notre Dame Press, 1977, pp. 36, 59–60, 71–72, 74 and 76. Also see Stillman Drake, *Galileo Studies.* Ann Arbor, University of Michigan Press, 1970, p. 35.
6. James Weishepl, "Galileo and his Precursors", in: E. McMullin (ed.), *Galileo, Man of Sci*ence. New York: Basic Books, 1968, p. 96.
7. H. Eves, *Introduction to the History of Mathematics* (Rev. Ed.). New York: Holt, Reinhart & Winston, 1964, p . 142.
8. A. Reymond, *History of the Sciences in the Greco-Roman Antiquity.* London: Methuen (1927). Tr. by Ruth G. DeBray, p. 71.
9. J. D. Bernal, *Science in History* (2nd ed.). New York: Cameron, 1956, p. 293.
10. Carl B. Boyer, *A History of Mathematics.* New York: Wiley, 1968, p. 273.

11. G. Sarton, *Introduction to the History of Science*. Vol. I Baltimore: The Williams & Wilkins Co., 1927, p. 422.

12. Stillman Drake, op. cit., p. 22.

13. Stillman Drake, "Velocity and Eudoxian Proportion Theory", Physics, 1973, 15: 49–64.

14. G.J. Allman, *Greek Geometry*. Dublin, 1889, p. 133.

15. Alexander Pogo, "Egyptian Water Clocks," Isis 25, 403–425, 1936.

16. Silvio Bedini, "The Instruments of Galileo Galilei," in: *Galileo, Man of Science*. (E.A. McMullin, ed.). New York: Basic Books, 1968, p. 258.

17. Sarton, op. cit., p. 721.

18. Thomas Kuhn, *The Copernican Revolution*. Cambridge, Mass.: Harvard University Press, 1957, p. 135.

19. Sir Thomas Heath, *Aristarchus of Samos*. London: Oxford University Press, 1913, pp. 94, 304–306.

20. Gomperz, *Griechische Denker*. Quoted in Heath, op. cit., p. 125.

21. Heath, op. cit., p. 258.

22. Giorgio Abetti, *The History of Astronomy*. New York: Henry Schuman, Inc., 1951, p. 21.

23. Sir Thomas Heath, op. cit., p. 259.

24. Westfall, op. cit., p. 434.

25. Kuhn, op. cit., pp. 136, 141.

26. Francis R. Johnson, *Astronomical Thought in Renaissance England*. Baltimore: The Johns Hopkins Press, 1937, p. 96.

27. E.A. Burtt, The *Metaphysical Foundations of Modern Physical Science*. New York: 1925, pp. 40–44.

28. J.L.E. Dreyer, *History of the Planetary Systems from Thales to Kepler*. Cambridge: 1905, pp. 306–308.

29. John North, "The Medieval Background to Copernicus", in: A. Beer (ed.), *Vistas in Astronomy Vol. 17*. Oxford: Pergamon Press, 1975.

30. Otto Neugebauer, "On the Planetary Theory of Copernicus", in: A. Beer (ed.), *Vistas in Astronomy Vol. 10*. Oxford, Pergamon, Press, 1968, pp. 89–103.

31. Sarton, op. cit., p. 602.

32. Fritz Krafft, "Nicolaus Copernicus and Johannes Kepler: New Astronomy from Old Astronomy", in: A. Beer and P. Beer (eds.), *Vistas in Astronomy Vol. 18*. Oxford: Pergamon, 1975.

33. R.S. Westman, "Continuities in Kepler Scholarship", in *Vistas in Astronomy Vol. 18. (see* Ref. 32).

34. Fritz Krafft, "Keplers Beitrag zur Himmelphysik", in the series "Arbor Scientiarium: Beitrage zur Wissenschaftgeschichte" (Verlag, Dr. H.A. Gerstenberg, Hildesheim, 1973).

35. Westfall, op. cit., p. 100.

36. Boyer, op. cit., chap. 17.

37. Eves, op. cit., p. 149.

38. James Gow, A *Short History of Greek Mathematics*. New York: G.E. Stechert & Co., 1884 (1923 reprint), pp. 107–108.

39. Eves, op. cit., p. 151.

40. Quoted by Westfall, op. cit., p. 510.

41. Quoted by Westfall, op. cit., p. 434.

42. Westfall, op. cit.. p. 434.

43. J.E. McGuire and P.M. Rattansi, "Newton and the Pipes of Pan", Notes and Records of the Royal Society of London, 21, (1966). p. 110.

44. McGuire and Rattansi, op. cit., pp. 108–143.

45. William Wilson (tr.), *The Writings of Clement of Alexandria*. 2 vols. Edinburgh: T & T Clark, 1868.

46. Sir Thomas Heath, *Greek Astronomy*, New York: AMS Press, repr. 1932, ed., 1969, p. xx.

47. George G.M. James, *The Stolen Legacy*, New York: *The Philosophical Library*, 1954. Reprinted by Julian Richards Associates, Publishers, San Francisco. 1976.

48. Otto Neugebauer, *A History of Ancient Mathematical Astronomy*, Part 1, Berlin: Springer Verlag, 1975. p. 559

49. Neugebauer, ibid., p. 3.

50. E.C. Krupp (ed.), *In Search of Ancient Astronomies*. New York: McGraw–Hill, 1978, p. 203.

51. George Sarton, *A History ol Science: Ancient Science Through the Golden Age of Greece*. New York: W.W. Norton, 1952, p. 30.

52. Quoted by Van der Waerden, op. cit., p. 37.

53. René Taton (ed .), *History of Science: Ancient and Medieval Science*. New York: Basic Books, p. 35.

54. Taton, ibid., p. 39.

55. Sir Thomas Heath, *Greek Astronomy*. New York: AMS Press (1969) reprint of 1932 ed.), p. xv.

56. Van der Waerden, op. cit., p. 40.

57. James, op. cit., p. 13.

58. Sir Thomas Heath, *Aristarchus of Samos*. Oxford: Oxford University Press, 1913, p. 220.

59. E.A. Parsons, *The Alexandrian Library*. Amsterdam: The Elsevier Press, 1952, p. 145.

60. Heath, *Aristarchus of Samos*, p. 48 (see reference citing the authorities Martin and Berger).

61. Heath, *Greek Astronomy*. New York, 1932, p. xxvi.

62. Quoted by Heath, *Aristarchus of Samos*, p. 131.

63. Gow, op. cit. p. 131.

64. Sarton, *History of Science: Ancient Science through the Golden Age of Greece*, op. cit., p. 200.

65. Heath, *Aristarchus of Samos*, pp. 101–105.

66. Norman Lockyer, *The Dawn ol Astronomy*. Cambridge, Mass.: The MIT Press, 1964.

67. Heath, *Aristarchus of Samos*, op. cit., p. 313.

68. Van der Waerden, op. cit., p. 37.

69. Heath, *Aristarchus of Samos*, op. cit., p. 299.

70. George Sarton, *A History of Science: Hellenistic Science and Culture in the Last Three Centuries B.C.*, Cambridge, Mass.: Harvard University Press, 1959, p. 54.

71. Heath, *Aristarchus of Samos*, op. cit., p. 302.

72. B. Hessen, "The Social and Economic Roots of Newton's *Principia*", in: *Science at the Crossroads*, ed. by Gary Wersky, London: Frank Cass, 1978, (reprint of 1931 ed.).

MATHEMATICS AND ENGINEERING IN
THE NILE VALLEY

Beatrice Lumpkin

For thousands of years, the Nile Valley was the Main Street of the civilized world. Especially in mathematics and the natural sciences, Egyptian scholars played a major role in building the foundations of our modern science. Yet the full scale of this African contribution is either little known, or attributed to other peoples. This paper will give a brief outline of the 4,000 years of Nile Valley pre-eminence in mathematics, with some reference to the engineering and technology which developed hand-in-hand with mathematics.

Many factors placed the Nile Valley in such an advantageous position. As Bernal points out, productive periods of science are based on a flourishing economy and technology.[1] And in the Nile Valley there was the needed combination of good physical resources and inventive people, people who were the first to grow food, to build brick houses and to develop writing.

Important stages that preceded the modern age in mathematics included the prehistoric, ancient, classical, Middle Ages and the Renaissance. In each of these periods, the mathematics of the Nile Valley played a leading role. In fact, the first task of the European Renaissance concerned the need to bring Europe up to the higher level of African and Asian knowledge, then expressed in the Muslim civilization.

The mathematical and scientific tradition of the Nile Valley was a continuous one. Yet in all the "standard" histories, Egyptian mathematics is dismembered into three parts, with only the first recognized as Egyptian. These texts arbitrarily bring ancient Egyptian mathematics to an abrupt end with the Greek conquest of the Egyptian state. The second part of Egyptian mathematics, from the founding of Alexandria in -332 (i.e., B.C.), up to 500, is not usually recognized as Egyptian, but as "Hellenistic." In this paper, I will use the more accurate term of "classical Egyptian."

The third era of Egyptian learning, also not recognized as Egyptian in the standard histories, is the Muslim period of the Middle Ages. As a whole, contributions of the Muslim culture are slighted in histories permeated by a Eurocentric bias—the belief that no one but Europeans made important contributions to knowledge. Almost completely left out, the work of African mathematicians and scientists of that period remains little known.

Continuity of Egyptian Science

The continuity and pre-eminence of Nile Valley mathematics and science is a concept based on historical fact. The language changed—Greek after Alexander's conquest and Arabic after the Muslim conquest. But the change in language did not represent a change of culture and tradition.[2] Historians have not been consistent in recognizing this continuity, as in Otto Neugebauer's *Exact Sciences in Antiquity:*

> Indeed mathematics of the Hellenistic period. and still more of the later periods, is in part only a link in the unbroken tradition which reached from the earliest periods of ancient history down to the beginning of modern times.[3]

Yet in another part of the same book, Neugebauer makes the highly prejudiced statement: "The role of Egyptian mathematics is probably best described as a retarding force upon numerical procedures."[4] Such an unhistoric judgment is much like faulting the inventor of the crystal radio for not inventing solid state television first.

The Beginnings

We must go back to the beginnings of the human race for the beginnings of science, because wherever there are humans, there is, already, the chemistry of fire. Wherever there are humans, there is mathematics, because every language has number words, and the concepts of logic needed for mathematics—the words "and", "or."[5] Since Africa is widely believed to be the birth place of the human race, it follows that Africa was the birthplace of mathematics and science.

Before the beginning of writing, people did record numbers. A fossil bone found near Lake Edwards, Zayre, was carved in year -8000 to make a very early record of numbers that may be a multiplication table,[6] a record of phases of the moon,[7] or even a game score.[8] The tally marks carved in the Ishango bone show numbers 3, 6, a space, 4, 8, then 10, 5, 5, 7 on one side. On the other side are 11, 21, 19, 9, 11, 13, 17, 19.

Although the Ishango bone was found in the Lakes region, the connection to the Nile Valley is immediate. The Ishango people have been traced, through their bone harpoons, down the length of the Nile valley, either by commerce or direct migration.[9]

By the earliest time of recorded Egyptian history, a 360 day calendar (with 5 holidays added) was well established. But there is little agreement

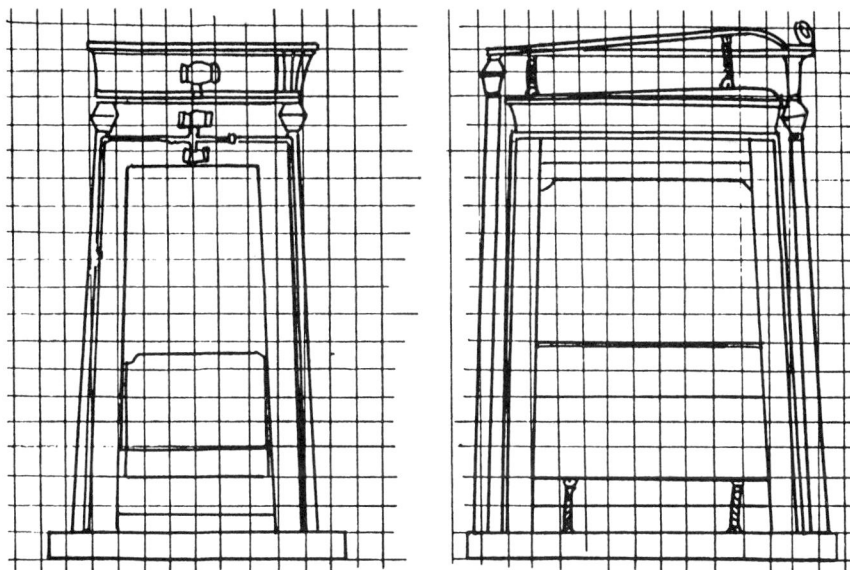

Front and side views of a shrine from Ghorab. (Adapted by Peggy Lipschutz from Clarke and Engelbach, *Ancient Egyptian Masonry*, (Fig. 48.) Cited as proof that Egyptians did draw objects from different aspects. Note the square grid used to preserve proportions during construction from the plans.

on the date of first use. From the astronomical information in the calendar, and based on the Sothic cycle of about 1,460 years (heliacal rising of Sirius) the start-up date of the calendar could be given as -4241 or -2773.[10] Struik argued for the later date, claiming that people, "slowly emerging from neolithic conditions," could not have developed such a calendar.[11] But available evidence argues for earlier dates. Agriculture began much earlier than -4241[12] giving "Stone Age" man both the incentive and the opportunity to make the astronomical observations necessary for a calendar. Indeed, Diop reminds us that many years of study of the star cycles were necessary before a calendar could be normalized.[13] Even the date of the origin of Egyptian hieroglyphs and the pharaonic institution has been pushed back in time, and southward in location, by the findings of Bruce Williams and his colleagues."[14]

The Glorious Ancient Egyptians

We may not know the full scope of ancient Egyptian mathematics, but fortunately a few primary sources survived the grave robbers. A few mathematical papyri, limestone chips and leather rolls outline many achievements of ancient Egyptian mathematics. The longest, written by the scribe

Ahmose, is known as the "Rhind Mathematical Papyrus", after the Scot who brought it to Europe. We also have books by Greek classical mathematicians in which they fully acknowledged their debt to Egypt.

The first cipherization of numbers took place in Egypt—a huge step forward for human science. Instead of single tally marks to represent numbers, as on the Ishango bone, hieroglyphic numerals used special symbols for powers of 10.

Egyptian arithmetic made use of the commutative, associative and distributive properties of multiplication. Egyptian multiplication needed no memorization of multiplication tables and was well suited to the additive nature of Egyptian numerals. For 32 × 19, they changed to 19 × 32 and proceeded to double:

−1	32	Using just the partial products checked
−2	64	to give 19 in the left column, we add:

4	128	1	32
8	256	2	64
−16	512	16	512
	total	19	608

Although problems always involved specific values, they were often followed by a statement of general procedure, a formula.[15] The derogatory claim that Egyptians were limited to solving practical problems and had no interest in the theoretical is refuted by the facts. Certainly, the Egyptian forerunner of the Mother Goose rhyme, "As I was going to St. Ives, I met a man with seven wives . . .", had no narrow, practical purpose. It is problem 79 of the Ahmose papyrus which lists: 7 houses, 49 cats, 343 mice, 2,401 spelt, 16,807 hekat, and the sum of 19,607![16]

Problem 79 seems, "just for fun." Its mathematical significance will be described later. But the path from ancient Egypt to Mother Goose went through Italy where Fibonacci, after study in Egypt, wrote: "Seven old women went to Rome: each woman had seven mules: each mule carried seven sacks: each sack contained seven loaves: and with each loaf were seven knives: each knife was put up in seven sheaths."[17]

Fractions

It is a measure of the advanced Egyptian technology that fractions became necessary very early. The vast construction projects for pyramids, irrigation works, temples and obelisks required accurate measurement of lengths, areas and volumes. Tens of thousands of workers received pay according to fixed rates and provisions had to be divided among members of

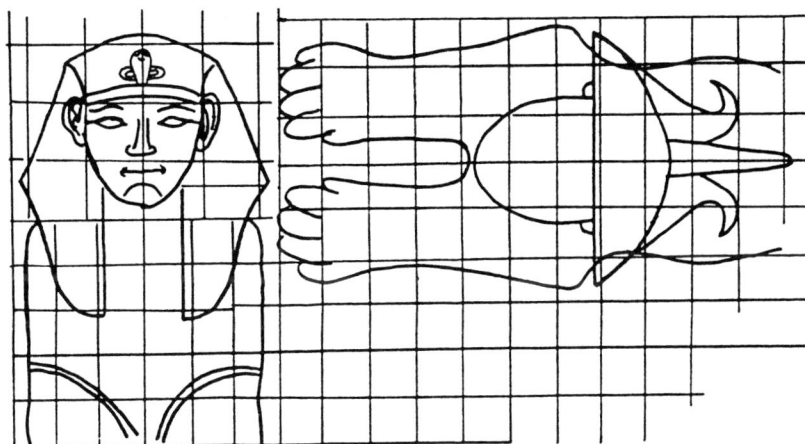

Working drawing for sculpture of a sphinx. (Adapted by Peggy Lipschutz from Heinrich Schafer, *Principles of Egyptian Art*. London: Clarendon, 1974, p. 329.) Common use of grid of squares led to concept of coordinates.

a work crew.

The concept of fraction was the concept of inverse of integers, or unit tractions of numerator one. Fractions were at the heart of the Egyptian arithmetic, according to Richard J. Gillings, a devoted encyclopedist of ancient Egyptian mathematics.[18] The scribes performed operations that were breathtakingly complex. For example, the proof in problem 33 of the Ahmose papyrus requires the addition of 16 + 1/56 + 1/679 + 1/776 + 10 + 2/3 + 1/84 + 1/1358 + 1/4074 + 1/1164 + 8 + 1/112 + 1/1358 + 1/1552 + 2 + 1/4 + 1/28 + 1/392 + 1/4753 + 1/5432. The sum is 37! The Egyptians used their equivalent of the least common denominator and red helping numbers (new numerators) to find the answer.[19]

Such complex problems were not easily mastered by some modem translators. Breasted judged that "Fractions. however, caused difficulty."[20] That may be true for some historians. But the virtuosity of the scribes turned their fractions into a very useful tool. These same Egyptian fractions were used by scientists for thousands of years after their invention, right up to the modern period.

Aha Calculus

Aha, or heap, was used as an abstract term for the unknown in an equation, leading historians to call Egyptian algebra, "aha calculus." Equations were solved by a method now called, "false position", which continued in use until the 20th century. A simple example from Ahmose asks for a quantity and its 1/7, whose sum is 19. To find the quantity, Ahmose assumed a false answer of 7. In this case 7 is a convenient choice as the least common denominator. But 7 plus 1/7 of 7 gives 8, not the desired 19. To get 19 from 8, we must multiply 8 by 19/8. Then the correction factor for the assumed false answer is 19/8. Use 19/8 × 7 to get 16 + 5/8, the correct answer. Of course, the Egyptians wrote 5/8 as unit fractions, 1/2 + 1/4."[21]

Until recent times, the rules used by Ahmose to convert common fractions to unit fractions were not seriously investigated. Gillings, the only "Western" historian to write a book-length study of "Mathematics in the Time of the Pharaohs", has proposed some possible formulas. Other scholars are now beginning to join this interesting study.

Problem 61B of Ahmose clearly states the Egyptian rule for finding 2/3 of any odd unit fraction: "The making of 2/3 of a fraction uneven. If it is said to thee, what is 2/3 of 1/5. Make thou times of it 2, times 6 of it: 2/3 of it this is. Behold does one according the like for fraction every uneven which may occur" (2/3 × 1/5 = 1/10 + 1/30).[22] With this statement, the scribe gave a general formula.

Series, Arithmetic and Geometric

Many Ahmose problems involved arithmetic and geometric series arising from wage scales and division-of-bread problems connected with the complex economy and class structure. These problems also shed light on one of the greatest Egyptian achievements, the organization and administration of thousands of people into coherent work forces encompassing many trades and professions.

Just to bring back the stone for a large sarcophagus, King Menthuhotep IV sent 10,000 people to the Hammamat quarry.[23] Then what were the numbers needed to build the huge pyramids? And what were the principles of organization used to coordinate the work teams, to assure a supply of materials and to feed tens of thousands of workers. How many bookkeepers did it take to divide the wages according to scales that went from the lowest to 35 times greater pay at the top?

Ahmose problem 64 asks how to divide 10 hekats of grain among 10 men so that there is a constant difference of 1/8 between portions. Ahmose solves this problem in arithmetic series by a method equivalent to our modern formula. (Arithmetic series have a constant difference between successive terms, for example, 5 + 10 + 15 + 20 + 25 etc.)

Steps	Ahmos	Formula
1. Find the average share	10/10=1	s/n
2. Subtract 1 from 10 to get the number of differences	9	n–1
3. Take half the given difference	$^1/_2 \times {}^1/_8 = {}^1/_{16}$	d/2
4. Multiply by the number of differences	$9 \times {}^1/_{16}$	d/2(n=1)
5. Add above to average share to find last, highest share, "L"	$1 + {}^9/_{16}$	L=s/n+d/2(n–1)
6. Alternate to steps 5, subtract $^9/_{16}$ from average share to find lowest term, "a"	$1 - {}^9/_{16}$	2=s/n-d/2(n–1)

Transposing in 6 gives the modern formula, s = n/2 (2a + (n–1)d). Ahmose's answers in modern terms were: 7/16, 9/16, 11/16, 13/16 . . . up to 1 + 9/16.[24]

Geometric series were also carefully studied. For example. Problem 79, 7 houses with 7 cats each, each got 7 mice, each of whom ate 7 spelts of grain, each of which would have produced 7 hekats of grain, was mentioned earlier. But Ahmose never wasted words. He only listed a second column which shows us further knowledge of geometric series:

1	2801
2	5602
4	11204
7	19607

Here 2,801 = 1 + 7 + 49 + 343 + 2401, according to Gillings.[25]

Long before the Ahmose papyrus was written, Egyptian mathematicians were already guiding the construction of pyramids, measuring the seked (cotangent) to guarantee that the pyramid would be stable. The first example of the use of rectangular coordinates comes from Egypt, a natural step beyond the square grids widely used to transfer art details in correct proportions. Of the thousands of construction plans, only a few have come down to us. One of these gives the height and horizontal spacing for constructing a curved surface, using the same principle of rectangular coordinates found in modern graphs.[26]

Had we not had the luck to find this one remnant, we might not have known that the Egyptians used rectangular coordinates in their building plans. The same is true of the Moscow and Berlin papyruses, known after the museums where they are now housed. Had we not had these papyrus fragments, we would have been unaware of the higher level reached in these problems which include second degree equations, and the formula for the area of a curved surface.

Berlin problem 1 asks for the size of two squares, the sum of whose areas equals a square of 100 square cubits, given that the side of the smaller square is 3/4 the side of the other unknown square.

If the unknown squares are of sides x and y, in modern symbols we have: $x = {}^3/_4 y$ and $x^2 + y^2 = 100$

Assuming the false position value of 1 for the side of the larger square, then the smaller would be $^3/_4$, and the sum of the two areas would be 1 + 9/16. Since it is the side, not area we are looking for, we need the square root of 1 + 9/16, which the Egyptians found correct to be 1-1/4 . Since the square root of the desired 100 square cubits is 10 cubits, the correction factor is 10 divided by 1-1/4 . We get the correct values for the sides, 8 and 6 cubits, by multiplying first 1, then 3/4 by the correction factor. The proof? Areas of squares side 8 and side 6 are 64 + 36 square cubits, and their sum is 100, as required.[27]

Geometry

This problem of the sum of two squares, equal in area to a third square, and sides 6, 8, 10, resembles an application of the "Pythagorean theorem. Another such relationship is built into the Egyptian measurements of length which include cubits, double remens equal to the diagonal of a 1-cubit square, and remens. Areas can be doubled by changing units from cubits to double remens, or halved by going from cubit to remen measure. These specific examples of Pythagorean triples indicate that Egyptians were conducting investigations that could lead to the formulation of the so-called Pythagorean theorem.[28]

Yet the style in Western historiography is to deny any possibility that ancient Egyptians contributed to the development of this theorem—that the sum of the squares of the sides of a right triangle is equal to the square on the hypotenuse. Some claim that the Babylonians were far superior because their clay tablet, Plimpton 322, contains a long list of Pythagorean triples. Of course, clay tablets of Babylonia proved more durable, although in their day they were less convenient than the Egyptian papyrus. The few, fragile pieces of surviving papyri give us only part of the achievements of ancient Egypt. Disparaging comparisons are not only unwarranted but detract from both the great African and Asian civilizations. And why is this theorem still known after Pythagoras when he came on the scene 1,000 years later?

The Moscow papyrus, although in poor condition, reveals two of the highest achievements of the ancient Egyptian geometers. The volume of a truncated pyramid, cut off at the top, was correctly found. Even more breathtaking, in Moscow problem 10, there is the correct formula for the area of a hemisphere, according to Gillings.[29] A possible method of measuring this area is illustrated in Lumpkin's, *Senefer and Hatshepsut.*[30] Another achievement was the accurate measurement of π as 3.16, compared to the modern 3.14 and the Biblical value of 3.

Classical Period of Egyptian Science

What happened to ancient Egyptian mathematics after the Greek conquest? It is the theme of this paper that ancient Egyptian mathematics did not die but blended into the new mathematics of the classical period, built on the base of the ancients. As Greek city states developed, a few Greeks had traveled to Egypt to study. Thales (c. -600) is credited with being the first to bring the study of geometry from Egypt to Greece. In all arrogance, some historians call Thales the first mathematician, as the first to give a deductive proof. Half a century later, Pythagoras spent 20 years in Egypt and also visited Mesopotamia before founding a school in Crotona, Southern Italy.[31] Democritus of Abdera (c. -400) also spent time in Egypt and boasted that not even the rope stretchers of Egypt surpassed him.

The Egyptian city of Alexandria, founded in -332, became the greatest center of classical mathematics. Most Egyptian mathematicians of the classical period wrote in the Greek language. But that did not make them Greek, any more than the current use of English by Japanese scientists makes them English or North American.

Alexandria, itself, was peopled by Egyptians and a few people from neighboring countries. George Sarton, the respected encyclopedist of the history of science, reminds us that, "Greek emigrants were too few in pre-Christian times and too little interested in science and scholarship to affect and change Eastern minds."[32] Then why, we must ask, is this period of Alexandrian science not credited to the African people of Alexandria, the people of the Nile Valley?

Euclid of Alexandria, one of the greatest mathematicians of this era, lived and died in Egypt. There is no suggestion that he ever left Africa. Yet he is pictured in textbooks as a fair, European Greek, not as an Egyptian. We have no pictures of these ancients, but we could at least visualize them honestly, in costumes, complexions and features true to their peoples and their times. George Sarton decried the historical forgery of fabricating pictures of mathematicians, but the racist aspect, representing Egyptians as Europeans, is even more serious.

Euclid's fame rests above all on his *Elements,* containing 13 books and 465 propositions.[34] The logical arrangement of this work is so masterful, that the *Elements* has dominated the teaching of geometry for 2,000 years. The deductive method of proof did more than add rigor to the largely experimental geometry of earlier Egyptians. With the deductive method, new theorems could be proved, allowing mathematics to progress beyond the immediate needs of the economy of that time. The practical side of mathematics continued, side by side with the theoretical.

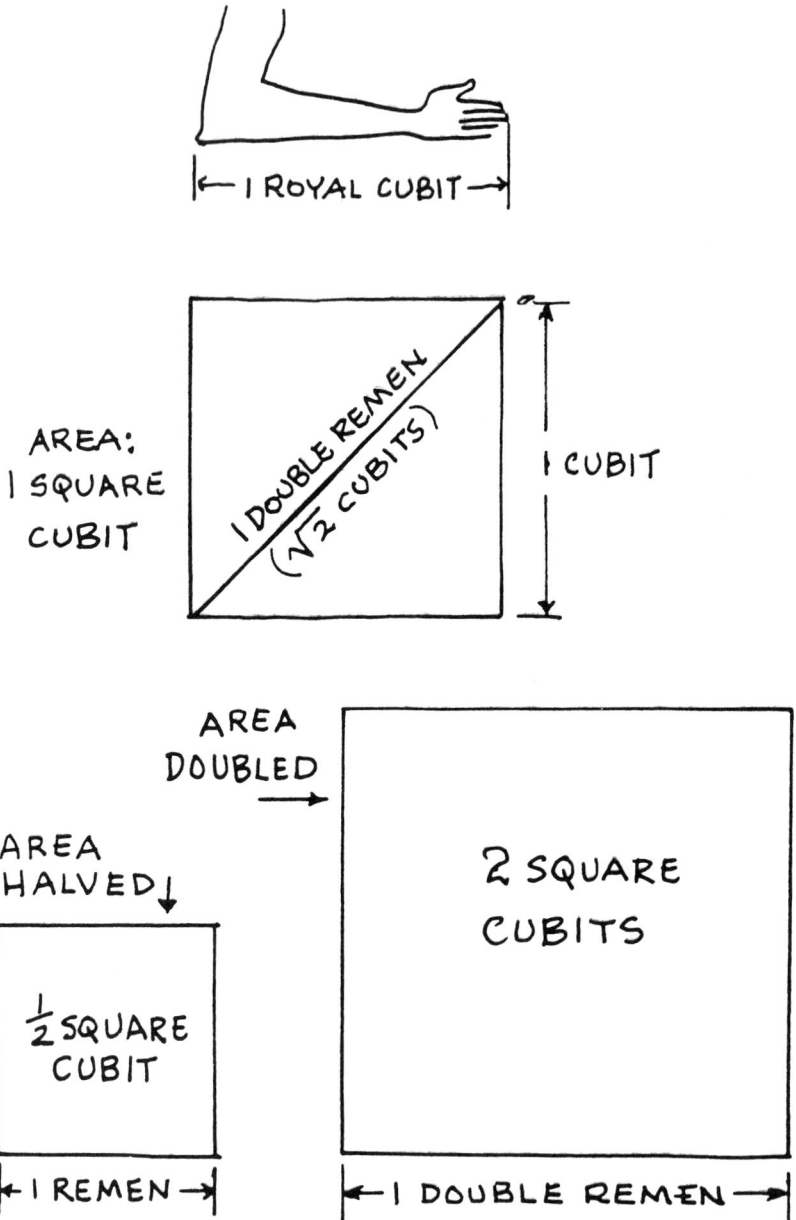

Egyptian Measurements. Relationships between cubit, double remen, and remen give an example of so-called Pythagorean theorem that $1^2 + 1^2 = (\sqrt{2})^2$ (From Lumpkin, *Senefer and Hatshepsut*, p. 55)

The first person to measure the circumference of the earth accurately, Eratosthenes of Cyrene, Libya, was also African born.[35] He measured the shadow cast by the sun in Alexandria the same day that the sun shone down a deep well in Syene, 500 miles south. The shadow showed an angle of 1/50 of a circle from zenith, directly overhead. Multiplying the 500 miles by 50 gave 25,000 compared to the modern 24,830 miles, an error of only .6 of 1%. Eratosthenes is also known for his "sieve" for prime numbers.

In trigonometry, Egyptians had always been pre-eminent, up to and including the Middle Ages. The ancients had used the concept of the seked or cotangent as a guide in building the pyramids. Menelaus of Alexandria (c. 100) laid the foundations for spherical trigonometry and its application to astronomy. He was followed by another great Egyptian, half a century later, Ptolemy of Alexandria, author of the *Almagest*. Known as an astronomer, his work in trigonometry alone would have assured his fame. To aid him in the extensive calculations needed for his astronomical tables, Ptolemy developed formulas for the sines and cosines of the sum and differences of two angles and half angles. His tables remained in use for 1,000 years. Ptolemy also improved on the excellent ancient Egyptian approximation of π with his value of 377/120, × 3.14167.[36]

In this same period, the mathematician and engineering genius, Heron of Alexandria, invented 100 machines and wrote extensive mathematical works. He is one Alexandrian often acknowledged as Egyptian, but for the wrong reasons. Eves follows other historians in describing Heron as Egyptian: "At any rate, his writings, which so often aim at practical utility rather than theoretical completeness, show a curious blend of the Greek and Oriental."[37] Indeed, isn't it strange that nationality or race should be deduced from the nature of a person's writings, rather than place of birth and homeland?

On the same grounds, Diophantus of Alexandria is judged to have been Egyptian, because his mathematical work had a practical orientation. Often considered "the father of algebra", Diophantus introduced efficient, algebraic abbreviations and proposed problems which inspired Fermat, the great 17th century mathematician.

Longer than any other city, Alexandria endured as a scientific center. Its last days of the classical period were highlighted by the short, brilliant career of Hypatia, a woman algebraist who held the chair of the department of philosophy at the University of Alexandria. In 415, a fanatical Christian mob brutally murdered Hypatia, literally tearing her apart. Some textbooks "picture" Hypatia as a white European, although she was born in Egypt, the daughter of Theon, also an Egyptian. Her prominence as a department chair was certainly in the Egyptian tradition of greater rights for women as compared to the near slave status of Greek women.

The Alexandria of Euclid, Ptolemy, Heron, Diophantus, Hypatia, Pappus,

Area of a hemisphere. The Moscow Papyrus correctly gives the area of a hemisphere as the area of two great circles of the sphere, or twice the area of the base of the hemisphere. This formula could have been checked approximately by counting the number of squares drawn on a large hemisphere and comparing the number of squares of the same size, drawn on the base (from *Senefer and Hatshepsut*, p. 126)

Menelaus, Theon, Proclus and many more, was Egyptian in every sense. Its economy was nourished by the productive agriculture of the Nile as well as the commerce between the Nile and the Mediterranean. Its population was Egyptian, and the number of immigrants, as Sarton said above, was small. As for all the Egyptians named Ptolemy in the first century, if they were

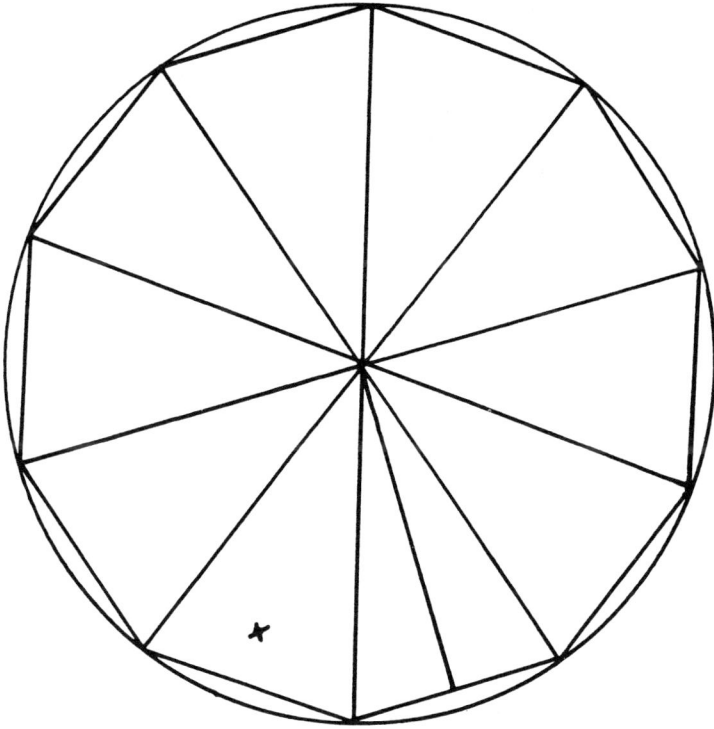

Abu Kamil's decagon (with construction line added). Area, 100; unknown side
x^7 **3.6**

descended at all from Alexander's general, after 15 generations they were Egyptians, in every sense of the word.

Egyptian Mathematics in the Middle Ages

With Hypatia murdered in 415, and the death of Proclus of Alexandria in 485, any possible later works of the Alexandrians have not survived. But by the year 750, Islam began to revive centers of learning and Euclid's *Elements*, Ptolemy's *Almagest* etc. appeared in Arabic. In the Nile Valley, a new center of learning arose in the city we call Cairo. But in Europe, little if anything was left of the mathematical schools. For lack of anyone to read and understand the great classics, even the books were lost.

In the 9th century, a textbook on Muslim arithmetic and algebra was brought into Europe from North Africa. It introduced the Europeans to Arabic numerals. Laws were passed forbidding their use, but the spread of Arabic numerals could not be stopped. The Arabic-Hindu numerals were vastly superior to the Roman numerals then used in Europe. Our word for algebra was taken from the name of this famous text, *Al-jabr wa'l muqabalah.* From the author's name, al-Khwarizmi, came our word for "algorithm", a mathematical procedure.

Al Khwarizmi stated that his purpose in writing his book was to serve the practical needs of the people concerning matters of inheritance, legacies, partition, lawsuits and commerce.[38]

Just a few years after Khwarizmi, a more advanced algebra was written by a man called, "the Egyptian calculator", al-Hasib Abu-Kamil Shiya ibn Aslam ibn Muhammad al-Hasib al-Misri (850–930). His work influenced mathematicians for centuries and was copied wholesale by Leonardo of Pisa (Fibonacci), 300 years later. Yet few today know the name of this great African mathematician, Abu Kamil.

New features of Kamil's work included use of several variables— Khwarizmi was restricted to one—a study of equal roots of quadratic equations, and especially the use of irrational numbers as terms of proportions, roots and coefficients of equations. For example, to solve the system:

$$x + y + z = 10$$
$$xz = y^2$$
$$x^2 + y^2 = z^2$$

Kamil used the false position value of $x = 1$. This lead to

$$x + y + z = 1\tfrac{1}{2} + \sqrt{1\tfrac{1}{4}} + \sqrt{1\tfrac{1}{2}} + \sqrt{1\tfrac{1}{4}}$$

Since the right side should have been 10, Kamil set up a proportion to find the correction factor needed.[39] And all of this was done with words, without the advantage of modern symbols, square root signs, etc. Diophantus, an earlier Egyptian, had introduced symbols for squares, cubes, etc. but his lead was not followed until much later. Kamil called the unknown, "the thing", and its square, "mal". Than x^4 he called mal mal, x^6, mal mal mal, etc.[40] Diophantus' work in indeterminate equations was the subject of other work by Kamil, his *Book of Rare Things in Arithmetic.*[41]

Kamil presented 20 geometric problems in *The Decagon and Pentagon*, a work copied extensively by Fibonacci, 300 years later.[42] In one problem Kamil asks for the side of a regular decagon whose area is 100—a specific value. Yet his method is general and his approach is almost entirely algebraic. Step by Step, Kamil finds the unknown side X from $x^5/_84 = 1600 - \sqrt{2,048,000}$, (approximately 3.6).[43]

Just a few years after Abu Kamil, Egypt came under the rule of the Fatimids (969–1171). The power of Egypt extended from North Africa to Syria and Western Arabia. There was a general surge of rapid development, economic as well as cultural. Windmills were built in Egypt and other new devices came into use. All of the sciences flourished; "Chemistry, medicine, pharmacology, zoology, botany and mineralogy knew an extraordinary development," wrote Yushkevitch, the Soviet historian of mathematics.[44] Cairo, founded in 969, became the capital and the site of a Science Academy, the Dar el Hikma, or House of Wisdom.

A very well equipped observatory was built on the Mukattam heights. There Ibn Yunus, probably the greatest Muslim astronomer, according to al-Battani and Abu'l Wafa, worked on his famous Hakimi Tables which included observations of eclipses and conjunctions of planets.

Yunus improved on the work of Ptolemy, the Egyptian astronomer of 900 years earlier. In trigonometry, Yunus was the first to use the prosthapherical formula: $\cos A \cos B = \frac{1}{2}(\cos(A+B) + \cos(A-B))$.[45]

For those who doubt that something called prosthapherisis could really simplify anything, Yunus' formula converts multiplication to addition, a simpler operation.[46] Indeed Yunus' method was used by the famous Danish astronomer, Tycho Brahe (1546–1601) and became known to Napier in Scotland. Then Napier used this principle to invent logarithms.[47] Yunus was able to calculate the sine of 1° accurately to 5 decimal places. So accurate were Yunus' calculations, that he succeeded in developing a table of sines for angles differing by just one second.[48]

At the same Cairo Science Academy where Ibn Yunus worked, the Iraqui-born ibn al-Haytham (died c. 1039) did the crowning work of his career. Haytham was famous for his work in optics. Less well known, but of the greatest importance, were Haytham's contributions to mathematics.[49] He developed a formula for the sum of a series of 4th powers which enabled him to evaluate the equivalent of $\int_0^a t^4\, dt$. His original work in geometry was developed by other famous Muslim mathematicians, especially Omar Khayyam and Nasir Eddin. They laid the basis for modern non-Euclidean geometry which describes the curvature of space. It is a fact that Saccheri, the European pioneer in this field in the 18th century, used the work of Muslim mathematicians. The "Saccheri quadrilateral" closely resembled ibn Haytham's quadrilateral of 700 years earlier.[50]

Important discoveries were still made by Muslim mathematicians (the term "Muslim" here is cultural, not religious) as late as the 15th century. Al Kashi in central Asia, developed decimal fractions although Stevin is given credit for their popularization.[51] Al Qasadi of Granada, who died in Africa in 1486, did remarkable work in bringing symbols into algebra, before this development began in Europe. He used the first letters of the Arabic words to show unknown, square, or cube and a symbolic equal sign. The symbolization was so advanced, that Yushkevitch believes there were other Muslim mathematicians, before Qasadi, who began this development.[52] Yet this outstanding work has remained practically unknown here and is still available only to the Arabic speaking world.

In summarizing the contributions of the African Muslim mathematicians, especially those of the Nile Valley, an author is overwhelmed by an embarrassment of riches. These facts have led some historians to revise the standard Euro-centric evaluation—that the Muslim mathematicians added nothing new, and served only to preserve the classics of the Greek mathematicians. Such bias is expressed by Morris Kline, that mathematics, "finally secured a firm grip on life in the highly congenial soil of Greece and waxed strong for a brief period . . . With the decline of Greek civilization, the plant remained dormant for a thousand years . . . when the plant was transported to Europe proper and once more imbedded in fertile soil."[53]

Other writers, for example, J.F. Scott, admit that Muslim mathematicians "did more than preserve; they made some significant contributions of their own."[54] But two pages later, the same writer, in the same book declares that, "The debt which the west owes to the Arabs for their part in preserving and transmitting Greek science is very great. It must not be forgotten, however, that preservation is one thing; creation is something different. Mathematics for its development requires the creative faculty, and there is little evidence of this in the many centuries which separate the decline of Alexandrian science and its revival in the West."[55]

Such unhistoric views are refuted by the same Europeans who borrowed so heavily from the culture of Egypt in the Middle Ages. For example, Leonardo Fibonacci of Pisa wrote:

> All that was studied in Egypt, in Syria, in Greece, in Sicily, and in Provence . . . I investigated very carefully . . . I wanted to write a work of 15 chapters, with nothing capital left without a demonstration and this I did so that the science might be easily understood, and *the Latin people should no longer be deprived of it.* [56]

Conclusion

When Fibonacci wrote these words, Egypt, compared to Italy, was more advanced in science and culture. But unfavorable changes during the rule of the Turkic Mamelukes and the Ottomans slowed down Egyptian development.[57] With the strengthening of feudal structures, the economy of the prosperous Muslim states retrogressed and scientific output declined. While the growth of capitalism and industry was being stifled in Egypt, the merchant capitalists in the city states of Europe were gaining power. Western Europe was also spared the damaging invasions suffered by North Africa and Western and Central Asia.

Still there was a rough parity between Western Europe and many African states in the 15th century. This equality was destroyed, and the economies of African countries were devastated, by the slavery and colonialism that followed. Not only did mathematic and scientific output come to a halt with the disruption of the Nile Valley economy, but even the memory of these achievements was almost destroyed by a flood of misinformation and racism, let loose to justify slavery and imperialism. This historical account reveals just a part of the mathematic and scientific genius of the people of the Nile Valley. Now suppressed, this genius will be free to produce again when there will be peace and freedom from imperialist oppression. Here, the true history of the achievements of the Nile Valley civilization can play a liberating role by restoring the sense of continuity and identity with a great past, pointing to a great future. In particular, knowledge of the mathematical achievements can help allay "math anxiety" among the descendants of the Nile Valley peoples in Africa and in the Americas.

Notes

1. J.D. Bernal, *Science in History, Vol. 1,* (N.Y.: Cameron, 1954), p. 23.
2. Dirk Struik, *A Concise History of Mathematics,* (N.Y.: Dover, 1967), p. 69.
3. Otto Neugebauer, *Exact Sciences In Antiquity,* (N.Y.: Dover, 1957), p. 146.
4. ibid., p. 80.
5. Karl Menger, lecture on History of Mathematics, I.I.T., 1970.
6. Claudia Zaslavsky, Africa Counts, (N.Y.: Prindle, Weber and Schmidt, 1973), p. 18.
7. Alexander Marshack, *The Roots of Civilization,* (N.Y.: McGraw Hill, 1972), p. 364
8. Ruth Helen Washington, "The Game Hypothesis of Notations on the Ishango Bone", *Journal of African Civilizations,* Vol. 4, No. 1, pp. 102–6
9. Sonia Cole, *The Prehistory of East Africa,* (N.Y.: Macmillan, 1963), p. 251.
10. Carl Boyer, History of Mathematics, (N.Y.: Wiley, 1968), p. 683.
11. Struik, op. cit., pp. 24–5.
12. Pred Wendorf and Rushdi Said, "Palaeolithic Remains in Upper Egypt", *Nature,* Vol. 215, July 15, 1967, pp. 244–247.
13. Cheikh Anta Diop, *The African Origin of Civilization,* (Westport: Lawrence Hill, 1974), p. 22.
14. Bruce Williams, "The Lost Pharaohs of Nubia", *Journal of African Civilizations,* Vol. 4, No. 2, pp. 38–42.
15. Richard J. Gillings, *Mathematics in the Time of the Pharaohs,* (Cambridge: M.I.T., 1973) p. 232.
16. Arnold Buffum Chace, *The Rhind Mathematical Papyrus,* (Reston: NCTM, 1979), pp. 136–7.
17. Quoted by Boyer, op. cit., p. 281.
18. Gillings, op. cit., p. 3
19. Chace, op. cit., p. 75.
20. James Breasted, *History of Egypt,* (N.Y.: Bantam, 1967 edition), p. 85.
21. Chace, op. cit., p. 67.
22. Ibid., p. 124.
23. Somers Clarke and Engelbach, *Ancient Egyptian Masonry,* (London: Oxford), pp. 32–3.
24. Gillings, op. cit., pp. 173–5.

25. Ibid., pp. 167–9.
26. Clarke and Engelbach, op. cit., pp. 52–3.
27. Gillings, op. cit., p. 161.
28. Beatrice Lumpkin, "The Egyptians and Pythagorean Triples", *Historia Mathematica*, Vol. 7, No. 2, p. 186–7.
29. Gillings, op. cit., pp. 198–9.
30. Beatrice Lumpkin, *Senefer and Hatshepsut*, (Chicago: DuSable, 1983), p. 126.
31. Howard Eves, *An Introduction to the History of Mathematics*, (N.Y.: Holt, Rinehart and Winston, 1969), p. 52.
32. George Sarton, *A History of Science*, (Cambridge: Harvard, 1959), p. IX.
33. George Sarton, "Iconographic Honesty", *Isis*, Vol. 30(1939), p. 226.
34. Eves, op. cit., pp. 114–5.
35. Boyer, op. cit., p. 176.
36. Ibid., p. 187.
37. Eves, op. cit., p. 157.
38. Ali Abdullah Al-Daffa, *The Muslim Contribution to Mathematics*, (Atlantic Highlands: Humanities Press, 1977), p. 53.
39. Adolf P. Youschkevich (Yushkevitch), *Les Mathematiques Arabes*, (8th–15th centuries), translated from Russian to French, Vrin, Paris, 1976, p. 59 Translations quoted are my translation from the French. B. Lumpkin.
40. Mohammad Yadegari and Martin Levey, Abu Kamil's *"On the Pentagon and Decagon"*, (Tokyo: History of Science Society of Japan, Supplement 2, 1971), p. 3.
41. Yushkevitch, op. cit., p. 66.
42. Yadegari and Levey, op. cit., p. 1.
43. Ibid., p. 31.
44. Yushkevitch, op. cit., p. 5.
45. George Sarton, *Introduction* to *the History of Science*, Vol. I, (Baltimore: Carnegie, 1927), p. 717.
46. *Encyclopedia of Islam*.
47. Boyer, op. cit., pp. 340–3.
48. Yushkevitch, op. cit. p. 148.
49. Gordon and Jeff Deboo, "Ibn al-Haytham, Pioneer Physicist of the Middle Ages", *Arab Perspectives*, Vol. 2, Nov. 1981, p. 13.
50. Dirk Struik, "Omar Khayyam as Mathematician", *The Mathematics Teacher* Vol. 51 (1958), pp. 280–5.
51. Boyer, op. cit., p. 268.
52. Yushkevitch, op. cit., p. 104.
53. Morris Kline, Mathematics in Western Culture, (N.Y.: Oxford, 1953), pp. 9–10.
54. J.F. Scott, History of Mathematics (London: Taylor and Francis, 1960), p. 61.
55. Ibid., p. 63.
56. Ettore Caruccio, *Mathematics and Logic in History and Contemporary Thought*, translated by Isabel Quigley, (Chicago: Aldine, 1964), p. 159.
57. Paulus Gerdes, *A Matematica Nos Paises Islamicos*, (Maputo: Tlanu, 1984). p. 13.

NILE VALLEY ORIGINS OF THE SCIENCE
OF THE MIND

Na'im Akbar

Despite the impressive technological advancement of modern Western man relative to his own history, he ranks far behind the Ancient African people of KMT (Egypt) both technologically and spiritually. Part of the reason for this mental devolution is the limited conception of human potential that one finds in Western science. Western man's limitation is a disaster for his captives, who are the descendants of the people of Ancient Kemit. The possible advancement of Western man and the redemption or "renaissance" of African man is contingent upon rediscovering those concepts of human development which inspired the ascension of the people of Ancient Africa.

The originators of modern thought, as it emerged from its genesis in the Nile Valley, were the early and indigenous people of Northern Africa: Black people! It is important to be explicit about the race of these fathers of civilization, not because the fathers emphasized race as the basis of their greatness, but because the subsequent thieves of Kemitic civilization intentionally concealed the racial identity of their teachers in order to take credit for Africa's accomplishments and to deny her (Africa's) heirs the dignity of knowing their true ancestral legacy. So, we affirm the Blackness of those Ancient Masters in order to redeem the orphans of these authors of civilization. The certainty of the origin of those authors of civilization has been well-documented by Diop (1967), Garvey (1923), James (1976), Ben Jochannan (1971), Muhammad (1965), Rogers (1961) and Williams (1976). Beginning to assert the source of this higher knowledge of humanity and of the universe becomes for African people what James (1976) referred to as a "philosophy of redemption." Just an awareness of the source is redemptive, not to mention the knowledge itself which is transformative. James (1976) observed:

> This proposition (Greeks were not the authors of Greek philosophy, but the Black people of North Africa, the Egyptians) will become a philosophy of redemption to all Black people, when they accept it as a belief

and live up to it. . . . Our philosophy of redemption is a psychological process involving a change in behaviors. It really signifies a mental emancipation in which the Black people will be liberated from the chain of traditional falsehood, which for centuries has incarcerated them in the prison of inferiority complex and world humiliation and insult.

Western Psychology

Psychology is a Greek word revealing its most recent origins among the Greek students of the Ancient African masters. "Psyche", frequently identified with a Greek goddess of the same name actually means "soul". According to Massey (1974) the word P*syche is* actually derived from the Egyptian in which *Khe* is the soul and *Su* is she; hence the feminine nature of the Greek *Psu-khe.* Without the article "P", *Sakhu* means the "understanding, the illuminator, the eye and soul of being, that which inspires." Not only is the study of the mind derived from ancient Egypt, but even the word used to characterize that study.

The serious handicap of this Western development is the devastation wrought by the distortions of the Divine Sciences as they were taken from their original teachers and forms. We will not review the steps in the devolution of Western conceptions of Ancient African science as this has been well-documented by Diop (1967), James (1976), Ben-Jochannan (1971) and Williams (1976). A recent review by Wade Nobles (1982) is particularly relevant to understanding how psychology has suffered from this distortion by the Western mind.

For purposes of contrast, let us briefly review some of the Western assumptions about the study of man as he is currently defined in the Judeo-Christian, Euro-American psychology. We are aware of wide diversity among the various "schools" of Western psychology and our description merely summarizes the pervading ethos. We are aware that increasing numbers of Western-trained scientists are raising similar concerns about the limitations of Western mental science. Euro-American psychology approaches its study of man in the following ways:

1. Man is viewed as an object and the emphasis is upon objective methods for studying him.
2. Quantification is the only acceptable measure of reality.
3. The material world is viewed as essential and the essence of man is material.
4. There is no superior power or purpose beyond man.
5. The observable activities of a person are the critical dimensions of his being.
6. Concepts such as soul, spirits, revelations or any non-observable phe-

nomena is viewed as superstition or delusion and has no relevance to understanding man.

7. Life and consciousness are identical with physical processes.
8. Man's individuality is paramount and there is no transpersonal awareness.
9. Man is a product of biological determinants, personal experiences and chance.
10. There is no "correct" order for man's development, he survives against odds by adaptation to his environment.
11. Morality and values have no meaning outside of personal experience.
12. Death of the body is death of the mind and one need not attend to life before or after the body.

Such an orientation to the study of the human being results in what Schwaller de Lubicz (1978) calls "a research without illumination." He observes that "this indecision colors everything, art as well as social organization, and even, in many cases, faith."

In addition to these characteristics which, as we shall see, stand in stark contrast to the Ancient conception of man, there is another problem which has served to distort the Western study of mind (man). This problem is rooted in the need of Western scholars to dichotomize reality and assert their superiority and to discredit the source of their knowledge. This distortion resulted in two rather serious problems for the Western scholar. One problem was his fear of the matriarchy and the need to inferiorize women. This is a problem with deep and ancient roots in Western culture, but this fear of women and feminine power resulted in the need to sharply delineate themselves from characteristics identified as feminine. The further need to control those forces led to a derogation of femininity and feminine characteristics which resulted in a limited view of the whole human form that was always present in the masculine and feminine *neters* or principles constantly interacting in the Kemitic Cosmos.

The other problem affecting the European distortion of mental science was a pervasive racism which has permeated the interaction of Europeans with African people and African knowledge. As Diop (1967) has pointed out: "the common denominator which characterizes the mindset of Egyptologists (as repeated in their various theses about ancient Africa) is their seeming desperate necessity and unrelentless attempt to refute ancient Africa's Blackness." Egypt has been summarily lifted from the African continent in the intellectual view of most scholars. Egypt in modern parlance is identified as the "Middle East" and rarely as Africa. What's even worse, the effort to displace the origin of Egypt's genius outside of Egypt altogether, has served to further the conspiracy of exclusion. Diop (1967) observes:

> As Egypt is a Negro Country, with a civilization created by Blacks, any
> thesis tended to prove the contrary would have no future. The protago-
> nists of such theories are not unaware of this. So it is wiser and safer to
> strip Egypt, simply and most discretely of all its creations in favor of a
> really White nation (Greece).

Such racist intention by Aryan scholars led to the need to dissociate
themselves from any qualities which were undeniably Black. The fundamental error of dichotomizing man's make-up into mind and body and
eliminating the spirit altogether was done in glory of the material or the
physical. Therefore, the spiritual or non-material world was relegated to the
practitioners of the "Dark Sciences" and essentially given to the dark races,
but not without degrading such involvements as superstitious, primitive (in
the sense of uncivilized) and unscientific (i.e. ignorant). On the other hand,
the physical and material was the source of thought, action, intellect and
science. Therefore, the material was superior and its practitioners (The
Aryan races) were a superior people. (Again, a lengthy review of this development in a 1983 paper by Wade Nobles entitled "Standing in the River,
Transformed and transforming: (The (Re) Ascension of Black Psychology"
is recommended for more detail on this issue.) Suffice it to say that the
racist motive to distinguish themselves from the African teachers and to
place themselves above their conquered mentors was fundamental in fueling
the distortions which came to characterize Western Psychology. Many reviews of the distinctions between Western and African Psychology over the
last two decades are recommended as an extension of this discussion which
space will not currently accommodate. See: Akbar (1981, 1984), Asante
(1980), Baldwin (1976), Clark (1972), Jackson (1979), King (1976), and
Nobles (1980).

The Psychology of Ancient Kemit

The wisdom of Ancient Kemit is like a vast tapestry of amazing complexity. Each thread of the tapestry has been carefully woven such that every
thread is defined by every other and the tapestry holds together in its wholeness only because every thread is present. No thread can be unravelled
meaningfully without destroying the tapestry. Such is the task which faces
anyone who seeks to explore any "thread" of the knowledge of Ancient
Egypt. As Schwaller de Lubicz (1977) observes:

> Excavations and philological studies supply the Egyptologists with
> abundant material for a knowledge of the life, beliefs and theology of
> Ancient Egypt. An encyclopedic amount of work is available to the
> researcher. Nevertheless, Pharaonic Egypt remains unknown in terms of
> its true science, its contingent psychospiritual knowledge and its philo-
> sophical mentality.

In short, the task that we have set for ourselves is an impossible one for even the Egyptologist of advanced knowledge. The other confounding factor is that our approach to knowledge within the Western context, is fragmentary and rational which automatically eliminates the holistic, suprarational and symbolic knowledge which typifies Egyptian thought. The most that we can hope to accomplish is to focus on a small design in this massive tapestry and hope that by analogy and induction we may come to appreciate something of the comprehensiveness of the Egyptian understanding of the mind.

Let us be clear, though a psychology of Ancient Egypt does not exist in any explicitly identifiable sense, it is important to realize that man was viewed as the fundamental metaphor for all higher Truth. The gods (*neters*) and most importantly the Pharaoh, all stood as symbols of profound truth. So, clearly the understanding of man (mind) was viewed as paramount in the science, the wisdom and the theology of Ancient Egypt. The study of religion, science (principles of nature), mathematics, psychology and government was the study of man. Contrariwise, the study of man (mind) was the study of religion, etc. The threads of the tapestry are inseparable. Schwaller de Lubicz (1967) describes the Egyptian view of the man as microcosm:

> Man is a microcosm in the sense of a tree in relation to the seed potentially containing it; the potentiality is its macrocosm, since the seed includes all the possibilities of the tree . . . The seed will develop these possibilities, however, only if it receives corresponding energies from the earth and sky. Even more so, man—who bears within him the total seed of the universe, including the seed of spiritual states—can identity with the totality and gain nourishment from it. The relationship of this microcosm with the macrocosm is . . . a unity depending only upon his degree of perfection as a human being relative to man as the final achievement foreseen by the cause.

The dictum (now correctly identified with its source) of "man know thyself," is the fundamental principle of the psychology of Kemit. James (1976) observes:

> The doctrine of self-knowledge, for centuries attributed to Socrates is now definitely known to have originated from Egyptian Temples, on the outside of which the words "man know thyself," were written.

James goes on to describe the Ancient Egyptian doctrine of self-knowledge by observing:

> Self-knowledge is the basis of all true knowledge. The mysteries required as a first step, the mastery of the passions, which made room for

the occupation of unlimited powers. Hence as a second step, the neophyte was required to search within himself for the new powers which had taken possession of him.

Essentially, we find in this doctrine of self-knowledge, a simplified description of the initial psychology of consciousness. Man's capacity to know himself was established as a fundamental human characteristic and in pursuit of that knowledge of oneself one was in pursuit of knowledge of all things. Again, in her description of Kemitic thought, Schwaller de Lubicz (1967) observes:

> ... the universe is only consciousness and presents only an evolution of consciousness from beginning to the end—the end being a return to its cause. This implies evolution of an innate consciousness toward the psychological consciousness that is consciousness of the innate consciousness, the first step towards the liberated consciousness of physical contingencies.

The question of consciousness is fundamental for understanding the Ancient Egyptian conception of human psychology. Initiation into the mysteries was not only a system of education but a metaphor for the total development of the human soul throughout life and death. This system of education (or more appropriately, "initiation"), was a formalized system of evolving consciousness of the person which was the nation (symbolized in the Pharaoh) which was the entire cosmos.

What was to be known in this pursuit of consciousness? The initiate was instructed that he must know "self" and self in the conception of the Ancients (as well as modern) Africans meant "soul." The kind of consciousness which had to be developed was, therefore, of much greater depth than the "brain consciousness" which most Westerners have reference to when they speak of "consciousness of self." Such consciousness, Schwaller de Lubicz (1981) describes as no more than a "a mental projection of what a man believes himself to want and do." The soul in its various dimensions as conceived by the Ancients is the most explicit description of the Egyptian conceptualization of human psychology. Therefore, a description of these components of the psyche (soul) will constitute the core of this discussion with its implications for the "natural" form of the human being.

Ancient Kemitic Dimensions of Self (Soul)

The soul is the fundamental subject of study for these wise men of Ancient Kemit. As Schwaller de Lubicz (1978) observes:

> The tombs of the leaders of this people (from Ancient Egypt) are consecrated to their profession of faith in the survival of the soul ... The

West labels this attitude of wisdom a state of science that is 'still mystical.' But the Egyptian technique and their symbolic attest to a realistic sense and to faculties of reasoning, contradicting the view held that this epoch is a "primitive, mystical" age.

Unfortunately, any science which delves into understanding the real "psyche" (soul) has come to be seen as "mystical" in Western scholarship. It was precisely these components of the person which have been discredited and excluded from the Western study of the mind which has resulted in its limitations. It is the inclusion of these elements in the studies of the Ancients which has given that science its power and permanence.

There is some inconsistency in the translation and identification of the components of the soul among various Egyptologists. Table I presents a comparison of how various writers have described the way that the world's earliest psychologists characterized the dimensions of man. Generally the dimensions which are identified are all similar to Massey's (1974) list: (1) *Ka(Kha)*, (2) *Ba*, (3) *Khaba*, (4) *Akhu*, *(5) Seb, (6) Putah*, (7) *Atmu*. These seven souls constituted the natural form of the human being's psychology as well as his evolution. The challenge to man was to become knowledgeable of these souls and achieve a crystallization of them into an Eighth or Divinely permanent form.

The *Ka* is described by Massey (1974) as "the soul of Blood." This psychic dimension is the formal element of the person which gives form to substance and creates matter. It is formative or the foundation of the abstract personality structure which has a formal structure capable of ultimate disintegration and return to the elements from which it came unless it is Osirified or mummified. The structure would have to become Divinely or permanently set (which is the symbol of the Mummy) as an eternally preserved form of the person. The body is usually identified as the symbol of the *Ka* though the *Ka* soul was certainly transcendant. Budge (1960) describes the *Ka* as "the thread of connection between man's tangible and intangible being."

The *Ka* is refined through the other dimensions of the soul, but it has a multiple expression of its own. Schwaller de Lubicz (1981) identifies these three manifestations of the *Ka* as:

1. *Divine Ka*—the original *Ka* which is the creator of all the others.
2. *Intermediate Ka*—*Ka*s of nature, mineral, vegetable and animal.
3. *Inferior Ka*—individualized Ka; inherited characteristics of psychological consciousness. Consciousness of the *Ka* evolved from the Inferior to the Divine Ka.

TABLE 1
A Comparison of the Ancient Kemitic Conception of the Dimensions of the Soul (Self) as Identified by Four Prominent Egyptologists

Massey (1974)	James (1954, 1971)	Budge (1960)	Schwaller de Lubicz (1981)
Ka—formal structure that would return to the elements; soul of blood	Ka—abstract personality of the man to whom it belongs possessing the form and attributes of a man with power of locomotion.	Ka—double or inner self which comes into being with each person and follows him throughout life. It is the thread of connection between man's tangible and intangible being.	Ka—Formal element which gives form to substance and creates matter. 1. original Ka—Creator of all the others. Divine Ka. 2. Kas of nature, mineral, vegetable and animal. Intermediate Ka—personal consciousness. 3. Individualized Ka, Inherited characteristics of psychological consciousness; Inferior Ka.
Ba—Breath of life; Eternal, invisible energy that runs through all visible functions. Essence of things.	Ba—the heart-soul dwells in the Ka. It has the power of metamorphosis and changes its form at will.	Ba—a combination of intelligence and spirit which leaves the body at death.	Ba—most spiritual element in man; it is his link with the Creator. It is free, unfixed and unaffected by the human being whose only link with it is a link of consciousness. 1. Ba is the cosmic soul in all constituents of the world (Universal soul); 2. Ba—the natural soul stabilized in the bodily form; 3. Ba—represented by bird with human head is symbol of human soul which comes and goes between heaven and earth.
Khaba—veil of the vital principle produced emotion and motion; sustains the sensory perceptions, total harmony and circulation of the blood shade soul.	Kaibit—Shadow. Associated with Ba. It has the power of locomotion and omnipresence.	Khabit—the shadow or soul of the blood.	Khabit—astral or etheric body, ghost or shadow. Holds the records of all pictures or imaginings in our universe.

TABLE 1 (cont.)

Massey (1974)	James (1954, 1971)	Budge (1960)	Schwaller de Lubicz (1981)
Akhu—Seat of intelligence and "mental perception." Attributes of judgment, analysis, and mental reflection all of which could be dedicated to service of higher being.	*Ab*—The heart, the animal life in man that is rational, spiritual and ethical. Associated with the Ba and undergoes examination in the Judgment.	*Hati*—represents the heart or conscience and understanding.	*Inferior Ka* (see above).
Seb—manifested at puberty; self-creative power of the human being. Ancestral soul. Procreational soul.	*Khat*—the concrete personality, the physical body which is mortal.		*Inferior Ka.*
Putah—"first intellectual father," marked the union of the brain with the mind. From its attainment the intellect governs conduct, Intellectual soul	*Sahu*—body in which the Khu or spiritual self dwells. All mental and spiritual attributes of the natural body are united to the new powers of its own nature.	*Sahu*—the spiritual body.	*Ba*—natural soul.
Atmu—the Divine or eternal soul. Represented as parenthood which symbolized the full creative power and perpetual continuation.	*Khu*—spiritual soul which is immortal. It is immortal. It is closely associated with the Ba (heart-soul) which is immortal.	*Khu*—the pure spirit or Horus—the highest expression of the personality, the perfect spirit of Christ consciousness.	*Divine Ka*—"Father of the father of the *Neters*" (Spiritual Witness).

Schwaller de Lubicz (1981) observes:

> A man ignorant of his own spiritual world has little or no contact with his Divine *Ka*. His personal *Ka* is brought down to the whole of his lower *Kas*; therefore after death, he will become his own shade or ghost . . . the quest for spiritual springs of action and the enlargement of consciousness, can modify the character of his "personal" *Ka* until the spiritual faculties are awakened and it makes contact with the Divine Ka.

The *Ba* called the "Soul of breath" by Massey (1974) is the second division of the psychic nature. It represented the transmission of the invisible energy source (like electricity) which runs through all visible functions. The Ancients believed that there was only one power, which was symbolically represented as "the breath," and, that this power or breath was transmitted from the ancestors to the descendants. They believed that this power or energy has always existed and will always exist. The *Ba* was in effect the vital principle which represented the essence of all things.

The *Ba* as represented by a bird with a human head is the symbol of the "human soul" which comes and goes between heaven and earth. It is the most spiritual element in man for by its divine nature it is linked with the Creator. It is incommensurable, and indivisible, free, unfixed and unaffected by the Vicissitudes of the human being whose only link with it is a link of consciousness. Schwaller de Lubicz (1981) also, divides the *Ba* into three aspects:

1. *Ba* (universal soul) the spirit of fire which gives life to the world in all its parts. The spirit of *Ba* is in all constituents of the world and in its final perfection .
2. *Ba* (natural soul) stabilized the bodily form (Ka), and its character is Osirian, that is, it is subject to cyclic renewal.
3. *Ba* as the human soul described above as represented by the bird.

The *Ka* by assimilating the universal *Ba* generates a new being which is the individualized soul which remains divine, incorruptible and therefore immortal. In fact the definitions of *Ba* and *Ka* must always be relative to each other, since they can only refer to one aspect in its relation to the other. The *Khaba* is the shade or covering soul, corresponding to the popular notion of the ghost. It is the astral or "etheric" body. It is related to the Akasha, the world or state which holds the records of all the pictures or imaginings in our universe. The *Khaba* (called *Khabit* or *Kaibit* by some writers) produced emotion and motion. It was further thought to be responsible for sustaining the sensory perceptions and the phenomena of color, total harmony and the circulation of blood.

The *Akhu* is the fourth division of the psychic nature and is described as the seat of intelligence and mental perception. It was in the area of the *Akhu*, the Ancients believed, that the whole mystery of the human mind was to be comprehended. The mind was in fact, an entity in and of itself and only during physical life was the mind the instrument of the human spirit. The concerns of the mind were primarily the survival of its own thinking processes. The *Akhu* was characterized by attributes like judgment, analysis and mental reflection, all of which could be trained and disciplined so as to be dedicated to the service of the higher being. The intelligence was considered to be located in the heart and it was considered to be not only rational but also spiritual and ethical. In the Ancient Kemitic Judgment drama it undergoes examination and is weighed on the scale of justice against a feather in the presence of Osiris, the great judge of the unseen world.

The *Seb* is the soul of pubescence in that it doesn't manifest itself in humans until puberty or adolescence. The evidence of the presence of the *Seb* was the power of the human being to generate his own kind. The *Seb* is in effect the self-creative power of Being.

The *Putah* was the intellectual soul or the "first intellectual father." Unlike the *Akhu*, the *Putah* was associated with the mental maturity of the individual and marked the union of the brain with the mind. It was the *Putah* which established the fact of the person and from the moment of its manifestation or attainment it was believed that intellect (i.e., will and intent) alone governed conduct. The maturity of the *Putah* represents the person's ability to reproduce intellectually.

The *Atmu* as the seventh division of the psyche was considered the divine or eternal soul. In some texts it is identified with the seventh creation, the god *Atmu* who inspired the breath of life everlasting. In ritual this division of the soul is represented as parenthood which symbolically stood for the presence of full creative powers and perpetual continuation.

Some writers, such as Massey, identify an eighth form of the soul which represents a synthesis or crystallization of the other seven. Massey (1974) refers to it as "Horus" or the Christ." It is the same as the "Divine Ka," described above by Schwaller de Lubicz (1981) and by Frankfort (1946). This component is described as enwrapping and serving as the essence of all the divisions of the soul and was the *Ka* of God. The Ka was the divine spirit which endowed all things and which survived past the physical life of the individual. The *Ka*, it was thought, had magical powers and could cause the dead to live again (the resurrected Christ) and could even enter a mummified being, animate it internally and cause it to have a continued inner life or existence.

Conclusion

This discussion has focused on just one aspect of a multi-faceted and complex system which describes the human psyche according to Ancient Kemitic tradition. As we cautioned from the outset, the entirety of the Kemitic cosmology is actually a comprehensive description of the Psyche of man. The amazingly complex theology of Ancient Kemit represents a series of allegories which define the workings of nature and most importantly the genesis and implied potentialities of man. These myths and symbols actually transcend the empirical conclusions of Western Science and describe man, not only on the basis of what he does but what he is.

We chose to look at the psychic dimensions as the Ancients described it because in that system we find a summary of what the human being is. By implication we can more effectively describe the properly functioning human being and can actually see the distinctions from the African perspective. Each of the components of the septenary soul which we have described has implications for understanding the "nature" of the human being.

The fundamental conclusion about human nature as implied by the description of the *Ba* and the *Atmu*, as well as the Divine *Ka* is that the human being is essentially connected with the Divine and with everything else in nature. There is continuity in all that is, having its origin in the Creator. This is consistent with the African psychologists (Akbar 1976; Baldwin, 1976; Jackson, 1979; Nobles, 1980 and X, et als, 1976) who have suggested the principle of consubstantiation as expressed in the idea "I am because we are and because we are, therefore I am," (Mbiti, 1970) as fundamental to understanding the African psyche. We have identified that this same concept called *Ba* in Ancient Africa is called *dya* by the Bambara people and the *Okra* by the Akan people of Ghana and more generally "soul" by African-American people, showing a continuity in this Ancient Kemitic conception of the human being among African people. This is in contrast with the dualistic and materialistic conception of the Euro-American psychologists who would be appalled at even admitting that "psyche" once meant soul even to them.

The *Ka* on the other hand brings balance to the picture of the human being and shows that the human being is not only of "heavenly" material but also of "earthly" material. There is implicit in this system, a recognition that the human being has a connection and an involvement in the earthly sphere. He has a physical component that is tangible, but this is a dimension and not an exclusive view of the person. The Ancients were able to construct impressive physical structures, feed their citizenry with advanced technology, master physics and physical medicine while understanding that all of those structures were transient in comparison with the higher being.

The *Kaibit* suggests that man has access to Universal knowledge from the so-called "Akashic records." Man can reach into the recesses of his own consciousness and retrieve the world's most valuable knowledge. This eliminates the apparent inequity in knowledge when it is assumed to emanate from outside.

Intelligence is multiple in its dimensions: rational, spiritual and ethical. The intelligent person is not simply one who has mastered a technique but is prudent enough to know when and how to apply that technique. The intelligent one is not one who is capable of performing independent of his moral and spiritual obligation to the rest of humanity. The *Akhu* and *Putah* give a conception of intelligence which requires self-mastery, and service to ones higher being in order to be considered intelligent.

Seb reminds the person that his nature is not only one which permits reproduction, but is procreative and self-creative. The human being is equipped not just to reproduce himself, but to re-create and then perpetuate his creation.

Ultimately, the human being becomes the fullness of what he is from his inception and that is a Divine form reunited with his Divine genesis. Through realization of one of Ancient Kemit's most consistent motifs (that is) transformation. The person transforms the raw material of his transient form and self-consciously forms and is transformed to the higher being from which he sprang.

> The deceased cries, "Do not take my soul!" *(Ba)* "Do not detain my shade!" (Khaba) "Open the path to my shade, and my soul, and my intelligence (Akhu) to see the great God on the day of reckoning souls."
> —From the Coffin Text

References

Akbar, N. Africentric social sciences for human liberation. *J. of Black Studies*, 14(4), 1984,395–414.

Akbar, N. Our destiny: Authors of a scientific revolution. *The Fifth Conference on Empirical Research in Black Psychology.* Washington, D.C.: Howard University Institute for Urban Affairs, 1981.

Asante, M. & Vandi, A. (eds.) *Contemporary Black Thought.* Beverly Hills: Sage, 1980.

Baldwin, J. Black psychology and black personality. *Black Books Bulletin,* 4(3), 19.

Budge, E.A.W. *The Book of the Dead:* An English translation of the *Papyrus of Ani.* New Hyde Park, New York: University Books, 1960.

Ben-Jochannan, Y. *Africa: Mother of Western Civilization.* New York: Alkebu-lan Books Assoc., 1971.

Clark, C. Black Studies or the study of black people in Jones, R. (ed.) B*lack Psychology* (1st edition). New York: Harper & Row, 1972.

Diop, C.A. *The African Origin of Civilization: Myth or Reality.* Westport: Lawrence Hill & Co., 1967.

Frankfort, H., et al. *The Intellectual Adventure of Ancient Man,* Chicago: University of Chicago Press, 1946.

Garvey, A.J. (ed.) *Philosophy and Opinions of Marcus Garvey.* New York: Universal Publishing House, 1923.

Jackson, G. The origins and development of Black Psychology: implications for Black Studies and human behavior. *Studia Africana,* 1(3), 1979, 270–293.

James, G.G.M. *Stolen Legacy.* San Francisco: Julian Richardson Assoc., 1976 (1954).

King, L. et al. Af*rican Philosophy: Assumptions and Paradigms for Research on Black Persons.* Los Angeles: Fanon Center Publication, 1976.

Massey, G. *A Book of the Beginnings,* Vol. 1. Secaucus, N.J.: University Books, Inc., 1974.

Massey, G. *Gerald Massey's Lectures.* New York: Samuel Weiser, Inc., 1974.

Mbiti, J. *African Religion and Philosophy.* Garden City: Doubleday and Co., 1970.

Muhammad, E. *Message to the Black Man.* Chicago: Muhammad Mosque of Islam, No. 2, 1965.

Nobles, W.W. African Philosophy: Foundations for Black Psychology in Jones, R. (ed.) *Black Psychology* (2nd ed.) New York: Harper and Row, 1980.

Nobles, W.W. Ancient Egyptian thought and the development of Afrikan (Black) psychology. Presented to "The First Annual Ancient Egyptian Studies Conference: The Social Life Area." Los Angeles, February 24–26, 1984.

Nobles, W.W. Standing in the river, transformed and transforming: The re(ascension) of Black psychology, Unpublished manuscript, 1982.

Rogers, J.A. *Africa's Gift to America.* New York: Helga M. Rogers, 1961.

Schwaller de Lubicz, I. *Her-Bak: Egyptian Initiate.* New York: Inner Traditions International, 1978.

Schwaller de Lubicz, I. *The Opening of the Way.* New York: Inner Traditions International, 1981.

Schwaller de Lubicz, R.A. *The Temple in Man.* New York: Inner Traditions International, 1977.

Schwaller de Lubicz, R.A. *Symbol and the Symbolic.* New York: Inner Traditional International, 1978.

Williams, C. *The Destruction of Black Civilization.* Chicago: Third World Press, 1976.

THE SYMBOLISM OF THE CROWN
IN ANCIENT EGYPT

Richard D. King

The historical origin of the twin pillars of modern European-African psychiatry, biological psychiatry and psychoanalytic depth psychiatry, can be directly linked to a common historical parent, The Science Of The Mind or The Way Of The Heart of ancient Egypt.[1] This premise arose from the observation of the crown, jewels, and tableaux found in the tomb of the 18th dynasty pharaoh Tut-ankh-amun (?-1349 B.C.E.).[2-10] These items of material evidence are excellent examples of symbolic references to a historical stream of ancient African philosophical thought that runs from the predynastic Egyptian period, Memphite cosmology, through dynastic Egypt and later postdynastic heirs of Egypt, Dogon cosmology. The evidence cited is not new, having been in the hands of investigators for over fifty years. Rather, it is the order in which the facts are arranged that is both new and very old, the meaning given to the evidence, an acknowledgement of a greater whole from which these ideas are abstracted. For it is an Afrocentric corpus of thought, an Afrocentric world view on the part of the investigator that appears to be an absolutely critical focus and tool of analysis in an examination of the crown, jewels, and tableaus of the pharaoh Tut-ankh-amun. From such an analysis there may come an appreciation of more subtle issues relating to the pineal gland, melanin, light and depth psychology issues of the unconscious, dreams, and levels of consciousness.

The largely intact tomb of the Pharaoh Tut-ankh-amun was discovered in 1922 by Howard Carter and excavated over a six year period.[2, 3, 8, 12] A diadem crown was found atop the pharaoh's head which was covered in linen wrappings that extended over the entire mummy. Upon the mummy was a golden mask that was placed within one coffin and this was enclosed inside of two successive coffins. The three coffins were found inside of a quartzite sarcophagus. These four coffins were enclosed within four successive shrines. The surface of each of the four were covered with elaborate tableaus.

The right side of the second tableau of the second shrine contains a scene of a serpent passing rays of light into the forehead of the first of six human figures of Pharaoh Tut-ankh-amun. The next two human figures have rays of light entering their foreheads from a star anterior and above the head. The last three human figures have stars passing rays of light from star to star, each star in all cases being directly over the head of each human figure. In front of each of the six human figures are two columns with a human headed hawk-like bird standing atop the two columns. The bird stands in such a manner that its left foot rests atop the left column, right foot rests atop the right column and the body and human head of the bird is situated between the two columns (see Fig. 1).[9, 14]

Two of the jewels taken from the tomb of Tut-ankh-amun are symbolic replicas of the ancient Egyptian concept of the left eye and right eye.[4] The replica of the left eye (Fig. 2a) is framed by a serpent wearing the crown of Lower Egypt at the left corner and a vulture wearing the crown of Upper Egypt at right corner of the eye, whereas the replica of the right eye (Fig. 2b) depicts a scarab body of a hawk whose outstretched wings and front legs uphold a boat. Within the boat is an eye framed on each side by cobras with sun disks above each serpent's head. Above the eye there is a crescent shaped moon containing a moon disc with the figures of the ibis-headed moon god Thoth wearing the moon disc, the king wearing the moon disc, sun god Ra wearing the sun with a serpent uraeus. Importantly, the god Thoth is on the left, the king in the center and the god Ra on the right.

There were at least five crowns found over the head of the Pharaoh Tut-ank-amun in his tomb—diadem, mask, and three whole-body coffins. In all cases there is the same representation over the forehead of the king, the head of a serpent on the left and the head of bird, vulture, on the right (Fig. 3).[15] Both of these objects were placed in the mid forehead location above the level of the eye brows. The crown closest to the head, the diadem (Fig. 4), which was actually enclosed inside of the mummy's linen wrappings not only displays the midforehead serpent and bird but also the wave-form body of the serpent across the midline of the crown of the skull from front to back. Furthermore, the diadem crown has the head and body of two serpents attached at the back of the head with the head of the serpent positioned at about the site of the temple on each side.

Upon unwrapping the successive line wrappings of the head of the Pharaoh Tut-ankh-amun, after the diadem crown was removed there was found a golden serpent and bird crowning the mid-forehead brow location (Fig. 9),[16] The wings of the golden bird were outstretched and covered the frontal portion of the crown of the head. The body of the golden bird rests atop the center line of the crown of the head from front to back. Yet, even before the head of the pharaoh was unwrapped, the symbolic importance of the crown

---

Figure 1, 10, 11, and 13 have been omitted due to the uneven quality of the submitted photographs—Ed.

Figure 2A. From *Eyptian Mysteries: New Light on Ancient Spiritual Knowledge* by Lucie Lamay (Crossword, N.Y., 1981, p. 44).

of the head was clearly defined by the ancient Egyptian priests by their placing an extra pad of linen upon the top of the head. (Fig. 5.)[17] Last, directly on top of the pharaoh's head there was a skull-cap with golden beads arranged in the form of four serpents, (Fig. 6) two serpents with heads at about the middle of the crown of the skull and two serpents with heads over the temple regions on each side respectively. (Fig. 6).

It is well known and reported in European-African archaeological literature that the serpent was used throughout Lower or Northern Egypt as a symbol of the Goddess Uatchet. This was so most particularly in the city of Per-uatchet, the capital of the seventh nome. This city of Uraeus worship as well as the other sites of its worship were collectively known as Pe-tep, within which were two distinct divisions. The first group *Tep* was identified with Isis and Uatchet. Isis was the worshipped divinity. The other, *Pe* was identified with Horus and Uatchet. Horus was the primary deity. Uatchet was regarded as the goddess of the elements and months of the Egyptian year, Epiphi, and during later dynastic times, was given the name Ap-tavi. Thus, in time the serpent and crown with a projecting coiled serpent-like body became a political symbol for royal rulership of Lower Egypt.

In a similar fashion the bird as a vulture became a symbol for royal

Figure 2B. From *Egyptian Mysteries* (1981, p. 45).

rulership of Southern or Upper Egypt.[19] Nekhebet was the vulture Goddess
of the South. She was worshipped throughout Upper Egypt in the city
named Nekhebet by the Egyptians, which was, moreover, the capital of the
third nome. This same city was called Eilethyiaspolis and "Civitas
Lucinae", by the Greeks and Romans respectively. The shrine of the Goddess Nekhebet, is presently located in the current Arab village of El-Kab.
Nekhebet was also believed to be the daughter of Sun God Ra, the divine
wife of Khent-Amenti, the holy vulture, and Hathor.

Following the unification of Upper and Lower Egypt by the Lower or Southern Egyptian Pharaoh Aha or Narmer (4000?, 3200 B.C.E.) all rulers of unified Egypt wore the composite crown of Egypt (Fig. 7).[17] The crown contained the bulbous top of Upper Egypt and the coil of the crown of Lower Egypt. Certainly this was a great political event and an even greater psychological achievement to develop a real unified sense of shared commonality, purpose, and philosophical base between two previously antagonistic groups of Africans. Clearly, there is a strong suggestion of a similar process having taken place earlier in Upper Egypt with the collective name of Pe-Tep being derived from the unification of the two distinct divisions of *Pe* and *Tep*. Likewise, in Southern or Upper Egypt in pre dynastic times there had been a unification of at least three distinct divisions that worshipped the Gods Nekhebet, Sun God Ra, and the Goddess Hathor. It is of the utmost importance, with regard to the political unity of Africans in the past and present, to appreciate not only the political and military issues of such unification events but even more to consider the psychological basis that allowed mutual respect, synthesis, and flourishing of all parties involved in such a union. With this in mind, one may consider the symbolism of the crown of ancient Egypt. For, in reviewing the crown, shrine tableau, and jewels it is readily apparent that the serpent of Lower Egypt and the vulture of Upper Egypt were found to have other symbolic meanings than just political rulership over the two-geo-political units of Southern and Northern Egypt.

From a psychoanalytic perspective a symbol has been defined as an act or object that represents an unconscious desire which has been repressed or automatically forgotten without ever having become conscious to the observer.[20] Symbols are inherently linked to deep spontaneous unconscious psychological processes. In contrast, signs are linked to largely conscious processes in which the observer consciously and arbitrarily allows one thing to stand for another. For example, in the case of a sign, ten different observers may use ten different signs to represent the same item. In the case of a symbol, different observers may use the same symbol to represent a wide variety of different classes of objects because it somehow spontaneously occurred to them to use the same symbol. The serpent and vulture found in the central mid forehead position of the crown of Tut-ankhamun is a symbol in that it is linked to deep unconscious psychological processes that tie together seemingly unrelated items from a purely conscious perspective such as religion, political unification, rulership, sun, moon, psychology and brain anatomy.

To appreciate the psychological concept of symbolism it may be helpful to consider the issues of projection, collective unconscious, and the ancient Egyptian concepts of body, mind, soul, and spirit. First, the word symbol is partially derived from the word *ballein*, to throw. The process, to throw,

Figure 3. Private photo by author. Cairo Museum.

Figure 4. John West, *Serpent in the Sky: The High Wisdom of Ancient Egypt* (Harper & Row, N.Y., 1979, p. 47).

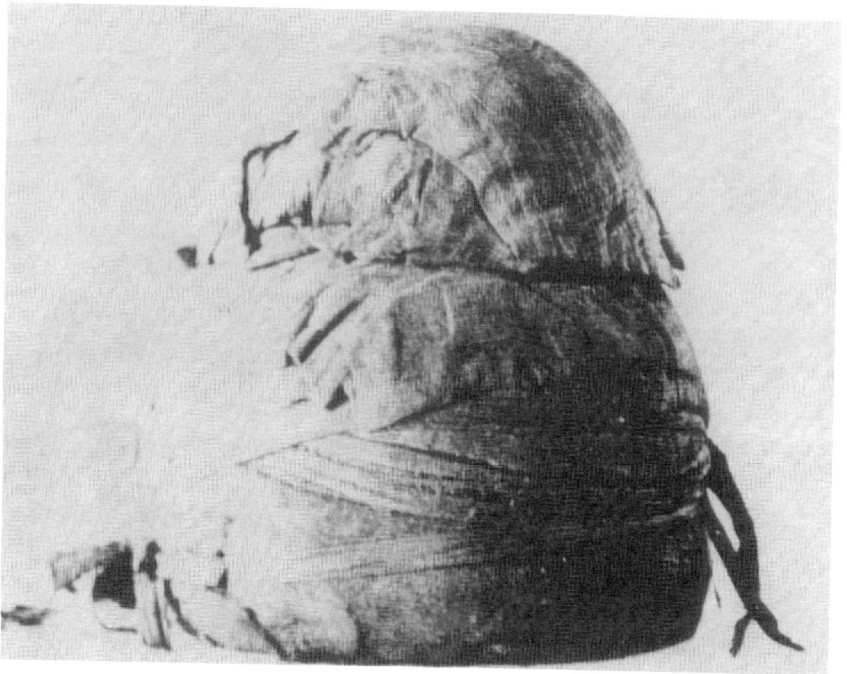

Figure 5. F. Leek, "The Human Remains from the Tomb of Tut'ankhamun" *Tut'ankhamun Tomb Series,* **V (Griffith Institute, Oxford University Press, 1972, plate X).**

speaks of a psychological state "projection," the unconscious act of ascribing to or throwing upon external things one's own ideas or impulses. What one sees externally as a good symbol to link together several seemingly unrelated items comes from a preexisting unconscious memory of an idea. There exists many different levels of the unconscious, one of which is the collective unconscious which contains the genetic memory of all that was ever known or experienced by one's ancestors. The collective unconscious is the living library, eternal memory bank that is hidden by ignorance or mental slavery but, unlike the physical libraries, was never destroyed. This concept was reintroduced by European-African psychiatrist C.G. Jung. Another concept, closely allied to the collective unconscious is the word archetype, the original pattern, or model, from which all other things of the same kind are made. C.G. Jung took the term "Archetype" from the Corpus Hermeticum (Scott Hermetica, vol. 1, 140, 12b) and from Chap. 2, Par. 6, of the *De Divinis nominibus* of Dionysius the pseudo-Aeropagite, which reads: "But someone may say that the seal is not the same and entire in all its impressions. The seal, however, is not the cause of this, for it imparts itself wholly and alike in each case, but the difference in the participants make the

Figure 6. F. Leek, "The Human Remains from the Tomb of Tut'ankhamun," plate XI.

impressions unlike, although the archetype is one, whole and the same."[4] However, Jung was drawn to the term archetype most of all by the writings of the African scholar St. Augustine, in particular St. Augustine's idea *Principales,* "For the principal ideas are certain forms, or stable and unchangeable reasons of things, themselves not formed, and so continuing eternal and always after the same manner, which are contained in the divine understanding. And though they themselves do not perish, yet after their pattern everything is said to be formed that is able to come into being and to perish, and everything that does come into being and perish. But it is affirmed that the soul is not able to behold them, save it be the rational soul." Thus, symbols may be used to tie together a number of seemingly unrelated items because there exists in the collective unconscious of the observer the memories of one's ancestors, their experiences and discoveries, as well as analyses and philosophical interpretations of all these things.

Ancient Egyptian priests or scientists defined not only the body and mind but also the soul and spirit. Additionally, the concepts of mind, soul and spirit were so important that this triune or trinity concept was a constant

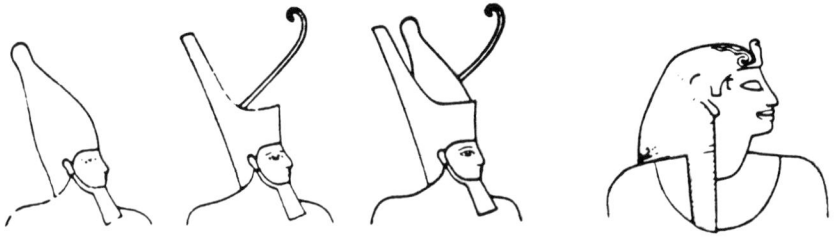

Figure 7. William J. Murname, *The Penguin Guide to Ancient Egypt* (Penguin Books, England, 1983, p. 47).

theme throughout many layers of their philosophical thought and scientific disciplines. There was a division of many things into three. There were three grades of students (neophyte, intelligence, sons of light).[23] Temple architecture comprised an outer court for public congregations, a middle hall for priests and nobles, and an inner middle chamber, adytum, Holy of Holies, solely used by the high priest.[24] There was the Goddess Isis (female), God Osiris (male), and God Horus (child, union of opposites).[25] An entrance to the temple was formed by a doorway in which the left pillar represented the masculine energy of creation, right pillar the feminine energy of creation, and the arch way that joined or united the two pillars or opposites represented the soul or self with the words written upon it, "Man Know Thy Self."[11] Thus, it is likely that Pharaoh Tut-ankh-amun's tomb with three successive coffins enclosed within a quartzite sarcophagus are symbolic replicas of the soul, spirit, mind, and body (the last being the quartzite sarcophagus). The three shrines which successively enclose the coffins and sarcophagus may represent the freedom of the spirit, soul, and mind of humans following the death of the physical body. "The Egyptian Mystery System" as George James in his book *Stolen Legacy* points out "had as its most important object, the deification of man, and taught that the soul of man, if liberated from its bodily fetters, could enable him to become godlike and see the Gods in this life and attain the beatific vision and hold communion with the Immortals." It sought "the liberation of the mind from its finite consciousness, when it becomes one and is identified with the Infinite. This liberation was not only freedom of the soul from bodily impediments, but also from the wheel of reincarnation or rebirth. It involved a process of disciplines (several liberal arts) or purification (ten virtues, negative confessions, Book of the Coming Forth by Day) both for the body and soul."[23] James further cited nine aspects of the soul as defined by the ancient Egyptians, of which four are central to the concept of spirit (Khu), soul (Ba), mind (Ka), and body (Khat). 'The *Ka* is the abstract personality of the man to whom it belongs, possessing the form and attributes of a man with power

O ← --- Pineal

Side View

U ← --- Pineal

Front View

Uraeus (Pineal)

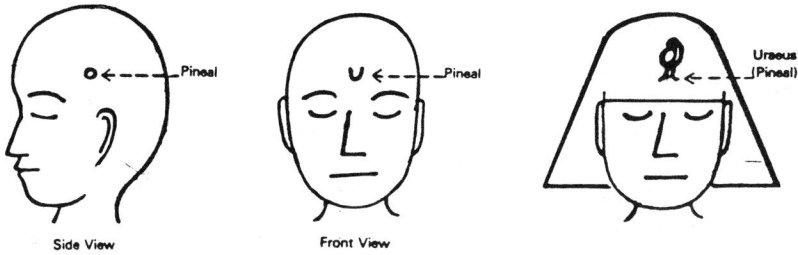

Figure 8. Richard King, "Uraeus: From Mental Slavery ot Mastership," Part III, *Uraeus* (vol. 1, no. 3, 1978, p. 26).

of locomotion, omnipresence and ability to receive nourishment like a man. It is equivalent to (Eidolon), i.e., image; the *Khat,* i.e., the concrete person- ality, is the physical body, which is mortal; the *Ba,* i.e., the heart-soul, dwells in the *Ka* and sometimes alongside it, in order to supply it with air and food. It has the power of metamorphosis and changes its form at will; and the *Khu,* i.e., spiritual soul, is immortal. It is also closely associated with the *Ba* (heart-soul), and is an Ethereal Being."[26] From these consider- ations it is possible that symbols not only arise from the deep unconscious of one's own present historical life, shared experience of one's genetic ancestors (Ba), but also the past reincarnations of one's *Khu* (spirit). The Ba and Khu are well known to have been symbolized by ancient Egyptians as birds[27] and indeed it was the Ba as a human-headed bird that was depicted atop the two columns in front of each of the six human figures of pharaoh Tut-ankh-amun in the second shrine tableau scene we referred to earlier.

Further, it is interesting to observe in the tomb of Tut-ankh-amun the jewels of the lateral eyes, for the moon rose on the side of the left eye as the sun descended on the side of the right eye, a position that can only occur if one is facing south, towards the Great Lakes ancestral homelands of the ancient Egyptians, Khui Land, and place of origin of those who later unified Egypt through military might, politics, but most of all knowledge.

One should consider even deeper questions by examining the crown, jewels, and tableau from the tomb of pharaoh Tut-ankh-amun. May it not be that these African people gave great thought to the symbolism of the color of their own skin and the physiological operations involved in maintaining such Black skin color in response to the radiation of the sun and the moon? What were the discoveries of these worshippers of the sun and moon on the relationship of the human form to light? The scene of the tableau clearly poses such questions, serpent passing rays of light into a midforehead site of the human figure, and stars passing rays of light into a midforehead site of two successive human figures. This is a crucial item of physical evidence of the African knowledge of biological psychiatry and depth psychiatry thou-

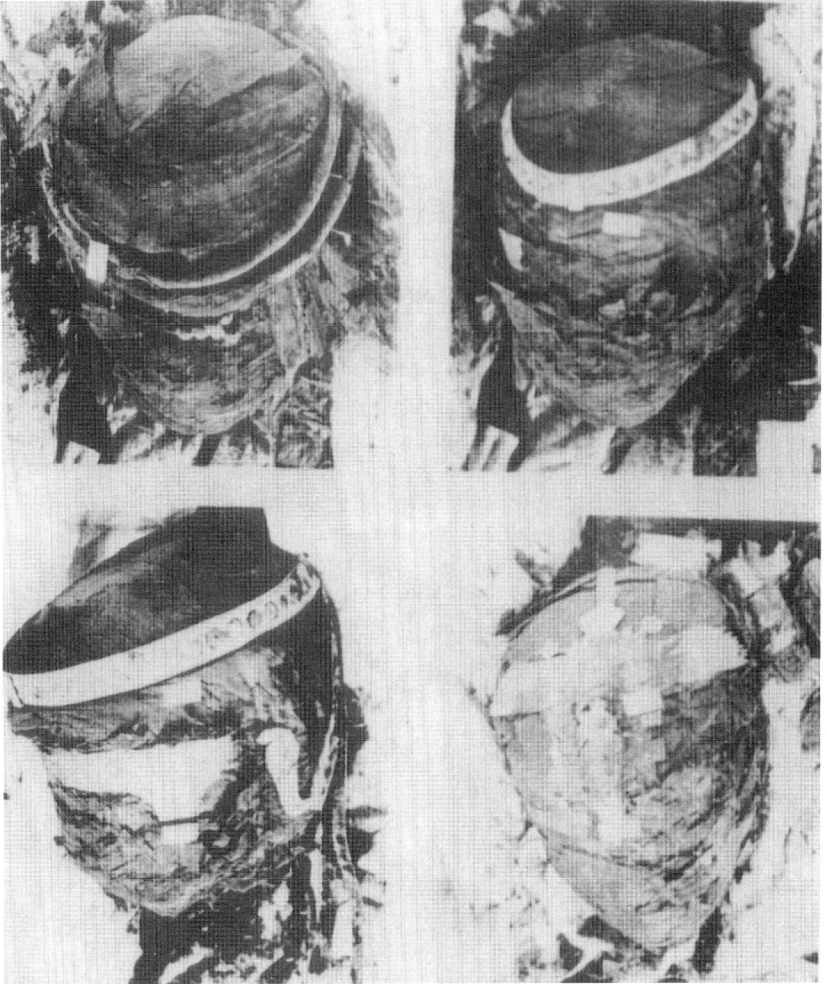

Figure 9. F. Leek, "The Human Remains from the Tomb of Tut'ankhamun," plate V.

sands of years before the rediscovery of the same bodies of knowledge by Europeans. This scene was probably already ancient and well known by the Africans when placed inside of Pharaoh Tut-ankh-amun's tomb in the year 1349 B.C.E., three thousand three hundred years before the European scientists Axelrod and Lerner rediscovered in the 1950's that the pineal was not a nonfunctional vestigial organ but an active brain endocrine gland that released the hormones melatonin and serotonin.[28–35] It was later found that the pineal gland, an organ long known to be located in the interior of the brain at a level above the eye brows and in the exact midline of the forehead, released the hormone melatonin into the blood during the hours of darkness, night, time of the moon (Fig. 8.). On the other hand, the hormone serotonin was released into the blood during the hours of sunlight, day, time of the sun. Furthermore, it has since been discovered that melatonin is actively involved in shifting levels of consciousness and access to the unconscious, such as dream states, rapid eye movement (or REM) sleep. Melatonin is now known to increase the flow of unconscious memories from the deeper levels of the mind-brain up to the cortex for conscious expression, whereas serotonin increases the flow of memories from the cortex down to the deeper levels of the mind-brain, memory storage.

Further evidence of the ancient Egyptian's earlier knowledge of site and function of the pineal gland is suggested by following the origin of the knowledge of the pineal in the early scientific literature of Greece, the first major European nation and one profoundly influenced by Africa. Herophilos (325–280 B.C.), deemed by Europeans as the "father of anatomy," has been held to be the first to discover the pineal. He was an anatomist at the University of Alexandria. However, it was the ancient Egyptians (Africans) who were the true discoverers of the pineal and the mothers and fathers of anatomy. According to George James, "owing to the practice of piracy, in which the Ionians and Carians were active, the Egyptians were forced to make immigration laws restricting the immigration of the Greeks and punishing their infringement by capital punishment, i.e., the sacrifice of the victim. Before the time of Psammitichus, the Greeks were not allowed to go beyond the coast of Lower Egypt but during his reign and that of Amasis (670 B.C.E.), those conditions were modified. For the first time in Egyptian history Ionians and Carians were employed as Mercenaries in the Egyptian Army. . . . In addition to these changes, King Amasis removed the restrictions against the Greeks and permitted them to enter Egypt and settle in Naucratis. About this same time (i.e., the reign of Amasis) the Persians, through Cambyses, invaded Egypt, and the whole country was thrown open to the researches of the Greeks. . . . The immigration of Greeks to Egypt for the purpose of their education, began as a result of the Persian invasion (525 B.C.E.), and continued until the Greeks gained possession of that land and access to the Royal Library, through the conquest of Alexander the Great (332 B.C.E.). Alexandria was converted into a Greek city, a centre of research (University and Library of Alexandria) and the capital of the newly created Greek empire, under the rule of the Ptolemies. . . . Concerning the fact that Egypt was the greatest education centre of the ancient world, which was also visited by the Greeks. . . . Plato in the Timeaus tells us that Greek aspirants to wisdom visited Egypt for initiation, and that the priests of Sais used to refer to them as children in the Mysteries." George James cited a long list of the fathers of Greek philosophy who, as students, had visited Egypt for the purpose of their education-

Thales (525 C.E.), Pythagoras, Democritus, Plato, and Aristotle. George James also stated that "any invading army would first loot the Royal Library of Alexandria and then would turn their attention to the Menephtheion at Thebes (Grand Lodge of Luxor, center of the world-wide African University system, The Mystery System). They would also visit the cities of Memphis and Heliopolis and likewise loot their libraries and temples. . . . The Greeks (i.e., Alexander the Great, Aristotle's school and the succeeding Ptolemies) converted the Royal Library of Alexandria into a research centre, by transferring Aristotle's school and pupils from Athens to this great Egyptian Library, and therefore the students who studied there received instructions from Egyptian priests and teachers, until they died out. . . . the subjugation of Egypt by Alexander the Great in 330 B.C. had checked the further development of Greek civilization on its native soil. . . . this school (University, Library of Alexandria) of philosophers, mathematicians and astronomers. Here for the next 700 years, science had its chief abiding place." Yet at the time of Herophilos (325–280 B.C.) the Greek capture of the Egyptian royal libraries had just taken place and scholars such as Herophilos had recently arrived in Egypt to study under the indigenous Egyptian scientists and to study and translate the preexisting books written earlier by these African scholars.

Thus, when we read of the discoveries of Greek scientists and philosophers from the time of Pharoah Amasis onward there exists the very great possibility that their discoveries were not their own but the teachings of their Egyptian professors. This would particularly be the case with Herophilos, *so called first discoverer of the pineal gland.* He actually resided in Egypt at the Greek University and Library of Alexandria, which had been formed from the confiscated vast libraries of ancient Egypt and the libraries of priest-scientists from the various colleges of Egypt. Importantly, *Herophilos localized the soul in the brain's ventricular system. Yet, upon viewing pictures of the unwrapping of Pharoah Tut-ankh-amun's head (Fig. 9)[16] there was found a golden bird laid across the top of the crown of the head with outstretched wings covering the front of the head and the body of the bird along the center line of the head. This may have been a symbolic statement of the actual African knowledge of the location of the soul being in the brain's ventricular system because the shape of the bird closely resembles the top-view appearance of the system, lateral ventricles similar to the outstretched wings, body similar to the third and fourth ventricles. The pineal gland is located anatomically at the posterior end of the third ventricle* and the pituitary gland is present at the anterior end of the third ventricle.[28, 31] Modern science has now discovered that though pineal hormones are released into the blood they are concentrated primarily in the cerebrospinal fluid (C.S.F.) that flows through the brain ventricular system.[41, 42] Again, *the symbolism of the bird found atop Pharoah Tut-ankh-*

amun suggest that such facts may have been known by Africans over 3,300 years before science's rediscovery of the same and 1,000 years before Herophilos. The third ventricle has long been called the vault of initiation. Certainly, it is most critical to consider that the ancient Egyptians not only knew of the psychological operation of what they term the spirit, soul, and mind but had also defined the physical location and perhaps physiological operation of this trinity.

Subtle and more direct indications of the original discovery of the location and importance of the pineal gland are indicated by several other sources. First, the Egyptians defined the purpose of education to be the freedom of the soul. The grades of students in their educational system were divided into neophyte, intelligence, and sons of light. The latter two higher grades of students were distinguished by their ability to develop Nous, mind or inner vision. This was the ability to have access to the greater mind, that 99% of one's mind that one is unaware or unconscious of, the personal unconscious mind, soul and spirit. Critically, to have inner vision suggests that one must also have an eye for inner vision, an inner or third eye. According to the ancient Egyptian myth, Horus fought his evil uncle Seth to avenge the death of his father Osiris. In battle Horus' eye was torn to pieces, but by magic Moon God, God of writing, assembled the pieces. This eye of Horus was the third eye, a regenerated or transformed eye (process of initiation), the sound eye, Udjat, the eye of magic.[35] An eye transforms light, spirit, into more dense forms of matter that have informational content such as neurotransmitters, indoleamines, and polypeptide hormones which have been rediscovered by modern scientists. Yet, we find several Egyptian references to the Eye of Horus' relationship to sunlight—I am Horus and I have come forth from the Eye of Horus (Uraeus-Pineal Gland). I am Uatchet (Uraeus, Eye of Horus) who comes forth from Horus. I am Horus and I fly up and perch myself upon the forehead of Ra in the bows of his boat which is in heaven (Book Of The Coming Forth By Day, Book Of The Dead). She (Uatchet, Uraeus or Pineal) riseth up on the left side of thy head, and she shineth from the right side of thy temples without speech; they rise up on thy head during each and every hour of the day as they do for their father Ra (sun), the bandage of Nekheb was laid upon the forehead of every carefully prepared mummy, and The goddess Uatchet cometh unto thee in the form of the "living Uraesu", to annoint thy head with their flames (Book Of The Coming Forth By Day, Book Of The Dead).[35]

The outstanding works by the modern African scholar Dr. Yosef ben-Jochannan, *The African Origins of The Major Western Religions,*[43] *Black Man's Holy Black Bible,*[44] *and We, The Black Jews*[45] have revealed how much the world's major religions, including Christianity have borrowed from the religions of Africans, particularly the ancient Egyptians. Thus, it should come as no surprise to find in Genesis 32:27–32[34] that it was at

Figure 12. Katherine S. Gilbert, Ed., *Treasures of Tutankhamun* **(Metropolitan Museum of Art, New York, 1977, p. 99).**

Peniel (pineal gland) that Jacob (mental slave, neophyte, dwelling in igno-rance, symbolic of the undeveloped unconscious or entrapped within the physical body (the contained mind, soul, spirit) met the Angel of God (soul, spirit). During the wrestling bout which ensued, he ascended from his former state of lower consciousness and was transformed into Israel (liber-ated mind, soul, spirit). It was at *Peniel* that Jacob saw God face to face and his life was preserved or renewed: "And Jacob called the name of the place *Peniel,* for I have seen God face to face, and my life is preserved." Phyloge-netically, the pineal gland is actually in humans a modified eye. In the lower life forms such as amphibians and reptiles, western fence lizard, the pineal is present as a parietal or third eye on the top of the forehead.[31, 35] In the higher life forms such as mammals the pineal withdrew into the head embrologically, converting from a physical eye into a light transducer which converts light into hormonal signals that can actually change the form and function of the physical body and levels of consciousness (spirit, soul, mind, body).

The pineal hormones melatonin and serotonin operate as hormonal keys that unlock the door to the unconscious mind, dreams. Melatonin is known to initiate dreams by activating the locus coeruleus. It is known that ancient Egyptians did practice dream analysis and hypnosis.[29, 30, 36] The recent rediscovery of the concept of the unconscious, hypnosis, and dream analysis, partially attributed to Sigmund Freud, should also be credited to the ancient Egyptians.[48–53] A photograph of the desk of Sigmund (Fig. 10)[49] does reveal a large number of Egyptian statues including one of the God Osiris, God of the Underworld or unconscious, confirming an Atrican knowledge of the unconscious thousands of years before the time of Freud.

A consideration of the pineal gland and melatonin does lead one to raise the question of ancient Egyptian symbolism in relation to the importance of their own Black skin color.[46, 47] Of the myriad of physiological functions of pineal melatonin there are at least two major roles that act directly upon physical Blackness, melanin. First, melatonin maintains and promotes the various shades of skin color by its effects upon the pigment cell, melanocyte, at the skin dermalepidermal junctions. Second, melatonin initiates dreams by its action upon the locus coeruleus.[54] The locus coeruleus is black because it contains large amounts of melanin, the same chemical that produces skin color which in this case is found within the very structure of the brain. Furthermore, the locus coeruleus is the twelfth and uppermost in a chain of twelve pigmented brain nucleii found in the brain stem. These are the substantia nigra with its associated nucleus brachialis pigmentosus and nucleus paranigralis. The other nine nucleii are either part of a neuromelanin column or adjacent to the neuromelanin column. They are: locus coeruleus, nucleus intracapularis subcerleus, nervi trigeini, mesencephasius, pontis centralis oratis, tegmenti pedennculoponticus, parabrachialis, medialis dorsomotor and retro ambigualis. The name locus coeruleus literally means black dot. Locus is a latin word, stlocus locum meaning point of dot. Coeruleus is derived from the Sanskrit word *caeruleus yamas* meaning black. Additionally, it should be noted that the symbol black dot as an actual image does appear in the Egyptian hieroglyphic name for the Sun God Ra.[47] The third eye or Eye of Horus contains the same symbolic image, black dot, as the black pupil through which light enters the eye of inner vision. Similarly, the entrance to the Egyptian temple usually had two obelisks, whose tops were crowned by the pyramidial point, the ben-ben or pyramidion, an all-black cap stone. Pyramids often contained a similar black cap stone, the pyramidion. Thus, it was the first point of the pyramid-temple site or obelisk-temple site to receive sunlight as the sun arose from darkness on each new day and symbolizing that light first enters through a doorway of darkness (pyramidion, pupil) when entering the temple of the human body.[47]

The symbolism of the crown should be placed in the context of the stream of African philosophical thought that stretches from the pre-dynastic Memphite cosmology through the post dynastic heirs of ancient Egypt, Dogon Cosmology. The Memphite cosmology is a stone inscription found at Memphis that had been rewritten by the Ethiopian-Egyptian Pharaoh Taharqa (690–664 B.C.E.) of the 25th dynasty who said he had copied the text from an ancient inscription of his ancestors. The language and arrangement of the text is of the form used at the beginning, before the dynastic period of Egypt. The text states that the Primate of the Gods Ptah (mind) was the first to emerge from the primeval waters of Nun in the form of a Primeval Hill. Closely following the Hill, the God Atom also emerges from the waters and sits upon the Hill.[11] The Hill is another name for the human body, whereas Atom can be correlated to the concept of the sun. Of course the top of the hill would be the human head. Symbolically this is the basis tor the Egyptian statement of the Eye of Horus, the Black doorway or pupil, pyramidion, eye on the mountain, through which light first enters the human temple or body. At this point one can be left in wonder, daring to glimpse the possible historical significance of such a statement and reflecting on the possibility that this is a very ancient memory. For this may have been a concept impressed upon the minds of early humans in the ancestral Great Lakes region of North East Africa in the watery regions at the base of the Mountain of the Moon. Similarly, the great emphasis of the Egyptians upon the crown of the head, the heaved up place or heaven, symbolically pictured as the winged scarab, whose body is like the crown of the skull when viewed from the top (Fig. 11). This may speak to an ancient African awareness of the importance of the enlargement of the cerebral cortex in man as compared to mammalian and primate ancestors. Nonetheless, the statue of Pharaoh Tutankhmun emerging from the primeval water of Nun (Fig. 12) is a direct reference to the Memphite Cosmology of religion, historical evolution of humanity, and daily experience of all humans in the drama of life, the struggle to free the spirit, soul, and mind through a conscious awareness of their operation and the liberation thereby from the body and unconscious state. For just as there was an original sea of the watery regions of the Great Lakes from which humanity did emerge in Africa, so too there exists an internal sea within the human body, the blood stream and cerebro spinal fluid of the brain's ventricular system.

This review of the symbolism of the crown, jewels and tableau of the ancient Egyptian African Pharaoh of the 18th dynasty, Tut-ankh-amun, has found evidence of the ancient African knowledge of the pineal gland. These ancient Africans appear to have had knowledge of the pineal anatomy, its psychological effects, and its physiological relationships with other parts of the brain's structure through the cerebrospinal fluid-filled brain ventricular system. Apart from being symbols of political power over a unified nation of African people they functioned on another level of meaning. They were symbols of potential psychological unity within the grasp of each citizen of the nation. It appears that these Africans knew that the pineal gland contained chemical keys that could unlock various levels of consciousness that would yield operative awareness of the personal mind, soul, and spirit. Furthermore, this triune concept of spirit, soul, and mind appear to have been central concepts found throughout various layers of their educational system. The stated purpose of their educational system was to free the soul from the finite consciousness of the body. Thus, it is reasonable to expect that such a people would have developed an extraordinarily elaborate symbolism around such issues.

References

1. Ghalioungui, Paul, *The House of Life, Per Ankh, Magic And Medical Science in Ancient Egypt,* B.M. ISRAEL. Amsterdam, 1973, p. 127.

2. Leek, F. Filce, *The Human Remains from the Tomb of Tutankhamun,* V, Tutankhamun Tomb Series, Griffith Institute, University Press, Oxford, 1972.

3. ben-Jochannan, Yosef A.A., *Tutankhamun's African Roots, Haley et al., Overlooked?,* Alkebu-lan Books and Education Materials Association, New York, 1978.

4. Lamy, Lucie, *Egyptian Mysteries, New Light on Ancient Spiritual Knowledge,* Crossroad, New York, 1981, pp. 44, 45.

5. West, John Anthony, *Serpent in the Sky: The High Wisdom of Ancient Egypt,* Harper & Row, New York, 1979, p. 17.

6. Gilbert, Katherine Stoddert Ed., *Treasures of Tutankhamun,* Metropolitan Museum of Art, New York, 1976, p. 99.

7. Murname, William J., *The Penguin Guide to Ancient Egypt,* Penguin Books, New York, 1983, p. 47.

8. Romer, John, *Valley Of The Kings,* Michael Joseph Ltd., London, 1981, pp. 245–76.

9. Piankoff, Alexandre, *The Shrines of Tut-Ankh-Amon,* Bollingen Series XL, Princeton University Press, 1977, pp. 128–31.

10. Budge, Ernest A. Wallis, *Tutankhamen, Amenism, Atenism and Egyptian Monetheism,* Bell Publishing Company.

11. James, George G.M., *Stolen Legacy,* Julian Richardson Associates, San Francisco, 1976, pp. 139–51.

12. ben-Jochannan, Yosef A.A., *Black Man of the Nile and His Family,* Alkebu-lan Books and Education Materials, New York, 1981.

13. Griaule, Marcel, *Conversations with Ogotemmeli,* An Introduction To Dogon Religious Ideas, International African Institute, Oxford University Press, New York, 1965, pp. 16–23.

14. King, Richard D., Private photograph, Cairo Museum, Cairo, Egypt, Group Lecture Tour with Dr. Yosef ben-Jochannan, 1983.

15. Private photograph, Cairo Museum, Cairo, Egypt.

16. Leek, op. cit., plate V.

17. Leek, op. cit., plate X.

18. Leek, op. cit., plate XI.

19. Budge, E.A., Wallis, *The Gods of the Egyptians,* Volumes I and II, Dover

Publications, New York, 1969.

20. Guralink, David B. and Friend, Joseph H. Eds., *Webster's New World Dictionary of the American Language,* The World Publishing Company, New York, 1968, p. 1477.

21. Jacobi, Jolande, *The Psychology Of C.G. Jung,* Yale University Press, New Haven, p. 39.

22. Ibid, p. 40.

23. James, op, cit., p. 27.

24. James, op, cit., p. 32.

25. James, op, cit., p. 68.

26. James, op, cit., pp. 123–124.

27. Lamay, op. cit., pp. 24, 25.

28. Reiter, Russel J., *The Pineal Gland* vol. I–III, CRC PRESS, Inc., Boca Raton, Florida, 1981.

29. Wurtman, Richard J., Moskowitz, Michael A., "The Pineal Organ, Part I," The New England Journal of Medicine, 296:23, 1977, p. 1329.

30. Wurtman, Richard J., Moskowitz, Michael A., "The Pineal Organ, Part II," *New England Journal of Medicine,* 296:24, p. 1977.

31. Smith, Ivor, "Indoles Of Pineal Origin: Biochemical and Physiological Status," *Psychoneuroendocrinology,* Vol. 8, no. 1, 1983, pp, 41–60.

32. Reiter, Russel J., "The Pineal Gland: An Intermediary Between the Environment and the Endocrine System," *Psychoneuroendocrinology*, Vol. 8, no. 1, 1983, pp. 31–40.

33. Cardonali, David P., "Molecular Mechanisms of Neuroendocrine Integration in the Central Nervous System: An Approach Through the Study of the Pineal Gland and Its Innervating Sympathetic Pathway," *Psychoneuroendocrinology,* Vol. 8, no. 1, 1983, pp. 3–30.

34. King, Richard D., "Uraeus: From Mental Slavery to Mastership," *Uraeus,* Vol. I, no, 3, 1978, pp. 22–35.

35. King, Richard D., "The Pineal Gland Review," Fanon Center Publication, Los Angeles, 1977.

36. Hobson, J. Allan, Mc Carley, Robert W., "The Brain as a Dream State Generator: An Activation Synthesis Hypothesis of the Dream Process," *American Journal of Psychiatry,* 134:12, 1977, pp. 1335.

37. Carman, John S., et al., "Negative Effects of Melatonin on Depression," *American Journal of Psychiatry,* 133 :10, 1976, pp. 1181.

38. Moskovitz, Charlene, Moses, Hamilton, and Klawans, Harold L., "Levodopa-Induced Psychosis: A Kindling Phenomenon," *American Journal of Psychiatry,* 135:6, 1978, p. 669.

39. Reiter, Russel J., *The Pineal Gland,* vol. I, CRC Press, Inc., Boca Raton, Florida, 1981, p. 3.

40. James, op, cit., pp. 41–51.

41. Mess, B, et. al., *Melatonin, Cerebrospinal Fluid, Pineal Gland Interrelationships, Brain Endocrine Interaction II, The Ventricular System,* Karger, Basel, 1975, p. 335.

42. Barr, Frank E., *Melanin and the Mind-Brain Problem,* Institute for the Study of Consciousness, 2924 Benvenue Ave., Berkeley, California, 1982.

43. ben-Jochannan, *African Origins of the Major Western Religions,* Alkebu-Lan Books, New York, 1970.

44. ben-Jochannan, *The Black Man's Religion,* Alkebu-Lan Books Associates, New York, 1976.

45. ben-Jochannan, *We The Black Jews,* Alkebu-Lan Books Associates, New York, 1982.

46. King, Richard D., "Black Dot, Part I," *Uraeus, Vol.* 2, no. 1, 1980, pp. 18–32, 43.

47. King, Richard D., "Black Dot, Part II," *Uraeus, Vol.* 2, no. 3, 1982, pp. 4–22.

48. Sulloway, Frank J., Freud, *Biologist of the Mind, Beyond The Psychoanalytic Legend,* Basic Books, Inc., New York, 1979, p. 366.

49. Engelman, Edmund, Berggasse 19: *Sigmund Freud's Home and Offices, Vienna 1938:* The Photographs of Edmund Engelman. With an Introduction by Peter Gay. Captions by Rita Ransohoff, Basic Books, New York, 1976.

50. Mac Hovec, Frank J., "Hypnosis Before Mesmer," *American Journal of Clinical Hypnosis,* Vol. 17, no. 4, p. 215.

51. Tompkins, Peter, *The Magic Of The Obelisks,* Harper & Row, New York 1981.

52. Shadow, Kenneth, *Cults of the Shadow,* Samuel Weiser, New York, 1976.

53. James, op, cit., p. 134.

54. Jouvet, M. and Delorme, F., "Locus Coeruleus and Paradoxical Sleep," C.R. Soc. Biol (Paris), vol. 159, 1965, pp. 895–899.

55. Olswezki, J. and Baxter, D., *Cytoarchitecture of the Human Brain,* Stern and Birjelow, editors, J. Rodgers, New York, 1954.

56. Bazelon Mary and Feinchel, Gerald M., et al., "Studies on Neuromelanin I, A Melanin System in the Human Adult Brainstem," *Neurology,* vol. 17, 1967, pp. 512–19.

57. Marsden, C.D., "Pigmentation in the Nucleus Substantiae Nigrae of Mammals," *Journal of Anatomy,* vol. 95, 1961, pp. 256–262.

58. Feinchel, Gerald M. and Bazelon, Mary, "Studies on Neuromelanin II, Melanin in the Brainstems of Infants and Children," *Neurology,* vol. 18, 1968, pp. 817–820.

59. Schere, H.J., "Melanin Pigmentation of the Substantia Nigra in Primates," *Journal of Comparative Anatomy,* vol . 71, 1939, pp. 91–95 .

60. Lewis, Charlton T. and Short, Charles, *Harpers Latin Dictionary, A New Latin Dictionary,* American Book Company, New York, 1907, pp. 262, 1074.

61. Rev. Means, Sterling, M., *Ethiopia: The Missing Link in African History,* 1945.

62. Dury, Victor, *Ancient History of the East,* vol. 1, p. 21.

63. Mookadi, Badha K., *Hindoo Civilization,* p. 33.

64. Rashidi, Runoko, "Ancient India. The Eastern Bastion Of the Ethiopian Empire," Lecture, Amenta Conference, Compton, California, August 1981.

65. Russell, G.V., "The Locus Coeruleus," Tex. Rep. Biol. Med., Vol. 13. 1955, pp. 939–88.

66. Finch, Charles, Lecture, Amenta Conference, Compton College, Compton, California, October 1983.

67. Gilbert, op. cit., plate 22.

KEMETIC CONCEPTS IN EDUCATION

Asa G. Hilliard III

> *As to the man without experiences, he does not listen, he does nothing at all. He will see knowledge where there is ignorance, he will see profit where there is loss; he makes all kinds of errors, taking always the side opposite to what is praiseworthy. In that way, he lives on what is perishable. His food is evil speech, as to which he marvels. He lives everyday on what the wise know to be mortal, flying from what is best for him, because of the multitude of efforts which present themselves to him each day.*
> —Chapter 41, *Book of Ptah-Hotep*
> (Myer, 1990, pp. 294–5)

Long before the colonization of the African continent by European nations, and long before the first recorded invasions of the African continent by any nation outside the continent, Africans had developed the most sophisticated system of education to be found in early records. Those records show that the African system of education, especially its classical expression in ancient KMT (later called Egypt by the Greeks), was the parent of other systems of education, especially early European education in Greece and Rome (James, 1956; Babbitt, 1969).

> Witness to this also that the wisest of the Greeks: Solon, Thales, Plato, Eudoxus, Pythagoras who came to Egypt and consorted with the priests, and in this number some would include Lycurgus also. Eudoxus, they say, received instruction from Chonuphis of Memphis, Solon from Sonchis of Sais, and Pythagoras from Oenuphis of Heliophis. Pythagoras, as it seems, was greatly admired, and he also greatly admired the Egyptian priests and, copying their symbolism and occult teachings incorporated his doctrines in enigmas. As a matter of fact, most of the Pythagorean precepts do not at all fall short of the writings that are called Hieroglyphics ...
> —Plutarch

Long after invasions of and colonizations in ancient Africa by outside nations, Africans maintained sophisticated systems of education. They maintained sophisticated systems appropriate to their environment even under harsh rural conditions. We can still see some of those systems today in traditional communities. It was these systems that were the priority targets of colonizers. Only when they were destroyed would Africans be weakened and confused to the point of serious vulnerability (Griaule, 1972; DuBois, 1969; Ngubane, 1979; Jahn, 1961; Erny, 1973).

Much of the present indigenous African education system is a part of a "secret" oral tradition, as was the case in Ancient KMT (Harley, 1970; Griaule,1972; James, 1976; DuLubicz, 1978). Knowledge was "secret" only in the sense that advanced technical ideas and skills would be taught only after a rigorous program of study had been mastered. This was nothing more than a recognition of something important about the learning process. It would mean little to give "secret" knowledge to an unprepared learner. He or she would not understand it.

Over the full course of African history, a number of African civilizations and nations were destroyed by external conquests (Ngubane, 1979; Williams, 1974; Rodney, 1974; Padmore, 1969). This has led such writers as Armah (1979), to describe in Two Thousand Seasons, the nearly 2,000 years of destruction and decline of African nations, mainly by outside invaders.

Any examination of education in Ancient KMT must take into account this relationship of Africa to the rest of the world, especially to its conquerors. Yet because of the traditional ignorance, neglect, defamation, and destruction of African history and culture by outsiders over centuries, the reclamation and restitution of African history today is a very difficult task.

Education Under Black African Rule

Within the time available to me today, my main purpose is to present a brief description of parts of the education system of ancient KMT when it was under native African leadership. While the population of KMT was somewhat mixed ethnically and racially even in the early kingdoms, it was southern black African leadership that founded KMT and governed it during its golden ages. For example, out of thirty dynasties or kingdoms, it was during the first seven dynasties that most of the pyramids were built. It was during the 18th dynasty that the most magnificent temples and tombs were built. It was during the 25th dynasty that there was a restoration of ancient ways. These were native African dynasties. Generally we may say that the native dynasties were Dynasties One through Twelve, Dynasty Eighteen, and Dynasty Twenty-Five. The Nineteenth and Thirtieth dynasties did have large scale building programs that imitated earlier native African culture. They added nothing new. Rameses II of the nineteenth dynasty did increase the scale of some architecture during his rule, but it was in essence the same type of architecture that his predecessors had created.

Operating Framework

The following statements will set forth the operating framework for this article. The limitations on the length of this presentation preclude a detailed review of supporting documentation for each of the following points. However, a more detailed treatment of evidence for these assertions has been presented elsewhere (Hilliard, 1984).

- According to archaeological finds, the oldest hominoids in the world lived in Africa several million years before they appeared anywhere else in the world. Most of the bones of ancient man were found in sites that cluster around that great central eastern African lake Nyanzaa (named Lake Victoria by the Europeans) on the equator. Only in the last one million years do we find that hominoids were on other continents.
- The oldest recorded civilization to date is Nile Valley civilization.
- The oldest nation on record to date was the Nubian nation Ta Seti, located to the south of KMT. Remember also, it was a king of the south or Upper KMT that united KMT and founded its First dynasty.
- KMT was Africa s greatest recorded African classical civilization.
- KMT was the natural extension of inner-African culture.
- There was in ancient times and there remains today a cultural unity between KMT and the rest of the African continent.
- The native African populations were a Negroid people.
- Ancient African nations influenced other civilizations worldwide.
- KMT was a black African nation during its most important development periods .
- Africans in the African diaspora, including the Americans and the Carribean retained and still retain varying degrees of African culture. That culture is reflected in family patterns, language, religious belief systems, artistic creativities, etc.

Sources of Evidence

While few historians have written specifically about Kemetic education, there is a good deal of direct and indirect evidence that helps us to bring a good picture of it into focus. The sources of evidence include the following:

- Sacred texts written in mdw ntru (renamed Hieroglyphics by the Greeks): Pyramid texts, papyri, coffin texts, etc.

- Monuments: Pyramids. tekenu (renamed obelisks by the Greeks), stellae.
- Carvings.
- Paintings.
- Pottery.
- European "classical writers," some of whom were eyewitnesses (Greek and Roman).
- The ancient and contemporary cultural practices of inner-Africa (religion, family practices, symbolic structures, educations, etc.), when compared to those of ancient KMT are very similar.

Foreign (Asian) Invasions as the Destruction of High Culture

Given the brief time that is allotted to this presentation, I have decided to begin my description of Kemetic education at one of the peak periods of its development, the New Kingdom, the 18th Dynasty. This was the Kingdom that included Thutmoses III, the great conqueror; Akhenaton, the world's first apostle of nonviolence and who is falsely regarded as the originator of the idea of monotheism; Hatshepsut, the most famous woman to rule KMT or any other ancient nation as a "King;" and the popular but inconsequential young pharaoh "King Tutankamen." These were native Africans who, led by Sequenenre the Southerner of the late 17th dynasty, had expelled the Asian Hyksos invaders from KMT and reestablished African rule.

It is very important to note that these Asian Hyksos invaders, also called shepherd kings, represented a dramatic interruption in the creative Kemetic cultural traditions. They were alien and made no recognizable lasting contribution to the culture of KMT, even though they ruled for five dynasties.

> These invaders, now generally called Hyksos, alter the designation applied to them by Josephus (quoting Manetho), themselves left so few monuments in Egypt that even their nationality is still the subject of much difference of opinion: while the latent character of their supremacy for the same reason, are equally obscure matters. The documentary materials bearing on them are so meager and limited in extent, that the reader may easily survey them and judge the question himself . . . (Breasted, 1937, p. 29).

> The Hyksos left no literary evidence of their occupation of Egypt. Indeed, they left practically no large monuments at all. What we know about them has been painfully gleaned from a host of scarabs—those beetle shaped amulets so characteristic of Egypt—cylinder seals, and a few other isolated objects; a tiny sphinx with royal head and a semetic face in the act of clawing to death an Egyptian: a dagger with remarkable representations of animals on the handle: a fragmentary writing pallet. . . . Perhaps the only truly monumental relics of the invaders are several blocks from a stone building found at Gebelein, a few miles

south of Thebes, which contained the names of the Kings, Khyan and Apophis Owoserre (Steindorff, 1957, pp. 25–26).

After this long cultural lull, the native 18th Dynasty came as a revival of the African culture of the first twelve dynasties, and indeed the culture of the predynastic period.

Kemetic Education

The center of 18th dynasty government was at Wa-Set, or Wo-Se', meaning in Kemetic "The Septer." Wa-Set was renamed "Thebes" by later Greek invaders. It was renamed "Luxor" by still later Arab invaders. In Wa-Set were two gigantic temples that contained the most highly developed education systems on record from ancient times.

One temple, the Southern Ipet (place), now called by the Arabic name the "Temple of Luxor," was located in the south of the city of Wa-Set. It was connected to the largest temple of ancient times, the Ipet Isut, called Karnak by the Arabs. These magnificent buildings existed long before there was a Greece, and even longer before Greeks would conquer KMT under Alexander the Great. Nearly a thousand years after the Greek invasion, the essentially Asiatic Arabic population under Islam would take over KMT.

Ipet-Isut meant "the most select of places," or "the holiest of places." It was both a center of religion and education, since the two could not be separated in the minds of the Kamites. It housed an elite faculty of priest-professors. It has been estimated that at one time there were more than 80,000 students at all grade levels studying at Ipet Isut University (Abdullah, 1984). Temples were at the center of religion, politics, and education.

Ipet-Isut was like all other lesser temples in KMT's Nile Valley. Every temple had a faculty and a library (Hurry, 1928). This was true, not only in the 18th dynasty or New Kingdom, it was also true in the oldest Kingdoms as well, kingdoms that flourished, before the invasions. For example, libraries were an important part of Old Kingdom culture.

> In one of the tombs at Gizeh, a great functionary of the sixth dynasty . . . takes the title of "Governor of The House of Books." This simple mention thrown incidently between two or more elevated titles would be sufficient in fault of others coming to show us the extraordinary development at the time of Egyptian civilization. Not only had they a literature, but that literature was also large enough to fill libraries, its importance was so great that to one of the functionaries of the court was especially attached the preservation of the royal library. . . . In a later writing, Professor Maspero says this liberation was of the time of Shepseska. He was the sixth King of the fourth dynasty . . . (Myer, 1900, p. 20).

The faculty were called Hersetha or "teachers of mysteries," and were divided into departments (Myer, 1900), as follows: (1) Mystery Teachers of Heaven (astronomy and astrology); (2) Mystery Teachers of All Lands (geography); (3) Mystery Teachers of the Depths (geology); (4) Mystery Teachers of the Secret Word (philosophy and theology); and (5) Mystery of Pharaoh and Mystery Teachers who examined words (law and communication).

Ancient KMT was a high-tech society. It required literal armies of educated people. The first step in the formal process of general education was training as a scribe, a highly honored profession. The route to sacred or secular office was through the scribal schools.

Scribes began their work by copying existing great works. The Mdw Ntr (Hieroglyphics) expressed the great ideas of the age. There was no Dick, Jane, and Spot here—no Mickey Mouse and Donald Duck, no Cinderella, and Jack and the Beanstalk, no Goldilocks and the Three Bears. Scribes were introduced to serious matters from the outset. Though they may not and probably did not understand fully what they were copying initially, gradually they came to know the greatest historical and spiritual tradition in the history of mankind.

The process of education was not seen primarily as a process of acquiring knowledge. It was seen as a process of the transformation of the learner who progressed through successive stages of rebirth to become more godlike. Disciplined study under the guidance of a master teacher was the single path to becoming a new person.

The education system was an open admission system that was not tied to heredity.

> There is not a son for the Chief of the Double White House: there is not an heir for the Chief of the Seal (Myer, 1900, p. 165).

The "Double-White House" was the Pharaoh's capital. In other words, in order to be educated, the Pharaoh's children, like all others had to follow the difficult path of hard study on their own. For example, Amenhotep, son of Hapu, was of lowly birth. However, he is identified as the architect-priest who designed the basic plan of the great temple of Ipet-Isut (White, 1970, p. 86).

Kemitic educators were first and foremost serious students of natural phenomena, especially in the native African dynasties. It was the long, painstaking study of everything in nature that led Kamites and other Africans to the belief in the essential unity of all things in the universe, and to a belief in one supreme God. This belief was held in KMT from earliest times. According to the great Egyptologist, E.A. Wallis Budge, who studies all the ancient Kemetic literature, the study of that literature reveals that there was never a time when Kamites did not believe in one Great God (monotheism). This God was nameless, incomprehensible, and self-created (Budge, 1973, p. xxiii). Kamites believed that any facet of nature could be studied to cover principles of nature's operations, or put another way, aspect of God. This allowed for the use of many natural objects as symbols of divine principles. It was the ancient Kamites' attempt to live in harmony with nature's principles, or God's manifestations (not many gods or polytheism), that led them to develop the earliest moral teachings and forms of worship to institutionalize those teachings.

Anyone who reads the ancient texts will detect the universal preoccupation of native Africans with the sacred. The overall aim of education is exemplified by the NTRU (diving principles) Tehuti and Maat. Tehuti (renamed Thoth by the Greeks) was the masculine wisdom principle of God. Tehuti also represented writing and learning. Maat was a feminine principle of God and represented truth, justice, and righteousness. By following such pathways as these and others, Kamites hoped to become more like the Supreme Creator, who was hidden.

Some students of ancient KMT have described the education system as "practical," as lacking in a desire to pursue "knowledge for its own sake," as if the "pursuit of knowledge for its own sake" represented a higher and more advanced concept than "practical" education. Kemetic education can be described as *functional,* a blend of *theory and practice,* a *wholistic* education. I remain unconvinced that "education for its own sake" or "learning for the love of learning" is a more lofty goal than education to become more like the Supreme Creator. Put another way, should education be for its own sake or for God's sake?

The European Response to Kemetic Education

Ancient KMT was conquered first by Asians, later by Europeans and finally by an Arabic-Asian population. However, under Greek rule, beginning with Alexander the Great in 323 B.C. and lasting through the Roman Ceasars to the time of Roman Emperor Justinian circa 6th century A.D., a strange thing happened. Before the Greek invasion, Greek students and settlers had been going to KMT for years to learn religion, architecture, and the arts and sciences. For example, the Parthenon on the Acropolis is merely a late copy of African architecture like the Southern Ipet and Ipet Isut Temples which had been developed in KMT at such places as Wa-Set. Yet even after winning their wars with KMT, Greece and Rome became and remained captives of Kemetic culture, especially its religion and education, for nearly 650 years!

It took years of calculated struggle for Romans to destroy Kemetic education. These struggles were initiated by rulers with such edicts as those issued by Theodosius, 380 A.D., and Justinian, 527 A.D. They had to burn down African temples or universities, and destroy or tame the priest-professors to destroy the leadership of KMT. Kemetic religion and education was led by a priesthood that was not Roman. Emperors from Constantine on wanted no foreign leaders as competition, especially for the minds of the people. Christianity became a state religion with a native Roman leadership.

All over KMT today, one can see the results of Greek and Roman conquerors' efforts to copy the culture that they conquered. They rebuilt African temples (church/schools) and joined the African religion. They carved their own images on the African temples. They showed themselves being blessed by African Gods, wearing African clothes and performing African ceremonies. A visitor to KMT today must wonder as he or she gazes on the many massive African temples that were rebuilt by the Europeans, why did they go to such trouble? Noble Europeans even had their bodies mummified in the African way! They took home the African religion of Isis, Osirus, and Horus. It remained very popular and prominent until suppressed by the royal edicts. Even then the influence of Africa remained. For example, the city of Paris, France is named for Isis (Par Isidos or Place of Isis). Notre Dame Cathedral is actually built on the site of the older Temple of Isis!

The last Kemetic college, Philae at the First Cataract, was closed under orders from Justinian in 527 A.D. After this, the classical education of KMT died out or went underground.

Many of the Kemetic educational concepts did not die. They remained in more or less disguised form in the education systems of European conquerors. George G.M. James, in *Stolen Legacy* (1956), has examined traditional histories of philosophy and has shown as did Plutarch (Babbitt, 1969), that many of these authors acknowledge that the wisest of the Greeks were students of African teachers in Kemetic universities. They were given a *liberal arts* education which became the prototype for later Greek and Roman education systems. In Greece, "the Trivium" of grammar, rhetoric and logic were practiced. In Rome, "the Quadrivium" of arithmetic, astronomy, geometry, and music were added. Taken together, these were the "seven liberal arts," the foundation of western higher education. They also remain in the traditional education systems of Nile Valley migrants to all other parts of the African continent.

Conclusion

Our reasons for looking at the ancient Kemetic system of education are many. The following reasons are but a few of them:

- Kemetic education is our best window on ancient African education continent-wide.

- Kemetic education is the parent of "western" education and therefore it must be understood if ancient and modern western education is to be understood.
- Kemetic education is a system that can and, in my opinion, should provide guidance for the organization of the education of our people today.

Morehouse men, African Americans have been asked over the years to sit as spectators in silence, in awe, in wonder, and in admiration of the ancient and modern cultures of other peoples. We have not been asked to follow that ancient African dictum, "Man, know yourself!" Were we truly to know ourselves, we would be able to use our own traditions and experiences as the basis for creative problem solving in today's world. To do otherwise is to become cultural schizophrenics, split personalities, trying vainly as DuBois has said, to view the world through the eyes of others, who look on us with amused pity and contempt, "while we chase gods not our own" (Bengu, 1975).

Many of those who view us thus have been partners in the design of an educational process that has withheld from us our birthright, a knowledge of ourselves. It has been said, "He who steals my purse steals trash. But he who steals my good name, steals that which does not make him rich but makes me poor indeed." But "'truth crushed to the ground" will rise again. In the words of Gerald Massey:

> Truth is all potent with its silent power
> If only whispered, never heard aloud
> But working secretly, almost unseen,
> Save in some excommunicated book;
> 'Tis as the lightning with its errand done
> Before you hear the thunder

Morehouse Men, you have a special opportunity and a special responsibility—an obligation. It is not enough for you to be bright and competent. You must also have purpose and direction. It is not enough for you to "make it" on your own—to save yourself. As the character Abena says in Armah's novel, *Two Thousand Seasons* (1979), "There is no self to save without the rest of us." Morehouse Men, Know Yourself!

References and Selected Bibliography

Abdullah, Mahmoud (1984). Egyptologist and Tour Guide. Seti I Travel, Luxor, Egypt.

Aldred, Cyril (1965). *Egypt To The End of The Old Kingdom.* New York: McGraw-Hill.

Armah, Ayi K. (1979). *Two Thousand Seasons.* Chicago: Third World Press.

Babbitt, Frank C. (Translator) (1969). *Plutarch's Moralia,* volume 5 Cambridge: Harvard University Press.

Bengu, S.E.M. (1975) *Chasing Gods Not Our Own* Pietermaritzberg, Natal Republic of South Africa: Shorter and Shooer.

Breasted, James Henry (1937) *A History of Egypt from the Earliest Times to the Persian Conquest* New York: Charles Schribner's Sons.

Budge, E.A. Wallis (1977) *The Dwellers on the Nile.* New York: Dover Publications (first published 1926).

Budge, E.A. Wallis (1973). *Osiris and the Egyptian Resurrection.* New York: Dover Publications (first published 1911).

Cerny, Jaroslav (1947). *Paper and Books in Ancient Egypt.* London: published by H.K Lewis & Company, Ltd. (for the University of London)

Diop, C.A. (1978). *Cultural Unity of Black Africa* Chicago: Third World Press.

DuBois, Felix (1969) *Timbucktu the Mysterious.* New York: Negro Universities Press (first published 1896).

Erny, Pierre (1973). *Childhood and Cosmos.* New York: Black Orpheus Press.

Freud, Sigmund (1967) *Moses and Monotheism* New York: Vintage (first published 1939.

Gay, John, *Red Dust Tracks on the Road.*

Graves, S.P. (1913) *Education Before the Middle Ages.* New York: McMillan.

Griaule, M. (1975) *Conversations with Ogotemneli.* Oxford: Oxford University Press.

Haskins, R.W. (1844) *The Arts, Sciences, and Civilization, Anterior to Greece and Rome* Buffalo: A.W. Wilgus.

Hilliard, Asa G. III (1984). *Pedagogy in Ancient KMT.* Paper presented to the Ancient Egyptian Studies Conference, Los Angeles.

Hurry, J.B. (1928). Imhotep: Vizier and Physician of King Zoser and Afterwards the Egyptian God of Medicine. London: Oxford University Press.

Jackson, John G. (1974) *Introduction to African Civilization.* Secaucus, N.J.: Citadel Press.

Jahn, Jahneinz (1961) *Muntu: The New African Culture.* New York: Grove.

James, George G.M (1976) *Stolen Legacy.* San Francisco: Julian Richardson.

Laurie, S.S. (1902). *Historical Survey of Pre-Cristian Education* London: Longmans, Green and Company.

Myer, Isaac (trans.; 1900) *Oldest Books in The World: An Account of The Religion, Wisdom, Philosophy, Ethics, Psychology, Manners, Proverbs, Sayings, Refinement, Etc., of the Ancient Egyptians.* New York: E W Dayton.

Mertz, Barbara (1978) *Redland, Blackland: Daily Life in Ancient Egypt.* New York: Dodd Mead Company.

Mokhtar, G. (1981). *General History of Africa To Ancient Civilizations of Africa.* Berkeley, California: University of California Press.

Lamy, Lucie (1981). *Egyptian Mysteries: New Light on Ancient Spiritual Knowledge.* New York: Crossroads.

Montet, Pierre (1964). *Eternal Egypt.* New York: New American Library.

Padmore, George (1969). *How Britain Rules Africa.* New York: Negro Universities Press (first published 1936).

Rodney, Walter (1970) *How Europe Underdeveloped Africa.*

Schwaller de Lubicz R.A. (1978) *Symbol and The Symbolic.* Brookline, Mass.: Autumn Press.

Schure, Edward (1973). *The Mysteries of Ancient Egypt: Hermes/Moses.* Blauvelt, New York: Multimedia Publishing Corporation (first published 1889).

Smith, William A. (1955). *Ancient Education.* New York: Philosophical Library.

Smith G. Elliott (1916). *The Influence of Ancient Egyptian Civilization in The East and in America.*

Steindorff, George and Keith C. Seele (1957). *When Egypt Ruled the East.* Chicago: University of Chicago Press.

Turner, Lorenzo (1942). Some Contacts of Brazilian Ex-slaves with Nigeria, West Africa, *Journal of Negro History,* vol. 27, no. I, pp. 55–67.

White, J.E. Manchip (1970) *Ancient Egypt: Its Culture and History* New York: Dover.

Williams, Chancellor (1974) *The Destruction of Black Civilization.* Chicago: Third World Press.

Wilson, John A. (1956) *The Culture of Ancient Egypt.* Chicago: University of Chicago Press.

EDITOR'S CORNER

THE VOODOO GALLERY:
AFRICAN PRESENCE IN THE RITUAL
AND ART OF HAITI

Ivan Van Sertima

The paintings of Haiti (though the same may only be said of rare pieces of its sculpture) can stand among the marvels of modern religious art. In 1949, five years after Haiti's first art gallery—*Centre d'Art*—opened, Jean Paul Sartre, the great French philosopher and critic, visited Haiti. "This is the first time in a decade," enthused Sartre, "that a visit to a museum of paintings has opened a new experience to me."[1] A year earlier, the spokesman of the French surrealist movement in poetry, André Breton, declared that Haitian art would "ventilate the world."[2] This art, therefore, entered the mainstream of the modern world less than 40 years ago. Hence it is seen by some as a young art: primitive, naive, a miraculous baby. But it is a mistake to date such a phenomenon of sensibility to the phase of its efflorescence and formal recognition. For Haitian art is not a child of the forties: it has its roots in the centuries.

It was born in the flame and darkness of the *houmfor*—the sacred temple of the voodoo priests. While there are brilliant Haitian paintings, to be sure, that owe their inspiration to experiences and influences outside the context of voodoo, there are few indeed untouched by the myths and symbols, the objects, the forces, the ideas, even the organizational principles, of this complex ritual cult. The object of this essay is to explore the nature of the relationship between voodoo and Haitian art.

In the preface to *Haitian Art,* Ute Stebich speaks of its beginnings in the Voodoo temples. She identifies this initial phase as "folk art" but points out that, while this provided the basis for most self-taught artists, they eventually moved away from these beginnings.[3] Not that folk art, as she terms it, disappeared, for it still continues to flourish on the walls of the voodoo

This essay is based on a trip to Haiti in January, 1981, sponsored by the African-American Exchange Program and partially financed by the National Endowment for the Humanities.

temples, on tap-taps (the Haitian taxi-cabs) on shop signs, in decorations on houses and in cemeteries.

The movement away from these beginnings, of which she speaks, is a movement, I presume, from certain naive or basic expressions to sophistications of color, form and organization, to subtler tapestries of theme and symbol, not a movement away from the spell of the *houmfor*. I think it would be of interest to look, first of all, at what I would label as "primary" paintings, that is paintings which are straightforward pictorializations of Afro-Haitian spirits (loas) hougans and mambos (the voodoo priests and priestesses) scenes from the stage of the ritual itself, and all the sacred paraphernalia—bells and rattles, conches and drums, candles and crucifixes, the ritual ground paintings of the Fon and Kongo known as the vèvè, the beaded and sequined flags and bottles, the painted calabashes, the stuffed and tasselled knapsacks and feathered dolls. These may serve as guides through the first room of the voodoo gallery of art.

Walking through this gallery one comes upon the master of the voodoo

Figure 1. *Le Grande Maitre* (AAEP photo—Musee d'Art Haitien)

gods—*Le Grande Maitre*—(see Figure l) A strange, double-faced presence with a third eye like an interior beam of light in the middle of his forehead. He wears a crown, is protected by wings that seem to float in the heavens above him, and he holds in his hands what appears to be a sacrificial cup where blood or fire fountains. Below him and beside him are the familiar emblems of voodoo—the snakes of Damballah, the drums that summon the loas, the vèvè or sacred cosmograms which are the family crests of the loa.

Every loa, like Damballah for example (Figure 2) is associated with a particular vèvè. In the original paintings we may observe his particular colors (green and pink) and the ritual drawings on his garments. These elements distinguish him as the Dahomean serpent god as much as his serpentine staff. We may also observe the open or unpolarized fluidity of his features, pencilled in such shadowy and deliberately ambiguous outline that he may be either African or European. This powerful spirit, brought down the *poteau-mitan* or center pole of the *houmfor* by the drums and the dances and the singing, by the signalling of his colors and his ensign, may descend

Figure 2. *Damballah,* by Andre Pierre (AAEP photo—Musee d'Art Haitien)

Figure 3. *The Zombies.* **Baron Samedi, lord of death, leading the lost souls (AAEP photo—Musee d'Art Haitien)**

upon you at the designated ritual point not as a pure African ancestral essence but fused with the shadow of St. Patrick, possessing you in both or either forms or personalities.

Doors open into the rooms of other cultures and races in the gallery of voodoo, where, as Robert Thompson puts it, "One universe abuts another." Damballah may fade into St Patrick while St Peter may stand, as the African god of the crossroads (Papa Legba) stands, between the loa and the living. But there are some figures in the Afro-Haitian pantheon for which there are no Euro-Christian counterparts, like the Loa or Lord of the Graveyard, Baron Samedi (Figure 3). He is the figure, as rumor has it, that looms largest now against the mental landscape of modern Haiti. He is associated not only with death, but with all forms of oppression and terror. In some portraitures he leads the zombies, people robbed of all freedom, driven through the darkness like dead souls.

But the terror of tyranny, of which so many outsiders speak, the terror of the military police, whom we saw parade with a beautiful and deadly efficiency on the *Champs de Mar*, is as distant from the lives of most people as the palace of Duvalier, so brilliant and nebulous in the white haze of the sun that it looks like the film of a castle projected against the mountain from the clouds. A more intimate and familiar terror is the hunger that haunts the street, the hunger and uncertainty that drives people into another world and

state, another dimension of feeling, where material poverty partly evapo-
rates through one's penetration of an enchanted universe.

In that universe the ancient shell of the *lambi* tolls to summon the
friendly spirits of one's ancestors to possess one with the power and transcendent freedom of the dead. There the rattle of the asson or the ringing of
bells by the houngan or mambo to invoke the spirits is louder than the stamp
of military heels beating in staccato against the asphalt like a volley of shots
across the square.

Figure 4A is a mambo (voodoo priestess). The drawing (Figure 4B) is a
detail of the lower part of Figure 4A, identifying the asson or rattle and
demonstrating the fusion of the Christian cross and the African ritual
ground-painting or vèvè. A talisman or charm-bracelet adorns the right
hand, while a bell, used to summon the loas, lies at the side. It seems both
the bell and the asson are sexually stylized here by Hector Hyppolyte (the
artist-priest) to suggest balance and fusion.

In Figure 5 we have a different kind of mambo. one who works both with
the right hand and the left. The left-hand, which seems here to be casting a
spell, is the hand used for black magic. The lambi at center is used to
summon the spirits in this case. This conch-shell was once a medium of
communication between the African slaves when the drums were banned.
The tree, which the loas use as a door into the human world, may be seen at
left, accenting this emphasis on the darker side of voodoo. Harold
Courlander, in *The Drum and the Hoe, i*nsists that this activity is peripheral

Figure 4A. *Mambo* **(Voodoo Priestess), by Hector Hyppolyte (AAEP photo— Musee d'Art Haitien)**

Figure 4B. Detail of 4A (Ritual Objects)

Figure 5. *Voodoo priestess practicing black magic.* Conch-shell or *lambi* in center is used to summon the god. Note use of left hand. Left-handed emphasis is a sign of black magic. (Photo by Van Sertima—Nader Galleries)

to the main body of voodoo.

> Though the making of *pouins* and magic (ritual magic) and *ouangas* (aggressive magic directed against individuals) is within the realm of the cult priest's activities, these things are part of Vodoun only in a subsidiary sense.
>
> Magic lurks on the periphery of Vodoun. It has little or no place in the placating of the deities or the dead. It concerns the relationship of the living with each other and with *loupgarous* [female vampires] and *baka* [demons]. Although cult rituals include various pouin and magic ceremonies, the cult priest draws upon magic as he draws upon other mystic arts and fields of learning—leaf doctoring, divination, Catholic ritual, and Masonic symbolism . . .
>
> But the respectable cult priest does not dabble in "black" magic—

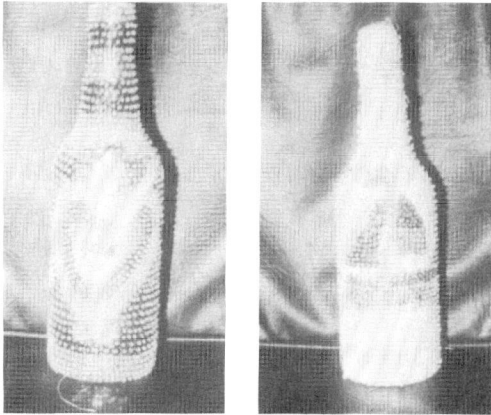

Figures 6A and 6B. *Voodoo bottle* (Monosiet collection)

Figure 7. *Voodoo doll* (Photo by Robert Thompson)

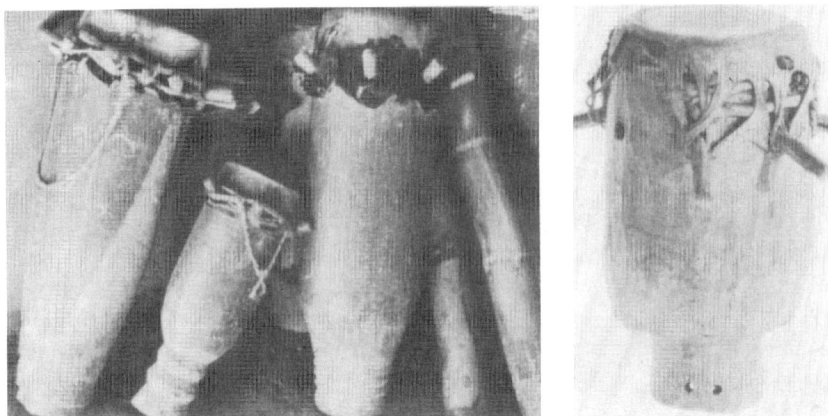

Figure 8A. *Voodoo drums, Rada and Petro, compared with African drums* (Photos by Robert Thompson) *Rada drums from Mariani in the Port-au-Prince area* (Fig. 8A) *are stylistically similar to the drum for the Fon smallpox deity* (Figure 8B). The latter instrument was collected by Claude Savary in Bécon-Hounli Quarter, Abomey, in 1973 for the Musée d'Ethnographie, Geneva.

the kind that maims or destroys human beings. One who does so is said to "work with two hands."[4]

The representation and decoration of ritual objects is the focus of intense artistic endeavour. Witness the beaded and sequinned bottles which house the breath of spirits and which invisibly smoke with that sweet strangled fermentation of fine liquor when opened (see Figure 6) the voodoo dolls

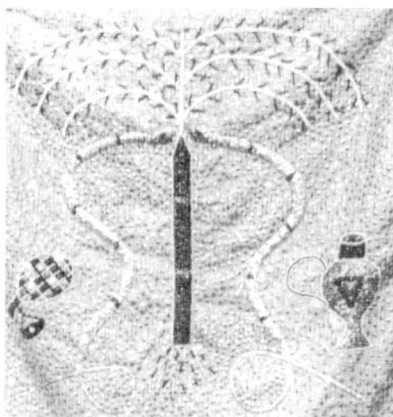

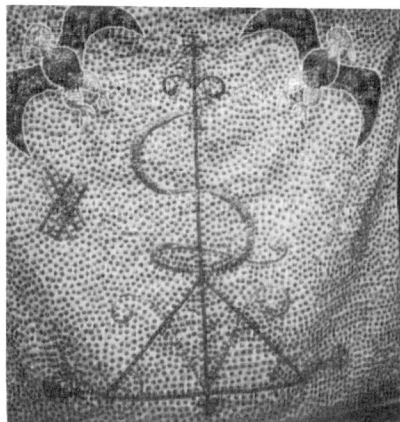

Figure 9A. *Vèvè on tapestry—Damballah-Wedo.* This vèvè is the family crest of the loa, Damballah (Photo by Van Sertima)
Figure 9B. *Vèvè on tapestry—Azagon loco.* This vèvè is the family crest of the loa of the wind.

(Figure 7) the flags (see Monosiet, Figures 9 & 10) and the drums (Figures 8A–8D) where the Rada and Petro are visually contrasted with their African counterparts.

The flags of voodoo, unlike European flags, are not the standard bearers of armies or nations but of deities. The vèvès of loas are embroidered on these flying banners. Robert Farris Thompson, in his brilliant essay, "The Flash of the Spirit: Haiti's Africanizing Vodun Art" sees the flag of the Voodoo shrine as "The most interesting Afro-Haitian textile." In his view the flag unfolded into a new form in the Caribbean, part of "the dialectic of Haitian vodun art, a continuous linking of tradition with developmental brilliance . . . Even European-looking media like the sequined flags paraded in the temples of vodun, inwardly were illumined with the determination of one people not to be structured wholly within another people's formal language. For these were more than military ensigns—they were presences and

Figure 10. *Drawing the vèvè* (**first stage**) (**AAEP photo**)

Figure 11. *Drawing the vèvè* (**final stage**) (**AAEP photo**)

Figure 12. *Women possessed falls on the vèvè sign drawn in flour on the ground.* (AAEP photo)

heralds of the coming of the gods, beaded or appliqued with the signatures of syncretic spirits, culmination of an encounter of African and European sensibilities."[5]

Drum design, as the examples show (8A–8D) did not change very much in their transplantation from Africa to Haiti and Thompson claims that this goes beyond superficial identities in material and design to "method of

Figure 13. *The Three Kings* (AAEP photo) Nader Collection

tuning" and "similarities of meter, tempo and attack." There are Rada and Petro drums, representing the two major branches of voodoo. The *Rada* is for agricultural rites and derived from the Yoruba/Dahomean ritual complex whereas the *Petro* or Petro-Lemba is Kongo/Angola influenced—Lemba for a North Kongo cult of that name; Petro from Pedro, a messianic figure who emerged from the south peninsula of what is now Haiti.[6]

The vèvè to me, however, is the most fertile of forms among all the voodoo ritual objects and designs (see my photographs of the vèvè on tapestry at 9A and 9B).

My special interest in vèvè led to a heated debate with Dr Philippe-Lerebours, a scholar of Haitian art and culture, who was our guide and informant through the George Nader complex of galleries. Dr Lerebours struck me as someone who felt the African presence was given far too much attention in the study of Haitian painting and that the embrace of other influences and elements, particularly the European, was more important. He flatly claimed that the origin of the vèvè lay in France, not in Africa, and that the Haitian revolution was not wholly inspired by African voodoo leaders but was in some way a reverberation of the French revolution. I shall return to the latter claim later in this essay but, with respect to the vèvè, Lerebours insisted that similar geometric and artistic designs could be found on doors and gateways in France even before France began taking slaves

Figure 14. *Baptème Voodoo*, by Andre Pierre (AAEP photo) Nader collection

from Africa into its provinces.

I countered this claim on two levels. First of all, I pointed out that the major encounter between the two cultures (French and African) did not occur as late as he believed. France was invaded twice from Africa and opened to elements of African influence, since the invading armies involved indigenous African types carrying their cultural habits, even as it involved so-called "Punic" types (first invasion) and Berber-Arab types (second invasion). Recent skeletal studies in Carthage[7] show that the population at the time of Hannibal's march into Spain and France was largely Africoid and that the "Punic" type associated with the Phoenician capitals of Tyre and Sidon were practically non-existent in Hannibal's Carthage. The Afro-Carthagenian types included peoples from the interior of central Africa who could have taken some of their ancient ritual habits with them (for this custom of drawing on the ground to signal and summon the gods is a ritual of great antiquity among both Central and West Africans). Africans reached as far into France as Tarascon in the third century B.C.[8] In the eighth century A.D. the Moors (a mixed bag of racial types but including many Africans) got through as far as Tours, 140 miles from Paris.[9] Even if one were to concede that the medieval French designs and those found among Africans in Haiti bore some similarities this did not automatically make Africa or Haiti the borrower and France the source.

A stronger argument lies in the work of Robert Farris Thompson, who not only presents the visual parallels in Africa for the Haitian forms but also cites their parallel function. Thompson has shown that these "ritual ground paintings" take their name from an archaic Fon term for the palm oil used in the making of ground paintings for the deities. "They take their structure from Fon and Kongo traditions of sacred ground painting, with the dominant influence of cruciform patterning from Kongo and Angola normally most evident. The cross is the starting pattern, usually, to which are added important sub-motifs or "points."[10]

It may be the cross or it may be some of the sub-motifs that suggested to Dr Lerebours that the vèvè was a European influence. For, in the process, "Latin Catholic attributes, the sword of St Jacques Majeur, the hearts of the Mater Dolorosa and even the compass-on-the-square of Freemasonry have come to be interspersed along the prevailing cross-shaped axes of the majority of vèvè ground signs."[11]

I think, however, there is something very revealing in this dialogue, that goes beyond the question of the origin of vèvè. That is, the instinctive rejection of things African by many Haitian and Caribbean intellectuals because of an association of the African with the primitive or the tribal or the simple. On several occasions, during discussions of Haitian paintings— *The Three Kings* for example (Figure 13), in which I pointed out that the Feast of the Epiphany grew out of the Festival of the Nile River and that the

January 6 celebration of both festivals was no coincidence,[12] and again, *Baptème Voodoo* (Figure 14) by Andre Pierre, in which I noted that there was river baptism in Africa before the arrival of Christian missionaries[13]—I found Dr Lerebours advancing a European origin and influence for these rituals and concepts without first considering the possible merger in Haiti of European and African parallels. It seemed important to him to disassociate as many African motifs and influences as possible from the best in Haitian art under the illusion that this would enable it to be seen within a larger and more respectable global or individual framework than what voodoo provided.

This notion, that voodoo, or the African base, is a restrictive critical tool, springs, I believe, from a profound inability to see beyond the superstition and appalling poverty of the peasants to the dynamism and universality of a cosmology that organizes and integrates effectively what could remain shattered and polarized in the psyche of a gravely disrupted world.

This fear of Africa, in general, though rooted in a misconception of what is essentially African, and this fear of voodoo, in particular, which has led so many Haitian governments to try and suppress it, cautions us away from our own potentially facile polarity of vision, the tendency to see Haitian voodoo as a flower that once bloomed in the cultivated garden of African religious ideas. The difference and discontinuity between the Dahomean voodoo (or vodun) cult and the Haitian ritual can illuminate for us the historical roots of the Haitian sensibility as well as the dialectic or tension of symbol and belief which elude the interpretation of major art critics (Lerebours, Stebich) and anthropologists (Simpson, Métraux) when faced with the more complex canvases of Haitian ritual drama or Haitian art.

Voodoo is derived from vodun which means "spirit" in the Dahomey serpent cult but the Haitian adopted a Bantu word "loa" to stand for spirit while voodoo (vaudou/vodun) became the word for the cult as a whole. This, in itself, is significant, as I pointed out in an earlier essay "Ritual Man in the Caribbean."

> The inability to see the line of discontinuity more clearly has led to other theoretical confusions and a misunderstanding of some of the statements made by informants in the field. Thus Simpson (1970) is confused by the apparently ambiguous relationship of the loa to the saint because he does not appreciate the significance of the discontinuity between the use of the word *loa* (which is Bantu) and the largely West African Yoruba-Dahomean ritual complex .
>
> He reports that "the situation is complicated by the fact that those who believe the *loas* and saints are on friendly terms and those who maintain they are enemies, sometimes talk about the *loas* and saints as if they were identical." . . . There is no contradiction and complication here. This is as it should be. The use of *loa* (alien to the traditional West African vodun cult) breaks down the fixed category of spirit entities

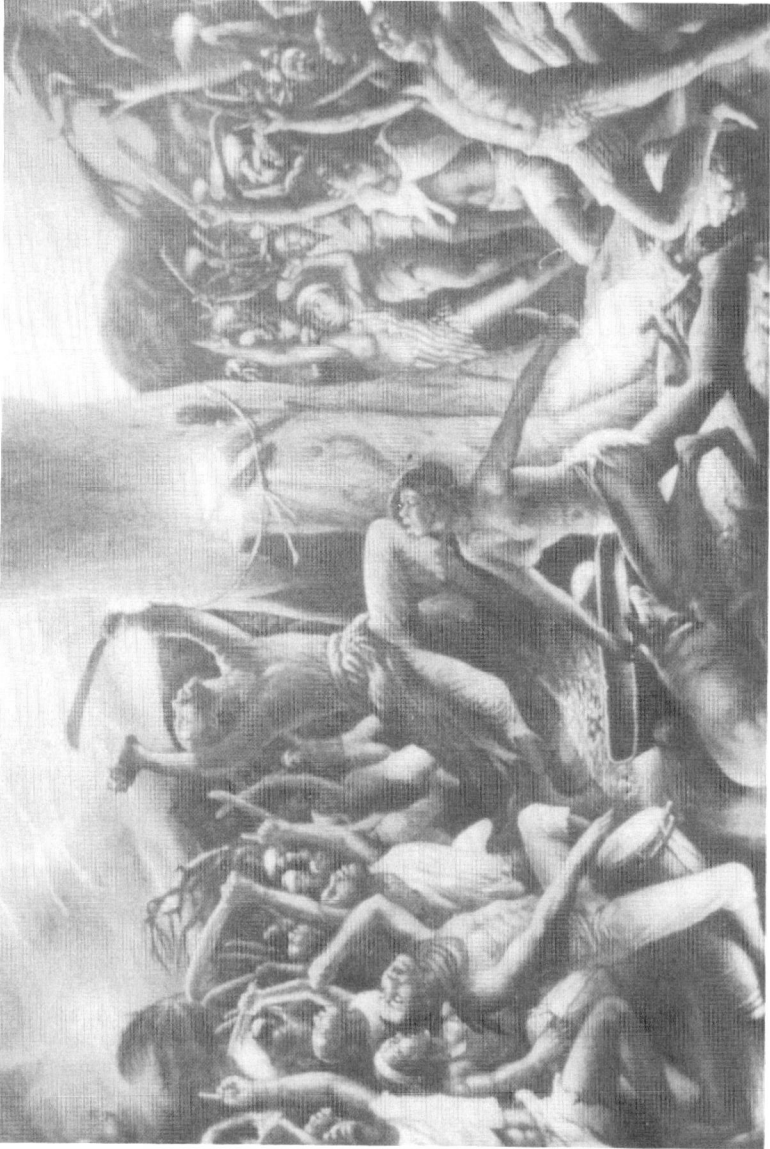

Figure 15. *Ceremonie de Bois Caiman*, by Ulrich Jean Pierre (AAEP photo)—National Museum of Haiti. This is the voodoo ceremony of August 11, 1791, at which Boukman presided. It is considered to be the beginning of the Haitian revolution.

and allows for both a dimension of opposition and identification. The *loa* plays complementary roles in people's thinking. This, after all, is true to the psychological and social reality of the Caribbean, where the theme of revolt (opposition to the saints) and the theme of accommodation (identification with the saints) are separate and simultaneous phases, which indicate a perpetual oscillation within the Caribbean psyche.

Loa, because of its symbolic vagueness (it means breath, shadow, soul, in Bantu) embraces the shifting fluid meaning of the spirit categories. What appears, therefore, as an imprecision, an irregularity or a caprice is a conscious/unconscious innovation to restore simplicity and order in an area where there is a great proliferation of spirit-entities from other tribes and cultures.[14]

Another important aspect of difference between African and Haitian voodoo is the fact that in the Caribbean it was always secret and subversive whereas in Africa it was a conservative phenomenon. "From the beginning," I wrote "we must appreciate that the ritual act of Afro-Caribbean man was an act outside of the established social order. While *Vodun, Shango, Myal* etc. may have enjoyed tribal or state legitimation in traditional Africa they were secret and suspect movements in the slave and colonial arena. They were played out in the shadow of the wings rather than on the center-stage of society. They were dialogues with submerged selves, with the banned ancestor, and I.M. Lewis has referred to them as "cults of deprivation".[15] In this respect they contrasted with the cults from which they derived, cults which had formal and collective sanction. As Erika Bourguignon has pointed out, "the Fon-Yoruba group of cults were not marginal societies ... but cults of worship linked to the power structure and establishment"[16] ... The significance of this needs to be stressed for it profoundly affected the form and function of the transplanted rituals. Even when, in the main, form remained the same, the inner life of the phenomenon was not the same. African and Caribbean ritual proceeded from a different dynamic."[17]

The revolutionary dynamic residing in voodoo was of a twofold nature. First, it broke down tribal boundaries and opened up closed systems of thought into a more universal and fertile medium. Second, it prepared the ground for a successful revolt against slavery, even though, to give due respect to Lerebours' thesis, the emergence of progressive elements in France—an internal crisis—may have eased the way for the triumph of external rebellions.

The cult began to take definite form in Haiti between 1750 and 1790. In less than 40 years, voodoo, under the influence of revolutionary leaders, blended essentials from several tribes and religious beliefs. Its very formation was the consequence of a bridging process. Tendencies toward accommodation (particularly with respect to the Euro-Christian elements) were to deepen in time (in the nineteenth and twentieth centuries) but in the latter half of the eighteenth century lack of historical material makes it difficult to see the emphasis on accommodation as an historically separate and distinct phase from the phase of revolt for, from the time we hear of Voodoo as an effective cult, it is already an "hybrid religion," suggesting the linkage of tribes and diverse ritual beliefs which enabled revolutionary leaders to integrate their followers into a politically effective unit.[18]

It was Boukman who made voodoo into a force that destroyed the French hold on Haiti. He also gave the final shape to modern voodoo or rather (since there is no final shape) instituted rites closest to the acts of the modern cult (the Petro rite in particular). It is important to note here that although the Petro-Lemba branch of Haitian voodoo is derived from Lemba of the Kongo, the rite in itself is largely a Haitian invention. The agricultural rites of Rada (Yoruba-Dahomean) is a more conservative celebration and invocation of the spirits and do not involve the violence and aggression one finds in the Petro rite. Here, I repeat, we are witnessing something both African and native (i.e. Caribbean). There is no scene in African traditional voodoo to rival the scene on August 11, 1791 (see Figure 15).

"In the midst of thunder and lightning, an old Negro woman appeared, danced wildly, sang and brandished a cutlass over her head. Finally, the silent and fascinated crowd saw her plunge the cutlass into the throat of a black hog. The slaves drank the animal's blood and swore an oath: "Let the whole world know that between slavery and death we have chosen death. We shall fight until we are free or the last one amongst us will die."[19] The voodoo scene is captured in all its spectacular terror by Ulrich Jean Pierre in one of the finest of Haitian historical paintings, of which there are few. It is not a romantic rendering. Lightning actually began to flash and thunder broke as Boukman was speaking.

Voodoo gave both the unity and the courage to the Haitian forces to defeat the French, Spanish and British armies. It is only the blindness and insensitive smugness of an intellectual middle class that can ignore the heroic stand of the Haitian peasants and speak of the French revolution inspiring the Haitian. The African never needed to be taught the desire for freedom by an oppressed European proletariat and its rebellious intelligentsia. The fire had struck before. It was only that in 1791 it was not the occasional sparking of hatred and anger but a huge conflagration. It was voodoo that made this possible. Even in the staged voodoo ceremony I witnessed under the hougan, Max Beauvais, one could see the passion and power of the possessed that must have swept like a wave of mortal terror over the spirits of the invading armies.

To this ceremony I must make brief reference if only to point up a problem in ethnographic studies of a phenomenon that baffles the senses and upsets all one's familiar notions of the natural and leaves one puzzled but still skeptical. In the ceremony under the supervision of Max Beauvais we saw two women and one man possessed. In the possession dance we saw them extinguish a roaring fire with their bare feet and the man consume burning coals with his mouth smoking. This scene was photographed, admittedly under difficult conditions (it was night and the stage was dark) but nothing whatever appeared on the contact sheets, only the scenes before and after the fire-eating. We decided to put this down to technical incompetence since we do not believe in the efficacy of magic but our Haitian informants took for granted that the loa's appearance on the stage radiated vibrations that made the conventional reflections of the image impossible. We do not intend to comment on this, save to say that the two photographers on the team were startled since they are both professionals. We present an apologia for the missing film in the form of an evocative postcard which shows a woman tied to the poteau-mitan as the fire rises beneath her (see Figure 16).

The incredible transformation of the human witnessed in a possession ritual, the almost unnatural intensification of energy that produces a quality of tension, vibration, rhythm (call it what you will) and what appears to be a brief but miraculous immunity to conventional forms of injury, must have been a decisive factor in the revolution. A slave who would inwardly tremble before the passing shadow of his master, would, in the transfigured

Figure 16. Woman standing tied to *poteau-mitan* (center-pole of voodoo temple) as fire rises beneath her. (Reproduction of Haitian postcard by Cliché P. Chareton)

state of voodoo possession, leap at his guns as though the bullets were as dust. Thus did 15,000 blacks under the houngan Ducoudray hurl their bodies against the white dragoons and the national guard at Croix des Bouquets. Thus were the finest armies of Europe driven back into the sea in spite of their materially superior armor and the lust and fervor of imperial illusions. Ulrich Jean Pierre, in another of his remarkable historical paintings (Figure 17) depicts the general upheaval that followed in the wake of the oath of Bois Caiman on the Boukman plantation.

Not only did Europeans fear this revolutionary power. The Haitian leaders knew well that a peasantry armed with such a psychological weapon was potentially dangerous. Haitian independence, therefore, though won with the help of voodoo, did not make the cult an arm of the establishment. It remained subversive. Toussaint, Dessalines and Christophe feared it and fought it. Other leaders tried to compromise with it until Francois Duvalier (the most powerful of all houngans and one of the leading experts on voodoo) finally succeeded in subverting it. He made the other houngans his tools, suppressing the opposition. That is probably where voodoo stands today, a tamed force, although it would have been impossible for us to test the validity of that assertion.

What interests us far more is how the metaphysic of voodoo, uniting

Figure 17. *Uprising of the slaves*—Scene from the Haitian revolution which followed the voodoo ceremony on the Boikman plantation. By Ulrich Jean-Pierre (AAEP photo)—National Museum of Haiti.

Figure 18. *Erzulie Dantor*, by Celestin Faustin (Reproduced from *Haitian Art*)—Brooklyn Museum catalog.

African, European, and to a lesser extent American Indian, elements (celts of the "Ceramic Indians" representing *zemi* appear as cult objects in some voodoo shrines)[20] manifested itself in increasingly complex and highly individual canvases of the great artists. Out of the body of works we selected for photographs—the product of a prolific generation—there is one *oeuvre* in particular, that of the painter, Celestin Faustin, which I would like to discuss since I feel there is no other in modern Haitian art which fuses so brilliantly the tensions and contradictions of African voodoo and Euro-Catholic influences.

Celestin Faustin is considered the most extraordinary of Haitian painters and although his major figures and symbols are drawn from voodoo "his fantastic, seemingly irrational imagery is painted with traditional Western pictorial devices and portrays space and three-dimensional corporeality."[21] Faustin was named after his grandmother Celestina, who exercised a lasting influence on his life and who herself was profoundly influenced by voodoo. It is said that through her constant communication with the loas she learned that her grandson was claimed from birth by Erzulie Dantor and so she ascribed his exceptional gifts and success to the power of this goddess

Faustin's anonymous biographer in *Haitian Art* concludes from this familial background that "on the one hand, Faustin is attracted and fascinated by the religious fervor of his ancestors . . . on the other hand revolted by it and would like to refuse to accept their beliefs. His paintings are statements of that ambivalence."[22]

Dr. Lerebours, who introduced me to the paintings of Faustin, gave a sexual explanation for the conflict in his work. Faustin, he suspects, is a latent homosexual and the pull towards Erzulie and away from her, which dominates so many of his canvases, and the peopling of these with hybrid monsters, sometimes with both the breasts of woman and the penis of man, expresses this quest for sexual identity.

Ute Stebich, in her critical comment on one of his paintings (see Figure 18) provides yet another type of explanation. Although she attempts to deal with the specific images and symbols of this particular canvas and does so with partial success, she indulges in statements which I find uncharacteristic of such a sophisticated critic. She compares a black Erzulie (Erzulie Dantor) with a white Erzulie (Erzulie Freda) thus: "As Dantor is black, hardworking, active and endowed with a strong character . . . Freda is white, passive and interested only in her own comfort and luxury."[22] These are racial clichés which I do not think do justice to Faustin or to voodoo philosophy.

One must confess that there are elements of the family conflict (biographer) sexual conflict (Lerebours) racial conflict (Stebich) in his work. Looking at it simply on this personal level, however, does not illuminate very much. Faustin's genius and the universality of the voodoo world-view, which is an inheritance of his imagination even if it is partially rejected by his intellect, places his symbols within a larger dimension, while personal conflicts and contradictions may help him organise these in such a way that they express both individual and collective dilemmas.

In Figure 19A—*Entre deux Femmes*—there is a dark woman at the side of the bed (left). The figure in darkness symbolizes some force that attracts him away from the lighted woman at center. But this central figure or goddess weaves a web for him. The strands of the web hover over his contemplative figure (at right). The web represents the pact she has with him. The counter-attraction (mysterious dark force, unconscious drive) cannot prevail against the goddess and so it flees (left of painting) in defeat and despair. To see the lighted figure as "white" and the counter-force as "black" *in a racial sense* would be a gross misreading of Faustin. In Figures 19B and 19C we see the drama played out again with different images but Erzulie is still the central image (black now, and again not as expression of any racial statement). Note that in all of Faustin's works the use of *skeletal trees with myriad roots and branches* serve both to divide and link the narrative units of the painting. This in itself is a symbolic statement.

Erzulie does stand for the African heritage or the voodoo principle, whether in a lighted or darkened form. Skin color shifts in the representation of the *loas* in voodoo painting, as witness two paintings by Louis Joseph

Figure 19A. *Entre deux femmes* **by Celestin Faustin (AAEP photo)—Nader collection**

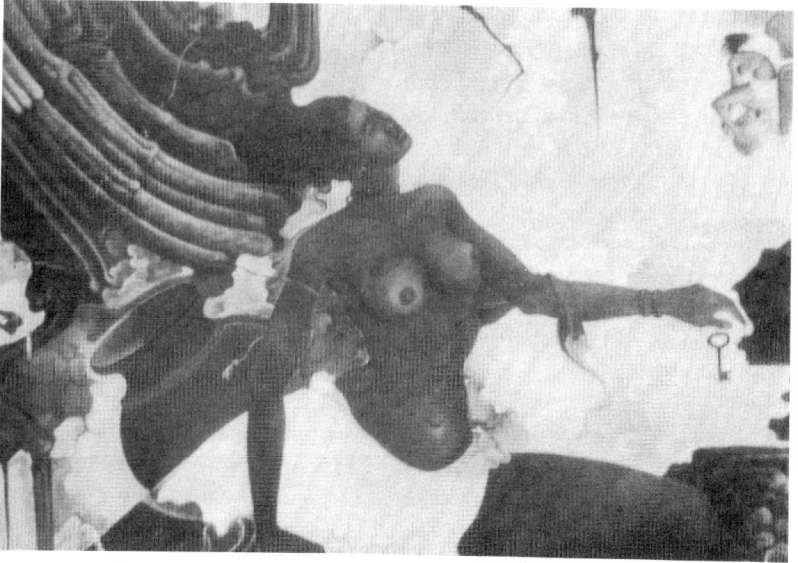

Figure 19B. *Erzulie series,* by Celestin Faustin (AAEP photo)—Nader collection

Figure 19C. *Erzulie series,* by Celestin Faustin (AAEP photo)—Nader collection

Figure 20A. *Agoué and La Sirène* (AAEP photo)—Nader collection

Figure 20B. *Agoué, La Sirène and Aida* (AAEP photo)—Nader collection

overleaf, where Agoué (loa of the sea) and La Sirene (one of his wives) are black in the first (20A) but the sea-loa is light-skinned, La Sirene is a mix of races and Aida is black in the second (20B). This fluid shift of skin color transcends the polarization of race and allows the occasional identification of African loa with European saint and vice versa. Integration of races at a social level may be rare since color has become a corollary of economic and social status but this integration on an interior level is a very real fact and must not be forgotten in a study of the Haitian imagination, his ritual and his art, lest it lead to superficial analyses and interpretations.

Voodoo is the best guide at the moment through the galleries of Haiti. We do not mean to suggest, however, that because it served us so well as an integrating framework and a critical guide, it is the only key. We do injustice to the range of Haitian painting by leaving that impression. But we must point out that voodoo, as a window on Haitian art, opens wider vistas than we have been able, in spite of our emphasis and focus here, to suggest. For example, one of the first paintings that struck us in the restaurant of Le

Figure 21. *Fruit sellers,* by Jacques Louissant (AAEP photo)—La Relais Restaurant

Figure 22. Selecton of six from *Ten Gourds,* by Andre Pierre—Reproduced from *Haitian Art* (Brooklyn Museum catalog)
These painted gourds were used as ritual objects in ceremonies. Each is devoted to the *loa* (African god or spirit) depicted on it, either figuratively or as a vèvè. Top left—*Legba,* loa of the crossroads. This is his vèvè. Top center—*Ogun,* loa of war and power. He is connected with fire and iron. This is his vèvè. Top right—*Papa Zaca,* loa of agriculture and fertility. He is depicted in his characteristic peasant suit, standing in a field of corn, his favorite food. Bottom left—*Damballah,* loa of life and wisdom. Bottom center—*Agoue,* Loa of the sea. Boat and fish are his attributes. Bottom right—*Loco,* Loa of vegetation, guardian of sanctuaries, also loa of discipline.

Relais where we dined on our first evening in Port-au-Prince, and which we thought then was irrelevant to voodoo, turned out to be influenced by the cult, not in terms of explicit theme or symbol, but in the organization of space.

The painted gourd, so African in its origin (see Figure 22 above—decorated gourds) dominates Jacques Louissaint's work. In the scene previous (Figure 21) fruit-sellers in the marketplace are capsuled in a gourd and all the forms and faces fit into this gourd-shaped world like unhatched forms in an egg. One finds echoes of this even in modern African painting, as in the work of Skunder Bogghosian.

The spirit of Papa Doc still broods over the scene. One of the remarkable paintings in the National Museum bear witness to his power as a houngan.

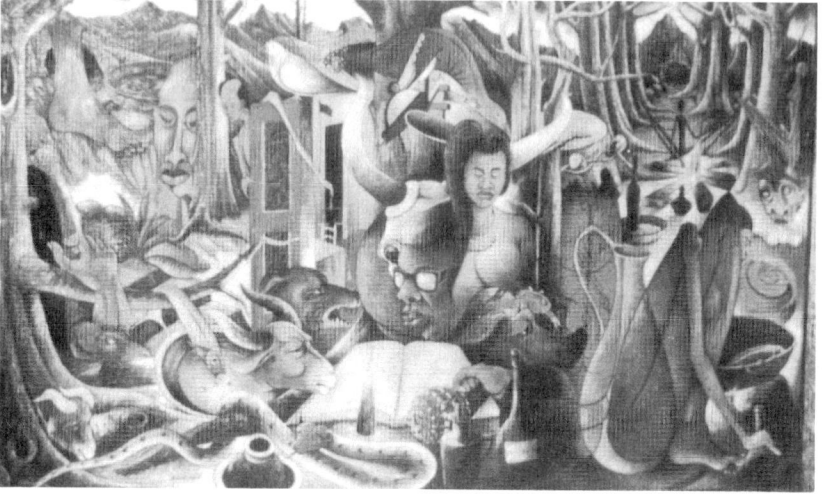

Figure 23. *Doc Avie*, by Jacques Enguerrand Gourgue. "Papa Doc" Duvalier, the leading houngan of his day, in center of voodoo paraphernalia (Photo by William Branch)—National Museum of Haiti

Figure 24. Peasant in Central Square, Port-au-Prince, Haiti (AAEP photo)

In Figure 23, a painting by Jacques Enguerrand Gourgue (Doc Avie) Duvalier's head dominates the center while the canvas is crowded with the paraphernalia of voodoo power. In the sculpture of the peasant in Central Square, however (Figure 24) resides a power greater than a congregation of *loas,* dormant now, perhaps, but once invincible against the world's armies. Within the crook of its arm Duvalier's palace looks like a wraith, a cloud that darkens the land for a moment and then passes.

Notes

1. Preface to *Haitian Art* (edited Ute Stebich), p. 7. Brooklyn Museum, New York, 1978. I have taken a slight liberty in the translation here. Sartre's actual words were: "C'est la premier fois depuis '39 qu'une visite a un museée de peinture m'aporte une experience nouvelle."

2. On Feb 13, 1948, André Breton visited the *Centre d'Art* in Port-au-Prince. He bought 12 paintings by the Voodoo houngan and artist, Hector Hippolyte. He wrote the following in the guest book (quoted, like Sartre above, in *Haitian Art* by Stebich:

>La peinture haitienne boira le sang
>>du phénix
>et, des epaullets de Dessalines,
>>ventilera le monde.)

3. Stebich, ibid, p. 11.

4. Harold Courlander, *The Drum and the Hoe: The Life and Love of the Haitian People* (Berkeley and Los Angeles: University of California Press, 1960), p. 13.

5. Robert Farris Thompson, "The Flash of the Spirit: Haiti's Africanizing Vodun Art" in *Haitian Art*, p. 27.

6. Thompson, ibid, pp. 27, 28.

7. S. Gsell, HAAN IV, p. 177 quoted in Ivan Van Sertima's "The African Presence in Early Europe," *Journal of African Civilizations, Vol.* 3, No. I, April, 1981, pp. 21–30.

8. Edward Scobie, "The Black in Western Europe," *Journal of African Civilizations*, Vol. 3, No. 1, 1981, p. 47.

9. Idem.

10. Thompson, op. cit., p.33.

11. Idem.

12. Mario Valdes, "The Black Wiseman in European Symbolism," *Journal of African Civilizations*, Vol. 3, No. 1, April 1981, pp. 67–85.

13. George Eaton Simpson, *Religious Cults of the Caribbean,* Institute of Caribbean Studies, Puerto Rico, 1970. p. 288.

14. Ivan Van Sertima. "Ritual Man in the Caribbean," Masters thesis. pp. 48, 49.

15. I.M. Lewis, "Spirit Possession and Deprivation Cults" in *Man* (1966), pp. 307–329.

16. Erika Bourguignon, "Ritual Dissociation and Possession Belief in Caribbean Negro Religion" in *Afro-American Anthropology* (eds. Whitten & Szwed), The Free Press, New York, 1970, p. 91.

17. Van Sertima. op. cit., p. 2.

18. Ibid. p. 89.

19. The first part of this quotation describing the ceremony comes from Maya Deren's *Divine Horsemen: The Voodoo Gods of Haiti* (New York, Dell Publishing

Co. Delta Books, 1970, pp. 62–63), but the actual oath itself (which may be a romantic rendering) from the caption of the Ulrich Jean Pierre painting in the National Museum of Haiti.

20. Irving Rouse, "Roots: Pre-Columbian" in *Haitian Art,* pp. 22–25.

21. *Biographies* in Haitian Art, pp. 158–159.

22. Stebich, *Haitian Art*, p. 92.

"Lorenzo Turner and Melville Herskovits demonstrated the sense of it decades ago, and black linguists in the vein of Turner like Ivan Van Sertima (Rutgers) have kept the argument alive in current times."
NEW YORK TIMES BOOK REVIEW
—September 7, 1972

"Ivan Van Sertima presents an incisive analysis of the influence of African languages on the language of African descendants, and he refutes one of the common myths about the so-called bankruptcy of black language."
THE AMERICAN JOURNAL OF SOCIOLOGY
1972

MY GULLAH BROTHER AND I:
EXPLORATION INTO A COMMUNITY'S LANGUAGE
AND MYTH THROUGH ITS ORAL TRADITION

Ivan Van Sertima

> *I, for one, coming from the coastlands of Guyana in South America, have never met a Gullah from South Carolina or the Georgia coast. A vast ocean lies between us which we have hardly crossed, my Gullah brother and I, since the days of the Middle Passage. Yet when I read Gullah in the folktales . . . something turns on in me like a second ear, something reechoes the words and structures of that dialect within me like a submerged speaker and tongue. What, you may ask, is that something? What is really moving and playing, like a drummer in shadow, behind me?* [Van Sertima, (Black Life and Culture in the United States (ed. Golstein) 1971, p. 13]*

Those words are taken from an article I wrote four years ago when I first came to America. Since then I have visited the Sea Islands twice, in 1970 and 1971. I have recorded the voices of the Gullah of Johns Island in their homes, in their churches, in their workplaces, and on their farms. I have even sat in on the private councils of a revolutionary group centered in Charleston but spearheaded by men of Johns Island. I have listened to the songs of the Gullah, to their stories of the vanished past, to the trickster tales of Rabbit and Tortoise which still run like a river of legend across the banks of the Black world from the old Guinea coast to Guyana. I have looked closely at the relationships between their form of Black English and my own and the way in which we have both been profoundly affected by an African ancestral grammar. And through all these years I have been haunted by a sense of familiarity which I sometimes find strange and by a sense of strangeness which is oddly familiar. It is the way I feel when I come upon a member of my own family from whom I have been long separated, the strangeness that grows from distance in time and space, the familiarity that is native to a common brood and blood.

I use the terms native and familiar because their English is an English which is not far removed from the one I have used as an oral alternative in the Guyanas and which still runs subterraneously, surfacing occasionally from under the English I now formally speak and write. When I say, therefore, that the Gullah is my brother I am not merely being romantic and sentimental. Africa is not only the common womb out of which the Gullah and I have sprung. It is still, through the golden thread of the oral tradition, binding a chain of tenuous but persistent vestiges and roots. We are not yet fully severed—my Gullah brother and I—from that ancestral trunk or constellation of roots. Transplanted as we are, we have branched into what we have joined here, we have grown into what we have known here in this hemisphere, but through the veins of our psyche there circulates still an ancient and potent sap. Hence, as I follow the trail of the oral tradition in the Sea Islands, I am not simply seeking a forgotten pathway into exotic survivals but a master key into the maze of my own related past, the labyrinth of my complex inheritance, the half-buried roots and branches of my dismembered self.

For this purpose of exploration and recovery of the threads of traditions I could not have picked a better area than the Sea Islands. These islands off South Carolina and the Georgia coast are unique in all North America. Unlike the mainland states of the United States, they maintained a massive black presence throughout their history and absorbed and Africanized the Europeans rather than being absorbed and Europeanized by them. Thus there are Whites in the Gullah islands who have grown up speaking Black English.

So minimal in fact was this White presence that even in the early days of slavery some of the overseers had to be selected from the Blacks. Is it any wonder, therefore, that here, in these islands, stretching 300 miles across Atlantic space and 300 years across American history, we find the purest form of Afro-English and African-influenced art, craft, mythology, ritual behavior, religious music, motor habits, proverbs, chants and riddles, naming systems, family patterns, and even some economic associations with West African prototypes? What is even more significant but seldom recognized is that the language of the Sea Islands has affected not only the language of the Blacks in the South but that of the Whites also who owe not only some of the vivid proverbs and images, the lyrical sweep and speed of narrative (captured so powerfully by Twain and Faulkner) to these Black islands, but also some of the lilt and tonal quality of their curiously accented speech.

Research into the language and life of the Gullah has been going on for a long time. This research has spawned a stubborn brood of misconceptions.

It would be interesting to list some of these, though they reveal more about the prejudice and ignorance of scholars and the racist climate of inquiry into Black life and culture over the past half century in these United States than they do about the Gullah themselves.

John Bennett was among the first of the researchers into the Gullah language. As early as 1908 he spoke of its "quick, crackling sounds" caused in part, he declared, "by excessive laxity of pronunciation, in part by the elision of every sound of which language may be shorn and still remain articulate." He compared the rapid-fire speech of the Gullah to the gabbling of ducks.

In 1939 George Krapp (and I think his surname is apt) dismissed any consideration of African influence on Gullah and merely echoed Bennett who saw all the peculiarities of the dialect traceable to the tongue of "low-bred redemptioners, humble Scotch, Scotch-Irish and Irish-English deportations." It would be folly to deny the influence of these immigrants, for it is true that it was their English that the Gullah first encountered on this continent and reworked and transformed, but it is amazing that this fiction of Gullah being simply a quaint preserve of the illiterate peasant English of the seventeenth and eighteenth century should have persisted to this day. As late as 1940, Mason Crum, author of the most comprehensive work on the Gullah before the coming of Lorenzo Turner (1939), remarked "Gullah is more truly English than much of the English spoken in America today." Again the surname Crum is apt, for in this major work *Gullah: Negro Life in the Carolina Sea Islands* he serves up the crumbs of both the old (Bennett, 1908; Krapp, 1939; Johnson, 1930; Gonzalez, 1922) as well as the new (Stoney & Shelby, 1930) theories of the Gullah. Stoney and Shelby, in their work *Black Genesis,* published in 1930, highlighted the African influence on Gullah language, although they could only come to grips with it at a superficial word level, which revealed very little since the African words in popular Gullah use are few. They, however, were the forerunners of Turner. But Crum, receptive though he was to what they had to say about the African influence, still spoke of Gullah as "a wreck of the King's English," albeit to him a fascinating and exotic wreck.

It is important to understand what is happening here. In Crum a new sentimental and parental-protective attitude toward the Gullah Negro emerges. Times had changed. He could boast in his book, with a proud and whimsical nostalgia, of having drank milk from a Black mammy's breast. What he was doing in making extreme claims for the Englishness of Gullah was what researchers were doing as late as the 1960's when equating Black dialects of America with those of lower-class Whites. I quote a statement from an earlier article of mine which helps to illuminate the latter day liberal motives behind this approach:

It has been said that the forms of English spoken by black people in America owe nothing to Africa at all, that in fact Black forms of English are no different from dialects of English spoken by lower-class white groups, and that all the non-standard elements in Black English can be traced to an earlier English used and dropped by American settlers or still partly in vogue among lower-class American whites. Strangely enough, this theory was advanced in America by linguists who thought they were doing the blacks a great favor. They were putting forward this theory of the non-difference between white and black dialects of America to prove that, where language was concerned, the blacks were no different from the whites. This was their misguided but well-intentioned attempt to establish equality among the races. They believed that this could only be done by denying diversity among the cultural subgroups of America, as if the very existence of difference in the use of English by blacks indicated their inferiority, and only the denial of that difference could establish their claim to equality with the users of standard English. Integration of the black and white elements of America meant for them the standardization and uniformity of peoples, rather than the coexistence of diverse but equally valid culture-groups. They sought to negate ethnic and cultural plurality which is America's greatest heritage [Van Sertima, 1971, p. 16].

Let it be said in Crum's defence, however, for he is full of contradictions, that he was convinced of what he calls "the African spirit" behind the body of the dialect. In one breath he is saying "nowhere on this continent can a purer African culture be found," in another he presents a count made by Guy Johnson (1930) of standard, corrupted and archaic English words from a glossary of Gullah prepared by Gonzalez (1922) to prove that only one-half of 1% of Gullah is African. Even Stoney and Shelby (1930), who confidently proclaimed Gullah as "the strongest linguistic connection between America, the Caribbean, and Africa, linking two hemispheres and two eras" found themselves at a loss to prove their hypothesis when it came down to a count of surviving African words.

Turner (1939) discovered thousands of these words. He went beyond the popular speech of the Gullah to their secret naming systems which were modeled upon the West African tribes and language groups from which the Gullah came. But while it is true that these words may with diligence be unearthed from under the popular face of the dialect, it is not the real crux of the matter. It is in fact peripheral to our main concerns in any serious study of Gullah language and culture. For while I may show, through Richard Allsopp's study (unpublished), that there are scores of African words still in popular use in my Guyanese dialect, and through Lorenzo Turner's work, that there are thousands of African words secreted in the alternative names of the Gullah people, and while I may also point to a number of African words in popular American speech which we have come to take for granted as being of English derivation or indigenous Americanese, all I would be saying is that we were once in Africa and picked up a few things as tourists pick up hello's and goodbye's in foreign parlance, flitting through alien spaces like birds of passage. This would be far too obvious and too facile. Our inheritance is not, as Stoney and Shelby thought, a few rhymes, games, systems of counting, tricks of the tongue, or a sprinkle of African words in common use. These are in fact surface exotica—stones and shells. The African spirit behind the body of the Gullah dialect and culture is not so easily found and not so easily lost. I quote from myself again:

> ... forgetting these words, since it is true that the main vocabulary of American blacks is non-African, the crucial African element to watch is not vocabulary at all, but a grammatical base, a syntactical structure. It is the African structure underlying the top layer of Anglo-Saxon words which accounts for the peculiar combinations, patterns, and transformations in the speech of peoples as far apart as the Guyanese of South America, the Gambians of West Africa, and the Gullahs of Georgia [Van Sertima, 1971, p. 17].

Turner, of course, established this. He was the turning point in studies of the Gullah. He was the only linguist to take the trouble to acquaint himself with the West African linguistic background of these people. He could therefore speak with authority and authenticity on their language which no other linguist before him could do. He was also the first Black scholar to do serious work in this area and (racial considerations aside) his Blackness helped. To no White observer before him, for example, did the Gullah ever confess their non-English names. We may still go to Ambrose Gonzalez (1922) and Charles Colcock Jones (1888) for excellent recordings of Gullah folktales; for social studies of the Sea Islands in general we may still read Mason Crum (1940) with profit and for a Sea Island in particular—St. Helena—we should look again at Guy B. Johnson (1930). But for any genuine insight into the interaction between African memory and inheritance and the American reality, particularly with respect to language, we can turn to no one but Turner (1939).

It is also time to turn another road in Gullah studies and go beyond Turner. It is now 40 years since his first major field work was done in these Sea Islands. What has happened? Those of us who must follow through have several tasks cut out. It is necessary to keep the work of Turner up to date. Has the African influence on Gullah grammar changed dramatically in these 40 years? In my own work I have asked myself that question. It is necessary to probe beyond the syntax of the language to the history and culture of the people, to use their oral tradition to ask much larger questions. How did they see their own world, for so far nearly all their social histories have been written by their masters, with the perspectives and emphases of their masters? How did they work and play and farm and fish and struggle and suffer and make love and rear children and pass on their tales and beliefs and customs? What do they think, not only of the vanished times but of the new day that is breaking in the South? These questions are essential because, more than any other people, our history, their history, lies in voices, oral treasuries, conversations, talking books. To go among the Gullah with one's ears wired is to run a blind man's fingers across a history of islands written in Braille.

I have tried to respond to all these questions and concerns, to see the oral tradition in its sociocultural, mythological, and linguistic aspects. My visits to these islands have been brief, my informants few, but the time was intensively spent and the old men and women I spoke with well chosen for the purpose. I try to trace, through the answers they gave to my questions, aspects of their early lives which I feel go beyond the personal and evoke the larger social background not only of the island but of the era from which they have come. I then go on to deal with their folktales of which there are many collections but few analyses. Finally, and very importantly, I seek to demonstrate the African presence in the Gullah language, not on a lexical but on a grammatical level, to prove that on that level Gullah has not lost any of its significant elements since the studies of Turner.

The old men and women of the islands were my informants. I ignored the youth save the radical wing of young adults in Charleston who had grown up on these islands. This was a deliberate choice on my part, for, where the oral tradition is concerned, it is written on a wrinkled parchment of skin and heard in a feeble voice. The vigorous shout, the smooth, bright face of youth is an empty book.

One of my informants was a 70-year old man called Guinea. I thought at first that this might be an African name and that it referred to the Guinea coast. The truth was he had come by that name through an extraordinary circumstance that said as much symbolically of the Negro's life as his own. He was so weak from malnutrition in his first years that he could not carry his weight on his legs. He could not stand straight or walk. His parents used to dig a hole in the ground (he showed us the hole) and bury him up to the thighs. They did this in the hope that it would make his legs grow firm and straight. As he stood there, half-buried in the ground, he watched the free and easy movement of the birds. He actually learned to walk by a close study of the guinea bird from which he took his name. But learning to walk was the beginning of a new disaster. He walked right into trouble. As soon as his legs grew strong they were clamped into chains. In an interview with Guinea, the story of his life in prisons and in a chain gang in the South began to unfold:

GUINEA: Looky heah, looky heah. I kin show all dese heah (lifts pants leg to reveal shackle scars). I wasn' no Uncle Chaalie, tho'. Ain' gonna be none uh dat. I radduh, I radduh all dis leg go.

> See ... shackle weah dat out, shackle weah dis out. Guard shoot me by duh head, try to get away. Evytime a slow train come in I try to ketch im, I have shackle on, but I try to ketch im, I wudden give up! ... Ah had duh shackle heah den ah had a ball between muh leg, an den de shackle come ovuh heah, den I tote duh ball all day, walk ri' down wi' duh res' to prison. But I didden give up. I say, "I bawn a boy, Chaalie, an I suppose to catch hell, Ah reckon."
>
> VAN: How long have you been in prison?
>
> GUINEA: Oh, 'bout seventeen, eighteen yeah, sumpin like dat ... off an on. But evytime I do sumpin, I plan to go to jail because I know my people po an no need kill dem cuz dey ain' got fifteen cent, an' if I go to jail I foll up my aam an fine out what time deh feed ... What I do make duh time, an try to make it back home. I don' write nobody no lettuh. You know what I write my people an say? "Doan sen me no hat. I take de hat off so fass. De white people doan like yuh weah no hat on. Juh sen me some long drawers an' some cigarette. S'all I need." De day I get home all the loving faces I leave I meet dem again.
>
> VAN: Did you have any visitor, like your wife or your children?
>
> GUINEA: O no, I doan know nuttin about dat, nuttin abow dat.
>
> VAN: You didn't? Why?
>
> GUINEA: Weh, you see, people you love an' been roun' all togedduh, you haat break til dat take five yeahs off yuh life, mo den time you got. So if de Judge give you ten yeah, you be sho' make you ten yeah, doan leh none o' you close relation come see you. An I feel bettuh ... Doan wan' none o' duh people come heah, see me. What deh got, sen it deh. Doan come.

We found Guinea had remained militant and hardy in spite of nearly a century of extreme poverty and punishment. He was out there in the van with a group of young activists in Charleston, the members of COBRA, the Committee for Better Racial Assurance. It lived up to its name. It struck with a quick bitter force at racial injustice. Guinea had helped in the organization of a strike and he was in and out of jail but was now challenging the law with a just purpose, fighting for his civil rights. As Bill Saunders, the head of COBRA, put it, "Any time anybody needed to be arrested, Guinea was right there going to jail." Prodded by Saunders, he recounted to us some of the highlights, or rather the lowlights, of his boyhood. It seems, of all his deprivations it was his crude, improvised clothing that humiliated him most. In his consciousness it was a second skin he would have given a great deal to discard:

> GUINEA: An I woiked wit croakuh suit on ... my mudduh an fadduh din have no money. I have croakuh. Deh make duh croakuh pans, duh croakuh coat. If I wanna play I have to play in dat croakuh pans ... you see dis bag? Is sack. I weh it.
>
> SAUNDERS: What you people call burlaps.

GUINEA: Deh wash it off clean, deh wash it off clean. Den deh make a
         coat an' a pans fuh me. An I is duh ony chile my muddah an'
         fadduh evuh'd. Deh din have no money atall. I leave home
         wen I was eleven year ole, doan know weh I going.
SAUNDERS: Tell them what you did after you left there, Guinea.
GUINEA: O, I went to stealing an' gambling an' doing evything else,
         selling tricks . . .

In his final lament for the life of hunger and denial he had led, Guinea
returned to the indignity of his croaker suit which he mentioned in the same
breath as the days he had wandered across the island like a stray dog,
foraging for food:

> Now yuh know, I cudden suffuh no mo dan I was suffrin den,
> cudden suffuh no mo dan I suffuh. I veah croakuhs. I eat today an'
> didden eat tomorrow.

Against this life one may contrast another—that of Alice Wine—also of
Johns Island, a life perhaps equally cruel and oppressive in some respects,
but distinguished by a sense of proud independence and self-sufficiency.
Alice Wine nourished this spirit of pride and independence through her
proprietary relationship to the land. She worked it hard but not as a labor
hand or a servant of the White folks. Rather, unlike the homeless and root-
less Guinea, as someone who could say "is me own place, me Daddy place."
She was up from four in the morning to scrape a living from this land:

ALICE WINE: I live on a faam, on me own place, me Daddy place . . . plan'
         potato, plan' peas, plan' cawn, plan' rice an' plan' mos'
         evyting . . . I wuk wit hoe, hoe potatos an' diffrin stuff like
         dat, you see. Hafta wuk. Wen I come home from school in de
         even time, I hafta wuk, an' befo' I go to school I hafta wuk,
         an' aftuh I come fum school I hafta wuk.
VAN: Did you ever have time to play games?
WINE: Weh doan know nuttin bow dat.
VAN: No kind of games?
WINE: No kinduh game.
VAN: It was all work, work, work?
WINE: All wuk.
VAN: You would get up very early in the morning?
WINE: Yes, lawd, fo' clock . . .

From Alice Wine, as old and sturdy as old Guinea, we learned a lot about
the way the islanders struggled to make a living on the land, how they
farmed and fished in the summer and lived off their bank of cured and
corned provisions in the winter:

> WINE: We doan nevuh wuk wen wintuh comes. We nevuh come out
>   in wintuhtaam.

VAN: So where would the food come from?

WINE: Come fum ow gaaden, my Daddy, we raise evyting. We raise rice, cawn, an de cawn bring you grits an flowuh an cawnmeal, des right. Hocks go anyway you wants em to go. An das tree paat right deh. An is grits an cawnmeal (no, das two paat fo to sell) an duh hocks go someplace else. We raise rice an rice an uh nex i' be peas an nex it be potato an you have you turnip an you cut off duh leaf an bank it like potatos an yuh have you turnip an you cut off duh leaf an bank it like potatos an yuh have dat in yuh baan. Din you go to duh creek an den you get plenty fish an you cawn dem an you put it to dry an wen deh done dry yuh out it in a barrel, den you have yuh fish, den yuh have yuh fish. Den yuh have yuh cow, 'e give yuh milk. Den yuh have yuh chicken. 'e give you eggs. an' den wheel on back, you take yuh cow milk an make buttuhs. Den you wheel on back again, you kin kill a cyaf an' cyo' it. Den you wheel on back, you kill a hog an' make buttsmeat out of it . . .

At one stage she compared this food-banking operation to the winter planning of the ants:

WINE: We reduce food jes like de ants reduce dem own in de summuh. In de summuh de ants reduce dey food an bank em in de urt an wen cole day come, deh doan come out. So dats wat de ole people was doing wi' deh children. Dey plant plenty uh potatos an bank it up, an peas, an put em in duh barrel, an turnup, dey sweeten dat in duh bank, an duh hog, deh cyo' it, an Daddy go in de crick an git duh fish an cawn em. We dry em out on duh bode (board). We nevuh buy nuttin . . . I injoy my *time coming* but not now. Kuh dis is no good now.

We found this insistence that *time-comin* (the Gullah phrase for youth and the past) was in every way better than the new times, the recent times, strange. We felt that this was an ultraconservative judgment and that it had to do with age, which looked back to its youth through eyes softened by nostalgia, however filled with terror and anguish the past had been. Also, we felt it was a defence against her children who were departing from cherished customs and traditions. We questioned her closely on this:

VAN: So what about those hard days in the fields getting up at four in the morning?

WINE: I radduh do dat kuz you doan wuk in sunhot but is vip an strappin vip behine you now kuz dese people put you in de feel rung seven o'click in de mawnin, knock off you a' twelve, putch you back deh one, knock off you six. Dat ain no business fuh me, see. I caan larn nuttin like dat . . . In my *time comin'*, usetuh git fawty cent a day an five dolluhs in de white people kitchen.

VAN: How much is it now?
WINE: O, deh git eight uhr nine dolluhs a day now but wat good it is?
Ain' a bit mo bettuh den I make my fawty cent a day kuz duh
tings ah so high. Das right. Din you cud git a yaad o' clawt jes
only fuh tree cent uhr five cent a yaad wen now you hafta pay
a dolluh an' two dolluh a yaad. So I radduh go back dan dis
time.

I radduh go back dan dis time! Alice Wine was not unique in this, of
course, but none of our other informants felt so strongly that the young
people of the islands had fallen away completely from ideals they cherished,
that the world had changed for the worse.

Isabella Simmons did complain of the "seeing story" (television) competing with the "hearing story" in the same tone of regret as Alice Wine had
complained of "you be laughing at me wen you see buttsmeat an' grits." But
many were open to the winds of change blowing across these islands and
did not see it as a necessary threat to what was essential in their traditions.
Some were out there in the vanguard with the young, fighting their new
battles, like Guinea for example, one of the fangs of COBRA, who could
boast at 71, "way I feel now its a fo'ty seven, good as I feeling." Some
tolerated considerable movements in consciousness toward a new life in
their young, while continuing to initiate them into some of the styles and
values of the old, into what was still relevant and crucial in their oral and
cultural inheritance. Such was the case of Jane Hunter, the great grandmother of Johns Island. It was in the Hunter home, surrounded by her
grands and great-grands, who listened to her every word intently, that we
felt a renewal of faith in the perpetuity of these traditions.

We sat for hours as she spun tale after tale of Brer Rabbit and Brer
Cooter, the ancient Bantu tricksters Hare and Tortoise, which the oral tradition had for centuries preserved. They were still the popular tales of these
islands and were told in an English nearer to the original Gullah than we had
heard so far in conversations. I quote from one of these—Bruh Rabbit an
Mistuh Wolf:,

Duh Rabbit an duh wolf was fren, dey was two fren, an deh was a
big dance. Mistuh Wolf girlfren was havin a big dance da night an Bruh
Rabbit had love duh Wolf girl more den he does his girl. So Rabbit go
an tie up he leg lukkuh e got a broke leg an e kun walk.
(Wolf) 'e say "Ol fren," say, "you going to duh dance tonight?"
(Rabbit) e say, "O man, I doan tink I make it, kuh I go a' fall an hurt
me leg an I haaly kin walk." 'E say, "I tell you sumpin, ol fren," 'e say,
"if you let me ride you back paa duh way, en wen I ah-us (almost) get
to duh house . . . "
"Den you get off quick. Doan let my girl see you ride my back
now."
All dat time duh Rabbit done gone tell duh Wolf girl dat he gonna

ride Mistuh Wolf to duh dance tonight. Duh girl say, "O no, not Mistuh Wolf, not Mistuh Wolf. You nevuh ride my boyfren back."

Well duh Rabbit doan tell, doan say he give im ride cause 'e had a sick leg, an he say (to Wolf) "Yeah, I promise, datsa promise. Yeah, I promise yuh dat I get off yuh back befo yuh get to my girlfren house."

An duh Rabbit put two what yuh call spur on 'e foot an he jump on duh Wolf back an'e say, "Walk slow now".

"Now mine me yuh promise, get off my back fo yuh git to dat girl house."

"Datsa promise, Mistuh Wolf." An all dat time de music was playin, an duh Wolf an Rabbit way till des mos' get but a few step from duh Wolf do' an 'e put duh two spur in duh Wolf side and 'e push right in duh do'.

An all duh girl say, "O no, o no dat ain't Mistuh Wolf dat ain't Mistuh Wolf' say "you no muh boyfren. Come on, Mistuh Rabbit, dance wit me." An Rabbit had duh whole houseful uh girl.

Brer Rabbit in this story outwits Brer Wolf, riding on his back to ultimate possesion of all they both desire. In the real world it would be Wolf who would win out in this struggle but in the world of dream the defencelessness of the Rabbit and the inherent predatory viciousness of Wolf are reversed. It is important to understand the profound relationship between the Rabbit's act and the slave's dream. It is important also to understand how it is that the Rabbit in Black American mythology is associated not only with mischievous and immoral but even criminal acts which would normally outrage but awaken instead in his listeners an enormous fascination and respect. This is not, as would appear on the surface, simply a child's story told for a child's amusement. Behind the disarming naivéte of the tale lies the complex psychology of the oppressed.

These trickster figures, of course, were born in another world, not a world of the slave and the free but a world, nonetheless, which, like all societies, is composed of the rulers and the ruled, the strong and the weak, the powerful and the powerless. These tales owe their original inspiration to the mythological imagination and architecture of fantasy in Africa. The surface features or motifs that appear (objects, creatures, incidents) in the new geographic and cultural environment of the South give the traditional African bones of the tale a new fleshing. The underlying structures, however, are the same. Why have these African animal archetypes survived and persisted in these islands? What new function do they serve and in what new forms and shapes are the African tale types expressed among the Gullah and the Blacks of the South?

An analysis in depth of the main elements in African folktales will show that the animals are involved in a shadow drama of the human world. They are dream figures through which personality traits, values, or power relations of groups—commoner and king, slave and master, the weak and the strong, the powerful and the suppressed—may be reflected in a dreaming drama of the social world, within which dream and drama the figures are invested with a fluidity and metamorphic quality denied them in the more rigidly structured social world, so that they often seem to reverse and overturn their given social role or condition. It is this capacity of the dream figure (animal archetype) to overleap and overturn an oppressive social condition that makes the personae of the tales (Rabbit, Tortoise, etc.) take on a heroic cast and revolutionary function.

This role reversal and revolutionary function of certain African folk heroes account for their enormous popular appeal among the Black communities of the New World. Like the Caribbean Annancy, the Gullah Rabbit plays the role of outlaw and con-man. Neither subscribes to the laws and moral values of their society. Secretive, elusive, cunning, deceptive, sometimes cruel and treacherous, they are in the role of the Transcendent Criminal, avoiding through their legendary agility of wit the onerous and unfair burdens imposed upon their fellows, always one step ahead of Brer Wolf and Brer Tiger, the predatory lords and overseers of the jungle.

The amoral character of these folk heroes do not represent in any sense the character of the Gullah or the Blacks of the Caribbean. In the Gullah Rabbit and the Caribbean Annancy we are face to face with what I would call a Black innocence. Whatever they may do in the tales can never outrage us, not because they are simply tales, not because their nonhuman personae remove us from an easy identification with their personality, but because theirs is an evil that liberates rather than oppresses. We love them in spite of their evil; we may even love them for their evil, for they assume aspects of evil in order to elude and conquer a condition of evil.

In their original African home and culture these figures took on other functions that are ignored, minimized, or forgotten among the Gullah and the Blacks of the New World. Their functions in this hemisphere have become restricted to a treachery and guile aimed at transcendence over impotence and servility within a highly oppressive order of relationships. It would be interesting to look at some of these functions and the reasons why they have been neglected or ignored in transplantation. The trickster in Africa is not only involved in tricking the lords of the jungle—Tiger, Elephant, Lion—the class of the mighty and powerful. He is involved in playing tricks on the rulers of Heaven itself, stealing fire or food for his fellows under the noses of the Gods. We seldom find him in such a role in the New World. Trickster is also involved in a revolt against the mores of his own group—committing taboo acts, acts of outrage which release him from the confines and boundaries laid down and observed by his peers. Here, he is the Individual in revolt against the Collective. Rarely do we find him in such a role among Afro-Americans.

Such functions of the Trickster were a luxury in a slave and colonial society, for the lords of the plantation were the Gods themselves, in terms of the laying down of the boundaries of behavior, and the individual personality was a remote probability within a dehumanized and deracinated collective.

So deep, so intense, so total indeed was this negation in real life that the role of the Trickster in the life of dream among Afro-Americans was nearly always recreative, transcendent, overpowering, and triumphant, rarely self-destructive, regressive, or anarchistic in a primal sense. We could hardly afford this. We, Afro-Americans, needed no vision of chaos to relieve our impatience with stable structures and immemorial orders. What we needed (at least in the past) was a new order through Black lawlessness which would negate the old order of White lawlessness that had negated and outlawed us.

But the Trickster figure has a duality of function in other societies. To put it in Paul Radin's words, "He is at one and the same time creator and destroyer, giver and negator, being duped as often as he dupes [Abrahams, 1968, p. 171]." In only one or two tales among Afro-Americans is the trickster tricked or duped. A rare example of this comes from tales told to us by Jane Hunter in our Gullah field trip of 1971:

> *Duh Rabbit en Duh Patrid* (Partridge)—1971
> Duh Rabbit en duh Patrid, dey was two great fren. So one day Patrid take her head en stick he head unduh he wing, went to Rabbit house.
> [Rabbit] say, "Ol fren, watcha doin?"
> Say, "Oh, I ain't doin nuttin but sittin in duh sun."
> Say, "Oh, wheahs you head?"
> Say, "Man, I leave my head home fuh my wife to shave."
> All dat time he had his head unduhnea' his wing. Rabbit run in duh house, say, "Ol Gal," he say, "Come on to chop my head off."
> 'E say, "No, Mistuh Rabbit. If I chop yuh head off, you'll die."
> Say, "No, I won' eidduh, cause Mistuh Patrid leave he head home fuh his wife to shave en so why caan I leave my head fuh you to shave?"
> So all his wife, all duh res wuh (what) he wife tell him, (he) say, "If you doan chop my head off, I'll chop you head off."
> So das two fren now. Das why you fren is duh one who gets you, enemy who come na accoshu (accost you). Buh if yuh get hurt, it (you) kin get hurt from fren. So he go en bawl his wife, bawl. Duh wife take duh big knife en chop 'en 'e chop 'e head off.
> So Patrid had a pretty girlfren. Rabbit had a very pretty girl, en Patrid wife wasn' as goodlookin as Rabbit wife. Patrid had a love fuh Rabbit wife, see? En dats duh only way he coulda get Rabbit wife by doin im some haam. So when duh lady gone en chop duh rabbit head off, rabbit pitch off yonduh en die.
> En duh Patrid take 'e head from unduhnea' he wing, say, "Wing, nuh foolin, nuh fun. En wing, no lovin, no gettin love." En den he had two wife, had his wife en duh Rabbit wife.

What has seldom been remarked upon is the fact that West African arche-types, like Annancy, are almost the exclusive inheritance of the Caribbean and the Guyanas whereas East African or Bantu archetypes (Hare, Tortoise) feature largely in tales of the Gullah and the American South. Speculation on the reasons for this have led into all kinds of blind alleys but it is at least clear why these African folk figures play the roles of trickster and underdog.

Observe closely the qualities of Hare (Rabbit). He occupies a disadvanta-geous position in the animal world. Extremely vulnerable, without a heavy hide, claws, beak, or sting, his fragility is counterbalanced by an extraordi-nary sensitivity (huge antennae for ears) and a lightning nimbleness (fleet-ness of foot). Though he may seem, therefore, an easy prey to the larger animals, the potential for outmaneuvering them belies his apparent fragility. In the body and spirit of Hare, therefore, is crystallized a subtle and delicate radar for scanning the potential peril (which he averts) and the potential possibility (which he exploits) in a given situation—a situation usually (in those tales most native to the tradition) of menace from the Mighty. A typical tale told by Uncle Remus is that of Brer Rabbit and Brer Lion, in which Rabbit is invited to offer up his life for Lion's supper and is so adept in his survival strategy that Lion dies wrestling with his own fearful shadow.

In a review of the Uncle Remus tales, Bernard Wolfe (1949) sees these not only as manifestations of the Black man's protest against the system and his sadistic delight in sabotaging the schemes or outraging the morality of his overlords, but also as manifestations of the White man's guilt and his masochistic delight in seeing the Black man (in his guise as the Rabbit) overcome, outrage, or negate him. Wolfe observes that the little White boy, Marse John, listens to Uncle Remus, the old Negro, with a mixture of fear and admiration and that this admiration (which he finds to be particularly strong in Joel Chandler Harris, the Southern White collector of the tales) corresponds to a certain vicarious identification of the White man with the Black: "For Harris as well as for many white Americans the Negro seemed to be in every respect the opposite of his own anxious self: unworried, gregarious, voluble, muscularly relaxed, never a victim of boredom . . . un-ashamedly exhibitionistic, devoid of self-pity in his condition of concen-trated suffering, exuberant . . . [Wolfe, 1949, p. 896]."

Wolfe, however, feels there is an ambivalence in the feelings of Whites in the South about these stories. They are not only harassed by guilt accompa-nied by a desire to revel in the Negro's hatred of them, but also by a protective instinct to shield themselves from their own masochistic uncon-scious. They have, therefore, attempted to drain these stories of their own aggressive potential, saying, for example that "the Black man makes all the animals behave like a lower order of human intelligence" as the Black man feels "he is in closer touch with the lower animals than the White man."

Wolfe sums this up in his article "L'Oncle Remus et son lapin" *Les Temps Modernes,* May, 1949:

> The Remus stories are a monument to the ambivalence of the South. Harris, the archetype of the Southerner, went in search of the Negro's love and claimed that he had won it (the eternal grin of Uncle Remus). But at the same time he was striving for the Negroe's hatred (Brer Rabbit) and he revelled in it, in an unconscious orgy of masochism— punishing himself. . . . certainly no one is *compelled* to read stories of Negroes who make love to white women (*Deep are the Roots, Strange Fruit, Uncle Remus*), of whites who learn they are Negroes (*Kingsblood Royal, Lost Boundaries, Uncle Remus*), of white men strangled by black men (*Native Son, If He Hollers Let Him Go, Uncle Remus*) . . . [p. 898].

Franz Fanon (1952) also sees these fables as "working off the black man's aggression" and this aggression being justified by "the white man's unconscious [which] gives it worth by turning it on himself." What I find rather strange is that this aggression is of a gentler nature in America than what we find in the Caribbean tales of Annancy. Is it diluted by passing through (most of it anyway) the filter of Chandler Harris, the Southern White collector, and his creation, the old gentle Negro, Uncle Remus? Is it that the contradiction between the White man's masochism and his protective instinct did in fact temper the heat of the Black man's aggression in the figure of Rabbit? There is no easy answer to these questions. But it has often been remarked that while Brer Rabbit in the American South is merely mischievous, Annancy in the Caribbean is a venomous and malignant creature.

Assuming this to be the case, I venture to suggest that the spider in the folk mythology of the Caribbean has taken on the configuration of the mudcrab (whom he so closely resembles). He can be as vicious as the crab struggling in a barrel of crabs to get out of his cramped position. He must move against all and everything in order to free himself. Whereas in Africa we sometimes see Annancy functioning on behalf of the collective we often find this creature in the Caribbean callously following his individual bent, his very attempt to free himself of the system involving an outrageous assault on both the oppressor and the oppressed. The collective had some functional reality in traditional Africa but in the colonial limbo the common mass had no relationship to the sources of social control and power. Like the crab coming out of the barrel one could only succeed at times by climbing with a relentless viciousness upon the backs of other crabs.

The tortoise is another symbol of the underdog in Bantu mythology. In fact he is more popular than the hare in some parts of East Africa. His main virtue is his capacity to endure for he can live longer without food than any other animal. He moves with a painstaking slowness, but with the sureness of the sun in motion across the streets of the world, and this impresses itself upon the Bantu mind as the unrelenting and invincible doggedness of an elemental force. The brooding silence and secrecy of the tortoise also invest him with a suggestion of craft and cunning and mystery. He hides his innards under a shell in the way the Black had to hide his true face and feelings in the Americas under shells and veils and masks of deception in order to carry and conceal the horror at the heart of his daily life.

In the final section of this presentation I would like to deal with the linguistic aspect of our Gullah research. Lorenzo Turner has done the definitive job in this field, establishing the African background for most of the features in Gullah which distinguish it from Standard English. Our task, therefore, has been made much easier. We were concerned to discover whether these distinctions were still in force, whether Gullah had appreciably changed between Turner's tape-collecting expeditions in the late 1920's and early 1930's and ours nearly 50 years later in the early 1970's. A list of distinctions between Gullah and Standard English is presented hereunder, their African origins outlined, and these distinctions are illustrated by sentences or phrases from our 1970, 1971 tape transcriptions. The list clearly shows that, whatever surface transformations in Gullah may have occurred through urban impact upon the islands in the past half century, the important African influence—the influence on grammar—remains the same as in Turner's day.

These distinctions, it should be borne in mind, are not only of relevance to the Gullah dialect of the Sea Islands but may be found also for the most part in forms of Black English throughout the Caribbean and many such distinctions preserved in the urban Black dialects of North America, where only half of them are still in popular use, but in the English-speaking Caribbean and Guyana the parallels are as many and as close and establish Gullah as a crucial link in the interhemispheral chain of Black English forms. This list, therefore, though primarily prepared as an index of distinctions between Gullah and Standard English, may in fact be viewed as a tentative outline of a Black English grammar.

1. In Gullah there is an absence of gender distinction, that is, the distinction between masculine, feminine, and neuter is not expressed in the pronouns "he," "she," and "it." Thus Jane Hunter, in her story of the Rabbit and the Partridge, uses *his* and *her* indiscriminately to refer to the Partridge: "so one day Partridge take *her* head an' stick *he* head unduh *he* wing." Also, in her story of *Mannuhs an' No-Mannuhs,* when the old lady calls on the bad boy (No-Mannuhs chile) to cut her some firewood, we find the referents "e" and "im" for the Standard English "she." Thus, "so dehs two brudduh en *a ole lady* live way pon duh hill en '*e* say, *im* say "Son . . . ah . . . comere, cut piece o' wood fo me.' "

West African languages have other methods of indicating gender rather then relying on pronoun case. In both of the examples just quoted it is obvious from the context that the Partridge is feminine and that it is the old lady, not one of the boys, who is speaking. Sometimes, as in Ga and Yoruba, a word meaning "woman" or "man" would be prefixed to the noun (or in Kimbundi, Mandinka, and Fante, added to specific nouns) to indicate gender. We find this practice carried forward both in the Caribbean (one day Brer Annancy sen *gal Annancy* fe go a Brer Deat' yaad) and in Gullah (de snake gone en structid dis *chillun gal*).

Gender distinction by reference to pronouns is also absent from Bantu languages. In Swahili, for example, *a-na-kuja* could mean he, she, or *it* (an animal) is coming. The prefix *a*, which is equivalent to the English pronoun *he, she, it* would vary to indicate the class of the subject—living creature or tree, something large or long (giant/snake), something expressing a collectivity (teeth/eyes), an abstract quality (beauty/folly), an inanimate object (chair), or a very small thing (baby)—all of these sophisticated niceties of distinction, but *not* gender. Turner says practically nothing about Bantu in his study but it should be noted here that, while the West African linguistic influence is the most relevant the Bantu complex cannot be completely ignored. Many Black slaves of North America came from the Lower Congo, which is within the Bantu culture complex. In fact, the Gullah examples quoted above are taken from tales which have their origin in Bantu folklore.

2. In Gullah, the plural marker used in Standard English is absent. Almost all Gullah nouns have the same form in the plural as in the singular. Plurality may be expressed by number only, as in the following examples:

(*a*) "an' das *tree paat* right deh . . . no, das *two paat* fo' sell (Wine)."
(*b*) "den you cud git a yaad o' clawt jes only fuh *tree cent* uhr *five cent* (Wine)."

Plurality may also be expressed by a qualifier (like the pronoun "dese" or "dem") or a type of phrase (houseful o' gyurl) that indicate clearly that more than one of something is involved:

(*a*) "each one *dem milepos'* you get to, you breaken ah egg an' it tun a blessing fa you (Hunter)."
(*b*) "I forget all *dem ting* now (Wine)."

Many West African languages use the same noun form for plural and singular as Gullah does. Ibo and Kongo are among these. Ga and Yoruba form plurals by adding qualifiers (like the pronouns *these* and *them*) or numerical adjectives (*two, three*) before or after the noun. Another method of indicating the plural is found in Ewe where the third person pronoun (them) comes after the noun. This is quite frequent in the Caribbean (an *Crab dem* cudden hear Annancy at all). Our tape expedition turned up examples also in the Gullah islands ('an each one *dem milepos'* you git to, you break *one dem* egg).

3. In Gullah there is no possessive marker. Possession is expressed by the juxtaposition of the possessor to the thing possessed:

> (*a*) " 'an Rabbit have love de *Wolf gyul* mo dan he does his gyul (Hunter),"
>
> (*b*) "De gyul say, 'Not Mr. Wolf, not Mr. Wolf, you nevuh ride my *boyfriend back*' (Hunter)."

Several West African languages, such as Ibo, do not use possessive markers. In Ibo the noun's position in the sentence shows whether it is in the possessive case. Ewe has no possessive case in the name of relationships. Again, where Standard English makes a distinction between nominative (he, she) and possessive (his, her) forms of personal pronouns, the nominative and possessive forms in Gullah are the same. Thus we have

> (*a*) all duh res' wuh *he wife* tell im;
>
> (*b*) duh Patrid take *'e head* from unduhnea' *he wing*.

This sameness in nominative and possessive pronouns may be found in Ibo, Ga, Yoruba, and Ewe. A qualification, however, should be noted here. Miss Hunter shifted from Standard to Gullah frequently in her use of personal possessive pronouns. Even when she did this, however, the primary rules of Gullah emerged strongly. Thus in her sentence—*Patrid take her head stick he head undernea' he wing*—the initial pull to Standard English as she began her story gave way to the stronger inner drift toward Gullah, which not only canceled out the use of a personal possessive like *her* but also the gender distinction implicit in its use.

4. Gullah frequently does not display the same past tense marker used in Standard English. A Gullah verb is often the same in both present and past tenses. Standard would have given us, in the following sentence, the past tense forms *got, broke, jumped, shot,* and *killed:* "Nex milepos' he get dere, he break de egg, a man jump out, shoot im an' kill im. Das wat he get fo be bad (Hunter)."

Other clues in the Gullah sentence may indicate the past tense. Phrases like "in my time-comin" or "yestuhday" and "lass mont" may carry the time information or a Gullah word like *binnuh* may be placed before the verb to indicate the past tense (as well as the perfect and pluperfect). Thus, *You binnuh walk een briah patch since you bawn.*

Looking to Africa again for grammatical roots, one finds that tense may be expressed not by something added to the verb, as is usual in English (jump-*ed*, kill-*ed*), or an alteration in the form of the verb (got, broke, shot), but by another verb or noun in what we may call a "verbal complex." This is the case in Ewe. We also find a number of West African languages, like Yoruba, where the past and present verb forms are the same.

5. In Gullah there is the absence of the third person singular present tense marker: "*What bark heah bite yonder?* (Hunter)" for "What bark(s) here and bite(s) there (Standard)."

Ewe, Fante, Yoruba, and Ga are among West African languages where the verb forms remain unchanged through the singular and plural number.

6. In Gullah the definite article is often absent. It is usually used to indicate something specific or to refer back to something previously mentioned. This use of the definite article almost exclusively for specificity and referentiality is characteristic of many African languages. Examples in Gullah are the following:

(*a*)   "*Shackle wear dis out. Shackle wear dat out* (Guinea)."

(*b*)   "*Das why you fren is duh one who gets you, na enemy who come accosh you* (Hunter)." Note here the presence of the definite article in the first half of the sentence and its absence in the second half. It is your friend who is the one to be careful of (specific); not enemies who accost you (general). It is your friend, of course, who is the enemy but that is already implied and needs no emphasis through the use of the definite article.

(*c*)   "*Is de same dance ri' now . . . they jes change rung, diffrunt name . . . Mash Potato, yes it is, das Charleston, Mash Potato das Charleston* (Hunter)."

7. There is a frequent absence of the copula—the verb "to be"—where it would normally occur in Standard English. The absence of the copula occurs in several types of constructions. I shall confine myself to a discussion of one of these, the construction which contains what is known as a predicate adjective:

(*a*)   "I know my *people poor*. I doan need kill 'em (Guinea)."

(*b*)   "Das why he *tail white* (Hunter)."

(*c*)   "Das why *you weak* today . . . *you wise* alright, *you wise,* got plenty o' sense (Wine)."

In these constructions, what in Standard would be called adjectives, "poor, white, weak, wise," are not linked by the copula "are" or "is" to the nouns "people, tail" or to the pronoun "you." In some West African languages "to be white" or "to be weak" would be one word in itself. The verb "to be" and the adjective "white" or "weak" etc. would be compounded. One word serving both functions of verb and adjective—*the verbal adjective*—cancels out the need for a link work or copula. Thus, in Fante the word *hwa* means "to be white," in Yoruba *dū* means "to be sweet," and in Mandinka *kidi* means "to be lonely." Within these verbs the concept expressed by *copula plus adjective* in Standard English is fully contained. This can account for most copula deletions in Gullah.

8. Gullah has no passive voice. Black English verb forms are always active. Take the following sentence from Alice Wine's description of preparations for winter: "Deh plant plenty o' potato an' bank it up an' peas an put 'em in de barrel an' turnip, deh sweeten dat in de bank an' potato, deh sweeten dat in de bank an' de hog, deh cyo' it (Wine)." In Standard this would in most cases be expressed thus: "Plenty of potatoes and peas and turnips are planted and banked in barrels. Potatoes are sweetened in the barrel banks and the hog's meat is also stored and cured there."

West African languages which have no distinctions in voice include Ewe, Yoruba, Twi, Fante, and Ga.

9. The Gullah use a number of words which, although they resemble English words in sound, function in Gullah in the way their African equivalents would function. For example, the word *go* means "to" or "toward" after a verb of motion (Rabbit, he jump off an' *run go* home). In Ewe the word for go (yi) when following a verb of motion also means "to" or "toward." Also, in both Ewe and Fante, the word for *go* or *go away* means "and" or "in order to" if it connects two verbs. The same is found in Gullah. "Once a man have tree daughter. Dem go *go* pick wacky."

The word *fa,* which is sometimes confused with the dialect distortion of *for* (fo', fuh), is from the Twi language and may be translated as "intend to, choose to, must" according to its context. It is another word in this category of English-looking words with African-type functions in Gullah but we can quote no good examples of this from our tape transcriptions though they abound in Turner's work.

The use of *sɛ,* however, even after the word "say" or "tell," which would seem to the untrained ear to be simple duplication occurs in several of Jane Hunter's stories: " 'E give bote o' em fo' eggs an' *tell em say,* 'On duh way going, dehs fo' milepost, an' each one dem milepos' you git to, see, yuh break one dem egg.' "

Sɛ (or say) here really means *that.* The sound sɛ, when occurring in Gullah after a verb of saying, thinking, or wishing, always means "that." This use of sɛ is common in some West African languages, including Twi and Ibo. Its resemblance to an English word explains why it has been retained in common speech while functioning in the way a similar sound functions in certain African languages.

10. Gullah uses what may be called the double negative or the multiple negative, that is, negation is expressed not once, as in Standard English, but twice or several times at various parts of the sentence. Thus,

(*a*) "Dat *aint no* business fo me. *Cyaan* learn *nuttin* like dat (Wine)."
(*b*) "I *doan* write *nobody no* letter (Guinea)."
(*c*) "Jesus *didden* need *no* baptize but he let John baptize im in de river (Hunter)."

The double or multiple negative arises out of the presence of several negatable elements in the verb or verbal complex in African languages. Negative inversion is also another feature of Gullah which has its roots in African languages but our tape expedition turned up no example. *"Don't no-body know* wat Nixon got on dose tapes" would be an example of this but it is not a very common construction.

11. Gullah frequently duplicates words also in conversation and, particularly in narrative, words and phrases are often repeated. This may be done, as in West African languages, for emphasis, for rhythm, and in sermons, testimonials, and prayers, as an oratorical device.

(*a*) "O yeah, *looky heah, looky heah,* I kin show all dese heah (Guinea)."
(*b*) *"You eat it, you eat it, you eat it* kuz you dere an' you cyaan get nuttin from home . . . you eidduh take dat or jes *lay down dere, lay down dere* an' die (Guinea)."
(*c*) *"He driving, he driving going* home an' he didden pay no attention, look back in de cart at de fish an' dat rabbit put everyone dat ole man fish *in de bush, ri' in de bush* (Hunter)."

12. Gullah sometimes places the adjective after the noun as in West African languages, like Fante, Ewe, and Twi: "I radder do dat kuz you doan wuk in *sunhot* (Wine)."

13. Gullah maintains the same order in interrogative and declarative sentences. A shift in intonation, as in West African languages (such as Ibo, Kikongo, and Efik) is all that is needed to indicate that a question is being asked as against a statement being made. Thus:

(*a*) "O, deh give you eight uhr nine dollah a day now but wat good it is? (Wine)."
(*b*) "Why 'e say dat? I askin you a question now, why the Bible say, 'weak an' wise?' (Wine)."

14. The subject or object is stated in Gullah, then repeated by the use of a personal pronoun, then a statement is made about the subject. This word order is common in Yoruba, Ewe, Kimbundu, and Kongo languages:

(*a*) "Then you *cow, he* give you milk . . . you *chicken, he* give you egg (Wine)."
(*b*) "So old *Rabbit, he* jump off and run go home (Hunter)."

15. In Gullah we find the use of groups of words for the standard English equivalent of a noun, verb, or adverb:

(*a*) "In my *time-comin* all chillun have a sutten 'mount o' work to do evvyday (Guinea)."
(*b*) "But is bettuh time *down yonder* dan is dere now (Wine)."

This is particularly true of phrases expressing time, as the above for the past, and *rebel time* (a Turner example) for the era of slavery. Others, like *crack e teet* (smile) *jes az it come out 'e mout* (verbatim) are concrete images as opposed to more formal abstractions. To what extent the greater tendency to image-making is African influenced and to what extent it is a natural preference and response to an unfamiliar word or a too formal or impersonal a concept it would be hard to say. In Guyana, for example, even in fairly formal parlance, I would prefer to say "I'm going to see "the eye-man' " rather than the oculist or optometrist. This is not only preferable on grounds of simplicity but a concrete image is immediately projected. Image-making on a far more extended scale than one would find in Standard English is a feature of Gullah and all Black English dialects.

16. Gullah makes use of the habitual tense which has no equivalent in Standard English. It indicates an habitual action. To convey the same concept in Standard English would necessitate the addition of a qualifying word or phrase:

(*a*) "*We be out trying* to keep up with everything that's going on (Bill Saunders)."
(*b*) "De 'umble chile, das da one *be honorable* (Hunter)."
(*c*) "I doan feel like *be going* to the barber all da time so's I leave me head home for my wife to shave (Hunter)."

The habitual tense has its roots in West African languages and in the Bantu languages of East and South Africa. These languages place more emphasis on the "mode of action" than on the "time of action." Rather than focusing on whether a verb tense (time) is past, present, or future they focus on whether the action indicated is habitual, completed, conditional, or obligatory.

There are a number of other distinctions which may be noted, such as the way the comparative and superlative degrees of the adjective are formed in Gullah, the basic or indicative form (big, for example) remaining unchanged in the comparative (big mo'nuh or mo'dan) and the superlative (big 'pass alla). No good, illustrative example from our field trip is available but Turner has noted the basic form of the adjective does not change in certain West African languages and the verb meaning to surpass ('pass) is used with the basic form of the adjective to express comparative and superlative degrees in Ewe, Twi, Fante, Ibo, Kimbundu, Mandinka, and Kikongo.

We could also point to other features of Gullah like the elision of sounds at the end of some words (*doan* instead of don't, *cyan* instead of can't, for example) because of the tendency of African languages to follow a vowel/consonant/vowel pattern and to avoid a clustering of consonants, particularly in final position. These, however, are phonological rather than syntactic considerations and take us into an entirely new field.

While in the Gullah Sea Islands we observed African influence in the art and craft of basketmaking, walking sticks, iron cooking pots, fishing nets, and stools, and African influence on cuisine, herbal medicine, folk beliefs, and riddles. We observed also the impact of African music and motor behavior on the rituals of the church, but these observations we feel were far too brief and superficial to form the basis for any authoritative statement or analysis. Other investigators, like Dr. Herman Blake, head of the Kinte Oral Tradition Project on Dafuskie Island, are now conducting extended and intensive investigations into these and other cultural areas. On a recent visit to St. Helena island as a consultant for the Kinte Project, I learned of plans for the development of a Gullah museum to preserve the history and tradition of these islands. We need not fear, therefore, the total loss of Gullah art and artifacts which have been kept fairly intact over the last three centuries. No museum, however, is needed for the oral tradition. It is a tradition very much alive in the way the Sea Islanders speak and in the way also many of them think, a tradition enshrined in the language and mythology of the folk, a tradition which, in spite of its many locations and variants in the Black world, has a common root, a common ground in the linguistic and mythological structures of Africa.

Acknowledgments

Tape recordings upon which this work is based were done on Johns Island and James Island, and in Charleston, South Carolina in the fall of 1970 and 1971. These trips were financed by the Dean's Fund, Douglass College, Rutgers University.

The tape recordings were put into broad and phonetic transcription by my research assistant, Mrs. Elizabeth Farrah, a speech therapist and phonetician, with the help of a grant awarded me by the Rutgers Research Council in 1972.

References

Abrahams, R. Trickster, the outrageous hero. *In* T. Coffin (Ed.), *Our living traditions.* New York: Basic Books, 1968. P. 171.

Bennett, J. Gullah: A negro patois. *The South Atlantic Quarterly,* 1908, 7, 332–347.

Crum, M. *Gullah: Negro life in the Carolina sea islands.* Chapel Hill, N.C.: Duke University Press, 1940. Reprinted by Negro University Press, 1968.

Fanon, F. *Black skin, white masks.* (Translated by Charles Markmann.) London: Paladin, 1970. P. 125. Originally published as *Peau noire, masque blancs,* Paris: Editions de Seuil, 1952.

Gonzalez, A. *The black border.* Columbia, S.C.: The State Company, 1922. Reprint, The State Printing Company 1964.

Johnson, G. B. *Folk culture of St. Helena Island, South Carolina,* Chapel Hill, N.C.: University of North Carolina Press, 1930.

Jones, C. C. *Negro myths from the Georgia coast.* Boston: Houghton-Mifflin, 1888. Reprinted by The State Co., Columbia, 1925. Reissued by Singing Free Press, Book Tower, Detroit, 1969.

Krapp, G. P. The English of the American negro. *American Mercury,* 1939, 2, 190–195.

Stoney, S. G., & Shelby, G. M. *Black genesis.* New York: Macmillan, 1930.

Turner, L. D. *Africanisms in the Gullah dialect.* Chicago: University of Chicago Press, 1939. Reprinted by Arno Press, New York, 1969.

Van Sertima, I. African linguistic and mythological structures in the New world. In R. Goldstein (Ed.), *Black life and culture.* New York: Thomas Crowell & Sons, 1971. Pp. 12–35.

Wolfe, B. L'Oncle Remus et son lapin. In *Les temps modernes.* Paris, 1949.

TRICKSTER, THE REVOLUTIONARY HERO

Ivan Van Sertima

The word *revolutionary* in my title is not lightly chosen. It has a double significance. The revolutionary role of the Trickster figure in the folk imagination is related in the first place to the longing of a powerless group, class or race for social or political change, for transcendence over an oppressive order of relationships. This may be expressed in folk tales by symbolic acts of sabotage or revenge by a weak or vulnerable or despised figure (Brer Rabbit, say) against an apparently stronger or more powerful opponent (Brer Wolf, Brer Bear, Brer Tiger, say). But I speak also of the revolutionary role of Trickster in a more radical and complex sense, a role Trickster played among aboriginal Africans and Americans, a role related to the profound and often obscure longing of the human psyche for freedom from fixed ways of seeing, feeling, thinking, acting: a revolt against a whole complex of "givens" coded into a society, a revolt which may affect not only an oppressed group, class or race but a whole order—the settled institutions and repetitive rituals of a whole civilization. I will explain more clearly what I mean when I come to deal with Trickster in this complex role. All I want to point out at the beginning is that the purpose of my paper is to show how the Trickster functioned in the African folk imagination—the main roles he played—and how those roles were recast and redefined by Afro-Americans under the unique social and psychological pressures of the New World.

In their original African home and culture these figures took on other functions that are ignored, minimized, or forgotten among the Blacks of the New World. Their functions in this hemisphere have become restricted to a treachery and guile aimed at transcendence over impotence and servility within a highly oppressive order of relationships. It would be interesting to look at some of these other functions and the reasons why they have been neglected or ignored in transplantation. The trickster in Africa is not only involved in tricking the lords of the jungle—Tiger, Elephant, Lion—which are symbolic of the class of the mighty and powerful. He plays tricks on the rulers of Heaven itself, stealing fire or food for his fellows under the noses of the Gods. We seldom find him in such a role in the New World.

Trickster is also in revolt against the mores of his own group—committing taboo acts, acts of outrage which release him from the confines and boundaries laid down and observed by his peers. We may find him, for example, on the eve of battle when the warriors have withdrawn from their families and are ritually forbidden to go in unto their wives before the clash, slaking his lust to the full in a village of husbandless women. This is an imaginative way of escape from the collective pressure upon the instinctual life of individual man.

We also have Trickster as pre-social man, that is, a figure which pre-shadows social man. *It* is man before the forms society made and dressed him in, man as free spirit, original energy, pure primal power before the limitation and rigidity of any social or ritual artifice. Such a form can imaginatively go back to beginnings, to the unstructured chaos of origins, in order to free the human psyche to explore new orders and forms.

Such functions of the Trickster were a luxury in a slave and colonial society. So deep, so intense, so total indeed was the negation of power in the real life of the African-American that the role of the Trickster in the life of dream was nearly always overpowering and triumphant, and never self-destructive, regressive or anarchistic in a primal sense. Blacks, barracooned in the slave plantations and colonial ghettoes of the Americas, could hardly afford this. They needed no vision of chaos to relieve their impatience with stable structures and immemorial orders. What they needed (at least in the past) was a new order through black lawlessness which would negate the old order of white lawlessness that had negated and outlawed them.

Thus, the role of Trickster as underdog, as representative of an oppressed group or class or race, became almost the only role or function transplanted here. I think the choice of animals for tricksters in Bantu culture (Rabbit and Tortoise) and in West African culture (Annancy, the Spider) is most revealing. Let us first observe the archetypal qualities of the Bantu pair.

Rabbit occupies a disadvantageous position in the animal world. Extremely vulnerable, without a heavy hide, claws, beak or sting, his fragility is counterbalanced by an extraordinary sensitivity (huge antennae for ears) and a lightning nimbleness (fleetness of foot). Though he may seem as easy prey to the larger animals, the potential for outmaneuvering them belies his apparent fragility. In the body and spirit of Rabbit, therefore, is crystallized a subtle and delicate radar for scanning the potential peril (which he averts) and the potential possibility (which he exploits) in a given situation—a situation usually (in those tales most native to the tradition) of menace from the Mighty. A typical tale told by Uncle Remus is that of Brer Rabbit and Brer Lion, in which Rabbit is invited to offer up his life for Lion's supper and is so adept in his survival strategy that Lion dies wrestling with his own shadow.

The tortoise is another symbol of the underdog in Bantu mythology. In fact he is more popular than the hare in some parts of East Africa. His main virtue is his capacity to endure, for he can live longer without food than any other animal. He moves with a painstaking slowness, but with the sureness of the sun in motion across the streets of the world, and this impresses itself upon the Bantu mind as the unrelenting and invincible doggedness of an elemental force. The brooding silence and secrecy of the tortoise also invest him with a suggestion of craft and cunning and mystery. He hides his innards under a shell in the way the black had to hide his true face and feelings in the Americas under shells and veils and masks of deception in order to carry and conceal the horror at the heart of his daily life.

Some interesting tales are told of Tortoise. Perhaps the best known is that of the Great Race, but to me the most significant is the tale of the Famine, of which there are innumerable versions. During the Famine the animals searching for food come across a tree, previously unknown, full of ripe fruit. They send messenger after messenger to the owner of the tree to ask its name. The name of the tree has a mystical significance (the fruit cannot be picked or made to fall without its precise utterance), but the messengers all forget it. Only the tortoise remembers, and he lifts the curse of hunger from the land by felling the fruit. But though he is the only one in the jungle who can summon a total awareness of origins (the name of the tree being the name of the tribal ancestress), the other animals turn on him and refuse him a share of the fruit. The tortoise in some versions is smashed to pieces and is put together again by the ants. On regaining his pristine strength he uproots the tree, with all the animals eating their fill in its branches, and they perish in the Fall.

The psychological value of this tale to Afro-Americans hardly needs to be underscored. The slave in the Americas may identify the smashing of the tortoise to pieces with his own dismemberment and fragmentation, the denial of its due share in the fruits of life with his own social deprivation, and its Samsonian uprootment of the tree on the recovery of its strength as a prophetic indication of his ultimate release in a cataclysmic act of vengeance and revolt.

It is strange that there are so many collections of Afro-American folktales and so few analyses of the significance of the animals in these tales. Grave misconceptions abound. One commentator sees the fairy tale as a flower of civilized societies and the animal tale as the relic of primitive tribes. Another finds it difficult to understand how the African can humanize animals in these tales and yet retain a clear distinction between the animal as creature and the animal as symbol of man. Yet others, closer to our times, refuse to accept the obvious influence of African trickster figures upon the folk mythology of Afro-Americans. It is clear that this is a field as rich in its accumulations as it is poor in its theoretical premises.

An analysis in depth of the main elements in these African folktales will show that the animals are involved in a shadow drama of the human world. They are dream figures through which personality traits, values, or power relations of groups—commoner and king, slave and master, the weak and the strong, the powerful and the suppressed—may be reflected in a dreaming drama of the social world, within which dream and drama the figures are invested with a fluidity and metamorphic quality denied them in the more rigidly structured social world, so that they often seem to reverse and overturn their given social role or condition. It is this capacity of the dream figure (animal archetype) to overleap and overturn an oppressive social condition that makes the personae of the tales (Rabbit, Tortoise, in Black America, Annancy the Spider in the Caribbean) take on an heroic cast and revolutionary function.

This role reversal and revolutionary function of certain folk heroes account for their enormous popular appeal among the black communities of the New World. Like the Caribbean Annancy, the black American Brer Rabbit plays the role of outlaw and con-man. Neither subscribes to the laws and moral values of their society. Secretive, elusive, cunning, deceptive, sometimes cruel and treacherous, they are in the role of the Transcendent Criminal, avoiding through their legendary agility of wit the onerous and unfair burdens imposed upon their fellows, always one step ahead of Brer Wolf and Brer Tiger, the predatory lords and overseers of the jungle.

The psychological value of the Trickster's role in the Caribbean slave society has not escaped all investigators, though they have been led into certain conclusions that are inconsistent with a full appreciation of Annancy's real function and meaning. Rex Nettleford, for example, in an introductory essay to *Jamaican Song and Story,* makes the following observations:

> *In Jamaica this descendant of the West African semi-deity seems to take on special significance in a society which has its roots in a system of slavery—a system which pitted the weak against the strong in daily confrontations . . . It is as though every slave strove to be Annancy and he who achieved the Spider-form became a kind of hero . . . This picaresque character misses no chance for chicanery . . . as though he lives in a world that offers him no other chance for survival . . . to cope with an unstraight and crooked world one needs unstraight and crooked paths.*

It would seem clear from this passage that Nettleford understands the profound relationship between Annancy's ACT and the slave's DREAM.

Yet in the very same passage, he commits the error of associating, in a very literal way, Annancy's characteristics with features of the Jamaican character.

Annancy . . . expresses much of the Jamaican spirit in his ostenta-
tious professions of love, in his wrong-and-strong, brave-but-cowardly
professions of bluff, in his love for leisure and corresponding dislike for
work, in his lovable rascality . . .

Here are echoes of the slaveowner's slander of the naturally resentful and reluctant slave: "dislike for work," "love for leisure," "cowardly," "lovable rascality." This patronizing attitude is unworthy of such an astute critic as Nettleford. The "black" character of Annancy does not represent the character of Jamaicans in that sense at all. Jamaican children, brought up within a puritan ethic, utter an oath of purification—*Jack Mandora me no choose none*—when they narrate Annancy stories, the oath being a plea to the doorman at heaven's door to absolve them of responsibility for Annancy's wickedness. What we are really face to face with in Annancy is what I would call a black innocence. He is loved and lovable because his "evil" liberates rather than oppresses. He assumes aspects of evil in order to elude and conquer a condition of evil.

Finally, and most importantly, we must return to the function I highlighted at the beginning of this paper, the most complex and yet the most revolutionary function of the Trickster figure. In aboriginal African and American tales we sometimes find the Trickster emerging as a Fool or Idiot Extraordinary, functioning with the power and freedom of a god and yet displaying an astonishing innocence of its power and capacity, even of its fundamental nature, like a new-born babe. Paul Radin has cited tales* in which this figure appears with its penis wrapped around its head, its right hand at war with its left, its proportions formless or undetermined. This incredibly vital and yet incredibly vulnerable creature demonstrates the god-like power to alter its amorphous shape as well as the baby-like propensity to see itself, as for the very first time, with no given assumptions about its limitations, extensions and capacities. What is the meaning of this? Why should the generative organ of this creature (symbol of creative power?) be so large that it cannot be comfortably coiled and contained within its accustomed lair? And why should it be so ignorant that it has to learn from scratch, like any creation at birth, to organize and utilize its power?

This power, I believe, is the pristine potential of the human before he is squared and squeezed, boxed and beaten, drummed and driven into a shape that would fit the patterns of a particular culture, time or place. This innocence is the child-like nakedness of man before he is clothed and straight-jacketed by the ritual fabric and collective costume of a particular society. This role of Trickster expresses the profound and obscure longing of the psyche to shed the familiar coat and dress of a particular order or civiliza-

---

*These tales, which some folklorists do not classify as Trickster tales, are, in fact, organically related to the basic themes of that configuration.

tion and return to an examination of origins so that it may rediscover the springs of original energy. That energy is the source of change. The need at times for such change underlines the psychic or psychological value of such tales.

I am highlighting this function for although it seems to have been lost in transplantation it may in fact have had no relevance to the African-American until now. He is no longer a separate, suppressed part of Western civilization but, in this latter half of the twentieth century, reenters the mainstream, no longer simply an underdog protesting the group or race or class in power, but becoming a power in his own right, sensitive to the fundamental malaise that afflicts the whole civilization. Thus it is that an African-American novelist, Wilson Harris, a writer of very complex and original fictions, has recently introduced this figure and function of the Trickster in a novel, *Companions of the Day and Night* (Faber and Faber, London 1975).

In that novel the Trickster functions as he does in the aboriginal African and American tales as a kind of god or super-conscious Being. He is a god in the sense that all the creations of the world through which he moves seem also to move through him. They are not separate or divisible from him. They are extensions and complements of his own self, the limbs and organs of one body of which he is the heart and brain, the center of Consciousness. He is the Organic Creation before its separation and division into diminutive capsules of individual personalities, times, cultures. This is what Radin means when he speaks of "original energy". That is what I intend to imply when I speak of the freedom and power of a god. The object of this highly imaginative exercise is to demonstrate the capacity of the human spirit and substance to recreate itself, to feel its way toward a Consciousness that breaks down and breaks through apparently fixed and frozen, partial and polarized, states of being and belief. The revolution implied here is a revolution of the imagination, a revolution in consciousness, a fundamental revision and reassessment of static and ritualised modes of seeing, thinking, feeling, which may afflict a whole civilization, regardless of whether one is in the black or white race, the capitalist or communist camp, the group of the ruler or the ruled. This is, in effect, the ultimate conflict between man's *freedom* to remake himself and the world he has already made, which *imprisons* him in the tightly woven fabric of its ritualised reflexes, ideologies and institutions.

It is not an easy concept to explain but to simplify it further is to run the risk of misrepresenting the subtleties of the fable and its extraordinarily apt and skillful application to the American and global reality in the novel. What it demonstrates is that what often passes for arbitrary invention and imaginative sport or absurdity in these ancient tales contains the most explosive seeds of wisdom. It is like the dreams which rise with such apparent effortlessness from the depths of our daily lives as we are suspended in the flickering twilight of our sleep, watching the strange theatre of the psyche unfold. The Trickster is one of the main characters on the stage of that theatre.

In *Companions of the Day and Night,* this figure returns to a fiction of the Americas to illumine the danger of collapse in a social order or civilization. It is a signal of pressures in the human psyche for a new creature to evolve, powerful and yet baby-like, original and yet formless (The Trickster God and Fool). It is the need for a revolutionary quality of the imagination to evolve among us, an imagination which seeks to rethread the basic fabric of the inner (and ultimately the outer) world, so much of which we take for granted. We are at a point where there are terrifying urges everywhere for change but the impulse expresses itself more as a sentiment or protest reflex than as a genuine fundamental thrust for a revision of mental structures, a revision of the human itself. Both the rebel and establishment ideologies seem locked in the same fixed, programmed ways of seeing, feeling, thinking and acting. The world has become a place where, in Matthew Arnold's phrase, "ignorant armies clash by night." The Trickster emerges as a counterbalance to that nightmare, an eye or light in the heart of a gathering but not implacable darkness. Fluid and free, a principle of revolutionary energy at war within forms that seek to contain it, it is able to see from within, act from within, move from within the roots of its world, to *re-root* that world, so to speak, to point the way forward to a new course, a new possibility, a new human person.

Sources

1. Harris, Joel Chandler, *Nights with Uncle Remus; Myths and Legends.* Boston, Houghton Mifflin Company, 1911.

2. Harris, Wilson, *Companions of the Day and Night,* Faber and Faber, London, 1975.

3. Jekyll, Walter, ed., *Jamaican Song and Story.* New York, Dover Publications, Inc., 1966. See introductory essays.

4. Radin, Paul. For this reference, see R. Abrahams "Trickster, the outrageous hero" in T. Coffin, (ed.) *Our Living Traditions.* New York: Basic Books, 1968, p. 171.

5. Van Sertima, Ivan, "African Linguistic and Mythological Structures in the New World" in Rhoda Goldstein (ed.) *Black Life and Culture in the U.S.* New York, Thomas Crowell & Sons, 1971, pp. 12–35.

6. Van Sertima, "My Gullah Brother and I: Exploration into a Community's Language and Myth through its Oral Tradition," in T. Trabasso and D. Sears (eds.) *Black English: A Seminar,* Lawrence Erlbaum Assocs. New Jersey, 1976. pp. 123–146.

7. Van Sertima, "Into the Black Hole: A Study of Wilson Harris' *Companions of the Day and Night"* . . . The essay on *Companions* . . . was submitted to the Nobel Committee in 1976, on behalf of the candidacy of the novelist, Wilson Harris. It was published later that year in the Journal of Commonwealth Literature (ACLALS) Fourth Series, No.4, Mysore, India, pp. 65–77.

INTERVIEW AND OVERVIEW
DR. IVAN VAN SERTIMA
(1991 INTERVIEW)

Kwaku Lynn Interviews Ivan Van Sertima

Dr. Kwaku: It's been a number of years since you wrote *They Came Before Columbus.* What kind of personal and intellectual growth have you experienced since writing that book?

Dr. Van Sertima: Well, *They Came Before Columbus* taught me a lot about the prevailing climate of prejudice which inspired the many attacks that were leveled against it. The attacks are becoming fierce again, now that they see the book is beginning to make its mark. For example, it's now* in its sixteenth printing. I am thinking of bringing out, once again, the collective work I edited in 1986—*The African Presence in Early America*—which presents important new data. My contribution would be much larger than it was before.

A great deal has happened over the last fourteen years. What the reaction to *They Came Before Columbus* taught me is that it does not matter how well documented, how well supported may be the new facts one presents to the world, the old habits of thinking about the African does not easily change. It is important that the vision of the African be changed, our old-fashioned vision of the African ancestor.

I began to realize the reason why it was so hard for people to see the African on any other plane before the European arrived except that of the primitive, the static primitive. Most primitives do not easily make transcontinental, trans-oceanic movements. It took thousands of years for the very early primitives to move across the spaces of Africa, across the spaces of Europe, across the spaces of Asia. By conceiving of the African as a relatively static primitive, it is hard to accept that he could be on a continent other than his own, unless someone brought him there. Especially when a vast and virginal ocean stands between. Where, therefore, it is claimed, that he not only made contact with distant civilizations but influenced them, it

---

*Entered its 21st printing in 1994.

would start a momentous controversy. I realized that I would first have to revise, in the mind of millions, the popular vision of the African.

That is why I got involved in the *Journal of African Civilizations,* which has produced more than a dozen volumes, nine of which are titled. I am now working on the tenth. I have stretched tentacles into Europe, into Africa, into the Caribbean, all across America, to draw from the very best of our scholars. *We,* and I really mean *we,* have developed a kind of school. It has made a tremendous difference.

There's the book *Blacks in Science: Ancient and Modern,* which is now accepted by nearly a hundred schools and universities. There is *African Presence in Early Europe, African Presence in Early Asia* (co-edited with Runoko Rashidi), *African Presence in Early America, Great Black Leaders: Ancient and Modern, Black Women in Antiquity, Great African Thinkers* (co-edited with Larry Williams), *Nile Valley Civilizations, Egypt Revisited, Golden Age of the Moor.*

Now what that has done is to make people aware that the African we have been dealing with, the African we've been focusing upon, or rather the African that our Eurocentric vision has created, is one-sided and false. The African we were taught to envision as the true African is the peripheral creature of the forest zone or the colonized survivor of the slave trade.

The more sophisticated centers of Africa were shattered, the great achievements of mainstream Africans were ignored. So we have a comparison between the mainstream European and the primitive African. Even people of African descent have come to the conclusion that what is special about the African is his simple, raw humanity, his exotic little rituals and costumes, etc. They are not aware, for example, of his scientific tradition. Most people have been made to think that it was the European, because of his so-called theoretical and abstract thinking, who alone learned to master and transcend nature.

When we go back in history, we begin to realize that this is not true. We have found, within the last twenty years, African astronomical observatories, one going back in Kenya three hundred years before Christ. Of course, in Egypt, it's much earlier than that. In the areas we usually call South of the Sahara, we have found an observatory 300 years before Christ. On the basis of the alignments of this observatory, these early Africans built one of the most accurate of prehistoric calendars.

We found steel-making machines that were in advance of Europe. We have found *tetracycline,* used 1400 years ago in Nubia. We only started to use that in the 1950's. We found the use of *aspirin* among the Bantu, centuries before us. We found Africans developing vaccines before us. A *smallpox vaccine* was brought here by the African slave Onesimus, as reported by his master, Cotton Mather. We find Africans were performing eye cataract surgery long before other people. The Arabs report this performed in Mali in the 14th century. We find Africans giving us *physostigmine,* still used in the treatment of glaucoma. We find what is probably the first drug to treat hypertension and psychotic disorder—*reserpine*—developed by Africans.

We find their navigation was far more sophisticated than we had come to assume. Carthaginian-type vessels were found on the Niger. Phoenician and Egyptian-type vessels were found on the African edge of the Indian ocean. We find the Chinese reporting Africans bringing elephants to them in ships, two hundred years before Columbus.

Our whole vision of the African, his capacity, his potential, his ability to move and to affect and to influence other peoples, all that had to be changed. All that had to be revised before people could look again at the hypothesis of an African presence in early America. And it is *not* just a mere hypothesis. A vast body of evidence has accumulated, and in this discussion I would like to deal more systematically with some of that evidence.

Dr. Kwaku: Before we get to that evidence, because of this new school you have been eminently involved in pioneering, do you see another level of consciousness and understanding emerging, in terms of the African point of view in this country and other parts of the world, because of what you and others have been doing for years?

Dr. Van Sertima: Something is happening that is very, very significant. I want to point to two major developments. There is a very serious growing movement now to rethink the curriculum in many of the major educational systems in this country. I have been advising teachers in the major school systems of various cities—St. Louis, Cleveland, Columbus, Detroit, Indianapolis, Portland, Atlanta, Boston, Newark, etc. I spent a whole week last summer teaching the basics of this new revision of history to three hundred and fifty teachers in the St. Louis system, both white and black. This goes across the boundaries of race, across the board.

All of us have to be affected by this. It is not just a Black thing. It affects Blacks more than anybody else, of course, because they have been practically excluded from history. Everybody has to become aware of this revision of history. The disrespect for us, the kind of prejudices that have built up upon that disrespect and contempt, is what is at the root of racism. It is no sense talking about man being equal when we have history books that show us repeatedly that that is not true.

The concept, the idea, the vision of equality, cannot be based simply upon liberal cliché or Biblical fantasy. We have to realize that it is rooted in hard historical realities. The movement in Atlanta, in Portland, Oregon, in Detroit, in Grand Rapids, in Columbus, in St. Louis, in New York, in New Jersey, in Maryland, in Washington, D.C., these are just a few I know of and have been involved in. It makes us aware of a new movement, a real attempt now to change the traditional curriculum.

There is resistance in certain places, and here is where I want to sound a note of caution. There is so much that has been developed in these years by this school, responsibly developed. There is no need for people to make up things or to ride upon half-known or half-sure things. There is a body of hard evidence about great achievements of Africans and African-Americans upon which we can build this new curriculum.

The curriculum is not simply Afrocentric. That term is being misused. Our so-called "Afrocentricity", or rather our new vision of the African, which is what this Afrocentricity should be about, should be used to counter and correct Eurocentricity. Eurocentricity has brought so much falsehood into our present curriculum. But you cannot exchange a biased Eurocentricity for a biased Afrocentricity. This shift of vision must be corrective. The Afrocentric vision comes as a corrective, so that you get nothing that is exclusively Eurocentric or exclusively Afrocentric. You get a balancing, which brings you closer to the truth. You cannot totally capture the truth, but you can come closer to a more balanced truth, as a result of this corrective vision.

I want to make that quite clear, because some people are saying "Why are you exchanging an Eurocentric for an Afrocentric curriculum?" It is not an Afrocentric curriculum. It is an Afrocentric perspective, which helps us to correct the present Eurocentric curriculum, so we get something broader, fairer, more *all-inclusive.* We get a more inclusive curriculum. The word inclusive is used, because instead of excluding us and merely including the achievement of others, or excluding their achievements and saying we did it all, it becomes all-inclusive. It pulls the various elements or fragments of the human condition together. We have been pushed out of it altogether. We are the invisible chapter of history. That is one of the foundations of racist thinking.

Dr. Kwaku: You mentioned two significant developments. There is the curriculum of inclusion being debated across the country. What is the second one?

Dr. Van Sertima: The second is something that is beginning to happen in Europe. I know there have been some significant upheavals recently in Russia, then there is the fall of the Berlin Wall, the end of the Cold War, which many of us seem to think is just a passing phase. It's no passing phase. A new Europe is being born and that new Europe is very conscious of the fact that, even though it may seek economic models from the West, it is very much aware of the kind of stifling prejudices, racist prejudices, that bedevil the West.

The Europeans are holding a conference, for example, in the Netherlands. I am invited to attend this. I am invited to this, so that the participants can have a new vision of the third world. A new vision of history, particularly of Africa. I want you to be aware of the change that is occurring, not only here in America but in the world. The Russians, (let us pray their movement does not come to a sudden halt) the Russians have spent the last year revising their history curriculum. They actually banned history exams for a year so that they could bring into being a more all-inclusive curriculum, that could include more objective truths and not repeat the Stalinist falsehoods of the past.

Dr. Kwaku: So you think it's not just on the grassroots level, people like myself and others, who are just interested in learning our history and culture, to correct what has been taught to us, but things seem to be moving into the mainstream, where established educational institutions and nations want to correct and change what has been done in the past?

Dr. Van Sertima: And both have to go together. Do not expect the mainstream curriculum is going to go far enough. It's going to take time and it's going to be the source of many battles. That is the great battle of this decade.

We have to carry on our own thing as well, carry on a subterranean movement under the conventional structures of the system. We have to make our people aware of these things and to be inspired by them. Not to be inspired by mere hollow chauvinistic boasts, but inspired by a genuine awareness of achievement, so they can emulate that achievement. So their children do not have to feel they only half-belong to the world. They do not have to feel as though they're just on the backside of the world, as it were. It is very important that we all be aware, particularly our people.

People of African descent should become very much aware of what is going on. Very much aware of these developments, of this record of achievement. It is affecting us profoundly. It's not only the ignorance of this that is making people despise us, push us aside and treat us as second-class citizens, but our ignorance of it makes us also treat ourselves in a certain way. It has affected the way we approach everything.

For example, one has seen many instances where there's a new enterprise or a new type of publication. Our people may think it is good enough, simply because it's a Black thing, regardless of whether it is operating on the lowest level. In other words, mediocrity has become the ideal. They do not realize that we are *not* a second-class people, we are *not* a mediocre people.

When you go back in history to the great West Africans, the West African at his best, the Egyptian at his best, during the ancient Black dynasties, the black-dominated period (and I'm not talking about modern Egypt, which is an entirely different thing), if you see these people at their best, you will see the passionate quest for excellence. Their legacy of excellence, their ideal of excellence, is so remarkable. When I first went to Egypt, I particularly wanted to find one of the things they had been building centuries ago, an obelisk, which they had abandoned because it had a slight flaw. It would have taken centuries for the flaw to make a difference, but it had to be perfect. It had to be as perfect as they could make it. That is the kind of mind, that is the kind of imagination so critical to us in this time.

Dr. Kwaku: In the history of Africans in this country, there was an era of Reconstruction after the Civil War, where we made a lot of progress, setting up businesses, getting into the political system and so forth. Then there was a backlash, called the Era of Redemption, to take all this back. Do you anticipate, in this new intellectual, academic wave of inclusion, there could be a backlash or an intellectual era of redemption, to try to take back all the things you and other scholars have been working toward over the years?

Dr. Van Sertima: That is always possible in history. It is for us to become vigilant. It is for us to push on with such great force that such a backlash either does not occur or, if it occurs, it does not have any lasting effect. You see, one has to be always careful in any movement, in any revolution. One has to be always careful about the old flesh creeping back. Look what happened in Russia. All these great liberals, everybody got so excited. Look what's happening today in Eastern Europe.

In the liberal wing, which had a chance to harden itself, consolidate itself and push forward, serious divisions occurred. It could be it was just the nature of the society and the time. I am not blaming anybody, but there is always the possibility for backlash. Backlash seems to have come.

The vigilance of the group that is fighting for a new life, for a new deal, the vigilance of that group is critical. One doesn't just fall back and say "OK, everything is going fine now. At least they are changing the curriculum." That is why I say, hand in hand with the mainstream shifts, there must come a subterranean group arming itself with these facts. If anything happens in the mainstream, they could push forward again, they could keep this thing alive. One cannot predict the future, because there is always a danger. One has to be vigilant.

Dr. Kwaku: You mentioned in the beginning, you wanted to focus on some of the evidence, rather than just dealing with boasting and glorifying. Some of the evidence of scholarship that has been done in the past few years.

Dr. Van Sertima: Let me, for example, deal with the subject that I have become most associated with, *They Came Before Columbus.* One of the things I may not have mentioned, with as great a force in the past as I do now, is the fact that even though we have to build up the evidence by going into many disciplines, most people seem to think there was no documented evidence. They think, nobody wrote about this, that nobody mentioned these early African explorers. In fact, at least a dozen people, who came during the time of Columbus, saw or heard first-hand reports of Blacks among the Native Americans.

Christopher Columbus, himself, was the first person to suggest there were blacks in America before him. He said that when he was in Haiti, Native

Americans came to them and told them there were Black-skinned people who came from the east and south-east in large boats, trading in gold-tipped metal spears called "guanin." Samples of these spears were sent back by Columbus on a mailboat to Spain.

They were inspected by Spanish metallurgists who found that they were identical, not similar, identical in terms of the ratio of gold, silver and copper alloys found in spears then being forged in Guinea. Ferdinand Columbus, the son of Columbus, wrote a book about his father, Christopher, in which he said his father told him he saw "Negro" people north of the area we now call Honduras.

Vasco Nunez de Balboa, in September 1513, the day after he claimed to have discovered the Sea of the South, was coming down the slopes of Quarecua when he saw two Black men among the Native Americans. They were very different from the natives and so he asked them where did these Black men come from? They said they did not know. All that they knew was that these blacks were living in a large settlement nearby. That's in the Isthmus of Darien, which we now call Panama. They were in this large settlement and they were waging war with them. Lopez de Gomara reports that these Blacks Balboa saw were identical with the Blacks of Guinea.

Peter Martyr, the first major historian of America, tells us that they found Africans living in the mountains. He called them Ethiopians. It was the word generally used for people with burnt skin—that is, black people. He was not talking about modern Ethiopians. He said that they were probably shipwrecked long ago and had taken refuge in these mountains.

Rodrigo de Colmanares reports that one of the pilots of Balboa said he saw Blacks east of the Gulf of San Miguel. Riva Palacio reports on Blacks off Tegucigalpa, on the Nicaraguan-Honduran border. L'Abbé Brasseur de Bourbourg says that there were two distinct people who were indigenous to Panama. One of them, the Mandinga, the other, the Tule. The Tule is the redskinned type with straight black hair, the Native American; the other, the African type.

Apart from all this, the Smithsonian Institute discovered two African skeletons in the United States Virgin Islands in St. Thomas, at a place called Hull Bay. When they dug up these skeletons, they said they were in a layer or stratum dated 1250 AD, which is more than two hundred years before Columbus. They said that these were the skeletons of African males in their thirties. They said their incisor teeth were filed, which was a peculiar dental ritual, used by some pre-Columbian Africans. They said in addition, there was a pre-Columbian Indian ornament, a Native American ornament, around the forearm of one of these skeletons. Yet, when they took them in the lab, to date them, they couldn't date them. They found an interference which didn't make sense. I'm not allowed to talk about what caused that interference. It is secret and has nothing to do with the subject.

Going into the Virgin Islands, I found at the bottom of the Reef Bay Valley on St. John's, a pool. Carved on the side of this pool, along the water line, I found a dot and crescent script. It was deciphered by Dr. Barry Fell, formerly a professor of Harvard. A shadow has fallen over Fell. A great deal of criticism has been levelled against his work. I therefore had the decipherment checked out with the Libyan Department of Antiquities. They gave the almost identical reading Barry Fell had given me.

It was the Tifinagh branch of the Libyan script. It was used by the Tamahaq Berbers. It was used also by a people in medieval Mali. It was used by a people in southern Libya. These were all mostly dark-skinned peoples. It read: "Plunge in to cleanse yourself. This is water for purification before prayer." They have found so far seven examples of this type of inscription, with the dot and crescent formation, across the United States. The one I discovered was deciphered. Mine was the longest one found.

Apart from that, there is the botanical evidence. The Portuguese, who entered Africa half a century before the Columbus journey, found cotton growing plentifully on the Guinea coast. They assumed it naturally to be an African cotton. They took it and planted it in the Cape Verde, *in 1462.* Note the date! They planted it in 1462, 30 years before Columbus. A study made in the 20th century established it as an American cotton. How could an American cotton get into Africa before Columbus, one must ask, unless there was a crossing. Now this cotton is gossypium hirsutum var. punctatum. It was only found growing in the Caribbean and South America, not in Africa. It is not indigenous to Africa. It cannot get to Africa without a human crossing.

There are certain things that can cross from Africa to America without humans. The bottle gourd, for example. It has a thick shell and it can fall from a tree or a boat into one of the currents. There are three currents that take things from Africa to America. The gourd could fall into one of the currents and come to the Americas. Salt water doesn't affect it. But that is not the case with cotton. Cotton cannot cross in the current without losing its potency. An African jack bean also got into South America. This jack bean (canavalia virosa) intermarried with an American jack bean (canavalia plagiosperma), producing a new world jack bean (canavalia piperi).

This is long before Columbus. Then there is banana/plantain. This is not an African plant. It is Asiatic. But it is found on the Atlantic side of South America, not on the Asian side. It had come into African trade since the 12th century. The Arabs introduced it into Africa. But they found it in the graves of South America. The burials in these graves were pre-Columbian. They also found widespread cultivation of the plantain (the banana's sister) along the Amazon coast, when they came in. Orellana reported it. It had nothing to do with the later post-Columbian introduction of the banana and plantain. The bananas in South America all have African names.

Dr. Kwaku: One of the things a lot of people are interested in are the pyramids. They say, "Well, we see these pyramids in Mexico. We've seen these large heads." Can you establish what the exact relationship of those things are to African culture or African people?

Dr. Van Sertima: Here, we are dealing with a much earlier period and a different type of African voyage. Remember this was not a once and for all affair. The currents that traversed the Atlantic, that moved from Africa to America, are massive and they've been continuous in the Atlantic Ocean for thousands of years. Voyages of intent as well as voyages of accident occurred over a long period. The period I've been talking about so far is the late pre-Columbian voyages, dating from the early 14th century right down to the time of Columbus himself, when people began to sight these Blacks among the Native Americans.

The early voyages, the early contacts, some of them are very important. They are not just simple shipwrecks. They involved a substantial body of people. The more significant of these is found among the Olmec, the very earliest of American civilizations. This had nothing whatever to do with the Mandingo voyages. It is absolutely removed in time by centuries. These very early voyages involved Egypto-Nubian types or other African types affected by Egypto-Nubian civilization. They occur between 948–680 BC. We know that because the first sequence of stone heads begins to appear in ceremonial centers, in the Olmec world, and the first pyramids also begin to appear.

I want to make something quite clear. The American pyramids were *not* built by Africans. They were initially influenced by them. The first pyramids that appear in America appear in a strange coupling on the same platform. They appear linked to the first sequence of stone heads, with both African and Mongoloid-type features. Not all of the stone heads can be classified as African, although they have broad noses and very full lips. Some of them are definitely African, especially the Tres Zapotes head with braids and another one in the a sort of Osirian pose, practically lying on his chin, showing no helmet, only a crown or tuft of hair.

The hair evidence is very important. Sometimes you could have an Asiatic type with broad features, like the African, because the African type entered Asia very early. Fortunately, you have lots of terra cotta, that is, clay sculptures of Africans in which the texture of the hair, even the coloration of the skin, is projected. You also have skeletal evidence, where the bones of the face, the texture of the bone, the brow ridge, the nasal aperture, the nasal fossae, the structure of the jaw, all sorts of things in combination, indicate the Africoid type, as distinct from the Native American.

Now to talk about the pyramids. The first pyramid to appear in America has no predecessor in America. It appears right on the platform where the first sequence of stone heads appear. That is, at La Venta. It is on a north-south axis. That in itself is very unusual, because all the major ceremonial centers and pyramids in Egypt, and Nubia, are on a north-south axis. Never before, in America, was any ceremonial center built on a north-south axis. Never before in America had a pyramid appeared.

Now all of a sudden (and just where the first sequence of stone heads appear) we have a miniature step pyramid, as well as a conical pyramid. Some experts say, "Ah, that's not a conical pyramid, it's a fluted cone." If you go and look at it now, you're going to find deep depressions, of course. You see, it has a cone, but it has deep depressions. They say it's a fluted cone, it's not a pyramid. That's nonsense. The reason it has deep depressions is because it was built of clay, not brick or stone as were the pyramids of Egypt. The Americans didn't have that much stone, not in that area anyway, where they built the first one. It's built in the swamps. The sides would naturally fall in with time, as do most earthen hills.

There are no more fluted cones in America after that. So if they planned it as a fluted cone in order, as the experts say, to represent a volcano, where are the other fluted cones? And if the pyramid at one end of the platform is meant to represent a volcano, then what is the step-pyramid doing at the other end of the same platform? Is that then a baby volcano? Again, experts have argued, "In America the pyramid is a temple; in Egypt it's a tomb." That is not true. The tomb and temple combination is reflected in both complexes of pyramids. Not only that, the greatest pyramid in America, the one at Teotihuacan, although not built by the Omecs, but influenced by them, has roughly the same base. It's off by one meter and some experts are now allowing that meter for mistakes in the reconstruction. It has roughly the same base, as the Great Pyramid of Egypt. It also has moveable capstones, like the one in Egypt. It was also used as a geodetic marker. It has all the relationships and functions you find in the greater pyramids of Egypt.

But, apart from the stone heads, there are thousands of terra cotta, clay sculptures of Africans. The Americans left tens of thousands of terra cotta bodies and heads. That is what survives, the remarkably life-like clay sculptures, so we have pictures of them. We can't say "Oh, because they didn't have the camera, we don't know what they looked like." We know what they looked like. Most of them did *not* look like Africans, so the African type, when it appears, stands out. When Dr. Andrzej Wiercinski went down into the graves, in the dry areas where the skeletons survived, places like Tlatilco, Cerro de las Mesas and Monte Alban, he was able to make significant cranial measurements that show you have a type here that is very distinct from the native type, that had come in and crossbred with the native type.

Dr. Kwaku: There is all this evidence to establish the relationship. Why do you think Africans were so influential during that time?

Dr. Van Sertima: Well, Africa obviously is not as influential as it was before the slave trade. Remember, Africa is no longer what it used to be. Africa is an exploded world, an exploded star, a shattered continent. It is only in this century, within our own lifetime, that it has started to stumble back into any kind of coherent, independent form. Even independence has not yet truly come to Africa. The richest part of Africa is not yet indepen- dent. So bear in mind, you can't compare modern shattered Africa with the Africa that was.

There is no place on the globe, at the moment, where the African figure has the kind of power and prominence the old Egyptians had, when Egypt was dominated by Africans. There is no empire in Africa, at the moment, that has the cohesion and the power such as we find in the medieval period in places like Mali or Ghana. Bear in mind, we are dealing with the African before the crash of their world, OK?

It's very important to deal with that, because one of the things you come to realize is that consciousness, once it preserves the past and the best of the past in us, feeds us with something precious and lasting. We lose when we believe that the past has nothing to do with us.

What is remarkable about the Jews is that they preserved the past, even though they were shattered and almost destroyed. Millions of them were wiped out. The only thing that kept them together was the bond of their history, whatever reservations one may have about the politics or policies of the present Jewish state (I'm not interested in the politics of the moment). I am dealing now strictly with the human spirit and how it preserves itself. How people remake themselves. The only thing that preserved them, that enabled them to hold their center, was their memory of the past. The preser- vation of the past, the glorification of the past, the consolidation of the past. They could go back to something that was thousands of years before their shattering, before their explosion into fragments, before their being scat- tered over the earth. Before the attempt to destroy them. They could go back to that and hold this, like a light before and within them, until they became, in spite of their small numbers, a central force in the world.

That is something you have to understand. Just because something hap- pened thousands of years ago, does not mean it is insignificant. In fact, the past is more significant than the present. The present, after all, is a passing fluid thing. Only the major events of the present are going to really leave any marks. The past however, has already left the blight or the bloom of major events. That is the nature of the universe.

Every major sound and light event in the universe is preserved. We photographed a doomed star that exploded a hundred and sixty thousand years ago. Yet, we photographed it, because the light of that event, the mark of that event, is still with us. It is still traveling through the universe. Even the sound of what people call the Big Bang, the birth-boom of the Universe, the sound behind all sound—Bell Labs picked it up some years ago. It is still with us. We can actually hear the echo of that primal explosion that occurred in the beginning of time.

Dr. Kwaku: You did something very significant a few years ago. You made a presentation to Congress, or to the committee that organized the five hundredth year of Columbus' so-called discovery. They changed the terminology from "discovery" to "voyages." Can you give us an idea of what you said, that made it so significant for them to change their terminology?

Dr. Van Sertima: I appeared on July 7th, 1987, before a Congressional Committee that was overseeing the work of the Christopher Columbus Quincentenary Commission. I was called upon to show due cause why they should not refer to Columbus' accidental stumble into the Caribbean as a "discovery." I pointed to the fact that Columbus was the first to suggest there were Africans in the Americas before him. The African voyage is significant. I also pointed to the fact that the International Congress of Americanists, meeting in Barcelona as early as 1964, had ruled "there cannot now be any doubt that there were Old World visitors to the New World, before 1492." I pointed to the testimony of nearly a dozen Europeans who had come into the New World in the first phase of the European contact period.

I pointed to other things. I pointed to a map that shows the correct latitudinal and longitudinal coordinates between the African Atlantic coast and the South American Atlantic coast, with certain prominent Caribbean islands drawn in, long before Columbus. They could not have been drawn at the time of Columbus or even two hundred years after 1492. Nobody in Europe could plot latitude and longitude in that way. In fact, one hundred and fifty years after the death of Columbus, encyclopedias in Europe reported that longitude had not been discovered and was probably undiscoverable. In the short time allowed me—twenty-five minutes—a range of things were presented to that Congressional Committee that indicated to them that it was insulting to use the word "discovery." It was not only insulting, it was inaccurate.

One of the things my testimony led to is the Chairman advising the commission (I'm not sure they are going to follow that to the letter, but they were strongly advised) *not* to use the word "discovery." One of them, in fact, got very angry. He left the chamber. He did an interview with the *New York Times* and reported the next day, "Even if Columbus was not the first to discover America, he was the first person to go back and give a press conference." So he chewed on that. He got his jollies out of that.

What was equally serious, I also managed to get the Bahamas into the commemoration. They just wanted to include mainland United States. Also, they did not want to have any Native Americans on the commission. That emerged as a result of my testimony, the discovery that there were no

Native Americans on the commission. There was only one Black, I think. If there was any, there was only one. I do think somebody mentioned there was one. So that meant a larger, more multicultural, diverse kind of commemoration of the fusion of Old World peoples in the New World, rather than a celebration of the mythical discovery of America by Columbus.

Dr. Kwaku: There have been reports, one by a historian who traveled during that period, Las Casas, there is another side of the Columbus story, the annihilation and genocide of the indigenous people. Can you speak a little bit on that?

Dr. Van Sertima: Well, everybody knows the movement, the massive continuous movement of Old World peoples here, led to the destruction of the Native American civilization. One of the things I would like to touch on, is what happened to the Native American. Today, we only find him in the reservations or we find him in certain other areas of America.

One of the things a lot of people don't understand is why Montezuma, who ruled a great empire, was so easily defeated by Cortes. The ragged army of Spaniards, under Cortes, who landed here in 1519, could not defeat the Aztecs, who were the Native American power at the time. It was impossible. What Cortes saw in the center of America startled him. Here again we have the same general ignorance about what Americans were doing as we have about what Africans were doing. When Cortes saw their pyramids and their palaces, their aqueducts and their zoos and their running baths, and their floating gardens [the chinampas, the most advanced agricultural techniques then in the world], he said "I have not seen its like anywhere."

The reason why Cortes defeated Montezuma, is that several tribes (or rather small nations) were being oppressed by the Aztec, the ruling power. They therefore joined with the European to defeat Montezuma. In the same way Europeans joined with the Africans, under Hannibal, to defeat the Romans. Some unseasoned European troops joined with the Africans to defeat their own European Rome. The Romans after all, were an imperial power oppressing other European peoples. It had nothing to do with race. The reason why Cortes won, had to do with the fact that he could draw upon the support of the dissident tribes pitted against Montezuma.

Dr. Kwaku: We can talk about this particular topic all day, but we want to move to some other areas, particularly those personally related to you. In the last few years you have been doing this work. What would you say are some of the highlights?

Dr. Van Sertima: Well, one of the things I've been excited about is the emergence of some of the most remarkable scholars out of Africa. I was very pleased by the tremendous respect accorded me by Cheikh Anta Diop, and later by Theophile Obenga. Cheikh Anta Diop very much wanted me to bring out his latest book *Civilization or Barbarism*. He had already given the rights to the French. The most he could do was to give me permission to have two major chapters of his work translated and published in my journal. I am very happy about that.

The book I wrote, or rather edited, on Cheikh Anta Diop, had quite a profound effect. I was assisted by Larry Obadele Williams. Larry Williams did a remarkable job. While a lot of people were just going around enjoying themselves during Diop's visit here, Larry Williams collected everything he could. He made photographs, collected tapes, all sorts of things about Diop which were very helpful. There were interviews that were extremely important in giving us a vision of Diop. Diop was profoundly affected by the Morehouse reception and honor. That was the last great moment of his life.

When he went home, his wife wrote and told me he talked about that all the time until he died. That was a marvelous thing. That was one of the great high points, because Diop really was the most important African in this field. I am very impressed by Theophile Obenga also. I was surprised that God had sent us another contemporary soul to light the way. Theophile Obenga is the true successor to Diop. He gave me his whole manuscript in French. I had two major chapters translated. It was rather expensive, so I couldn't do the whole book. I brought it out in *Egypt Revisited*. That has been one of the great high points.

The other high point is the participation of European scholars in our venture, like Basil Davidson, John Pappademos, etc. They are not Eurocentric even though they are European. These are two different things. There are Black scholars who are Eurocentric, like Frank Snowden. Many of the major figures in this field: Claudia Zaslavsky, the mathematician; John Pappademos, the physicist; Martin Bernal, the linguist and classicist, and Basil Davidson, a very remarkable historian, are among the best Europe has produced on Africa. All of these people found a platform in my journal. They represented a new wave of European. Not the European interested in putting the African down, excluding him, but rebuilding him by struggling against the prejudice of their disciplines, and even (as in the case of Davidson) their own early prejudices.

Dr. Kwaku: Going in the opposite direction, what has been some of the lowest points and biggest disappointments you've had to face?

Dr. Van Sertima: Well, I don't want to dwell on those things because every struggle has its anguish. I sometimes have been pained by statements made by African-Americans or Africans who are still Eurocentric, and who, instead of revising their thinking, would go out of their way to destroy what we are doing, and keep us where we have been before. I don't want to call names, but I have sometimes been very pained by that. I also was very pained by the attack of the New York Times, which was so unfair. There was no proper discussion of the subject and it led a lot of people to dismiss the whole thing. It has taken years to fight one's way back.

But the negatives have been my greatest help. That is the one lesson I learned over the years. The negative is very important. Sometimes it's more important than the positive. Sometimes, if something is highly successful instantly, it makes you facile. If something meets great negatives, it can be even better in the end. Unless it is destroyed, it is far better that it meets with negatives. The negative makes you go back and check out everything. You find a whole lot of new things. If before, you came with a revolver, the next time you come in with a cannon. The time after that, you come in with a nuclear bomb.

So the negatives are very important. To know the enemy is larger than you think, more formidable, makes you go back and build a bigger arsenal. The negatives made me realize, for example, how very alone I was. How necessary it was that we have a community of scholars. It welded a great many of us together, people whom I had never met or known.

When I wrote *They Came Before Columbus,* there was not a single writer, who later wrote for the Journal, that I knew personally. Not one. I did not even know who John Henrik Clarke was until he came to speak at the book party of *They Came Before Columbus.* I was not aware of anyone here who was doing anything. I did not know Asa Hilliard. I did not know Charles Finch. I did not know any of these people. So it built, for me, a community. Being attacked in that way built a whole community that was really very critical.

Dr. Kwaku: Why do you think there are still African-Americans still holding on tightly, will almost defend to the death this European perspective of theirs, and in the process, harming our own progress?

Dr. Van Sertima: You see, if as a child and all through your adult years you have been accepted for doing a certain kind of thing, and the people who have tried to do something else have been crucified, it would take something very extraordinary, something tremendously traumatic, for you to change. Some people are good enough to keep quiet, they just fade away.

I have known one or two scholars, and here I can't call names, who attacked me at first, then found through their own researches, I was on the right track. They were so upset they never said anything. They quietly died. It is not until you look at their posthumous papers that you find they made discoveries that brought them around. They preferred to be silent, until death, than say they found x.

People deal with these things in different ways. I myself have pointed this out over and over. I wasn't born with any revolutionary vision of the African. All the prejudices, all the Eurocentricities that had become part of the flesh and blood of man's thinking, in the Western world, were part of mine. I only began to wake up in my thirties. All through my twenties, all through my teens, all of the falsehoods about African people, like myself, people of African descent, all of these fictions I believed. I believed in them as one believes in the Bible. I mean, those were like biblical truths to me.

It is only with trauma, real trauma, real tremendous internal upheavals, personal catastrophes, my going to Africa when I was thirty-two, which led me to swing around. Even the actual revolution in the Caribbean and in Africa, which had a temporary effect on me, I suppressed. It came up in me again to dismember all of these myths I had, which had become a foundation of my life. It had been a foundation for centuries for billions of other people.

Dr. Kwaku: I remember hearing in one, maybe a couple of your lectures, you mentioned you were lecturing in England and your brother was there. Afterwards, he questioned you on why you were doing all this African stuff and so forth. Then he saw you years later. After the lecture, he had tears in his eyes. Is this similar to what you are talking about, that transition?

Dr. Van Sertima: Things that happened in his life made him see the truth, the larger truth of what I was saying. He had been traumatized by his experience, so he jumped out of his shell and was able to transform himself. I think it is very important to note that people are not to be dismissed because they are locked into this sort of thing. One still has to attempt to change them, you know. This change has to occur at various levels in various minds.

Dr. Kwaku: Do you think, among scholars, that ego, jealousy, envy plays a role in some of these attacks?

Dr. Van Sertima: Oh yes. I know that is something which happens in everything. You find, for example, people who feel you are getting too much attention, that your ideas and so forth are becoming too popular or are affecting other things. Sometimes it's just a plain bread and butter issue. They feel that if they were to say your kind of thing, they would lose their jobs. All of that plays a part.

Dr. Kwaku: I've heard you mention this, and other scholars I've had the opportunity to talk with, and other writers, have said this on a consistent basis, that this is a very lonely battle. You stand alone many times. Where does that come from?

Dr. Van Sertima: To follow up on some of the things one discovers calls for a lot of thinking. You can't think easily if your life is a "social" thing. A lot of people are very surprised they can get in touch with me. They may speak with me for a moment on the telephone, but I don't have a social life. I don't go to parties. If there is a reception for a talk, etc., I'll go. I meet very few people face to face.

Some of the people who have written for me, some of the people with whom I have had the most profound relationships I have never met. Like Diop, for example. I never met Diop until about a year before his death. I had long correspondence with him. I spoke with him on the telephone, but I never saw him for ten years. Not until it was absolutely necessary to meet him face to face.

I met him in London, then I met him in Atlanta, when he came over here at the big celebration for him. Yes, it is very important to realize that in order to pursue certain things in life, it is very important to be alone. When I was doing *They Came Before Columbus,* I saw no one. I forbade meetings. I would see my chairman and colleagues once a month, at faculty meetings. For about six to seven years, I met no one properly.

Dr. Kwaku: Do you feel this internally? Do you regret, well, I don't want to say regret, but do you miss having a social life and doing some of the other things people do just to have fun while living on this earth?

Dr. Van Sertima: I am very fortunate in some respects. I have a remarkable wife. She takes care of half of my business. She is busier than I am. She often goes to bed at one or two in the morning. She is not my secretary because she has as much work to do in her business as I do in mine. The one thing I do regret is that so much of my time is spent on little things. I do not get as much time for research without having to separate myself. For example, I spend about five hours a day on mail, in addition to my full time lecturing, my research, etc. It is all very well for people to say, "But why don't you have a secretary?" I do have a secretarial assistant, but you have to directionalize things. Otherwise, the whole thing falls down.

You have to make all the big decisions about what book is being published this year. Who will participate. Who has expertise in this or that. How can a secretary do that? How can a secretary discover who knows about the music of the Moors? These are areas that are not charted. They are virginal areas, you know. It calls for a lot of exploratory work you have to do yourself. Who decides what is going to be the issue? What is the most feasible issue? Who decides what your interest is going to be? Who decides where the experts in the new area you are exploring are? You can't get that from a secretarial assistant.

Dr. Kwaku: You have done work on the Moors. Can you briefly tell us what is the significance of the Moors?

Dr. Van Sertima: The Moors were to have a profound influence on Europe. Europe was in a kind of Dark Age when the Moors (that is, the Africans and Arabians) invaded. During that period some of the most significant developments occurred. What we call the European Renaissance, should really be called the World Scientific Revolution. That was the beginnings of the gun, for example. The gun is not European. The father of the gun is the firestick, which the Moors brought into Europe. There were developments in mapmaking. There were developments in trigonometry. There was the transmission of early Egyptian geometry. There was the beginnings of algebra. There was the beginning of optics. There were windmills, crankshafts, worm and pinion gears operated hydraulically. Chess. The beginning of the lighting of city streets. The beginning of hot and cold water systems. All these things, I don't want to give away the book on the Moors. There were so many surprising things, I don't want people to just pick up a few bits and pieces. You have to look at it. The impact of the Moors on Europe, on the edge of the new thing that was to happen in Europe.

Europe was to seize the initiative. Europe was to conquer these places. Europe then took on the head of this, when in fact, it wasn't Europe's thing. Europe was a part of this, but Europe had drawn heavily upon the world. Its number system came from the Arab and Hindu. It truly is Arab and Hindu. It's not just Hindu, as some people thought. Even I thought that until I began to study it in depth. I have a whole pilot-guide now on Arabic-Hindu numerals, which enables me to see exactly what the Hindu gave and exactly what the Arabs gave. Exactly what was changed.

Some of these things one had only understood superficially. Now, one has begun to understand them in depth, to try and find out where certain things come from. I had to start all over again, after months of work. I had to start a section called "The Egyptian Precursors," because I began to realize that many writers on the Moors had excluded Africans. Not just the European historians, but some Arabs had actually assumed the African had nothing to do with this and that what the Arab invader of Egypt was starting with was the Greek heritage, not realizing the Greeks took a lot from the Egyptians. While there were certain refinements and extensions, of course, which are due to Greek genius, it was not merely a transmission of Greek heritage, but a critical part of the ancient African heritage.

One had to really probe deeply to begin to realize this was a truly multicultural tradition. Elements were coming in from all over the world to build the World Scientific Revolution, which we have come to believe was simply a European thing.

Dr. Kwaku: Many of the young scholars today look up to you very highly. I mean, respect you, respect your work. What message do you have for the young scholar starting out, sort of following in the trail you've left for them, still here and still active. I don't want to give anybody the impression you are leaving us or anything like that, but what advice do you have for the young scholars of today?

Dr. Van Sertima: First of all, realize you have a far greater advantage than I had. You have before you a body of work which was not available to us in our time, until rather late in our lives. Also, a word of caution, please do not accept everything. Do not assume that merely because someone is of your own race, everything they have to say about what Africans or people of African descent did is true. This revolution has to be built up responsibly, on a body of hard facts. You have to look very closely at evidence. You have to become self-critical. It's important that you do.

Life is not simple. The simpler you are, the more you are involved in the simplification or facile falsification of things. The harder life will become. The more it will surprise you. The capacity to look at things with great care is not just critical to the scientific mind. It's critical to human development. The more facile you become, the more simplistic you become, the more difficult your life will become because you will slip and fall over in the very darkness you have created.

Since you have this body of material now before you, you do not have to go through the terrifying searches some of us have had to go through. Examine it closely so you can build upon a hard base. Do not become chauvinistic. It is very important that those people who are against us or those people who are not of us, learn to respect us, learn to respect these discoveries. It is equally important you also become aware they had their achievements too.

We have got to lay emphasis on our achievements, of course, because we have been excluded from history for centuries. Therefore, nobody is to accuse us of being racist, simply because we emphasize what we have done. They would have good cause to accuse us of being racist if we tried to denigrate everything they have done. Let us be able to see clearly what claims were false and what claims were valid.

We should try to see with a critical clarity, although the truth can never be total, try to see with as much caution and clarity as possible, what claims we have made that are false and what claims we are making that are truly valid.

Dr. Kwaku: One last question I want to throw to you. It came to me as you were talking and seems to be a question that comes a lot from our sisters. They say that they hear you and they hear other scholars and say, "Well, good. I appreciate that, but they never say anything about relationships, about African men and women in this country and in other countries. What does scholarship have to do with our relationships?" Do you have any response to that?

Dr. Van Sertima: You see, one of the things that leads to extremely difficult relationships (and this is not something that is going to vanish overnight) is self-contempt. This is very deep among African-American and African-Caribbean people. Our historylessness (and by that I mean our assumption that we have no significant history), our lack of belief in ourselves, our lack of belief in having something of value, something substantial of value to support us, leads to all sorts of anxieties, angers, insecurities that are bound to affect relationships. No relationship, therefore, in a highly troubled psyche, a shattered psyche, no relationship with people who nurse or nurture troubled or shattered psyches can be easy relationships. That is why it is so critical to use history to rebuild, to bring a healthier wholeness to that psyche. So even though, directly, no one could come and tell you, "Well look, if you study this history you are going to have a better relationship," the study of history can give you a sense of wholeness. Can give you a different quality of mental health. It will, almost inevitably, lead to healthier relationships . . .

One of the problems we have by the way, is our misunderstanding of polygamy. This misunderstanding can flatter and foster gross male chauvinism. African polygamy is a complex thing. It is not a ticket to sexual license and lechery. This was a social institution that was less of a sexual than a protective or social welfare type of institution. First of all, not everybody could be polygamous. You had to be fairly prosperous. You had to be able to support the unhusbanded females in your harem. You are not necessarily sleeping with all of them. The protective institution may include, for example, your unmarried sister and your widowed mother. You would not even dare to dream of touching them.

Incest is far more serious in Africa than in any culture in the world. You could be executed for incest. Incest is so serious, it extends beyond the immediate family. You cannot even marry your cousin. Sometimes in some places, you cannot even marry someone in your own clan. Incest was only allowed in ancient times as a royal prerogative, in those extreme situations when it became connected with certain religious assumptions about divine royal blood. The blood of the pharaoh was the blood of God, because he was the representative of God on earth. Those are religious exceptions and oddities. In the polygamous institution, women who are not yet married would become the responsibility of a prosperous man. He is not necessarily sleeping with them. Polygamy grew out of a certain stability, a certain economic stability or prosperity.

Whereas here, when the Black man was brought here, our women were kept fairly close to the children most of the time, and some of them became concubines of their European masters, forced or tempted into sexual liaisons. The man was sent wandering all over the place. Liaisons developed, at times, between him and women in other places. Those plural liaisons, or his so-called polygamous behavior in America, grew out of something totally different from the situation in Africa. Not out of prosperity and stability, but out of insecurity. Men should not use this and say, well the Africans are polygamous, therefore, that is why I am polygamous. Those things are not genetic, they are not even fixed cultural imperatives. They are responses to social situations, changing rapidly in our times. That is sometimes the source of great distress.

On the other hand, you have the woman who may pride herself on the fact that the West African woman had a certain measure of independence in relation to her man that was often comparably greater than the woman in the traditional European family. In this particular American context, because of the wandering Black man or the unemployed Black man, whose economic opportunities were sometimes less, she has sometimes been in the unusual position (unusual in terms of our convention) where she becomes the chief breadwinner. All sorts of tensions develop in those relationships. You have to see, therefore, the unhealthy or unhappy types of relationships between men and women, particularly Black men and Black women, as part of all sorts of social situations and crises.

It's not confined to us by the way. Marriage at the moment is undergoing a revolution. Many people have never investigated the fact that there is a dramatic increase in the break-up of marriages among whites. There has been a tremendous shift to single-family households headed by women, not only among "Blacks" but "Whites." If you see the latest statistics, you would be utterly surprised how much of that is happening. You have a relationship that has been stretched to its limits. The battle for woman's equality on all levels has led to all sorts of redefinitions of marriage. This has profoundly affected all of us. *The family is in crisis.* It is not only the Black family.

One has to see in what way the new historical information that can heal or help to heal the black psyche can be used to help the family. I just want to end by saying, that to think this historical information stands as a separate area of knowledge and that it can only peripherally impinge on relationships is not true. It's just that nobody could come and map out your relationship for you. They can give you certain information that can change your consciousness. A changed consciousness automatically remaps its relationships.

Dr. Kwaku: Well, Dr. Van Sertima, I want to thank you so much for sharing this time with us. All of us always appreciate the knowledge you are giving to us. I think it does help us personally and collectively. So, on behalf of myself and all of us who love and appreciate you, thank you very much, again, and we hope to see you again sometime real soon.

Dr. Van Sertima: Thank you very much Kwaku.

HISTORY AS A GUIDE TO
MODERN POLITICAL ACTION

Ivan Van Sertima

I conclude this address, ladies and gentlemen, with both an inspirational note and a salutary warning. We are on the brink of great change in this country as well as great danger. Nothing major should be done, nothing major attempted, without great thought, without great caution. We should drink deep from the well of our history but in a way that nourishes rather than simply titillates us, poisons us, or divides us. History is a critical complement to contemporary reality and it is particularly helpful to those who have lost their way in the world because the footprints of their past have vanished or been erased. But let not history stand like the ghostly twinkle of a long dead star on the horizon of our consciousness. It should be a dynamic beam of light in daily motion across the sky of our minds. It should charge us not only with a surge of new pride but the electric energy of creative action. For it to animate us thus, it will demand, it will most certainly demand, a corresponding animation of consciousness. History is a window through which we see only half of ourselves. The other half may be quickened into life by the image of the twin we see looking back through the window. Let us, however, never fool ourselves that there, in the mirror of time, we can see our totality and therefore know not only where we have been and what we have done but also what we must do now to get where we think we are going.

History does not provide, and should not be seen as providing, save in a few isolated instances, a tried and tested program of action for contemporary situations. What may have worked in 2000 B.C. may lead to disaster in 2000 A.D. What failed in 2000 B.C. might work marvels in 2000 A.D. We learn the lessons of the past to alert us to a range of human situations and sometimes to mistakes which we would otherwise have to repeat ourselves in order to learn from them. History enables us, therefore, to act with greater caution and wisdom in the future. But we must constantly and simultaneously be aware of the many new variables that have entered the

From Address to the National Council of Black Studies – Republic of Guyana, South America – June 4, 1994 world. The emotional infantilism which still divides and imprisons man, his racial or tribal antagonisms, may not have changed very much but the world we live in has changed. It is no longer a neat conglomerate of separate and sovereign entities. What happens in Bosnia is not just between the Muslims, the Croats, and the Serbs, what happens in Haiti is not just between Aristide and the junta of General Raoul Cedras, what happens in Rwanda is not just between the Tutsi and the Hutu, what happened in Chernobyl was not just a Russian disaster. Our modern world is intimately intersected and connected. We are living in the same global house. The voice of my most distant neighbor is just a radiowave or light-wave away.

Contemporary reality calls for an updated program, therefore, a subtletisation of liberation strategies. Consciousness of history is a critical part of this. Relating it to the complexities of the modern world is equally critical. We cannot say, as we have done, with an earlier and understandable innocence, that when we know what we have done wrong in the distant past we can make sure we shall not do it again. For what may have been dead wrong 500 years ago may be a workable strategy in our time. What we can learn from history, however, is to have, through a more total vision of our past, a truer and more total sense of ourselves, a better ground upon which to build our lives, a more informed and illuminated base upon which to make decisions about the role we should play in our family, our community, our country and the world. Too many people believe that the emotional boost this new history can bring to some of us will be enough. It will not be.

The vision of our former stature in the world must penetrate our consciousness so deeply that it begins to transform the degrading and dwarf-like habits of our present thought and action, habits which have crippled our progress for too long. This heightened awareness of the best in our past can stimulate and inspire and heal us but it must blend intelligently with a maturing vision of the living present if it is to be of practical value. Unless the two dimensions—the past and the present—are fused creatively, we shall dance forever to the tune of slogans, we shall be titillated by the vulgar drama of history rather than be galvanized into new thought and action by the current of lightning, the current of insights, springing from the past. . . .

BIOGRAPHICAL NOTES

Akbar, Na'im

Dr. Na'im Akbar is a Clinical Psychologist in the Department of Psychology and Black Studies at Florida State University. He received the M.A. in Psychology and Ph.D. in Clinical Psychology at the University of Michigan. Dr. Akbar has been appointed to the Editorial Board of the *Journal of Black Psychology*, the National Council for Black Child Development and the Health Brain Trust of the Congressional Black Caucus. Articles by and on him have appeared in *Jet, Black Books Bulletin, Journal of Black Studies,* and the *New York Amsterdam News.* His published writings are *The Community of Self* (1976), *Natural Psychology and Human Transformation* (1977) and *Chains and Images of Psychological Slavery* (1983).

Ampim, Manu

Manu Ampim is a historian and primary researcher on African and African American culture and history. He taught in the Department of History at Morgan State University. Currently he is the Historian at the San Francisco African American Historical and Cultural Society, and a Ph.D. candidate in African Studies at the Western Institute for Social Research.

He has researched intensively in North Africa, Europe, and North and Central America. Most recently, from 1989–1991, he has conducted independent research at nearly all of the major museums, institutes, and libraries in Europe and America which house ancient Egyptian artifacts. While conducting this research, he travelled to eleven European countries, over twenty U.S. collections, and to a large number of sites in Egypt. His research findings are forthcoming.

Ampim is the author of *Critical Issues in the Current Africentric Movement, volumes I–II.* For further information write: Advancing The Research, c/o Manu Ampim, P.O. Box 31207, Oakland, CA 94604-7207, or call (415) 239-5530.

Blackburn, Regina

Dr. Regina Blackburn is an African-centric writer and educator. During the last ten years she had taught at several major colleges and universities including, Scripp's, California State University Northridge, and LeMoyne-Owen. She is currently an English instructor at California State University Long Beach and Santa Monica City College in Southern California. In 1987 she completed an extended educational tour of Egypt. She is currently working on a book focusing on the struggles of African women in America.

Brooks-Bertram, Peggy

Dr. Peggy Brooks-Bertram, M.P.H., Dr. P.H. is a graduate of The Johns Hopkins University School of Hygiene and Public Health and she is near completion of a second doctorate in American Studies at the State University of New York at Buffalo. She is co-founder of Concerned Parents and Citizens for Quality Education, Inc., a parent advocacy organization funded by the New York State Education Department and President of Jehudi Educational Consultants.

Dr. Bertram has extensive experience in the areas of public health, public education, African history, American Studies, curriculum development and community organization. She has designed and taught the course "Trying to Stay Well in the Master's House: The Effects of Racism, Sexism and Classism on the Mental Health of African American Women" through the State University of New York at Buffalo American Studies program.

She writes a weekly column on education for the Buffalo Challenger, a local newspaper in Buffalo, New York. She was the co-producer and host of a local television program, entitled "Education in Review," a program which provided a forum for educators and parents to discuss local, national and international issues in education. Her internationally known guests included former Congresswoman Shirley Chisholm, Geraldine Ferraro, Sarah Weddington, Asa G. Hilliard, and many others.

She is recognized as an extraordinarily motivational speaker who demonstrates expertise in a broad range of subjects, including health, history, education and social problems such as community violence, institutional racism, sexism, stress reduction and the politics of education. She is a poet, playwright and historical dramatist. Her literary creations focus on African civilizations with particular emphasis on the Kushite dynasties of Ancient Kmet. She was one of the featured playwrights at the First International Womens Playwright Conference, sponsored by the State University of New York, where her play, *The Dynasty of Kush*, was performed before women playwrights from thirty-one countries.

She is the author of numerous poems for children including *Africa on My Stairs*, a 5-volume collection of illustrated children's poetry designed to teach and entertain children using the countries of Africa. *Africa on My Stairs* was featured at the world famous Albright Knox Gallery in Buffalo, New York. She has lectured to many universities, colleges and professional organizations in the United States, Canada and Cairo.

Chandler, Wayne B.

Wayne B. Chandler is an Anthrophotojournalist and Co-Chairman of What's A Face inc. He has done extensive research into the origins of race and ancient civilizations and is co-producer and writer of A People's History To Date—4000 B.C. to 1985 and 365 Days of Black History, Parts I and II. Through the photo archives of What's A Face Inc. Mr. Chandler and his associate Mr. Gaynell Catherine have been instrumental in unearthing key photographs relating to the African presence in the Olmec civilization, as well as the civilizations of ancient India, Southeast Asia, Egypt, and China. He is a committee member of the Historian Roundtable and has lectured in various locations in the U.S. He was visiting lecturer at the University of D.C. from 1978–1983 and instructor at the prestigious Ananda Institute from 1982–1986. In 1984 he helped implement the program Genius Transformation which proved that when under-privileged children are exposed to proper historical information, along with diet and exercise, their psychological perspectives undergo a radical change for the better. From 1987 through 1989, he was working with archaeologist Dr. Edward Otter on various excavations of pre-historic Indian sites in the southeast and midwest. He has been involved with the Journal of African Civilizations since 1985 and his contributions include "Jewel in the Lotus: The Ethiopian Presence in the Indus Valley Civilization" (1985); "The Moors: Light of Europe's Dark Age" (1986); "Trait-Influences in Meso-America: the African-Asian connection" (1987); "Hannibal: Nemesis of Rome" (1988); and "Of Gods and Men: Egypt's Old Kingdom" (1989). Current project is a collaboration with Creative Fox Associates in the production of "Strangers in Their Own Land," a five part documentary involving Drs. Van Sertima, Runoko Rashidi, Asa Hilliard III, and Alexander Von Wuthenau. Any comments regarding chapters published or unpublished are gladly welcome. He may be reached at P.O. Box 928, Adelphi, Maryland 20783.

Crawford, Keith W.

Dr. Keith W. Crawford earned a B.S. degree in Biology from Cornell University and a B.S. degree in Pharmacy from Temple University. He completed a residency in Clinical Pharmacy at the National Institutes of Health Clinic Center and earned a doctorate in Pharmacology from the Uniformed Services University of the Health Sciences in Bethesda, Maryland. He is presently a Research Associate at the National Institute of Health in Bethesda and a lecturer at Howard University School of Medicine. He had published numerous scientific and clinical research studies.

In addition to researching ancient African civilizations, he is particularly interested in African religions and traditional African medicine. He serves on the Board of Directors of the International Organization of Traditional Medical Practitioners and Researchers (I.O.T.M.P.R.) He has written a series of articles dealing with Afrocentric perspectives on Holistic Health in the African Market Newspaper.

He is the Director of the Kujichagulia Youth Empowerment Program, an Afro-centric self-esteem development program for adjudicated adolescent males. He lectures frequently and has appeared on numerous local television programs.

Finch, Charles S.

Charles S. Finch, M.D. is a board-certified family physician who is currently Assistant Professor of Community Medicine and Family Practice at the Morehouse School of Medicine. Dr. Finch completed his undergraduate training at Yale College, his medical training at Jefferson Medical College, and his Family Medicine Residency at the University of California, Irvine Medical Center. He has worked as an epidemiologist for the Center of Disease Control and was formerly a clinical preceptor at the Duke-Watts Family Medicine Clinic in Durham, North Carolina. He was the founder and chairman of the Raleigh Afro-American Life Focus Project between 1981 and 1982 and is a co-founder and Co-Convener of Bennu, Inc. of Atlanta. He is an Associate Editor of the *Journal of African Civilizations* and author of "The African Background of Medical Science," "The Works of Gerald Massey: Studies in Kamite Origins," and—with Mr. Larry Williams of Bennu, Inc.—the co-author of "The Great Queens of Ethiopia," all published in the *Journal of African Civilizations*. In addition Dr. Finch has visited Senegal, West Africa where he has begun studies on the empirical basis of traditional West African medicine. On his most recent visit, he interviewed Dr. Cheikh Anta Diop.

Hilliard, Asa G., III

Asa G. Hilliard is the Fuller E. Calloway Professor of Urban Education at Georgia State University, Atlanta, Georgia. He holds a joint appointment in the Department of Educational Foundations and the Department of Counseling and Psychological Services. Dr. Hilliard served previously as a department chairman and as dean of the School of Eduction at San Francisco State University. He is a graduate of the University of Denver with a bachelor's degree in psychology, a masters in counseling and guidance and a doctor of education degree in educational psychology. He has had experience as a teacher, administrator, researcher and lecturer throughout the United States and in several foreign countries, including a six-year period of professional service in Liberia, West Africa.

King, Richard D.

Richard D. King, M.D., is a physician presently engaged in the private practice of psychiatry in San Francisco. He was trained at Whittier College, University of California at San Francisco Medical Center, Los Angeles County; University of Southern California Medical Center; and the Langley Porter Neuro-phychiatric Institute of the University of California at San Francisco Medical Center. He continues to seek an education in Ancient African Philosophy through Black Gnostic Studies of Los Angeles, California. Presently, he is a member of the Board of Directors of the Aquarian Spiritual Center of Los Angeles, Assistant Professor of Black Studies, San Francisco State University, and Vice-President of the Black Psychiatrists of America. Formerly, he was a scholar in residence at the Franz Fanon Research and Development Center, Charles Drew Post Graduate Medical School, Martin Luther King Hospital, Los Angeles, M.H.C.D. program Staff College, National Institute of Mental Health, and a member of the medical school admissions committee of the University of California at San Francisco Medical Center. His primary research interests are Ancient African psychology, Pineal gland, and melanin, with publications in the journal *Uraeus* (From Mental Slavery to Mastership, Black Dot: Archetype of Humanity), *Sepia* and the Fanon Center publications.

Lumpkin, Beatrice

A retired Associate Professor of Mathematics, Malcolm X. College, Chicago, Professor Lumpkin has written on the Afro-Asian foundations of mathematics and science for *Freedomways*, the *Mathematics Teacher, Science and Society, Historia Mathematica*, and *Journal of African Civilizations*. As a mathematics consultant, she participated in the Multi-Ethnic Curriculum Project of the Portland Public Schools and the Chicago Board of Education Intercultural Project. She is the author of *Young Genius in Old Egypt*, and *Senefer and Hatshepsut*, novels featuring Egyptian mathematicians.

Pappademos, John

Dr. Pappademos received his Ph.D. in theoretical elementary particle physics in 1964 from the University of Chicago. Since then he had been teaching at the University of Illinois at Chicago, except for the academic year 1980–1981, when he was a visiting professor at the University of Crete, in Greece. He is the author of several articles and a monograph on the history, philosophy, and social aspects of science.

Patten-Van Sertima, Jacqueline

Jacqueline Patten-Van Sertima is photographic consultant, art director and cover designer for the *Journal of African Civilizations.* Mrs. Van Sertima also established the Journal's audio arm, Legacies, Inc. As director, she produces companion audio cassettes to each volume of the *Journal of African Civilizations* as well as of various presentations made by Dr. Van Sertima and colleagues.

As a photographer, Mrs. Van Sertima has won international distinction for her hand-painted photography and its significant contribution to social awareness. Listed in the Cambridge W*orld Who's Who of Women* for "distinguished achievement," their *International Register of Profiles* and their *International Who's Who in America* and *Personalities of America* for "outstanding artistic achievement and contributions to society." Mrs. Van Sertima received her B.S. degree in Psychology/Sociology and M.S. in Education from Hunter College, New York.

Rashidi, Runoko

Runoko Rahsidi is an historian, research specialist, writer, and lecturer with a pronounced interest in the African foundations of world civilizations. As a lecturer, he has made major presentations at 52 different colleges and universities in the United States, as well as in Egypt, India, England, and France. From 1981 to 1984, he was African History Research Specialist at Compton Community College.

Since 1982, Rashidi has been an important contributor and editorial advisor to the *Journal of African Civilizations.* In 1985, Runoko Rashidi edited with Ivan Van Sertima the *African Presence in Early Asia.* A revised and expanded edition of the *African Presence in Early Asia* (the most comprehensive work on the subject to date) was published in 1988. Rashidi is the author of *Introduction to the Study of African Classical Civilizations,* published in 1993 by Karnak House of London, England.

Mr. Rashidi has been described as the world's foremost authority on the African presence in Asia. On October 8, 1987 he formally inaugurated the "First All India Dalit Writers Conference" in Hyderabad, India, and delivered a major address on "The Global Unity of African People." For information contact: Runoko Rashidi, 4140 Buckingham Road, Suite D, Los Angeles, CA 90008; or call (213) 293-5807.

Reynolds-Marniche, Dana

Dana Reynolds-Marniche is a specialist engaged in writing, lecturing, and researching about the world traditional cultures, and problems in the

Western study of ancient history and African civilizations. She spent a semester in 1984 at the L'Ecole du Louvre studying art history and the archaeology of ancient Europe. In 1985 and 1986, she was a translator of Egyptological texts from French to English for Dr. Zahi Hawass, Director of the Inspectorate for Giza Antiquities in Egypt. In 1988, she completed the program for the Masters in Social Sciences at the University of Chicago, where she concentrated on the history, archaeology, and anthropology of the ancient Sahara and North Africa. Since 1990, she has taught anthropology and sociology courses, including World Cultures Through New York City Museums at the College of New Rochelle, Cultural Anthropology and World Civilizations at Jersey City State College, and Sociology of the Family as an adjunct instructor at Glassboro State College. In 1991 and 1992, she served as research assistant for Dr. Charles Hamilton at Columbia University. Over the last three years she has been the research assistant for T.C. McLuhan, whose newest book on world cultures is slated to be published by Simon and Schuster in 1994. She is the author of the essay, "The African Heritage and Ethnohistory of the Moors: Background to the Emergence of Early Berber and Arab Peoples, from Prehistory to the Islamic Dynasties."

Van Sertima, Ivan

Ivan Van Sertima was born in Guyana, South America. He was educated at the School of Oriental and African Studies (London University) and the Rutgers Graduate School and holds degrees in African Studies and Anthropology. From 1957–1959 he served as a Press and Broadcasting Officer in the Guyana Information Services. During the decade of the 1960s he broadcast weekly from Britain to Africa and the Caribbean.

He is a literary critic, a linguist, and an anthropologist and has made a name in all three fields.

As a literary critic, he is the author of *Caribbean Writers*, a collection of critical essays on the Caribbean novel. He is also the author of several major literary reviews published in Denmark, India, Britain and the United States. He was honored for his work in this field by being asked by the Nobel Committee of the Swedish Academy to nominate candidates for the Nobel Prize in Literature from 1976–1980. He has also been honored as an historian of world repute by being asked to join UNESCO's *International Commission for Rewriting the Scientific and Cultural History of Mankind.*

As a linguist, he has published essays on the dialect of the Sea Islands off the Georgia Coast. He is also the compiler of the *Swahili Dictionary of Legal Terms*, based on his field work in Tanzania, East Africa, in 1967.

He is the author of *They Came Before Columbus: The African Presence in Ancient America*, which was published by Random House in 1977 and is now in its twenty-first printing. It was published in French in 1981 and in the same year was awarded the Clarence L. Holte Prize, a prize awarded every two years "for a work of excellence in literature and the humanities relating to the cultural heritage of Africa and the African diaspora."

Professor of African Studies at Rutgers University, Van Sertima was also Visiting Professor at Princeton University. He is the Editor of the *Journal of African Civilizations*, which he founded in 1979 and has published several major anthologies which have influenced the development of a new multi-cultural curriculum in the U.S. These anthologies include *Blacks in Science: Ancient and Modern, Black Women in Antiquity, Egypt Revisited, Egypt: Child of Africa, Nile Valley Civilizations, African Presence in the Art of the Americas, African Presence in Early Asia* (co-edited with Runoko Rashidi), *African Presence in Early Europe, African Presence in Early America, Great African Thinkers* (co-edited with Larry Williams), *Great Black Leaders: Ancient and Modern* and *Golden Age of the Moor*.

Professor Van Sertima has lectured to more than 100 universities in the U.S. and has also lectured in Canada, the Caribbean, South America and Europe. He defended his highly controversial thesis on the African presence in pre-Columbian America before the Smithsonian which will be publishing his address in 1994. He also appeared before a Congressional Committee on July 7, 1987 to challenge the Columbus myth.

A Series of Historical Classics

The Journal of African Civilizations, founded in 1979, has gained a reputation for excellence and uniqueness among historical and anthropological journals. It is recognized as a valuable information source for both the layman and student. It has created a different historical perspective within which to view the ancestor of the African-American and the achievement and potential of black people the world over.

It is the only historical journal in the English-speaking world which focuses on the heartland rather than on the periphery of African civilizations. It therefore removes the "primitive" from the center stage it has occupied in Eurocentric histories and anthropologies of the African. The Journal of African Civilizations is dedicated to the celebration of black genius, to a revision of the role of the African in the world's great civilizations, the contribution of Africa to the achievement of man in the arts and sciences. It emphasizes what blacks have given to the world, not what they have lost.

BOOKS

Add $7.50 per book foreign airmail.

___African Presence in Early America	$15:00
___African Presence in Early Asia (out of print)	
___African Presence in Early Europe	$20.00
___Black Women in Antiquity	$15.00
___Blacks in Science: ancient and modern	$20.00
___Egypt Revisited	$20.00
___Egypt: Child of Africa	$20.00
___Golden Age of the Moor	$20.00
___Great African Thinkers - C.A. Diop	$15.00
___Great Black Leaders: ancient and modern	$20.00
___Nile Valley Civilizations (cancelled)	

Postage for above books:
$1.75 per order of single book.
.75 more for each additional book.

___They Came Before Columbus		$23.00
(For this particular book, please make checks payable to	postage	$ 2.50
"Ivan Van Sertima".)		

Date_____

Name_____

Address_____

City/State_____

Zip_____ Tel. No._____

Check and money orders should be made payable to:

"Journal of African Civilizations"
Ivan Van Sertima (Editor)
Journal of African Civilizations
African Studies Department
Beck Hall
Rutgers University
New Brunswick, New Jersey 08903

A Listener's Library of Educational Classics

Legacies, Inc., the audio arm of the Journal of African Civilizations, was established by Mrs. Jacqueline L. Patten-Van Sertima in answer to a genuine need and many requests from parents and teachers across the country. They needed a widespread, easily accessible and responsible medium of communication. It not only had to serve as a learning tool, but as an informational vehicle for educational strategies that hold promise for our youths. They also needed a dynamic and expedient way to absorb and disseminate information as well as a bridge to parents whose time for relearning and participation in the educational process was limited. So, in keeping with the highly controversial needs of the times, Legacies, Inc. was born.

In most of our audio cassette tapes, you will be hearing the voice of Dr. Ivan Van Sertima, founder and editor of the Journal of African Civilizations. His untiring fervor has made learning for everyone an exciting adventure through time. The lectures, by a variety of speakers, are brilliant, stimulating, passionate and absorbing. It is the drama of forgotten peoples and civilizations, brought to you through an unusually fresh and liberating vision of the human legacy.

Audio Tapes

___African Presence in Early America & Address to the Smithsonian	$10.00
___African Presence in Early Asia - R. Rashidi & Van Sertima	$10.00
___African Presence in Early Europe	$10.00
___African Presence in World Cultures	$10.00
___The Black Family - J.H. Clarke & Van Sertima	$10.00
___Black Women in Antiquity	$10.00
___Blacks in Science: ancient and modern	$10.00
___Egypt Revisited	$10.00
___Golden Age of the Moor - R. Rashidi & Van Sertima	$10.00
___Great African Thinkers - C.A. Diop	$10.00
___Great Black Leaders: ancient and modern	$10.00
___The Legacy of Columbus - Jan Carew	$10.00
___Re-Educating Our Children	$10.00
___Socialization of the African-American Child - Asa G. Hilliard	$10.00
___They Came Before Columbus	$10.00
___Van Sertima Before Congress	$10.00
___Egypt: Child of Africa	$10.00

Date_____

Name_____

Address_____

City/State_____

Zip_____ Tel. No._____

Check and money orders should be made payable to:

"Legacies"
Jacqueline L. Patten-Van Sertima
347 Felton Ave.
Highland Park, New Jersey 08904

Please include postage:

1 tape	1.00
2 tapes	1.70
3 tapes	2.15
4-10 tapes	3.00
11-16 tapes	4.35

Please Note: *Tapes cannot be purchased through bookstores or other vendors.*

The Eg. Fertility Rite? Postscript   pg 26-27
on 43, 1943 – "fertility dance" ~~written~~
                discussed as
                        (its the vase from Brussels
                        with 2 warriors - one with
                                shield.

NOTES

modern parallels for Ancient Eg.
Tatooing - pg. 71 SN and R. 29/1948

Iron in the Napatan + Meroitic Ages
                        Wainwright SN + records
                                vol. 26 / 1948.

the Nuer of the upper Eg Nile province'
pg. 183 ~~to~~ S. N and Records vol. 6
                        1923
H. C. Jackson.

Two decades ago- ebony spears was
common, band with thong on shaft
    inserted in

g. 180 - 181 - sacred spear - prayed to and
housed in a special hut - (diefied spear?)

ear of Hemeka- Ivory prob. from Sudan- Djer Expedition?

Breasted A History of Egypt NY 1912 P. 127
Under Sahure Snefern- Sahure " 2,600 staves of
                costly wood" brought from ex to his

Avis hotel 0171
8th + 9th   387-4321
                  £43.50

NOTES   Turn room-
        private
        facilities 10th →

' Kush "
' Africa in Antiquity " main library
                      B059.6/A16
Shabaka Ivories

_____

Sudan notes + records D. Anthrop. Ar
                            2
                        Ground
                        reading
                        room.
                        Area 2

             257032

" The Aliab Dinka uprising and its
suppression - " Sudan notes + Records 4
                                    196?
R. O. Collins, pg. 77
English occupation, Dink violence usuall
involved cattle, women + revenge
British tried to stop/curb violence, to no a
Oct. 30, 1919," Aliab Dinka spearmen, 3,000
attacked a police station at Minkammon
after attack military stations of British
see 78-79

" An early manuscript on the Dinka,
written by a member of this tribe,
edited + translated by Fr. E. U. Toniolo
- pg 112-113